YUCATAN
& MAYAN MEXICO

*'A very particular combination
of street life, tricycle taxis, unhurried pace, bright flowers and
fruit, women in embroidered huípiles and solid colonial architecture.'*

Nick Rider

About the Guide

The **full-colour introduction** gives the author's overview of the country, together with suggested **itineraries** and a regional **'where to go'** map and **feature** to help you plan your trip.

Illuminating and entertaining **cultural chapters** on the Maya, local history, culture, food and everyday life give you a rich flavour of the country.

Planning Your Trip starts with the basics of when to go, getting there and getting around, coupled with other useful information, including a section for disabled travellers. The **Practical A–Z** deals with all the **essential information** and **contact details** that you may need while you are away.

The **regional chapters** are arranged in a loose touring order, with plenty of public transport and driving information. The author's top **'Don't Miss'** ⚀ **sights** are highlighted at the start of each chapter.

A **language and pronunciation guide**, a **glossary** of cultural terms, ideas for **further reading** and a comprehensive **index** can be found at the end of the book.

Although everything listed in this guide is **personally recommended**, our author inevitably has his own favourite places to eat and stay. Whenever you see this **Author's Choice** ★ icon beside a listing, you will know that it is a little bit out of the ordinary.

Money

Because the Mexican peso is a relatively unfamiliar currency in international terms, prices quoted in this book are given in US dollars, except where explicitly stated otherwise.

Hotel Price Guide (*see also* p.104)

Luxury	Over $140
Expensive	$80-140
Moderate	$45-80
Inexpensive	$25-45
Budget	Under $25

Restaurant Price Guide (*see also* p.111)

Expensive	Over $22
Moderate	$8-22
Budget	Under $8

About the Author

Nick Rider lived in Spain for several years and wrote a PhD on Spanish history before first travelling in Mexico. He has written extensively on Spain, and for Cadogan has also written *Short Breaks in Northern France*. In preparing the current book he scaled the flanks of the Tacaná volcano, looked for coatis at Chacchobén, refined the pleasures of counting pelicans against the sky and met many great people.

4th Edition published 2009

01 INTRODUCING YUCATAN & MAYAN MEXICO

Top: Dzibilchaltún

Above: Dock at Puerto Morelos

Every country has its stereotypes. Mexico conjures up more than most: big sombreros, cacti, moustaches, mariachis, half-asleep men sitting against walls, tequila, enchiladas, tropical colour, romance. But there is much, much more to Mexico than the old stock images allow.

The variety of scenery is tremendous, a whole continent of different terrains and climates. Another feature of Mexico is what can only be called 'density of culture'. What does this mean? It means that Mexico is a world of its own, one in which patterns of behaviour are distinctive and highly developed, often downright cranky, strongly defined by tradition and culture. In its history as an independent country Mexico has never been seriously swayed by any foreign theory or political movement. Although Mexicans have often looked over their shoulders to see what the rest of the world thought of them, the nation's triumphs and disasters have always been home-grown. It has its own music, its own food, its own religious cults. And within this self-sufficiency, the human diversity from place to place is immense, an extraordinary richness. This is a country where every new town, every new area, brings a sense of discovery and its own surprises. It is not bland, and not a place you can second-guess.

If this can be said of the entire country, it is even more the case in the south. Big sombreros have scarcely ever been worn here, except to please the tourists. Mexico's five southernmost states have always been distinct from the rest of the country. Here 'density of culture' is multiplied 100 times by the presence of the Maya, in the past and in the present. They bring a special element into play, with

Above:
San Cristóbal de las Casas

Opposite:
Palenque Temple of
Inscriptions

reactions and ways of doing things that easily challenge the preconceptions and habits of industrialized visitors. Rather than any threat, in the Yucatán you encounter an almost gracious courtesy and kindliness now hard to find anywhere else, a rare, seductive atmosphere that needs to be experienced. Few people transmit tranquillity as well as Yucatecans. There are still many twists and paradoxes in the ways of local people, which only adds to the fascination. And as a setting there is a unique set of landscapes, from dazzling coral reefs, pure-white beaches and turquoise seas, through the cave-riddled limestone brush of the Yucatán to rainforest, swamps and high Alpine mountains in Chiapas. Wherever in the five states you choose to sling your hammock, you can easily sway gently for a long, long time without tiring of the view.

Top Ten Places to Visit

1 Exploring dazzling reefs off Cozumel, Puerto Morelos or Akumal, see pp.158, 169, 186
2 Tulum and the model of a tropical beach, p.193
3 Sian Ka'an, for mangroves, lagoons, wild nature and total tranquillity, p.202
4 Chichén Itzá, the ancient Maya at their most awe-inspiring, p.224
5 Mérida, the white city, p.253
6 Uxmal, the most refined creation of Maya architecture, p.299
7 Calakmul, a giant lost city in a forest teeming with life, p.367
8 Old Campeche, within its bulwarks and Spanish city walls, p.380
9 Palenque, its palace and pyramids and their remarkable stories, p.436
10 The atmospheric Spanish mountain city of San Cristóbal de las Casas, p.481

01 Introduction

Where to Go

The regional chapters of this guide are ordered roughly following the route of a traveller entering the Yucatán and southern Mexico through Cancún, its modern gateway.

Cancún, the Islands and the Riviera Maya covers the great tourism hub of Cancún itself, booming Playa del Carmen, the 130km of Riviera Maya beaches and coral reefs down to Tulum and the islands of Isla Mujeres and Cozumel, but also includes less well-trodden spots such as tiny Holbox island, the vast wildlife reserve of Sian Ka'an and, just inland, the Maya ruins of Cobá. Moving west, **Yucatán State** hosts a spectacular wealth of attractions: the languidly gracious colonial capital of Mérida, charming old towns where Maya and Hispanic cultures are seamlessly intertwined such as Valladolid and Izamal, bird-filled mangrove lagoons at Río Lagartos and Celestún and many of the greatest remains of the ancient Maya, in Chichén Itzá, Uxmal and a remarkable number of fascinating smaller sites.

Southern Quintana Roo and the Río Bec is one of the most intriguing, idiosyncratic parts of the Yucatán, containing the just recently accessible beach retreats of the Costa Maya and the fabulous Chinchorro reef, an exquisite lake (with Spanish castle) at Bacalar, the quirky state capital of Chetumal and one of the richest regions in Mexico for Maya ruins. The Río Bec sites and the great city of Calakmul are surrounded by a rain forest reserve that's home to some of the Yucatán's rarest wildlife.

Roads from the Río Bec and Yucatán state converge on **Campeche State**, with the most complete Spanish walled city in Mexico in Campeche city, a long, curving coast facing the opal Gulf, ultra-placid villages and remote, little-visited Maya ruins.

Leaving the Yucatán peninsula, the sultry delta state of **Tabasco** has a vibrant tropical capital in Villahermosa and extraordinary relics of the Olmec and Maya civilizations at Parque La Venta and Comalcalco.

Finally, **Chiapas** is almost a continent in itself, with an extraordinary range of landscapes and settings to explore: the great Maya jungle cities of Palenque, Yaxchilán and Bonampak, the Lacandón rain forest, then an abrupt climb up to the cool Highlands and the gorgeous old Spanish city of San Cristóbal de las Casas and mountain villages of the Maya, perhaps going on to jewel-like lakes at Montebello before an equally abrupt descent down to the torrid temperatures of the Pacific coast. Around the state there are extraordinary places to stay in stunning, remote natural locations, from forest cabins to haciendas.

Above: Flamingoes at Río Lagartos

Below: Yucatán hacienda hotel

Chapter Divisions

200 kms
100 miles

N

Gulf of Mexico

Isla Holbox

Isla Mujeres

Cancún
08
CANCUN, ISLANDS & RIVIERA MAYA

Mérida
09
YUCATAN STATE

Cozumel

Campeche

10
SOUTHERN QUINTANA ROO & THE RIO BEC

Isla del Carmen

11
CAMPECHE STATE

Ciudad del Carmen

Chetumal

Xcalak

12
TABASCO
Villahermosa

VERACRUZ

Caribbean Sea

BELIZE

OAXACA

13
CHIAPAS

Tuxtla Gutiérrez

San Cristóbal de Las Casas

GUATEMALA

HONDURAS

Tapachula

EL SALVADOR

Pacific Ocean

Above: Beach near Tulum, Caribbean Coast

Below: Cancún, the Hotel Zone

Beach Dazzlers and Coral Marvels

Even people who would not normally set foot on a beach from one year to the next find the Yucatán's cool, ultra-soft white sands irresistibly seductive – beach freaks, of course, need no such enticement – while the marine life just below the surface provides an added hypnotic attraction.

- **Cancún**: the big one; for banana boats, paragliding and every other beach entertainment on tap, p.124
- **Holbox**: no reefs, and facing the shallow Gulf of Mexico rather than the Caribbean, but ideal for serious relaxation, p.152
- **Cozumel**: family-friendly beaches and a coral wonderland full of brilliantly-coloured fish not far offshore, ideal for snorkellers, p.158
- **Puerto Morelos**: a laid-back haven where you can snorkel easily among luminous shoals of snapper and angelfish, p.169
- **Playa del Carmen**: coolest spot on the Riviera, with hip beach clubs for hanging out and excellent dive operators, p.174
- **Akumal**: perfect curving bays of clean white sand, where turtles breed in summer, p.186
- **Tulum**: the archetype of a tropical idyll – one of the wonders of the world, and king of beaches on the Riviera, p.193
- **Celestún**: one of the best Gulf Coast beaches; stay over after the day's tours have left to enjoy stunning sunsets, p.284

Above:
Chichén Itzá: Chac Mool
and El Castillo

Tracing the Maya

Over more than a thousand years, the Maya created a civilization of enormous complexity and diversity and left behind thousands of ruins and relics, from isolated temples to massive pyramid-cities. Never think that if you've seen one ruin you've seen them all: the range of styles, and what each site tells us about Maya society, is remarkable.

- **Tulum**: flagship of the small east-coast communities that flourished just before the Spanish Conquest, and the only Maya city built above a beach, p.193
- **Ek-Balam**: a mysterious city with a unique architectural style and some of the finest of all Maya carving in the giant monster-mouth tomb called 'The Throne', p.222
- **Chichén Itzá**: the most dramatic and awe-inspiring of Maya cities, p.224
- **Uxmal and the Puuc Cities**: absolute 'must-sees', the most elegant and sophisticated of all Maya architectural styles, p.299
- **Mayapán**: the last major Maya centre, abandoned only in 1440, p.324
- **Kohunlich**: an enthralling site known for its unnervingly serene *Mascarones* or carved heads, in a fabulous setting amid giant palms, p.356

• **Becán and Chicanná**: the most complete Maya walled city, and some of the most dramatic monster-mouth temples, pp.362–366

• **Calakmul**: once the largest of all Maya cities, forgotten for centuries deep in the forest, p.367

• **Comalcalco**: a demonstration of Maya ingenuity – the only Maya city built out of bricks, made from sand and seashells, p.424

• **Palenque**: the magnificent forest city whose inscriptions have yielded up the story of King Pakal and his dynasty, p.436

• **Yaxchilán and Bonampak**: two spectacular sites deep in the Lacandón forest with extraordinary murals, the only large surviving Maya paintings, p.459 and p.465

• **Toniná**: a science-fiction city, with multiple levels of temples, giant steps and dark alleys climbing up a mountainside, p.477

Clockwise from top: Toniná; El Castillo, Chichén Itzá at the equinox; Carving at Ek Balam

Itinerary 1: Introduction to the Ancient Maya

Anyone with a real interest in Maya sites will not want to limit themselves to the 'star-sights'. A week is just enough to visit a range of sites around the Yucatán peninsula.

Day 1 Arrive in **Cancún** and as a first call visit the compact site of **El Rey**, on Cancún island itself.

Day 2 Drive west to Valladolid and make a detour north to see the extraordinary carvings of **Ek-Balam** before going on to one of the giants, **Chichén Itzá**. Spend the night at one of the hotels nearby.

Day 3 Stop in **Izamal** – where Maya pyramids emerge between the buildings of the Spanish colonial town – and then continue on to **Mérida**. Visit the **Anthropology Museum** in the afternoon.

Day 4 Begin early with a visit to **Dzibilchaltún**, and then turn south again towards the Puuc Cities. See **Oxkintok** before turning back onto the main Puuc road at Muna for **Uxmal**, **Kabah**, **Sayil**, **Xlapak**, **Labná** and the **Loltún** caves. Spend the night at **Santa Elena**.

Day 5 Head south into Campeche state on the Hopelchén road, visit the **Xtacumbilxunaan** cave, and look out for a turn east for **Santa Rosa Xtampak**, a fascinating, remote ruin. Continue on to **Campeche** city, via a stop at the ruins of **Edzná**, and go straight to the **Fuerte San Miguel** museum to see one of the finest collections of Maya artefacts.

Day 6 Start as early as you can for the four hour drive to the **Calakmul** entry road, from where there's another one hour drive to the ruins of the largest of all Maya cities. Afterwards, visit the fascinating smaller sites along the Highway: **Balamkú**, **Chicanná**, **Becán** and **Xpuhil**. Spend the night at **Chicanná**.

Day 7 Head east along the Highway stopping at **Kohunlich** and **Dzibanché-Kinichná** before heading north to **Tulum** (about 6hrs), one of the last Maya centres, before heading back to Cancún airport.

Above:
Uxmal relief;

Below:
Mayapán

01 Introduction | Itinerary

Natural Worlds

Southern Mexico has a unique range of landscapes, above and below ground, which are home to an equally rare mix of animal life. Visit mysterious, deep 'sinkholes' called *cenotes*, entrances to a vast labyrinth of caverns, great expanses of mangrove and silent lagoons, the overwhelming greenness of the Tabasco deltas, lush tropical forest and the massive ridges and peaks of the Chiapas Highlands.

- Snorkel alongside whale sharks off **Holbox**, p.155
- Swim in the *cenotes* **near Tulum**, entrances to some of the world's longest underground rivers, p.196
- **Sian Ka'an**, where fresh- and seawater meet to create bizarre currents in the mangrove channels, p.202
- Look for spider monkeys around the lake at **Punta Laguna**, p.210
- The cathedral-like cenote at **Dzitnup**, p.221, and the village swimming-hole at **Yokdzonot**, p.240
- Follow pink lines of flamingos at **Río Lagartos**, p.242
- Awesome caverns that the Maya saw as gateways to the underworld, at **Balankanché**, p.239, and **Loltún**, p.316
- Exploring **village *cenotes* south of Mérida**, silent pools in the woods that provide delicious relief even on the hottest day, p.297
- **Calakmul**, the largest rainforest reserve in Mexico, p.367

*Below:
Lacanja, Lacandón forest*

*Opposite, clockwise
from top:
Cenote near Tulum;
Caverns at Loltún; Chaca
Tree, Sian Ka'an*

• Sparkling rivers, rapids and scarlet macaws in the **Lacandón forest** of Chiapas, p.455

• The multiple shades of blue of the lakes of **Montebello**, p.510

• Limitless views and astonishing biodiversity in the mountain **coffee *fincas*** of the **Soconusco**, p.529

Above:
Fiesta in San Cristóbal de
las Casas

The Feel of Local Life

Beaches and Maya monuments may first grab the attention, but an essential part of any visit to southern Mexico is to spend some time just getting in touch with everyday life, its tricycle taxis and shaded patios, its special pace, colour and charm. Here are a few of the best places in which to savour different facets of life in Yucatán and the other southern states.

- **Puerto Morelos**: the town that (almost) manages to let the Riviera pass by, p.169
- **Valladolid**: centre of all comings and goings in eastern Yucatán state, p.214
- **Izamal**: the 'golden city', tranquility in yellow-painted form, and the model of an unhurried, friendly Yucatán country town, p.246
- **Mérida**: the Yucatán's gracious old capital is a stunner, where long, straight streets conceal glorious plant-filled patios, p.253
- **Santa Elena**: an ideal base from which to explore Uxmal and the great Puuc ruins while seeing the modern Maya go about their business too, p.309
- **Señor**: spend a day at this former rebel village to get an individual introduction to Maya life today, p.333
- **Campeche**: stroll around the varicoloured streets of the old town, taking a look in through the giant grill windows, p.380
- **Villahermosa**: another side of Mexico – visit during the April *Feria*, as this brash, modern city lets its hair down, p.412
- **Lacanjá**: where the Lacandón Maya are adapting to modernity, and a natural base for visiting Yaxchilán, Bonampak and the forest, p.455
- **San Cristóbal de las Casas**: the fascinating, multi-layered capital of the Chiapas Highlands, p.481
- **Chamula and Zinacantán**: the two villages where the intricate culture and traditions of the Highland Maya can be experienced most vividly, pp.501 and 503

Clockwise: Handicrafts display, Izamal; Renovated colonial houses, Campeche; Daily market in San Cristóbal de las Casas

Itinerary 2: Two Weeks' Highlights

Day 1 From Cancún, drive to **Valladolid**, take a walk around to get a feel of a Yucatecan town, and then stop off at **Dzitnup** for a swim in the giant cave-*cenote*. Drive to one of the hotels at **Pisté**.

Day 2 Get up early to visit **Chichén Itzá** before the crowds. Then, drive back to Valladolid and stop off at **Ek-Balam** for a far less well-known, but spectacular, Maya ruin. Carry on north and stop at **Río Lagartos** for the night.

Day 3 Another early start to see flamingos and other birds at the best time of day, on a boat trip from **Río Lagartos**. Then head inland through backcountry Yucatán to **Izamal**, one of the most engaging of all Yucatecan country towns, with the largest of all the region's Spanish colonial monasteries.

Days 4 and 5 Leave Izamal and drive on through the countryside via a stop at **Aké**, where a strange Maya ruin is inseparable from the hacienda village. Arrive in **Mérida** and spend a day looking around the city, its museums, markets and street life.

Day 6 Drive south out of Mérida following signs for Uxmal, with a stop at the '*hacienda*-museum' of **Yaxcopoíl**. Visit **Uxmal** and stay at **Santa Elena** or in one of the nearby *hacienda* hotels.

Day 7 Tour the rest of the **Puuc Route**, with some of the most impressive of all Maya ruins, in woods full of birds: **Sayil**, **Xlapak**, **Labná** and the caves at **Loltún**. Then turn back down the same road, and at the junction near Sayil turn south for Campeche on the back road through the little town of **Hopelchén**, via stops at the **Xtacumbilxunaan** cave and a detour to the ruined city at **Edzná**. Stay in **Campeche**.

Day 8 Walk around the old city, its Spanish walls and bulwarks, and drive or get a cab up to the Fortress-museum of **San Miguel** south of the city, for superb views and remarkable Maya artefacts.

Day 9 Start early for the drive to **Palenque** (5–6hrs). Visit Palenque ruins in the afternoon.

Days 10 and 11 Drive down the *Fronteriza* road to **Lacanjá** (3hrs), book into the best *Campamento* there, then visit the nearby **Bonampak** murals that afternoon and cool off in one of the clear pools near the Lacanjá river. Then the next morning, drive to **Frontera Corozal** and take a boat to the ruins of **Yaxchilán**.

Day 12 From Palenque drive to **Chicanná** or **Xpuhil** in the **Río Bec** area, and visit the Maya sites of **Becán**, **Chicanná** and **Xpuhil**.

Day 13 Drive back to the **Calakmul** reserve, to see the forest and the ruins. Finish in time for lunch, and then drive to **Tulum** (6 hrs).

Day 14 Time for a much-needed rest on Tulum beach so long as you're getting an evening flight out of Cancún (2 hrs).

Above:
Colonial monastery,
Izamal

Below:
Rainforest route to
Calakmul Maya ruins

CONTENTS

01 Introducing Yucatan & Mayan Mexico 1
Where to Go 6
Itinerary 1 11
Itinerary 2 16

02 The Maya 19
The Land 20
The Eras of Mesoamerican Civilization 22
Academics and Adventurers: the Changing Image of the Maya 22
Origins and the Olmecs 28
Classic Maya Society: Dynasties and City States 29
Religion, Mythology and the Stars 32
The Calendar and Numbers 36
Maya Warfare 38
The Ballgame 39
Art and Architecture 40
The Terminal Classic and Chichén Itzá 41
The Maya Collapse 42
The Postclassic Maya 44

03 History: Conquest and After 45
First Contact 46
The Conquest of the South 47
The *Encomienda* and the Cross: Colonial Society 49
Colonial Backwaters 51
Independence 53
The Caste War and the Talking Cross, 1847-1901 54
The Empire and the *Porfiriato* 56
The Revolution, 1910-40 59
The *Priato* 62
Mexico since 2000 63

04 Topics 65
Cenotes and Caves 66
Colonial Builders and Missionary Churches 67
Ecotourism: What Is It? 68
Maya Textiles 71
Wildlife and the Natural World 73

05 Food and Drink 77
Eating Out 78
The Food of Southern Mexico 80
Drinks and Drinking Habits 81
Fantastic Fruit 83
Mexican Menu Decoder 83

06 Planning Your Trip 87
When to Go 88
Climate 88
Festivals and Fiestas 88
Tourist Information 90
Embassies and Consulates 91
Entry Formalities 91
Disabled Travellers 92
Insurance and Health Precautions 93
Money and Banks 93
Packing 94
Getting There 95
By Air 95
By Road 95
Getting Around 96
By Air 96
By Bus 97
By Car 99
By Ferry 101
By Taxi 101
Travelling to Guatemala, Belize and Cuba 101
Where to Stay 102
Tours and Tour Operators 105

07 Practical A–Z 107
Children 108
Crime and Security 108
Eating Out 110
Electricity 110
Entertainment 110
Health and Emergencies 111
Internet
Language and Communication 111
Media 112
National Holidays 112
Opening Hours 113
Photography 113
Post Offices 113
Shopping 114
Sports and Activities 116
Telephones 118
Time 118
Tipping 118
Toilets 119
Visiting Archaeological Sites and Museums 119
Water 120
Women Travellers and Sexual Attitudes 120

The Guide

08 Cancún, the Islands and the Riviera Maya 121
Cancún 124
The Hotel Zone 129
Ciudad Cancún 133
The Islands 142
Isla Mujeres 142
Isla Contoy 147
Isla Holbox 152
Cozumel 158
The Riviera from Cancún to Xcaret 169
Puerto Morelos 169
Punta Maroma and Punta Bete 173
Playa del Carmen 174
Xcaret 185
The Southern Riviera 186
Tulum 193
Muyil 202
Sian Ka'an and Punta Allen 202
Cobá 206
Punta Laguna 210

09 Yucatán State 211
Valladolid 214
Cenote Dzitnup and Cenote Samula 221
Ek-Balam 222

Chichén Itzá 224
Around Chichén Itzá 239
Northern Yucatán and Río
 Lagartos 241
Izamal to Mérida 246
Izamal 246
Aké 251
Mérida 253
Around Mérida 284
Sisal and Celstún 284
Dzibilchaltún 287
Progreso and the North Coast
 290
Uxmal, the Puuc Cities and
 Southern Yucatán 294
The Camino Real to
 Campeche and Oxkintok
 295
Uxmal and the Puuc Route
 297
Uxmal 299
The Puuc Road 309
Ticul and the Southern
 Yucatán Towns 320

**10 Southern Quintana
Roo and the Río Bec 329**
The Land of the Talking Cross
 331
Felipe Carrillo Puerto 332
The Costa Maya 336
Around Laguna Bacalar 341
Chetumal 345
Excursions from Chetumal
 349
Into Belize 353
Mayan Sites in Southern
 Quintana Roo 353
The Río Bec 359
The Calakmul Biosphere
 Reserve 367
Balamkú 373

11 Campeche State 375
The Camino Real and the
 Campeche Petenes 378
Campeche 380
Edzná and the Chenes 393
Edzná 393
Hopelchén and the Chenes
 Sites 397

South from Campeche 401
The Gulf Coast Route 402
Inland through Escárcega
 404

12 Tabasco 405
The Centla Coast 411
Villahermosa 412
Around Villahermosa 423
Yumká Nature Park 423
The Road to Comalcalco 424
Comalcalco 424
Western Tabasco 428
The Sierra de Tabasco 429
The Rivers Region 431

13 Chiapas 433
Palenque 436
Palenque Town 440
The Ruins of Palenque 442
Misol-Ha and Agua Azul 453
Yaxchilán, Bonampak and the
 Lacandón Forest 455
Lacanjá and Frontera Corozal
 455
Yaxchilán 459
Bonampak 465
The Highlands 471
Ocosingo, Toniná and Laguna
 Miramar 477
San Cristóbal de Las Casas
 481
Around San Cristóbal: the
 Highland Villages 499
Around Comitán and the
 Montebello Lakes 506
The Montebello Lakes 510
Tuxtla Gutiérrez 512
Around Tuxtla 518
Pacific Chiapas 521
Tapachula 523
Izapa 527
Into Guatemala 529

Reference

14 Language 530
15 Glossary 534
16 Further Reading 535
17 Index 537

Maps and Plans

Yucatán and Mayan Mexico
 inside front
Chapter Divisions 7
Mayan and Olmec Sites 21
Cancún, the Islands and the
 Riviera Maya 122
Cancún Hotel Zone 131
Ciudad Cancún 135
Isla Mujeres 143
Isla Town 144
Cozumel 159
San Miguel de Cozumel 162
Playa del Carmen 178
Tulum Ruins 195
Cobá 207
Yucatán State 212–3
Chichén Itza 228
Mérida 255
Dzibilchaltún 289
Uxmal 301
Kabah 310
Sayil 313
Labná 315
Mayapán 327
Southern Quintana Roo and
 the Río Bec 330
Chetumal 347
Kohunlich 357
Becán 363
Chicanná 365
Calakmul 371
Campeche State 376
Campeche 383
Edzná 395
Tabasco 406–7
Greater Villahermosa 414–5
Central Villahermosa 419
Comalcalco 427
Chiapas 434
Palenque Town 441
Palenque Ruins 444
Yaxchilán 461
Bonampak 466
Chiapas Highlands 473
San Cristóbal 483
Tuxtla Gutierrez 513
Tapachula 525

The Maya

The Land 20
The Eras of Mesoamerican
   Civilization 22
Academics and Adventurers: the
   Changing Image of the Maya 28
Origins and the Olmecs 29
Classic Maya Society: Dynasties and
   City States 32
Religion, Mythology and the Stars 36
The Calendar and Numbers 36
Maya Warfare 38
The Ballgame 39
Art and Architecture 40
The Terminal Classic and Chichén
   Itzá 41
The Maya Collapse 42
The Postclassic Maya 44

02

When the first Spanish expeditions reached the Yucatán peninsula, they thought it was another isolated Caribbean island. Mexico's tropical south has always followed its own history, its own dramas. Fundamentally, the peninsula and Chiapas to the south were the home of the Maya, very distinct from the cultures of 'Mexico' proper across the isthmus of Tehuantepec, but extending east into modern Guatemala, Belize and Honduras. In art, architecture and trade, in their knowledge of astronomy, the Maya were the most sophisticated of the cultures of ancient America; they were also the only really literate American culture, with a complete writing system, and thanks to the huge progress made in deciphering Maya hieroglyphs since the 1970s they are now the only pre-Columbian people with a history of names, dates and individuals rather than just an anonymous archaeological record. After the Conquest, while Indian communities were decimated or driven to extinction throughout central Mexico, the Maya and their culture survived more strongly than any other indigenous group in Mexico and Central America. They continue very much alive today.

One of the most remarkable things about the Maya is that our image of them is not some fixed, established text, but has been transformed over the last 40 years, and is still developing. More has been learnt about the ancient Maya in the past four decades than in the previous century and a half, and a great many of what were once seen as accepted facts about them have been put up for grabs. This shifting image only reflects the variety and complexity of Maya communities themselves. Maya centres were not all of the same size and style, but changed and developed over centuries. Nor were there only a few giant – and now famous – sites like Palenque or Chichén Itzá; rather, these cities were part of an extraordinary patchwork of communities of different scales and histories, a complete civilization. This density and richness give the Maya a very special fascination.

The Land

A very special physical setting has provided the background to all human habitation in the region. The whole Yucatán peninsula is one giant slab of very ancient limestone, jutting out into the Caribbean. This Yucatán shelf retains scarcely any surface water. In its northern half it is almost completely flat, and there is not a single surface river north of Champotón, on the Gulf of Mexico, and the Río Hondo, now the frontier with Belize to the east. In contrast to this surface flatness the whole of the slab is riddled with cave systems and underground rivers, access to which is sometimes possible through natural sinkholes called *cenotes* (*see* **Topics**, p.66). The soil on top of the limestone is very thin: the Spanish Friar Diego de Landa marvelled that 'Yucatán is the land with least land that I have ever seen', and that in many places it was not possible to dig even a shallow trench without hitting bedrock. The natural vegetation this land supports, often called jungle, is more like a huge, dry, brushlike wood, with trees 5–6m high. This landscape is full of strange phenomena, with many species of trees and plants that are unique to the Yucatán.

For an agricultural people this land imposed special demands, as well as being imbued with a sense of mystery. The whole of the Yucatán and Chiapas has a similar tropical seasonal pattern of a long dry season (roughly November to May) followed by a shorter rainy season, but in the peninsula the rains are less reliable than in many tropical regions, and at many times there have been catastrophic droughts. For the lowland Maya, water was a divine substance, and awaiting the rains and then keeping or maintaining access to their waters before they ran into the rock, through *cenotes* or ingenious artificial cisterns and watercourses, was a constant obsession.

In the southern half of the peninsula the land is more uneven, with thicker soil, and slightly better watered, as it runs into the great plain of the Petén, which extends across northern Guatemala and into Chiapas to the west. Rainfall here is heavier and more consistent, and the Yucatán brush gives way to denser and denser forest, and real rainforest in the Chiapas lowlands and southern Campeche (although today vast areas of these regions have been deforested). The most important Classic Maya

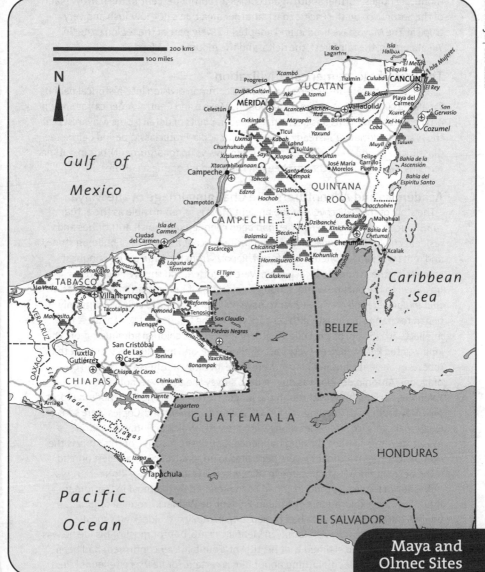

Maya and Olmec Sites

centres – Palenque, Calakmul, Tikal – grew up in this forest region, although it is likely that at that time (around 1,500 years ago) the area had more of a savannah climate than it has now, one more amenable to agriculture. To the west it is also crossed by giant rivers running off the mountains to the south towards the Gulf of Mexico, the Grijalva and the Usumacinta. These rivers come together in a wide, swampy delta which makes up most of the state of Tabasco. The radical contrast in the whole Maya region comes south of Palenque, as the terrain rises abruptly into the Highlands of Chiapas and Guatemala. Temperatures are far lower, pine woods replace tropical forest, and the soil, if thin, is often very rich, in cool, green valleys between massive mountain ridges. Further south again comes an abrupt descent to the narrow plain of the Soconusco on the Pacific coast, another area that's hot, low, lush and very tropical. The Maya have lived in and adapted to every part of the region – the dry Yucatán plain, the rainforest, the delta, and the mountain valleys.

The Eras of Mesoamerican Civilization

Since the 19th century experts have used a common division into historical periods for all the cultures of Mesoamerica (modern Mexico and Central America), as shown on the facing page. This has been challenged in points of detail (some Mayanists call the first era 'Formative' instead of Preclassic, or add a 'Protoclassic' period before the Classic, and boundaries between periods are always up for argument), but in outline remains a universal shorthand when referring to pre-Conquest cultures.

Academics and Adventurers: the Changing Image of the Maya

The story of the rediscovery of the ancient Maya is as remarkable as the actual ruins. Once the different territories had been conquered, Spanish authorities and resident *criollos* lost interest in the ruined cities except as sources of building stone, and most were abandoned to the forest. Reports from the time of the Conquest connecting these ruins to local people were forgotten, and they were entirely unknown to the outside world. Among local whites, it became an established truth that *Indios* were too primitive ever to have built such things as cities. Things only began to change in the late 18th century, when King Charles III tried to inject the intellectual curiosity of the Enlightenment into Spain's colonial administration. The king wanted knowledge of every part of his empire, and instructions went out that reports of ancient ruins in Chiapas were to be investigated. In 1787 a captain of dragoons, **Antonio del Río**, was duly sent to survey the utterly remote site of Palenque, hacking his way through the jungle. He compiled the first modern report on a Maya ruin, with drawings by his artist Ricardo Almendáriz. Copies were sent to Guatemala, Mexico and Spain, along with artefacts which are now in Madrid's Museo de América. Then nothing happened. One of the features of this story is the number of times documents were deposited in imperial archives and left unread.

The next significant stage came in 1822, when an edition of Del Río's report was published in English in London. It had been prepared by the most extraordinary figure in Maya exploration, **Count Jean-Frédéric de Waldeck**, from an original bought from a traveller who had picked it up in Mexico. Waldeck was most probably born into a Jewish family in Vienna, in 1766, but for most of his life he was a French citizen, and claimed that his title of 'Count' (never confirmed) had been given him by Napoleon. Nothing about him is certain, for he was a teller of tales

Eras of Mesoamerican Civilization

Archaic	**prior to 1800 BC**	Hunter-gatherers begin settled agriculture and ceramics-making in about 2000 BC
Early Preclassic	1800–900 BC	Olmecs create the first city-civilization, centred on San Lorenzo (Veracruz)
Middle Preclassic	900–300 BC	La Venta takes over as main Olmec centre First settled Maya communities on the Pacific coast, in the Guatemalan highlands, the Petén and in Belize.
Late Preclassic	300 BC–AD 250	The first era of a distinctive Maya civilization. Maya writing system and Long Count calendar developed.
Early Classic	AD 250–600	Great flourishing of Maya civilization. Period of greatest influence of Tikal in the Petén, prior to 562.
Late Classic	600–950	Apogee of Maya civilization. 562–695, ascendancy of Calakmul in the Petén; 650–800, intensified warfare between southern city-states. After 700, in the 'Terminal Classic', rapid growth of communities in northern Yucatan. In the 9th century, the 'Maya Collapse' leads to rapid abandonment of the southern cities. Maya civilization survives for another 200 years in the north, but by around 910 the Long Count calendar has been abandoned. 850–950, ascendancy of Chichén Itzá in northern Yucatán.
Early Postclassic	950–1200	Maya culture fails to revive in the south.
Late Postclassic	1200–1530	After final collapse of Chichén, Mayapán becomes last 'capital' of Yucatán Maya. Trading communities expand on east coast. Small city-states form in southern highlands.

about himself of Baron Münchhausen proportions, creating clouds of mystery wherever he went. However, by publishing Del Río's text and illustrations he did reveal the existence of Maya ruins for the first time to a world beyond the Maya regions themselves or the Spanish bureaucracy. To pursue his new interest in 1825 he moved to Mexico, and after more adventures tried to get its government to pay him to study the ruins at Palenque. Aged 67, he spent a year there in 1832–3, holed up in great discomfort with his Indian mistress in the building now known as the 'Temple of the Count'. Returning to Europe, he published a series of drawings and an account of his travels in 1838.

It has been the fate of the Maya to be the object of other people's fantasies. Waldeck and other early travellers to Palenque shared the colonials' assumption that the local Indians were incapable of building the temples themselves, certainly not without help. Captain del Río suggested Greeks or Romans could have travelled this far. Waldeck himself developed a complicated theory according to which the now-

Mr Stephens and Mr Catherwood

John Lloyd Stephens and Frederick Catherwood are inseparable from any account of the Maya lands and Maya cities. Stephens' books, *Incidents of Travel in Central America, Chiapas and Yucatán* (1841) and *Incidents of Travel in Yucatán* (1843), superbly illustrated with Catherwood's engravings, revolutionized knowledge of ancient American ruins and first made them known to a wide public.

They were an odd pair. Stephens was born in 1805, the son of a wealthy New York businessman. After qualifying as a lawyer at Columbia he became something of a man about town, and dabbled in politics. Campaigning in support of Andrew Jackson in 1834 he caught a throat infection, and it was suggested he travel for his health. Like most men of the Romantic era he was eager to visit Rome and Greece, but unlike others he kept on going to Egypt, Syria and Palestine, becoming the first American ever to visit Petra, before returning via Turkey and Russia. He had not intended to be a writer, but unknown to him some of his letters to a friend had been shown to a publisher, who at once declared them worthy of a wider public. At a time when few Americans could travel so far, Stephens' first book, *Incidents of Travel in Arabia Petraea*, already with his easy-going style, made him an immediate celebrity.

In London on his way home two more things happened that would change his life forever. First, he met Frederick Catherwood. Reserved, intense and fanatically precise, he had none of Stephens' social connections nor his social graces. Born in Hoxton in east London in 1799, he showed great drawing ability from childhood and was apprenticed as an architectural draftsman. After working around Britain he spent ten years travelling in Greece and the Middle East, drawing cities and ancient sites. Back home without money, he exhibited his drawings at 'Burford's Rotunda' in Leicester Square, a display of pictures of exotic places which in those pre-photographic days was a big attraction, and it was at one such show that he met Stephens. Secondly, Catherwood showed Stephens Waldeck's edition of Del Río, bringing to his attention the existence of unexplored pyramids and temples in Mexico. These two dissimilar personalities shared a passion for ruins and an awareness of the questions left unanswered in Del Río's report, and a new double act was born.

On their first trip, from 1839 to 1840, they travelled through British Honduras, Honduras and Guatemala, up through Chiapas to Palenque and then by ship to Mérida and Uxmal. Stephens had with him credentials as US Ambassador to the Confederation of Central America and conscientiously made side-trips to Nicaragua and Costa Rica. Their first book was a huge success, selling as much as best-selling novels of the time in America and Europe. On the strength of it they thoroughly explored the Yucatán peninsula in 1841–2, this time with no diplomatic responsibilities, for their still more successful second book. After that it was suggested they try Peru, but Stephens had to attend to family business and got wrapped up in a scheme to build a railway across Panama, dying there of one bout of malaria too many in 1852. Catherwood published a beautiful separate edition of his engravings in London in 1844, and worked with Stephens in Panama before he also died, when his ship sank crossing the Atlantic in 1854.

One of the great attractions of the books is Stephens himself: endlessly good-natured, curious, perceptive, enthusiastic, full of a rather preppy charm and always willing to be distracted by a fiesta or 'charming young ladies'. In the background there is the obsessive figure of Catherwood, making his infinitely detailed drawings in atrocious conditions and through recurrent attacks of 'fever'. A great many passages begin 'Leaving Mr Catherwood at the ruins...', where he stayed alone for days and weeks with his hammock and camera obscura while Stephens explored the surrounding villages and their village characters. On several occasions he nearly died, but would not give up, and their first journey only ended when Stephens found Catherwood collapsed by his drawing-board at Uxmal. The result was images of an extraordinary precision.

Stephens' greatest achievement stemmed from his generosity of spirit, aided by the research of Yucatecan scholars such as Juan Pío Pérez: leaving aside the prevailing racism, he and Catherwood were able to see what was in front of their noses, that the builders of the ancient cities had been the region's native people. They effectively 'discovered' the Maya for the outside world: when they set out in 1839, they had only vague references to ruins in Copán, Palenque and Uxmal. They provided the first detailed descriptions of these cities and Chichén Itzá, and brought the first news of scores of other unknown sites. Not the least compliment paid to them is that, of all the gringo books on Mexico, Stephens' rate consistently among those best regarded by Mexicans themselves.

extinct American civilization was the work of wandering Greeks, Egyptians, Jews and Indians from India. He was a trained artist (he said he had been taught by David in Paris), but in his drawings he shamelessly distorted his material to fit his theories, adding in Classical details and even elephants. To publish his book Waldeck wangled finance out of another eccentric, Lord Kingsborough, who was obsessed with an idea that the ancient American cities were built by the Lost Tribes of Israel. In the mean time another traveller, '**Juan Galindo**', an Irish adventurer (real name unknown) serving as a soldier with the Central American Confederation, visited Copán and Palenque and made the radical suggestion that local Indians and the builders of the cities were the same people, but he died fighting in 1840. This was the state of knowledge before John Lloyd Stephens' first book on the region appeared in 1841.

After Stephens the next great figure in Mayanology was the **Abbé Charles Brasseur de Beaubourg**, a French priest who worked in Mexico and Guatemala in the 1850s. He discovered and published the manuscript of the *Popol Vuh* (*see* p.32), and then in 1862 found Bishop Landa's *Relación* (*see* p.51) in a library in Madrid, where it had been lying ignored for three centuries. Once this was published it became impossible to deny the connections suggested by Stephens. The information in Landa also made it possible to begin understanding what was then the only known Maya manuscript, the *Dresden Codex*, believed to have been sent to Charles V by Cortés, and which had reached Germany via Vienna. With the rapid growth of interest in the subject, two more, the *Paris* and *Madrid* codices, came to light in Europe in the 1860s (a fourth, the *Grolier*, appeared in a private collection in the 1970s and is now in the Anthropology Museum in Mexico City). From the 1860s to the 1890s three explorers, **Desiré Charnay**, **Alfred Maudslay** and **Teobert Maler**, French, English and German, took the first photographs of Maya ruins. At the same time academic Mayanism began with the work of the great German scholars **Ernst Förstemann**, Keeper of the Royal Saxon Library and so of the *Dresden Codex*, and **Eduard Seler**. Förstemann worked out the basics of the Maya calendar and the Mayas' astronomical knowledge.

Archaeological excavations of Maya sites began with the first expeditions from the Peabody Museum in Harvard in the 1890s. During the 1900s **Edward Thompson**, US Consul in Mérida, bought the site and *hacienda* of Chichén Itzá, and began his amateur excavations by crudely dredging the great *cenote*. Then, in 1914 a young Harvard academic called **Sylvanus Morley** persuaded the Carnegie Institution to fund ongoing research into the Maya. For the next 40 years, led by Morley and his British deputy and friend **Eric** (later Sir Eric) **Thompson**, the Carnegie dominated the field, particularly with their excavation of Chichén Itzá in the 1920s. Their discoveries were enthusiastically publicized by Morley, which is one reason why 'Mayan' features became so prominent in kitsch Art Deco around the same time. They were not the only people working on the Maya, for excavations were also undertaken by the Dane **Frans Blom**, who worked for Tulane University in Louisiana and went on to found Na Bolom in San Cristóbal de Las Casas, and the extravagant and unscrupulous British explorer **Thomas Gann**, supposedly one of the models for Indiana Jones. By the 1930s the nationalist culture of the Revolution also led Mexicans to take an interest in their own past at last — and sparked a strong desire to end its appropriation by foreigners – resulting in the foundation of the **INAH**, the National Institute of

Anthropology and History. One of its great early successes was the excavations at Palenque led by **Alberto Ruz Lhuillier**, and the discovery of the tomb of Pakal in 1952.

By this time a certain image of the Maya had become established. The early studies were all based on the major buildings of the largest Maya ruins and the codices, and the first great achievements of Mayanism were all to do with deciphering numbers and the complexities of the calendar. The rest of Maya inscriptions remained impenetrable. On this basis eminent figures such as Morley presented a picture of the Maya that had great appeal to their scholarly minds: in contrast to the Aztecs, who, as the Spaniards had chronicled, were bloodthirsty and militaristic, the Maya appeared as the cultured Greeks of ancient America, a rather ethereal, pacific people ruled by astronomer-priests who spent their time in abstruse calculations and observations of the stars. Morley also put forward the existence of an 'Old Empire' (roughly the area around the Classic cities in the Petén and Chiapas) and a later 'New Empire' (northern Yucatán), terms which still turn up in some books, although it is well established that neither empire ever existed. Another broadly accepted idea was that the Maya cities were not real cities at all, but only 'ceremonial centres', temple complexes with a permanent population of only a few hundred priests and nobles, to which scattered villagers came only for special ceremonies and rituals.

Simultaneously a belligerent debate had gone on in both institutes and academic journals (beautifully described in Professor Michael Coe's *Breaking the Maya Code*) over whether Maya glyphs could ever be read as text in any language, in the way Egyptian hieroglyphs had been. Several writers claimed to have found a key to the glyphs – Brasseur, Cyrus Thomas – only to be shot down by eminent figures such as Seler or Eric Thompson, who maintained that Maya inscriptions were purely ideographic symbols, without any relation to spoken language, and referred only to the calendar, numbers and astronomical calculations. This was a central assumption underlying the idealized, other-wordly vision of the Maya.

This image, however, would be eaten away at from the 1940s, and has been turned on its head since the 1970s. In 1952 a Russian named **Yuri Knorosov** published an article saying that by studying the codices he had worked out a viable system for reading Maya glyphs, based on the idea that they were neither purely ideographic nor phonetic symbols, but a combination of both, rooted in actual Maya languages. Thompson, who dominated Maya studies after the death of Morley in 1948, had spent years in the dust of archaeological sites, and was a ferocious anti-Communist; the idea that a Russian who had never set foot in Central America could see something he didn't appalled him, and for the next 20 years anyone in the western academic world who suggested that Knorosov had a point was battered with all the capacity for sarcastic malice that an English public school education can give you.

Nevertheless, the 'abstract' vision of the Maya would also be undermined by evidence harder to dismiss. Belief in Mayan pacifism was shattered by discoveries such as the murals at Bonampak in Chiapas (*see* p.465), which show bloody battles and human sacrifices, and in the 1960s **Heinrich Berlin** and a member of Thompson's own Carnegie team, **Tatiana Proskouriakoff** (born in Russia, but American), demonstrated that many Mayan monuments referred to historical events and not simply the calendar. What has been called the 'great decipherment' really began, however, in 1973, with the first Palenque *mesa redonda* (round table) organized by

Mayan Spelling, or the Lack of it

Mayan names and terms are regularly being reinterpreted, so there are different forms and spellings to choose from. For example, it was long thought that the first king of Palenque was Balam-Kuk, 'Jaguar-Quetzal', but experts now tend to think he was the other way round, K'uk-Balam or 'Quetzal-Jaguar'. Some writers also use a set of standard spellings for all Mayan languages developed in Guatemala (with which Campeche becomes Kampeche). However, this is scarcely ever seen in Mexico. For convenience, this book uses the most common current archaeologists' interpretations of historic names, while sticking with the most widely used (if inconsistent) Mexican spellings for places and terms, but you will often see alternatives.

what could be called the hippy generation of Mayanists. These informal gatherings brought together academics such as **Floyd Lounsbury**, **Peter Mathews** and **David Stuart** with others who were not professionals in the field, like artist **Merle Green Robertson** and art teacher **Linda Schele**. Starting from Knorosov's basic idea and an assumption that the language of the glyphs was related to modern Yucatec or Chol, they began the laborious process of reading Maya inscriptions. One of their first successes was to make out the name of the greatest king of Palenque, Pakal. The decoding of Maya inscriptions has accelerated ever since. Inscriptions and carved stelae have revealed a complex interplay of dynastic history and religious beliefs, providing an incomparably fuller image of Maya society.

For years this approach continued to meet with resistance, but since the 1980s not only Palenque but other cities have been given substantial 'histories'. Simultaneously with the 'decipherment' has come a major acceleration in archaeological investigations using modern techniques – such as satellite mapping – which have opened up lesser-known, smaller sites alongside those that have been famous for decades, and focused on the material minutiae of Maya life as much as major buildings. These studies have revealed, firstly, a far higher number of substantial settlements than was ever previously recognized, and secondly that the 'ceremonial centres' were actually sprawling agglomerations with complex systems of water management and agriculture, supporting populations of thousands.

Much of what has been considered 'enigmatic' about the Maya stems from the fact that they do not fit into any of the habitual stages of history invented to describe Europe or Asia. Their sophistication in some areas seems belied by an apparent primitiveness in others. Strictly speaking, the Maya lived in the Stone Age. They began to work metals very late, when gold and silver reached them from South America, and then only on a small scale. Like all the pre-Columbian American cultures they did not use the wheel, although in the Anthropology Museum in Villahermosa there are some ancient wheeled trolleys – as children's toys. To know about the wheel but not use it seems deliberately perverse. However, many of the most basic advances in Old World civilization came about due to continual intercommunication between Europe, Asia and Africa: the domestication of the horse, for example, began in Central Asia and spread towards Europe, and metals, crops and foods moved in similar ways. In ancient America, on the other hand, there were only two great centres of civilization, Mesoamerica and the Andean region, with relatively limited contact between them. Left largely to its own resources, Mesoamerica is rich in some things but surprisingly poor in others. In the Mayan region, there are no useful metals, nor a single native animal that could be used as a beast of burden – without which wheeled carts give only a limited advantage. The most intriguing 'enigma' about the Maya is that they developed amid very special circumstances. They 'progressed' less by technical innovation than by complex social organization and the mobilization of collective labour.

Origins and the Olmecs

The earliest human inhabitants of the Mayan region were primitive hunters and gatherers who moved across from Asia and south through North America in the Ice Age, spreading to every part of the American continent by about 14,000 BC. Exactly where and when agriculture began in the Americas is still hotly debated, but it seems likely that it started in central Mexico in around 5000–4000 BC with the domestication of maize (corn), always the staff of life on the continent. It would be joined by other staples: beans, squashes, chillies. The next fundamental advance came in around 2000 BC with the invention of *nixtamal* flour, a mixture of maize and white lime powder, boiled together and ground on a *metate* grinding stone. By itself, maize is deficient in some nutritional values, especially amino acids; the creation of this minerally enhanced flour was essential for settled agriculture to be able to support an expanding population. Whether in *tamales* or *tortillas*, *nixtamal* has been consubstantial with civilization in Mesoamerica throughout its history.

Just as inseparable a part of the region's life over millennia is the *milpa* slash-and-burn cultivation system of the maize farmer. A *milpa* is a corn patch. With a new *milpa*, the vegetation is cut down around January, and then burnt off in the spring months to prepare the soil for planting, which has to be timed to the arrival of the rains. Each *milpa* can only be planted for a few seasons, after which the farmer moves on to a new patch, leaving the old one to regenerate. The time this takes varies: in good soils some *milpas* can be used for ten years and left for only five, but in the dry Yucatán, plots can often be planted for only three years and then must be left for an equal time or even more. *Milpa* cultivation imposes an unavoidable schedule – to miss the rains is suicidal – which has always set the rhythm for Maya village life.

These elements of village life were in place by about 1800 BC. The first great civilization to create large centres in Mesomerica, ruled by a powerful élite, were the Olmecs. They are a mysterious people, discovered only in the 1920s; they left no writing system that has been decoded, and much about them is still unknown. They emerged in apparently unpropitious territory, the river deltas and swamplands around the base of the Gulf of Mexico, which in later centuries were avoided by other cultures as disease-ridden; however, the delta region provided easy river communications, and abundant food, in fish and the produce of its rich soils. The first great Olmec centre was **San Lorenzo** in Veracruz, which grew up around 1600–1500 BC and disintegrated for reasons unknown some 500 years later. It was surpassed by **La Venta** in western Tabasco, flourishing from about 900 to 400 BC, the greatest monuments from which are now in the Parque La Venta in Villahermosa.

Straddling – unlike later pre-Conquest civilizations – central Mexico and the Maya region, the Olmecs were the 'mother culture' of the whole of Mesoamerica. Many traits of Maya civilization are already visible in the Olmec: a polytheistic religion involving astronomical observations and a cosmos divided between the heavens, this world and the underworld, with constant contact between them; a ritual ballgame played in two-sided courts; and cities built around temple-mountains as a sacred 'base' for the community, for these were Mesoamerica's first pyramid builders. For the Maya and nearly all the region's later cultures, civilization was always seen as 'centred' at the foot of a mountain, and, like the Olmec, they sought to recreate this cosmic pattern in symbolic form with their own pyramid-mountains. Parts of the Maya calendar may also have been of Olmec origin. A recurrent image in Olmec temples is the jaguar, as a godlike, awesome symbol of cosmic forces.

The Olmecs had a unique, dramatically dynamic style of sculpture, seen at its best in the giant heads from La Venta now in Villahermosa. They also began the tradition of mobilizing huge collective efforts in the creation of monuments. These heads are all made of giant blocks of basalt, which is nowhere to be found in the delta around the site. The rock had to be brought from the Tuxtlas mountains in Veracruz, over 200 kilometres to the west, on wooden rafts or dragged on rollers over the ground. Major buildings, similarly, must have required the work of thousands for decades to be completed. On a smaller scale, the Olmec were also Mesoamerica's first skilled workers in jade, seen in small figurines left as tomb offerings. Nevertheless, their civilization disintegrated, in a collapse more mysterious than that of the Classic Maya a thousand years later, and their centres were abandoned some time around 400 BC.

Classic Maya Society: Dynasties and City States

It is a curious feature of Maya history that most people see it backwards. The most-visited Maya sites – Chichén Itzá, Tulum, San Gervasio on Cozumel – all date from the last centuries of Maya civilization. Very few people visit the oldest proto-Maya ruins, **Izapa**, outside Tapachula near the Pacific coast, from about 300–200 BC, or **Kaminaljuyú**, now mostly buried beneath Guatemala City. From there Maya culture moved northwards: **El Mirador** and Tikal in the Petén were already monumental cities in the 1st century AD, and early buildings have even been found in the north, at **Acanceh** and **Yaxuná**. The early Maya evidently took a great deal from the Olmecs, whose influence spread south along the Pacific plain, a communications channel throughout history, but among the 'unknowns' of Mesomerica is when a clear division can be drawn between them, and when a full-blown Maya culture can be said to exist. The chief pillars of Classic Maya civilization, the *ahau* system of dynastic kingship, the Long Count calendar, glyph writing, styles of architecture, were all established by around AD 250. Recent studies, though, have traced them further back, and stress the continuities between the Preclassic and Early Classic eras. The oldest known Long Count date inscription, from **Chiapa de Corzo**, is from 36 BC.

In their inscriptions the Maya showed an awareness of themselves as distinct from other, non-Maya peoples. However, they were never politically united, but divided, like Ancient Greece, into a mass of local polities or city states, over 60 of them by the Late Classic. They varied greatly in size and power, and a few dominated whole webs of smaller communities as 'overkings', via a range of relationships from loose alliances to direct subordination. The greatest of all these 'superpowers' of the Maya world were **Tikal** and **Calakmul**, whose rivalry over centuries is one of the central conflicts of Classic Maya history. Far from being peace-loving, Maya states of all sizes were continually warring and forming alliances with each other. A fractious disunity can almost be said to have been the Achilles heel of the Maya throughout their history.

The earliest Maya agricultural communities were made up of groupings of extended families or patriarchal lineages. Within each community, there was little inequality. One reason for the belief that Maya sites were only 'ceremonial centres' was that it was never understood how this simple society could have grown and how *milpa* agriculture alone could have supported large populations. However, excavations in the forests around the great pyramid-temples have shown that they were surrounded by hundreds, often thousands, of smaller structures, most of them basic *na* huts. Modern aerial and ground surveys around many Maya centres have also shown webs of man-made raised fields and vegetable gardens, ringed by drainage ditches. Instead of developing new techniques, which were scarcely available, given the lack of new crops, materials and useful animals, the Maya developed slash-and-burn and garden agriculture to the very limits of their potential.

As they grew, each of the Maya centres came under the rule of a single hereditary king or lord, called an ***ahau*** (also spelt *ahaw* or *ajaw*), assisted by warrior-nobles called *sahalob* (singular ***sahal***; in Yucatec, the ending -*ob* indicates a plural). The institution of the *ahau* served to justify inequality to a society that had traditionally rejected it, by setting up a web of mutual obligation. The *ahau* was far more than just a ruler or the representative of God on earth: he was the actual centre of the religious life of the community, an awesome figure whose survival, together with that of his lineage, and the performance by them of spectacular rituals, were essential for the wellbeing of everyone. In return for this service the *ahau* and *sahalob* called on the populace for regular efforts in building and other labours – which, as far as anyone knows, were made voluntarily. The *ahau* and his royal lineage 'became' in effect the community. Dynastic rule by the *ahauob* can in many ways be called the defining element of Classic Maya civilization, with which it began and ended, and around which many of its other characteristics revolved: the purpose of most glyph inscriptions, for example, is to laud and commemorate different rulers (and so their version of history is often questionable). Few societies have ever glorified power and their rulers more than the Classic Maya.

Lords and nobles were, naturally, men, but the enormous emphasis placed on lineage meant that women of royal blood were also accorded great respect, especially if they married into neighbouring royal houses. The most complete surviving image of Classic-era court life we have, the murals of **Bonampak**, shows sacrifices, rituals and celebrations in which royal women play a prominent and honoured part. They could also sometimes exercise great power, when a dynasty found itself short of a male heir or a matriarch had to keep control for a young son.

The ritual accession of a new *ahau* was an event of enormous importance in the life of a city, nearly always commemorated in monuments. When a centre had some kind of alliance or subordinate relationship with a larger patron this would be mentioned too, and it is through these inscriptions that the intricate network of 'overkingship' has been traced. Calakmul was for many years better known for the extraordinary geographical range and number of its vassals than for the city itself. This system was highly intricate, since there were many degrees of alliances, and an *ahau* who had vassal-cities could in turn be subordinate to someone else. It was also inherently unstable, since a city could renounce its established alliances and seek the support of a new 'overking', risking fierce retribution from its former patron.

Like most Native American peoples the Maya did not have much of an idea of the individual ownership of land, but only of its products. Farmers could make their *milpas* anywhere in their centre's lands, but then had to pay tribute to the élite. As communities grew so too did trade, between Maya communities and with other non-Maya peoples in central Mexico and to the south. From Chiapas and Guatemala came jade, amber and obsidian, the natural black glass in high demand for jewellery, weapons and sacrificial knives. The Petén produced cotton, and the Yucatán honey and salt, from salt-beds in the north-coast lagoons. Feathers and flowers had huge value, as symbols of wealth and natural abundance. All areas produced ceramics, and there was a steady trade in slaves, with captives taken in war. Most valuable commodity of all was cacao, the source of chocolate, consumed by the Maya in a variety of mostly savoury drinks, not as solid food. In Classic-era carvings and ceramics, chocolate is shown as one of the most prized luxuries of the élite, and food for the gods; cocoa beans featured in many rituals, and were an essential part of aristocratic wedding gifts (this tradition, 'democratized', survives in many Maya communities to this day, though in Classic times most Maya peasants probably never tasted chocolate in their lives). So valuable were cocoa beans that they began to be used as the region's first form of money (to be joined, not much later, by types of seashell). Cacao's value was boosted by scarcity: it grows naturally In only two parts of Mesoamerica, the Tabasco deltas and the Pacific plain from the Soconusco to Guatemala, and despite efforts to grow it elsewhere supplies remained limited.

Chocolate dependency helped shape Maya history and economics. The Tabasco deltas were also home to the Chontal Maya, also known as the **Putunes**, and their privileged access to cacao was a prime factor in the rise of this group, otherwise regarded as primitive by other Maya. Taking their canoes around the coasts or up the Usumacinta river, the *Putunes* were the great transporters of the Maya world, and in the Late Classic gained in power and influence over older, more settled communities further inland. Trade also led to considerable contact between the Maya and central Mexico, beginning in the 4th century AD when **Teotihuacán** in the Valley of Mexico – then the largest city in Mesoamerica – had great influence over Tikal.

Important though this trade was, the numbers involved were probably limited, and it is likely around 80 per cent of the Classic Maya still worked the land. Most of the goods were high-value luxuries, used only by the élite, and the amounts traded were limited to what could be carried in canoes or on men's backs. Father Landa wrote of the Conquest-era Maya that 'the occupation to which they are most inclined' was that of merchant, but – while this is one of the big 'open question' areas of Maya research, still not resolved by recent discoveries – any 'merchant class' seems to have been less prominent among the Classic Maya, certainly compared to warriors. This is why, while the idea they were just 'ceremonial centres' of priests is now untenable, some experts still refuse to call Maya states 'cities', preferring the more neutral 'centres'. Compared to ancient communities in Greece or the Middle East, for example, it seems Maya centres were politically over-developed – with the numbers of lords and all their scribes and hangers-on – but economically under-developed, in their dependence on basic agriculture. This would have great consequences for the fragility of Maya society as it came under massive strain, from the late 8th century onwards.

In their heyday, Maya centres also got rich just by the exercise of power. A city that was subordinate to another had to pay tribute to its *ahau*, so one with many vassals, like Calakmul, could grow enormously wealthy. Many images on ceramic vases show reclining lords accepting bundles of cloth or cacao and other foods from lesser lords. *Ahauob* and *sahalob* lived well; examination of their remains has shown that most were significantly taller and more robust than the peasants around them. Along with these noble lineages, which spread into 'clans' of several hundred each by the 780s, other privileged groups included the scribes. Maya glyph writing was, clearly, a means of communication, but it was never a general system of literacy. Writing was the work of a prestigious caste, who may themselves have been related to lordly houses. Each scribe was expected to make personal touches to his inscriptions, as a magical work of art – another reason why they are so enormously difficult to decipher. Among the Postclassic Maya there was also a caste of priests alongside the nobility, but it seems that in earlier eras these roles were absorbed into each other.

The opulent way of life of the élite included ornate jewellery, finely worked clothing and rich foods. The condition of the rest of the population is harder to determine, but in good years, at least, they too seem to have enjoyed a fairly benevolent standard of living. Knowledge of daily life among the Maya from archaeological remains is supplemented by observations made by the Spaniards among the Postclassic Maya. Father Landa – a generous observer when he saw things in the Maya he approved of – praised greatly the hospitality shown to all strangers (outside of war), and the way Maya farmers helped each other at planting time. He also noted that the Maya washed frequently – unlike any *conquistador* – and loved fine scents, decorating houses with 'very curious and well-worked' bouquets of flowers and herbs. In many palace complexes there are sweat baths (*temazcal*), a Maya tradition that survives today. The Maya enjoyed lavish celebrations, at which men, above all the élite, drank themselves into infinity on fermented chocolate, a kind of mead called *balché*, or *pulque*, made from the maguey cactus. This relentless drinking was an inseparable part of celebration, but also had mystical significance; stranger still, intoxicants were also taken in the form of enemas. They were among the world's first smokers, using raw tobacco that made a much stronger drug than modern tobacco. Ideas of beauty were distinctive: a high, sloping forehead was a mark of aristocracy, and babies' heads were placed in a kind of wooden clamp during the first months of life to induce it. Teeth filed to points were attractive in women, as were cross-eyes, to encourage which small balls were tied to girls' heads, dangling over their noses. Warriors were elaborately tattooed.

Despite its wars, Maya society continued expanding through the Classic era, and the 8th century saw a leap in population and a new wave of settlement-building in central and northern Yucatán. Population estimates of Maya 'cities' have regularly been revised upwards: now widely accepted are figures of the scale of 70,000 for Palenque or Calakmul, 60,000 for Tikal, 25,000 for Uxmal. The total may have been over ten million, much more than the same land has supported since then.

Religion, Mythology and the Stars

The Maya had many gods and complex beliefs, but they were all based in one mythology and vision. An essential source on all Maya myths is the *Popul Vuh*, the 'council book' of the Quiché Maya of Guatemala, written down after the Conquest in

Quiché but with the Latin alphabet, and discovered by a Spanish priest, Francisco Ximénez, in the 18th century. There are many differences of detail, but the basic elements of the *Popol Vuh* stories have been traced in every area of Maya culture.

The Maya believed there are three levels of existence, the heavens, the middleworld that we inhabit, and the dark underworld, *Xibalba*. The central creation myth begins with 'everything in suspension, everything in calm, in silence' in the featureless primordial sea, and only the two creator-gods, called Tepeu and Gucumatz in the *Popol Vuh* but translated as **First Mother** and **First Father** from Classic inscriptions (Maya myths prefer pairs to single figures, and tend to include male and female principles). They create the universe several times. In the first creation the gods create the animals, but find that they do not praise or nurture them. They next create men out of mud, but they are too soft and dissolve in water. They then make men of wood, but they are too stupid. In their anger the gods send in a great flood, and the wood-men run into the trees, becoming the monkeys. In the fourth creation, this one, the gods make men of maize, which satisfies them.

The beginning of this final creation is the central era of Maya myth, when the story of the **Hero Twins** (*see* p.34) takes place. In Classic-era versions, once the Maize Gods have been resurrected at the Ball Court by their own sons, they grow to adulthood and awaken three sleeping old gods, two of whom, the **Paddler Gods**, take the Maize Gods in a canoe across the primordial sea to the place of creation. There they rise up out of a crack in the back of a Cosmic Turtle, and direct the old gods to set down three stones as the first 'Hearth of Creation' at the centre of the new universe; 542 days after that they finish their work by sending different gods to set up the four sides of the new creation and raise up the great world-tree the *wakah-kan* (*yaxché* in Yucatec), between them, to separate the heavens from the earth and form a central axis of the universe. The cosmos having been centred, creation could begin.

In the Long Count calendar the laying-down of the stones was held to have taken place on a date corresponding to 3114 BC, on 13 August, and the raising of the tree in 3112 on 5 February, two dates (give or take a few days) which always had tremendous significance for the Maya. In their book *Maya Cosmos* the late Linda Schele and David Freidel argued convincingly that this image of a world-tree corresponds to the shape of the Milky Way as it moves through the night sky, as seen from Maya territory in mid-August and early February. The three setting-stones represent the belt of Orion, and are still represented in the three hearthstones that are a part of the cooking fires in many Maya homes – a typical Maya transition in scale from the intimately domestic to cosmic vastness in one leap. Obviously, these observations were not actually made in 3114–12 BC, but they could be confirmed each year in the Classic era.

As the prime axis of existence the world-tree is the principal conduit between this world, the heavens and *Xibalba*, and the centre of the four cardinal points (*bacab*, *bacabob* in Yucatec), each one of which is associated with a specific colour and different cosmic forces: east (red), south (yellow), west (black) and north (white). The *ceiba* (silk-cotton tree) was held to symbolize the *wakah-kan* and represent spiritual powers. At the same time, the idea of the world-tree, often shown crossed by a bar or a vision serpent representing the Paddler Gods' canoe, means that the cross is as much a Maya as a Christian symbol, something that disconcerted the Spanish missionaries greatly and has caused enormous confusion ever since.

Playing Ball with the Lords of Death

The era of myth at the dawn of the current creation is the realm of the 'Hero Twins', another Maya pair, called Hunahpu and Xbalanqué in the *Popol Vuh* but probably Hun-Ahau and Yax-Balam in the Classic era. They have many adventures, but their central story begins with an earlier set of twins, Hun-Hunahpu and Vucub-Hunahpu. They are great ballgame-players, and play so continuously that they disturb the Lords of Death below the ground. The Lords summon these elder twins down to Xibalba, where they defeat them in a ballgame and kill them. The decapitated head of Hun-Hunahpu is hung in a tree, until a daughter of one of the Lords of Death, defying her father, goes to look at it. The skull spits in her hand and impregnates her. Fleeing from her father's rage the princess, Ixquic, runs from Xibalba into the Middleworld and takes refuge with the first twins' mother, in turn giving birth to the Hero Twins.

As they grow up, their grandmother, mindful of the elder twins' fate, hides their ballgame equipment, but Hunahpu and Xbalanqué make a deal with a rat to show it to them, and become dedicated ballplayers. Like their father and uncle they disturb the Lords of Xibalba, who summon them downstairs. The twins play the ballgame continually with the Lords of Death for days, while each night the Lords submit them to a series of tests. To their fury, the fearless twins outwit them every time, until the Lords decide to burn them. Hunahpu and Xbalanqué, though, are two steps ahead, and instruct two seers to tell the Lords to dispose of the twins' remains in a special way. The twins then go along with the Lords' next trick and jump into a flaming pit.

The Lords of Xibalba, following the seers' instructions, grind the twins' bones into dust and cast them into a river. A few days later, the twins revive with the faces of fish. They return to Xibalba disguised as wild carnival dancers, and perform all kinds of amazing feats, including decapitating and reviving each other. So excited are the Lords by this dance they beg to be killed and revived themselves. The twins naturally oblige, but do not revive them – thus triumphing over the Lords of Death. They then revive their own father and uncle, Hun-Hunahpu and Vucub-Hunahpu, who are buried beneath the Ball Court of Xibalba. In the *Popol Vuh* Hunahpu and Xbalanqué leave them beside the Ball Court to be honoured for ever after, but in the Classic myth they are reborn as the Maize Gods, who go on to create our universe (see p.33).

The story of the Twins is full of archetypically Maya ideas of regeneration after death, and of a son regenerating his own father. Another striking feature of the myth is that the twins defeat their enemies by wit and cunning, never brute force.

The movement of the stars is of course cyclical, and this was only one of many endlessly repeated cycles that the Maya saw in the universe. With a certain sense of ecological insecurity characteristic of Native American religions, they conceived creation not as stable but as requiring regular human intervention to sustain it and guarantee the cycle of regeneration. The gods were not simply almighty beings, for gods and men were mutually dependent: the gods created humans to praise 'and nurture them' because they needed to as well as wanted to. Hence the importance of sacrifice. The gods sent humanity life-giving rain; humans gave sustenance to the gods in offerings of food and, above all, blood. Maya religion was very physical, and fluids – semen, spit, blood – were considered to have great power.

Gods and spiritual forces were also multifaceted and contradictory, and could be benevolent or threatening at different times: 'God loves me' is not an idea the Classic Maya would ever have thought they could rely on. Contact between men and supernatural beings and forces was also possible, and unavoidable, at all kinds of levels. The three elements of existence, if often seen as separate 'levels', sometimes appear more like parallel planes, with only thin barriers between them. In the Maya conception, the whole world is alive: every part of the environment, animate or inanimate, possessed some degree of 'soul' or spiritual energy, and certain places, such as caves or mountains, were particularly important as points of contact with the Otherworld. The world was full of such power points and places. For example, the giant caverns of the Yucatán were naturally seen as the very gates of *Xibalba*.

Maya religion was essentially shamanistic, focused around making mystical contact with the gods and conjuring up supernatural forces to the community's aid via these power points. Hence the enormous importance of the *ahau*, the great shaman of the city and in his own person the community's link to the Otherworld, who became, in ritual, a form of the world-tree itself. It was essential for the very continuity of the city that the *ahau* and his lineage performed the central rituals, and above all gave their own blood, for royal blood was the most powerful sacrifice of all. In blood-letting rituals, royal women passed cords spiked with thorns through their tongues, while the *ahau* – and sometimes other members of his family and *sahalob* nobles – made cuts in his penis and other parts of the body. Strips of bark paper were inserted into the cuts to soak up the blood, and with them attached the *ahau* danced in an ecstatic trance in which he made contact with his ancestors – another instance of the son regenerating the father – and the gods. Apparently, as in mystical rites elsewhere in the world, they felt no pain (and there's no record of what was done to bind the wounds). At the end of the dance, the paper strips were burnt amid clouds of incense to carry the blood to the gods. The same rituals also included the sacrifice of prisoners, who ideally needed to be royal captives from other cities.

Closely associated with these beliefs is the image of the **Vision Serpent**, a two-headed creature shown held by or at the feet of an *ahau* in many Classic-era stelae, and an obsessive image in cities such as Uxmal. This was a conduit from this world to the Otherworld and the gods, which the *ahau* 'opened up' through his trance. In some cases it appears that men actually danced with live snakes. Another aspect of the Maya conception of the soul is the idea that everyone has a 'spirit companion', called a *way*. In ritual dancing, it was believed that people could actually become their *way*, often seen as an animal or mythological beast.

These shamanistic rituals required a suitable space, and the creation of such spaces was one of the Mayas' central activities. As Octavio Paz noted, pre-Columbian traditions were fed by a strong formal sense of order. Underlying much of religion was a desire to maintain order in the universe and so keep it safe for human habitation, against a tendency for it to sink back into primeval chaos. If the gods were regarded as having 'centred' the universe at the moment of creation, Maya builders sought to repeat the same act time and again, in structures that mirrored directly the cosmic order. Hence the sometimes astonishingly intricate alignments of major buildings with the movements of stars and planets, and the often rigid, rhythmic geometry of Maya cities. Mesoamericans – and the Maya above all – were obsessive city-builders because the 'centring' of a community around a ceremonial core was seen as essential for settled life. Maya temples were built as mountain-like pyramids or with entrances like mythical monsters not simply as symbols but because they actually took on the powers of their natural models, as sacred objects in themselves. In the same way that caves or trees could be points of contact with the Otherworld, so too could power points be created, and the dedication rituals of a temple – bringing it 'alive' with spiritual forces – were vital moments in sustaining a community and linking it to the general pattern of creation.

02 The Maya | Religion, Mythology and the Stars

Within this overall religious scheme there was room for a varied pantheon of gods, seen as divine energies with more than one earthly manifestation. In the Postclassic Yucatán **Itzamná**, inventor of writing and god of medicine, was the foremost god, while his wife **Ixchel** was the most important female deity, goddess of fertility, childbirth and weaving. Another god prominent in the dry north was the long-nosed **Chac**, god of rain and lightning. Palenque had its own set of patron-gods, the 'Palenque Triad'. As good polytheists, the Maya had no problem in absorbing alien gods. In the Early Classic the central Mexican war god **Tlaloc** was imported from Teotihuacán, and in the Postclassic the Mexican feathered-serpent god **Quetzalcoatl** was introduced into the Yucatán with the name **Kukulcán**. Legends across the Maya lands referred to Kukulcán as a historical figure, but his image also blended in with the older Maya concept of the Vision Serpent. As a god Kukulcán became the centre of a major cult in Postclassic Yucatán, and the focus of a hereditary caste of priests.

The Calendar and Numbers

If the Maya marked out space, they also marked out time. Seen as a series of repetitive cycles, for the Maya it was a dimension almost as solid as physical space, just as much a part of the structure of the universe. They observed and recorded the passage of time and the movements of the sun and stars obsessively, and their calendrical, astronomical and mathematical knowledge, gained through enormous collective effort (the Maya records of the movement of Venus were based on observations made over 384 years, all with the naked eye or only primitive instruments) is one of the most remarkable features of Maya civilization. Each phase within the calendar was associated with different omens and auguries, and the periods at the end of the main cycles and the beginning of a new one were thought unstable, and marked by ceremonies as important as those to dedicate a temple.

The calendar was expressed in the Maya bar-and-dot numbering system. It uses only three symbols, a dot for one, a bar for five and a shell symbol, often more like a bean, for zero (the Maya being, with the Arabs, the only peoples to have invented the concept of zero). Larger numbers were calculated on a vigesimal basis, in multiples of 20. Whereas our numbers increase in value by a factor of ten from right to left (as in 1,234), Maya numbers were written in vertical columns, increasing by a factor of 20 from bottom to top. So, in a column of numbers (see p.38), if the bottom row is two dots above a bar this means seven, in the next row up three dots indicates 3 x 20 = 60, a five bar in the next row means 5 x 400 = 2,000, and two dots in the next line means 2 x 8,000 = 16,000. The total number corresponds to 18,067. Taking 20 and not 10 as a base means this system moves rapidly into very large numbers.

The Maya had three different calendar cycles. The simplest was the 260-day **Short Count** or *tzolkin*, believed to be of Olmec origin and the oldest Mesoamerican calendar. This combines numbers from one to 13 (seven, nine and 13 were special numbers for the Maya) with a sequence of 20 day-names, as in *1-Imix, 2-Ik* and so on. Once the first 13 is completed the sequences are out of step, and it takes 260 days for the same number-day combination to come round again. The *tzolkin* cycle intermeshes with the *haab* cycle or 365-day year. It is also called the 'vague year', because it does not allow for the fact that the solar year does not correspond to 365 days (the reason we have leap years); Maya astronomers were aware of this but seem to have disregarded it. The *haab* year is divided into 18 months of 20 days each.

*Glyphs for the 18 months in the 365-day count, and the **uayeb**, the 'unstable' five days at the end of a year*

This left five 'loose' days at the end of a year, the *uayeb*, a time thought unlucky and full of potential dangers. Hence, if a day in our calendar has three identifiers in a year (Thursday, 14 May), a Maya day has four, such as 5 *cauac* 11 *yax* (*tzolkin* number, *tzolkin* name, number in a *haab* month, name of the *haab* month). It takes 52 vague years or 18,980 days for any combination of all four elements to come round again. This 52-year cycle is known as the **Calendar Round**, and was common to all Mesoamerican cultures. To this day elements of it, such as the *tzolkin*, are still used by the Highland Maya and other indigenous communities.

The limitation of the Calendar Round was that, with only a 52-year cycle, it had no way of differentiating between events in successive cycles, making dating events through the centuries impossible. The Maya compensated with their most awesome exercise in mathematics, the **Long Count** calendar. Since the oldest known Long Count date is from non-Maya Chiapa de Corzo, it seems likely it was first invented by an earlier culture, but it was only the Maya who fully used and developed it, and then only in the Classic era. In the Long Count (sometimes called the Initial Series), 20 *kins* (days) make up one *uinal* (month). Eighteen *uinals* make a 360-day *tun* or year. The system then goes back to 20: so 20 *tuns* make a *katun*, and 20 *katuns* a

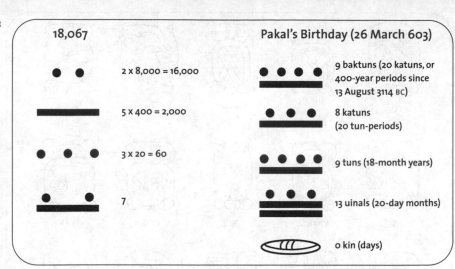

The Maya numbering system, using columns of bars and dots to represent numbers and dates.

baktun, or close to 400 conventional years. The *baktun* is the largest multiple usually written, but there are plenty more available, into infinity. A period of 13 *baktuns* (around 5,200 years) represents a **Great Cycle**, of enormous importance in the movement of time. According to the 'Thompson Correlation', established by Sir Eric Thompson and now almost universally accepted, the current Great Cycle began on or near 13 August 3114 BC, also the date of the current creation of the earth. All dates in historical time therefore fall within it. This is why it is possible to date Classic-era monuments with such precision: so many were rigorously inscribed with Long Count dates. The ending of a *katun* was particularly important, an occasion for ceremonies and blood-letting rituals to ensure the wellbeing of the city in the new era.

With their several multiples, Long Count dates were written in columns of five numbers or more. The day on which the great Lord Pakal of Palenque was born was 9.8.9.13.0 into the Great Cycle, or 26 March AD 603 (*see* above). The calendar also made it possible for Maya scribes to place mythological events and prophecies within unimaginable caverns of time, with calculations of baroque intricacy. A stela at Cobá recording the current creation places it in a cycle that amounts to some 41 thousand, million, million, million, million years. How much the Maya believed in these immense wheels within wheels is uncertain, but they served to express the vastness of the universe. Another feature of the Long Count is that the present Great Cycle is due to end on 23 December 2012. New Agers with an interest in the Maya predict something drastic for that day. It could be a whole new cycle of creation. Optimists can draw consolation from the fact that the combination of calendrical elements is so complex (since the Long Count was always used in association with the Calendar Round, and there are other factors such as the movements of Venus to be taken into account) that establishing one set of omens for the date seems near impossible.

Maya Warfare

Ideas of Maya warfare are another area where accepted notions have been revised several times over. For Maya cities warfare was a religious imperative. Waging war was an essential proof of the continuing power, physical and supernatural, of an *ahau* and his followers, and vital to secure royal captives to use as sacrifices. However, it is clear the Maya also went to war for more conventional reasons: to grab their neighbours' lands, wealth and sources of tribute. A successful warrior-state gained in vassals and allies, and grew rich from the inflow of tribute; a ferocious *ahau* like Bird-Jaguar IV of Yaxchilán almost obsessively proclaimed his own victories and prowess in battle on monuments and inscriptions around his city. Conversely, a defeat like those of Calakmul in 695 or Palenque in 711 could lead to a collapse in prestige and support, so that a city could rapidly become impoverished.

Early Maya wars seem perhaps to have been quite ritualized, and often to have ended once one side felt it had taken enough captives to be considered the winner, prestige being more important than taking territory. The limitations of Maya agriculture also made it difficult to maintain armies for any length of time. Over time, though, wars clearly became more bitter and more destructive. They intensified in number and their consequences in the Late Classic, especially with the struggle between **Tikal** and **Calakmul** and their many allies, almost as titanic a conflict in the Classic Maya world as that between Rome and Carthage in the ancient Mediterranean. In 562 a massive defeat of Tikal by an alliance of Calakmul, Caracol and Naranjo established Calakmul as the most powerful state in the Petén; then, from about 650 a resurgent Tikal challenged this ascendancy with a see-saw series of wars that culminated in the victory of 695, which left Calakmul grievously wounded. After 700, as Classic Maya civilization reached its peak in wealth and population, conflicts continued to multiply in many areas, above all along the Usumacinta and in the Petén, an intensification in warfare that was clearly linked to the imminent Maya Collapse (*see* p.42). It also appears that conflicts in the south were an important factor in causing groups from defeated cities to migrate northwards to new cities such as Uxmal and Chichén Itzá.

All these wars took place within the overall context of Maya belief, and attacks were often timed to coincide with movements of Venus. The intensification of warfare led to 'revenge wars', as a dynasty avenged the humiliation of an ancestor, and placed strains on Classic kingship, causing some *ahauob* to relinquish significant power to their nobles. The history of the Classic Maya reveals a web of intrigue, alliances and betrayal as intricate as anything in Renaissance Italy.

The Ballgame

Centuries before the invention of professional soccer, the Maya already knew all about sport as a representation of broader dramas. The Mesoamerican ballgame was played by the Olmecs and has been traced in Archaic-era settlements in Oaxaca, making it older than pyramids or temples. It is found in every one of the region's ancient cultures. As the story of the Hero Twins shows (*see* p.34), it was charged with meaning: in a world where everything was laced with omens and cosmic powers, it represented a chance to defy the forces of destiny. In Maya cities, ball courts were at the heart of the network of power points that formed the city's ceremonial core.

No one knows exactly how it was played. In general, there were two main types of ball court in Mesoamerica. The most normal Classic-era Maya ball court is relatively small, with sloping parallel banks either side of a flat central channel. It was probably played by only two opposing players, or perhaps in doubles or threes. Scoring was probably a matter of getting the ball out of the opponent's end of the court, and it was also essential not to let the ball touch ground in the central channel, although it could be bounced off the sides. In all forms of the ballgame, players could not touch the ball directly with hands or feet: instead, they had to use shoulders, backs, buttocks and especially hips. They wore thick leather helmets, pads and belts to protect them as they threw themselves around the court, but injuries must have been common. In the later, central-Mexican variant of the game the ball court is much bigger, with flat sides and large stone rings jutting out from the middle of each side. It was probably played between teams of seven, with scoring a matter of getting the ball through one of the rings. This version of the game was introduced into the Maya area in the Terminal Classic, and is represented by the greatest court of them all, the Great Ball Court of **Chichén Itzá**.

Yet another endless subject for debate is whether defeat always meant death for the loser. It seems possible the game was played both as sport and solemn ritual. It is certain, though, that ball courts were also places of sacrifice. Held to represent the crack in the Cosmic Turtle through which the Maize Gods emerged to begin creation, they were among the gateways to *Xibalba*. Several Classic-era images, such as the hieroglyphic stairs at Yaxchilán, show an *ahau* playing the game with the heads of captives. Royal prisoners were possibly brought to the ball court for one last combat. Whether they could go free if they won is unknown.

Art and Architecture

Maya large-scale architecture is intensely theatrical. The role of major buildings as symbolic, sacred spaces, continually reproducing cosmic structures and 'mimicking' natural features, meant that they were often more than anything giant stages for the performance of public ritual. As hot weather architecture, too, the spaces they enclosed – plazas, patios – could be as important as the buildings themselves. Behind the awe-inspiring façades, rooms and interiors could be surprisingly plain.

The veneration of the *ahau* also made large parts of Maya cities giant monuments to their rulers. One consequence of this was the practice of building on top of existing buildings. *Ahauob* felt it necessary to continue the work of their forefathers and demonstrate their own sacred powers by commissioning their own monuments. Temples were built next to other temples, and pyramids built over existing ones, sometimes only completed a few decades earlier.

Maya building techniques were a mixture of the simple and the sophisticated. Most structures were built up by amassing together crude rubble work with a simple form of concrete, which was then clad in smooth or elaborately carved facings in stone or stucco. A characteristic feature was the 'Maya arch', a flat-sided upturned V topped by a flat coping stone. The Maya never discovered the true arch, and the rooms that could be built with the Maya arch, if sometimes long, were narrow. The builders of Chichén Itzá created larger spaces by placing Maya arches on top of pillars, but these were unstable, and have all collapsed. Also, the Maya arch could only support a certain amount of weight, which is why the Maya were never able to build true buildings of more than one storey. The apparently multi-storey buildings they did produce were created by building up solid masses at the back to support the upper floors, slightly pyramid-style. Maya-arch roofs could support a 'roof comb', monumental stone screens that rose out of the top of buildings, clad in carved stucco. One feature that has been lost is that buildings were bright coloured: walls were mostly painted red, and carvings accented in brilliant blues and yellows.

Temples and pyramids are the most famous Maya buildings, but élite residential complexes have been identified. The **Palacio** at **Palenque** is the most famous and complete Maya palace, but there are many others, especially at **Sayil**, **Kohunlich** and **Comalcalco**. Most follow a similar pattern, with small rooms around connecting patios. Much of court life went on in the open air in these patios, some, where traces of food preparation have been found, the domain of servants. Again, a major feature that can no longer be appreciated is their colour: the irreplaceable Bonampak murals are the only substantial surviving wall paintings (except, maybe, for murals recently found at Palenque), and leave you breathless as you think what might have been.

What most homes of humbler people were like can be deduced without any archaeological knowledge. Look in any Yucatán village and you can see examples of the *na*, the stick and palm-leaf hut that has housed ordinary Maya people throughout history, surrounded by a *jacal*, a family enclosure for cooking, keeping animals and other daily tasks. Cities or not, Maya centres were not orderly urbanizations: instead, they were mixtures of clusters of *nas*, stone buildings, fruit gardens, open spaces and *milpas* straggling into the forest. Nor were they all uniform, for there were some with a concentrated core within a perimeter wall, like **Becán**, and others spread over a wide area, like **Cobá** or **Dzibanché**. Some – notably **Kohunlich** and **Dzibanché** – have a high number of small stone buildings, suggesting, surprisingly, that even non-aristocrats may have lived in them. Maya builders deployed their techniques with great ingenuity and variety, and could build in brick (**Comalcalco**) or out of a mountainside (**Toniná**). Some of the most distinctive styles (which overlapped) are outlined on p.42.

As well as buildings, another feature of most cities was the stela or standing-stone. Elaborately carved with reliefs and inscriptions, they formed the historical and ceremonial record of a city. Stelae are common in most southern cities, but much less so in the north. If much Maya architecture has a geometrical simplicity, Maya carving often abhors a vacuum, covering surfaces with entangled shapes.

Maya public art and architecture stresses the awesome, but another element in Maya art is that 'genres' are not separated, and it's possible to find details of ordinary life shown alongside imposing cosmic rituals (very noticeable at Bonampak). Images of daily life are most often seen on smaller objects, especially ceramics. Vases were painted with scenes of Maya eating, smoking, writing and receiving guests, as well as mythology and ceremony. Separate mention is owed to the **Jaina figurines**, clay figures that were placed in graves on **Isla Jaina** off the coast of Campeche. Superbly vivid and naturalistic, they depict every part of Maya society, and include a wider range of images of women than any other type of Maya art.

The Terminal Classic and Chichén Itzá

The greatest Classic cities – Palenque, Calakmul, Tikal – were all in the Petén and the Usumacinta valley. It used to be thought northern Yucatán was scarcely inhabited before about 800, when southern migrants supposedly arrived to found Morley's 'New Empire'. Modern research has indicated that in fact there was a high level of settlement in the north throughout the Classic era, with major centres such as **Dzibilchaltún** and **Cobá**, which was linked to Calakmul. It is true, though, that the

Distinctive Styles of Maya Architecture

Petén: A 'root style' of Maya architecture, out of which later styles developed. Centrepieces of Petén cities are pyramid-platforms built up in horizontal layers, often with rounded corners, decorated with stucco masks, stelae and roof combs. Pyramids are often grouped in 'acropolises', with a 'triad' of one huge and two smaller pyramids forming a plaza open on one side.

Puuc: Uxmal and the Puuc cities have the most refined of all Maya architectural styles, with an elegant, very 'modern' sense of geometry and a dynamic contrast between plain walls and carved friezes. Buildings that appear abstract in form 'mimic' humbler structures: the small drum pillars or 'colonnettes' at the base of walls represent the stick walls of a basic *na*, and roof friezes often have a line of moulding (an *atadura* or binding) that represents the ropes around a thatched roof.

Chenes: In the Chenes region of Campeche extravagant carved decoration takes over entire façades of buildings. Temple entrances are made into the mouths of giant gods and cosmic beasts.

Río Bec: The most theatrical of Maya styles. The Río Bec cities of southern Campeche have tower-like pyramids with near-vertical false staircases on their main façades. They were never actually meant to be climbed (there was an easier access at the back) but they increased the temples' awesomeness for the crowds below.

200 years after 700 witnessed an effervescence of Maya culture in the north, in what is known as the 'Terminal Classic', with a rapid growth of cities from **Uxmal** and the **Puuc** hills – with few settlements before 700 – through the **Chenes** to the **Río Bec**. This produced some of the greatest Maya architecture, notably at Uxmal.

Around the same time, a new community appeared in the Yucatán: **Chichén Itzá**. Chichén's Mayan-ness is one of the oldest debates for Mayanists. The first visitors to the site immediately noted the architectural differences between it and other Maya cities, and its similarities to central Mexican styles. It used to be fairly accepted that the larger, 'new' part of Chichén was built by an alien people called the Toltecs, who invaded the Yucatán after their capital of Tula, north of Mexico City, was overthrown around the year 1000. They were said to have created a hybrid 'Toltec-Maya' culture, and in idealistic visions of the Maya were held responsible for bringing bloodthirsty practices such as mass sacrifice to the Yucatán. By the time of the Conquest, legends told that Chichén's founders had been led by a great king called Kukulcán; however, the same figure turns up as coming to lead the Quiché Maya, far to the south, in the *Popol Vuh*, and Kukulcán-the-mythical-king obviously blended in with the Mexican serpent-god of the same name. Later, some theories claimed, another alien people called the Itzá followed the Toltecs, and took over the city in its final years.

This image has been comprehensively challenged. The argument is still not over, but investigations have traced 'Mexican' influences at Chichén ever further back in time and stressed the continuity in its history, and it now appears to have always been a mixed community, in which Mexicans and Maya lived side by side (*see* p.224).

Chichén was very different from earlier Maya cities. Instead of a single *ahau* it had a collective government called a *multepal*, with power rotated between the heads of several lineages. This enabled it to mobilize greater resources and gave it greater flexibility than its neighbours and rivals. After defeating Cobá in about 860, Chichén dominated the Yucatán with few challengers for nearly a century, becoming one of few Maya cities semi-acknowledged as a regional 'capital'.

The Maya Collapse

Classic Maya civilization reached an opulent peak during the 8th century, with a boom in population and building in the south, at the same time as the great late flowering of the Terminal Classic was developing in the Yucatán. Then, over the next 150 years, city after city ceased to build, gave up marking the major ceremonies, and was abandoned to be reclaimed by the trees. Archaeologists trace the irregular fall of the Classic Maya by the last dates recorded in the Long Count calendar: 795 at Bonampak, 799 at Palenque, 810 at Calakmul, 879 at Tikal.

The 'Maya Collapse' is one of the great enigmas of history, and there are theories to explain it for all tastes (including extraterrestrials). Some stress the effects of warfare, others climate change and overpopulation, others rebellion by the Maya masses. But most evidence suggests a spiralling combination of disasters.

With their thin soils and irregular water supplies, the Maya lands are an ecologically delicate and not naturally highly productive area, and their productivity had been stretched to the maximum. Population had grown rapidly, and studies indicate that by the late 8th century it had reached, or exceeded, the limit the land could support. Forensic-archaeological excavations undertaken at Copán in Honduras show strong evidence of malnutrition among the lower classes and even the élite at the end of the Classic era. As food ran short, overused land became less productive, and farmers extended slash-and-burn *milpas* further and further into the forest – accelerating soil erosion, and ultimately reducing the amount of usable land. It was really no surprise the 'Collapse' came so soon after the greatest years of many centres, for with the peak in population and wealth other things peaked as well – the demands placed on the land, the number of aristocrats, warriors and scribes who expected to be kept in luxury, the effort peasants were required to give over to building temples and palaces – stretching the 'cosmic bargain' between the élites and the Maya masses to the limit. Strong evidence also suggests that from the early 9th century there were periods of drought of unprecedented intensity, which in some places may have detonated all these crises-in-waiting and pushed Maya civilization to the edge.

As hardship grew, the peoples of the cities looked to their *ahauob* lords to provide answers and regain the favour of the gods. Rather than any new strategies, the most common response was the traditional one of raiding one's neighbours. Ever-more destructive wars were one more factor in the crisis. The Maya were also threatened by barbarians on the fringes, such as the Putún Maya, raiding up the Usumacinta and into the Petén. For a society that had tried to nurture and sustain a balance with the universe, to be hit by so many disasters to which the sacred *ahau* had no response was profoundly undermining. The individual stories of centres such as Palenque or Yaxchilán reveal that, as crises grew, once-all-powerful dynasties shared power with lesser noble houses to shore up their rule, but this was a double-edged sword. The fall in prestige of the *ahau* is visible in many Late Classic carvings, announcing a generalized disintegration of confidence in dynastic rule.

It now appears there were actually two, separate stages in the 'Collapse'. The first, most famous and most dramatic, was the fall of the *ahau* dynasties, which happened remarkably quickly, as the halt in monument building and the 'last dates' indicate. So much of Classic Maya civilization had revolved around the *ahauob*, that when they fell a great part of Maya art and written culture, the Long Count calendar and most of the caste of scribes and scholars went with them. Later communities still used glyph writing, but in a much more limited fashion. Classic-era vases frequently show scribes with bark books, of which there must have been hundreds, but none have survived. However, this breakdown at the top did not necessarily mean the whole community fell apart at the same time. Recent studies suggest sizeable numbers of people lived on around some centres for decades, and some noble lineages still built new temples and residences, as earlier lords had done. Nevertheless, environmental degradation did not let up, and, given the flimsy economic base of Classic Maya cities, without the dynastic core there was little to hold them together. The second, more gradual, but final stage of the Collapse followed over the next 200 years, as populations broke up, the survivors wandered off into the forest, and whole cities were entirely abandoned.

None of this can be stated with absolute certainty, but it appears likely the Maya were destroyed by a part-self-induced ecopolitical catastrophe, demonstrating that such things can happen – as has been picked up by modern writers comparing the Collapse with current ecological dangers. Millions died through wars, famine, revolts and drought. Huge areas were left nearly empty. The last known Long Count dates are from opposite ends of the Maya world, Uxmal (907) and Toniná in Chiapas (909).

The Postclassic Maya

The great collapse did not affect every area at the same time, and through the 9th century, as city after city crumbled in the south, centres in northern Yucatán continued to trade, build and fight each other. From about 900, though, the Collapse arrived there too, with a still more intense drought to add to the effects of overpopulation. The Puuc cities, always environmentally fragile, were the first to be abandoned, from around 930 onwards. Decline was never as drastic as in the south, and Chichén Itzá lingered on, but dwindled in size and wealth from 1000 to 1050.

Maya culture stayed semi-silent for some 200 years, until the minor revival of the Postclassic began around 1200. Confined to the north – in the south the Collapse was terminal – Postclassic culture was less sophisticated than that of the Classic Maya. In the calendar only the 52-year round was used. The northern cities had never had as many written inscriptions as those in the south, and after the collapse there were scarcely any, although Maya glyphs were still used in bark books. However, trade expanded, and it was in the Postclassic that the Maya began to work gold, copper and other metals, brought from Mexico or modern-day Colombia and Panama. From around 1350 there was an impressive growth in coastal trade centred on East Coast settlements such as **Tulum**, and one theory goes that had the Spaniards arrived 50 years later they would have found the Maya further advanced in a commercial-cultural renaissance, and harder to conquer.

Chichén Itzá seems to have survived as some kind of entity into the early Postclassic, for according to the Mayan chronicles written after the Conquest it was not finally overthrown until the 1190s, by newly founded **Mayapán**, last 'capital' of the Yucatán Maya and the last major Maya city. In style, Mayapán was based on Chichén, as if its builders sought to evoke former glories. It too had a type of *multepal* government, as the lords of Mayapán, the *Cocom* clan, were only first among equals among several *halach uinicob* or 'first men'. Here the Maya past enters conventional history, as events in the downfall of Mayapán were recent enough to be told to the Spaniards. Around 1440 the lineage of the High Priests, the *Xiu*, led a revolt against the *Cocom*, and the city fell apart. The *Cocom* withdrew to their lordship at Sotuta, the *Xiu* to theirs at Maní, and the Yucatán broke up into a patchwork of bickering chieftaincies.

History: Conquest and After

First Contact 46
The Conquest of the South 47
The Encomienda and the Cross:
  Colonial Society 49
Colonial Backwaters 51
Independence 52
The Caste War and the Talking Cross,
  1847-1901 54
The Empire and the Porfiriato 56
The Revolution, 1910-40 59
The Príato 62
Mexico since 2000 63

03

The Maya south of Mexico has remained very distinct from the rest of the country since the arrival of the Spaniards. Under Spanish rule the region was outside the Viceroyalty of 'New Spain' ruled from Mexico City: the Yucatán (meaning the whole of the peninsula, before its division into three states under Mexico) under its own administration; Chiapas as part of Guatemala. Both became part of an independent Mexican Republic out of economic convenience and as a result of a series of what were more-or-less accidents, while the Yucatán flirted with complete independence for years. Mexican history is full of statements that could end 'except in the south'. In the 20th century the Mexican Revolution, economic development and modern communications increasingly integrated the Yucatán states and Chiapas with the rest of the country, but the south remains in many ways a world apart.

First Contact

In February 1517 **Francisco Hernández de Córdoba** sailed with three ships and 110 men from Cuba, conquered by the Spaniards a few years earlier, to explore the unknown lands to the west. Driven south by a storm, they made the first Spanish landfall on or near the Mexican mainland at Isla Mujeres, where they saw statues that they took to be female figures – leading them to give it the name 'Island of Women' – and some gold ornaments. From there they followed the Yucatán coast to Kin Pech (Campeche) and, looking for water, put into the bay at Champotón, by the first river they had found. While on shore they were attacked by the warriors of the lord of Kin Pech, Moch-Cuouh. Many Spaniards were killed, Hernández de Córdoba himself was wounded, and they were forced to turn back. Nevertheless, this first news of the existence of monumental buildings, real cities and gold in the Americas was electrifying, both in Cuba and in Spain. The following year a second expedition set out under **Juan de Grijalva**, who landed on Cozumel and continued down the east coast to the Bahía de la Ascensión, passing, awestruck, the cliff-top temples of Tulum. Turning back, they retraced the coast westwards: after another clash with Moch-Cuouh at Champotón, they discovered the Laguna de Términos – which led them to think the Yucatán was an island – and the mouth of the river that now has Grijalva's name, before reaching the Panuco river in modern Veracruz. There they first encountered the Aztec Empire, which then dominated all of central Mexico, and saw a rich range of goods including precious stones, fine fabrics and gold and silver.

In February 1519 a third expedition left Cuba under **Hernán Cortés**, with 11 ships, cannon, 400 men and some 50 horses. They too landed on Cozumel, where they were approached by a group of Indians in canoes, from which a solitary figure ran toward them yelling *'Dios, Santa María y Sevilla'* ('God, Saint Mary and Seville'), to avoid being shot. This was **Jerónimo de Aguilar**, a Spanish priest who had been shipwrecked on the Yucatán coast in 1511, and who immediately became invaluable to Cortés as an interpreter. Ignoring the Yucatán and drawn west by tales of gold, Cortés sailed round the peninsula, avoiding Champotón, to land at Xicalango on the Laguna de Términos. The Spaniards defeated a local chieftain, and as part of the booty Cortés was given **La Malinche** (*see* p.48), the former princess who was to prove still more important than Aguilar in the events that followed. In April Cortés founded the first Spanish settlement on the mainland at Veracruz, from where within two years his pocket army would destroy the Aztec Empire and set in stone Spanish rule in the New World.

When the Apollo astronauts landed on the moon, they knew vastly more about where they were going, and had incomparably more back-up from home, than the first Spanish *conquistador* columns as they wandered into the Americas. The wild, greedy bravery involved in their epic journeys at times seems incomprehensible. Small bands of only a few hundred men – down-at-heel aristocrats or soldiers ready to gamble everything for wealth and glory – marching across completely unknown territories, they were frequently terrified. This atmosphere of panic was one element in the savage violence often used against native peoples who resisted.

The Conquest took place differently in the two main areas of Mayan Mexico, Chiapas and the Yucatán, a pattern that has continued ever since.

The Conquest of the South

The first part of the south conquered by the Spaniards was the Pacific plain of the Soconusco, the only part of the Maya lands dominated by the Aztecs, who had seized it to secure its fine-quality cacao In 1523, Cortés' troublesome and brutal lieutenant **Pedro de Alvarado** passed through on his way to conquer Guatemala. The following year another column, led by **Luis Marín** – and which included the great chronicler of the Conquest, Bernal Díaz – headed into Chiapas from Veracruz, and after skirmishes at Zinacantán and Chamula discovered the Valley of Jovel, where San Cristóbal de Las Casas now stands. They were entranced by the valley, pronouncing it an ideal site for a Spanish colony. The true conquest of Chiapas would be undertaken in 1528 by **Diego de Mazariegos**, who defeated the Chiapa, a non-Maya people who then inhabited the western valleys around modern Tuxtla Gutiérrez, and whose warriors supposedly flung themselves into the great gorge of the Sumidero rather than accept defeat. Mazariegos founded the first Spanish town in Chiapas, Chiapa de Indios (now Chiapa de Corzo) on the site of their former capital, and then Ciudad Real de Chiapa (San Cristóbal), a lonely outpost surrounded by Tzotzil Maya villages.

The Yucatán, by contrast, was strangely neglected for several years, while most *conquistadores* headed for the wealth of central Mexico. The Spanish Conquest functioned on a high-risk, semi-private enterprise basis. A noble or commander would secure a royal warrant to explore and conquer some uncharted territory. He himself, though (perhaps with other 'investors'), had to bring together the men and ships necessary and meet all their costs, with only the prospect of first pick of the spoils of conquest and an eventual title and salary as Governor-for-Life as recompense. No one showed much interest in the Yucatán, until at the end of 1526 **Francisco de Montejo** secured from Emperor Charles V the title of Governor and *Adelantado* (literally 'he who goes before', or 'first promoter') of the territory. Montejo was a minor noble from Salamanca in Castile, who had made himself rich in Cuba and Santo Domingo, and then served on the expeditions of Grijalva and Cortés before returning to Spain for some years. His 'fleet' reached Cozumel in September 1527 and landed on the Yucatán mainland at Xel-Ha – where tourists now snorkel in the lagoon – to found the first Spanish settlement next to the Maya town, calling it 'Salamanca de Xel-Ha' in honour of the Adelantado's birthplace. Leaving 50 men there, he then made a six-month expedition into the peninsula, meeting continual resistance and conquering no territory. Returning to Salamanca he found only ten men alive, the rest having gone down with disease, but met up with reinforcements sent from Santo Domingo. With them he sailed to Chetumal,

Guerrero and La Malinche: Two Sides of a Coin

Gonzalo Guerrero and Cortés' aide and mistress Malinche are two emblematic figures in the Conquest of Mexico. Guerrero was an ordinary seaman and soldier who was one of 13 Spaniards shipwrecked on the coast of Yucatán, probably somewhere near Tulum, in 1511. Most soon died as sacrifices, but two, Guerrero and the priest Jerónimo de Aguilar, were kept alive as slaves. Their luck began to improve when they came into the hands of Nacanchán, lord of Chetumal. Aguilar was only given fieldwork, but Guerrero made himself useful to his new lord, using his knowledge of European war to advise on tactics in inter-Maya conflicts. From a slave he became a trusted warrior, and married one of Nacanchán's own family, possibly his daughter. When Spanish ships were seen off the coast in 1519 and Aguilar urged that they should escape to find them, Guerrero refused to go, no matter how much the priest argued with him and warned he could lose his eternal soul. Condemned by Cortés as a traitor, he is thought to have played a decisive part in later Spanish defeats at Chetumal, Champotón and other battles in the Yucatán. He is believed to have died in about 1536, fighting the Spaniards in Honduras.

La Malinche, on the other hand (real name probably *Malintzín*), was a princess from Jalisco in west-central Mexico. Captured in war, she was made a slave and passed between owners in Yucatán and Tabasco before she was given to Cortés. She spoke Nahuatl and Yucatec, while Aguilar spoke Yucatec. Between them they gave Cortés a key to the Aztec Empire. Malinche's role went well beyond that of an interpreter, learning Spanish and being credited with advising Cortés on how to trick and defeat the Aztecs. She also had several children with the conqueror.

As symbols Guerrero and Malinche have been regarded very differently in modern Mexico, *machismo* playing an obvious part in the interpretations. A giant statue of Guerrero and his Maya family stands outside modern Chetumal, proclaiming the town as the *Cuna del Mestizaje* or 'cradle of racial mixing'. His decision to stay with his family is presented as a manly choice, a noble gesture of early multiculturalism. There are no monuments to La Malinche, although she does figure in *Cortés y La Malinche*, a powerful image by the great mural painter José Clemente Orozco. Traditionally she is Cortés' whore, selling herself for Spanish baubles. As the ultimate humiliation, she was discarded by Cortés when he went back to Spain to be made a *marqués* and marry a high-born Spanish woman. *Malinchismo* is part of the special terminology of Mexican nationalism, a contemptuous word used to condemn a supposedly uncritical acceptance of anything foreign.

In the motivations of the original individuals, though, there was plenty of ambiguity. According to Bernal Díaz, when Aguilar argued that they should go to meet Cortés, Guerrero answered, 'I have a wife and three children... you go with God, for I have tattoos on my face and holes in my ears [the marks of a Maya warrior]; what will the Spaniards say about me when they see me like this?', suggesting a fear of the consequences of returning, and a sense that he had just gone too far ever to go back. Malinche for her part was already a slave, and it appears that, baptized as 'Doña Marina' and accorded considerable respect, she was treated better by the Spaniards than she had been at many times in her life, certainly until Cortés left her. Either way, as figures of myth these two represent different sides of *mestizo* Mexico's very complex attitudes towards its origins.

where he was again defeated by the Maya, this time probably led by **Gonzalo Guerrero**, and from there down the coast to Honduras, establishing that the Yucatán was not an island. Then, accepting failure, he withdrew his surviving men and sailed back to more profitable service under Cortés in Tabasco.

At the end of 1531 the Adelantado Montejo, who still held 'exclusive rights' to the Yucatán, decided to try again, taking with him his illegitimate son, a tough young soldier also called **Francisco de Montejo**, *El Mozo* ('the boy'). They landed by the Champotón river – an essential source of water – and again met strong resistance, taking Campeche only after fierce battles during which the Adelantado himself was wounded. Montejo el Mozo then made one of the reckless marches that so often brought results for the Spaniards, leading a small detachment right across the peninsula to the ruins of Chichén Itzá, where he tried to found a Spanish 'capital'.

However, the Yucatán Maya lords, completely against the grain of their usual quarrelsomeness, offered concerted resistance, and the divide-and-rule tactics that had been so fruitful for Cortés failed to function. The Montejos were bottled up in Campeche and Chichén, their men began to desert them, and in 1534 they gave up, and withdrew. Once again, the Adelantado had gained no return from a very large investment, and he went back to serve as Governor of Honduras and, later, Chiapas.

In 1540 the Adelantado delegated his powers to El Mozo to have one more try. This time he had with him yet another **Francisco de Montejo**, *El Sobrino* ('the nephew', as the Adelantado was his uncle). In the interim the Maya had been weakened by disease – the Spaniards' most effective advance guard – and drought, and had fallen back into fighting against each other, with a bitter dispute between the *Cocom* and the *Xiu*. Nevertheless, initially they still gave effective joint resistance to the invaders. The Montejos again landed at Champotón and Campeche, fortunately finding that the belligerent old lord Moch-Cuouh had died, although they still had to fight off repeated attacks. From there Montejo el Sobrino struggled north to establish himself in the ruined Maya city of Ti'ho, where he was joined by El Mozo. They and their 200 men were then surrounded in a months-long siege, which reached its climax in June 1541 with frontal attacks by thousands of Maya, slashed down in ranks by gunfire, until one murderous day when Maya morale seemed to collapse, and their force began to break up. The Spaniards had thought themselves doomed, and took their survival as clear evidence of divine intervention. Shortly afterwards **Tutul Xiu**, Lord of Maní, came to the Spanish camp to accept Catholicism and the rule of the kings of Castile, thus breaking the Maya front. Disunity let the Maya down, and the local lords could be picked off one by one. Mérida was founded in the ruins of Ti'ho in January 1542 and, over the following year, Montejo el Mozo defeated the most important of the Maya lords, **Nachi Cocom** of Sotuta. By 1546 the Yucatán was considered sufficiently subdued for the Adelantado Montejo to return to take up his governorship, only to meet a major Maya revolt, which took months to overcome.

The Yucatán Maya had resisted the Conquest longer and more effectively than any other major pre-Columbian culture. Moreover, some Maya remained outside Spanish control for years to come. The Itzá kingdom on Lake Tayasal in the Guatemalan Petén had been visited by Cortés himself in 1525, when he passed through on his way to Honduras, but resisted all attempts to conquer it until 1697.

The *Encomienda* and the Cross: Colonial Society

Once a territory was under Spanish control, *conquistadores* were rewarded by means of the *encomienda* system, under which they were given lands and 'entrusted' (*encomendado*) with authority over all the Indians in an area, with the right to demand labour from them. In practice this gave near-absolute power, and there were many instances of Indians being worked to death. At the same time, churchmen were arriving in the colonies to carry out the 'spiritual conquest' of the American population. Different areas were allotted to different Catholic orders: the Yucatán to the Franciscans, Chiapas to the Dominicans. They began by building monasteries – Maní, Izamal and Sisal (Valladolid) in the Yucatán, San Francisco de Campeche, Santo Domingo in San Cristóbal in Chiapas – from which to spread out into the countryside.

Conflicts arose between the two 'arms' of the Conquest. Monks complained that *encomenderos* even begrudged their Indians the time to go to Mass. The new landed gentry argued back that all the priests wanted was for the Indians to work for them, on building churches and keeping them comfortable, although some priests, above all the Bishop of Chiapas, **Bartolomé de Las Casas** (*see* p.486), defended Indians with intense dedication. *Encomenderos* defied the Church and royal governors with violence. Neither the Spanish crown nor even the Church hierarchy necessarily sided with humanitarian priests, but Charles V had already decided more order was needed in his empire. *Encomiendas* were stripped of most of their political powers, and their owners compensated with hereditary estates. However, this still left them with immense power, and in backward areas – such as Yucatán and Chiapas – parts of the *encomienda* system persisted till the end of the colonial era. The Yucatán was to be governed as a separate *Audiencia*, only vaguely linked to the Viceroyalty of New Spain in Mexico, while Chiapas was to be a province of the Audiencia of Guatemala; in practice, each region was largely self-contained under the crown.

In most of Mexico these conflicts took place against a dramatic backdrop: the disappearance of the Indian. According to one estimate, there was an indigenous population of 25 million in Mexico, before the Spaniards arrived, while one of the lowest calculations gives 12 million. By the 1630s there were only some 750,000 left, a decline of at least 93 per cent. Bishop Las Casas claimed huge numbers were massacred or worked to death by the *conquistadores*, but few believe that even at their most brutal they could have been wholly responsible. As with the Maya Collapse centuries earlier, a complex of disasters built up. Agriculture throughout Mexico rested on a delicate balance: when Spaniards grabbed much of the best land for stock-raising or growing cash crops, this had a catastrophic effect on food production. Food itself was requisitioned by the new masters, and men were marched off to work in building or mines, robbing the fields of hands. The dwindling of the labour force was noted and laws issued against overexploitation, but numbers still fell and so African slaves were brought in. Of fundamental importance was disease. In its isolation, America had had few diseases. With the Europeans came measles, typhus, flu and above all smallpox, to all of which indigenous people had no resistance. One viceroy of Peru said that Indians stopped having children out of pure depression. The shrinking of indigenous America took place at different rates in each place, but together amounted to the greatest population collapse in world history. In Mexico, many Indian communities were confined to remote pockets, while great areas were taken over by an increasingly *mestizo*, mixed-race, society.

Except in the south. Once again, no one knows precisely why, but in the Yucatán and Highland Chiapas population loss, while significant, was far less acute, between 25 and 50 per cent. Diseases seem to have had less effect in the Yucatán woods and the Highlands. Of the greatest importance was the fact that in the south there was, as local *conquistadores* soon came to rue, 'no other wealth than the Indian'. To their immense frustration they realized they had drawn the short straw in the Conquest, and that in the Yucatán and Chiapas there were neither precious metals nor other great riches. After a while they accepted that their best source of wealth was simply to extract tribute in food and labour from the Indians. For this to be provided, Maya village farming had to continue, and with it much of the traditional way of life.

This had profound cultural consequences. Across Mexico, even many surviving Indian communities were gradually obliged to learn Spanish. In the south, many

Father Landa's Bonfire

Father Diego de Landa (1524–79), first head of the Franciscans in Yucatán and second bishop of the province, is responsible for a great deal of what we know and do not know about the Maya. In 1566 he wrote a 'report' for his religious superiors entitled *Relación de las Cosas de Yucatán* ('Account of the Affairs of Yucatán'), a painstaking account of every aspect of Maya life before the Conquest, based on his own acute observations and long conversations with (or interrogations of) Maya aristocrats. Rediscovered in the 19th century, it also contained information that provided the basis for any understanding of the Maya calendar and, later, the unravelling of the Maya glyphs. He also defended the Maya against *encomendero* abuses. However, it was the same Landa who as Provincial of the Franciscans learnt in 1562 that large numbers of the Maya, including many he had instructed in religion himself, were continuing 'idolatrous practices' in secret. Enraged, he organized a giant *auto-da-fé* in front of the monastery at Maní, at which 'idolaters' were beaten, humiliated and tortured to the point of death. He also brought together every Maya idol, pot or other artefact he could find and destroyed them all, and, as he wrote, 'we found a great number of books [written] in their letters, and because there was nothing in them but superstition and falsehoods of the devil we burnt them all, which had an extraordinary effect on [the people] and caused them great sorrow'.

Today, there are only four Maya manuscripts in existence. Mayanists never know whether to thank or curse the man in the same breath.

Maya had little contact with the colonizers much of the time, and the opposite happened: as Spaniards and 'Mexicans' continually complained, outside the towns even *mestizos* spoke Mayan languages to get by. Some Yucatán communities kept up their traditional chronicles, the books of *Chilam Balam*, in Yucatec but in Latin script, and sometimes the old Maya aristocracy continued to lead their communities, as *batabob* or headmen. Deprived of opportunities for trade, they became little richer than other villagers, but were still accorded great respect. In religion, there were severe penalties for lapses into 'idolatry', but the Church never had enough manpower to keep a constant control over the religious life of the rural Maya. This left plenty of room for the development of 'syncretic religion', the often bizarre mix of Catholic and Maya belief and ritual so characteristic of the south.

The Spanish Empire operated on a caste system, in which political status depended on both race and birth. In central Mexico, this tended to develop into something of a class society, with an important division between élite *criollos* (Mexican-born whites) and a lower class of *mestizos* and Indians. The south remained more colonial, with a major gulf between *ladinos* (all Spanish-speakers, white or *mestizo*) and a surviving Maya world with many traditions intact.

The great hubs of the *ladino* world and Spanish administration were the colonial cities. These followed a set plan, which was laid down in the *Leyes de Indias* of 1523: a rectangular grid running out from a central plaza, with a cathedral on the east side and a government palace next to it around the corner. This arrangement appealed to the methodical mind of Charles V. In the first two centuries after the Conquest, only whites were allowed to live in the central streets of each town. Outside of them were *barrios* reserved for black ex-slaves or *mestizos*, and beyond them were Indian settlements. A sharp division between Spanish-speaking towns and a Maya countryside appeared by both accident and design.

Colonial Backwaters

As the Conquest faded into memory, the Yucatán and Chiapas settled into their places among the less prominent parts of Spain's empire. A constant problem for the governors of the Yucatán was the continuing independence of the Itzá Maya in the

Petén. Spanish authority was even pushed back, for in 1636 a revolt forced the evacuation of Franciscan missions along the rivers of modern Belize, leaving a space later occupied by British pirates. Not until 1697 was Governor Martín de Urzúa able finally to conquer Tayasal. Other thorns in governors' sides were the pirates who had lodged themselves in Belize and the renowned buccaneer haunt of Tris, the Isla de Carmen on the Laguna de Términos. To resist them a 'castle' was built at Bacalar, and Campeche, attacked time and again, was given massive fortifications. Indians were still obliged to offer services to landowners and contributions to the Church, and were held subject to *ladinos* in many other ways. When this pressure became too great there were sporadic revolts, the largest in Chiapas in 1712 and Yucatán in 1761.

The pace of life accelerated a fraction in the 1760s, after King Charles III ascended the Spanish throne. New-broom governors were sent to distant provinces to modernize the administration. In colonial capitals like Mexico City wealthy *criollos* chafed at being subordinate to Spanish economic controls, and in towns like Mérida groups met to discuss 'advanced' ideas. Ironically, Charles III's reforms probably acted as a spur to opposition, irritating the *criollos* by interfering in their affairs while also giving them more awareness of the possibilities of independence.

Independence

Nationalist sentiments were only tentatively expressed until Napoleon conveniently kidnapped the Spanish royal family in 1808. This had a huge impact in central Mexico. *Criollos* demanded they be represented in the regency that took over government, but were resisted by Spanish-born *peninsulares*, who had monopolized power in the old colonial system. This argument among the wealthy was thrown into sharp focus in 1810 when **Father Miguel Hidalgo**, a free-thinking *criollo* priest in the town of Dolores, launched his *grito* ('cry'), calling on all Mexicans to throw off the inequalities of Spanish rule. It's unlikely he intended to launch a social upheaval, but a ragged army of poor *mestizos* and Indians flocked to join him, and massacred whites irrespective of origin in Guanajuato and Guadalajara. Faced with the prospect of a rebellion of the dispossessed, *criollos* and Spaniards drew together to resist the revolt, with bloody reprisals. Hidalgo was executed, and after King Ferdinand VII was restored to his throne in 1814 the rebels were worn down in a fierce guerrilla war.

Then, the situation was stood on its head once again. In 1820 radical army officers in Spain took over the government and issued a series of liberal decrees, against slavery and the power of the Church. Revolution was now coming from the centre of the Empire, so Mexican conservatives had a whole new motive for independence. In an extraordinary about-face the Mexican-born commander of the royal army, **Agustín de Iturbide**, made contact with the surviving guerrilla leaders and called on them as patriots to accept his authority in an independent Mexico. Quite naïvely, they agreed. Mexican independence, like that of much of Latin America, thus arrived branded with a profound ambiguity, a combination of revolt from below and a move by a colonial élite precisely to defend their privileges. Many still believed in monarchy and in 1822 Iturbide proclaimed himself Mexico's first 'Emperor'.

The south stood on the margins of these dramatic conflicts. In Chiapas politics were all but nonexistent until the Spanish Empire began to crumble around it. When they heard of Iturbide's new monarchy, the deeply conservative élite of San Cristóbal (then still Ciudad Real, the 'Royal City' of Chiapas) declared their intention to renounce the authority of Spain and Guatemala, and take Chiapas into Mexico. Their predominance in local affairs was opposed by the *ladinos* of the Soconusco and the growing town of San Marcos Tuxtla, who took up the cause of Guatemala or Chiapan independence. After ragged fighting, an equally disorderly referendum in 1824 decided that Chiapas was to be part of Mexico. In the Yucatán educated *ladinos* were more self-aware. When the vacuum appeared in government after 1808 a group of liberals called the **Sanjuanistas** (because they met in Mérida's church of San Juan) emerged to demand reform; then, after Ferdinand VII's restoration, local conservatives reasserted themselves through repression. As elsewhere, the situation was confused by the liberal coup in Spain in 1820. In late 1821, as news arrived of Iturbide's conversion to independence and it became clear Spanish power was collapsing, the Governor Marshal Echéverri himself called a meeting of important local citizens to discuss the Yucatán's response. It was decided to declare the Yucatán's sovereignty, with a grudging 'conditional' adhesion to Mexico. Then the last Spanish governor departed amid declarations of affection from all the leading figures in the peninsula, in one of the most peaceful transfers of power ever seen.

This was very atypical of the next 50 years in the peninsula and Mexico. Iturbide's 'Empire' lasted less than a year before it went down in the first of many coups. The political argument was generally described as being between Centralists, In favour of a strong Mexican state (frequently led by **General Antonio López de Santa Anna**), and Federalists. The former were normally seen as more conservative, and linked to the Catholic church. Some brave souls evoked the principles of the French Revolution, but many of these revolts and uprisings revolved as much around crude power conflicts between generals, local bosses and city élites. The political system was rudimentary, and in whole areas of rural Mexico the real system of power was *caciquismo*, the domination of administration, law and much else by leading landowners. The mass of the population had only walk-on parts in their disputes.

For most of the next century politics in Chiapas consisted of little more than squabbles between the leading families of San Cristóbal and Tuxtla, each of them looking for allies outside the state. The Yucatán, which still covered the whole of the peninsula, including the modern states of Campeche and Quintana Roo, had a much more spectacular history. Since many white Yucatecans regarded Mexico as almost as foreign as Spain, there was strong opposition to Centralism, but bickering also arose between Mérida and Campeche. Uprisings, coups and incidents sparked up all around the peninsula, and in 1838 a Federalist revolt against Mexican interference in Tizimín led to the Yucatán declaring its independence. This was the situation when John Lloyd Stephens (*see* p.24) arrived in 1840, finding it led by men who were aware of the Yucatán's limited prospects as an independent state but didn't know what else to do with it. In 1842 Santa Anna sent an army to bring the unruly province back under control, but after several battles and a siege of Campeche, the Yucatecan forces covered themselves in glory and were victorious. The dictator was obliged to accept a peace that left the Yucatán only very loosely linked to Mexico, which was soon fully occupied with the national calamity of the Mexican-American War.

If political life was chaotic, things also changed in other areas after independence. Most *ladinos* could agree that now the country was theirs it was necessary to develop it, and the obvious way to do so was by extending into the countryside the principles of the market and laissez-faire economics they had heard about from Europe and the USA. An argument emerged that has resounded ever since, as modernizers identified one special feature of Mexico, the village system of collective landholding, which had survived from pre-Columbian times, as an obstruction to progress. Landowners increasingly took over common lands. At the same time, since Indians had theoretically become equal citizens, they could also be taxed more than ever before. For Indians, then, conditions could get worse with independence.

The Caste War and the Talking Cross, 1847–1901

In 1841 John Lloyd Stephens wrote that he had never seen a people as accepting of 'the most abject submission' as the Yucatán Maya. This only shows how difficult it is to interpret Maya quietness. A few years later the Maya burst out of their placidity in the most organized, most far-reaching indigenous revolt anywhere in the Americas since the Conquest, and came within an inch of retaking their land for themselves.

Under Spanish rule Indians had never been allowed to have military weapons or serve as soldiers. The post-independence faction-fights, however, required cannon fodder, and some of the Yucatán's generals began recruiting among the Maya, in particular for the revolt of 1838 and the war against Santa Anna. They were promised remission of taxes and the money contributions paid to the Church, and guaranteed rights to common lands. Such was the contempt with which *ladinos* regarded Indians that they clearly felt they could say anything to them without any concern for delivering on their pledges. The Maya felt they had been lied to too often.

In January 1847, after one more political squabble, Maya troops in Valladolid ignored their officers and rioted, killing over 80 people and sending shock waves throughout the peninsula. It was noticed that Indian soldiers had not handed in their weapons after the wars, and rumours were heard of meetings between local *batabob*, especially **Cecilio Chi** of Ichmul and the highly respected **Jacinto Pat** of Tihosuco, and that the Maya had acquired more arms from traders in Belize, then British Honduras. One of the conspirators was executed, which, however, only provided the final provocation to action. On 30 July Chi and his men descended on Tepich, south of Valladolid, and murdered the entire *ladino* population, and more attacks followed immediately.

With the news that a *Guerra de Castas*, a 'Caste War' or race war, had begun, a wave of terror ran through *ladino* Yucatán. Vicious reprisals were taken even against the still-peaceful western Maya. The Yucatecan militias, however, were unable to hold back the revolt. Columns sent into the forest to find the rebel Maya were ambushed, and their paths were blocked, as they were picked off with machetes. Town after town was surrounded. *Ladino* Tihosuco was taken in October 1847, and Peto in February 1848. A peace was briefly negotiated with Pat that would potentially have freed the Maya from the most hated *ladino* impositions, but it fell apart amid distrust on both sides. In March the order was given to evacuate Valladolid, colonial capital of eastern Yucatán, after a two-month siege. Some 10,000 people were in the town – whites, *mestizos*, loyal Maya, troops and civilians of all ages – and it took them three days to reach safe territory, in desperate panic, as militia units collapsed and Maya guerrillas slaughtered a third of the column. Appalled, **Santiago Méndez**, Governor of the Yucatán, sent identical letters to Spain, Britain and the United States, offering sovereignty over the Yucatán to whichever country would save its civilized population from their fate. The USA, then still at war with Mexico proper, briefly showed interest, but decided against further involvement. Towns closer and closer to the capital fell to the Maya, and even Campeche was attacked, as *ladino* morale fell apart. Mérida was crowded with refugees, who were strung out along the road to Sisal, looking for any boat willing to take them to Cuba, Veracruz or anywhere else. At the end of May 1848 the new State Governor **Miguel Barbachano** wrote a proclamation ordering Mérida to be evacuated, but was unable to distribute it because the printers had already left.

Then the Maya went away. In one of the most extraordinary episodes in this whole drama, winged ants appeared, indicating the early arrival of rain. To the village Maya this meant that it was time to begin their year's planting, without which they could not eat, and so they went home. Some *batabob* argued with their followers to stay, but the general opinion was that they could just as easily come back at the end of the year. Saved at the eleventh hour, however, the Yucatecan militias regained confidence, and set off in pursuit. In order to plant, the Maya had to come out into the fields, where they were vulnerable. Outside aid finally came for the *ladinos*: if there had been no takers among the major powers, there was one country ready to send troops and arms – Mexico, if only the Yucatán would come back into the national fold. There was still savage fighting, but gradually the Maya were pushed back, from Peto in October and Valladolid in December 1848. The Mayas' chronic inability to act together played its part in their defeat: Cecilio Chi was killed by one of his lieutenants, apparently in an argument over the *batab's* wife, and Jacinto Pat, ablest of the Maya leaders, was murdered by a fellow chieftain. The rebel Maya lost any sense of political direction, and retreated into the forests south of Valladolid.

The Yucatán Caste War was of a totally different order from the political skirmishes of the era, an explosion of the tensions and hatreds of three centuries. The Maya massacred *ladinos*, while Yucatecan troops exterminated and burnt out entire Indian communities. After the war, imprisoned Maya were sold to Cuba as slaves to restore the Yucatán state finances. The effect of the war can still be seen on the map of Yucatán: the eastern 'frontier', an area of growing *ladino* settlement before 1847, was to remain depopulated for the next 100 years. The system of independent village leadership by *batabob* that had survived since the Conquest was fatally undermined, leaving the 'pacified' Maya more vulnerable to the demands of *ladino* landowners. The war also knocked the swagger out of white Yucatecan nationalism: there were no more serious independence attempts, and a few years later the old Audiencia of Yucatán was divided as Campeche became a separate state.

Moreover, the war was still not over. Many of the Maya had accepted defeat, but there were still thousands of rebels in the woods, and they were soon to regain a sense of purpose. The rebel Maya had not abandoned Christianity as they understood it; rather, they denounced the Church and the whites as bad Catholics. Their defeat caused profound confusion, as if God and the spirits had turned against them. Then, in late 1850, one of the Maya bands, led by a renegade *mestizo* called **José María Barrera**, declared that they had found a 'Talking Cross' by a remote forest *cenote*, a traditional shrine. The Cross told the Maya that God had not abandoned them, that if they followed the instructions of the Cross they would be invulnerable to bullets, and that one day the Cross would lead them to victory. *Ladinos* who heard of this immediately said it was a ventriloquist's act masterminded by Barrera, but within traditional Maya beliefs the idea that a sacred object should 'speak' was perfectly admissible. The scattered rebel bands became a messianic cult. They founded a town around the shrine of the Cross, **Chan Santa Cruz**, 'Little Holy Cross', a typical combination of Maya and Spanish – which is now Felipe Carrillo Puerto.

Every year, columns of soldiers were sent south into the territory of the *Cruzob* (the followers of the Cross) without achieving any significant victory. On several occasions they took Chan Santa Cruz, but the Maya just fell back, closed the paths behind the troops and cut away at them bit by bit. At other times the Maya emerged to attack and take Tihosuco, the Yucatecan army's main forward base, or make raids deep into pacified territory. The only Spanish town in the southeast, Bacalar, had been taken by the Maya in 1848, and then retaken by the army. In 1857 the Cruzob seized it for good, so that they had the whole Belize frontier to themselves. In Mérida the idea gained ground that, if it was too expensive to destroy the Cruz Maya, it might be safe just to ignore them. After one last major campaign in 1866 under Maximilian's empire, when Tihosuco was besieged by the Cruzob, the frontier town was abandoned, and the Maya were left to themselves for years at a time.

The area the Cruz Maya carved out for themselves extended from the Belize border to Tulum. At Chan Santa Cruz they built their 'church', the **Balam Na** ('Jaguar House'), and developed a comprehensive religion and system of authority, a combination of Maya tradition, Catholicism and 19th-century military organization. They enjoyed an on-off relationship with the authorities of British Honduras, whose traders continued to sell them arms. On more than one occasion they applied to join the British Empire. The passage of time, though, together with epidemics and internal disputes, brought a fall in both Cruzob numbers and morale. Things turned against them in 1895, when the regime of Porfirio Díaz decided the situation was intolerable and signed a treaty with Britain recognizing its ownership of British Honduras in return for a serious attempt to prevent gun-running across the border. Perhaps as important as patriotic concerns was the soaring US demand for newly invented chewing gum, the natural ingredient of which, *chicle*, is found in huge amounts in the *sapodilla* trees of Quintana Roo. For the first time, the Cruzob's wilderness was potentially valuable, and *chicle*-tappers were pushing at the Cross's frontiers. The Díaz regime's real intent was evident: instead of just supporting the Yucatán state government against the Cruzob, the President separated off the whole east coast of the Yucatán as the new Federal Territory of Quintana Roo, amid ineffectual protests from Mérida politicians, giving Mexico City direct control of its potential resources.

In 1901 General Ignacio Bravo and a large army marched into Chan Santa Cruz to reassert Mexican sovereignty. The Cruzob fled to the forest, but no longer had the resources to resist. The story did not end there, though, for in 1915 Salvador Alvarado, Revolutionary Governor of the Yucatán, decided that the Mexican Revolution had no interest in imposing itself on the Maya and withdrew his troops. It did not definitively come under government control until 1930, and even then some Cruzob retreated north of Felipe Carrillo Puerto, from where they still reject Mexican authority.

The Empire and the *Porfiriato*

While the Yucatán was paralysed by its Caste War, in Mexico history had moved on. In 1854 there was an uprising of more substance than those of other years, bringing to power a group of liberals led by **Benito Juárez**. He was the first Indian to govern Mexico since Moctezuma, although ironically some parts of his great programme, the *Reforma*, were profoundly destructive of traditional Indian life. Juárez' government was the first to give Mexico some of the institutions of a modern state, and in the Constitution of 1857 set out to remake the country in line with the doctrines of 19th-century liberalism, changing, they hoped, a nation of élites and peasants into one of citizens and independent farmers. The mass of legal privileges and inequalities left from Spanish times was abolished. In the countryside, village lands were to be divided up and sold off as private plots. Freedom of speech and education, and separation of Church and State, were guaranteed. Mexico's intensely conservative Catholic Church, accused of having meddled in politics and held the country back ever since independence, lost its lands, much of its wealth and its special legal powers.

This provoked a Catholic-conservative revolt, and another bitter civil war. Juárez was victorious, but in 1861 he suspended payments on Mexico's massive foreign debts. As there was no IMF around to impose terms in such circumstances, a Spanish, British and French fleet appeared off Veracruz to demand payment. The Spaniards and British withdrew after an agreement had been reached, but the French stayed, and against dogged resistance installed the Austrian **Archduke Maximilian** as Mexico's second emperor. In Mexican patriotic rhetoric this has always been presented as a foreign invasion, but in fact the idea had been put into Napoleon III's head by Mexican conservatives, whose belief in monarchy had been intensified by 40 years of chaos, and who had just lost the civil war. In the Yucatán the Empire was actually very popular among the battered white and *mestizo* population, who seemed genuinely taken by its promise of stability. In 1865 Maximilian's Belgian Empress María Carlota was lavishly welcomed in Mérida. In the same year, however, the American Civil War ended, and it was made clear to Napoleon III that the USA would not tolerate permanent interference in Mexico. French troops were withdrawn, and without them the Empire, which had never won control of the whole country, crumbled. Still the Yucatán stayed loyal, and it was even suggested that if Maximilian could escape there Mérida could be a new capital of the Empire. In May 1867 news arrived that the Emperor had been captured by the Republicans in Querétaro, but even then Mérida fought on for another month, as the last redoubt of an empire that no longer existed.

Reinstated, Juárez remained president until his death in 1872. Mexico briefly fell back into a round of rebellions and minor incidents, until in 1876 power was seized by one of Juárez' generals, **Porfirio Díaz**. His reign, the *Porfiriato*, would last 34 years.

Porfirio Díaz is remembered for the one statement all Mexicans can agree with, '*Pobre México, tan lejos de Dios, y tan cerca de Estados Unidos*' – 'Poor Mexico, so far from God, and so close to the United States'. In his lifetime he also enjoyed an excellent press internationally, as a model leader of a 'backward' nation ('third world' not having been invented). To the financial markets, he was a man you could do business with. First, he imposed order, establishing his authority over local bosses and ending Mexico's reputation for chaos. Secondly, Díaz, a tough soldier, surrounded himself with highly educated, business-minded men known as the *científicos*, 'scientists', who set out to bring rational progress to the country. All kinds of commercial development were encouraged, and foreign investment welcomed.

That Díaz' authoritarian regime might conflict with the spirit of democracy was openly acknowledged: the great problem of Mexico, it was widely stated, was its ordinary people, who were lazy, stupid and lacking in enterprise. For the nation to move forward, the Mexican masses had to be dragged into the 19th century.

In the countryside, it became clear that the laws of Juárez' *Reforma*, intended to fill the country with small farmers, could also allow big landowners to amass even larger estates. The abolition of legal inequalities had not altered the real balance between rich and poor, while the freeing up of land made it easier for it to be bought and sold. As commercial agriculture boomed, whole villages might find their lands had been sold from under them without them ever being aware of it. Whole states came into the hands of a few dozen families. This was quite right, in the *científico* view, since big landowners would make the land productive, whereas villagers would only misuse it.

The Díaz regime had some phenomenal successes, in its own terms. Its time in power coincided with the great late-19th-century expansion in the world economy. By 1910 Mexico's foreign trade reached ten times its level of 1876, with a huge expansion of cattle ranching, cash crop production and mining. It acquired railways, oil was discovered and industry appeared – textiles, iron and cement works. Debts were paid off, and the Mexican government was treated with respect abroad. At times Mexico had one of the highest rates of growth in the world.

However, this, and the acquisition of astronomical wealth by some individuals, was not incompatible with worsening poverty among the mass of the population. This is a trick Mexico has pulled off more than once. A boom in cash farming disrupted food production, and drove up prices. Industry was limited to a few places – Mexico City, Monterrey – and wages were pitifully low. Statistics from the *Porfiriato* are astonishing: in one estimate, the standard of living of the poor in 1910 was under half what it had been at the time of Hidalgo's revolt a century earlier. Since then Mexico's booms have often failed to touch the depths of poverty in the country.

No part of Mexico witnessed a greater transformation in the Díaz era than Yucatán. It was at last discovered that the peninsula could produce something valuable: **henequen**, a cactus used to make sisal twine and rope. From the 1850s the value of *henequen* exports increased continually, and the crop, *el oro verde* ('green gold'), dominated the State. This was Yucatán's 'gilded age' when, from a backwater, it became the wealthiest state in Mexico. The state had its own *científico* sub-regime, under Olegario Molina, one of Díaz' firmest supporters, with a particularly blatant amalgam of political power and personal wealth: not only was *Don Olegario* state governor from 1902 to 1910 and later Federal Secretary for Development, but he and his family were also the greatest *henequeneros* of them all, at one time controlling over 60 per cent of the Yucatán's crop. Meanwhile, Yucatán *haciendas* were extended by grabbing village lands. Many Maya estate workers were kept in debt slavery: a sum of money was advanced to the worker that he could never pay off, so that he was as bound to the estate as under the old tribute system.

Modernization also came to Chiapas during the *Porfiriato*. A *científico* governor, Emilio Rabasa, sought to set progress in motion with roads, schools and telegraph lines. Commercial agriculture began with coffee and sugar in the north and the Soconusco, and many destitute Maya from the Highlands were lured to work on lowland estates, where debt bondage was even more common than in the Yucatán.

The Revolution, 1910–40

Mexico has had many revolutions but only one Revolution. The great upheaval that began in 1910 is the founding moment of the modern country. Entire books are written, though, attempting to define what it was about. As in 1810, leaders set movements in motion without any real awareness of the forces they were dealing with, events slipped out of anyone's control, and the final outcome was a strange composite that emerged out of the contributions of different elements, some of whom were in outright conflict with each other. No single group came forward to dominate it. The Revolution was intended to bring democracy to Mexico, to create a state that responded to and did not despise its people. It was nationalistic, in politics and culture, an intense reaction to the denigration of everything uniquely Mexican under Díaz. It was expected to modernize the country, in the interests of the whole nation and not just an élite. It was to bring agrarian reform, to give land and security to the country's millions of peasants. International -isms – anarchism, communism – had a little influence, but the Revolution's major tendencies – *Maderismo, Zapatismo, Villismo, Carrancismo* – were home-grown and derived from different leaders' names. They did not issue theoretical statements. At times it could seem like an elevated debate, at others a brawl in a *cantina*. As so often in Mexico, power struggles, egos and personal loyalties could be as prominent as political agreements or differences.

It began very modestly in 1910, as Díaz, then nearly 80, was getting ready for one more rigged election and his seventh presidential term. A mild, wealthy liberal called **Francisco Madero** began a campaign of opposition around the simple constitutional demands of clean elections and a ban on re-election to office. Díaz swatted him aside, but Madero didn't give up. The context of the campaign changed utterly, and the Revolution began, when all sorts of groups previously ignored by politics revolted in support of Madero: tough cowboys in the northern border states, among them a former bandit, **Pancho Villa**, and village Indians in the southern state of Morelos, led by **Emiliano Zapata**, who had been dispossessed of their lands by sugar planters. In May 1911 Díaz gave up and retired to Paris, and Madero was elected president. This was only the end of the beginning, for the next months saw an explosion of political activity. Zapata's movement issued their *Plan de Ayala*, demanding the immediate return of land to the villages. Madero did not comply, and they continued their rebellion. He increasingly relied on the army to keep order, but the generals despised him. In February 1913 he sent the army commander **Victoriano Huerta** to suppress a coup by the old dictator's nephew, Félix Díaz. Huerta changed sides, had Madero arrested and murdered, and made himself president with a government of old Díaz *científicos*.

In former times, that would have been that, but in the new situation Huerta's brutal act brought forth a wave of opposition. As the country descended into chaos, there were two main centres of resistance: the north, where **Venustiano Carranza**, Governor of Coahuila, led a 'Constitutionalist' alliance with Villa and generals **Alvaro Obregón** and **Plutarco Elías Calles**, and Zapata's growing 'Army of the South'. There were major differences between all the Revolutionary armies, but especially between these two main groups. Zapata's movement was an irregular army of Indians and peasants, led by an Indian who acquired an aura of absolute, unbreakable honesty. Joined by some anarchists and urban revolutionaries they took over *haciendas* and attempted a peasant revolution in Morelos, Guerrero, Oaxaca and Puebla. The northern chiefs and *comandantes* (except for Villa, a strange amalgam) were mostly middle-class ranchers and soldiers, enemies of 'privilege' but no socialists. They had no set views on land redistribution, but seized the estates of anyone who opposed them. Another characteristic of the Revolution emerged: that Revolutionary power could be a very quick way of getting rich. High idealism, brutality and staggering corruption often combined in the same people. One thing most of the northern leaders could agree on was an intense opposition to the Catholic Church, which had supported Huerta and was regarded as an arm of the élite that had consistently held the country down.

By mid-1914, Huerta's counter-revolution was defeated, but fighting broke out almost immediately between Carranza and an alliance of Villa and Zapata. After another year Villa's forces had been broken, but the Zapatistas fought on in the south.

Since chaos was in the essence of the Mexican Revolution, each state had its own story. In the Yucatán, bursts of rural violence in 1910–11 revived memories of the Caste War and so frightened both liberal and conservative politicians that they closed ranks again, which kept the Revolution at bay for another five years. The Molina clan still dominated the economy, largely undisturbed. The Revolution finally arrived in March 1915 with an army sent by Carranza under **General Salvador Alvarado**. A stern radical moralist who imposed the Revolution by decree, Alvarado closed all churches in the state. He also ended debt slavery and imposed a single, state-run authority to market *henequen*, and with the profits proposed to build 1,000 schools. In the whole south the Revolution's main bridgehead was the state of Tabasco. In Chiapas the cause of Madero was first taken up by some of the most conservative sectors in the state, who had felt excluded under Díaz, and who bizarrely incited the Maya of Chamula to revolt for them by insincerely promising land and an abolition of taxes, as in Yucatán in the 1840s. Led by a Chamula known as *Pajarito* ('bow tie'), the Indians advanced on Tuxtla Gutiérrez in July 1911, but were beaten back as all *ladino* factions agreed it was better not to allow the Maya a role in political disputes. In 1914 a Carrancista army arrived in Chiapas to impose Revolutionary control, the opening to years of violence and abuse of power.

In late 1916 Carranza called a national convention to agree a new constitution and give the Revolution some shape. Zapata's followers were not represented, but their persistence meant that peasant demands had to be acknowledged. **Article 27**, stated there would be limits to individual landholdings in each state, and that land would be redistributed to be worked as smallholdings, or collectively. The thrust of the 19th century reforms that had tried to destroy communal village landholding was reversed. Article 27 was vague as to what this might mean in practice, but the Indians' most basic demand was enshrined in law.

By 1919 the Zapatistas were virtually defeated, and Zapata himself was lured into a trap and murdered by followers of Carranza. Then, since Revolutionary *caudillos* could never stand each other for long, a rift grew between Carranza and Obregón, when the former seemed to be planning to prolong his reign, in contravention of the ban on presidential re-election, a key principle of the Revolution. Forced out of Mexico City, Carranza was assassinated by yet another chieftain in 1920. It was under Obregón (President 1920–24), and Calles (1924–8), both from Sonora near the Arizona border, that the consolidation of the Revolution really began. They made overtures to Villistas and Zapatistas. Obregón began the practice of granting favours to selected labour unions, in return for loyalty as political power bases. The Revolutionary state adopted a belligerently radical style, especially in its clash with the Church. This diverted attention from the absence of any clear position on the property system, for the Sonorans were supporters of 'national capitalism', not communists.

Within the archipelago of states, all sorts of experiments were still possible. The Revolution had made little use of political parties, but the Yucatán after 1917 saw the rise of the **Partido Socialista del Sureste** (Socialist Party of the Southeast), led by a former railwayman who had fought with Zapata, **Felipe Carrillo Puerto**. In 1922 he was elected state governor and, himself a *mestizo*, caused astonishment by giving his inaugural address in Yucatec. He also required that all official documents be signed in red ink. Beyond these rhetorical flourishes, Carrillo Puerto distributed land to 35,000 families, expanded roads and schools, founded the Yucatán's university and even introduced family planning, although further plans were limited by the declining profitability of the *henequen* trade as the world found other sources of rope. Carrillo Puerto was assassinated in one more factional putsch in 1924, but his work meant that the Revolution brought tangible benefits in the Yucatán sooner than in many parts of the country. Tabasco, meanwhile, became the fiefdom of the Partido Socialista Radical under **Tomás Garrido Canabal**, who sought to eradicate religion, drawing down worldwide condemnation from Catholics such as Graham Greene. In Chiapas, on the other hand, events were still dominated by power squabbles, and many of the Revolutionary reforms went unnoticed in large parts of the state.

In 1928, as his term came to an end and the question of the presidential succession reared its head again, Plutarco Elías Calles decided more institutions were needed to demilitarize the Revolution, give it final stability and prevent the same old crises every four years. He proposed that all the many elements identified with the Revolution: regional parties like that in Yucatán and local bosses, should unite in a single party, the **Partido Nacional Revolucionario**. Together they formed what was called the *familia revolucionaria*, irrespective of their differences. If the PNR was sufficiently inclusive its election would be guaranteed, and for additional continuity presidential terms would be extended to six years, a *sexenio*. Instead of presidential succession being fought over in the streets, it would be sorted out in smoke-filled rooms. The official party, one of the Mexican Revolution's abiding features, was born.

The high-water mark of the radical Revolution came in the term of the most revered of Mexico's modern presidents, **Lázaro Cárdenas**, 1934–40. He was originally a protégé of Calles, but unlike his old boss had a genuine commitment to land reform. Over 17 million hectares were distributed, and an elaborate structure of state bodies was set up to help communally owned villages, called *ejidos*, farm successfully. Cárdenas took special interest in the Yucatán, where 25 per cent of estate lands was divided up. Against furious opposition in the USA and Britain he also nationalized the railways and oil, winning the admiration of all Mexican patriots. The Cárdenas years were also the high point of the cultural transformation of the Revolution, as reflected in the paintings and murals of Rivera, Siqueiros, Orozco and Frida Kahlo. Previously, Mexico had turned its back on its pre-Columbian heritage, but now it gloried in it, and made it the base of a new national mythology.

It was also at this time that official interest was first shown in pre-Columbian relics. While Cárdenas was a radical in many of his policies, though, he also built up the PNR, renamed the **Partido de la Revolución Mexicana**, as a centralized, professional party of power. In 1946 the PRM in turn became the **PRI**, the strangely titled **Partido Revolucionario Institucional** or 'Institutional Revolutionary Party'.

The *Priato*

Under its different names the PRI remained in power for 71 years, from 1929 to 2000, one of the longest political reigns in history. Many Mexicans thought that it would never end. The PRI regime was a peculiar institution, which liked to describe itself as 'expressing' the Mexican Revolution and, like the event itself, requires interpretation. Mario Vargas Llosa called it 'the perfect dictatorship', because it was never quite perceived as one. Dissidents were rarely prevented from decrying the party in print, and the PRI saw that rather than create martyrs it was better to flood out criticism with adulation from its own friendly media. If active opposition arose the PRI acted like a sponge, acknowledging some complaints, ignoring others, and finding protest leaders some place in the labyrinth of party organizations, where they gradually shut up. If this failed, election rigging or the iron fist were still there as last resorts.

Straddling the centre ground, the PRI was able to be all things to all men, maintaining a bizarre pseudo-Marxist-nationalist style in its labour unions, while simultaneously helping some of its other friends to amass some of the largest private fortunes on the planet. With a divided opposition to its right and left, for decades it could present itself as the only viable option for government. Ever since Obregón, the primary role of the web of Mexican 'official' unions had been to ensure support for the party. All kinds of jobs were organized through PRI-affiliated unions, and for millions there was the unspoken fear they might be out on the street if they lost the favour of the local PRI boss. This system supported a huge party and union bureaucracy, with a pervasive atmosphere of corruption.

Like the Revolution, the PRI did not have a set ideology, but its dominant attitudes changed over time. Of the four impulses behind the Mexican Revolution – democracy, nationalism, modernization and land reform – the last was a priority only in the Cárdenas years. If Cárdenas was the most celebrated of modern Mexican Presidents, ultimately more influential was **Miguel Alemán**, in power from 1946 to 1952. Mexico did well out of the Second World War, producing goods for the Allies. At the same time PRI tariff policies kept out imports, and Mexican industry expanded into a growing market. Under Alemán it was made clear that nationalism and modernization, through industrialization, were the main objectives, and growth more important than any social programme. Giant state enterprises played a major part in industry, in cooperation with 'national', Mexican, business, and politicians and officials were constantly involved in granting concessions and contracts. All this gave hugely expanded scope for corruption. Nevertheless, for a long time this programme seemed successful: the Mexican economy grew consistently from the 1940s to the 1960s, and for once this was reflected in better living standards for ordinary people.

In the countryside, the great estates of the Díaz era had been swept away, but the *ejido* system failed to satisfy the hopes pinned on it at the time of Cárdenas. The over-complex structure of credit banks and organizations, intended to help *ejidos* work as modern farms, was underfunded and infected with the same corrosive corruption as the rest of the administration. Without support it was ever more difficult for *ejido* farmers to keep up with changes in agriculture; moreover, in the interests of modernization, state and national governments consistently favoured commercial farmers over *ejidos*. Article 27 remained in the Constitution and with it the *ejido*, but as something of a nostalgic anomaly within an expanding commercial agriculture. Where conflicts arose over land, abuses of power were still common.

In the late 1960s, Mexico's long post-World War summer ended as the economy stagnated and production failed to keep up with accelerating population growth. In the 1970s respite came with the rise in the oil price, and another brief boom. Then, in 1982, an oil glut set off a massive economic crisis. Political opposition grew, and the PRI's ability to control elections started to slip. It began to lose state governorships to the conservative, free-market **Partido de Acción Nacional (PAN)**. In the 1988 election, opposition centred around the left-wing **Cuauhtémoc Cárdenas**, son of the great president. Most independent observers believed he won, but against huge protests, the official victor was the PRI candidate, **Carlos Salinas de Gortari**.

Salinas enjoyed a better press in the USA than any Mexican leader since Porfirio Díaz. For years, US economists and business figures had battered at Mexico's crypto-Soviet economy of state enterprises, arguing it formed a block to growth. Salinas agreed, and reversed the traditional economic policies of the PRI, privatizing banks and industries, ending state subsidies and opening Mexico to foreign investment. Though his admirers didn't make much of it, this did not mean a total departure from PRI traditions, for many privatization beneficiaries were close friends of the president. Foreign business flowed in, and Mexico once more had one of the highest growth rates in the world. The pinnacle of Salinas' achievement was the NAFTA agreement, binding Mexico into the US economy, for which it was necessary to amend the sacred Article 27 on the inalienable status of *ejido* land. Then, on New Year's Day 1994, the **Zapatista** rebels appeared in Chiapas. Once again, it was noticed, a Mexican boom had failed to make more than a dent in underlying poverty.

Salinas' choice to succeed him, **Luís Donaldo Colosio**, was assassinated, and his own brother, **Raul Salinas**, was accused of contracting the murder of a PRI rival. Scandals emerged one after another, revealing a level of corruption that astonished even a cynical Mexican public. The monolithic PRI was falling apart.

The PRI President elected in 1994, **Ernesto Zedillo**, promised to negotiate a solution in Chiapas, but played for time while permitting a massive military build-up in the state. In 1997 the PRI lost its majority in the federal congress, and Cuauhtémoc Cárdenas was elected mayor of Mexico City for the left-wing **Partido de la Revolución Democrática (PRD)**, a fundamental break in a system built on one-party rule. Zedillo, to widespread surprise, resisted pressure from old PRI bosses known as *dinosaurios* (dinosaurs) to deploy the full range of dirty tricks, and undertook to ensure the 2000 presidential election was the cleanest in Mexico's history.

Mexico since 2000

On 2 July 2000 PAN candidate **Vicente Fox** was elected president, finally bringing PRI, one-party rule to an end. Many said that only with this changeover of power, 90 years after the revolution, could Mexico really be called a democracy. Fox won support with his call for change, liberalization and a clean break with the old system. More changes came in each state. In Chiapas, at the end of the same year, the notoriously hard-line local PRI lost the governorship to a multi-party alliance led by a liberal lawyer, **Pablo Salazar**. In 2001 the Party also took over the Yucatán state government from one of the old PRI dinosaurs.

Mexicans got used to their new political panorama remarkably quickly. In place of the PRI regime there is a three-party system (of the PAN, the PRI and the PRD), but one with a great deal of cynical horse-trading. Mexico is now fully part of the global economy, with only a few pillars of the old PRI protectionism left (such as the state oil monopoly), but this has brought new problems. President Fox had promised to settle the Chiapas conflict 'in 15 minutes' but failed to press home a proposed agreement in the face of right-wing opposition. The administration fell back into the policy of letting the 'crisis' run on in slow motion, and since 2002 the Zapatistas, the federal government and Chiapas state have ignored each other (see p.472).

In 2005, as the Fox presidential term neared its end, a new standard-bearer for the left emerged in the shape of the former PRD mayor of Mexico City, **Andrés Manuel López Obrador** (or AMLO, for short), an abrasive populist whose appeal soared with promises at last to challenge Mexico's glaring inequalities of wealth. As PRD presidential candidate for 2006 he called on everyone interested in real change in Mexico to give him their support, including the Zapatistas, in order to bring about a second, more genuine 'new beginning' for the country. After long consideration, Subcomandante Marcos and the Zapatistas declared that instead they would spend 2006 touring Mexico in the 'Other Campaign', making contact with other radical groups throughout the country and pouring scorn on all politicians, AMLO included, as dishonest manipulators. The rift this caused between the Zapatistas and the mainstream left has still not healed. In the event, the July 2006 election was the closest in Mexican history – so Marcos' intervention may have been significant. Out of over 41 million voters, the margin of victory of PAN candidate **Felipe Calderón** over López Obrador was just 0.58 per cent, and that only after weeks of recounts and appeals. López Obrador refused to accept the result, denounced it as a fraud and staged a separate inauguration as 'the Legitimate President of Mexico', but this did not win sufficient support and led to a crisis in his own party – many in the PRD regarded this 'Presidency' as irresponsible and overly driven by AMLO's egomania.

After such a marginal victory, new President Calderón sought to broaden his mandate by incorporating elements of López Obrador's social and environmental programmes into his policies. Most controversially, he also set out to affirm the government's authority with a determined challenge to the power of Mexico's drug cartels in the northern states, relying on the army to reinforce ineffectual police forces. However, the cartels, pumped full of cash by North American and European drug users, and with an ample supply of weapons bought in the USA, came back with the attitude that, if you want a war, you can have it, and we'll win it. Gun-related deaths multiplied, notoriously in grotesque multiple murders, and cartels staked out border towns such as Nuevo Laredo as no-go areas for federal authorities. The administration's campaign has had significant successes, but this can lead to more violence, as cartels fight for higher stakes. Contrary to an impression often given by international media, this is not remotely the situation across the whole of Mexico, and in the south, especially, its everyday impact is limited (see p.108), but it obviously places the Mexican state under severe strain.

Topics

Cenotes *and Caves* 66
Colonial Builders and Missionary
 Churches 67
Ecotourism: What Is It? 68
Maya Textiles 71
Wildlife and the Natural World 73

04

Cenotes and Caves

The features that make the Yucatán landscape unique are usually noticed little by little: the immense flatness of the scrub, which can make it seem dull, superficially; the thinness of the dusty soil if you kick the ground, revealing that you're standing on one giant ledge of rock; the total absence of rivers, streams or other surface water. Instead, water can be found beneath the surface, in kilometres of caverns within the limestone shelf, accessible only through natural sinkholes in the rock, called *cenotes*.

The word is a Hispanicized version of the original Yucatec, *dzonot*. They can be small water holes with just room enough to pass a bucket through, or huge chasm-like pools, often because a cavern roof, eroded over centuries, has collapsed to open the *cenote* to the skies; in many cases a seemingly narrow entrance can lead into magnificent giant chambers and underground rivers. Until modern machinery allowed wells to be dug or blasted, every Yucatán village needed to be attached to a *cenote*, and the major Maya cities were built near the largest pools. Where there were no or only inadequate *cenotes*, in the Puuc hills, artificial ones had to be created to retain water in the form of enormous man-made cisterns called *chultunes*. In the Chenes region of Campeche (*chen* means well), where the water table is much further from the surface, the Maya could only obtain water by going into caverns hundreds of metres below ground, as at the Great Well of **Bolonchén de Rejón** (*see* p.399). As sources of life-giving water and entrances to the underworld, *cenotes* had a special place in the cosmic vision of the Maya, but they are in any case innately mysterious. Some seem like bottomless pits into the centre of the world – the famous **Sacred Cenote** at Chichén Itzá, is a prime example – while others that look to be placid pools in fact extend far below, into chamber after unexplored chamber.

They're also magical places in which to swim, with echoing walls, shafts of sunlight and underground water that's wonderfully cool, clean and fresh. **Dzibilchaltún** and the unmissable **Cenote** Dzitnup outside Valladolid are both superb for swimming. In addition, since the attractions of *cenotes* have become more widely known, a greater number of other, once half-hidden village *cenotes* are being opened up to visitors, such as **Cenote** Yokdxonot and others south of Mérida (*see* p.297). As the extent of the Yucatán's labyrinth of subterranean watercourses has become appreciated, *cenotes* have attracted a growing number of divers, and the area inland from the Caribbean Riviera is now one of the most important in the world for cave diving (*see* pp.189–90). The **Ox Bel Ha** cave near Tulum, of which some 172km have been explored, is one of the longest underwater cave systems in the world.

As well as *cenotes* filled with water, the Yucatán limestone is riddled with other cave systems. To the Maya all caves had special significance, and the earliest signs of human presence anywhere in the peninsula have been found in the astonishing caves of **Loltún** near the Puuc hills, with a record of uninterrupted human use dating back to before 3000 BC. The smaller but better-known caves of **Balankanché** near Chichén Itzá do not have quite such a long history, but still contain extraordinary relics, while to the west, at **Calcehtok**, another huge cavern near the Maya ruins of Oxkintok holds the added mystery that it is still scarcely visited at all.

Colonial Builders and Missionary Churches

Colonial churches and old patio houses seem as embedded into the scenery of southern Mexico as Maya ruins, and can appear almost as ancient, a legacy in stone of Spanish rule. The churches, especially, are the product of a remarkable adaptation of European styles to the New World. The introduction of Christianity was carried out almost like a military campaign by the missionary orders entrusted with the Yucatán and Chiapas, the Franciscans and Dominicans respectively. Both had professional priest-architects, principally Friar Juan de Mérida for the Franciscans and Pedro Barrientos for the Dominicans. Each order, however, built in very different ways.

In each region the first large, permanent Spanish buildings were monasteries, the main bases for the missionary friars. In the Yucatán, **Maní**, the Assumption in Mérida (since demolished), **Izamal** and **Sisal** in Valladolid were all built under the direction of Juan de Mérida. As well as a chapel they all included a plain, massive cloister and an equally solid well-head, built over a natural *cenote*. The first rudimentary churches built to hold services for newly converted locals were *capillas de indios*, Indian chapels, consisting effectively of only one solid wall, a kind of arch containing the altar, coming away from which was a roof of wood and palm leaves to give some shade to the congregation. If these altars were free-standing they were called *capillas abiertas*, 'open chapels', of which one remains remarkably intact, in the middle of the Maya ruins at **Dzibilchaltún**. In the monasteries *capillas de indios* were set into the outside walls, in order to 'deal with' as large a number of Maya as possible. This can be seen very clearly at Maní. Another feature of these monasteries was the *atrio* ('atrium'), a great open space in front of the façade that enclosed the Maya brought together for open-air services at the *capilla*. The best example is the huge *atrio* at Izamal. One other characteristic is that they were nearly all built over old Maya temple platforms. This was partly to take advantage of the existing stones, but it also came out of a desire to show the superiority of the new religion in 'taking over' a sacred spot. Building was undertaken by local Maya, who had to give one day's work a week to the Church, as they had given labour services to their communities in building temples.

As far as architectural style is concerned Friar Mérida and his Franciscan colleagues, in line with the tradition of their order, seem to have been austere and practical men with little interest in visual embellishments or current fashions. Although they were working from the 1540s onwards, their buildings are based in a much older Spanish rustic Gothic, and some, such as the **Hospital de San Juan de Dios** in Mérida, are distinctly archaic. Superficially, the early Franciscan churches of the Yucatán bear a resemblance to late-medieval European churches; however, they have very few of the details or decorative features found in even the simplest Gothic churches. Instead, they are up-and-down, slab-sided holy blockhouses, intended to give the true religion a presence every bit as solid as Maya pyramids. The effect is one of austerity and solidity rather than gracefulness, further increased by the grey Yucatán stone.

After the initial, post-Conquest burst of activity the resources devoted to church building fell rapidly. There was no further wave of church construction until the mid-17th century, the greatest period for colonial religious art in the Yucatán, which saw the building of notably more elegant churches, especially in southern Yucatán towns such as **Teabo** or **Texax**, many with Baroque altarpieces or mural paintings.

The architecture of the Dominicans in Chiapas was always more sophisticated and less puritanical. Their first major building, Pedro Barrientos' monastery of Santo Domingo in **Chiapa de Corzo**, reveals a far greater awareness of the styles of the Renaissance, with a light, elegant cloister. They also made clever use of Spanish styles such as *mudéjar* (Moorish-influenced) brickwork and Plateresque decoration, so called because it was seen as reproducing the effects of silverware (*plata*) in stone and plaster. The Chiapas Dominicans also had more contact with the extravagant colonial Baroque of Oaxaca and Guatemala. Consequently their buildings, with their ornate, often exuberant decoration, provide a radical contrast to those further north.

Several of the largest Dominican buildings have fallen into ruin, but there are plenty left in **San Cristóbal de Las Casas**. The summit of 'Chiapanecan Baroque' is the church of Santo Domingo itself, especially its extraordinary 17th-century façade. The Dominicans' openness to decoration combined perfectly with the tastes and customs of the Highland Maya. The Cathedral of San Cristóbal is painted in ochre, terracotta, white and black, and Spanish heraldic motifs are coupled with Maya flower designs. San Cristóbal's churches have more Baroque altarpieces than any other city in Mexico.

Ecotourism: What Is It?

Ecotourism is one of the buzzwords of modern travel in Mexico. Everywhere you go, local authorities and private agencies are eager to signal their *proyectos ecoturísticos*. This word, though, has two distinct meanings. Sense one involves enabling people to see and experience wildlife, rainforests, reefs and other natural environments remote from centres of development. Sense two refers to sustainable tourism, developing facilities for travellers in such a way that they do not disturb delicate ecological balances. They are often confused, but it's possible for these meanings to be seriously (or completely) at odds with each other, since taking tour groups into remote areas can involve providing infrastructure – plumbing, roads, 24-hour water – on a scale that amounts to a major transformation.

Sense one is the way the word is usually understood in Mexico. You can find the *ecoturístico* label attached to dinky nature parks with a morose caged jaguar, production-line boat trips, restaurants that are a bit out of the way, just about anything, in fact, that's in any way different from lying on a beach in Cancún. Most Mexican developers, geared up for big-money beach tourism, don't adapt smoothly to the low-level implications of sense two. Nevertheless, with the growing interest in ecotourism, many once inaccessible places across southern Mexico have become visitable, from village *cenotes* and mangroves to the Lacandón forests, and most – especially the most remote – can be visited with low-impact, small-group trips.

To avoid disappointment, it's best to be aware of the potential tension between meanings one and two. Like any marketing term, ecotourism can be completely empty, or mean something, and it's open to a great deal of manipulation. Also, the balance between the two sides of ecotourism is complex and shifting. Projects with genuinely idealistic objectives may have to cut low-impact corners just to get going.

There is an argument that the most ecofriendly thing one can do for the jaguar and its environment is stay at home. But even ecotourism projects that don't entirely satisfy purist standards can contribute to remedying worse problems. In the Río Bec region of Campeche there are now hotels that enable you to visit the Maya ruins and wildlife reserve of Calakmul in comfort, where a few years ago there were only basic huts. Naturally, this involves a significant change in the life of the area, but one impulse behind the introduction of tourism has been to give an alternative to constant erosion of the forest. If it becomes a resource, bringing in visitors, then local people have an incentive to preserve trees rather than just cut them down. Leaving the forest alone as if the people did not exist is not an option.

One reason why rigorously low-impact sustainable tourism schemes are rare is that they are very expensive, so that in rural Mexico 'community-based, low-impact' tourism can be a contradiction in terms. Solar energy, composting drainage and so on require such an investment that the obvious way to recoup it is to charge high-end prices. However, country people are themselves ever more aware of the need to safeguard their natural world, and many of the village tourism schemes now up and running (see pp.187, 334) work – within the limits of their resoures – in ways that seek to avoid and even counteract any environmental damage. And, even if they don't meet every low-impact criteria, their use of resources is necessarily small scale.

Ecological Problems in the Region

Any consideration of ecotourism intersects with the real problems in the ecology of southern Mexico. In tropical conditions, delicate and volatile environmental problems cease to be discussion points and become apparent to the naked eye.

The galloping, ever-mutating development of the Riviera Maya inevitably produces environmental stresses. The Yucatán peninsula is a unique, and uniquely delicate, natural setting. The thin, dry limestone slab, the intricate maze of *cenotes* and fresh-water cave-rivers just beneath it, the fringe of beach, mangroves and lagoons around the coast and the coral reefs just offshore are all interconnected, and interdependent. The vibrancy of the reefs is fed by nutrients from the land, filtered through the mangroves. One problem created by Riviera growth is simply in **land management**. Critics of the Riviera (or those who just dislike it on taste grounds) tend to target their ire at Cancún, but the big city is at least one, compact place, and actually has quite functional local infrastructure. More damage is now caused by the spread of giant all-inclusive resort complexes, marching down the coast seemingly ready to fence off any vacant beach. The worst are set right on the shoreline, and to build them mangrove is essentially filled in with solid earth and concrete. This cuts off the flow between land and sea that is a central element in the coast's natural balance.

Part of the same problem is 'beach manipulation'. The soft sand of the Riviera shifts naturally, and beaches regularly change shape after storms – or can be stripped away, as after Hurricane Wilma. However, since Wilma some resorts no longer wish to accept this natural shift, and have sought to stabilize 'their' beach frontage by inserting sections of powdered stone called *sacsab* or even geosacs (giant plastic bags filled with cement), sometimes trying to mould open beaches into private bays. This, again, is harmful to marine life, especially turtles that try to breed on the beach.

Drainage is another related problem, for ballooning new towns as well as the resort complexes. Because of the porousness of the soil, the closeness of the water table to the surface, and the way in which – as divers have discovered – its water-filled caverns are connected to each other and the sea, drainage systems here should be especially secure. However, few complexes or resort towns have waste treatment systems adequate for the growth of human numbers here in the last 20 years. Tourists and Riviera residents also generate vast amounts of **garbage**, and the region is desperate to find an alternative to the inadequate inland landfill sites.

A specific issue is **golf courses**. To be blunt, the Yucatán is one of the worst places in the world to build them. Most tropical golf courses are ringed by barrier chemicals and pesticides to keep naturally invasive vegetation off greens and fairways. In the Yucatán, yet again due to the porous rock, these can very quickly filter through to the water system and the sea. Yet, 12 courses are open or nearing completion. Essentially, if you have any concern at all for nature in the Yucatán, you don't play golf here.

All these related factors – and a few more, such as the growth of **cruise traffic** off Cozumel – have contributed to serious **reef loss** and the depletion of marine life. First-time visitors can still be dazzled by the life and colour underwater, but this loss has been recorded by all divers with long-term knowledge of the area. Local NGOs such as the CEA or CINDAQ monitor waste flows (*see* above), and promote public information campaigns. After years of ignoring these issues, local authorities have no alternative but to tackle the garbage problem, and are beginning to approach waste management seriously, so that it actually seems possible that traditionally weak local laws in these areas may be made at least a little more relevant. Action on controlling building within a kilometre of the shoreline, though, seems further off. Some NGOs encourage certification schemes for non-environmentally-damaging resorts. Visitors can themselves help in this (as well as by not playing golf) by looking at Google Earth, and avoiding resorts built on the beach. They can also minimize reef damage by acting sensibly when diving, swimming or snorkelling, above all by avoiding touching coral, and not going in the sea covered in sun lotion.

Away from the Riviera, and further south, the foremost long-term problem is **deforestation**. Until the 1960s Tabasco, for example, was almost covered by swamp and forest; since then the state has lost 95 per cent of its forest cover and now consists overwhelmingly of cattle pasture and fruit farms. A similar process has been seen in Campeche and Chiapas. There are two major forces behind it: the acquisition of land for ranching, and the clearing of land by poor village farmers. For years, as ranchers grabbed good lowland terrain for their cattle, poor farmers and *ejidatarios* were more or less encouraged to move into supposedly 'vacant' national lands in

Contacts and Information

For local ecotourism tour agencies, *see* p.106.

Amigos de Sian Ka'an, *www.amigosdesiankaan.org*. Extensive information (in Spanish) on Sian Ka'an and Yucatán ecology.

Centro Ecológico Akumal, *www.ceakumal.org*. Monitors the Riviera environment and promotes conservation, especially of turtle-breeding beaches (*see* p.191).

CINDAQ, *www.cindaq.org*. A group set up by divers to explore and plan the vast underground aquifer beneath Quintana Roo, and work to ensure its conservation.

Eco Travels in Mexico, *www.planeta.com/mexico*. A useful resource, with a range of links and information.

Pronatura Yucatán, *www.pronatura-ppy.org.mx*. Conservation organization with varied programmes.

RARE, *www.rareconservation.org*. US-based specialists in developing community-based ecotourism, with several projects in Mexico.

SAVE, *www.saverivieramaya.org*. Activist group that opposes environmental abuses on the Riviera, run from Villas de Rosa dive hotel, Akumal (*see* p.191). Also produces well-documented reports.

forest areas such as the Lacandón jungle. Today political responses are more varied, but the pace of change is slow. Anywhere new roads have been built in the last 30 years, such as Highway 186 in Campeche or the *Carretera Fronteriza* south of Palenque, settlements have appeared and forest has been cleared.

Several areas are now **Biosphere Reserves**. The Biosphere concept aims to ensure a sustainable environment taking into account every aspect of an ecosystem – fauna, forest, local communities – rather than just a 'wildlife reserve' ignoring human use. There are eight in the region: Sian Ka'an, Banco Chinchorro, Ría Lagartos, Celestún, the Campeche Petenes, Calakmul, and in Chiapas El Triunfo and Montes Azules.

Maya Textiles

If the growing of corn has traditionally been a semi-sacred function for Maya men, weaving has been the sacred role of women. Ixchel, goddess of fertility, was also the goddess of weaving, and was often shown with her loom in Classic-era images. By tradition, Maya men in Highland Chiapas will not marry a woman who cannot weave. From the point of view of women themselves, weaving is an essential skill that enables them to supplement their income and gain some independence.

The same word, *huípil*, is used throughout Mayan Mexico for the main items of women's traditional dress, but means different things. In the hot Yucatán – where embroidery, not weaving, is the main traditional skill – it refers to the light cotton shift dress that is one of the region's emblems. A variation for special occasions is the *terno*, which unlike the one-piece *huípil* has three parts, a lace-edged underskirt, the main skirt and, most richly embroidered, a smock-like yoke around the neck. *Ternos* are exquisitely worked, and always worn with bright flowers in the hair. MACAY museum in Mérida (*see* p.264) has a display of fine Yucatecan embroidery.

The real repository of weaving skills is Highland Chiapas, where, like most things, it comes with a greater sense of tradition. The basic implement is the backstrap loom, the *telar de cintura*, as seen in ancient Jaina figurines of women weaving. It consists of two wooden end-rods, between which the main threads are stretched. One end-rod is attached, by a cord looped around both ends, to a post or tree; the other is fixed to a strap around the woman's lower back. She works kneeling, moving backwards and forwards to alter the tension in the loom, using the only other parts of the loom, five spacing rods, to separate and weave the threads. If it's too dark to weave, Highland women move on to embroidery or the *petet* or spinning wheel.

Though all Highland women weave, not all do so to the same standard. In each village there are women admired for their special skills. Recently, since tourist sales became a big source of income – and given that Indian weaving is always under-priced – there has been a strong incentive to produce more and more simple pieces for quick sales, while neglecting more time-consuming traditional techniques. Cooperatives, the most important of them Sna Jolobil and J'pas Joloviletik in San Cristóbal de Las Casas, have been set up with the aim of promoting the survival of best-quality weaving, and to establish the principle of a fair price for Indian women's work. Another question is the use of synthetics. The Maya love colour, and when cheap lurex and other synthetic threads became available they took to them with glee, abandoning the laborious process of producing natural dyes (which turned out duller). The Maya, however, have always adapted to new materials, and the wool and sheep of Chamula and Zinacantán were themselves introduced by the Spaniards.

The most traditional garment made by Highland women is also called a *huipil*, here meaning a loose blouse – essentially two pieces of cloth sewn together at the top and sides, with holes for the head and arms – with richly brocaded panels around the neck at front and back. They also produce belts, shawls, men's smocks, embroidered blouses and mats and other decorative pieces for the home. Skirts are made of heavy, plain black wool. In contrast to the Yucatán there is no arbitrariness in the designs of Highland weaving. Each community has its own, easily identifiable style, and after a brief time in San Cristóbal recognition of people from surrounding villages becomes immediate: the embroidered blue or white blouses of women from Chamula, the brilliantly bright shawls and flower-embroidered smocks of Zinacantán, or the red and white *huípiles* of Chenalhó. In each community there are legends that the First Mother – a common way of referring to Santa Lucía, Catholic patron saint of weavers, and a modern manifestation of Ixchel – taught the village's women their designs.

Within the set styles, though, there is leeway for each weaver to work the pattern and display her skill, and no specific design is ever repeated. The main patterns and shapes in each style all have symbolic meanings: like so much in Maya culture, they mirror the Maya conception of the universe. Diamonds are the most common feature, representing creation between the four *bacabs* or cardinal points, and centred on an inner diamond symbolizing the sun, Jesus Christ and the *yaxché* or world-tree, three elements intertwined in the universe of the Highland Maya. Similar diamonds can be seen on the robe of Lady Xoc on an 8th-century lintel at Yaxchilán. Some *huípiles* can almost be read as texts: sequences of diamonds correspond to the months and days of the *haab* calendar, and stylized shapes indicate vultures or monkeys – symbols of uncontrolled nature – and other animals. Each woman also has a personal motif with which she 'signs' her weaving, often coupled with a family motif.

The finest weaving of all is reserved for the special *huípiles* that dress the saints in village churches. These are never discarded, but once a year are removed and washed, and new, bright *huípiles* are placed over the old ones. They thus represent a museum of centuries of weaving. At times when weaving skills have been lost – as when the Maya have come under strong pressure to adopt non-Indian customs and dress – they have been revived by praying to the saints, and by studying their *huípiles*.

Wildlife and the Natural World

Birds

The abundance of birds that this land possesses is marvellous in extent, and of such diversity, that it does great honour to he who filled it with them, as a blessing.
Father Diego de Landa, *Relación de las Cosas de Yucatán*

Landa, Stephens and many other travellers have been equally awestruck by the exceptionally rich birdlife of the Yucatán, with some 500 species present at one time or another during the year. Many are permanent residents – including several species unique to the peninsula – and the Yucatán's position and combination of woods and mangrove wetlands also make it a favourite wintering ground for birds from North America. To the south of the peninsula, tropical woodland blends into the high forest that runs (or ran, until a few years ago) from southern Quintana Roo into Chiapas, the home of exotic, colourful birds such as toucans and parrots.

The full range of birds is extraordinary, and many can be seen just by looking around. The most universal bird here is the **great-tailed grackle** (in Mexican Spanish *zanate*), a relative of the blackbird with a long thin tail. There are a few hopping around, and the call of the *zanate*, a long, rising whistle that seems unnervingly human, is a constant background sound of the Yucatán. Another inescapable presence is the *zopilote* or **black vulture**, the great garbage-picker of Mexico. All around the coast the **brown pelican** is very common, perched on mooring posts or floating against the wind. The most famous birds of the Yucatán are its **flamingos**, which are easy to locate as you're taken to see them. There are two main flamingo breeding grounds, at Río Lagartos and Celestún (*see* p.244 and pp.285–6).

In the dry Yucatán woods, frequently-spotted birds are the **Yucatán jay**, the brilliant-blue **indigo bunting** (*azulito*, little blue bird, in Spanish) and vivid yellow and black **orioles**. Also still not hard to find is the *chachalaca*, a wild relative of the turkey. Its name comes from its unmistakable clucking call, and it's more often heard than seen. Winter visitors include **tanagers**, little, luminous-red birds that dart in front of your car on country roads. The wetlands and mangroves are home to a beautiful variety of American **herons** and, in winter, most non-Arctic species of American **duck** and **goose**. The margins of mangroves, beach and sea are the best place to see the magnificent **frigate bird**, a commanding presence, usually high up floating on the wind, that justifies its name with its fierce bill and long crooked wings.

Further south, the true tropical forest of the southern peninsula and Chiapas is under heavy pressure from deforestation, and the birds that remain most numerous are those that adapt best to patches rather than undisturbed swathes of forest. Only when the trees are above a certain height do they provide a home for the most

Places To See Birds

Northern Yucatán

Under your own steam you can see plenty of water and sea birds around the Quintana Roo coast, especially at Puerto Morelos, Holbox, and from Tulum to Punta Allen. There are aviaries at Playa del Carmen and Xcaret (*see* p.185). In Yucatán the Toh-Yucatán Bird Festival is held in Nov–Dec. For information contact Ecoturismo Yucatán (*see* p.106) or check *www.yucatanbirds.org.mx*.

Campeche Petenes: northern Campeche has huge stretches of wetlands (*see* p.378).

Celestún and **Río Lagartos:** most people only visit to see flamingos, but these lagoons are also home to many other birds. The lagoon east of Progreso similarly hosts flamingos and a range of wetland and sea birds, especially winter migrants, and at Uaymitún there is a (free) viewing tower (*see* p.292).

Isla Contoy: this island sea-bird reserve is most easily visited from Isla Mujeres.

Maya sites: an attraction of less-visited Maya sites is that they're great places for seeing birds. Among the best are Dzibilchaltún, smaller Puuc sites (Xlapak) and Cobá.

Sian Ka'an: the best single place for wetland birds, a must for birders (see pp.202-3).

Southern Peninsula and Chiapas

Calakmul: Mexico's biggest rainforest reserve, and the best place to see forest birds and wildlife in southern Yucatán (*see* pp.367-8).

Lacandón Forest/Pico de Oro: the largest area of undisturbed rainforest, in the southeast corner of Chiapas, still contains substantial numbers of macaws. At Pico de Oro there are cabins at **Las Guacamayas** (*see* p.470).

Maya Sites: great opportunities to see birds: **Dzibanché** and **Kohunlich** are spectacular for this, and among the places where you have the best chance of seeing wild toucans.

Palenque, Bonampak, Yaxchilán: parrots and hummingbirds are easy to spot in Palenque, but for rarer birds it's better to take the trip to the latter two sites, deep in the forest.

El Triunfo: this huge reserve in the remote southern sierras of Chiapas is the only place to find some of the region's rarest birds: curassows, guans and quetzals. Access is difficult, but trips (for several days, with real hiking) can be arranged (*see* pp.520-1).

spectacular tropical birds, such as **toucans**, their smaller relative the **aracari** (*tucancillo*, little toucan, in Spanish) and, now rare, scarlet and blue **macaws**. Scarcer still is the **quetzal**, the enormous tail feathers of which were treasured by Maya kings. In Mexico it is now found only in the high forests of the Sierra Madre in Chiapas. Small, bright green **parrots** are common, as are tiny **hummingbirds**.

Animal Life

Father Landa suggested the Almighty had blessed the Yucatán with so many birds partly to compensate for the shortage of useful animals – no beasts of burden, no cattle – which seemed so strange it led him to ponder what the divine intention could have been. In fact, the region has pretty near as much variety of life on the ground as it does flying above it. In Tuxtla Gutiérrez there is a complete zoo, the Zoomat, with the peculiarity that its several hundred species are exclusively natives of the state of Chiapas. It's just that most of the region's animals are not very user-friendly from a human point of view. Many are also nocturnal, and go unnoticed most of the time; hence any sighting of them is particularly special.

The most often-seen animal in northern Yucatán is the **iguana**. They are very common at Maya ruins, where crannies in old walls form ideal nesting-places. Some are huge dragons, but they're completely harmless. Tiny **geckos** are even more common, and are very useful to have around, as they gobble up mosquitos.

Other animals are more elusive, but the Yucatán woods contain **white-tailed deer**, **collared peccaries** (the Mesoamerican wild boar), **armadillos**, **coatimundis**, **grey foxes** and an extraordinary range of rodents such as *tepezcuintles* (paca, in English), *agoutis* and *guaqueques*. All are more common the further south you go, and in Calakmul some are quite plentiful. The rarest animals are likely to be found only in reserves or remote forest areas. There are **tapirs** in the remotest parts of the Calakmul reserve and Chiapas, but you will have to work very hard to find one.

The one animal most people want to see is the **jaguar**, spotted or black, symbol of cosmic power to the Olmecs and Maya. They are still reported across the whole region, from the Lacandón forest to Sian Ka'an, and even in the woods inland from Playa del Carmen, but they've no liking for humans and you will be very lucky to see a wild one. Jaguars are only one of an ample range of wild cats, all as rare or rarer. The **lynx**, **ocelot** and **puma** are the most well-known, but there are also engaging (or undeniably cute) smaller cats such as the *leoncillo* (jaguarundi in English) and *tigrillo* (margay). **Monkeys** are much easier to find. There are two kinds here, spider monkeys (*mono araña*) and howler monkeys (*mono aullador* or *saraguato*). Spider monkeys are still quite widespread; the bigger howlers are more reclusive, but can be seen and heard in Punta Laguna, Calakmul, Río Bec and, especially, at Yaxchilán.

Spectacular animals of southern Mexico include three types of **crocodiles**, alligators and caymans, all of them usually called *cocodrilos* by locals. Not especially numerous but wide-ranging, they still turn up around Río Lagartos (whose name, Lizard River, refers to their earlier abundance there) as well as in Sian Ka'an and the Sumidero gorge, near Tuxtla Gutiérrez. Other reptiles few people try deliberately to see are **snakes**: rattlesnakes, several more venomous species and a huge range of innocent smaller snakes. The chances of being bitten by a dangerous one are minimal unless you work at it. They are most active by night, at dawn and dusk, and after rain. Walking by day in the dry season you are unlikely to come across one, and if you do it will probably slither away faster than you can run in the opposite direction. To be doubly sure, avoid walking through undergrowth where you can't see what's on the ground, don't walk in the brush at night, and keep to clear paths.

Lastly there are **insects**. Most people find them an irritation, and in forests and mangroves they make life dire if you don't have repellent, but the sheer range is astonishing, and as night falls in the forest the cacophony of bizarre sounds they produce is something no amount of description prepares you for. Most do not bite. Bugs with more serious bites are the *tábano* (horse fly) and the African killer bee, a nasty import, but even they are not very common. More dangerous than most bugs are **scorpions** (bites require medical attention, but are not immediately life-threatening), but in the dry season you rarely find them by accident. Far more attractive are the 40,000 species of **butterflies**, sometimes seen in huge swarms.

Sealife and the Reefs

The 'Great Maya Reef' (or Cozumel Reefs) along the east coast of the Yucatán is the second-largest coral reef system in the world after the Great Barrier Reef in Australia. In Mexico, it stretches over 300km, from Contoy to Banco Chinchorro. The reefs are

Places To See Wildlife

Since it's sadly against the odds you'll catch sight of a *leoncillo* in the wild, you may settle for the region's zoos and animal reserves. Of these, the best are **La Venta** in Villahermosa and the **Zoomat** in Tuxtla Gutiérrez. In second rank lie **Xcaret**, and **Yumká** (also near Villahermosa). There are a few small wildlife parks, especially near Cancún.

In northern Yucatán, there is a good chance of seeing wild animals at **Punta Laguna** (especially monkeys), **Sian Ka'an** and more remote Maya sites. **Calakmul** is the best place to see animals, especially rare species. Crocodiles are easily seen in the **Sumidero**. All rarer species, above all big cats, are more active in the rainy season. This, though, is when you need to be most wary of snakes and scorpions, and when mosquitos and bugs cause most torment.

most concentrated and closest to the surface between the islands and the mainland: between Isla Mujeres and Cancún, on the west coast of Cozumel, and off Puerto Morelos and Akumal across the Cozumel channel. There is a separate, older reef system in the Gulf of Mexico 100km northwest of Yucatán, Arrecife Alacranes or Scorpion Reef, which can be visited with a few Mérida-based agencies (*see* p.274).

Coral reefs are among the most fragile ecosystems, and the deterioration that has followed the growth of the Riviera is already noticeable in some areas, particularly inshore reefs closest to Cancún. Nevertheless, huge stretches are still full of life. Off Puerto Morelos you can get a good idea of the sheer wealth of undersea life just by sticking your head in the water, with no need for tanks; you'll see fine-veined fan coral, luminous shoals of fish like **butter hamlets** and yellow-tailed **snappers**, **queen angelfishes** or striped **sergeant-majors**. There are also several species of **sharks** and **barracudas**, and the sea off Cabo Catoche is one of the world's largest feeding-grounds for the huge (but entirely harmless) **whale sharks**. Whale-shark watching trips are run from Holbox. Regarding the natural safety question, shark attacks are all but unknown in the region, and barracudas scarcely attack people unprovoked in clear water like that around the Maya reef. They prefer to eat other fish.

Dolphins are quite common in deeper waters offshore. Dolphin shows and pools where you can swim with them are big business on Isla Mujeres, at Xcaret and other locations, but there are objections to them. One of the best places to see dolphins un-penned is Holbox.

The Caribbean coast of Quintana Roo is also a major breeding ground for giant **sea turtles**, though they have suffered an appalling reduction in numbers (to under 5 per cent of the figure of 50 years ago). They were long hunted by the Maya, but this is now illegal, and even poaching is now rare. Hunting has been less of a factor in their decline than the fact that the turtles' favourite egg-laying beaches are smack in the middle of the main tourist areas. Where the turtle beaches are properly protected (the largest is at Akumal) signs instruct you to keep your distance. There are turtle breeding and repopulation programmes at Xcaret, Akumal and Isla Mujeres.

Still rarer, but not under such immediate threat, is the **manatee**, a big aquatic mammal related to the African sea cow, a kind of mangrove seal, that's one of only three such species in the world. The north end of Chetumal Bay is a reserve for these gentle animals, and trips can be made to look for them from Chetumal, but there's no guarantee they'll actually cooperate.

For a list of **bird** and **wildlife guides**, *see* **Further Reading**, p.536.

Food and Drink

Eating Out 78
The Food of Southern Mexico 80
Drinks and Drinking Habits 81
Fantastic Fruit 83
Mexican Menu Decoder 83

05

Mexican food is familiar just about everywhere: *tacos, burritos, guacamole* and the rest. Much less well known is that the dishes served in the vast majority of Mexican restaurants across the world are from just one part of the country, along the US border (if not actually Tex-Mex). Mexico, though, is a big place, and every part of the country has its own traditional dishes. Differences are especially marked in the south, and the food of the Yucatán, *cocina yucateca*, is widely considered the finest and most distinctive of all Mexico's regional cuisines. Rich use is made of fruit, turkey, fragrant seasonings, and the excellent fish and seafood from the Gulf and the Caribbean. The flavours that linger in the memory are those of lime and coriander.

Eating Out

All across Mexico, eating is a very public, social activity. Every town has its crop of restaurants: smart tourist or upscale **restaurants** (relatively scarce except in certain areas), comfortable places with lofty roof-fans, or plainer, rough-and-ready eating houses with plastic seats with beer logos on the back. Even in small towns or villages there is nearly always at least one very cheap *lonchería* or *cocina económica* (literally 'cheap kitchen'), and some open in the evening as well as for *lonch*. In towns, market areas always offer a cluster of *cocinas económicas*, open for breakfast and lunch only, which are invariably the cheapest places to eat. For immediate immersion in local life, eat there. Anywhere called a *restaurante* usually has beers to go with the food, while *loncherías* and *cocinas económicas* normally have no alcohol, only colas and juices. Throughout this guide restaurants are divided into three price categories (*see* p.111).

One peculiarity of eating in Mexico to be noted: still more than in most countries, paying more does not necessarily get you a better meal. In many smarter restaurants, higher prices will be reflected in fancier décor, fussier service and so on, but the fare on offer may still be routine, while in contrast some simple, far cheaper place nearby may have considerably better food, especially if it's a fresh seafood specialist. And it's notorious that some of the best, tastiest, freshest Mexican cooking comes from *cocinas económicas* and even street-stands. Price and appearance are just no guide to food quality, which gives Mexican dining an original pot-luck quality.

In restaurants of all grades you may be presented with a menu that's surprisingly long, offering local and 'Mexican' – meaning central-Mexican – dishes. In more basic places it can be a good idea just to ask ¿*qué hay de bueno hoy*? ('what's good today?'), which should bring forth the freshest thing they have rather than forcing them to put together some more complicated dish. By the coast, you often get great fresh fish.

Sit-down restaurants only make up part of the range of eateries. Mexicans are among the world's greatest **snackers**. Around the *plazas* and main streets of every town there are stands and hole-in-the-wall shops selling **tacos**, **tortas** (bread rolls) and a range of **antojitos** (aptly translated as 'something you want on a whim'); nearby, women and old men sell peeled fruit, potato crisps or ice creams. On Sundays and

Know Your Chillies

Down here the *jalapeño*, familiar in Tex-Mex food, is considered a bit of a softy. An enormous range of chillies is available: among the most common are *chile güero* ('pale chilli') or *xcatik* (its Mayan name), mild and used in the actual cooking of dishes; *chile poblano*, the most widely used medium-strength chilli, used in milder *picantes*; the hotter *serrano* and *jalapeño* chillies, which figure in a lot of central-Mexican dishes; *chipotle*, a dried, hot chilli used as seasoning; and, most powerful but most beloved of all in the Yucatán, the tiny, explosive green chilli *habanero*. Taken straight, chopped *habaneros* are used to make the most thermo-nuclear *picantes*, but dried, ground up and mixed with other herbs and spices they also feature in mixed seasonings like *achiote* powder and *recado negro*, in which case their influence is much more subtle.

fiesta days the number of food-stands trebles again. Should you get into *tortas* and *taco*-stands, this is a very cheap way of eating. In cities and the main tourist centres, international fast-food chains are now well established. Pizza has been thoroughly adopted across all five states, often with Mexican touches such as *jalapeño* peppers.

Mention apart goes to a special venue, the **cantina**. Spanish *conquistadores* related that in all Mesomerican cultures men drank themselves senseless to make contact with the other world. Heavy drinking remains a Mexican male cultural phenomenon. The *cantina* has been the traditional place to do it, and in every town there are still some that fit the old, shabby model, with saloon-style swing doors that put off outsiders. However, there are also now some, notably in cities, that – while still suitably atmospheric – are cleaned up, relaxed and far more comfortable. A historic *cantina* is a 90 per cent male institution, but more 'refined' ones are women- and family-friendly, especially at weekends. This makes it easier to sample the great *cantina* snacks, **botanas**, the local equivalent of Spanish tapas. Traditionally, around four different ones are served with each drink, and get slightly bigger with each order. They're enormously varied, from cucumbers in lime to *ceviches*, tamales or grilled fish, and often more impressive than many restaurant dishes. Tradition also dictates you're only charged for the drink, not the food, so this is an astonishingly cheap as well as fun way of eating. *Cantinas* traditionally only open during the day, till 5–7pm.

Eating times are pretty flexible, but distinctive too. Mexicans get up early, and **breakfast** is a main meal. Most restaurants open by 7am and people often go out for breakfast, especially in the more sultry cities. Get into the habit and the egg, sauce and bean-rich Mexican wake-ups, with fruit on top, are a great way to get set up for the day. The Yucatecan main meal of the day is traditionally the **comida fuerte**, a hefty lunch begun around 2pm (and especially leisurely on Sundays). This is why many of the best traditional restaurants in Yucatán state and Campeche – like cantinas – **only** open for long lunches, from 11am or noon to 6–7pm; bear this in mind if you want to try the best local food. At midday many cheap restaurants offer a set menu or *comida corrida*, for $3 or less. After the *comida fuerte*, the evening **cena** (dinner) is commonly a far smaller affair, at around 9pm. However, foreigners accustomed to eating in the evenings find this impossible to deal with, and in cities and resort towns most restaurants follow more 'international' timings. In smaller places, there are also plenty of places open in the evenings, but they often close early, around 9pm. Just as flexible as meal times are meal sizes, as you're rarely obliged to eat a set number of courses.

The Food of Southern Mexico

Yucatecan cooking has several characteristic dishes that appear all across the peninsula, and many rarer specialities. Staple **meats** are pork, chicken and the most common bird in the Maya farmyard, turkey, which is leaner and more flavoursome than the fattened festive fare served up in the USA or Britain. Beef is common in some areas, particularly in northern Yucatán around Tizimín; it's generally far thinner than prime steak, but when good it's very tasty. There is also a rich variety of fragrant **soups**, most often taken as a first course; outstanding among them is one of the great Yucatecan classics, *sopa de lima*, actually a chicken soup sharpened with lime, which when done well has a unique, superbly delicate flavour. The most common **fish** are red snapper, grouper and grey mullet, but they are less widespread than **shellfish**, which in coastal areas are virtually the staple diet.

One feature of Yucatecan food is that it is not necessarily hot. This is because hot spices (called simply **picante**) are not added in the cooking of many dishes, but served on the side in little bowls. The red sauce is (relatively) mild, the green one is a blaster. Most locals will spoon on at least a little, for the Yucatán is actually known for having the most powerful chillies and hot spices in all Mexico (*see* 'Know Your Chillies', p.79).

Skilful **marinades** are integral to many Yucatecan classics, giving them a distinctly tropical colour and tone. Lime juice features frequently, often with coriander and a touch of *achiote*, as do the Yucatán's distinctive bitter oranges (*naranjiles*). Marinating is one of the prime techniques used in intricate dishes such as *poc-chuc* or *pollo oriental de Valladolid*, in which some seven to ten seasonings are combined with two fruit juices to achieve the final result. Fish and seafood are often served in the form of a *ceviche*, raw but marinated in lemon or lime juices with coriander, and usually eaten as a refreshing, simple salad with chopped onions, peppers and tomatoes. Otherwise, fish is generally served simply: either plain-grilled, in breadcrumbs or fried in garlic.

Meat or fish dishes nearly always come with a variety of **accompaniments**, such as salads, sliced onion, guacamole, skinny French-fries (especially with steaks) and one of the basics throughout Mexico, red kidney beans (*frijoles*), usually served in a refried mass. They can also be eaten in a kind of broth, usually as a starter (*frijoles charros*). Another culinary staple is, of course, the staff of life of Mesoamerica, **maize**. Corn *tortillas*, made fresh every day, are served hot and soft (the most usual) or as crisp, dry chips, and a basket of them has traditionally appeared on the table with just about every meal. Sadly, since the rocketing of maize prices in the last few years real maize tortillas have become increasingly rare in many restaurants, and may be replaced by wheat tortillas or even bread. If you want the luxury of maize tortillas, ask for *tortillas de maíz* and be prepared to pay a little extra. The best traditional breads in the south are found in Yucatán state and Chiapas.

While *cocina yucateca* is the best-known cuisine of the south, other areas have their own specialities. **Campeche** has perhaps the most subtle cooking, a variation on Yucatecan food but with delicious fish, rice dishes and distinctive sauces featuring coconut and chillies. **Tabasco** too has very individual cuisine, especially using native river fish such as the *pejelagarto*. **Chiapas** has different styles in every region: around Tuxtla and the Pacific the most prominent dishes are *tamales*. **Highland Chiapas** shows the traces of a colonial society: the diet of the rural Maya has traditionally been a mix of *tortillas* and beans, while the food of the *coletos*, the Spanish-speaking people of San Cristóbal de Las Casas, is still close to that of Spain, with very Iberian sausages and great bread. Many menus have a section for *platos mexicanos*, central-Mexican classics such as *fajitas* and *enchiladas*. Even these will differ from familiar Tex-Mex variants: you're bound to come across *mole*, a wonderful savoury chocolate sauce seasoned with chilli and spices, often ignored in 'international' Mexican food.

Vegetarians do not fare well with traditional dishes: nearly all include some meat or fish and if you don't eat eggs either, you could be really stuck. Soups and snacks offer more possibilities than main dishes. However, there are dedicated vegetarian restaurants in many cities, and elsewhere restaurants that offer a good choice of animal-free dishes, such as the **100% Natural** chain, with branches in Cancún, Playa del Carmen and Mérida Dishes to look out for include those containing *chaya*, a vegetable similar to spinach that is extraordinarily good for you, and also tastes good.

Desserts are not a highlight of Mexican cooking and the range featured in books rarely turns up on menus. As everywhere in the Hispanic world, *flan* is universal, and there are good ice creams (*helados*). Apart from that, it's best to go for the fruit.

Drinks and Drinking Habits

Mexico has an export in which it leads the world – **beer**. Corona is the globe's best-selling label. Foreigners often drink this light beer near-automatically, but others with more body are Superior, Dos Equis (XX) Lager, Modelo, Carta Blanca, Sol and Tecate. There are also slightly more expensive, finer-quality versions, such as Bohemia or Modelo Especial. The Yucatán's own brewery, Cervecería Montejo, also produces a good lager (Montejo Especial). As well as lagers there are good Mexican dark beers: Negra Modelo, Dos Equis Negra and Yucatán's brown ale, Montejo's León Negra. One thing Mexicans do not usually do is drink beer with a piece of fruit in the bottle, nor do they always drink straight from the bottle. This is a Californian invention; in real Mexican bars beer is served with a glass, and if you want fruit you have to ask for it. Two variations on beers that are popular are a **chelada** (or *chela*) beer with a shot of lime and a salted glass, and a **michelada**, the same plus tabasco sauce and dashes of spicy seasonings (there are many different recipes, according to taste).

For years press comments abroad have suggested the quality of Mexican **wines** (*vinos*) is improving. This is news to most wine-buyers inside the country: about the best Mexican wines are those of the Cetto label from Baja California, but others still fail to impress. Good Chilean, Spanish and US wines are available in upscale restaurants, at relatively high prices. Mid-range restaurants will only have a few 'national' labels, if any, and except on the coast cheaper restaurants scarcely ever have wines at all. In any case, wine doesn't go very well with Mexican and Yucatecan food.

The most famous of Mexican drinks is, of course, **tequila**. It comes from hair-on-the-chest Jalisco in central Mexico, but a big choice is available everywhere. There are hundreds of tequilas, and should you wish to embark on a tasting, Riviera barmen will be happy to assist. There are three basic 'grades': *blanco* is clear, has not been through any ageing process, and is allowed to 'rest' in barrels for a maximum of 30 days after being distilled; *reposado* is aged for 2–11 months in oak barrels; *añejo* is aged for 1–5 years. In general, as it ages a tequila gets darker, stronger, but more subtle in flavour. Some tequila lovers consider fine *añejos* overly refined, and prefer a good *reposado*. The most traditional way to take tequila is now a rather self-conscious ritual. It's served straight in a small glass (a *caballito*), and on the bar are bowls of salt and lime or lemon slices: you lick a pinch of salt from your fingers, knock the tequila down in one and suck the juice from a slice of fruit. A variation is to alternate tequila and sips of tomato juice spiked with chilli (a *sangrita*). Alternatively, you can sip the tequila, not shoot it, and many people just take it in margaritas. Another cactus-based drink is **mezcal**, from Oaxaca, stronger, coarser and famously with a worm in the bottle.

The most traditional booze in the Yucatán is actually **rum** (*ron*), still the favoured hard drink at country *fiestas*. There are many brands of Yucatecan rum, which is cheaper than tequila (but really cheap non-label village rum is to be avoided, even by the most adventurous). There are also drinks of pre-Conquest origin, such as **xtabentún**, a mead-like Maya liqueur made with fermented honey, aniseed and herbs. A 'legendary' drink of Highland Chiapas is **posh**, but you'll never see it advertised. This is the home-distilled cane hooch of the Highland Maya, traditionally drunk to open the doors of perception. It is made (illegally) in every village, and those in the know with a little asking can usually find the local distiller, often an old lady (take a plastic bottle if you want to buy). It's actually a pretty coarse rum, but not dangerous.

Non-alcoholic drinks: much of Mexico's large **coffee** crop has often gone for export and in the Yucatán especially, coffee-culture has been peculiarly absent: cafés with decent fresh coffee are now sprouting up in Mérida in good part due to foreign influence. In some cheap country places if you ask for coffee you will still be offered '*agua para café*', a cup of hot water, and a jar of instant coffee for you to add. A natural exception is the Riviera, both due to tourists and the many people there from coffee-devoted states like Veracruz. Tabasco and Chiapas have more of a coffee tradition. An older Chiapas tradition is **pozol**, a cold drink of unfermented maize liquor, sometimes with cocoa powder added. Those used to it find it enormously refreshing, but it's an acquired taste. **Juices** (*see* opposite) are available in all towns and cities, and then there are **colas**. If Latin Americans ever want to deal a blow to *gringo* power, all they have to do is boycott Coke and Pepsi for one week. They are everywhere, even where nothing else is available. Sadly for the other brand, the generic name for a cola is *una coca*.

Fantastic Fruit

It would be a great blow for human values if someone would replace the national anthem, *Mexicanos, al grito de guerra* ('Mexicans, at the war cry'), with a hymn to the nation's **fruit**. It is the Yucatán's greatest symbol of abundance, and it is wonderful. Tropical fruits abound, but others that might seem completely familiar are just as, if not more, impressive. You've had pineapples before, but not like these pineapples.

Fruit can be taken chopped up on a plate, bought from street sellers, or as juices. There are specialized **juice shops**, labelled *juguerías* or just *jugos*. Juices in turn come in three ways: as straight juice (*jugo*, normal for orange juice); as a **licuado** – with the fruit put through a blender and mixed with a little water (a *licuado de agua*) or milk (a *licuado de leche*); or as an **agua**, with the juice diluted with water and ice (both nearly always of purified water). Some local fruits, such as the *mamey* and *guanábana*, are unimpressive when eaten but make very enjoyable *aguas*. Others are only available as drinks, such as *agua de jamaica*. Made with an infusion of dried flowers of the *jamaica*, a type of hibiscus, it is diluted to make an exceptionally refreshing, healthy drink; *agua de tamarindo*, tamarind water, is similar. *Agua de chaya*, an infusion of the Yucatecan vegetable, is another that's virtually a health-food concentrate, best mixed with a little lemon. Not a juice, but sold in juice shops, is **horchata**, a speciality of Tabasco: this is not the same as the Spanish nut-drink of the same name, but is made with rice, cinnamon and milk. A speciality of Chiapas is **tascalate**, a mix of ground maize, cocoa, cinnamon, sugar and *achiote* that is beaten into water or (better) milk.

As well as in *jugos* shops, *aguas* (but not *licuados*) are also on offer in **paleterías** and **neverías**, ice-cream shops, a vital local service. At their best they sell beautifully fresh home-made ice creams in many fruit flavours, in pots (*copas*) or on a stick (*paletas*). There are also ice-cream chains, which while not bad are not the same thing.

Mexican Menu Decoder

Restaurant Basics

carta/menu menu
lonchería cheap, basic restaurant, which won't normally serve alcohol
menu del día/comida corrida set meal
mesero/a waiter/waitress
¿Tiene una mesa (para dos, cuatro)? Do you have a table (for two, four)?
el menu (o la carta), por favor Can I see the menu, please?
¿Qué hay? What have you got?
¿Qué hay de bueno hoy? What's good today?
¿Hay una lista de vinos? Do you have a wine list?
la cuenta/la nota bill (check)
la cuenta, por favor Can I have the bill (check), please?

¿Puedo pagar con tarjeta de crédito? Can I pay by credit card?
cambio change
propina tip

General Terminology

almuerzo lunch
cazuela large, earthenware cooking pot
cena dinner
copa glass, wine glass
cuchara spoon
cuchillo knife
desayuno breakfast
ensalada salad
hielo ice
al horno oven-baked
pan bread
pan dulce sweet rolls
pimienta pepper
plato plate, dish

postres, dulces desserts
sal salt
servilleta napkin
sopa soup
taza cup
tenedor fork
torta sandwich made with a small roll
vaso glass

Meats

arracheras thin steak, fast-grilled in strips
asado/a roast
carnitas deep-fried pork
chicharrones deep-fried belly pork
chorizo spiced red sausage, of Spanish origin but found in most parts of Mexico, and especially Chiapas
chuleta chop
cochino/cochinita pork
jamón ham
lomo, lomitos loin of pork
longaniza pork sausage, not especially spicy, that was originally Spanish. There are variants in both Yucatán and Chiapas.
pavo/guajolote turkey
pollo/gallina chicken
puerco pork
res/carne de res beef, steak
tasajo dry-cured beef (common in Chiapas)
tocino bacon
venado venison, deer

Fish and Seafood

almejas clams
atún/bonito tuna
calamares squid
camarones prawns/shrimp
cangrejo large crab
caracol conch
cazón hammerhead shark/dogfish
corvina/corbina sea bass
esmedregal black snapper
huachinango/pargo red snapper
jaiba small crab
langosta spiny lobster
lenguado sole, flounder
lisa/mojarra grey mullet
mariscos shellfish (general)
mero grouper
ostiones oysters
pámpano pompano
pez espada swordfish
pulpo octopus
sierra mackerel
tiburón shark

Vegetables and Basic Ingredients

aceite (de maiz) oil (corn oil)
aceitunas olives

achiote stock-like Yucatecan seasoning made from a mixture of dried herbs and chillies
aguacate avocado
ajo garlic
alcaparras capers
arroz rice
azúcar sugar
calabaza pumpkin/courgette
canela cinnamon
cebolla onion
chaya spinach-like leaf vegetable
chía chaya in Chiapas
chícharos peas
chipilín strong spinach-like vegetable used in several traditional dishes of Chiapas
chirmole or chilmole a traditional Maya seasoning mix made with dried, ground and roasted chillies, dried ground pork stock and coriander, mint and other herbs. Used in *relleno negro* (black sauce) and other dishes.
cilantro coriander/cilantro
clavos cloves
comino cumin
elote corn cob
frijoles red beans
frijoles refritos refried beans
guacamole avocado mashed into a purée with lemon/lime juice, coriander and a little chilli
hongos mushrooms
huevos eggs
jicama a local gourd-like root vegetable, between a potato and a pumpkin
jitomate tomato
lechuga lettuce
mantequilla butter
miel honey
mole (poblano) spicy savoury chocolate sauce
nopalitos nopal cactus, similar to palm hearts
papas potatoes
papas fritas chips/french fries
pepino cucumber
pepitas, pepita de calabaza pumpkin seeds
pimienta ground pepper
pimientos peppers
   morron red,
   verde green
queso cheese
rabanitos radishes
totopos broken-up, fried *tortilla* chips
zanahoria carrot

Fruits and *Agua* Ingredients

chicozapote/zapote the fruit of the *sapodilla* tree, from the sap of which comes *chicle*, the raw ingredient of chewing gum. Its texture is slightly custardy when eaten straight, but it is a delicate flavour in juices or ice cream
coco coconut
durazno peach

fresas strawberries
guanábana soursop, a kind of custard apple
guayaba guava
jamaica a type of hibiscus flower, dried and used to make *agua de jamaica*
lima lime
limón lemon
mamey a member of the mango family, but smaller and not as sweet
mango mango
manzana apple
melón melon
naranja orange
naranjil/naranja agria small bitter orange
papaya papaya/paw paw
piña pineapple
plátano banana
  hoja de plátano banana leaf
sandía watermelon
tamarindo tamarind
toronja grapefruit
uvas grapes

Drinks
agua mineral mineral water
  con gas/sin gas fizzy/still
  agua para café water for instant coffee
  agua purificada purified water
café coffee
cerveza beer
coca cola
jugo juice
leche milk
licuado milkshake
raspado mixture of juice and crushed ice
refresco soft drink
vino wine
  tinto red
  blanco white

Glossary of Dishes
The following are some of the dishes that you will find most frequently in this region.

Breakfasts
Chilaquiles: heavy casserole of slivers of crisp *tortilla* baked in a cheese sauce with tomato, onions, spices and strips of chicken or turkey.
Huevos estrellados/fritos: fried eggs.
Huevos mexicanos/a la mexicana: scrambled eggs with peppers, chilli, onions and *chorizo*.
Huevos motuleños: *tortillas* topped by refried beans, fried eggs, a mild-chilli tomato sauce, peas, ham and grated cheese; often served with pieces of fried banana on the side.
Huevos rancheros: *tortillas* topped by refried beans, fried eggs, and spicy tomato sauce.

Huevos revueltos: scrambled eggs; usually includes a little onion and sweet pepper.
Platillo de fruta: a plate of mixed fruit.

Southern *Antojitos/Botanas* (Snacks)
Chalupas: crisp, boat-shaped *tortillas* with a filling of refried beans and different meat and vegetables; typical of Chiapas.
Coctel de camarones (de calamares/de langosta...): in the Yucatán, seafood cocktails are served in a light, vinaigrette-style dressing with loads of coriander.
Garnachas: small *tortilla* snacks, similar to *panuchos*, in Tabasco and Chiapas.
Panuchos: small *tortillas* with a coating of refried beans, rapidly fried, then topped with chopped tomato, onion, lettuce, avocado, medium-hot chilli and strips of chicken or turkey, previously cooked with a little *achiote* and bitter orange juice.
Papadzules: chopped hard-boiled eggs in a sweet pumpkin-seed sauce, served in rolled *tortillas*, often with tomato sauce on top; meat-free, but very filling.
Salbutes: like *panuchos*, but with a thicker, spongier base instead of standard *tortillas*. The double act of *panuchos* and *salbutes* turn up everywhere in the Yucatán, and women sell them from trays at small-town bus stations.

Mexican *Antojitos/Botanas* (Snacks)
Enchiladas: large, rolled soft *tortillas* with different fillings and sauces. Southern *enchiladas* are usually served with cheese and savoury chocolate *mole* (called *enchiladas suizas*) rather than tomato sauce.
Quesadillas: small soft *tortillas*, folded over with cheese and sometimes other fillings inside, and grilled or fried; usually served with a choice of sauces.
Tacos: rolled *tortillas* filled with meat, fish or whatever else is available; there are as many types as there are things to fill them. At *taco* stands you are given the *taco* complete, rolled up in paper; in sit-down *taquerías* (where the basic order is normally three *tacos*) all the ingredients are brought to your table, and you assemble them yourself.
Tacos al pastor feature chilli-spiced pork, compressed into a mass similar to a Turkish doner kebab, and then charcoal-grilled (*al carbón*); cheese, guacamole, onions and other extras are usually added.
Tostadas: round *tortillas* fried crisp and served open with a great variety of toppings (like *panuchos*). *Taquerías* also serve *tostadas*; *gringas* are meat and onion *tostadas* topped by melted cheese.

Southern Soups and Main Dishes

Cochinita pibil: pork marinated in *achiote*, lime and bitter orange juices, then wrapped in banana leaves and oven-baked in an earthenware dish. Pure Maya in origin (most traditionally baked in a hole dug into the ground, covered in hot stones), this is the Yucatán's most famous dish, served as a main course or a *taco*-ingredient. *Pollo pibil*, made with chicken, is similar.

Crepas de chaya: large soft crèpes (made with wheat flour, and so not maize *tortillas*) with a stuffing of cooked *chaya* and garlic, and a light cheese sauce.

Fríjol con puerco: a casserole of black beans, chopped pork, onion, tomato, lemon, coriander and hot chilli, served with rice.

Manitas de cangrejo (Campeche): crab claws cooked with chillies and onions, and served with salad. Campeche also has many other variations on seafood dishes.

Mondongo kabik: powerful stew of chilli, fruit and offal, maybe recommended to anyone who really wants to kick sand in the face of health warnings. Anything called *mondongo* is made with guts; the northern Mexican equivalent is *menudo*.

Pan de cazón (Campeche): hammerhead shark, chopped up with spices, served between cooked *tortillas* with tomato sauce.

Pavo en relleno negro: boned pieces of turkey (or chicken) in a rich, thick, black sauce made with very finely minced pork, herbs, spices, chilli, peppers and grated hard-boiled egg.

Poc-chuc: pork marinated in bitter orange juice and then cooked with onions, garlic and herbs, served with black *fríjoles*. Believed to have been invented in Los Almendros restaurant (Ticul), but now a standard across the peninsula.

Pollo oriental de Valladolid: chicken (or turkey) pieces on the bone casseroled with onion, garlic, mild and hot chillies and cloves, then quickly oven-roasted in a baste of oil and bitter orange juice, and then served all together. Typical of Valladolid and the east (*oriente*) of the Yucatán, hence the name.

Puchero: a rich stew made with two or more meats – typically pork and chicken – and pumpkin, carrots, rice, bananas, bitter limes and oranges, *habanero* chilli and herbs.

Sopa de lima: not just a lime soup: shredded chicken, strips of fried *tortilla*, tomato, sweet peppers, oregano, garlic and lots of lime, which infuses into the meat. A gentle, very satisfying dish.

Tamales: steamed maize dough stuffed with meat, beans, and any one of a whole variety of vegetables, chillies and seasonings, then baked in corn-husk or banana leaves.

Mexican Dishes

Caldo tlalpeño: soup of chickpeas, vegetables and chicken.

Carne a la tampiqueña: char-grilled beef with assorted accompaniments: guacamole, refried beans, *quesadillas*, onions and salad.

Fajitas: strips of meat or seafood, pan-fried and served sizzling hot for you to create your own *tacos*; the *tortillas*, onions, beans, guacamole and other necessaries are all provided on the table.

Machaca: shredded beef or pork with peppers, tomatoes, onions, medium chillies and herbs.

Pescado a la veracruzana: any fish cooked in a tomato, caper and olive sauce.

Pollo con mole: fried chicken in thick chocolate *mole* sauce; usually spicy but not searing.

Pozole: from Jalisco, a butch stew of chickpeas, tomatoes, chillies and pork or offal. Very cheap, if you like that sort of thing.

Puntas de res a la mexicana: strips of beef, char-grilled and served with tomatoes and onions.

Planning
Your Trip

When to Go 88
  Climate 88
  Festivals and Fiestas 88
Tourist Information 90
Embassies and Consulates 91
Entry Formalities 91
Disabled Travellers 92
Insurance and Health Precautions
  93
Money and Banks 93
Packing 94
Getting There 95
  By Air 95
  By Road 95
Getting Around 96
  By Air 96
  By Bus 97
  By Car 99
  By Ferry 101
  By Taxi 101
Travelling to Guatemala, Belize and
  Cuba 101
Where to Stay 102
Tours and Tour Operators 105

o6

When to Go

Climate

The whole of the Yucatán and Chiapas is below the Tropic of Cancer, and the region's climate follows the usual tropical pattern of a dry season building up in heat from roughly late October to May, and a rainy season from June to early October, although in recent years the weather has become noticeably more volatile. If you want to see wildlife, it's actually better to come in the rainy season, but the downside is that along with creatures you do want to see there also emerge some you probably don't (bugs and snakes), and dirt roads in remote areas may be impassable.

There are also major differences in climate from one area to another. Broadly speaking there are three climatic zones across this region. The whole of the **Yucatán peninsula** is hot, with dry-season daytime temperatures climbing from a mild high-20s°C (about 80°F) in January up to 38°C (100°F) by May-June, but dry, with humidity rarely much over 70°. **Tabasco, southern Campeche**, the lowlands of **northern Chiapas** around Palenque and the Pacific coastal strip of the **Soconusco** are real rainforest territory – or were, before huge swathes were cut down. Temperatures are a few degrees higher than in the peninsula, and the atmosphere is often steamy. In both these zones temperatures are cooler at night, but not by a great amount. In the third zone, **Highland Chiapas**, the mountain air is crisp and cool: around 18°C (65°F) by day Dec–Jan, and rarely much above the mid-20s°C (75°F) at any time. Temperatures drop sharply at night. Rainfall is particularly heavy in June and September, but the weather is erratic.

Hurricanes

The Atlantic hurricane season officially runs from June to November, but within that time major storms are naturally unpredictable. Should your visit be disturbed by a hurricane warning, the best thing to do is simply get to somewhere else. Otherwise, Mexico now has some of the best anti-hurricane precautions in the Caribbean, especially in Cancún, where many buildings have the orange sign of a *Refugio Anticiclón* (Hurricane Shelter). Visitors are warned well in advance of any dangers.

Climate Calendar

Mid-December–February

Temperatures throughout the Yucatán, and in most of the rainforest areas, are ideal: hot but not oppressive. In the Highlands, it can get pretty cold at night. This is the peak tourist season.

March–June

The heat picks up, but it's still a good time to travel around. The number of fellow travellers drops from February (except around the equinox in Chichén Itzá, and during Easter). Prices are also off-peak, except at Easter. The truly hot *seca* ('dry spell') starts in late May. In Highland Chiapas the weather from February to early May is superb.

Mid-June–September

July and September are usually the rainiest months. In the Yucatán peninsula the rain is by no means continuous, temperatures are high, and in Cancún and on the coast the July/August period is actually busy. In the forest and highland areas the rains are much heavier, and travel may be difficult, and tours cancelled, due to the state of the roads.

October–mid-December

The rains tail off in most areas. This is when the Yucatán gets fewest visitors, but the hurricane risk is usually negligible after September, and once the rains are done the weather is delicious; plus, nowhere is crowded, and prices are at their lowest. Come from mid-Nov to early Dec, and you can have the best of all worlds.

Festivals and *Fiestas*

We are a ritualistic people.
   Octavio Paz, *The Labyrinth of Solitude*

Paz, the great collective psychoanalyst of modern Mexico, is just one of many writers who have pointed to the immense importance of *fiestas* throughout the country. Every town or village has at least one major festival each year, nearly always on the day of its patron saint, and different districts, churches, trades or just groups of people (the blind, students) all have their own patrons too. The *fiesta* is one of the essential features of Mexico, the ultimate synthesis of the

Calendar of Events

January

1 Jan *Año Nuevo* (New Year's Day). Celebrated with parties and parades in the main cities.

6 Jan *Día de Reyes* (Feast of Three Kings, or Epiphany). Children all over the Hispanic world receive their Christmas presents; *Fiesta Mayor de Tizimín* (**Yucatán**). In Tizimín, Three Kings is also the town's Saint's day.

Mid-Jan *Festival Internacional de las Artes*, Mérida. Music, theatre, film, traditional arts.

20 Jan *San Sebastián*. Main *fiesta* in Chiapa de Corzo (**Chiapas**), the most colourful festival of *ladino* (non-Maya) Chiapas. Also celebrated in San Juan Chamula.

23 Jan *San Ildefonso*. The patron saint of Tenejapa, **Chiapas**.

February

2 Feb *La Candelaria* (Candlemas). Night processions (with hundreds of candles) and *fiesta* entertainments. Celebrated all over the **Yucatán** and, especially, in **Campeche**.

Late Jan/Feb *Carnaval*. Most spectacular in Mérida and Campeche, where it's the biggest *fiesta* of the year, but there are events in most **Yucatán** towns, and growing carnivals in Cancún and Cozumel.

Late Jan/Feb *Carnival of San Juan Chamula* (**Chiapas**). The most remarkable of Highland Maya festivals (*see* p.506).

March

21 Mar *Equinox* at Dzibilchaltún and Chichén Itzá (**Yucatán**). The only annual 'celebration' that could be called 'pre-Columbian', if it was not a modern revival. Events at Chichén are getting too big, with around 100,000 visitors.

Mar–April *Semana Santa*. Holy Week is low-key in much of the **Yucatán** and **Quintana Roo**, but celebrations are elaborate on Cozumel. Further south, Easter is a much more important celebration. There are processions and in San Cristóbal and other towns in **Chiapas**, and a typical mix of rituals in the outlying villages.

April–May

Late April–May *Feria de Tabasco*. The Tabasco State Fair takes over Villahermosa (**Tabasco**); not traditional or religious, but great fun.

3 May *Santa Cruz* (Holy Cross): major *fiesta* in Celestún (**Yucatán**), Felipe Carrillo Puerto (**Quintana Roo**) and other towns.

June

Early June (or late May) *Corpus Christi*. Another significant festival in that city of *fiestas*, San Cristóbal de Las Casas (**Chiapas**).

24 June *Fiesta* of St John the Baptist. San Juan Chamula's actual Patron-Feast (**Chiapas**).

July

16 July *Fiesta de la Virgen del Carmen*. The little oil town of Ciudad del Carmen (**Campeche**) throws a big *fiesta* for its patron on her day.

25 July *Santiago (Saint James)*. Yet more celebrations in Highland areas (**Chiapas**).

August

10 Aug *San Lorenzo*. Patron of Zinacantán (**Chiapas**), the best chance in the year to hear the Zinacantecos' unearthly festival music.

15 Aug *La Asunción* (Feast of the Assumption). An important religious festival in **Yucatán**; Oxcutzcab has a lively *fiesta* in the week preceding the Assumption, while Izamal sees religious celebrations on the day itself.

September–October

27 Sept–13 Oct *Cristo de las Ampollas* (Christ of the Blisters). A religious festival in Mérida (**Yucatán**), with devotional processions.

18 Oct *Cristo Negro*, Izamal (**Yucatán**). Charming, friendly festival, with processions.

November

2 Nov *Día de los Muertos* (Day of the Dead). The most famous of all Mexican *fiestas*, one of few events common to every part of the country, although it has local variations such as the *Hanal Pixán* in Yucatán, when families build little altars to evoke their dead in a very personal way. It's actually a three-day holiday, from the Eve of All Saints' Day (**31 Oct**), when dead children are especially commemorated, and going on through *All Saints'* (**1 Nov**) when the same is done for adults. Toys, sweets and multi-coloured decorations formed in the shape of skeletons and coffins can be seen in every child's hand, and families visit the cemetery to have a party with their own departed, a marking of the continuity between the living and dead that can be traced to pre-Columbian times. Foreigners are not likely to be invited along, but few can avoid being fascinated by the pink sugar skulls, death's-head garlands and other souvenirs, presenting death as an integral part of life.

Nov–Dec *Toh-Yucatán Bird Festival*. A week of bird-related tours and events, to mark the arrival of migrant birds in **Yucatán** (*see* p.74).

December

8 Dec *Immaculate Conception*. Very important in Izamal (**Yucatán**), with pilgrimages and ceremonies in the Virgin's honour.

12 Dec *Virgin of Guadalupe*. Major celebrations throughout Mexico; in preceding days, *Guadalupano* pilgrims run along roads, to the nearest shrine of the Virgin.

25 Dec *Navidad*. Celebrations everywhere throughout the Christmas period.

country's two primary traditions, Spanish Catholicism and pre-Columbian culture.

Local festivals are spectacular. In towns, the streets are garlanded in livid colours, there are even more food stands, balloon-sellers and crowds than on a normal Sunday and music is provided by traditional groups, *mariachis*, pop groups and salsa bands. Fireworks go off all over the place. Village *fiestas* are similarly colourful but more low-key, although they can be wilder. Since the *fiesta* is usually in honour of a saint, there is normally a religious procession on the main day of the feast.

A few *fiestas*, such as that of the **Virgin of Guadalupe**, are celebrated across the entire country. Most, however, are strictly local. It is in the heavily 'indigenous' southern states that local festivals show the strongest pre-Columbian, pre-Christian influences.

In the Yucatán (including Yucatán state, Quintana Roo and Campeche), **Carnival** is a major event, but curiously **Easter** goes by with relatively few ceremonies: for most people it's just the main break from work in the year, when just about everyone heads to a beach or somewhere cool. Local *fiestas* in honour of patron saints are most frequent between February and September. A feature of nearly all Yucatán small town fiestas is **bullfights**. This, obviously, is a Spanish introduction, but the links between the precise ritual presented in Madrid or Mexico City and the Yucatecan village affair can be pretty tenuous. For one thing, the bull (or, sometimes, cow) doesn't always die; it may be too valuable for that. Animal rights supporters are unlikely to find it much more acceptable, however, as instead the beast is just tormented for half an hour or so. It may be something of a consolation to know that, statistically, the 'bullfighters' are actually in greater danger of serious injury than the bull. Announcements of upcoming *fiestas* always appear in the *Diario de Yucatán*.

Among the Highland Maya of Chiapas, whose whole life is dominated by ritual, the notion of festival reaches another level still. They are the most vivid demonstration of the survival of the Maya past, an extraordinary synthesis of Catholic ritual and an ancient Maya essence that has been dream material for generations of anthropologists. The **Carnival of Chamula** is the most famous and most spectacular, but there are many more.

Tourist Information

Mexican tourist offices around the world can provide a wide range of information, but there are always local initiatives they are unaware of. In the 1990s Mexico and other governments in the region set up the *Mundo Maya* ('Mayan World') scheme for the joint promotion of the whole region, but very few joint projects have ever taken shape on the ground. Most information is still produced separately on a city/state basis.

Inside Mexico there are official **tourist offices** in all state capitals and main towns. Their staff may be helpful and well informed, or they may just be leaflet-pushers. At times they can be misleading, so check transport details with the relevant companies. They should at least be able to give you a free town map. Local private travel agencies can be as useful as tourist offices, and some are recommended in this guide.

Independent sources are usually better than tourist offices as places to look for background and local information. Always handy are the English-language magazines produced in each area, such as *Cancún Tips* in Cancún, the *Blue Guide* on Cozumel, *Yucatán Today* in Mérida and several others. They are distributed free in hotels, tourist offices, travel agencies and often restaurants.

The internet is also naturally an essential source, especially for information on specific activities and areas outside the main tourist centres. There are a great many general and specialist websites on Mexico, and Yucatán and the Maya region in particular: *See* **Useful Websites**, p.92, for a brief selection.

For information on specialist tours and guides in the region, *see* **Tour Operators**, p.105.

Maps

A peculiarity of travelling in Mexico is the difficulty of finding reliable maps, even those from the tourist office are of variable quality. Decent maps are given in free magazines (*see* above), but anyone exploring will probably want others. If you plan to drive around it's wise to stock up on maps in **Mérida**, as they are harder to find elsewhere. Mexican maps are often published by state, and show little or nothing of the next state over. The best available are the *Mapa Turística* series

Mexican Government Tourist Offices

For the UK and Ireland

Mexico Tourism Board: Wakefield House, 41 Trinity Square, London EC3N 4DJ, t (020) 7488 9392, *www.visitmexico.com*.

In the USA and Canada

t 1 800 44 MEXICO, *www.visitmexico.com*.

Canada: 1 Place Ville-Marie, Suite 1931, Montreal, Quebec H3B 2B5, t (514) 871 1052; 2 Bloor Street West, Suite 1502, Toronto, Ontario M4W 3E2, t (416) 925 0704; 1110-999 Hastings Street West, Vancouver BC V6C 2W2, t (604) 669 2845.

USA: Suite 1850, 225 N., Michigan Ave, Chicago IL 60601, t (312) 228 0194; 4507 San Jacinto Street, Suite 308, Houston TX 77004, t (713) 772 2581; 1880 Century Park East, Suite 511, Los Angeles CA 90067, t (310) 282 9112; 975 Sunset Drive, Suite 305, Miami FL 33143, t (786) 621 2909; 400 Madison Avenue, Suite 11C, New York NY 10017, t (212) 308 2110; 2829 16th Street NW, 4th Floor, Washington DC 20009, t (202) 265 9021.

published by the *Secretaría de Comunicaciones y Transportes* (SCT), but several were first done some years ago and have not been kept up-to-date. In this region, they cover Yucatán, Campeche, Tabasco and Chiapas. The best map for Quintana Roo is published by Ediciones Independencia, but it too has errors. Mexican states, especially Yucatán and Chiapas, often have new road schemes, and these are frequently not shown, even in the most recent maps.

Embassies and Consulates

As well as their embassies in Mexico City, many countries also have consular sections in Cancún and some other towns.

Belize: Belize Consulate, Av. Nader 34, Cancún, t (998) 887 8417; there is also a consulate in Chetumal (*see* p.351).

Canada: Mexico City: Canadian Embassy, C. Schiller 529, Col. Bosque de Chapúltepec, Mexico D.F., t (55) 5724 7900, *www.canadain-ternational.gc.ca/mexico-mexique*; Cancún: Canadian Consulate, Plaza Caracol II, 3rd Floor, Suite 330, Blvd Kukulkán Km 8.5, t (998) 883 3360.

Cuba: Cuban Consulate, C. 42 no. 200, Colonia Campestre, Mérida, t (999) 944 4215. It is not necessary to go in person in order to travel from the Yucatán to Cuba (*see* p.101).

Guatemala: Consulates in Chetumal, Comitán and Tapachula (for details *see* each town).

UK: Mexico City: British Embassy, C. Río Lerma 71, Col. Cuauhtémoc, Mexico D.F., t (55) 5242 8500, *http://ukinmexico.fco.gov.uk*. **Cancún:** British Vice-Consulate, Royal Sands Hotel, Blvd Kukulkán Km 13.5, t (998) 881 0100.

USA: Mexico City: US Embassy, Paseo de la Reforma 305, Col. Cuauhtémoc, Mexico D.F., t (55) 5080 2000, *www.usembassy-mexico.gov*; **Mérida:** US Consulate-General, C. 60 no 338-K, x 29 & 31 (by Av. Colón), t (999) 942 5700, *http://merida.usconsulate.gov*; **Cancún:** US Vice-Consulate, Plaza Caracol, 3rd Floor, Blvd Kukulkán Km 8.5, t (998) 883 0272; **Cozumel:** Villa Mar Mall, offices 8–9, on main plaza, San Miguel de Cozumel, t (987) 872 4574; **Playa del Carmen:** C. 1 Sur, x Av. 15 & 20, t (984) 873 0303.

Entry Formalities

Passports and Visas

Citizens of the USA, Canada, Britain, Ireland and other EU countries, Australia and New Zealand do not need visas to visit Mexico. US nationals **must** have a full passport or another authorized travel document (such as the US passport card) in order to re-enter the US; Canadian citizens can still enter Mexico with only a birth certificate and photo ID, so long as they do not pass through the US, but it's simpler to take a passport. On entering the country all visitors fill in a **Mexican Tourist Card**, which will be completed and stamped by an immigration officer with the length of your permitted stay. Keep the card in your passport, and give it up when you leave. If you arrive **by air** you will be given the form on the incoming flight, and airline staff will collect them at check-in when you leave.

If you **drive** into Mexico from the US you are not required to have a card in the *zona fronteriza* (*see* p.95) for stays of up to 72hrs, but if you stay longer or travel further you should ask for one from border officials. There is no charge for a Tourist Card if you arrive by air (the cost is included in the ticket), but if you enter overland from the US, Guatemala or Belize you will usually be charged 225 pesos (around US$16) for one.

Useful Websites

www.trace-sc.com: Mexico Channel, a comprehensive site for general and travel information on Mexico, with loads of links.

www.mexonline.com: Mexico Online, a similar site with useful travel information and links.

www.mexconnect.com: magazine site with good writing on every side of Mexico.

www.mexperience.com: Excellent UK-based site with a wide mix of travel and other information, and good travel booking links.

www.planeta.com/mexico: Eco Travels in Mexico, a good way to find out about less mainstream, small-scale and adventurous travel possibilities and tour operations.

www.differentworld.com: Online travel service specializing in more individual, special destinations, hotels and services in Mexico.

www.cancun.net: Cancún Online, with links and information on hotels, things to do and all other services in Cancún and the Riviera.

www.mostlymaya.com: Interesting site on everything to do with travel in Maya lands.

www.mayayucatan.com.mx: Yucatán state's official tourist information website.

www.yucatanliving.com: Lively, varied site produced by Mérida-based expats.

www.yucatantoday.com: The site of Mérida's English-language magazine.

www.travelyucatan.com: An enormous range of local information.

www.yucatanwildlife.com: Everything to do with local wildlife, and upcoming tours.

www.campechetravel: The official state tourism site of Campeche.

www.cozumel.net: a similar online guide to facilities on Cozumel.

www.locogringo.com: useful site for hotels and all other services on the Riviera Maya.

www.bill-in-tulsa.com: Hotels, fishing, diving and more in less well-trodden parts of Quintana Roo, especially Akumal and Xcalak.

www.turismochiapas.com.mx: Chiapas state tourism directory, in Spanish only.

www.mundomaya.com.mx: San Cristóbal-based site with information on a very varied range of services, activities, etc. in Chiapas.

This can take a little time, as you must pay the fee at a Mexican government bank and then go back to collect the card.

Standard Tourist Cards are valid for a maximum of six months, and immigration officers at Cancún, Mérida and Mexico City airports usually give 90 or 180 days to most visitors. However, if you come in from Belize to Chetumal, or Tapachula from Guatemala, you may only be given 15 or 30 days. If you want to stay longer, make this clear to the officer as you arrive, and if this doesn't work, apply for an extension in Cancún, at the *Instituto Nacional de Migración* (INM; *corner of Av. Nader and Av. Uxmal, t 884 1749; open Mon–Fri 9–1*). The staff are helpful, and generally give extensions to 90 or 180 days without much question. Apply early at 9am and you can often collect a new card before lunch. Offices in other cities are much slower. **Immigration offices** in other cities are listed in phone books under *Secretaría de Gobernación–Instituto Nacional de Migración*. It is particularly important to have a tourist card in order in Chiapas, because of heavier security checks (*see* Crime and Security, p.108).

Customs

On arrival visitors must fill out a **customs form** (given out on incoming flights). At airports, as you go through customs with your bags, you are asked to press a button at a thing like a small traffic light; if it comes up green, you walk straight through, if it's red, your bag will be searched. This is intended to guarantee that baggage checks are random. Periodically, extra checks may be made.

Departure Tax

On leaving Mexico, airline passengers are required to pay tax of around 500 pesos (US$36). Nowadays, this is nearly always included in the ticket price, but with a very few flights it's still necessary to pay in cash at check-in, so it's a good idea to have some cash with you (the fee can be paid in dollars).

Disabled Travellers

From a very low starting-point, the provision of special facilities such as ramps and handrails for disabled people in Mexico has improved in the last few years – at least in Mérida and Cancún, which now have wheel-chair ramps in many streets. Many state **museums** also have access ramps, and more are being installed. The lack of special facilities can also be compensated for in part by people's helpfulness: bus drivers and ferry crews often make great efforts to find space for a chair. Of **archaeological sites**, Chichén Itzá and Uxmal have smoothish walkways in main areas that are chair-accessible, but most have stony paths where the going is difficult. **Hotels** with fully-adapted rooms are scarce: the best to go for are big resort hotels in Cancún, Cozumel and the Riviera Maya, many of which do have good facilities. Smaller or colonial-style hotels tend to be less suitable, but some have good-size ground-floor rooms.

Useful Contacts

Cancún Accessible, Blvd Kukulcán Km 8.5, Cancún, t (998) 883 1978, *www.cancunaccessible.com*. The region's first agency with specialist services for disabled travellers: transport, rental of wheelchairs and other equipment, trip planning, and full advice on how best to enjoy the Yucatán.

Mobility International USA, 132 E. Broadway, Suite 343, Eugene OR 97401, t (541) 343 1284, *www.miusa.org*.

RADAR, 12 City Forum, 250 City Road, London EC1V 8AF, t 020 7250 3222, *www.radar.org.uk*.

Insurance and Health Precautions

It is essential to have full travel insurance when travelling in Mexico, covering all medical eventualities, including repatriation in an emergency, as well as theft, lost baggage, cancellations and so on. If you expect to do some adventurous activities while here, such as scuba diving, you may need extra cover, so check before you travel. With a decent travel insurance policy, if you need any kind of medical treatment, you can then use one of the good-standard private clinics found in many resort towns. For more on medical and emergency facilities, *see* p.111.

In normal circumstances (i.e. leaving aside exceptional events such as the 2009 swine flu scare) there are no obligatory **inoculations** for travellers in Mexico. However, as a precaution it's advisable to be immunized against polio, tetanus, typhoid, hepatitis A and, to really be sure, cholera. The risk of these diseases is low, but they are present in the area. In remote forest areas of Chiapas and southern Quintana Roo, Campeche and Tabasco there is a slight malaria risk, so to be extra sure take malaria tablets if you intend to go to these areas. Be aware, though, that they can cause secondary effects: those based on **chloroquine** tend to give the least side effects,

but check with your doctor on the varieties currently recommended. Malaria tablets must be taken for at least a week before you enter a risk area, and after you leave.

For more common, minor eventualities you should have a **first-aid kit**, with sticking-plasters and antiseptic wipes to deal with cuts and scratches, bite lotion, and your remedies for diarrhoea and stomach complaints. The risk of these hitting you is much exaggerated, but it's advisable to take along standard remedies (e.g. Imodium, Dioralyte), and rehydration mixtures to aid recuperation, although ideally it's better to survive an attack without them and build up resistance. If you have children with you, the need for medication will be greater.

For information on **Health Services** and **Pharmacies**, *see* p.111; on **Water**, *see* p.120.

Money and Banks

The Mexican currency is the **peso**, which since the 2008 financial crisis began has been at around 14 to the US dollar. The peso partly 'tracks' the value of the dollar, which means that for Europeans (with euros, and even sometimes with sterling) Mexico can appear relatively cheaper than it does to Americans (with around 20 pesos to the pound sterling, and about 18 pesos to the euro). *Because of the unfamiliarity of the peso, most prices in this book are quoted in US dollars.*

There are **coins** for 1, 2, 5, 10 and 20 pesos, and **notes** for 20, 50, 100, 200, 500 and 1,000 pesos. Each peso divides into 100 *centavos*, with little coins for 5, 10, 20 or 50. Confusingly, the most common symbol for the peso is the same as the dollar sign ($), but to differentiate this may be written after the amount (20$). In Cancún, Cozumel and the Riviera Maya prices are often given in US dollars as well as (or even instead of) pesos, and dollars are widely accepted, but note that if you pay in dollars you normally end up paying more: dollar prices stay close to a $1=10 pesos rate that hasn't been given by banks for some time.

If you are travelling to Mexico from Britain or anywhere in Europe take money in **US dollar** cash or travellers' cheques. Mexican **banks** usually give very bad rates against non-dollar currencies, or may even refuse to take them (euros, though, are now more accepted). Canadian dollars are changed quite readily.

Credit cards (MasterCard and Visa, less so American Express) are generally accepted in larger shops, dive shops and hotels of mid-range and above, and near-essential for hiring a car. They are less common in restaurants, and the street and market economy is cash-only. Most bank branches even in small towns have **ATM** cash machines. Most take all major credit cards, but some do not accept debit cards. Many Mexican ATMs also have a limit on the amount you can take out in one go.

Nowadays using ATMs is commonly the best and most popular way of getting cash while travelling in Mexico, as you get the best rates and avoid hefty bank commissions. **However**, there are still areas where banks and ATMs are very scarce, notably **Holbox**, the **Costa Maya** and the **Río Bec**, and where you can be stuck if the only ATM for miles suddenly runs out of cash. So don't rely solely on cards or ATMs, and have at least some dollars or travellers' cheques as back-up. If you expect to stay a while in these areas, consult with hotels on the best way to carry money.

Opening Hours and Changing Money

At **airports** there are exchange offices open whenever there are incoming flights, which tend to give very poor rates. Change only as much as you need to get into town, then go to a bank, an ATM or an exchange office. Medium-sized towns should have at least one bank, but city branches are more efficient and hassle-free. All banks exchange dollars in cash and virtually all will take travellers' cheques, although since these became less common banks can be even slower in handling them.

Bank hours are traditionally Monday to Friday 8.30am–1pm, but most branches, especially in cities, now stay open later, till 4/5pm or even 7pm, and open on Saturdays 9am–1pm. All banks are closed on Sundays and public holidays. Mexican banks sometimes refuse to change money at certain times: this is rarely signposted, so check ('*¿Se puede cambiar dinero/dólares?*') before joining the line; larger branches are usually best. Dollar rates and commissions vary, so it's worth comparing. In all tourist towns there are also exchange offices (*casas de cambio*), open every day.

Note: When changing money, make sure you're not left with only large-denomination notes (i.e. 500 or 1,000 pesos), which are hard to break for any transaction smaller than a hotel bill. Try to keep some change in coins.

Estimating Costs

Travelling costs depend entirely on what you aim to do, but the following may be helpful in making an estimate. There are three pretty clear price zones in this part of Mexico. Cancún and the Caribbean Riviera is one of the most expensive parts of the country, with prices often close to US levels. In the rest of the Yucatán peninsula and most other parts of the region prices are commonly about 70% of Cancún levels or less: they tend to decrease the further south you go. Most of Chiapas is another price zone, and much cheaper. These differences are most marked in hotel prices. On the Riviera they change a lot by season, with higher prices from around December to April and an extra spike for Christmas/New Year and Easter.

In the largest, middle zone, two people travelling together without package bookings can stay in pleasant inexpensive- to moderate- range hotels and eat in mid-range restaurants for about $50–60 a day each (for price guides, *see* pp.104, 111). On top of that are travel costs: $19 each for a first-class bus from Cancún to Mérida, or $40 a day for a hire car, plus anything you want to buy. It's possible to travel for a lot less, staying in cheaper hotels and taking advantage of the huge range of cheap food. Aim to spend $60–70 a day, and you can be very comfortable.

Packing

Clothing

Local attitudes to **clothes** are casual, but it's better not to expose too much flesh, especially if visiting churches. Topless and nude bathing are tolerated in a few places such as Playa del Carmen, Tulum and the Costa Maya, but elsewhere swimming costumes are not that skimpy. The Chiapas Highlands are usually the only area where warm clothing is needed, but it's useful to have long trousers and a long-sleeved shirt to minimize sunburn, scratches and bites when exploring forests and ruins. You will need a **sunhat**, but many people pick one up on the spot, with sunglasses and T-shirts.

Accessories

Sunblock, high-factor **suncream**, aftersun and **lip balm** are all available in Mexico. **Insect repellent** is best brought with you. The best kinds have the ingredient DEET. More natural equivalents are kinder on the skin and smell better, but unfortunately are not as effective. It's also advisable to take a basic **first-aid kit** (see 'Insurance and Health Precautions', p.93).

Among less obvious things worth acquiring ahead are: a **torch/flashlight**; a **snorkel mask** (expensive to buy/hire on site); and especially a **bath plug**, as many hotels strangely don't have them. It's customary to advise travellers to take a money belt, but many give up on them after finding the natives aren't hostile.

Getting There

By Air

Cancún is the main gateway airport for the whole of southern Mexico, but at present it has strangely few flight links to other airports in the region. If you wish to fly to other airports in the south, and especially Chiapas, it will be more convenient to change in Mexico City. Cancún does have excellent bus links with every part of the area (see pp.97, 98).

If you intend to take internal flights within Mexico during your stay, it's worth considering the **MexiPass** scheme (see p.97) before you go, as this can only be arranged from abroad.

From the USA and Canada

It is easy to get to the Yucatán from anywhere in North America. All the airlines listed (see p.96) have daily **scheduled flights** from various parts of the USA and Canada to Cancún. There are also direct flights to other airports in the region: **Continental** flies from Houston to Mérida, Cozumel, Ciudad del Carmen and Villahermosa and from Newark to Cozumel, and **Aeroméxico** from Miami to Mérida three times a week. Via Mexico City, there is an even wider range of flights.

With **charter flights**, the choice expands even more and it's not hard to find returns to Cancún for under $200. The best times for budget charters are Spring Break season (Feb–April) and summer. From Canada there are often Toronto–Mérida charters.

From the UK and Europe

There are currently no direct scheduled flights to Cancún from Britain. The best ways to travel there by scheduled flight are with a change in the USA or via Spain with **Iberia**, which has frequent flights from Madrid. The quickest route is via Miami (about 9hrs) with **American Airlines** or **Virgin Atlantic** (using **Mexicana** for the Miami–Cancún leg). Alternative routes that take a bit longer are via Philadelphia or Charlotte with **US Airways**, or via Houston with **Continental**. Prices for an economy return to Cancún via the US or Spain usually begin at around £450.

Travelling via Mexico City gives a far wider choice: with **British Airways** or **Mexicana** direct, **Air France** via Paris, **KLM** via Amsterdam (often has good deals), **Iberia** via Madrid, or **Aeroméxico** from Madrid or Paris.

It is still easy to fly direct to Cancún from Britain because of the many **charter flights**. It's possible to find prices around £350 return, especially in low seasons. Check flight websites for offers (see box, p.96).

Getting to and from Mexican Airports

Except in Cancún, which now has airport buses (see p.125), at Mexican airports only special **Transporte Terrestre** airport taxis and minibuses, with a distinctive paint scheme with a plane on the doors, are allowed to pick up passengers. Their fares are higher than those of standard cabs, but there's no alternative unless you or a travel agent have arranged for you to be collected. This only applies on arrival; when you are leaving, any local cab can take you to the airport.

By Road

To take a US or Canadian vehicle into Mexico beyond the *zona fronteriza* (about 20km from the border, except in Baja California and Sonora states, where special conditions apply) you must obtain a **Temporary Import Permit**, which must be kept with your Tourist Card (see 'Entry Formalities', p.91). AAA offices near border crossings have the forms required, and help members with paperwork. To get a permit you need the originals and two photocopies of the following: your passport or birth certificate; a Mexican Tourist Card (which you should obtain first); a current driving licence; and the

Major Air Carriers

From the USA and Canada

Aeroméxico, t 1 800 237 6639,
www.aeromexico.com.

Air Canada, t 1 888 247 2262,
www.aircanada.com.

American Airlines, t 1 800 433 7300,
www.aa.com.

Continental, t 1 800 523 3273,
www.continental.com.

Delta Airlines, t 1 800 241 4141, *www.delta.com*.

Mexicana, t 1 877 801 2010,
www.mexicana.com.

Northwest, t 1 800 225 2525, *www.nwa.com*.

United, t 1 800 538 2929, *www.united.com*.

US Airways, t 1 800 622 1015,
www.usairways.com.

From the UK and Europe

American Airlines, t (020) 7365 0777.

British Airways, t 0844 493 0787,
www.british-airways.com.

Continental, t 0845 607 6760.

Iberia, t 0870 609 0500, *www.iberia.com*.

KLM, t 0871 222 7474, *www.klm.com*.

Mexicana, t 0870 890 0040.

US Airways, t 0845 600 3300.

Virgin Atlantic, t 0870 380 2007,
www.virgin-atlantic.com.

Flight Websites

From the USA and Canada

www.bestfares.com
www.cheapflights.com
www.expedia.com
www.flights.com
www.lowestfare.com
www.orbitz.com
www.priceline.com
www.smartertravel.com
www.travelnow.com
www.travelocity.com

From the UK and Europe

www.cheapflights.co.uk
www.dialaflight.com
www.ebookers.com
www.expedia.co.uk
www.flightmapping.com
www.lastminute.com
www.traveljungle.co.uk
www.travelocity.co.uk

car registration papers, in the same name as the licence and passport. At a Customs (*Aduana*) post at any main border crossing, take these to the **Módulo de Control Vehícular** desk. Permits currently cost US$29.70. To get one you effectively also need a credit card, as your card details are taken as a guarantee against you selling the car in Mexico or overstaying the permit, in which case import duty and a fine will be charged on the card. The alternative to using a card is to leave a cash bond for around $400. The permit will name the drivers authorized to use the car, and be valid for six months (a dated sticker comes with it), during which time you can leave and re-enter Mexico as many times as you like. Because of the card guarantee, though, it's important that when the six months is up and/or you finally leave Mexico, you revisit a *Control de Vehículos* desk at the border to have the permit cancelled. Permits can also now be obtained at some (but not all) Mexican Consulates in the US, for a higher fee ($35). For an update on procedures (which sometimes change) and more useful info, check *www.mexconnect.com/travel*.

To get from the Brownsville border crossing around the Gulf Coast to the Yucatán takes about 30 hours driving, and so can be done in four days (or even three). Toll roads make the going quicker at times. Most people, though, make a trip of it, and allow at least a week.

It is not usually permitted to take any US-rented car into Mexico.

Insurance

You will also need Mexican **insurance**, since US and Canadian policies are not valid here. Again, the AAA assists members with tourist policies, and there are plenty of insurance company offices near every border crossing.

The following companies offer a range of short-term policies at reasonable rates:
Mexpro, t 1 888 467 4639, *www.mexpro.com*.
Sanborns Mexican Autoinsurance, t 1 800 222 0158, *www.sanbornsinsurance.com*.

Getting Around

By Air

Mexico has an extensive internal airline network, and all the state capitals and many other cities (in this region Cancún, Cozumel,

Ciudad del Carmen and Tapachula) have daily links to Mexico City. The deregulation of Mexico's airlines has led to the emergence of a number of (sometimes short-lived) low-cost operators and a bigger choice of flights and prices on popular routes, but there are fewer inter-regional flights (such as between Cancún and Chiapas, or Cancún–Mérida). Many places can only be reached via a change in Mexico City.

Small airports have been built at Palenque and San Cristóbal de Las Casas, but currently they have no scheduled flights. For Palenque, the most convenient airport is **Villahermosa**, a 2hr drive away; for San Cristóbal, it's **Tuxtla Gutiérrez** (a 1hr drive). A light-plane shuttle flies between Cancún and Cozumel, and there are airstrips at Playa del Carmen, Isla Mujeres, Holbox and Xcalak, used mainly by air-taxi companies operating out of Cancún or Playa.

Domestic flights can still be good for avoiding long land journeys, even if you have to make a detour through Mexico City. It's worth making the most of the **MexiPass** system (*see* below). In Mexico, look out for fare offers at travel agents.

By Bus

The bus system is one of the great wonders of Mexico, the glue that holds the Republic together. Wherever you are, no matter how remote the village, there will always be some kind of vehicle that will come chugging along to take you to the nearest town, from where there will be buses on to the nearest city – so that for the traveller there's scarcely anywhere that's impossible to reach.

Unless you hire a car, buses will be your main means of transport. There are different grades of buses, giving a choice of prices and comfort levels. In most cities first- and second-class have separate stations, but in most small towns stations are shared. When

---

Mexican Internal Flights

The MexiPass

Offered jointly by Mexicana and Aeroméxico, MexiPass gives foreign visitors discounts of 25–50% on internal flights. You can enter Mexico with any airline, but must book MexiPass tickets outside the country at the same time as you buy your main ticket, specifying routes you wish to travel, and take at least two domestic flights per person on the same trip (three, if coming from North America). European visitors can also get discounts on Mexicana flights between Mexico, the USA and Canada, and some other places in Latin America. For details, contact:

In the USA and Canada: t 1 800 531 7921.
In the UK: t 0870 890 0040.

Main Domestic Airlines

All airlines now offer online booking. All freephone numbers are those used in Mexico.

Aeromar, t 01 800 237 6627, *www.aeromar.com.mx.* Flies from Mexico City and Poza Rica to Villahermosa.

Aeroméxico, t 01 800 021 4010, *www.aeromexico.com.* One of Mexico's two main international airlines; domestically, in this region, it has flights between Cancún, Mérida, Villahermosa and Mexico City.

Aeroméxico Connect, t 01 800 800 2376, *www.amconnect.com.* The arm of Aeroméxico for lower-demand regional routes, with flights

between Campeche, Ciudad del Carmen and Tapachula and Mexico City. Also has some routes that miss out the capital: Mérida–Villahermosa, Mérida–Guadalajara and Ciudad del Carmen–Veracruz.

Aviacsa, t 01 800 284 2272, *www.aviacsa.com.* Flights between Mexico City and Cancún, Mérida, Chetumal, Villahermosa, Tuxtla Gutiérriez and Tapachula.

Interjet, t 01 800 011 2345, *www.interjet.com.mx.* Flights from Cancún, Ciudad del Carmen and Tuxtla Gutiérrez to Mexico City and Toluca (near Mexico City), at low fares.

Mexicana, t 01 800 801 2010, *www.mexicana.com.* The other of Mexico's big two airlines, with flights from the US and many other countries. Domestically, the main airline flies on busier routes such as Cancún–Mexico City.

MexicanaClick, t 01 800 112 5425, *www.clickmx.com.* Mexicana's low-cost arm mainly runs from smaller airports, with frequent flights between Mérida, Cozumel, Chetumal, Ciudad del Carmen, Villahermosa and Tuxtla Gutiérrez and Mexico City, and a has a popular daily international flight between Cancún and Havana. But, there are no flights between the regional airports, or between the regional airports and Cancún.

Volaris, t 01 800 122 8000, *www.volaris.com.mx.* Low-cost flights from Cancún to Toluca, Puebla and Guadalajara, and Mérida–Toluca.

asking directions, specify *la estación de camiones de primera clase* (or *de segunda*).

First-class buses are air-conditioned, modern and comfortable, with ample legroom, videos and (in most) on-board toilets. They run between main towns and cities, with only a few set stops on each route. Fares are pretty reasonable: Mérida–Cancún costs around $19–31. Baggage on first-class buses is rigorously checked in and out.

In Yucatán, Quintana Roo, Campeche and Tabasco the main first-class company is **ADO** (so the station may just be known as *el ADO*); in Chiapas it is **OCC** (Omnibus Cristóbal Colón, actually now a subsidiary of ADO). There are also some more companies, which sometimes have their own depots. As well as ordinary first-class there are extra-luxury services, the **ADO-GL** and top-range **UNO** buses; the chief differences are more legroom, free coffee or soft drinks, better toilets and better videos. First-class services are pretty punctual, and schedules can now be consulted online; otherwise, there is a timetable board in each station. Many towns now have **Ticketbus** shops, where you can buy first-class tickets without having to go to the station, and tickets can also be bought online, through Ticketbus or each company. It's not usually necessary to book first-class buses far ahead, except at holiday times, but is a good idea if you need to travel at a set time.

Second-class buses provide local services and often follow similar routes to those of first-class buses, but stop in just about every village and are 25–30% cheaper. 'Traditionally' they have been older and more basic than first-class buses, but in many areas second-class buses now have a comfort-standard not far below first-class, as in the air-conditioned **Riviera** and **Mayab** buses on the Cancún to Chetumal route. Buses like this may be called *intermedios*, as they stop frequently but offer an *intermedio* level of comfort. Second-class buses are essential for getting to smaller places, but taking them long-distance is usually not worth it, given the extra time involved.

It's not usually possible to book ahead for second-class buses, and they're more likely to be full; you just have to queue for a ticket. There are not usually any printed timetables; services are signed up above ticket windows. Baggage is not checked in; you place it

First-Class Bus Companies

Ticketbus, t 01 800 702 8000, *www.ticketbus. com.mx*. At Ticketbus shops, usually located in town centres, you can buy first-class bus tickets for the same price without having to go out to the bus station (especially useful in cities where the station is on the outskirts). A full list of Ticketbus outlets is on the ADO GL website (under *Puntos de Venta*). Ticketbus also takes online bookings, but it can be faster to use the company sites directly. All these companies are branches of the same group, and the phone number above is the same for all phone bookings.

ADO, *www.ado.com.mx*
ADO GL, *www.adogl.com.mx*
OCC, *www.occbus.com.mx*
UNO, *www.uno.com.mx*

yourself in side compartments or overhead racks on the bus. Watch your bags, especially in southern Campeche and northern Chiapas.

Colectivos, also known as *combis*, fill any gaps left by the other two. Villages not on a second-class bus route have at least one or two *combis* that run up and down to the local town, once or twice a day or more frequently. Other *combis* run long distances along the same routes as buses, but are even cheaper. In many places they are licensed as taxis, others are more 'informal'. *Combis* stop wherever anyone wants them to. They are now more organized in places, but to a great extent *colectivos* still form a word-of-mouth system. In towns, there are known places where *combis* from each village arrive and depart, often near markets. *Combi*-points may even have a battered sign, but the best way to find one for a particular village is to go around and ask: '*¿Por favor, dónde salen los colectivos para...?*' Similarly, at the other end you need to ask when there is a *colectivo* for town B and where it leaves from (usually the main plaza).

This is not a quick mode of transport, and being prepared to be told there isn't one for hours is part of the experience. When you squeeze into a *combi*, ask the driver how much it is to where you want to go, and, if you're at the back, pass the money to other passengers to hand forward. Change is passed back just as punctiliously.

Local Buses
Most cities have local buses. In fact, in some places it can seem the traffic is made up of

nothing *but* buses of all sizes. In most towns they do not have route numbers: instead their destinations are painted on the windscreen. To use them, identify a street or landmark to head for, and look for that. Fares are the same for each bus no matter how far you travel, rarely more than 3–6 pesos. Urban *combis* are cheaper. Some towns have bus stops with blue and white signs, but it's more usual to flag buses or *combis* down at street corners.

By Car

It's possible to get to just about anywhere in Mexico by bus – eventually. However, if you don't have infinite amounts of time, a car is an enormous asset. It is especially so if you wish to visit remoter parts of the coast or more out-of-the-way Maya sites, including some well-known ones such as those on the Puuc route: bus and *combi* routes answer the needs of local people, not tourists, so there may be very few that go near isolated sites.

Car Hire

To hire a car you must be over 21 and have a driving licence, your passport and a credit card. Many agencies give discounts if you pay in cash, but you will still need a credit card to use against a deposit. Some agencies still have VW Beetles (Bugs), but at most the lowest-cost models are now Chevy hatchbacks or Nissans, with the option of a/c. In Cancún and the Riviera many agencies offer small 4-wheel-drives, from $60 a day.

Most car rental agreements include collision damage waiver (CDW) insurance, but note that in Mexico, unless you take out expensive extra cover, this usually only covers the total loss of the car, not 'partial damage', i.e. the kind of bumps and knocks that are much more likely to happen. If you do have any kind of collision with another car, the usual way to settle it is with an exchange of cash, with no insurance involved.

Car hire is much easier in some places than others. The main concentrations of agencies are in Cancún and the Riviera, Mérida and Villahermosa, with a scattering of others in Chetumal, Tuxtla Gutiérrez and Tapachula. Car hire rates in Cancún are no longer all as expensive as they once were but, in general, if you intend to drive any distance it is best to go to **Mérida** and hire there. In Mérida there are small local agencies, such as **México Rent**

Distances/Driving Times

Times given here can only be averages: real driving times – naturally – depend not just on distance but the state of the roads (including the number of *topes, see* below, and villages), the terrain, and traffic. Journeys are far slower in the Chiapas mountains than in flat Yucatán.

Cancún–Mérida 320km/199 miles: 3–4hrs (*Cuota* motorway); 4–5 hrs (*180-Libre*).

Cancún–Chichén Itzá 200km/124 miles: 2½–3hrs.

Cancún–Tulum 131km/81 miles: 2hrs

Cancún–Chetumal 395km/245 miles: 5–6hrs.

Cancún–Xpuhil 516km/320 miles: 7–8hrs.

Cancún–Palenque 867km/538 miles: 12–13 hrs.

Chetumal–Xcalak 155km/96 miles: 2½–3hrs.

Mérida–Chichén Itzá 120km/75 miles: 2hrs.

Mérida–Uxmal 80km/50 miles: 1hr.

Mérida–Campeche 196km/122 miles: 2½hrs.

Mérida–Palenque 555km/345 miles: 7–8hrs.

Palenque–San Cristóbal 191km/118 miles: 5hrs.

Palenque–Villahermosa 145km/90 miles: 2hrs.

San Cristóbal–Tuxtla Gutiérrez 85km/53 miles: 1hr.

San Cristóbal–Tapachula 330km/205 miles: 7–8hrs.

Tuxtla Gutiérrez–Villahermosa (by Highway 187) 354km/219 miles: 4–5hrs.

a **Car** (*see* p.259), which offer the best rates in the region (from about $30 a day).

Cancún and **Playa del Carmen** have a great many rental agencies among which there are now some with rates from around $30 a day or less, but overall you still find the best deals in Mérida. Car hire is usually expensive in Chetumal and Campeche. For Chiapas and Tabasco, agencies in **Villahermosa** are a reasonable option. Local agencies also tend to keep their cars in better condition.

Driving in Mexico

Driving here presents no great difficulties, if a few peculiarities. Main roads are mostly in good condition; on secondary roads look out for potholes and sudden lurches in the road surface, which make it inadvisable to drive at night. You may have to negotiate a few dirt tracks, which may be slow but are usually passable in an ordinary car. The biggest peculiarity of driving here is the *tope*. This is a speed bump, but not as you know it. They may be gentle humps, or great ridges that, if attempted in anything other than first gear, will bring you down the other side with a crash. In towns, they double as pedestrian crossings. In many villages they are announced well ahead (signs saying 'Topes a 200m'), but in remoter places you can come upon them totally unawares. It's impossible to drive around Mexico without being caught out by at least one *tope*.

Flat tyres are a hazard, due to debris on roads and dirt tracks. When you hire a car, the agency should check the spare. If you have to stop for a flat, you are required by law to place a red warning triangle behind the car, which should also come with the car. In the next village there will almost certainly be a tyre repair shop, a *llantera* or *vulcanizadora*, which will fix the tyre and put it back on for 20–50 pesos.

Local road habits include a convention that, if two vehicles approach on a narrow road, the one who flashes lights first claims the right of way. Others relate to **indicators** and **turning left**. If you're behind a slow-moving vehicle and its winkers indicate left, this doesn't usually mean it is about to turn, but that it's clear ahead and you can overtake. Mexican drivers rarely indicate when about to turn, but may put on hazard warning lights as a sign some manoeuvre is imminent. There is also a special procedure for turning left on highways that have no central turning lane (especially on the Highway 307 Cancún to Chetumal road). Instead of moving to the middle of the road and just indicating, pull over to the **right**, with left blinkers on to tell cars behind you to pass. Then, when there's no traffic in either direction, turn left across the road.

Speed bumps aside, official speed limits are 80 to 110kph on main highways, 60kph in the outskirts of towns and 40kph or less in town centres. Fines can be levied on the spot. Also, Mexican police occasionally pull cars over, find things wrong with them, and threaten undefined prosecutions. This is the *mordida* ('bite'). If this happens, usual procedure is to say something like 'Tengo mucha prisa, ¿no se puede arreglar esto?' ('I'm in a hurry, can't we sort this out?'), and proffer 100–200 pesos. However, this is far less common than it's said to be, and most foreign drivers never have any such experiences. You will have to stop at army checkpoints (*see* p.110), but they are not usually very interested in foreigners.

Some roads are toll **motorways**. Most important is the *180-Cuota* part of the way between Mérida and Cancún. This is one of the least-used major roads in the world: the toll, about $25, is seen as too much by Mexicans. It's more interesting and cheaper to take the parallel old road, the *180-Libre*. At each end the roads are signed *Mérida-Cuota* and *Mérida-Libre*. There is a more useful *cuota* road south of Campeche to Champotón, and the *Supercarretera* from Veracruz to central Chiapas is also a toll road.

Parking is restricted in city centres, indicated by the kerb being painted yellow (sometimes red). Many hotels have car parks, and privately-run car parks are marked E or **Estacionamiento Público**. Streets with unrestricted parking are often staked out by an *aparcacoches*, a man with a red rag who stops traffic for you, waves you in and watches your car for a few pesos.

Petrol/Gasoline

All petrol/gasoline in Mexico is sold by the state oil company, **Pemex**. Prices are higher than in the USA but lower than European levels (about 60–70 US cents a litre). All Pemex stations sell unleaded (*magna*) and diesel fuel, and many have higher-grade unleaded (*premium*). Petrol stations (*gasolineras*) are easy to find around cities, and there's one in each town in Yucatán state. There are rarely any between towns on highways, and they are thinly distributed in many rural areas, above all in southern Quintana Roo and Campeche. It pays to know where they are, and fill up when you can. In villages without a *gasolinera* there's often someone who sells fuel unofficially from a tank; ask in shops if anyone has *gasolina*.

For a full tank, say 'lleno, por favor'. Some tips to note at *gasolineras*: it's not unknown for unwary tourists to be short-changed, or for attendants to start the pump with 50 pesos or so already on the gauge. This is not to say all staff will do this, but it's advisable to do what Mexicans do: get out of the car, and look at the pump. The attendant will then demonstrate that it's set at zero before turning it on. This also shows you know what you're doing, and discourages other scams.

By Ferry

Frequent passenger-only ferries run to **Isla Mujeres** from Puerto Juárez, north of Cancún, and to **Cozumel** from Playa del Carmen. The Isla Mujeres car ferry runs from Punta Sam, a bit further north of Cancún, and the Cozumel car ferry operates from Puerto Calica. There are also passenger launches between **Isla Holbox** and Chiquilá. For details, see each section.

By Taxi

There are taxis in all cities, towns and even villages. In smaller places, they blend into *colectivos* (see p.98). If you have a car to yourself, it's a taxi; if you share, it's a *colectivo*. In some towns – notably Villahermosa – where taxis are used by locals almost as much as buses, it's customary for cab drivers to stop to pick up as many people as they can fit in going the same way. The fare is a little less than if you had the cab to yourself.

Taxis do not usually have meters. Instead, in each area there are official set rates for journeys within a town, to the outskirts and so on. This could be expected to create problems, but with one big exception usually works well on trust: in towns like Villahermosa or Chetumal with few tourists drivers rarely overcharge you, even though they realize you don't know what the official rates are. The exception is Cancún and the Riviera. Cancún cab drivers have a reputation for trying out inflated rates on any foreigner. It's useful to know the current rates (see p.128): they're posted at taxi stands at the bus station and Puerto Juárez, and listed in free magazines. The other rule is always to agree the price **before** you get in, and be firm in rejecting anything outrageous.

In Mérida the council has introduced taxis with meters (*taxímetros*). They are usually cheaper than cabs that still use set rates, but all Mérida taxis are relatively expensive, with minimum fares around 30 pesos ($2.70). In most places taxis are cheaper: in most towns, the standard fare is 15–20 pesos or less. In Cancún rates are cheap for trips within Ciudad Cancún, but more than double for anywhere in the Hotel Zone or to the airport. Cabs will travel long distances if you agree a price first. For a group, this can be cheaper than taking a bus. For **airport taxis**, see p.95.

Travelling to Guatemala, Belize and Cuba

Guatemala

The main border crossings into Guatemala are in Chiapas at **Ciudad Cuauhtémoc** and on two roads from **Tapachula**. Direct international bus services run only from Tapachula. At Ciudad Cuauhtémoc, except with the Maya Shuttle service from San Cristóbal, you must get a Mexican bus to the border and a Guatemalan one on the other side. There's also a popular route from **Palenque** to Frontera Corozal, where you take a boat across the Usumacinta river to Guatemala and then another bus to **Flores** (for the ruins of **Tikal**). There are also buses to Flores from **Chetumal** via Belize. For details see relevant chapters.

Citizens of the USA, Canada, Britain and most EU countries, Australia and New Zealand do not need visas to enter Guatemala for up to 90 days. US citizens must have a full passport. Taking a US- or Canadian-registered **vehicle** into Guatemala requires a temporary import permit, which should cost about $20.

Belize

The crossing-point between Mexico and Belize is at **Subteniente López**, just west of Chetumal. Belizean buses run frequently from Chetumal. It is not usually permitted to take a Mexican rental car into Belize.

Citizens of Britain, other EU countries, the USA, Canada, Australia and New Zealand do not need a visa to enter Belize, but must have full passports, which are checked.

If you **enter Mexico** from Belize/Guatemala, you may be given only a 15-day Tourist Card; if you want to stay longer, go to the immigration office at Cancún (see p.92).

Cuba

The Yucatán is a popular jumping-off point for trips to Cuba. There are daily **MexicanaClick** flights between Cancún and Havana, and **Cubana** flights. The agency that sells you the ticket will also provide your Cuban **visa**, for around $20. You need only provide photocopies of your passport. For bargain trips to Cuba, try:

Cancún: Viajes Divermex, Plaza América mall, Av. Cobá, t (998) 884 5005, www.divermex.com.
Mérida: Yucatán Trails, C. 62 no. 482, x 57 & 59, t (999) 928 2582 (see p.274).

Where to Stay

There's a wide choice of hotels at different price and comfort levels in all cities and most towns of any size, and at some major archaeological sites (Chichén Itzá, Uxmal, Cobá) there are luxury-grade hotels. In more remote country areas and small towns accommodation is more scarce, and you may prefer to base yourself in the nearest larger town. In colonial cities such as Mérida, Campeche or San Cristóbal de Las Casasm hotels are often in charming old buildings with plant-lined patios; in more modern cities they tend to be more functional. Cancún and the Riviera have of course any number of big resort hotels, which are cheaper (and easier) to book from abroad as part of a package than by calling direct. Growing even faster are all-inclusive resort complexes, each with its own restaurants, pool, dive trips, beach etc.

Any hotel in or above the *moderate* range (*see* 'Hotel Price Guide', p.104) will provide ample comforts such as large beds, good bathrooms and air conditioning (although as everywhere there can be surprises). Places in the *inexpensive* range may similarly be charming, bright and very enjoyable, or decent value but plain and functional, often depending on the demeanour of the owners and how well the hotel is kept up. Below that there's the Mexican *budget* hotel, with rooms that, if they're clean, decently sized and with good light, can be perfectly pleasant, or may be pretty cell-like. All but the very cheapest hotels have bathrooms (toilet, basin, shower) in every room. All accommodation listed in this guide has been chosen to highlight attractive, enjoyable places to stay – or the only hotel in town, where that's the case.

Many hotels have rooms with a/c, which cost a little more. This can be a mixed blessing: it may be a relief at times, but the machines are often old and noisy, and the cheaper old-fashioned ceiling fan is more peaceful and can be just as efficient. Avoid rooms in *inexpensive–budget* places that are sealed boxes with a/c only; the best option is one with a/c and a fan, so you can choose.

It's advisable to book ahead during the high seasons (mid-Dec–Feb, at Easter and to a lesser extent July–Aug). In and around Cancún you should book at all times. At peak times in busier places (Isla Mujeres especially) don't expect any *inexpensive/budget* hotel to hold a booking beyond mid-afternoon. Ask to be shown a room before you take it, and if it's gloomy ask if there are any others with more light ('*¿Hay cuartos con más luz?*'). There are often larger, brighter rooms on upper floors at the same price. Another feature of Mexican hotels stems from the way Mexicans travel. Families and groups often take one room between them, and many hotels have big, multi-bed rooms, and have no objection to large numbers sharing for only a marginally higher cost, so that travelling in a group, if you don't mind bunking in, can be very cheap.

Hotel Price Ranges

In hotel prices, more than any other field, there are three different economies in the region covered by this book. **Cancún and the Riviera** are one of the most expensive areas in Mexico, above all in high season (mid-Dec–April), with a spike for Christmas-New Year and Easter. At these times it's difficult to get any room for much under $35, mid-range rates are around $60 and up, and big hotels have public rates of around $200. Prices have recently risen particularly in Tulum. There are always inconsistencies however, so it's worth checking around. At other times of the year Riviera prices drop, often by a lot.

In **most other areas** a lower set of prices applies, with variations. A fair number of places are available for $30–35 (or less), and hotels for $40–60 can be very comfortable. In **Highland Chiapas** prices drop again. A budget hotel in San Cristóbal de Las Casas means $15–25 a night, and magnificent colonial-style rooms can cost $60–70.

To avoid confusion the same price bands are used throughout, based on the middle one of the three ranges above. With this in mind, a hotel listed as *luxury* in Yucatán state will be more exceptional than one in Cancún.

Hacienda Hotels

The Yucatán state is peppered with *haciendas*, aristocratic estate-houses built from the 16th to the 19th centuries. In the last few years several have been beautifully restored as seductive upscale retreats, with exuberant gardens, high ceilings and wood beams, palm-shaded pools and restaurants on colonial-style verandahs, providing some of the Yucatán's most distinctive experiences.

Prominent in the *hacienda* revival was the Grupo Plan, which restored several in Yucatán state and Campeche (with a joint website, *www.thehaciendas.com*, and which are also marketed by Starwood Hotels in their 'Luxury Collection' *www.starwoodhotels.com/luxury*). Rooms at these *haciendas* cost from $200 a night. As well as staying at a *hacienda* you can rent a whole one, at **Hacienda Petac**. For details of Yucatán *haciendas*, see pp.272-3.

Following this grand example, some less opulent, but still attractive, *haciendas* have opened, such as **Santa Cruz Palomeque** or **San Pedro Nohpat** outside Mérida, **San Antonio Chalanté** near Izamal (for all, see pp.272-3) and **Hacienda Blanca Flor** (*see* p.381) in Campeche. There is also a more economical *hacienda* for rental, **Hacienda Yunkú**, north of Uxmal (*see* p.273). There's also a *hacienda* hotel near Comitán in Chiapas, the **Parador-Museo Santa María** (*see* p.511).

Guest Houses

For a more personal atmosphere than in the average hotel, Mérida features a growing clutch of old houses that have been turned into relaxed guest houses by resident owners. Some have kitchens for guests' use. Among the most attractive are **Cascadas de Mérida**, **Casa Mexilio, Hotel Marionetas** and **Hotel MedioMundo** (*all moderate*) and **Las Arecas, Casa Ana, Casa San Juan, Los Cielos** and **Luz en Yucatán** (*all inexpensive; see* pp.244-6).

In many places on the Caribbean coast there are medium-sized B&B lodges.

Hostels

The increasing (relative) cost of *budget* hotels has led to a revitalization of the youth hostel concept in Mexico, and several hostels have appeared with beds in dorm rooms for around US $10. Some are part of the local affiliate of Hostelling International (*www.hostellingmexico.com*) or Hostel Mexico (*www.hostelmexico.com*), others are independent. They're usually well kept and quite attractive, with new facilities, and often provide the best real-budget places to stay. Many also have double rooms, for $20 a night.

Cabañas and Palapas

You would be missing out if you visited the Yucatán and did not spend at least a couple of nights under a palm roof by a beach. A *palapa* is that palm roof, and can be a big shelter for sleeping under, a shade over a bar or just a sunshade on the beach; with walls beneath the roof, it becomes a *cabaña*. The original basic beach *cabaña* is just a stick and palm hut, the traditional Mayan *na* with sand floor, a simple mattress or hooks from which to sling a hammock, candlelight and mosquito net, with communal toilets and showers. The first great home of this *cabaña* was **Tulum** (*see* pp.198–201), where due to demand huts like this now go for $25 a day (per hut, not per person). There are still a few basic *cabañas* around Playa del Carmen, in some bays on the Riviera, and in south Quintana Roo near Mahahual. Budget *cabaña*-hotels also crop up in isolated spots on the coast, such as **El Cuyo**.

From these beginnings the *cabaña*-concept took off, and there are now two main grades of cabin: the basic model described above, and the smart *cabaña* with solid walls, tiled floors and comforts: excellent bathrooms and beds, roof fans and terraces on which to sit and watch the birds float by, reaching up to real seductive-luxury standard in many of the new *cabañas* recently built at Tulum, the **Shangri-La** at Playa del Carmen (*see* p.181), or **Xixim** near Celestún (*see* p.286). Tulum has many beautiful *cabaña*-hotels in this style, for which prices have leapt recently. Inland, nearly all 'ecotourism' projects (*see* p.106) also use *palapa*-style, low-impact accommodation.

Staying in Villages

Amid all the talk about ecotourism in this region there has naturally been discussion about low-level projects that directly involve and benefit local people. At present, though, the number of schemes in operation is small, leaving aside small-town cheap hotels, which by their nature tend to be run by locals.

In Yucatán state, you can stay in the middle of a Maya village at **Ek-Balam**, and with a rustic tourism scheme at **Yaxuná** (*see* pp.203, 224). Behind the Riviera there is camping space at **Punta Laguna**, and in south Quintana Roo the very Maya village of **Señor** now has a campsite (*see* pp.210, 334). In Chiapas there are several places to stay in the Lacandón village of **Lacanjá** (see p.469), and other communities with village tourism schemes, such as **Misol-Ha, Laguna Miramar, Las Guacamayas** and **Las Nubes**.

Hotel Price Guide

Prices based on the cost of a double room for one night.

Category	Mexican Pesos ($)	US Dollars ($)	UK Pounds Sterling (£)
luxury	Over 2,800$	Over $200	Over £135
expensive	1,720–2,800$	$120–200	£82–135
moderate	900–1,720$	$60–120	£42–82
inexpensive	430–900$	$30–60	£20–42
budget	Under 430$	Under $30	Under £20

Apartments and Renting Longer-term

Thanks to all the condominium-building on the Caribbean coast, there are many self-contained apartments and villas available, notably around Playa del Carmen and Akumal. Rental agents advertise on the internet. Rents can be very reasonable, especially outside the winter season. Long-term rents are a speciality in Puerto Morelos. In small places, you can find houses just by asking around.

Away from the Caribbean coast, Progreso, Chicxulub and other towns on the north coast are largely made up of beach houses that are used by *Meridanos* for only a few weeks each year. The rest of the time they're rented out. There are always places available in Progreso, and the same agencies may have places in Mérida as well. In Chiapas, a range of cheap rents is available in San Cristóbal de Las Casas.

Camping and Trailer Parks

On the Riviera there are organized camp sites, most with trailer parks as well, north of Cancún at El Meco, in Playa del Carmen and, especially, south of the town at **Paamul**. Many camp sites have spaces where you can sling up a hammock beneath a *palapa*. Inland, there are camp sites and trailer parks near Chichén Itzá and Uxmal, and a couple of very lovely, tranquil camp- and hammock sites on Lake Bacalar. Elsewhere, there are fewer camp sites than places where you can camp: beaches in Mexico are public property, and along the Tulum–Punta Allen road, the 'Costa Maya' down to Xcalak or the Yucatán sand bar, lovers of lonely places can stop more or less anywhere, but you will have to take everything with you (including bug repellent). In **Chiapas**, there are camp sites at Misol-Ha and Agua Azul, and you can camp in the grounds of some budget hotels in San Cristóbal de Las Casas. It is not advisable to camp anywhere in Highland Chiapas without prior permission, due to the political situation and the complex local system of landholding.

Tours and Tour Operators

For a select list of websites with general and specialist information, *see* 'Useful Websites', p.92. A great many **dive** hotels and other services in Mexico advertise directly on the internet. Simply search for *dive Mexico*.

Outside Mexico

Hundreds of agencies across the **USA** and **Canada** offer flights or all-in packages to Cancún and other parts of the region, and it's impossible to mention more than a few of the more interesting specialists here. An enormous range of flight deals is available on the web, and from February through to May an equally huge choice of low-cost Spring Break packages is offered to students.

Many large-scale **UK** tour operators – Kuoni, Thomson's, Unijet, Cosmos – include Cancún and the Riviera in their brochures.

In Mexico

Within Mexico there are many local, small-scale tour agencies and organizations that are a great help in getting around the remoter parts of the country and, in particular, provide a rapidly expanding variety of **environmental** and **adventure tours** (*see* p.106). Most of the UK-based **trek** companies offer 'Mayan Route' small-group tours, often combining the Yucatán with Chiapas and parts of Belize and Guatemala, with variations in the details.

Local Tours and Guides

In any town with a few tourists local agencies run tours to archaeological sites, nature reserves and so on. **Bus tours** are an easy way of seeing the region's treasures, above all if you don't want to hire a car, but in the most visited parts of the Yucatán they have notable limitations. They usually give you two hours at a major site such as Chichén Itzá, which is too short, and always seem to shepherd everyone round together at the hottest times of day. Also, while some tour companies offer fresh trips, many itineraries are unchanged and unimaginative, and rarely go near lesser-known Maya sites. Bear in mind that many big sites are easy to get to by yourself, giving you all the time you want; especially Chichén, on a major bus route.

It's best to be selective with tours, and use them for places otherwise hard to get to. At another extreme, if expense is a minor worry, there are **air tours**. The air-taxi services AeroCosta (Cancún), Aerobanana (Isla Mujeres) and Aerosaab (Playa del Carmen), run light-plane tours to Isla Mujeres, Chichén, Holbox, Xcalak and San Pedro, in Belize.

Where tours really come into their own is in **Chiapas**. The distances, and the state of many roads, make independent travel into many remote areas daunting and slow even if you have a car. The spectacular Maya forest sites of Bonampak and Yaxchilán are now far easier to get to under your own steam, but good tours are available from Palenque if you don't wish to drive yourself. In **Highland Chiapas**, you are strongly recommended to visit villages such as Chamula and Zinacantán with a guide from San Cristóbal, as they open doors for you that otherwise stay firmly shut.

Of the other kinds of trips available, some of the most valuable are **nature tours**, exploring the region's landscapes, wildlife and natural attractions. The Biosphere Reserve of Si'an Kaan, south of Tulum, can only be visited by guided tour (*see* p.202). Most such trips are run for a minimum of four or six people, so if there are fewer of you it's advisable to look around for other interested parties. This kind of trip blends in with using **local guides**. In many towns and villages there are men who make a bit of extra money by guiding visitors around local forests and ruins. A few have a surprising level of English, others none. They are a great help when exploring remote Maya sites. On the coast it's essential to hire local boat-owners (*lancheros*) to see wildlife. Several hours rarely costs much over $30 (but more, $50–75, with a boat), but you can cut costs by going as a group.

At the largest **Maya sites**, you will find officially licensed guides available for hire. They are impressively skilled linguists and often very informative; their tours last 1½ hours for a set fee of about $35. At more deserted sites you may be approached by local kids who will offer to guide you, even though they may show little knowledge of what they're looking at. If you wish you can pay them off with a few pesos in advance.

Ecotours

A growing number of agencies organize trips to see wildlife and visit the most remote areas. These are mainly day trips, such as visits to the flamingos at Celestún or Río Lagartos; areas for longer trips, often with one or more nights camping, are south Quintana Roo, Calakmul and Río Bec, and especially the Lacandón forest in Chiapas. *See* below, for some of the best specialists. More information can be found on related websites (*see* p.92).

Specialist Tour Operators

In North America

eXito, t 1 800 655 4053, *www.exitotravel.com*. Latin American specialists offering a wide variety of flight-only fares, hotel bookings, package trips, adventure tours and so on.

The Mayan Traveler, t 1 888 843 6292, *www.themayantraveler.com*. Small-group or individual ruins, culture and wildlife tours.

Maya Sites, t 1 877 620 8715, *www.mayasites.com*. Guides used by Maya Sites include leading experts in archaeology and culture. Other activities can be included in itineraries, and service is very personal.

Mayatour, t 1 954 889 6292, *www.mayatour.com*. Specialists in heritage and archaeological tours with comprehensive knowledge of the area. Also wildlife, diving, adventure and leisure tours.

Mexico Adventure, t (480) 820 5407, *www.mexicoadventure.com*. A full range of travel services.

STS Travel, t 1 800 648 4849, *www.ststravel.com*. Major student travel service with plenty of spring break deals.

In Britain

Bales Worldwide, Bales House, Junction Road, Dorking, Surrey RH4 3HL, **t** 0845 057 1819, *www.balesworldside.com*. Guided tours and tailor-made itineraries in Mexico, including classic tours of the Yucatán.

Cathy Matos Mexican Tours/Mexicana, 1st floor, Totteridge House, 1 Allum Way, London N20 9QL, **t** 0870 890 0040, *www.mextours.co.uk*. The leading Mexico-only specialists in the UK, with the widest range of tours, itineraries and contacts. UK reps for many *haciendas* and hotels, and UK agents for **Mexicana**, providing Mexipass discount passes (*see* p.97).

Cox & Kings, Gordon House, 10 Greencoat Place, London SW1P 1PH, **t** (020) 7873 5000, *www.coxandkings.co.uk*. Prestigious travel service providing bookings at *haciendas*, tailor-made itineraries and luxurious tours.

Journey Latin America, 12–13 Heathfield Terrace, London W4 4JE, **t** (020) 8747 3108/8315, *www.journeylatinamerica.co.uk*. One of the UK's best sources for flight-only deals, bespoke and organized tours and language courses.

South American Experience, Welby House, 96 Wilton Road, London SW1V 1DW, **t** 0845 277 3366, *www.southamericanexperience.co.uk*. Helpful specialists with small-group tours, tailor-made trips, flight-only deals and 'Soft Landings', flight deals with the first two nights' hotel included.

Trips Worldwide, 14 Frederick Place, Clifton, Bristol BS8 1AS, **t** 0800 840 0850, *www.tripsworldwide.co.uk*. An imaginative range: wildlife and heritage tours, fly-drive combinations and tailor-made itineraries.

Ecotourism and Adventure Tours

El Tour/Bike Mexico, **t** Canada (416) 848 0265, *www.bikemexico.com*. Very friendly Canada-based operation offering small-group cycle tours led by able, multi-national guides.

Explore Worldwide, Nelson House, 55 Victoria Road, Farnborough, Hants GU14 7PA, **t** 0845 013 1539, *www.explore.co.uk*. Small-group treks and other activities, including diving.

Funky Tours, Canada (514) 448 2416, *www.funky tours.com*. Small-scale operation whose small-group trips in Mexico, Guatemala and Belize have been warmly praised.

Legacy Tours, PO Box 8156, Spokane, WA 99203, USA, **t** (509) 624 1889, *www.legacy-tours.com*. Individual birding tours with expert guide.

Mesoamerican Ecotourism Alliance, 4076 Crystal Court, Boulder, CO 80304, USA, **t** 1 800 682 0584, *www.travelwithmea.org*. Works in partnership with local conservation organizations throughout Mexico and Central America; offers many specialist tours, including some to remote areas like El Triunfo in Chiapas.

VENT (Victor Emanuel Nature Tours), 2525 Wallingwood Drive, Austin, TX 78746, USA, **t** 1 800 328 8368, *www.ventbird.com*. Bird-watching specialists with tours to El Triunfo and other remote sites in Chiapas.

Diving and Water Sports

Scuba Voyages, 595 Fairbanks Street, Corona, CA 92879, USA, **t** 1 800 544 7631, *www.scuba voyages.com*. A big range of all-in scuba trips.

World of Diving & Adventure Vacations, 215 Pier Ave, Hermosa Beach, CA 90254, USA, **t** 1 800 463 4846, *www.worldofdiving.com*. Diving packages for all experience levels.

In Mexico

See also under each town.

Pronatura, *www.pronatura.org.mx*. No tours but the main Mexican conservation organization, and a good source of info.

Ecocolors, C. Camarón 32, SM27, Cancún, **t** 01 800 326 5577, **t** US and Canada 1 866 978 6225, *www.ecotravelmexico.com*. Birding, shark-watching, kayaking, cycling, camping and more in Quintana Roo and Yucatán.

Ecoturismo Yucatán, C. 3 no. 235, x 32-A & 34, Mérida, **t** (999) 920 2772, *www.ecoyuc.com*. The longest-established local wildlife and ecotour specialists, offering an enormous range of trips, car and bike hire and hotel bookings. Ecoturismo also supports many small village ecotourism schemes, and so is a good place to find out about some that are not widely known, and sponsors the annual **Toh Yucatán Bird Festival** in Nov–Dec.

Explora, C. 1 de Marzo 30, San Cristóbal de Las Casas, **t** (967) 674 6660, *www.ecochiapas.com*. Excellent agency that has adventure trips around Chiapas, and handles bookings for **Campamento Río Lacanjá**, near Bonampak. Offers rafting, kayaking and hiking (*see* p.469).

Journey Mexico, Av. Palenque 112, SM26, Cancún, **t** (998) 898 2237, in US and Canada **t** 1 800 513 1587, *www.journeymexico.com*. Leading adventure and ecotour specialists with options throughout Mexico, at varied prices: custom-made itineraries a speciality.

Mayan Quest, C. Sac-Xib 9, SM26, Cancún, **t** (998) 874 0254, *www.mayanquest.com*. Highly regarded agency: nature and birding trips in Sian Ka'an and Quintana Roo are specialities.

Red de Ecoturismo Yucatán, C. 56-A no. 437, x C. 29, Mérida, **t** (999) 926 7756, *ecoturismo.ac@ gmail.com*. Small organization set up to assist the various village ecotourism schemes – *cenotes*, *cabañas*, forest trails – that are opening up in villages around the Yucatán. Can also be contacted through Ecoturismo Yucatán.

Red de Turismo Indígena, **t** (55) 5676 1394, *www.rita.com.mx*. An association of local tourism schemes set up by indigenous communities throughout Mexico.

Yucatán Adventure, *www.yucatanadventure. com.mx*. Set up in association with **Hacienda Chichén** hotel (*see* p.237), this group works closely with Maya communities, and offers an exciting range of wildlife, village and *cenote* visits.

Practical A–Z

Children 108
Crime and Security 108
Eating Out 110
Electricity 110
Entertainment 110
Health and Emergencies 111
Internet 111
Language and Communication 111
Media 112
National Holidays 112
Opening Hours 113
Photography 113
Post Offices 113
Shopping 114
Sports and Activities 116
Telephones 118
Time 118
Tipping 118
Toilets 119
Visiting Archaeological Sites and
   Museums 119
Water 120
Women Travellers and Sexual
   Attitudes 120

07

Mexico Information

Time Differences
Country: –6hrs GMT; –1hr EST
Daylight Saving: early May to late September

National Dialling Codes
To call anywhere in Mexico outside your immediate area, dial 01 and then the area code, before the numbers shown in this guide. Area codes are shown with the listings information for each place in the guide. If a Mexican number begins with 1, it is usually a cell phone, and you will probably have to use access codes 044 or 045 instead of 01 before the number, with the same area code.

International Dialling Codes
To call Mexico: country code 52 + (area code) + (number)
To call from Mexico: Australia: 00 61; Ireland: 00 353; New Zealand: 00 64; UK: 00 44; USA and Canada: 00 1

Emergency Numbers
Common number for all services: in most areas, 066 or 060

Local Consulate Numbers
Canada: t (998) 883 3360; **UK**: t (998) 881 0100; **USA**: t (999) 942 5700/(998) 883 0272

Children

Highland Maya in Chiapas often ask why *gringos* never seem to have any children. Away from beach resorts, foreign children are seen relatively rarely; Mexican children, on the other hand, are everywhere.

Brave parents who venture into the Mexican interior with young children often find they represent a point of contact with locals that's lost to the childless traveller. Children get smiled at and indulged, and their parents are accorded added respect.

On a practical level, Cancún and the Riviera offer everything associated with a family holiday: hotel pools, water parks, rides and, of course, beaches. **Eco-theme-parks** like Xcaret are expensive, but give an enjoyable, very safe introduction to snorkelling in Caribbean lagoons. There are also **dolphin pools** (*see* p.76). Of the beach areas, Cozumel is one of the best for kids, with tranquil water and a lot to see just offshore. Away from the Caribbean

keeping kids entertained is more a matter of involving them in local sights. Big Maya ruins like Chichén have huge spaces for exploring, and Palenque is surrounded by real jungle. Villahermosa and Tuxtla Gutiérrez have great zoos, with hard-to-see local wildlife.

Travelling with a family it's specially recommended to **hire a car**, as long bus trips are perfect for getting kids bored. This will also work out cheaper than public transport.

Mexicans themselves often travel in big family groups, so virtually all **hotels** have at least a few very large, multi-bed rooms, which make travelling as a family and sharing rooms easy and economical. **Restaurants** will often try to cater for special requests. If your kids are inflexible, there are pizzerias (and burger chains) in most towns. As to drinks, local milk is thin, so if you need it stick to the best (most expensive) brands available in supermarkets. Try to interest kids in the local fruit juices; otherwise, Coke or Pepsi are always available.

Crime and Security

Is Mexico Dangerous?
There is a long-standing preconception, especially in the USA, that Mexico is a violent and dangerous place. This has naturally been magnified since President Felipe Calderón's government launched an open confrontation with powerful drug cartels in 2007, reflected in street fights between the army and cartel hitmen, intensified turf wars between the cartels, kidnappings and some horrifically grisly murders.

Despite all this, first-timers are still making their way to the Yucatán, perhaps with some trepidation. And then, a few hours after arriving, they wonder what everybody was talking about. It might seem paradoxical, but this is a very peaceful and tranquil place, and many of the Americans and Canadians who retire here cite the absence of crime as a prime reason for coming. A distinctive, gentle decency is characteristic of the Yucatán. The crime rate in most of the peninsula is actually very low. There are few firearms in circulation (one area in which Mexico's 'failed state' is quite successful), and violent crime of any kind is rare. Chiapas, even with its political problems (*see* below) now likes to be described as 'the most peaceful state in Mexico'.

The battle with the cartels is obviously a major crisis for the Mexican government, and nobody should play down the real problems. However, perceptions of this situation outside the country – above all as regards its effects on foreigners travelling there – have also been wildly distorted by sloppy and ignorant reporting in the international media, which has a tendency to treat the whole of this 2,000-mile-long country as if it were the same place. Ideas are carelessly thrown around such as the one that Mexico is soon to be a 'failed state' like Somalia, and the impression is allowed to fly that this is a place to avoid. Negative, often prejudiced perceptions are only reinforced when mixed in with entirely unrelated events in Mexico such as the swine flu scare.

The main flashpoints in the 'drug war' are border cities like Ciudad Juárez, Nuevo Laredo or Tijuana, parts of Mexico City and other northern cities such as Culiacán In the Pacific state of Sinaloa. There are incidents in other parts of the country, but in the Yucatán they have been very sporadic and have not affected tourists. It has long been known – since well before the current crisis – that remote places in Quintana Roo have been used as drug conduits between Colombia and the USA, and military checks on roads have been stepped up in an effort to control this traffic. But tourists will have no contact with this kind of criminal activity unless they go looking for it.

Fear of the crisis zone on the border, 1,800 miles away, is just not part of life in the Yucatán Peninsula and Quintana Roo, and attempts to suggest that it is are distorted. There really is no reason to be especially fearful of coming here. For some lively comments on the safety of Mexico travel and related issues, check www.playasonrisa.com/TravelAdvisory.html and www.bikemexico.com/fear.

As everywhere in the world, there are places where risks are higher, but these are more to do with petty crime than drug wars. Parts of Cancún City – away from the more touristy areas – have an edgy, urban atmosphere, and sadly there is a certain level of petty crime, assaults, beach thefts and so on around Playa del Carmen and parts of Tulum. There is a greater likelihood of street thefts in Tabasco and northern Chiapas, and robberies and car-jackings on empty country roads. But, so long as you keep to standard, sensible rules – stay where there are people around, watch your bags – it's easy to travel around without encountering problems.

Political Conflict in Chiapas

Since 1994 there has been an ongoing conflict in central Chiapas between the Zapatista rebels and the Mexican army, right-wing paramilitaries and others. It's wise to avoid predictions, for flare-ups are still possible, but at present the situation in Chiapas scarcely obstructs travellers at all.

The Zapatistas currently still control about 2,000 villages around Chiapas, but there are no formal contacts between them and any federal or state authorities. Instead, Zapatistas, their opponents and the army exist in a kind of eternal standoff, which neither side wishes to openly disrupt. The Zapatistas have never engaged in attacks on tourists or hostage-taking, or anything similar; on the contrary, they have relied on international public opinion as a major source of support, and now invite tour groups to visit Zapatista villages. The Mexican army, meanwhile, is concerned that tourists go on their way with the least unpleasantness. The shadowy right-wing paramilitary groups are less disciplined, but are not usually much interested in conventional tourists.

The 'conflict' still exists, but often in the form of small-scale land disputes, or when the army attempts to encroach on Zapatista villages, generally in remote places far from main highways and media attention. A constant feature of the Chiapas conflict is that it goes on almost in secret. The army and its allies are determined to ensure that, whenever confrontations and/or human rights abuses are likely to occur, they should do so away from any foreign attention – hence the contrary interest of the Zapatistas in having international observers in many situations, to deter incidents from developing. These volunteer observers are the only foreigners likely to be caught up in clashes, if they confront anti-Zapatista groups. Other foreign visitors in Chiapas are in a position of greater safety than locals, and San Cristóbal de Las Casas and the main villages visited by travellers are very peaceful. For more on the conflicts of Chiapas, see p.472.

Police and Military Checkpoints

If you are robbed or are a victim of any other kind of crime, report the incident to the police in order to get an official statement for an insurance claim. In Mérida, Cancún, Playa del Carmen and some other towns there are special **Policía Turística** units with English-speaking officers. *Cancún Tips* and *Yucatán Today* (see p.136) have handy lists of local emergency numbers.

You will also encounter **military checkpoints** on country highways, particularly in Quintana Roo. Their main function is to prevent drug trans-shipments through the peninsula. Don't be spooked: the soldiers cause little trouble to foreigners, and usually just ask where you're going and wish you well. They may look at your bags, ask you to open up your car and check your passport and Tourist Card (especially in Chiapas).

There are severe penalties for possession or transportation of marijuana or narcotics. Anyone caught in possession is usually refused bail. The safest thing, of course, is not to touch any.

Hustling and Begging

As in many countries where there are a lot of people with insecure incomes and plenty of tourists, many people try to make money by wandering around selling things to foreigners, especially in Mérida. Yucatecos, though, tend to be among the world's worst ever hustlers. If, in answer to the standard question, '¿Quiere hamaca?' ('Do you want a hammock?'), you say politely 'No gracias', or better 'Yo tengo una' ('I've already got one'), most will just say 'Bueno' and walk on. Alternatively, speak a bit of Spanish and the chances are they'll express surprise and start a conversation, thoughts of a sale apparently forgotten. Begging, again, is rarely aggressive. Street selling is more intensive in Chiapas, especially in Palenque and at Agua Azul, where kids selling crafts or fruit are far less ready to accept no for an answer.

Eating Out

Throughout this guide, restaurants are arranged in three **price categories** (see box, right), based on price per head for an average three-course meal with drinks. However, in Mexican restaurants there is no obligation to have multiple courses, so meals can easily work out cheaper. Bear in mind too that the *expensive* range is an open-ended one, so that while in Cancún there are places where you can easily spend over US $30 a head, in Chiapas it may be hard to part with much over $25 even in the best restaurant in town.

See **Food and Drink**, pp.77–86, for a menu glossary and information on Mexican cuisine, tastes and eating habits. For information on Tipping, see p.118, and on **Water**, see p.120.

Electricity

Electricity in Mexico works on a 110v system, as in the USA and Canada, with the same flat-pin plugs. Newer equipment has three- rather than two-pin plugs; adaptors from three to two pins can be bought in any *tlapalería* or ironmongers (in Calle 58 x 61 in Mérida there are several). If you wish to use British or European 220/240v equipment take a plug adaptor and (if required) a current adaptor, as these are impossible to get.

Entertainment

Every Mexican town has a few discos, and cities have air-conditioned cinemas that show Hollywood movies in English with Spanish subtitles. However, just as life on the street is often more interesting than anything you pay for, in Mexico a lot of live entertainment is on offer informally. Music can be found in all kinds of places; in bars and restaurants, or for hire in the troubadour style of the Yucatán trios or *mariachis*. It's also a community experience: as well as *fiestas* (see pp.88–90), many towns have free concerts, folklore displays or street dances in central squares on one day or more every week (usually Sunday).

There are also two specific kinds of spectacle in the region. The Spanish-style **bullfight** has a long tradition in the Yucatán, and is a feature of village *fiestas* (see p.90). There are bullrings in Mérida and Cancún.

Restaurant Price Categories

Prices based on the cost per person of a three-course meal

Category	Mexican Pesos ($)	US Dollars ($)	UK Pounds Sterling (£)
expensive	Over 280$	Over $20	Over £14
moderate	100–280$	$7–20	£5–14
budget	Under 100$	Under $7	Under £5

The other distinctive show is the **charrería**. A *charro* is a Mexican cowboy, in the classic wide *sombrero*, embroidered jacket and tight trousers with embroidery down the leg. Like other elements of typical Mexican-ness, *mariachis* and tequila, their home is Jalisco state in central Mexico, and in the Yucatán they're an imported article. Nevertheless, a *charrería* can be genuinely impressive. A kind of rodeo, it features horse-wrangling, steer-wrestling and displays of horsemanship by the *charros* and *charras* (whose feats can be even more impressive, since to remain ladylike they must ride side-saddle in flouncy skirts). There are *lienzos charros* (special grounds for the shows) outside most large towns, which hold *charrerías* on occasional weekends. Tourist offices have details.

Health and Emergencies

There are well-equipped, modern **private health clinics** in all main cities and resort areas, with English-speaking staff. If you need any kind of medical treatment these will be the best places to turn to, using your travel insurance. Clinics in the major cities are listed in relevant chapters in this guide; elsewhere, ask at hotels for recommendations.

Small towns and country areas have **public health centres** (*centros de salud*) which may lack some sophisticated equipment but respond perfectly adequately in emergencies.

If you need to **phone** for help, most parts of Mexico now use **t 066** as a central number for all emergency services (although some use **t 060**). However, it can be quicker to call the service you require direct; the local **Red Cross** (*Cruz Roja*) has ambulances on call. Numbers are in the phone book or hotels should be able to give them to you.

Pharmacies

Pharmacies are peculiarly abundant in cities and even small towns. In most places a few open 24 hours a day. They stock a wide range of goods including purified water, cosmetics, sanitary products, aspirins and a huge range of medicines, some of which are only available on prescription in other countries and should be treated with care. Local people often ask the advice of a pharmacist rather than go to a doctor. They also provide different forms of contraception, including condoms (*condones*).

Internet

Unsurprisingly, given the the the state of the postal system, Mexico is highly internet and e-mail conscious. Internet cafés are plentiful in cities and can even be found in small towns. They usually charge around $1 an hour, or $2.50 or so in places such as Playa del Carmen. Server connections can be volatile, but as elsewhere e-mail has become by far the easiest means of keeping in touch while travelling, and the most reliable means of making hotel reservations.

See box, p.92, for a list of useful websites.

Language and Communication

Around Cancún and the Caribbean strip it's really not hard to spend a week or even more without giving the slightest recognition to the Spanish language. The level of English falls dramatically, however, as soon as you head inland, and you will gain immeasurably on your trip if you can handle even basic Spanish. Local guides in forest areas rarely know more than limited English and, in any case, Mexico still operates far more of an oral culture than North America or Europe. Bus timetables are unreliable, street names are not signposted, opening times are nowhere to be seen: in all kinds of situations where you are used to reading or following signs, you have to ask.

Communicating Effectively

Communication here is not just a matter of the meaning of words, but of how you use them. Mexicans in general, but the Maya above all, are extremely polite and lay great importance on courtesy. Observing unhurriedly the old forms of courteous and ceremonious Spanish, and apparently strange practices such as preceding a question by a question ('¿Le puedo hacer una pregunta?', 'May I ask you a question?'), forms an essential bridge to being heard. The Yucatán Maya can appear impenetrable and stony-faced, but greet someone with a proper 'Buenos días' and you may be rewarded with the most dazzling of smiles. This is a more amiable and effective means of communication than the self-conscious, brash upfrontness that has grown up in Mexico's tourist zones. In Cancún and Playa del Carmen, many workers veer from traditional formality to the opposite extreme of forced, overdone and slightly self-defensive good cheer, with the 'Hey amigo d'you wanna beer?' that often comes over as just pushy.

The Joys of Getting Lost

Taking on board the need for a courtly style of speech doesn't mean your communications will all then be crystal clear. This stems in part from courtesy itself: rather than disappoint you by admitting they cannot help, people will often send you off somewhere with apparent certainty, even if they haven't a clue what you're asking for. Another trait is imprecision: no matter how well you define your question, as in 'Is this the road to the bus station?', the standard response will be 'P'allá', 'Over there' (from por allá) accompanied by an undefined hand gesture; whether this means p'allá to the left (izquierda) or p'allá to the right (derecha) can involve real mental gymnastics. Getting lost at least a few times is inevitable in Mexico. This also means you find yourself in all sorts of places you never thought to visit. It's best to enjoy it.

Learning Spanish and Local Languages

San Cristóbal de Las Casas and **Mérida** are the main centres for Spanish courses. Schools offer courses on a tuition-only basis if you want to find your own accommodation, or via homestays with local families for immersion in the language and closer contact with local people. Schools also run extra activities, such as cookery classes and trips to Maya sites, and some have courses in indigenous languages such as Tzotzil or Yucatec. For schools, see sections on these cities.

Media

Newspapers

An English-language paper is published in Mexico City, The News, and the Miami Herald has a 'Caribbean Edition' produced in Cancún with local news and features. They are most easily found on the coast and in Mérida.

There are swathes of Mexican papers. Most states have one main paper – Diario de Yucatán in Yucatán, ¡Por Esto! in Quintana Roo. In main towns, the Mexico City press goes on sale mid-afternoon: the erudite La Jornada is the main liberal paper; Excelsior is the most traditional, conservative heavyweight daily.

Television and Radio

The omnipresent means of communication in modern Mexico, TV can reach into the remotest village and very often the cheapest hotel. Local programming is dominated by Mexico's own telenovelas (soap operas), lurid crime reporting, movies and sport, especially football. As well as the main networks (Televisa, TV Azteca), cable and satellite TV have grown rapidly, so that in small hotels you can be surprised to find over 40 channels, with swathes of local services. Also usually included are US channels (CNN, ESPN), and Rupert Murdoch has a firm grip on Latin America with Sky channels and the Fox Sports Americas network, which (like ESPN en Español) frequently shows soccer games from the European leagues. Movies on cable channels are often shown in English, with Spanish subtitles.

National Holidays

The country's official holidays are important events in the life of the Mexican state, which observes them with parades and patriotic rhetoric, above all in the capital. On the ground, curiously, they attract nothing like the interest shown in traditional *fiestas*, and for many people are just a day off work. Exceptions are the Virgin of Guadalupe and Christmas, which are national and religious celebrations. In Holy Week, Easter Thursday, Good Friday and Easter Saturday are also official holidays. The only institutions that consistently mark national holidays are banks and government offices, all of which close.

1 Jan	*Año Nuevo* (New Year's Day)
5 Feb	*Día de la Constitución* (Constitution Day)
21 Mar	*Nacimiento de Juárez* (Birthday of Benito Juárez)
1 May	*Día del Trabajo* (Labour Day)
5 May	*Batalla de Puebla* (Battle of Puebla)
16 Sept	*Día de la Independencia* (Independence Day)
12 Oct	*Día de la Raza* (Discovery of America)
20 Nov	*Día de la Revolución* (Anniversary of the Revolution)
12 Dec	*Nuestra Señora de Guadalupe* (Our Lady of Guadalupe)
25 Dec	*Navidad* (Christmas)

Opening Hours

Shops generally follow a siesta pattern: they open early, are busiest in the morning and close from 1–2pm to 4–5pm, and then stay open until dark, around 9pm.

Set timings are not part of Mexican culture, so there are exceptions. In **cities**, several shops stay open all day, until late at night or round the clock. There are always one or two 24hr pharmacies. In **small towns** and villages, shops are often just open from morning till night. **Markets** get busy very early, and mostly close by 2pm. City shops usually close on Sundays, but in smaller towns Sunday morning can be the busiest shopping time of the week.

Churches are always opened at sunrise and nearly always closed in the afternoons, from about 12.30–1.30pm until 4 or 5pm, when they will be opened again until after dark.

For bank hours, *see* p.94; for museum and archaeological site hours, *see* p.119.

Photography

There are restrictions on the use of video cameras at archaeological sites (*see* 'Visiting Archaeological Sites and Museums', p.119). Otherwise photography in most of the region poses no special problems, although Yucatán village Maya tend to be shy of the camera. The major difference is in central Chiapas, where Highland Indians often actively dislike having their picture taken. Contrary to what tourists are regularly told this is not because they think cameras 'steal their souls'; their beliefs are more complex than that (for a different angle on the Highland Maya and photography, *see* p.502). However, they do resent involuntary photography as an intrusion. There is an absolute ban on taking pictures in the churches of villages such as Chamula and Zinacantán, as any guide will remind you.

With individuals (but not in churches, or at some ceremonies), this reluctance to be photographed may be overcome by politely asking permission, or offering a little money. If you're with a guide, they will tell you when you may and may not take pictures.

The other people you shouldn't photograph are soldiers at army checkpoints.

Post Offices

There are **post offices** (*oficinas de correos*) in all towns, and small offices that open a few hours a day in many villages. They sell stamps (*estampillas*), as does any shop with the sign *Expendio de Estampillas*. Post boxes are small metal boxes in two shades of blue marked *Servicio Postal Mexicano*; they're usually fixed to walls, but can be hard to find. Outside post offices there are big red boxes optimistically labelled *Buzón Expresso*, but post office staff tell us that mail in them is dumped in with everything else, so it goes no faster; at best, they have more frequent collections.

Receiving Mail

Post offices have a *poste restante*/**general delivery service** (*lista de correos*). Mail sent this way should be addressed to you with the post code, e.g. your name, Lista de Correos, CP 97000 Mérida, Yucatán, Mexico.

Sending Post

The Mexican postal service is cheap but very, very erratic: letters to North America or Europe might arrive in two weeks, or two months (businesses operate purely by courier or e-mail). For anything important it's best to use the **Mexpost** express courier service, run by the post office but efficient and reliable. Charges are higher than for regular post but still lower than those of commercial couriers. Packages within Mexico arrive the next day, to North America in about two days, to Europe in about three days to a week. In most cities there are Mexpost desks in the main post office, but in some places they have separate offices. It is not available at small post offices.

Shopping

The **market** is one of the very oldest of Mesoamerican institutions, and there are still many Mexican towns in which buying and selling seem to take up more time than any other visible activity. The Yucatán is also one of the world's great souvenir mines; Cancún itself can seem like one giant bazaar. Most people take away at least one T-shirt; more problems may arise with the supposedly traditional craftwork, as many items are now mass-produced, and often poor quality.

The two great places for finding genuinely original craftwork are **Mérida**, for panama hats, hammocks, and embroidery, and **San Cristóbal de Las Casas**, for the weaving of Highland Chiapas. Some towns have their own specialities: Valladolid embroidery, Ticul ceramics, Becal hats. In the main towns there are museum shops and official craftwork stores (usually a *Casa de Artesanías*) where you can see an array of high-standard local work. Their prices are higher than average, but they allow you to compare quality against the goods in markets and independent shops.

Books

For books in English, Amate Books in **Mérida** has a good selection, particularly on Maya art and history. The only full English-language bookshops are Alma Libre in **Puerto Morelos**, a *gringo* home-from-home, and La Pared in **San Cristóbal de las Casas**, which has more bookshops than any other city in the south. Many cities have official **Conaculta** bookshops (often attached to museums), which have beautifully illustrated books on Mexican archaeology and traditions, some in English.

Ceramics

Large quantities of earthenware pots are produced in Yucatán state, although many are not very skilfully made. The main centre is the little town of **Ticul**; its most characteristic pots are big water vessels, but local shops also offer smaller, finer pieces. There are also makers in Ticul who use pre-Conquest techniques.

In Chiapas, the remarkable town of **Amatenango del Valle** has a pottery-making tradition believed to date back 2,000 years. It is continued by women, using an open-fired technique to make pots and small figures. The **Lacandón Indians** of the forest near Bonampak have their own, basic ceramics tradition, but this is fast disappearing.

Clothing, Embroidery and Textiles

In textiles more than any other craft the two main areas with distinctive traditions are the Yucatán and the Chiapas Highlands. For more on this, *see* 'Maya Textiles', pp.71–73.

Across the Yucatán the *huípil*, a spotlessly white shift dress with bands of bright flower embroidery around the yoke and the bottom of the skirt, is still everyday wear for many women. Simple, light, loose-fitting and pretty, *huípiles* are ideal for a hot climate, and still worn by all ages from little girls to wizened old ladies. Market stalls and shops have a huge variety, from mass-produced models to dazzling *ternos* for special occasions. *Huípiles* seem to fit Maya women like an extension of the skin, but the jury is still out on whether *gringas* can look good in them. In response to modern demand it's possible to find blouses with *huípil*-style yokes, as well as embroidered handkerchiefs and tablecloths. Besides Mérida, Valladolid is famous for embroidery.

For men, the Yucatán's most distinctive product is the *guayabera*, a light, elegant shirt-jacket, with four pockets, that is accepted as tropical formal wear. Mérida is the main centre of production and sales.

Some shops in the region now use Mexican cottons and traditional fabrics in modern designs that make great, stylish hot-weather wear. Flapping in the breeze at stalls there are also multi-striped *sarape* blankets and throws, made in giant quantities in northern Mexico.

Other parts of the region have their own traditions. Campeche has its own, slightly sober variation on the Yucatecan *huípil*. In Villahermosa a few shops sell the traditional off-the-shoulder blouses and embroidered skirts of Tabasco (for that Rita Hayworth look).

Weaving is one of the strongest traditions of the Highland Maya of Chiapas. Each village has its distinct style, but in San Cristóbal, where Maya women come to sell their wares, they are often jumbled up together. Articles vary greatly in quality, from those created with the full array of traditional skills to others made for quick tourist sales. To get a feel for the best traditional work, it's a good idea to go first to a weavers' cooperative such as **Sna Jolobil** or **J'Pas Joloviletik** (*see* p.495). Prices are higher than on the street, but the weaving is of fine quality, and an objective of these cooperatives is to ensure that Indian women receive a fair price for their work. Blankets (suitable for throws or wall-hangings), belts, blouses (confusingly also called *huípiles*) and small decorative cloths are traditional products, but in response to demand you can now find tablecloths, table mats and napkins.

As well as in San Cristóbal, there are village markets in Chamula, Zinacantán and other communities. The non-Maya region towards Chiapa de Corzo has its own tradition in textiles, weaving bright *sarape* blankets.

Foods

All markets have plenty of stalls offering good picnic ingredients, especially very fresh, cheap **fruit**. Most things on show are not an option as souvenirs, but fans of ferocious food may want to take away some local **chillies**. Livid red and green trays of them, in many shades and varieties, flare in every market; as a rule, the smaller they are, the stronger. In Mérida and other Yucatecan markets you can buy local seasonings such as *achiote* and *chirmole* as powders already made up. Markets also have aromatic selections of fresh **herbs**. Small quantities of peppers and **spices** can usually be brought into Britain as long as they're in a sealed bag; US Customs are much more restrictive. For drinks to buy, *see* pp.81-2.

Hats, Hammocks and Shoes

The **panama hat** (known as a *jipi*) and other articles made from the *jipi* palm – bags, mats – are some of the Yucatán's best-known products. *Jipis* are available in all sorts of styles and sizes, and make the best sun hat for travelling. Any hat worth buying can be rolled up and packed, and should regain its shape naturally when unrolled. Panamas have traditionally been made in the town of Becal, but most of these are now shipped out directly to markets elsewhere, and you'll find a wider range of hats at low prices in Mérida.

The **hammock** is the second great Yucatecan product to take home. Once again, the best place to buy – by far – is Mérida's market area. For notes on hammock-buying, *see* p.276.

Equipped with sun hat and hammock, you may still be after hot-weather footwear. Hard wearing, cheap leather *huarache* **sandals** can be found pair upon pair in any market, and especially in Cancún, Mérida and Chetumal.

Jewellery

Cozumel specializes in jewellery stores aimed at cruise passengers, offering fine silver and settings of Colombian emeralds, Mexican opals and other gems at low (a relative term here) prices. There are also outlets on Isla Mujeres and in Cancún and Playa del Carmen. Most of the stock is international in style, but some feature pieces made with the region's **obsidian**, the deep-black, diamond-hard stone considered so precious by the Maya, and **jade**.

Amber is a traditional treasure of Chiapas. Many shops in San Cristóbal de las Casas offer fine amber and amber jewellery, and boys may come up on the street offering coarser pieces.

Markets and Bargaining

The markets of Mérida and San Cristóbal may be the most spectacular, but there are others in every city. An 'ordinary' Mexican market is remarkable in itself. It may not have much original craftwork, but will look, instead, to satisfy every possible need or desire. Two of the most extraordinary markets are in the border towns of Chetumal and Tapachula.

In most local markets bargaining is still common, especially for bigger articles such as hammocks. Like most public interactions here it's pretty relaxed, and a figure is usually agreed after only a few offers and counter-offers. It is not the norm to bargain in shops, but many will offer discounts if you show an interest in buying more than one of any item.

Useful Stuff and Mexican Junk

The market in Mérida is the best place for just about any practical item you might need, though Chetumal and Tapachula give it close competition. Plus, if you're not wedded to craftwork for souvenirs, consider the myriad options thrown up by day-to-day Mexican markets: plastic shopping bags, tablecloths, party decorations, giant fruit-squeezers and odd cooking implements.

Sports and Activities

Diving and Snorkelling

The late Jacques Cousteau brought the coral reefs of northeast Yucatán to the attention of the world in the 1960s, describing them as one of the richest undersea environments in existence. Cozumel is the largest dive centre, but others are **Cancún, Isla Mujeres, Puerto Morelos, Playa del Carmen, Akumal, Tulum** and smaller places. South of the main Riviera, off Xcalak, is **Banco Chinchorro**, a giant reef that's a growing draw for divers in the know. There are reefs of every grade of difficulty, from shallow, gentle waters to those strictly for experienced divers. The sea is beautifully clear, and the range of coral and marine life spectacular. Outside the Caribbean, off Yucatán state, there is another, ancient reef, **Arrecife Alacranes**, now also open to diving and snorkelling on a limited scale. For more on all reefs, see 'Sealife and the Reefs', p.74.

On the whole, **diving accidents** are pretty rare here, and extra measures have been brought in to improve diving safety, especially on Cozumel. Cozumel has a world-class divers' emergency centre and hyperbaric chamber (*24hr emergency line* t (987) 872 1430). Local dive-masters have their own contacts with it. There is also a well-equipped centre in Cancún (*24hr line* t (988) 892 7680).

Dive Shops and Courses

Most dive centres offer a full range of services, from 'resort courses' – an intro-duction to scuba for complete beginners – through certification courses to accompanied dives and equipment hire for already-certified divers. Most diving here is **drift diving** (you let the current carry you, rather than swimming), so it is very important to follow a guide.

You should only dive with an instructor with an international PADI or NAUI certificate. This is fairly academic, as you are unlikely to see anyone present themselves as a dive-master here without PADI or equivalent qualifications (or who doesn't speak English), but the number of clients entrusted to an instructor can vary: look for the lowest ratio possible, and with beginners' courses never accept more than four per dive-master.

Very roughly, 'resort courses' here **cost** from around $60–80 per person; four- or five-day basic certification courses from about $300; and a half-day two-tank dive for a certified diver about $45–60, with more complicated prices for extra tuition, special and night dives. Discounts and packages are always on offer for diving over several days or for groups. Schools are usually most expensive in Cancún, which is also where seas are most crowded. For better diving, head south to Puerto Morelos, Playa del Carmen or Akumal. Complete beginners will probably be best off in Cozumel, Isla Mujeres or Puerto Morelos, which have the best combination of shallow, tranquil reefs that still have plenty to see. However, you can take introductory courses at almost any dive centre on the coast, even in Xcalak.

Cave Diving

The Yucatán is one of the world's key centres for cave diving, in its thousands of *cenotes* or cave systems and underwater rivers (*see* p.66). The main area is just inland from the southern Riviera, behind Akumal and Tulum, with **Ox Bel Ha** cave, one of the longest underwater cave systems in the world. To go on a cave tour, divers must have at least basic open-water certification; cavern trips (still within sight of daylight) cost from about $80, underground cave dives from about $100.

Prices are lower if you make up a group. For more on cave diving near Akumal and Tulum, see p.189. If you're not already a diver but still want to sample the unique environment of a cenote, cave-diving centres and some other places offer snorkel tours of the upper levels of some caves (from about $25). More and more cenotes are also being explored in Yucatán state, from Mérida, and snorkel trips are available there too, in a more rustic setting than the Riviera (see p.263).

Snorkelling

If you don't want to be bothered with scuba tanks (and the cost), snorkelling is by no means second-best. The same centres that give scuba courses usually offer snorkel trips to inshore reefs (most for around $15–20) and rent snorkels; if you have your own you can just organize yourself. Cozumel, Isla Mujeres and Puerto Morelos are among the best places for easy offshore snorkelling. For a more expensive but no-effort alternative, there are the 'snorkel parks' of Xcaret, Xel-Ha, Tres Ríos and Yal-Ku in Akumal, which are very commercialized but can still be fun, especially for kids. Arrive early to avoid the crowds.

Fishing

Before Mexico's Caribbean coast was discovered by divers or sunbathers, the first to appreciate it were sport fishermen. **Deep-sea** and **inshore** fishing are possible. Deep waters offshore contain snapper, amberjack, bonito, kingfish, shark and barracuda (year-round) and sailfish, marlin, tuna and dorado (best Mar–June). The inshore waters further south, below Tulum, attract pompano, tarpon and are the richest **bonefish** grounds in the world.

Many dive centres, especially on Cozumel and Isla Mujeres, organize fishing trips, and there are fishing specialists with brokering agencies that arrange longer-term charters and packages. **Licences** are needed for deep-sea fishing, which brokers also obtain. On the mainland, Puerto Morelos is a good fishing base, and more expensive companies use Puerto Aventuras. A must for flyfishing fans are the fishing lodges on the Punta Allen road south of Tulum, the bonefishers' mecca.

The Caribbean coast is not the only spot to fish. On the Gulf Coast, fishing has tended to be more rustic, but some of the finest fishing grounds are off Holbox, where things are getting more organized, and good fishing guides are easy to locate. Elsewhere, some of the best undeveloped lagoons and friendliest fishermen are in El Cuyo and Río Lagartos.

Golf

The Riviera Maya is in the middle of a golf boom, with nine courses already completed and more under construction; there is also a long-established course outside Mérida (for a list, see www.golfinmexico.com). Golf courses are potentially a major environmental hazard in the Yucatán; see p.70.

Horse Riding

South of Cancún near **Puerto Morelos** there is a ranch, Rancho Loma Bonita, offering group rides on horseback, with guides, through forests and along the beach, swim optional; on **Cozumel**, Rancho Buenavista organizes similar tours. No experience is necessary.

In Yucatán, Hacienda San Antonio Chalanté near **Izamal** has horses for its guests. In Chiapas, several tour agencies in **San Cristóbal** run horseback treks up to Highland villages.

Sailing, Windsurfing, and Kayaks

Sailing boat hire is oddly underdeveloped on the Riviera. It's usually easiest to find boats for rent on Isla Mujeres and Cozumel.

Inshore **windsurfers** are better off: windsurf boards can be rented at many hotels, at several places along the beach in Cancún, on the southwestern beaches of Cozumel and on the beach at Isla Mujeres. They may also be available for hire from dive schools at Tulum.

If you prefer boats that let you slide silently through still waters there are places that rent **kayaks**. Kayak tours are available in Sian Ka'an, and many hotels at Xcalak have kayaks for exploring the lagoons. One of the best places for tranquil kayaking is the lake at Bacalar. Kayak and rafting trips are also available on the forest rivers of Chiapas, through Explora and at Las Guacamayas (see p.106).

Skydiving and Other Esoterics

You can **skydive** on to the beach at Playa del Carmen with Skydive Playa. In Cancún it is possible to **parasail** from AquaWorld, Playa Tortugas (which also offers **bungee-jumping**, from a crane) and other places along the beach. In Tulum, the latest extreme-sports craze along the beach is **kiteboarding**.

Telephones

In cities, tourist areas and nowadays many villages there are white **Lada** (for *larga distancia*, long distance) public phones, which operate with phone cards (a *tarjeta de teléfonos* or *tarjeta Lada*). They can be bought for 30, 50 or 100 pesos from phone company offices and shops with the blue and yellow *Ladatel* sign (pharmacies often sell them). In villages where there is still no phone box there is virtually always a local phone office (*caseta*), identified by the blue-on-white logo of the **Telmex** national phone company, and *Teléfono Público* or *Larga Distancia*. In them you write the number down, and it is dialled for you; they also send and receive faxes. The village *caseta* is an institution in rural Mexico, taking messages for anyone in the community, and naturally knowing everyone's goings-on.

Local calls are cheap, but charges go up steeply for anywhere defined as long distance (which can be just 2km outside a city) and are very expensive for international calls. These are best made from *casetas* or, in towns, from the many private phone centres (*locutorios*), where similarly you give the number and the call is dialled for you. They're still not cheap, so the best thing to do may be to have someone call you back at a hotel. In tourist places there are often separate black phones used only for making international calls with a credit card.

Mobile/cell phones are very widely used in Mexico, and there is now pretty good coverage around most towns; in some rural areas, mobiles arrived before land lines. All work on a 1900 band, as in the US, so European mobiles only work here if they have a tri- or quad-band facility. Charges for using a foreign cell phone here are very high, so if you need a phone it can be better to get a cheap local one.

Dialling Codes within Mexico

Whether using a phone box or a hotel or private phone, to call any number in Mexico outside your immediate area you must first dial an access code (**01**) followed by an area code (often referred to as *el lada*). Most area codes have three digits, while individual numbers have seven; the one exception is Mexico City, where the area code is **55**, and individual numbers have eight digits. The *lada* codes for each area are indicated throughout this guide. For Playa del Carmen, for example, the area code is **984**; to make a local call within the town you dial just the number, say 873 0176, but to call the same number from outside Playa you must dial 01 **984 873 0176**.

Any phone number that begins with 1 is usually a mobile/cell number. For these you may need to use the codes **044** or **045** instead of 01, but with the same area code, so a Playa number would be **044 984 117 5060**. Numbers beginning **01 800** are toll-free.

Time

Most of Mexico is on the same time as US Central time (six hours behind GMT). However, Mexico moves to daylight saving time in early May, a month after the USA and Britain, and back to winter time earlier in September, so that for part of April and September Yucatán is at the same hour as US Rocky Mountain time, seven hours behind British time.

Tipping

Tips are an essential supplement to low wages for many Mexicans. For **hotel porters** a usual tip is 3–10 pesos (depending on the hotel); it's also usual to leave something for the maid. It's a good idea to keep a stock of loose change (especially if you're driving), for all the other service providers for whom there are no fixed charges, such as windscreen washers, men who watch over your car, etc. Petrol station attendants do not expect a tip for putting fuel in your car, but it is normal to give them a few pesos if they've checked the oil, the tyres and so on. **Taxi drivers**, though, don't normally expect tips, except if they've gone out of their way, or helped with bags.

It's normal to tip in all **restaurants**, and at **bars** if you've had more than one drink. The going rate is 10%, although in Cancún and the Riviera waiters expect more. Wherever you are, tip more if the service has been especially good. A growing number of restaurants now add a service charge (usually 10%) to the bill, in which case you're not really expected to add more, though whether this actually gets to the staff is an open question.

Toilets

There are not usually any public lavatories in Mexican cities, but bars and restaurants have toilets. Ask for *los servicios* or *el lavabo*. There are also toilets at bus stations, and most first-class buses have on-board toilets. Museums of any size have decent toilets, and whenever the INAH makes an archaeological site more accessible they install toilets by the entrance. Otherwise, there's always the bushes, and in Cancún you're never too far from a shopping mall with spanking shiny toilet facilities.

Visiting Archaeological Sites and Museums

Usual Opening Hours: *daily 8–5.*

Virtually all archaeological sites in Mexico are administered by the **INAH** *(Instituto Nacional de Antropología e Historia)*. Most have a standard timetable, 8 till 5, although less prominent sites may open later and close a bit earlier, and/or are closed one day a week. Entry charges vary; admission to the most famous sites (Chichén Itzá, Uxmal) now costs around US $8.50 (plus $1 to park), but for smaller sites is usually $3–4. **Note** that the old tradition that admission was free for everybody to all sites on **Sundays** has ended; entry is now free on Sundays only for Mexican citizens and resident foreigners. Sundays have long had the disadvantage that, with so many locals making use of free entry, this is the day that major Maya sites get most crowded. Now that there's no saving to be made, it's best to leave your ruins-visiting to other days.

INAH sites have standard signs to look out for along the roads: blue with white lettering and a silhouette of a pyramid. Excavations are continuing at many sites and there are plans to open up more, so it is now possible to visit more Maya sites in Mexico than ever before. Among sites that have been opened up in the last decade are some of great importance, such as **Santa Rosa Xtampak** and the great city of **Calakmul**, both in Campeche. One side of these programmes is controversial, in that they often involve large-scale restoration work. The INAH, however, insists that only original stones are used in all restored structures, only after painstaking research.

There are Maya sites for all tastes in this region. The most visited are Chichén Itzá, Tulum and, some way behind, Uxmal and Palenque. Away from this well-beaten path, visitor numbers fall radically (especially mid-week), and there are awe-inspiring sites where you can wander undisturbed among the forests, birds and ancient stones, and get a real sense of exploration. Many are hard or near-impossible to reach without a car, often at the end of dirt tracks. Wherever you go, there will be an INAH watchman waiting with his book for you to sign. As-yet unsated ruins enthusiasts can also look out for sites not yet brought under INAH administration, some of which can be reached with local guides.

For an introduction to the Maya, it still makes sense to look first at the 'classics': **Chichén Itzá**, **Uxmal** and the **Puuc hill cities**, and **Palenque**. The two great Yucatán cave systems of **Loltún** and **Balankanché** are also easy to reach, and fascinating. Mention apart goes to **Yaxchilán** and **Bonampak**, two fabulous sites – the latter with the only surviving series of Maya mural paintings – best visited in a one- or two-day trip from Palenque. Less known but hugely impressive are **Cobá**, and the most important recent discovery in the Maya world, **Calakmul**. Others worth highlighting include **Mayapán**, **Ek-Balam**, **Kohunlich**, **Becán**, **Edzná** and **Toniná**.

Getting around a large site like Chichén Itzá or Palenque with any appreciation (and all the walking involved) requires at least a morning, and can easily fill a full day. At

Chichén, Cobá, Tulum, Uxmal and Palenque there are multilingual guides who take you round for about $35. Bus tours with guides are the easiest way to see these ruins, but they have their limitations (*see* p.104). At smaller sites the watchman may accompany you (a tip is in order). Most sites have slabs set into the ground with information in Spanish, English and the local Maya language. Larger sites have visitor centres with restaurants, shops and bookshops; at others there may be little or no printed material, nor refreshments. Some useful things to have are the site leaflets (5–8 pesos) published in Spanish and English by the INAH itself, although, like most local guide books, they are often out of date. They are oddly hard to find, too, but there are stocks at Uxmal and the museum in Mérida.

At any site, it's best to start early, to avoid the heat and any crowds. Take water, a sun hat, sunblock, and insect repellent.

There are no restrictions on photography (except where sites are still being prepared for opening), but you are required to obtain a permit at each site to use a video camera (normally around 45 pesos or $3). Staff at major sites check on this, but lone watchmen at smaller ones may not bother. And, at any site, don't even think of taking away any souvenir stones. Arrest is immediate and arranging bail and a lawyer very expensive.

The INAH also administers **archaeological museums**. Opening hours are similar to those at sites, but most are **closed on Mondays**; like the sites, they're no longer free to tourists on Sundays. The most important museums for Maya artefacts are in Mérida, Dzibilchaltún, Campeche, Palenque and Tuxtla Gutiérrez. Also interesting are the innovative museums in Chetumal, the site museums at Chichén Itzá, Uxmal, Comalcalco and Toniná and the local museum in Tapachula, and there are several small eccentric local museums.

Water

Traditionally, Mexican guide books come with a lengthy list of 'don'ts' related to water. This is another set of risks that are greatly exaggerated. The essential rule is to drink only purified water (*agua purificada*); this is not mineral water, just guaranteed clean. It is available from grocery stores, supermarkets, and all pharmacies, and is provided free in nearly all hotels above budget level. The standard of mains water has also improved a lot, and you're unlikely to catch anything from swallowing a bit of tap water while you wash. Most bars and restaurants use purified water to make ice, and as long as you exercise reasonable care when choosing foods like shellfish or meat, and steer clear of dirt-cheap *loncherías*, you should avoid most dangers.

Women Travellers and Sexual Attitudes

On the whole **women travellers** don't experience great difficulties in southern Mexico. Each experience will be different, but in general the pervasive *machismo* archetypically associated with Mexico is far less noticeable in the south: among Mexicans, Yucatecan men are associated with *suavidad*, 'softness'. Indian men are likely to be shy and keep their distance; for *mestizo* (mixed-race) men, women travelling alone or in pairs may be an object of fascination and vaguely suggest availability, but this doesn't mean they'll try to do anything about it.

Sexual come-ons are most likely in Cancún and Playa del Carmen. Some sexual assaults have been reported in Cancún and tourist hot spots on the coast. Wherever you are, it's best to follow the same sensible practice as in any country – avoid empty streets at night, and the isolated parts of archaeological sites. It is necessary to be more careful in northern Chiapas. Two women travelling together will rarely encounter harassment, and women can also enjoy advantages over male travellers in that they may have more immediate access to some areas of local life, such as the markets.

Attitudes to **homosexuality** are contradictory. As is evident on the street, a fair few foreign gay men come here to meet young Mexicans, but beside this is a strain of covert and overt, occasionally violent homophobia. There is a gay scene in Cancún and Playa del Carmen, but elsewhere it's fairly subterranean.

Cancún, the Islands and the Riviera Maya

Brilliant white beaches lining arc-like bays, lush tropical greenery and an impossibly turquoise sea make Mexico's Caribbean coastline one of the most beautiful in existence. One of its greatest features is the sand itself: made up of fine powdered fossils, it's wonderfully soft and doesn't retain heat, so that it's comfortably cool even when the temperature tops 35°C. Offshore in the always-warm sea lies one of the richest reef environments in the world, a paradise for divers and snorkellers, while onshore, behind the beaches and beneath the jungle scrub, there are awe-inspiring giant caverns and underground rivers. Relics of the ancient Maya are dotted along the coast, next to resort complexes or in still-quiet forest villages. And in the northeast corner stands Cancún, modern gateway to the Yucatán, economic motor of southeast Mexico, showcase of over-the-top 21st-century baroque hotel architecture and one of the ten biggest resorts on the planet.

08

Don't miss

⭐ **Vibrant inshore coral reefs**
Off Cozumel p.158

⭐ **Palms and dazzling white sands**
Punta Bete to Playa del Carmen pp.173-184

⭐ **Giant *cenotes***
Near Akumal p.186

⭐ **Majestic clifftop ruins**
Tulum p.193

⭐ **A vast mangrove reserve**
Sian ka'an p.248

See map overleaf

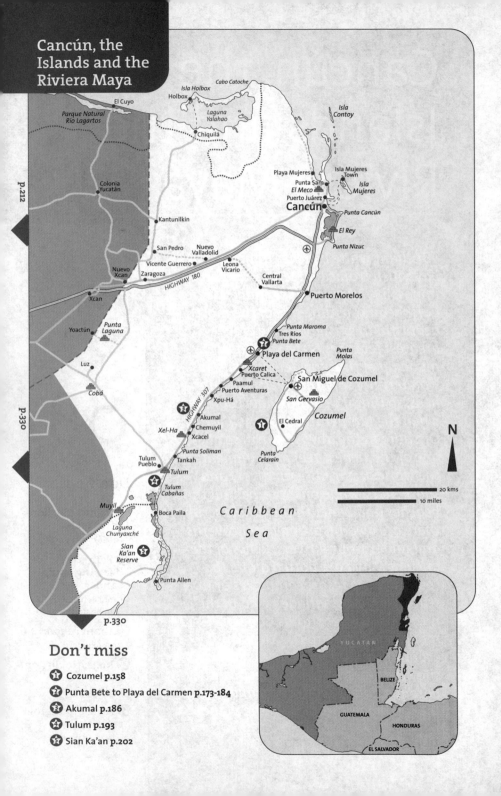

Cancún, the Islands and the Riviera Maya

Cabo Catoche
Isla Holbox
Holbox
El Cuyo
Isla Contoy
Parque Natural Rio Lagartos
Laguna Yalahao
Chiquilá
Playa Mujeres
Isla Mujeres Town
Colonia Yucatán
Punta Sam
El Meco
Isla Mujeres
Puerto Juárez
Cancún
Kantunilkin
Punta Cancún
El Rey
Punta Nizuc
San Pedro
Nuevo Valladolid
Vicente Guerrero
Leona Vicario
Nuevo Xcan
Zaragoza
HIGHWAY 180
Central Vallarta
Puerto Morelos
Xcan
Punta Maroma
Tres Rios
Yoactún
Punta Laguna
Punta Bete
Luz
Playa del Carmen
Punta Molas
Xcaret
Puerto Calica
Cobá
Paamul
Puerto Aventuras
San Miguel de Cozumel
HIGHWAY 307
Xpu-Há
San Gervasio
Akumal
Cozumel
Xel-Ha
Chemuyil
Xcacel
El Cedral
Punta Soliman
Punta Celarain
Tulum Pueblo
Tankah
Tulum
Muyil
Tulum Cabañas
Boca Paila
Caribbean
Laguna Chunyaxché
Sea
Sian Ka'an Reserve
Punta Allen

p.212

p.330

p.330

N

20 kms
10 miles

Don't miss

⭐ Cozumel p.158

⭐ Punta Bete to Playa del Carmen p.173-184

⭐ Akumal p.186

⭐ Tulum p.193

⭐ Sian Ka'an p.202

YUCATÁN

BELIZE

GUATEMALA

HONDURAS

EL SALVADOR

Belying its current image, until the 1960s this area was virtually deserted, home only to a few turtle fishermen, chicle tappers and some of the least 'Europeanized' Maya communities in the Yucatán. Then foreign archaeologists and a few hippies wandered down, discovered this lost paradise and decided to hang around. And then, in 1969, the Mexican government noticed the country had a Caribbean coastline, decided something should be done with it, and Cancún was born.

For the last decade we have been enjoined to call this 130km strip – from Cancún to Tulum, together with the islands of Isla Mujeres and Cozumel – the Riviera Maya. The transformation of the Mexican Caribbean from undiscovered remote spot to mega attraction is sometimes cited as a benchmark case of overdevelopment, of how not to do it. The statistics are overwhelming: the **Riviera Maya** has the highest population growth of anywhere in Mexico, while Playa del Carmen swells so fast it has left any available statistics way behind. The region's developers, Mexican and foreign, often seem chronically unable to say enough is enough.

It's a guidebook cliché to sneer at Cancún at this point, at how tacky it is, but Cancún's own astonishing growth is an old story compared with the spread of all-inclusive resort complexes, gobbling up the coastline down to Tulum. Assessments of the Riviera's future tend to go for all-or-nothing. Some say development here is like a careering train, which will race on, assuming it can pour in ever more people, until it runs up against a real disaster, such as irreversible damage to the precious reefs. Others are more optimistic, and say there's more rationality to the process, and that it will still be possible to give greater structure to local growth – imposed if nothing else by hard-to-avoid problems, like the failure of 'hidden infrastructure', such as the shortage of acceptable places to put the Riviera's mountains of garbage. And there are signs that new local authorities are now more aware they have to face some hard choices, and not just dismiss the questioners of continual building as obstructive killjoys.

No disasters have come as yet, and there are still plenty of beautiful places along this coast. Come here expecting somewhere out of the way of the modern world, and you'll be disappointed. But take Cancún, for example, for what it is – a brash, flash resort – and it's fun. Places like Isla Mujeres and Puerto Morelos retain a laid-back, beachtown atmosphere, and elsewhere you can find isolated, small-scale hotels looking on to miles of empty beach, and wonderfully clear *cenotes* to swim in, and Maya ruins at Cobá and Tulum – one of the most beautiful places on earth. Beyond Tulum is the Sian Ka'an reserve, where development is still held back. The Maya reefs are still full of life, and nobody has yet changed the colours of the sea or sand, where you can sit amid shadowy palms and watch dazzling canopies of stars.

Cancún

People are very nasty about the city of Cancún. Hotel proprietors along the rest of the 'Riviera' tell you with great self-esteem, 'of course, we're not Cancún'. The implication is that Cancún is big, brassy, 'oh, so tacky', Miami-South, a cross between a beach and a freeway. Well, Cancún is big and unsophisticated, and horrifies some people. But, to say something on behalf of the old place, consider these two points:

A few years ago Friends of the Earth put out the suggestion that people who were really concerned about the environment should take their holidays in established commercial tourist towns rather than forever demand new remote and 'unspoilt' places into which to extend airports and air conditioning. By these standards Cancún is the most eco-place in the whole Riviera. It is a purpose-built, industrial estate of fun, a specialized facility, to be made use of or not as you wish. It does not pretend to be anything else, or extend itself in disguise into the countryside.

Secondly, people often complain that Cancún is 'not the real Mexico', which presumably exists in some ideal adobe-state of immobile third-worlddom. In fact Cancún is the most Mexican city in the whole Yucatán, in that, in contrast to the very distinct, traditional Yucatecan culture of Mérida or Valladolid, people from all over Mexico live here. From being a necessary dormitory for chambermaids and gardeners, Ciudad Cancún has become a real city, population 600,000 and counting, gathering its own momentum as well as tourism. It has the *barrios*, bustle, street life, sense of chaos and some of the tensions of a modern Mexican city. OK, you say, this is not actually the Mexico we came to see. But you can't say it's not authentic. Mexicans take holidays too, and at some times of year foreigners share the beaches with crowds of locals and big family groups.

Having accentuated the positive, this is not to deny that Cancún can be an acquired taste. The Hotel Zone along Cancún island is forever being compared to Miami, but it has a lot of similarities with Las Vegas, being so new and pleasure-centred, with so much architecture that's downright silly, such as banana-shaped restaurant signs in luminous pink. Charm is not the strip's most obvious characteristic, and the traffic density, there and in the city centre, can be atrocious. Cancún is a bit like any modern city, in fact, although crime and similar signs of urban decay are still fairly small-scale.

Because Cancún is preeminently the main entry point to the Yucatán, most people find themselves spending at least a night here on arrival or departure. Even though it has over 29,000 hotel beds, it fills up. The busiest times are Christmas, winter and Easter.

Getting to Cancún

By Air

Cancún **airport** is 15km south of Ciudad Cancún, on the mainland parallel with the southern end of Cancún island. It now has **three terminals**, so it's important to know which one you need. All Mexican airlines, Air Canada and some other airlines (especially from Latin America) use **Terminal 2**; most US and European airlines use **Terminal 3** (**Terminal 1** is normally used only for charter flights). However, there are inconsistencies, so **always check** your terminal. A free shuttle bus runs between Terminals 2 and 3. In each terminal there are shops, services, ATMs and **money exchange offices**, which usually give poor rates; change as little as possible.

Getting to and from the Airport

Arrival in Cancún is rarely a triumph for Mexican PR – one can get the feeling things are deliberately set up to get jeg-lagged new arrivals to spend more money than they need to as soon as possible – but facilities have been getting more user-friendly. At both Terminals 2 and 3 the most prominent means of transport into town offered to passengers as they come through the gate, and who don't have a transfer arranged by a tour company, are the **airport minibuses** or *colectivos*, with big ticket desks in the arrivals halls.

These are large, air-conditioned 10-seater vans, which take each passenger to their hotel door (drivers expect tips). Fares, posted up at the ticket desks, are similar between different companies, at around $14 per person. You buy the ticket, and the vans are the other side of customs. Depending on where you're going, their drawback is that they go first through the Hotel Zone and then on to Ciudad Cancún, which takes an hour or more. Passengers going only to Ciudad Cancún are sometimes told a bus will take them straight there, but this is scarcely ever true, and *colectivos* are not obliged to leave until they have at least eight passengers, so that you can have an irritating wait. You can also take a whole van that will leave immediately, but this will cost from $35. Conventional, standard-size taxis are not usually available at the airport.

There is also an ADO **airport bus service**, even though it's partly hidden. It leaves from Domestic Arrivals at Terminal 2; from Terminal 3, take the free shuttle bus. At both Terminals there are ADO-Riviera desks which sell tickets and give directions to the bus. Buses run from the airport to the bus station in Ciudad Cancún 6.30am–12.40am, and to the airport 4.30am–11.45pm, once an hour before 8am and two or three times each hour after that. Journey time is 25min and the fare 40 pesos or $2.90, so if you're going to Ciudad Cancún this is the quickest and cheapest way to get there.

If you are heading not for Cancún itself but **Puerto Morelos** or **Playa del Carmen**, there is also an ADO bus from Terminal 2, once or twice an hour 8.30am–10.15pm daily (from Playa, 6am–8.15pm). Journey time to Playa is about 1hr; the fare is around $7. *Colectivos* also run to and from Playa more or less hourly (more at peak times) 8am–9pm; tickets are around $23 per person, or $70 for a whole van.

A hassle-free alternative to dealing with *colectivos* or buses can be to book your own transfer with a service like Cancún Valet or KinMont, which generally offer lower prices for advance bookings online.

When you're **leaving** Cancún, any city cab can take you to the airport (about $14 from Ciudad Cancún; $20 from the Hotel Zone) but, as usual, agree a price before you get in (*see* p.101, 'By Taxi'). Along Av. Tulum there are bus-stop signs marked *Aeropuerto*: ignore them; these buses are for airport workers and run only occasionally at inconvenient times. For transport from Playa, *see* p.176.

Airport Services

Cancún Airport, *www.cancun-airport.com*. The airport's official website now also offers *colectivo* and van booking online, but it's actually more expensive than private sites.

Cancún Valet, t 848 3634, *www.cancunvalet.com*. Efficient, friendly company providing airport pick-ups for $40 to Cancún, $65 to Playa, and other services.

KinMont, t 914 4040, from US and Canada t 1 888 811 4255, *www.airport-cancun-shuttle.com*. Prebooked vans from the airport, from $35 to Cancún, $60 to Playa.

Local Numbers for Leading Airlines

Aeroméxico, t 01 800 021 4000/(998) 287 1822.
American Airlines, t 886 0129.
Continental, t 886 0169.
Iberia, t 886 0158.
Mexicana, t 01 800 801 2030/(998) 892 1642.
MexicanaClick, t 01 800 112 5425.

By Bus

Cancún conveniently has only one station for first- and second-class buses, in the centre of Ciudad Cancún at the junction of Av. Tulum and Av. Uxmal. There are buses to most parts of the Yucatán and cities throughout Mexico, and only some are detailed here. As usual, they are run by different companies, but ADO has the most long-distance services.

Campeche (*6½–7hrs*): four ADO GL, seven standard first-class and several second-class daily, via Mérida. First-class fares $27–32.

Chetumal (*5–6hrs*): two ADO GL and regular first-class at least once an hour 5am–11pm daily, and frequent Mayab *intermedio* and second-class services. Most first-class buses and all others stop at **Playa del Carmen**, **Tulum** and **Felipe Carrillo Puerto**, and all *intermedio* and second-class stop at **Bacalar**. First-class fares to Chetumal $17–21.

Chiquilá, for **Holbox** (*3½hrs*): six Mayab *intermedios* daily (4.30am, 6am, 8am, 12.30pm, 1.30pm, 2.15pm). Fare about $6.

Mérida (*4¼hrs*): 12 luxury services (ten ADO GL, two UNO) daily, and normal first-class hourly 5am–2am. Fares $18–23. Second-class buses run hourly 3am–7pm, and slightly less frequently at night, several on the central Yucatán route via **Valladolid** and **Izamal**.

Mexico City (*22–26hrs*): four luxury and three regular first-class daily. Fares from $90.

Palenque *(13hrs)*: six or seven OCC or ADO first-class daily via Playa del Carmen, Chetumal and Escárcega 2.15–8.45pm, and one ADO GL (5.45pm daily). ADO GL and most OCC continue to San Cristóbal de Las Casas (17–18hrs) via Ocosingo, and some go on to Tuxtla Gutiérrez (see below) or Tapachula (24–26hrs). Fares $42–50 Palenque, $53–59 San Cristóbal, $71–74 Tapachula.

Playa del Carmen *(1¼hrs)* via **Puerto Morelos**: Riviera shuttle every 10mins 5am–11pm daily, and over 20 Mayab *intermedio* services; fare to Playa about $2–3. Mayab buses stop anywhere en route, and 13 continue on to **Tulum** and **Chetumal**. There are frequent *combis*, which in Cancún leave from two blocks north of the bus station on Av. Tulum.

Tuxtla Gutiérrez: two OCC, one ADO GL daily via Palenque and San Cristóbal *(19hrs)*; two more direct ADO GL *(17hrs)*. Fares $53–66.

Valladolid and **Chichén Itzá** (*2–3hrs*): nine first-class Mérida buses daily stop in Valladolid, one of which (9am) also stops in Pisté (for Chichén Itzá). All second-class Mérida buses (hourly, 3am–12.30am) stop at both; time to Pisté is 4¼hrs, and they can drop you at the ruins. Fares about $6–9 Valladolid, $8–12 Chichén.

Villahermosa (*12–13hrs*): 10 luxury and 15 ordinary first-class buses daily. Fares $44–53.

Orientation

Cancún is made up of two parts. The **Hotel Zone** (*Zona Hotelera* or *Zona Hoteles*) is the prosaic name for **Cancún Island**, the 23km spit of sand, looking like a giant '7' on the map, that encloses Laguna Nichupté and is held to the mainland by bridges at each end. It has only one road, **Boulevard Kukulcán**, measured by kilometre markers (used as locators in addresses, to distinguish one part from another). There are hotels, restaurants and attractions all along the strip, but the biggest concentration is around the angle of the '7', near Punta Cancún and the Centro de Convenciones.

Ciudad Cancún, often called 'Downtown', is the mainland city originally built to provide services for the hotels and somewhere for their employees to live. The north end of Blvd Kukulcán meets the town's north–south artery, **Av. Tulum**, which at one end runs up to the ferry landing at Puerto Juárez and at the other runs away to the airport and the coast road south. The centre of town is the stretch of Av. Tulum between two large roundabouts at Avenidas Cobá and Uxmal: the bus station, town hall, main banks and other essentials are on this block or within easy walking distance. Cheaper hotels, cheaper restaurants – in fact, cheaper anything – are all in Ciudad Cancún.

As a new city Ciudad Cancún has an addressing system that can be uniquely incomprehensible. It is made up of several wide avenues, most named after Mayan cities. The areas between them are called *Super Manzanas* or 'Super Blocks', each of which has a number. The smaller streets within the SM blocks are named or numbered too, but in some parts of town, especially north Cancún, this has taken a long time. Instead, addresses are given as lot numbers, as in SM 64, Mza 3, Lote 8, which is meaningless to anyone fresh off a plane. If you have such an address the only way to find your way there is to trust in a cab driver, and/or call ahead and find out if there are landmarks close by. Note that many named side streets are not through streets but only enclosed rectangles around a small block, so that exits next to each other on an avenue often have the same name.

Part of the folklore nowadays is Spring Break, a great American institution, which traditionally sees US college students have a wild time before serious exam business starts. Think Club 18–30, and multiply the numbers by several thousand.

Things to do in Cancún? Go with the flow. The city's reason for being, its beach, is one of the world's finest, a spectacular strand of white sand and surf running for miles. For a quick immersion in the Cancún experience, book a couple of nights here, see that view, and sample that other great Cancún institution, a pool with a swim-up bar. Have three margaritas and then roll mellowly backwards into the water, with your ears half-in and half-out. With luck they'll be playing some bouncy Mexpop that you can hear vibrating through the pool as you float around and look straight up at the perfect azure sky. It can be a transcendental experience. If you must have culture, Cancún has a theatre, a soccer team, and two Maya sites, at El Rey, on Cancún island, and El Meco, at Punta Sam.

History

In the afternoon we steered for the mainland, passing the island of Kancune, a barren strip of land, with sand hills and stone buildings visible upon it...
John Lloyd Stephens

History? There isn't any, surely. When Stephens and Catherwood came along this coast by boat in 1842, looking for Tulum, they were told there was not a single road through the entire great triangle between Valladolid, Bahía de la Ascensión and Yalahao (modern Chiquilá), and that the only settlement anywhere on the coast was a small *rancho* that had been the home of a retired pirate. It was, Stephens wrote, 'a region entirely unknown; no white man ever enters it'. And this was before the Caste War, which led non-Maya Yucatecans to keep even further away. Cancún and this coast had seen much greater human habitation many centuries earlier. Archaeological research has shown that there were fishing communities on Cancún island from the Preclassic period, around 300 BC. It was not, however, until the Late Postclassic in about 1200 that the town now known as El Rey was built, around the same time as other coastal communities such as Xcaret (Polé), Xel-ha and Tulum. They were important points on a trade route from the Gulf of Honduras around the coast to the Gulf of Mexico, bartering dried fish, cotton, honey and sea shells (a valuable commodity, with many uses) for obsidian from Guatemala, gold from Panama or cacao, grinding-stones and salt from western Yucatán. Small temples along the coast were often built as aids to navigation. This trade was fatally disrupted, however, when the Spaniards conquered the lordship of Chetumal in the 1540s. Deprived of their livelihood, the local Maya moved inland looking for places to farm, leaving the coast all but empty.

Getting around Cancún

By Air

Cancún airport is also a base for light-plane air tours, run mainly by **AeroCosta, t** 884 0383, *aerocosta2001@hotmail.com*, with sightseeing tours and an on-demand air-taxi service to Holbox, Isla Mujeres, Xcalak and other airstrips in the region. **Ecotour Taxi Aereo, t** 872 3424, *www.dolphinair.com.mx*, offers similar services at slightly lower prices.

By Bus

Cancún has user-friendly local buses. Routes R-1 and R-2 run up and down between the Hotel Zone and Ciudad Cancún almost 24hrs daily, from Av. Tulum and along Blvd Kukulcán; most go the length of the island and turn back by Wet'n'Wild, but some turn round earlier, so check with the driver. Buses are full in the mornings and early evenings, but come every few minutes. There's one fare no matter how far you travel: 6.50 pesos. Some R-1 and R-13 buses run from Av. Tulum (by the bus station) to the Isla Mujeres ferry at Puerto Juárez.

By Car and Bike

Petrol/gas stations are plentiful in Cancún. **Cycling** is not something associated with this city, but there is a cycle track (*ciclopista*) along most of Cancún island, with some gaps. Rental facilities are scarce, but many hotels have bikes for guests' use.

MTB Cancún, *www.mtbcancun.com*. Mountain biking enthusiasts who run tours, and rent bikes and equipment. Contact is by email.

Car Hire

There are any number of rental agencies, in hotels, malls and along Av. Tulum. Renting has been relatively expensive (from $45 a day, with hikes in high seasons), but good deals can be found, although you still get better rates in Mérida (*see* p.259). All agencies offer a range of vehicles including jeeps. If you don't have a car booked online, the best place to find cheaper agencies is Ciudad Cancún, especially on Av. Tulum and Av. Uxmal. Agencies usually stay open in the evenings, for clients wishing to book a car for the next day.

Prices are higher for cars picked up at the airport, as they include a special airport tax.

America Car Rental, Av. Yaxchilán 31, **t** 892 7017, *www.america-carrental.com*. Cars from $28 a day, or even less for longer rentals.

Easyway, Highway 307, near the airport, **t** 886 2464, *www.easywayrentacar.com*. Useful local agency with bargain rates, under $30 a day. Cars can be delivered to hotels.

Econo-Rent, Edificio Atlantis, Av. Bonampak, corner Av. Cobá, **t** 01 800 282 7875, *www.econocarrental.com*. Rates from around $35 a day, or less for longer rents.

By Taxi

Cancún has hundreds of taxis. As in most parts of Mexico, they do not have meters, and there is a complicated structure of official rates based on the idea that tourists can pay more than locals. Any journey within Ciudad Cancún is quite cheap (about $1.50), but trips are more expensive to or from the Hotel Zone ($5–10, depending how far you go). Similarly, a taxi to the airport from the Hotel Zone costs more than one from Ciudad Cancún, even if it's a shorter journey. Current rates are posted up at Puerto Juárez, the bus station and in many hotels, and listed in local free magazines (*see* p.136). Partly thanks to the system's complexities, Cancún's *taxistas* have a bad reputation for trying to scam confused tourists. This doesn't mean that all do, but it's best to be aware; the basic rule is always **agree the price before getting in the cab**

After the Caste War, the northeast corner of the peninsula was left as something of a no-man's-land for decades. In the 1900s, when the trade in *chicle*, the raw ingredient of chewing gum, finally brought in new population, Puerto Juárez was built as a ferry port to Isla Mujeres, but traffic was still never more than sluggish. Quintana Roo was so underpopulated it remained a federal territory rather than a state until 1974. A few sport fishermen and people seeking a very out-of-the-way retreat built houses in the area, but that was it until the great transformation began in 1969. There is a story put around that, once the Mexican government decided it should have a resort on the Atlantic as a counterpart to Acapulco, Cancún was chosen by a computer, as having the optimum combination of climate, proximity to major markets and so on. Perhaps of more immediate influence was the fact that the biggest building on Cancún island at the time was the holiday hideaway of Luis Echeverría, a leading figure in the PRI and later president of Mexico from 1970 to 1976. Echeverría was considered very left-wing in PRI terms, which means he was much in favour of Mexico's state enterprises and the party unions, and liked to talk about the Third World and goad the *gringo* by hobnobbing with Fidel Castro, but this didn't stop him from recognizing the deal of the century. He sold the island to the nation, and a public corporation, Fonatur, was set up to oversee the creation of the new resort. The first hotel opened in 1971, and the builders have been hard at work ever since.

The Hotel Zone

Cancún's two halves can be taken one at a time, or entirely separately, but since the beach was the start of it all it's only fitting to begin with the Hotel Zone. And an awesome sight it is. Cancún island is one of the great display cases of contemporary kitsch-pleasure architecture, a giant park in which architects have been let loose to create some of the largest buildings on the planet in a tutti-frutti of corporate-fantasy styles. As you travel along Blvd Kukulcán, the hotels give out a real mixture of signals: some retire behind imposing driveways and primped lawns, others are placed up front beside the street. The balconies of the Fiesta Americana Coral Beach drip with vegetation, while the two halves of the Sheraton Towers want to reach out and give you a hug. If leisure is a religion of the modern era, the builders of Cancún have followed up the sacred temples of the Maya with pyramids on a scale the ancients never dreamed of: a stepped pyramid with a three-pointed-star ground plan at the Caesar Park; three massive, squat pyramids at the 1,000-bed Gran Oasis. Other buildings take less note of their location. The French-owned Meridien mixes up Parisian Art Deco with a few Mayan motifs on top, while the Ritz Carlton is a picturesque combination of Italian Renaissance and US penitentiary architecture.

Apart from the hotels and prominent restaurants, the other landmarks of the Hotel Zone are its giant malls or plazas (not to be confused with squares) spaced out along the boulevard. **La Isla** at Km 12.5 is the most stylish and currently the most popular, a 'shopping village' rather than a mall, with little streets part-open to the skies along little canals, and a pretty walkway beside Nichupté lagoon.

Building in Cancún is a relentless, unstoppable force: once a place becomes a little worn it's commonly left to slide, then built over with something bigger. The greatest disaster in Cancún's history has been Hurricane Wilma in October 2005, which brought everything to a stop for a while, but this turned out to be only a temporary turndown; if anything, once the essential reconstruction was done, new building resumed at an even sharper pace. This tends to happen in Cancún, after hurricanes or financial crises, if perhaps with a cruder style (as seen in the box-like hotels taking shape along the southern stretch of the beach). There's no shortage of fantasy architecture, even so, and the giant towers of the Spanish-based Riu group's hotels near the Convention Centre have become landmarks with their overblown Las Vegas-baroque, awesomely floodlit at night.

The busiest section of the Hotel Zone is along the north side and running roughly down to La Isla. At Km 4 is another glossy attraction at the **Embarcadero** activities centre, with a giant rotating tower offering a panoramic view. In the same building there is also a small, colourful private folk-art museum, the **Casa del Arte Popular Mexicano**, and the **Teatro de Cancún**. For years this theatre had the same programme, a folkdance show for tourists, but one sign of Cancún's growth is that it now presents a varied mix of theatre (in Spanish!), comedy and concerts aimed at local audiences.

Embarcadero
Open daily
9am–11pm; adm.

Casa del Arte Popular Mexicano
Open Mon–Fri
9am–9pm, Sat, Sun
11am–7pm; adm.

The bend in the '7' around Km 8–9 is the hub of the strip and the site of the biggest clubs and bars, and so the spot where Cancún's nightlife is most dazzling. To give a public focus there is another giant mass in the same block, the **Cancún Center** convention centre. Before Wilma it also housed Cancún's archaeological museum, but this has been closed ever since the hurricane. It is promised that its compact but interesting collection will reopen at some point – here or in another location – but no reliable date has been set. One of its best exhibits is the stucco head from the ruins nearby, after which the site was named *El Rey*.

Beyond La Isla the traffic and the atmosphere become quieter as the road (and the cycle track) rolls down to **Punta Nizuc**. The area between the south end of the island and the Wet'n'Wild water park (where the buses turn back) is so far relatively empty, but there are always plans to build something in this city.

Cancún's Beaches after Wilma

Its magnificent sand strip is obviously the be-all and end-all of Cancún, but it has its problems. The very softness of the sand means that it shifts easily, especially during storms, and beaches here change shape naturally all the time. Hurricane Wilma in 2005 stripped away whole sections of Cancún beach back to the sea wall. An emergency beach-rebuilding programme was immediately set in motion, which involved teams of dredgers, hired at great cost from around the world, digging up sand off the sea bed to the east and depositing it back on the beach.

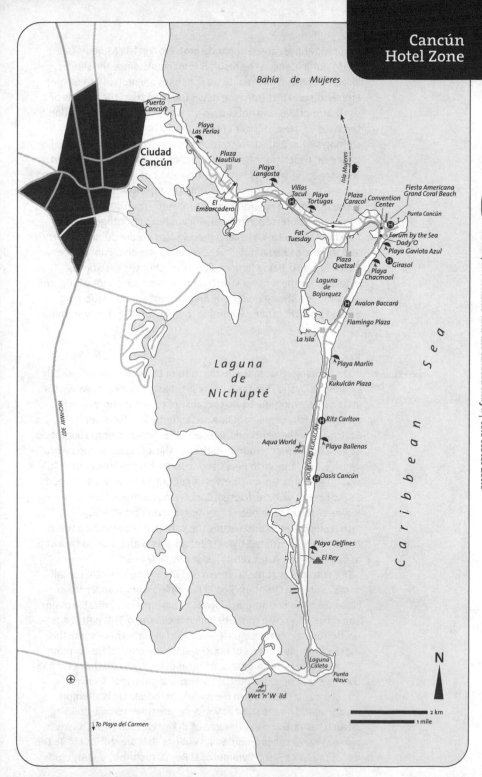

Bahía de Mujeres

Puerto Cancún

Playa Las Perlas

Ciudad Cancún

Plaza Nautilus

Playa Langosta

Isla Mujeres

Villas Tacul

El Embarcadero

Playa Tortugas

Plaza Caracol

Convention Center

Fiesta Americana Grand Coral Beach

Punta Cancún

Fat Tuesday

Forum by the Sea

Dady'O

Playa Gaviota Azul

Plaza Quetzal

Girasol

Playa Chacmool

Laguna de Bojorquez

Avalon Baccará

Flamingo Plaza

La Isla

Playa Marlin

Kukulcán Plaza

Laguna de Nichupté

Ritz Carlton

BOULEVARD KUKULCÁN

Aqua World

Playa Ballenas

Oasis Cancún

Caribbean Sea

HIGHWAY 307

Playa Delfines

El Rey

Laguna Caleta

Punta Nizuc

Wet 'n' Wild

To Playa del Carmen

N

2 km
1 mile

This may have caused separate problems on Isla Mujeres (*see* p.146), but in Cancún the result is remarkable: since the sand is local, it's of the same quality, and changes are pretty hard to spot. Problems stem less from the new sand than from the actions of some authorities and hotel-owners, who – like many others along the Riviera – are no longer prepared to accept natural beach shifting and as a quick fix to speed up reconstruction and 'stabilize' their own beach frontage, insert sections of *sacsab* or powdered limestone. Initially this is like coarse sand, but after it has been wet a few times it's as hard as rock, which is unpleasant underfoot and causes a range of environmental problems (*see* p.70).

While the hotels each have their own beach frontage, the beaches themselves, as everywhere in Mexico, are public property, and there are several public access points (*see* box, 'Public-Access Beaches', p.133). Being long and open, most of the east-facing *playas* along the longest stretch of the island have a lot of surf and sometimes a strong undertow, and are best suited to jumping around on rather than swimming (*see* 'Swimming and Swimming Safety', p.137).

El Rey

El Rey
By Km 17 on Cancún island; open daily 8–5; adm.

The buildings that make up the ruins of **El Rey** are not individually impressive by the standards of the great Mayan cities. However, it's still an interesting site to visit because of the clear impression it gives of a Maya settlement as a real community. Like other Postclassic settlements on this coast El Rey grew up from about 1200, as a subordinate community of the lordship of Ecab, the capital of which was to the north near Cabo Catoche. No one knows what it was originally called, and it owes its current name to a stucco head found here, now in the (closed) Cancún museum and labelled a 'king'. However, the site has been of considerable importance to archaeologists in reconstructing the pattern of Postclassic trade: it has been demonstrated that El Rey had links with places as far away as Colombia and Aztec territories in central Mexico.

The **entrance** is at the southern end of the site. Like other small communities in Quintana Roo, El Rey differs from grander Maya cities, with their multi-plaza layout, in having a recognizable main street running north to south, called the *Calzada*. This path leads north from the entrance past several small platforms – some the bases of temples, others of houses – into the main plaza. Forming its south side is the largest building at El Rey, a low platform with 18 columns that once supported a wood and palm roof, known as Structure 4 or **El Palacio**. In the middle of the square is a temple platform, and on the right as you enter are three temple buildings (**Structures 3a, b** and **c**). The head of 'El Rey' was found in 3b, which also has carved glyphs and wall paintings that are still visible. To the left of the three is the **Pyramid of El Rey (Structure 2)**, a fairly crude

Public-Access Beaches in Cancún

From the top of the '7'. Those facing north are the most popular.

Playa Las Perlas (Km 2): A small, quiet beach (except for the traffic on the boulevard), mostly surrounded by condo developments.

Playa Langosta (Km 5): Much bigger, a big stretch of sand that's good for swimming and about the busiest public beach, with restaurants and a boat landing stage.

Playa Tortugas (Km 7, by Fat Tuesday): Similarly big and busy, with plenty of attractions, and expensive ferries to Isla Mujeres.

Playa Caracol (Km 8): A narrow but pleasant beach on a sheltered mini-lagoon.

Playa Gaviota Azul (Km 9): Northernmost of the east-facing beaches, near the point, but a bit narrow and cramped.

Playa Chac-Mool (Km 9.5): A narrow beach with a simple, cheap bar and a few rather shabby shops; a bit like a little island unnoticed by the tourist hotels alongside it.

Playa Marlin, much further down at Km 13 (behind the Kukulcán Plaza): A big, open stretch of sand and surf.

Playa Ballenas (Km 14): Less attractive than Marlin, squeezed between two big hotels.

Playa Delfines (Km 17), near the El Rey ruins: About the best of the surf beaches, a tall, steep bank of sand with a great view. A favorite with locals.

Playa Mirador and Río Nizuc (Km 21–22): Right at the bottom of the island, by a creek connecting the lagoon to the sea: a tranquil little reserve where locals go to fish and have picnics.

pile that was built over an older base from the Terminal Classic. Excavations into it have revealed a tomb, almost certainly of the town's ruler, buried with offerings of copper vessels and conch, jade and coral jewellery.

The L-shaped building next to the Pyramid is another colonnaded platform (**Structure 1**), with a stone bench around the back wall. This too would have had a palm roof, and is thought to have been a fish market. Beyond it is another plaza, with another platform (**Structure 7**), probably a residential complex for the ruling lineage, and then more small temple and house platforms. Again, the small size of the squares is an indication of the limited size of El Rey, its population a few hundred at most. This scale also makes it easier to imagine comings and goings across the plaza.

Ciudad Cancún

Even people who really like Boulevard Kukulcán rarely suggest it's much good for strolling. For that you must go into town, where the streets and street life are more or less normal, despite an ever-increasing traffic density. The hub of the town is the tree-lined central section of Av. Tulum, with the bus station at the top and the Town Hall (the **Ayuntamiento Benito Juárez**, the official name of the municipality of Cancún) in a square on the east side. Av. Tulum also catches the most tourist movement. Walk down any of the streets on the west side such as Claveles or Tulipanes and you will come to a pleasant, park-like square in the middle of the SM 22 block called **Parque de las Palapas**, with a clutch of simple cafés and a big stage for occasional free live entertainment (especially at Carnival time). From there you can carry on through to **Av. Yaxchilán**, the night-time social hub of the city for Cancún locals, and so one of the best places to seek out good cheapish restaurants as well as cheaper, non-tourist-dominated nightlife. On the far side of Yaxchilán, Av. Sunyaxchén runs away to SM 28, which contains the post office and the **market**, sometimes called **Mercado 28**. By Mexican standards this is not an impressive market, but inside there is a collection of the cheapest restaurants in Cancún, packed with locals at weekends.

Atlante
www.club-atlante.com;
t 880 5151

To the west of the centre down Av. Cobá is the **Estadio Andrés Quintana Roo**, the ground of Cancún's soccer team, **Atlante**. A historic Mexico City team founded in 1916, it was bought for the city by some local businessmen in 2007.

Av. Tulum runs all the way through the city. North of the bus station it runs up to meet Av. López Portillo, the main road out towards Mérida on one side and Puerto Juárez on the other. If the Hotel Zone is the hub of tourist Cancún, this junction, **El Crucero**, is the heart of the Mexican city. Around it cluster the *taco*-stands, overstocked shoe stores, street-corner dentists, ice cream shops, crowds of kids and pharmacies characteristic of modern, working-class urban Mexico.

The coast north of the Hotel Zone has been fairly neglected but this is now another of Cancún's growth areas. A huge marina development·is underway around a creek east of the downtown area, labelled **Puerto Cancún**. This has been dogged by financial problems (one of its American promoters is in jail for fraud) but is still taking shape. Av. López Portillo leads after 3km to the Isla Mujeres passenger ferry at **Puerto Juárez**, with two docks, the old **Estación Marítima** and a new facility titled **Gran Puerto Cancún**. The road goes on another 3km to the car ferry at **Punta Sam**. Hotels and condo developments are also multiplying on the narrow beaches in this area, and north of Punta Sam is another big promotion, with golf course, dubbed **Playa Mujeres**. For ferry information, *see* 'Isla Mujeres', p.145.

El Meco

El Meco
Open daily 8–3; adm

A little south of Punta Sam is the Maya site of **El Meco**. It is older than El Rey, with parts dating back to AD 300, but it grew to a significant size at around the same time, after 1100. Compared to El Rey the site is small, but the buildings are bigger and the **Pyramid** (*closed off to visitors*) is taller and more solid. It is at the centre of three well-structured plazas, ringed by the remains of temples and palace complexes. The largest, **Palacio 12** in Plaza C, was a much more opulent structure than the similar colonnaded palace at El Rey. The chief interest of El Meco lies in its layout, but in Palacio 12 and the Pyramid steps you can still see decoration and animal carvings.

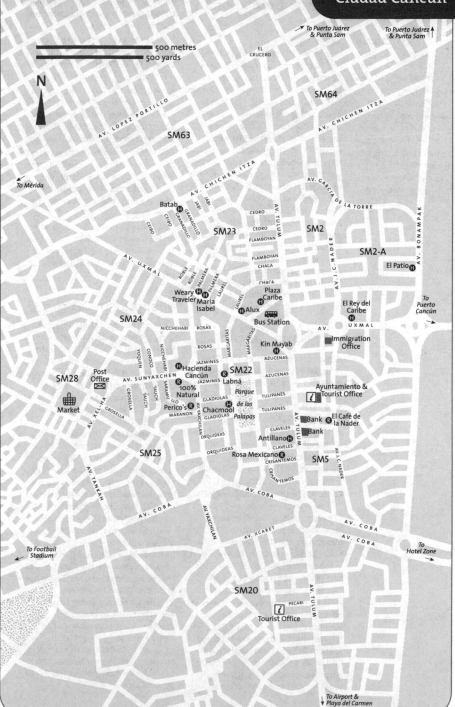

(i) **Cancún**
City Tourist Office,
town hall, Av. Tulum,
t 884 8073. Hidden
away off the lobby;
staff, mostly students,
are not well-informed,
but have loads of
leaflets. There are also
kiosks in La Isla and
Forum malls and by the
ferry in Puerto Juárez
(open Mon–Fri 9–3
and 6–8).

Tourist Information in Cancún

t (998-)

There are scores of tours, club nights, trips and so on advertised in Cancún at any time. Useful things to pick up are the free magazines *Cancún Tips* and *Cancún Nights*, available in hotels and shops as well as tourist offices (you're usually offered one in the airport as you arrive). As well as masses of ads they have current taxi rates, maps and discount coupons to soften the blow of Cancún prices. Also useful is the free *Hotel Guide*, which is not a guide but consists of discount coupons for hotels along the Riviera. An avalanche of information is online: *www.cancun.travel* and *www.cancun. net* are among the most useful sites. Along Av. Tulum there are **kiosks** advertising 'Information'. These are usually only interested in selling tours, tickets to bullfights and other attractions and time shares.

Services in Cancún

Banks: main bank offices are on the central stretch of Av. Tulum. All have ATMs and most are now open on Saturday mornings. There are also banks in the Hotel Zone near the Convention Center, in Flamingo Plaza and in Kukulcán Plaza. *Cambio* offices (*open Sun*) are plentiful on Av. Tulum.

Consulates and Immigration: Canadian Consulate, Plaza Caracol II, 3rd floor, room 330, **t** 883 3360; **US Consulate** (in the same building), Plaza Caracol II, 2nd floor, room 320–323, **t** 883 0272; **British Vice-Consulate**, Royal Sands Hotel, **t** 881 0100. The **Mexican Immigration Office** is at Av. Nader 1, **t** 884 1749 (*open Mon–Fri 9–1*), at the corner of Av. Uxmal. This is the best place in the region to get an extension to your stay (*see* p.92).

Health: The 24hr emergency number is **066**. Otherwise, the **American Hospital**, C. Viento 15, SM 4, **t** 884 6133 (off Av. Tulum, in the *super-manzana* south of Av. Coba) and **Total Assist**, C. Claveles 5, **t** 884 1092, off Av. Tulum, are private clinics with English-speaking staff and 24hr services.

Pharmacies are plentiful, and **Farmacia Unión**, on Av. Uxmal opposite the bus station, is open 24hrs.

Internet Access: Internet shops are especially abundant around the bus station: **Cyber-Office**, Av. Uxmal 19, has low rates.

Newspapers and Books: The Cancún edition of the *Miami Herald* is available at newsstands on Av. Tulum and in the malls. The best book and magazine store is **Fama**, Av. Tulum 27.

Police: The main police station is next to the Town Hall, Av. Tulum, **t** 884 1913. There is another in the Hotel Zone beside Kukulcán Plaza. Cancún has special 'tourist police' officers who speak English.

Post Office: Corner of Av. Sunyaxchén and Av. Xel-Ha (*open Mon–Fri 8–6, Sat, Sun and hols 9–12.30*). There is a **Mexpost** office (*closed Sun*) alongside the main building.

Shopping in Cancún

Cancún has thousands of places to shop, but how much you might want to buy is another question. Handicrafts here are often of production-line standard, and more expensive than in other parts of the Yucatán. The Hotel Zone's giant malls can be of most interest just for looking around and buying silly souvenirs. **La Isla** and **Kukulcán Plaza** are the most stylish, with big international fashion brands. **Jewellery**, made with Mexican silver, jade and imported gems, is a traditional buy in all the malls, but prices are now little different from international levels. **La Fiesta**, Km9, and **Coral Negro**, Km9.5, are cheaper, flea-market-type malls with jewellery and all sorts of Mexicana, with fine pieces as well as an awful lot of junk. The real signature product of Cancún is the **T-shirt**, and **Ki-Huic souvenir market** on Av. Tulum has enough to clothe a whole city.

There are shops offering tequilas and other Mexican alcoholic specialities in all the malls. Cuban cigars are another sought-after commodity; **La Casa del Habano**, Blvd Kukulcán Km 12.7, near Kukulcán Plaza, has by far the best stock of the genuine article.

Sports and Activities

Diving and Snorkelling

There are a few diving schools in Cancún, and introductory scuba trips are available at attractions such as Aqua World, but diving here is more expensive than at other places nearby, and since the Cancún reefs are in a poor state, you may well be taken from here to those same areas on a fairly long boat trip. It's usually more enjoyable to go straight to Puerto Morelos, Playa, Isla Mujeres or Cozumel. Two established dive shops are:

Ocean Sports, Av. Cobá 51, **t** 884 6034.

Scuba Cancún, Blvd Kukulcán Km 5, **t** 849 7508, *www.scubacancun.com.mx*. Lagoon snorkel trips can be made from Aqua World and other venues (*see* below).

Golf

Cancún Golf Club – Pok-ta-Pok, Pok-ta-Pok island, by Blvd Kukulcán Km 7.5, **t** 883 1230, *www.cancungolfclub.com*.

Hilton Cancún Golf Club, Hilton Hotel, Blvd Kukulcán Km 17, **t** 881 8000, *www.hilton.com*.

There is also a course at the **Gran Melia Cancún** hotel, Blvd Kukulcán Km 16.5. For some background on golf in the Yucatán, *see* p.117.

Swimming and Swimming Safety

Spaced out along the ocean sides of the island, Cancún's several beaches have different characteristics (*see* p.133). **Lifeguards** are posted along the long, east-facing beaches, which attract a strong swell. Look out for red flags: caution is especially recommended when a *norte* (north) wind is blowing. The beaches facing north, along the top of the '7', have calmer waters. Locals also swim in the tranquil lagoon on the other side of the island, where there are several landing stages, but foreigners seem to avoid it.

Other Watersports, Rides, Fun Parks

An essential Cancún tradition is getting around on the water by different means: try **wave runners** (jet skis), **water-skiing**, **banana rides**, **parasailing**, **kayaks** and **windsurfing**. Small-scale operations can be found all along the Kukulcán strip, especially around Playa Tortugas, but the two below are the largest. There are also regular **excursions** from Cancún to places out of town, especially Isla Contoy, Dolphin Discovery on Isla Mujeres and Xcaret. For these, *see* the relevant sections.

Aqua World, Blvd Kukulcán Km 15.2, **t** 848 8327, *www.aquaworld.com.mx*. The biggest fun-on-the-water venue, on the lagoon rather than the open sea: attractions include wave runners, sailing, scuba, fishing, 'jungle tours' with snorkelling at 'Paradise Island', a 'submarine ride' (not a sub, but a boat with a glass-sided hull) and lots to do for kids.

Wet'n'Wild, Blvd Kukulcán Km 23.5, **t** 881 3000, At the bottom of the island, this water park's main attraction is currently its **Dolphinaris** dolphin pool. The park around it has a relatively limited number of slides, rides and wave pools, but it's fun for kids.

Where to Stay in Cancún

Cancún's hotels can be expensive, but, with 28,000 beds, they offer nice surprises too. Those in the Hotel Zone are designed to be booked as part of a package, and peak-season public rates are often very high (some do not take non-agency bookings). If you want to stay by the beach you will nearly always get better deals by booking a package through a travel operator or online booking service rather than by reserving direct with the hotel. Many hotels too can only be booked on an all-inclusive basis. Independent travellers who need or want to spend some nights here nearly always stay in the simpler hotels in Ciudad Cancún.

However, it can be more enjoyable to cut your losses and splurge on a beach hotel to sample the Cancún experience, and even on an average budget this can be done. Rates drop a lot outside the winter, Easter and July–Aug peak seasons, and smaller hotels, especially, often have good offers for direct reservations, and are more flexible as regards all-inclusive service. It's worth checking for current offers, even in luxury hotels. The *Hotel Guide* of discount coupons (*see* p.136) is also useful.

With so many hotels in Cancún, this list can only be a selection. Those listed in the Hotel Zone are among those with distinctive qualities, and/or more amenable to individual travellers. It is always advisable to book ahead.

Hotel Zone

Luxury
Fiesta Americana Grand Coral Beach, Blvd Kukulcán Km 9.5, t 881 3200, *www.fiestaamericana.com*. If you want to go the whole hog in Cancún, then this giant pile might as well be it. It has a matchless location by Punta Cancún, a grand-hotel feel of real luxury its rivals find hard to beat, and sumptuous facilities: an exquisite garden pool, extravagant spa, fine restaurants and more. And in low seasons rates for many rooms drop into the *expensive* band.

Expensive–Moderate
Avalon Baccara, Blvd Kukulcán Km 11.5, t 881 3900, *www.avalonvacations.com*. Next to the same company's huge Avalon Grand all-inclusive and not far from La Isla, the Flamingo Plaza and other attractions, this hotel has a more intimate style than its neighbours (just 27 rooms) but still offers Cancún essentials like a fine pool with swim-up bar and soaring ocean views.

Cancún Clipper Club, Blvd Kukulcán Km 9, t 891 5999, *www.clipper.com.mx*. Faces the lagoon (near the Convention Center), not the sea, so no beach frontage, but it has comfortable, well-appointed rooms and a nice pool, and low prices for the Hotel Zone.

Villas Tacul, Blvd Kukulcán Km 5.5, t 883 0000, *www.cancunvillas tacul.com*. One of the first hotels opened on Cancún island, this retains a more tranquil style than more recent arrivals. It's made up of 23 self-contained villa-apartments in a lush garden, with its own beach and pool and other extras. The main hitch is

(★) **Hotel El Rey del Caribe >>**

that there's much more traffic noise than when the hotel was built.

Ciudad Cancún

Moderate
Hotel Antillano, Av. Tulum and C. Claveles 1, t 884 1132, *www.hotel antillano.com*. Reliable hotel handily located on the main drag, and accordingly popular. The rooms could do with modernization – and some are noisy – but they're spacious and comfortable, and there's a little patio pool. Rates drop to *inexpensive* off-peak. Book well in advance.

Hotel Kin Mayab, Av. Tulum, corner of Av. Uxmal, t 884 2999, *www.hotel kinmayab.com*. This hotel has a well-established niche thanks to its very handy location near the bus station. Rooms are functional but quite pretty and surprisingly quiet, and there's a small pool. Listed rates can seem quite high, but discounts are often available off-peak.

Hotel Kokai, Av. Uxmal 26, near Av. Nader, t 193 3175, *www.hotelkokai.com*. Attractive, unassuming mid-range hotel, next to the Rey del Caribe with a high reputation for good service. Light, spacious rooms, a pool, a friendly patio restaurant and lively bar (with music at weekends) are other attractions. Rates are borderline *inexpensive*.

Hotel Plaza Caribe, Av. Tulum and Av. Uxmal, t 884 1377, *www.hotelplaza caribe.com*. Right next to the bus station, but despite it being so central, behind the hotel's façade there are pretty gardens with a nice pool, a charming restaurant and pleasant rooms with ample comforts. Very good value, especially off-peak.

Hotel El Rey del Caribe, Av. Uxmal 24, corner Av. Nader, t 884 2028, *www.reycaribe.com*. Long-running, popular hotel that feels unusually peaceful for central Cancún, with rooms – a bit elderly, but pretty – around a lush garden with small pool. Breakfast (included) is served in the garden, and massages are available; the owners also make big efforts to meet high ecological standards. There's free WiFi in some areas, and rates are near the bottom of this band.

Suites Alborada, Av. Nader 5, t 884 1584, *www.suitesalborada.com*. Located behind the town hall, this apartment hotel has one- or two-bedroom suites, all with kitchens and a lounge area. Décor is modern rather than traditional, but they're very well equipped (WiFi throughout) and well maintained, and the owners, a family, are very attentive.

Inexpensive

Cancún's cheaper hotels are mostly a few blocks from the central stretch: the most economical (and more basic) are in the blocks north of Av. Chichén Itzá towards the Crucero. All hotels listed have showers en suite.

Cancún Inn-Suites El Patio, Av. Bonampak 51, t 884 3500, *www.cancuninn.com*. Distinctive guest house on one of the avenues away from the centre. Its 13 rooms (not really suites) are among the most comfortable in this price slot, basic breakfast Is included, and owners and their staff are attentive and welcoming. Traffic along Av. Bonampak can get noisy, but inside the house and its patio there's a nice tranquility. Bikes are also available to rent.

Hotel Alux, Av. Uxmal 21, t 884 0556, *www.hotelalux.com*. A good no-frills inexpensive choice only a few steps from the bus station. Its well-sized rooms all have a/c, fans, TV and good bathrooms, but prices remain very low. Word has got around, and it's often full.

Hotel Batab, Av. Chichén Itzá 52, t 884 3822, *www.hotelbatab.com*. One of a bunch of hotels on the north side of the city centre, in a functional '70s building; don't expect any frills but it's decent value for a short stay, with big rooms with a/c, TV and phone, and breakfast included. In peak seasons, rates go just into the *moderate* band.

Hotel Hacienda Cancún, Av. Sunyaxchén 39–40, t 884 3672, *hhda@cancun.com.mx*. Rooms (all with fans and a/c) are a bit small and dark at this long-running hotel, but the mock-'hacienda' décor is quite pretty, and its big plus is a nice pool in a pretty garden.

Budget

Security is often a problem in Cancún hostels. All provide guests with lockers, but check that the one offered is in good condition, and never leave valuables unattended.

Hotel María Isabel, C. Palmera 59, t 884 9015, *www.mariaisabelcancun.com*. Long-running favourite a short walk up Av. Uxmal from the bus station. Some of its 12 small but snug rooms, all with a/c, are very dark, but the hotel has an unfussily friendly feel, and needs to be booked well ahead.

Hostel Chacmool, C. Gladiolas 18, t 887 5873, *www.chacmool.com.mx*. Bright, deliberately hip hostel on Parque de las Palapas, with dorms that even have a/c (from $13 per head) and simple double rooms (from $30). Opinions differ on the quality of the 'fusion food' at the **Terraza Chacmool** restaurant, but breakfast is included, and there's free internet access. The Terraza and **Moonshine** rooftop bar stay open late and can be noisy, but the bar has a fine view of the *parque*.

The Weary Traveler, C. Palmeras 30, t 887 0191, *www.wearytravelerhostel.com*. Bright hostel spread over two buildings in adjacent streets, with dorm beds (around $10), some airily located on the roof, and double rooms (around $21). All rooms have a/c, breakfast is included (though you get it yourself, in the open kitchen) and there's free WiFi and internet access. It's clean, and staff are friendly. To find it from the bus station, turn right up Av. Uxmal. There's also a Weary Traveler 'Backpacker Info Center' opposite the bus station on Av. Uxmal. American owner John Kavanagh also has a similar hostel in Tulum (*see* p.201).

Eating Out in Cancún

Cancún has even more restaurants than hotels. Along the Hotel Zone boulevard you can find every cuisine (usually as filtered via the USA), and all the big noises of theme eating – the Hard Rock, the Rainforest Café. Cancún's tourist restaurants have a reputation for paying more attention to flashy décor than their sometimes anonymous food, and prices are around double the Yucatán average. In among them, though, there are places where the expense can be worth it for a special meal and, since locals eat out too, there is a bigger price range in eating places than in hotels. In Ciudad Cancún there are plenty of good local restaurants, and even by the beach you can still eat cheaply at cafés and *taco*-stands.

Expensive

This category is necessarily open-ended: whereas in many Mexican cities it's hard to spend much over $25 per person even in the best restaurants, in anywhere remotely smart here this is an average price.

Blue Bayou, Hyatt Cancún Caribe Hotel, Blvd Kukulcán Km 10.5, t 883 0044. Award-winning Cajun/Creole cooking, served in a pretty, soothing dining room.

La Destilería, Blvd Kukulcán Km 12.5, t 885 1086, *www.ladestileria.com.mx*. A showcase for traditional Mexican – not Yucatecan – food, with Cancún's biggest tequila selection, and a view over the lagoon.

(★) **Los Arcos** >>

La Habichuela, C. Margaritas 25, t 884 3158, *www.lahabichuela.com*. In a tranquil location in Ciudad Cancún next to Parque de las Palapas, this long-running place offers excellent traditional Yucatecan dishes, charmingly served in a lovely garden.

(★) **El Café de la Nader** >>

Labná, C. Margaritas 29, t 884 3158, *www.labna.com*. Some of the most refined and enjoyable cooking in Cancún can be sampled at this very comfortable restaurant, with the same owners as La Habichuela nearby (see above). Menus are based on Yucatecan and Mexican dishes, and highlight fresh fish and local ingredients.

(★) **Labná** >

La Madonna, La Isla, Blvd Kukulcán Km 12.5, t 883 2222, *www.lamadonna. com.mx*. Extravagantly over-the-top neo-art-nouveau décor, creative Italian and Swiss-based food and a balcony martini bar make this one of the Hotel Zone places with the best buzz.

Perico's, Av. Yaxchilán 61, t 884 3152, *www.pericos.com.mx*. Mexican theme restaurant that's a Cancún institution: for years taxi-loads of tourists have come here to sample an 'authentic' fantasy-*cantina* atmosphere, live music, waitresses in bandit-girl outfits and all. Go early or book to avoid queueing.

Moderate

On Av. Yaxchilán in Ciudad Cancún – the same street as Perico's (*see* above) – there's a clutch of fun Mexican restaurants, sports bars and other venues that are among the prime places for Cancún locals to go for a night out or Sunday lunch. They have shaded terrace tables and an ample choice from simple tacos to giant all-included buffets – plus live music on many nights, so if you get into the spirit you can join in singing all-time Mex-classics like Guadalajara and La Bamba.

Los Arcos, Av. Yaxchilán, corner C. Rosas. One of the most enjoyable places on the Yaxchilán strip, a bustling terrace with great meat or seafood grills and classic Mexican dishes in generous portions. Packed with locals on weekend nights: service is fast but friendly.

El Café de la Nader, Av. Nader 5. Behind the town hall, this attractive modern terrace café is a favourite meeting-point for middle-class Mexicans, especially for breakfast. The speciality is excellent Veracruz coffee, but the classic Mexican dishes are also very good.

Carlos'n'Charlie's, Forum by the Sea, Blvd Kukulcán Km 9. Cancún is a great home of the chain restaurant, and among its most prominent corporate identities is Grupo Anderson, a Mex-US group, which has four places in Cancún with similarly silly names: **Señor Frog's** (Blvd Kukulcán Km 9.5), the **Shrimp Bucket** and so on. They're very much a chain, but they know what they're doing: presenting standard Mexican dishes with the heat slightly taken off for *gringo* tastes, in a noisy, non-stop (often cheesey) party atmosphere, especially at Señor Frog's.

100% Natural, Av. Sunyaxchén 62, corner of Av. Yaxchilán. A Mexican chain to be taken note of by all vegetarians, and anyone else feeling like a lighter alternative to traditional Mexican fare: on the menu are excellent salads, sandwiches and light dishes made with fresh produce (vegetarian and non-), and fabulous juices and juice cocktails. Another branch is at Blvd Kukulcán Km 9.5.

Pabilo's, Av. Yaxchilán 31. Those in search of a more cultured ambience in Cancún should seek out this 'cafebrería' – a bookshop-café. Rather stylish, and popular with middle-class locals, it has soft sofas, good coffee, wines and snacks, and hosts art shows and other events. *Open Mon–Sat 5pm –1am.*

Rosa Mexicano, C. Claveles 4. Just off Av. Tulum, this pretty, slightly old-fashioned Mexican restaurant has enjoyable food and charming service, still uninfected by fake have-a-nice-dayism. *Open eves only.*

Sanborn's, Av. Tulum, corner of Av. Uxmal. Opposite the bus station is this branch of the famous Mexico City café (there are two more in Plaza Terramar and Plaza Flamingo). They're great for breakfast, and for insomniacs it's the best place to get a coffee and a snack and find café-style animation late-night. *All open daily 24hrs.*

Budget

Cancún's biggest concentration of cheap eating places and street food is in the central court of the **market** at the end of Av. Sunyaxchén. Its 20 or so restaurants, with outside tables under shady canopies, are not as basic as market *cocinas* in older Mexican cities, but they're more comfortable, and still cheap. Reflecting Cancún's Pan-Mexican population, every part of the country is represented: **Restaurante Veracruz** has Gulf fish and seafood, **El Rinconcito del DF** (Distrito Federal, or Mexico City) offers strong, classic Mexican food, and there's even **Cocina La Chaya**, with Yucatecan *chaya*-based dishes and vegetarian options. Go for Sunday lunch, when they're full of family groups, and you'll never again be able to say Cancún lacks Mexican atmosphere. A full meal can cost $6.

Other good places to look for cheap eats are the snack- and *taco*-stands in the middle of **Parque de las Palapas**, and **Calle Tulipanes**, with its line of unfussy bars and restaurants.

Gory Tacos, C. Tulipanes 26. Classic straight-forward *taquería* with countless fans for its juicy, fiery Mexican classics and cold beers.

Entertainment and Nightlife in Cancún

Live Entertainment

Naturally enough, there's loads of it. One fixture on the programme is **bullfights**, every Wed at 3.30pm, which include a preceding *charrería* (*see* p.111) and folk music display. Tickets can be booked from a stand on Av. Tulum, near the Ki-Huic market. There are also occasional full-scale *charrería* shows at the *Lienzo Charro* south of the city, information on which is available from the tourist office.

Another Cancún speciality are **theme dinner cruises** (Pirate's Night, the Columbus cruise, etc.), including live entertainment, dinner, disco, karaoke and other forms of fun for around $45 a head. Places like the **Hard Rock** and **Dady'O** often present live rock shows by US and international acts.

Mariachis and other Mexican traditional musicians can be seen in any number of restaurants. Folk-dancing shows, once a Cancún fixture, are now far more intermittent (although local freesheets sometimes still advertise them, which leads to a lot of confusion): the *Ballet Folclórico* is no longer in residence at the Convention Center, and the **Teatro de Cancún** only occasionally presents its *Voces y Danzas de México* show. Most of the time the theatre now presents a mix of music and theatre more tailored to local audiences.

Teatro de Cancún, El Embarcadero, Blvd Kukulcán Km 4, **t** 849 5580, *www.elteatrodecancun.com.*

Clubs and Bars

Hubs of Cancún nightlife are the Hotel Zone clubs, the biggest of which handily cluster together in the same block, near the Cancún Center at Km 9.5. They tend to be vast, with several spaces, a/c that's a miracle of modern science and hot body contests, bikini nights and similar to draw in the crowds. Clubbing here can be expensive: big venues like Coco Bongo have a one-charge, open-bar system, so a fairly high entry price ($35–$45) covers all drinks for the night, but

⭐ **Congo Bar >>**

keeping drinks flowing requires keeping the attention of your waiter (assigned as you arrive) with liberal tips. The way to cut costs is to take advantageof happy hours, discount coupons, and girls-go-free sessions and other promotions on slow nights.

If you want something more Mexican (and cheaper), head for Av. Yaxchilán in town, where there are buzzing places like **Buena Onda** disco and **El Gran Melao** salsa club.

Azúcar, Dreams Cancún, Blvd Kukulcán Km 9, t 848 7000. The best Latin dance club in town, a smart venue with an equally well-dressed, largely local crowd, and superb live bands. *Open Thurs–Sat only*.

The City, Blvd Kukulcán Km 9.5, t 848 8380, *www.thecitycancun.com*. Claiming to be the biggest club in Latin America, this giant has four floors, nine bars and a beach club for pool parties. Frequent theme nights, and (mostly) hip hop at weekends.

Coco Bongo, Blvd Kukulcán Km 9.5, t 883 5061, *www.cocobongo.com.mx*. Giant multi-level mega-venue that has long set the pace in Cancún and retains the crown as the most popular in town, with eye-boggling show nights and a funkily eclectic music policy.

Congo Bar, Blvd Kukulcán Km 9.5, t 883 0563, *www.congobar.com.mx*. Smaller venue (but still three floors, and a terrace open to the stars) with a more relaxed style than the mega-clubs (and lower prices). Hip and sexy, and as popular with young locals as tourists.

Dady'O, Blvd Kukulcán Km 9.5, 883 3333, *www.dadyo.com.mx*. Ever-popular with Spring Breakers, this mega-club has several sections: the main **Dady'O** is huge party disco; **Dady Rock** is smaller and has live bands; **Terrasta** is for reggae and related sounds; and **O Ultra** is the hip corner with house and trance.

The Islands

Each of the three inhabited islands around the Quintana Roo coast is distinct from the others. **Isla Mujeres** has retained a lot of its easy-going, beach village atmosphere, as well as being a diving centre. Tiny **Holbox**, around the cape north of Cancún, remains a more remote spot. **Cozumel**, the largest, has a more conventional feel, and is shared between package holiday-makers, cruise passengers and diving devotees.

Isla Mujeres

The 'Island of Women' is all of 8km long, a narrow, rocky strip running southeast from the small triangle that contains the only town. A fork of land on its west side encloses a sheltered lagoon, Laguna Macax. The best swimming and snorkelling beaches and diving reefs are all on the western, landward side; the ocean side is much rockier and more windswept, and the sea rougher. When Cancún was first being set up for mass tourism, the sleepy fishing community of Isla Mujeres was the first place on the coast discovered by backpackers. Development has picked up, but the little town with its sandy streets still has a lot of its laid-back, Caribbean, hippyish feel.

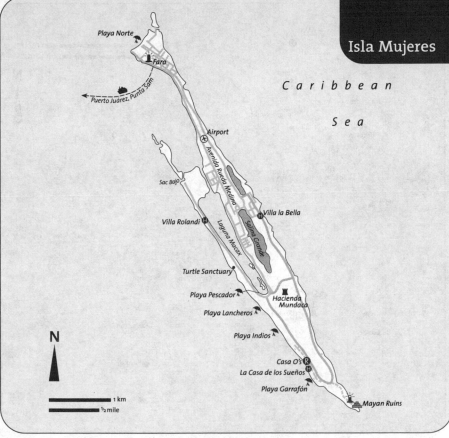

Playa Norte

Faro

Puerto Juárez, Punto Sam

C a r i b b e a n

S e a

Airport

Sac Bajo

Avenida Rueda Medina

Villa Rolandi

Villa la Bella

Laguna Macox

Salina Grande

Turtle Sanctuary

Playa Pescador

Hacienda Mundaca

Playa Lancheros

Playa Indios

Casa O's

La Casa de los Sueños

Playa Garrafón

Mayan Ruins

N

1 km

½ mile

History

As a monument in the town plaza recalls, this was the site of the Spaniards' first landfall anywhere in Mexico in 1517, when Hernández de Córdoba's expedition came upon the island after a storm. The idols that his men saw on the island which they recognized as figures of women (and so the origin of its Spanish name) were mostly images of Ixchel, Goddess of Fertility. It seems likely that Isla Mujeres was a secondary place of pilgrimage, associated with the shrine of Ixchel on Cozumel (*see* p.158).

After the Conquest the island was of little interest to the Spaniards, and was largely abandoned by its Maya inhabitants. However, its remoteness and the shelter of its lagoon did make it attractive to pirates, in particular the last of the great Caribbean pirates, the Louisiana-born brothers Jean and Pierre Lafitte. They made it a favourite refuge, but their career was brought to an end here when they were attacked by the Spanish navy in 1821. The brothers escaped, but both were fatally wounded, and one is said to be buried at Dzilam Bravo (*see* p.293). Isla's population grew a little more in the 1900s, when *chicle* tappers favoured it over anywhere on the mainland. The island's varied past and population – with a lot of contact with Cuba

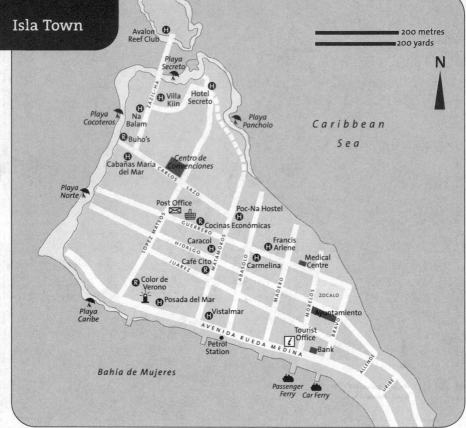

and the Caribbean – are reflected in the traditional houses still seen in some streets: brightly painted clapboard houses with porches, instead of the plain palm huts of the Yucatán.

Isla Town

The ferries leave you on Av. Rueda Medina, the main road along the western side of the town. A walk up the streets opposite and just to the right, Morelos or Nicolás Bravo, will take you to the main square, with the town hall and the church, which runs right through to the east side of the island, so narrow is it at this point.

Inside the town, Avenidas Juárez and Hidalgo, north of the Zócalo, are the nearest things to 'main drags', with the main restaurants and souvenir markets. This is also where most of the beach-squatters gravitate to after dark. On Guerrero, next to the post office, there's a tiny **food market**, and nearby on Av. Carlos Lazo is a rather fancy **Centro de Convenciones**, although it doesn't seem to host many events. Among the more modern buildings there are still a few old Isla houses with wooden porches and balconies, and a few doors

Getting to and around Isla Mujeres

By Air
Isla's **airstrip**, along the neck of the island south of town, is used for light plane tours by **Aerobanana, t** 872 5040, which also offers air-taxi transfers between Isla and Cancún.

By Sea
The most popular way of getting to Isla Mujeres is by **passenger ferry** from **Puerto Juárez**, 3km north of Ciudad Cancún. Several local buses (R-13, some R-1 buses) run from Av. Tulum to the ferry docks, and there are also *colectivos* (cab around $2). There are two ferry companies, with separate docks. **Magaña** fast ferries sail from the main **Estación Marítima** in Puerto Juárez every half-hour 6.30am–11.30pm daily (from Isla 6am–8.30pm). Journey time is about 15mins; tickets are around $3. The bigger **Ultramar** ferries run from the swankier **Gran Puerto Cancún** dock a short walk south (to the right) from the Estación Marítima. Boats leave Gran Puerto every half-hour 5am–11.30pm (from Isla 5.30am–12 midnight), and fares are competitive with those of Magaña, also at about $3. Ultramar also runs more expensive ferries ($7) about once an hour from **Playa Tortugas** in the Hotel Zone (9.30am–5.30pm from Cancún, 9am–4pm from Isla).

There are five **car ferries** each way daily from **Punta Sam** (8am–8.15pm from Punta Sam; 6.30am–7.15pm from Isla Mujeres). A car and two people costs about $25.

By Road
Isla Mujeres has the usual complement of **taxis**. A trip to the furthest point costs around $4 each way, or $15 for a 'taxi tour' all around the Isla. There are also *tricicleros*, tricycle-cart drivers, who will carry your bags anywhere in town (5–10 pesos), and an infrequent local **bus** service around town and down to Garrafón.

The number of vehicles is growing, but for getting around on your own, given Isla's size, cars are a bit excessive. The most popular form of transport is the four-seater **golf cart**. **Scooters** and **mopeds** are faster, but it is very easy and more peaceful to take an ordinary **bicycle**. The same shops normally rent carts, scooters and bicycles, and there are plenty around the town. Local authorities now impose fairly standard rates, so you won't find big differences in prices. The **usual rates** for golf carts are around $12 an hour, $50 for 24hrs; for scooters, $7 an hour, $25 for 24hrs; and for bikes $4 an hour, $12 for 24hrs. When renting you will need to pay in advance and leave a document or cash deposit, so take something else if you don't want to leave your passport. Go early in the day to have the best choice (some vehicles have been round the island many, many times), and check the machine over before you take it, especially the brakes and saddles on cycles. Take a hat and plenty of sun block too.

Mega Ciro's, Av. Guerrero 11, corner of Av. Matamoros. Carts, scooters and bikes.

Motorent El Zorro, Av. Guerrero between Matamoros and Abasolo. Mopeds and bikes only: low rates, but check bikes with care, as they have some real wrecks.

Rentadora Cárdenas, Av. Guerrero, between Abasolo and Madero. A big choice of carts and scooters, but no bikes.

---

from smart jewellery stores there are places like the 'Fishermen's Cantina', brightly painted with a perky and drunk-looking tuna. A big part of the town's charm – carried over on to newer, concrete buildings – comes from its lurid paintwork in candybox greens, pinks, reds and yellows, which are almost an Isla trademark. It's hard to take things very seriously in any place that's bright pink.

Around the Island
Av. Rueda Medina continues south down the island, past the airstrip, at the end of which there's a left turn across to the eastern side (still only half a kilometre away). A kilometre or so further, at the island's main crossroads, lies the entrance to Isla's best known monument, **Hacienda Mundaca**. Fermín Mundaca, who built a mansion here, is often described as a pirate, but he was actually

Isla Town Beaches

Playa Caribe: The long beach between the ferry landings and the lighthouse. Used by dive-masters and fishing guides, but not the most popular for beach-lounging.

Playa Norte and **Playa Cocoteros** (really the same beach): The main beaches along the 'top' of the island, and with many beach bars. They're sheltered and the water is very shallow, so they're excellent for easy swimming, but get crowded. Also, since sand dredging nearby to restore Cancún beach – at least, this is what many on Isla allege – these beaches have become less stable, and in some tides lose a lot of sand. Cement-filled plastic 'geotubes' may be laid to restrict erosion, which are pretty ugly.

Playa Secreto: At the eastern end of Playa Norte a little inlet that's shallower and more tranquil still, and so ideal for kids paddling, but also subject to beach erosion. A wooden footbridge runs across it to the Avalon Grand all-inclusive.

Playa Pancholo: A small beach further around the corner which, facing east, suffers from rougher seas. It can be dangerous; check whether the red warning flag is up.

something far less romantic. One of the last Caribbean slavers, he ran Africans to Cuba until in 1860 the British Navy's anti-slavery patrols prompted him to call it a day. According to legend he chose Isla Mujeres for his retirement because he was infatuated with an 18-year-old local girl, *la trigueña* ('the fair one'), and so built the largest house ever seen on the island in the hope it would impress her. She was not interested one bit, and married a young islander, leaving Mundaca to go mad and die an embittered man. The story is more interesting than anything at the site today, for only the entrance gate and a few ruins survive of the Hacienda. Its grounds have been made into an (often bug-filled) **park** with a little zoo with a jaguar, monkeys and other local wildlife.

park
open daily 9–6; adm

A sharp right turn at the crossroads will take you up the west side of the lagoon, a gentle run past a few restaurants, beach clubs, hotels and houses with boat landings. A little north of the turn is the **Tortugranja turtle farm,** a turtle-breeding and repopulation centre. As well as the tanks and pools in which sea turtles are bred and kept until big enough to be released into the wild, there is a good display (in Spanish and English) on turtle and reef ecology, and the inevitable souvenir shop. Further up is an 'eco-attraction' that people like or hate (*see* p.76), **Dolphin Discovery.**

Tortugranja turtle farm
open daily 9–5; adm

Back at the crossroads, the main island road continues to the right of Hacienda Mundaca leading to **Playa Lancheros**, the longest beach on Isla, with beachside restaurants visited by Cancún day trips, and where Isla's first really big resort hotel, the Isla Mujeres Palace, opened in 2007. The road winds on past other beaches to **El Garrafón** nature park, a user-friendly snorkelling centre similar to Xcaret or Xel-Ha (*see* pp.185 and 188) in a big natural pool in the reef. There is also another Dolphin Discovery centre. However, the pool itself is often crowded and reeks of suntan oil, and its coral is now pretty dead, especially since Wilma, making this the most disappointing of the facilities of this kind on the Riviera.

El Garrafón
open daily 10–5; adm

Getting to Isla Contoy

Tours to Contoy are offered by a great many dive shops and agencies in Isla Mujeres (around $40 per person) and some in Cancún, and good Contoy trips now run from Holbox (see p.155). From Isla Mujeres, a standard trip lasts a full day (journey 1½hrs each way), with (hopefully) some time to walk the path and snorkel in the lagoon (equipment provided); drinks and lunch are included. These trips, though, can be very disappointing: many are badly managed, and often all the boats arrive together, so you don't see many birds. You may be left on the beach for much of the day with the other tours, to drink and splash around. Check carefully with a tour operator when booking. More information and a list of recognized operators is on *www.islacontoy.org*, site of the semi-official **Amigos de Isla Contoy**.

Parque Escúltorico Punta Sur
open daily 7am–10pm; adm

From Garrafón it's only a short distance to the southern tip of the island, now marked off as the **Parque Escúltorico Punta Sur**. Beside the path to the point there's a 'sculpture park' of multicoloured modern works, often evoking Maya themes, leading to the older monuments at the tip, a lighthouse and a small **Maya temple** to Ixchel. Never very impressive, this crumbling cube was badly battered by Hurricane Gilbert in 1988, and a better reason for going to the point is the sweeping view of the ocean and the island behind you. The east side of the island is flat, bare and windblown, dotted with isolated clumps of private beach houses. Take drinks with you, as any shops or bars along this route are only intermittently open.

Isla Contoy

The uninhabited island of Contoy, 30km north of Isla Mujeres, is Mexico's most important seabird reserve. It has important populations of pelicans, cormorants and frigate birds, but there are also boobies, spoonbills and over 50 other species. Much of the island is made up of mangroves that contain many rare plants, and there are turtle breeding beaches. Around the island lie beautiful lagoons with intact reefs.

The areas open to ordinary visitors are the **visitor centre**, the main **lagoon** (with a fine beach), an **observation tower** and a path that runs past one of the main frigate-bird nesting lagoons. Controlled fishing is also permitted.

ⓘ **Tourist Office**
Av. Rueda Medina 130, t 877 0307, infoisla@isla-mujeres.net; near the ferry quay (usually open Mon–Sat 9–5).

ⓘ **Viajes Prisma**
Av. Rueda Medina 9C, t 877 0938. Tours, other travel agency services and air transfers to Cancún.

Tourist Information on Isla Mujeres

t (998–)
Isla Mujeres's free ads-and-information magazine, *Islander* (*www.isla-mujeres-mexico.com*) has maps and is available at the tourist office and in shops and restaurants. The best of several Isla-based websites is *www.isla-mujeres.net*.

Services on Isla Mujeres

Banks: HSBC, on Av. Rueda Medina by the ferry docks (*open Mon–Fri 8.30–6, Sat 9–2*). There are ATMs at the bank and on the town plaza, and several *cambio* offices on Av. Juárez and Av. Hidalgo (*open Sun*). ATMs quite often run out of cash on weekends.

Health: Dr Antonio Salas, Av. Hidalgo 18, t 877 0047, is an English-speaking **doctor** with a 24hr emergency service. The main **pharmacy** on Av. Juárez between Morelos and Bravo is also open late.

Internet Access: Plenty to choose from: **Net Café**, Av. Madero between Juárez and Hidalgo, has decent rates.

Post Office: Towards the beach, corner of Guerrero and López Mateos.

Shopping

Isla town has plenty of souvenir shops and markets, with goods from all over Mexico and Guatemala, including a lot of junk. **Casa Isleño II** on Av. Guerrero, off the Zócalo, has its own hand-painted T-shirts and locally-made shell and coral jewellery, and every Sunday afternoon in the plaza there's a **Gran Feria** market where island artists and craftspeople sell their wares. There are several **jewellery stores** offering fine gems at only slightly bargainish prices (**Van Cleef & Arpels** is on the corner of Juárez and Morelos). For general shopping, besides the market there are supermarkets on the Zócalo (**El Bético**) and on Matamoros by the waterfront (**Capricornio**).

Sports and Activities

Diving, Snorkelling and Watersports

Isla Mujeres, more than Cancún, is the best base for **diving** in the northern part of the Maya Reef. Prices are lower, and the local dive-masters have a far better reputation. Despite the intensification of traffic in the area, Isla still offers fine diving conditions. The **Manchones** reef is popular for beginners and basic dives, a very safe reef about 10m deep where there is an undersea cross. There are other deeper reefs nearby, many with wrecks, including that of one of the *conquistador* Montejo's ships sunk in 1527. A special attraction for more experienced divers is **Sleeping Sharks cave**, in a 20m reef northeast of the island, where an underground river flows out into the sea bed. The confluence of fresh and sea water is peculiarly attractive to reef sharks, and large numbers of them 'sleep' for hours on end on the cave floor (properly dealt with, they never attack anybody). For more on diving off Isla, check *mayanparadise.net/isladiveguide*.

Even more popular than scuba diving are **snorkelling** tours. Most boat outings go to the reefs off Sac Bajo, the little island at the northwest tip of Laguna Macax, or Manchones, where it's possible to see plenty of underwater life even without scuba equipment. On **Playa Norte** there are also beach huts that rent out pedalos, kayaks, windsurf boards, cheap snorkel equipment and more.

Sport **fishing** trips are also widely available. If you have your own **boat**, there are ample facilities at three marinas, one in town and two on Laguna Macax. For information on facilities and formalities, call the tourist office on t 877 0307 or check *www.isla-mujeres.net*.

Dive Shops and Agencies

The same shops and agencies frequently offer diving, snorkelling and fishing trips. An introductory scuba 'resort course' costs around $60, a two-tank dive for certified divers about $45; diving in Sleeping Sharks Cave from $60. Snorkel tours cost $15–25, and fishing trips from about $250–350 a day. All the shops offer good-value packages for certification courses and for dives over two days or more. From their building near the ferry landing, the local *Cooperativa de Lancheros* (boatmen) offer trips around the island for around $10 a head ($13 with snacks), for snorkelling or fishing.

Captain Tony García, Av. Matamoros 7A, t 877 0229, *capitantonys@ hotmail.com*. Very experienced local boatman offering fishing trips (from about $38 an hour) and snorkel tours (around $15 per person).

Coral Dive Center, Av. Matamoros 13-A, near Av. Rueda Medina, t 877 0763, *www.coralscubadivecenter.com*. Large, well-equipped agency with accessible rates. Also offers specialist courses (rescue, underwater photography) and sailing boat rental.

Enrique's Unique Dives, Av. Rueda Medina, between Madero and Abasolo, t 145 3594, *www.divingislamujeres.com*. Enrique Avila is one of Isla's most experienced dive-masters, and provides very personal service.

La Isleña, Av. Morelos, between Rueda Medina and Juárez, t 877 0578. A more basic shop with bargain snorkel tours and fishing trips.

Sea Hawk Divers, C. Carlos Lazo, near Playa Norte, t 877 0296, *www.isla-mujeres.net/seahawkdivers*. Friendly, reliable local operator with a full range of diving, snorkelling and fishing trips at rates. They have some attractive suites (with kitchens) and **rooms** (*inexpensive*) for clients taking courses or their excellent-value dive packages, which are available to anyone.

Where to Stay on Isla Mujeres

Big resort hotels have begun to appear here in the last few years, but most Isla hotels, in line with the size of the island, are still small and low-key. Nearly all are in town. Rooms fill up from Dec to early April and to a lesser extent in July–Aug, when prices are also at their peak. Between these times it's rarely hard to get a room, and prices drop, often by a full price band.

Luxury

La Casa de los Sueños, Ctra Garrafon, 8km south of town, t 877 0651, *www.casadelossuenosresort.com*. A discreet luxury hideaway on a bluff above the sea near the south end of Isla, with dazzling contemporary Mexican architecture. It's now only available as a private rental, of at least five rooms, for a minimum stay of five nights: guests have the hedonistic run of nine rooms, a spectacular pool and terrace overlooking the ocean, and the 'SpaZenter' for all kinds of pampering treatments.

Hotel Secreto, Playa Secreto, t 877 1039, *www.hotelsecreto.com*. Isla's foremost 'boutique hotel', praised to the skies by international travel magazines. Making a virtue of a small site, next to Playa Secreto, it promises something of the intimate feel of a private beach house. Its rooms, pool and garden restaurant are all extremely chic, though some find them a bit lacking in spaciousness. Service, however, is very charming, and in recognition of post-2008 economic circumstances prices often drop down to the *expensive* band ($125–175).

Villa Rolandi, Fraccionamiento Laguna Mar, t 999 2000, *www.villarolandi.com*. Under the same owners as Hotel Belmar in town, but much smarter, the Rolandi sits above its own beach on the west side of Laguna Macax, facing Cancún in the distance. Each room is beautiful, with sea views from the shower and a Jacuzzi on the balcony, and it has its own landing stage and yacht (sea transfers from Cancún are included). Rooms are normally taken on a semi-all-inclusive basis, with dinner (on a terrace with similarly great view) in the package. The hotel is aimed at couples, so no kids under 13.

Expensive

Cabañas María del Mar, Av. Carlos Lazo 1, t 877 0179, *www.cabanasdelmar.com*. Comfortable rooms in a main 'tower' building and two-room *cabaña*-style bungalows, with fridges, around a garden and small pool. All rooms have tempting hammocks. The beach's most popular bar, **Buho's** (*see* p.151), is nearby, and massages and health treatments are a speciality. Prices drop to *moderate* off-peak.

Hotel Playa la Media Luna, Punta Norte, t 877 0759, *www.playamedia luna.com*. Modern hotel sharing a road with the Secreto (*see* left) on the ocean side of Playa Secreto.Much of it faces a rocky open sea rather than a usable beach, but there's a fine pool and pretty **restaurant** (*expensive*). Accommodation ranges from 'rustic' (*moderate*, or even *inexpensive* off-peak) to very spacious rooms and suites with ocean views (*luxury–expensive*).

Na Balam Beach Hotel, C. Zazil-Ha 118, t 877 0279, *www.nabalam.com*. Mellow hotel among palm trees behind Cocoteros beach. Rooms all

⭐ Villa Kiin ≫

have sitting areas and balconies or terraces, but some are a little dark, and not all have direct beach access. It has a pretty pool, one of the island's best restaurants (see p.151), and yoga and meditation courses. Prices are in the *luxury* band mid-Dec–April.

Villa La Bella, Ctra Perimetral, t 888 0342, *www.villalabella.com*. Very attractive American-owned B&B lodge on the east side of the island, with a clifftop location just south of the town. The six rooms are all big and beautiful, and have great ocean views, and there's a lovely pool with terrace alongside where you can enjoy the fresh breakfasts. A personal welcome makes this a popular home from home.

Moderate

Hotel Francis Arlene, Av. Guerrero 7, t 877 0310, *www.francisarlene.com*. One of Isla's more individual hotels, with pastel-coloured, suite-style rooms. Some are fan-only, but most have a/c, fridges, balconies and big beds, some have kitchenettes, and top floor rooms are mini-apartments with big roof terraces. The patios are attractive and airy, and the whole place has a cosy feel. Rates are mostly inexpensive in low season.

Hotel Posada del Mar, Av. Rueda Medina 15-A, t 877 0044, *www.posadadelmar.com*. Big hotel on the waterfront by the lighthouse, pink and green (on the outside) and with 61 well-equipped rooms and ample suites *(expensive)*. Main pluses are the views from most of the sea-side rooms (rooms with no view are less attractive), and a pretty pool; some rooms can be noisy at night.

Maria's Kankin, Ctra Garrafón, t 877 0015, *www.mariaskankin.com*. An eccentric place set up in the 1970s by Frenchwoman Maria Llopet. Each of the nine beach-cabin rooms and suites is different, but all are big and have ample sitting space, fridges and other extras. There's also a beach and jetty, a **restaurant** (see right) and free bikes for guests. Maria's fans are those who forgive its quirks (the age of bits of it) to enjoy its pluses (the tropical-garden location).

Su Casa, Sac Bajo road, west side of Laguna Macax, t 877 0180, *www.sucasamexico.com*. Cluster of pretty beach houses on its own tranquil stretch of beach. The cabins are a few years old but have nice comforts, a kitchen and a double and a single bed.

Villa Kiin, C. Zazil-Ha 129, t 877 0045, *www.villakiin.com*. Individual hotel – better known by its old name, Casa Maya – that has one of the most attractive locations on Isla Mujeres, facing Playa Secreto lagoon. Rooms, some in the main house and some in *cabañas*, are decorated with traditional textiles; they vary a good deal in size and extras (some have a/c, some are on the beach, some are quite simple; no. 11 is best), so there are several prices as well. There's a comfortable lounge and open kitchen for guests' use. Prices vary more than usual between seasons.

Inexpensive–Budget

Isla Mujeres has plenty of plain-and-simple budget hotels, all in town. Virtually all vary in price from the low *inexpensive* band Dec–April to significantly cheaper at other times. You can book ahead, but don't expect these hotels to hold on to rooms for long at peak times; in winter, get to the island as early as you can, certainly by 1pm, to be sure of getting a room.

Hotel Carmelina, Av. Guerrero 4, between Abasolo and Madero, t 877 0006. One of Isla's most popular budget stand-bys, on three floors around a wide patio, so all the well-kept rooms have good light. Rooms with a/c are only a little pricier.

Hotel Marcianito, Av. Abasolo, between Juárez and Hidalgo, t 877 0111, *hotelmarcianito@hotmail.com*. Fresh little hotel with bright, well-maintained rooms with new fittings, helpful owners and low prices. Street noise is the only drawback.

Hotel Vistalmar, Av. Rueda Medina, corner of Matamoros, t 877 0209. Impossible to miss with its island colours of pink, yellow and green, the Vistalmar has a great view and a funky atmosphere that attracts a laid-back crowd (don't expect perfect quiet). The owners are also friendly, and it has a terrace **restaurant**.

Poc-Na Hostel, Av. Matamoros, corner of Carlos Lazo, t 877 0090, *www.pocna.com*. This backpackers' favourite has dorms of 8 or 14 beds, one women-only, others mixed, or you can camp in the grounds (by the beach). There are also double rooms with showers, some with a/c ($25–33). Bikes are available to rent, and there's free Net access. The bar-lounge is a social centre, and the hostel has its own beach bar on Pancholo beach.

Posada Soemi, Av. Matamoros, between Juárez and Rueda Medina, t 877 0122. Simple little hotel run by a charming elderly lady. Her fan-only rooms are plain but big, all with showers, and prices are low all year.

Apartment and Villa Rentals

Many people want to settle on Isla Mujeres for a few weeks at a time, and there are plenty of apartments and villas available for rent. As well as the general Isla websites, other good places to look for short-term rentals are *www.lostoasis.net* and *www.islabeckons.com*.

Eating Out

After Cancún, Isla Mujeres represents a return to something closer to normal Mexican restaurant style and – within the limits of the Riviera – prices, with the extra element of gringo-influenced health-food outlets.

Expensive

Casa O's, Ctra Garrafón, t 888 0170, *www.casaos.com*. One of Isla's best, a beautiful, stylish restaurant, with exquisite ocean views, superior modern Mexican food and a good wine list. It's next to Maria's.

Maria's Kankin, Ctra Garrafón, t 877 0015. Quirkily enjoyable, with an idiosyncratic blend of Mexican and French cuisine – great seafood – served on a lush terrace. Book ahead rather than just turn up.

Olivia – Sabores del Mediterráneo, Av. Matamoros, between Juárez and Rueda Medina, t 877 1765. Innovative restaurant opened by an Israeli couple, with inventive pan-Mediterranean

cuisine served in a pretty patio. *Open Tues–Sat 5–9.30pm*.

Zazil-Ha, Na Balam Beach Hotel, C. Zazil-Ha, t 877 0279. Fine fish and organic and vegetarian dishes, served in a garden or an over-neat air-conditioned dining room.

Moderate

Beachside eateries along Av. Rueda Medina tend to be overpriced, but are fine for watching the movement of boats and people. By day, Playa Norte bars like Zazil-Ha and Buho's are the place to be.

Aquí Estoy, Av. Matamoros, between Guerrero and Hidalgo. Isla's enormously popular, Italian-run takeaway fresh pizza bar.

Buho's, Cabañas María del Mar, Playa Norte. The most popular beach bar, with seats on swings dangling from the *palapa* roof, and Mexican snacks, salads and seafood.

El Café Cito, Av. Juárez, corner of Matamoros. A mellow healthfood café specializing in fruit and yoghurt breakfasts and vegetarian and wholefood lunches. *Open daily 7am–2pm, and some evenings in winter high season*.

Color de Verano, Av. López Mateos, near corner of Av. Rueda Medina. With surprisingly chic décor so close to the beach, this café-crêperie offers nice fresh crêpes and other light, French-oriented fare. *Closed Sun*.

Elements of the Island, Av. Juárez, between Matamoros and López Mateos, t 877 1715. Healthy wholefood breakfast or brunch guaranteed at this calm and comfortable café; they also have three very mellow, high-standard **apartments** to rent (*moderate*). *Café open 7.30am–1pm, closed Wed*.

French Bistro Français, Av. Matamoros, between Hidalgo and Juárez. Likeable place with a suitably beachcomberish air that presents French-oriented, global cuisine, and breakfasts made with flair. *Open mornings till noon and eves after 6pm*.

El Sombrero de Gomar, Av. Hidalgo, corner of Av. Madero. Enjoyable Mexican classics are the staples of this perennially popular spot, with a pretty and airy *palapa*-roofed balcony

Entertainment and Nightlife

Isla town's small size dictates that after dark there are three main centres of activity, the beach, the waterfront and the Zócalo, with Av. Hidalgo to connect them in between. By the waterside, on the corner of Av. Rueda Medina and López Mateos, there's **Jax** Bar & Grill, a big and noisy US-style dine-and-party venue. After midnight, options include **Nitrox Club VIP** on Av. Guerrero, Isla's most high-energy dance club, or the more mellow **Om Bar and Chill Lounge** on Av. Matamoros, with Brazilian, acid jazz and similar sounds, herbal teas and serve-yourself beer taps at each table.

Isla Holbox

Nowhere in Quintana Roo is unnoticed by tourism these days, but there is still a giant contrast between Cancún and Isla Holbox, a tiny sand-strip across Laguna Yalahao on the north coast west of Cabo Catoche. It has become better known, above all since the discovery of its whale sharks (*see* below), but so far it remains most of the time a delightfully friendly place of about 1,000 people, for many of whom the main business is stilll passing the time of day and a bit of fishing as well as catering to visitors. The pace of change has been gathering – Holboxers have had TV since 2003 – but even its largest hotels are small beer by Riviera standards. Holbox was badly battered by Hurricane Wilma, but bounced back with unfussy calm. With its sandy streets and empty beaches, it's a lovely place to forget the world for a few days.

On the way across to Holbox, look out for dolphins jumping in the lagoon; the sight of them, glistening in the sunlight, is an exhilarating introduction to the island. Holbox is a long narrow strip, running east–west, with the village near the western end. From the ferry landing on the landward side the one main street (Av. Juárez) runs straight across for about a kilometre to end at the beach on the ocean side. Along the way you pass the noisy generator that provides the place with electricity, and the little **plaza**. Streets run off between palms on either side (they have been given names, but as these are not signed up anywhere this is pretty irrelevant). At the ocean end of Juárez there's a leaning lighthouse, a jetty, the Faro Viejo hotel and bar, boats pulled up on the beach and sand and dunes running to the horizon. Facing the Gulf, Holbox does not have the crystal-turquoise waters of the Caribbean, but it's a gentle beach great for a relaxing swim, with sandbars that allow you to 'walk on water' for enormous distances out to sea. All along the beach are huge numbers of pelicans, frigate birds and terns, and scurrying flocks of turnstones and other wading birds.

West of the village there is only the airstrip and a few small, scattered *cabaña* hotels, which consequently are often splendidly secluded. The long beach east of the village is where, as Holbox experiences its mild 'tourist takeoff', a palm-roofed line of smartish hotels is extending along the shore. However, if you carry on past them on the track behind the beach toward Cabo Catoche (best done with a bike), you can find long, long stretches of beach with nothing but brush, sand, sea birds and the breeze.

Holbox has one drawback, though, which for some can be a major irritation: much of it is made up of mangroves, and its mosquitoes can be ferocious and unrelenting, especially around sundown and, as usual, whenever the humidity rises (let alone after rain). Take DEET.

Laguna Yalahao and Cabo Catoche

Holbox itself is only one of several islands around Laguna Yalahao (mostly uninhabited). On the next island west is **Ojo de Agua**, a magical place where an underground river brings fresh water up into the sea-water mangrove, creating a delicious pool for swimming and a very special mix of flora and fauna, and further south is **Isla de Pájaros**, home to or a nesting-spot for over 150 species of birds, including flamingos (from March to August). Trips can also be arranged to mangroves on the far side of the lagoon, where – at night – you might see some crocodiles. On the ocean side, boats can leave you for a day on deserted beaches east of the village, take you to **Cabo Catoche**, where the Gulf and Caribbean waters meet, or (for a higher price) continue round the cape to **Boca Iglesia**, where there are scarcely excavated Mayan ruins and an early Spanish chapel

Dolphin Spectaculars

Dolphin shows are among the most widely advertised – pretty much inescapable – attractions on the Riviera, Isla Mujeres and Cozumel. All operate to a pretty familiar format, with a show, when the dolphins do tricks with their trainers, and the chance to swim in a dolphin pool and maybe do some tricks yourself. Most are run by one of three companies, **Delphinus** (*www.delphinusworld.com*, t 998 206 3304), with locations at Dreams Cancún Resort, Riviera Maya (near Playa del Carmen), Xcaret, Xel-Ha and, shortly, near Mahahual further south; **Dolphinaris** (*www.dolphinaris.com*, t 998 881 3030), at Wet'n'Wild, Cancún, and Cozumel; and **Dolphin Discovery** (*www.dolphindiscovery.com*, t 01 800 727 5391) in Isla Mujeres, Cozumel and Puerto Aventuras. They are quite expensive: prices at Dolphin Discovery for a swim with dolphins begin at $69, at Delphinus (which has a higher reputation) around $98.

Dolphin pools are popular, but controversial: wild dolphins normally travel large distances, and 'performing' ones that are kept in small pools with barriers to prevent them leaving and trained to do tricks all day become prone to a range of diseases. Most captive dolphins live shortened lives. For the anti-pool case, see *Dolphins are Dying to Amuse You*, from the Animal Welfare Institute (*www.awionline.org*).

Getting to Holbox

You can reach Holbox via the little port of **Chiquilá**, 80km north of Highway 180, after a long drive from a turn just east of the Quintana Roo state line at **El Ideal**. This road has been improved and widened, making it far less bumpy and cutting down driving time to about 2½hrs. There are **gas stations** at Kantunilkín and Chiquilá. There are parking lots near the jetty where you can leave your car for $3–4 a day.

Passenger ferries (about $3 per person) leave Chiquilá about every 2hrs, on the hour, daily 6am–7pm, with returns from Holbox 5am–6pm (journey time 20–25mins). There are also *Primera Clase* ferries, supposedly a bit faster, with three to six a day 6.45am–3.30pm (7.45am–4.30pm from Holbox) but their schedule often varies. If you miss a boat there are always *lancheros* in Chiquilá who will take you across, and if four or more people get together this won't cost much more than the ferry. There's also a **car ferry** roughly twice daily, but only for local vehicles.

Second-class **buses** run to Chiquilá from Cancún (*3hrs*) and Mérida (*5½–6hrs*). Six leave Cancún daily (4.30am–2.15pm); going back, buses leave after the arrival of Holbox ferries at 5.30am, 7.30am and 1.30pm. From Mérida there is one bus nightly at 11.30pm, calling at Valladolid (2.30am) and arriving in Chiquilá at 5am; the return leaves at 5.30am after the first ferry of the day from Holbox. An alternative during daytime is to get off a Mérida–Cancún bus at El Ideal, and get a taxi from there to Chiquilá, which will cost around $23–30. There are also *combis* on the same route.

The opulent option is to go by **light plane**. Cancún's AeroCosta (*see* p.128) and Aerosaab from Playa del Carmen (*see* p.176) offer day tours and air-taxi transfers. Holbox hotels also arrange private car-and-boat (or sometimes air) **transfers** from Cancún.

Getting around Holbox

Once on Holbox, it's easy to get anywhere on foot or by cycle, and there are few motor vehicles (though the number is growing). The favourite form of transport is now the **golf cart**. Locals love them, and there are golf-cart **taxis** (note – some that hang around the boat landing are on commission from hotels, and may try to drag you off you to their best payers). Cart rental shops (*rentadoras*), are spread along the main street. Most have similar prices (around $8 an hour, $40 a day).

Bicycles are actually handier for getting to the places outside the village you're most likely to want to visit, and can also be hired. Most *rentadoras* also offer a range of tours by boat around the island, and fishing trips.

Rentadora Monkeys, Av. Juárez, south of the plaza. Slightly lower rates for golf carts, and motor scooters from $8 an hour, $40 a day.

Rentadora Willy, Av. Juárez, south of the plaza. Carts and a full range of tours. Divers and snorkellers can be catered for, and Sr Willy is one of Holbox's best fishing guides.

Tienda Dinora, Av. Juárez, on the plaza. The owners of Los Arcos (*see* p.157) have well-used bikes to rent, for $1.50 an hour, $7 a day.

Orientation

In response to its new fame, Holbox town has been given new **street names**, even though many people didn't use the old ones (and many streets didn't seem to have any). The street parallel to the beach across the plaza, on the sea side, is now Calle Damero. The one old name that people did often use was that of the main street across town from the ferry, **Avenida Juárez**, but this is officially now **Avenida Tiburón Ballena**, Whale Shark Avenue. However, most people still seem to call it Juárez, so we have done so here.

---

swallowed up in the forest, or to **Isla Contoy** (*see* p.147). The waters towards Catoche are also great for diving and snorkelling. Dolphin-watching trips are available all year; from June to August turtles breed on beaches near Catoche, and the summer phenomenon is the cape's whale sharks (*see* p.155). Holbox is also excellent for fishing, both deep-sea and fly-fishing, and the island is full of fishermen who double as expert fishing guides.

The Whale Sharks of Cabo Catoche

Just a few years ago it was first noticed that large numbers of whale sharks were gathering to feed off Cabo Catoche, from around May to September each year. The world's largest fish, whale sharks are usually around 15m long, and often bigger. They are absolutely harmless, feeding only on plankton and small fish. Exactly why they meet at Catoche is still not fully understood, but it may be linked to the special currents and food supply at the meeting of the Gulf and the Caribbean. These slow-moving, silent giants are usually solitary, so the experience of swimming with a group of them off Catoche is very probably unique in the world.

From a trickle of visitors, a fast-growing number of people now come to Holbox to see them. Most of the village *rentadoras* and guides offer shark trips in season, but as usual some of the best are available through Hotel Faro Viejo and Posada Mawimbi (*see* pp.156). The whale shark grounds, about 20km from Holbox, are now protected. Access to them should be strictly controlled, and in practice all the Holbox-based operators observe the essential rules: only a few boats go up to Catoche at a time, and take six passengers each, and only two people plus a guide can be in the water snorkelling with the sharks at a time. Operators from Isla Mujeres have also begun offering shark trips in season, but these are usually very carelessly run, and are best avoided. Shark-watching trips from Holbox cost around $80–90; they leave early in the morning, and the full trip takes about six hours.

Tourist Information and Services on Holbox

t (984–)

There is no 'official' Holbox website, but www.holboxisland.com and www.holboxtravel.com are useful. Take note: there is no bank on Holbox, nor another one closer than Cancún, Tizimín or Valladolid. Some hotels change money, but it's best to come prepared; ask hotels for advice.

Internet Access: Cyber Shark Internet, C. Damero, one block east of the plaza.

Pharmacy: Av. Juárez, just south of the plaza.

Post Office: Next to the town hall on the plaza.

Sports and Activities

Snorkelling, Diving and Water Sports

Snorkelling in Yalahao lagoon is wonderful, and most local guides offer snorkel tours and have snorkels to rent. Scuba diving options are limited: there is no air compressor on Holbox, so diving is only regularly possible with operators (mostly from Playa del Carmen, *see* p.179) who bring their own equipment. **Rentadora Willy** and other shops provide boats and guides for divers with their own gear. Of the hotels, **Posada Mawimbi** has the best scuba contacts, and owner Carmelo is a dive-master.

Holbox waters are also fine for **windsurfing** and – the latest craze – **kitesurfing**, and several hotels have boards for rent and/or can arrange kitesurfing sessions.

Dolphin and Whale-shark Watching and other Tours

Virtually the entire population of Holbox knows its way around the places to see dolphins, turtles, flamingos, sea birds and other attractions of the Yalahao lagoon, and many places in town – especially the golf-cart *rentadoras* (*see* left) – offer boats and tours. Particularly good trips (open to non-guests) are run by the **Hotel Faro Viejo** and **Posada Mawimbi** (*see* p.156), and other hotels have their own contacts. Most guides offer similar routes, but when you book tours ask around, for prices and where exactly the trip goes; guides are very flexible, and will cater trips to what you want to do. The most common tour is of **Laguna Yalahao** (Ojo de Agua, Isla de Pájaros), with snorkelling stops, for $12–25 per person – bigger groups pay less each. Longer trips, to see **dolphins** or to **Cabo Catoche** or **Contoy**, are more varied. All guides offer **whale-shark watching** (*see* above) in May–Sept. With these and other longer trips, it's very worth looking at the better-organized tours (such as Faro Viejo or Mawimbi), not the cheapest. In June–Aug night-time **turtle-watching** tours may also be available.

Many shops, *rentadoras* and hotels also rent **kayaks** for tranquil exploration, and many restaurants offer low-cost **kayak tours** of the lagoon and mangroves.

Fishing

Everyone on Holbox seems to know its fishing grounds too, but Sr Willy, of **Rentadora Willy** (*see* left) and his men are especially experienced fishing guides, for fly- and sea fishing. The **Faro Viejo** and other hotels also arrange fishing trips with local captains.

Holbox Tarpon Club, t 875 2144, *www.holboxtarponclub.com*. The business identity of Alejandro Vega, Holbox's most expert fly-fishing guides. Also has windsurf boards and sailing boats for rent.

Where to Stay on Holbox

Just about every Holbox hotel, except for the cheapest, has *palapa*-style palm roofs. Prices have gone up with Holbox's popularity, and it's now often hard to find attractive rooms for *inexpensive* (or lower) prices. But, rates vary a lot by season, and outside peak times (Christmas, Easter, July–Aug) good deals are available. If you want to settle in, *cabañas* and houses are available for longer rentals at low rates. Ads offering rooms (*se rentan cuartos*) are common: ask around for good ones.

Luxury–Expensive

CasaSandra, Playa Norte (east of town on the beach), t 875 2171, *www.casasandra.com*. Far the most sumptuous option on Holbox, a *palapa*-roofed beach mansion with an intimate, boutique feel. Suites are fabulous, with a very high wow-factor; rooms are a little more conventional but still extremely seductive. The hip **restaurant** (open to non-guests; *expensive*) has a Cuban chef, and the lounges and

terrace are ideal for relaxing. Plenty of tours can be arranged.

Villas Paraíso del Mar, Playa Norte, t 875 2062, *www.paraisodelmar.com*. Largest of the beach hotels, with 46 (still palm-roofed) suites of different sizes, and a fine pool. It doesn't have the laid-back feel of Holbox's smaller *palapa*-hotels (and many suites are lacking in sea views) but has more in the way of luxury-level comforts, so the choice is yours. Many rooms are *moderate* off-peak.

Xaloc Resort, Playa Norte, t 875 2160, *www.holbox-xalocresort.com*. Smart hotel with 18 *cabañas* in two groups of nine, each around its own pool. Not all rooms have real beachfront views, but all have terraces and combine spaciousness with island-retreat style. The **Maja'Che** restaurant (*expensive*) is one of Holbox's most attractive, and a full range of tours and activities is on offer. Rates for some rooms are *moderate* off-peak.

Moderate–Inexpensive

Casa Las Tortugas, C. Damero, by the beach, t 875 2129, *www.holboxcasa lastortugas.com*. Neighbour to the Mawimbi (*see* below), this beach *palapa* hotel has 11 rooms, between *cabañas* and a main house. They're very pretty and spacious (some sleep 3–4), and even rooms without direct sea views are colourfully attractive. There's an original 'tower-room' for contemplating the sea, and a beach-front **restaurant** (*moderate*).

Hotel Faro Viejo, Av. Juarez, at the ocean end, t 875 2217, *www.faroviejo holbox.com.mx*. The first 'proper' hotel on Holbox, the Faro Viejo nabbed the prime location at the sea end of the main street, and has its own jetty. It still has some of the nicest rooms: doubles or twins with balconies and sea view, or large suites with kitchenettes and terraces on the beach. There's a nice beachside **restaurant** (*moderate*), and the hotel offers excellent fishing, snorkelling, whale-shark watching and other **tours**. Rates go just into *expensive* at peak times, but deals are often available.

Posada Mawimbi, C. Damero, t 875 2003, *www.mawimbi.net*. One of

⭐ CasaSandra >

⭐ Posada Mawimbi >>

Holbox's most enjoyable places to stay, right on the beach with seven very mellow beach-bum-style rooms in a *palapa*-roofed house and cabin-suites with kitchens. The very friendly Italian owners are also divers, and provide some of the best **tours** on Holbox (available to non-guests): snorkelling, whale-shark watching, lagoon tours, fishing, kayaking and more.

Villas Chimay, 1km west of town by the beach, **t** 875 2220, *www.holbox.info*. Seven palm-roofed *cabañas* (some with room for up to four) in a fabulously peaceful location a healthy walk or bike-ride from town. Very prettily fitted out, with good bathrooms, they're designed to be fully eco-friendly, with solar and wind power and low-impact services, as is the **bar-restaurant** (*moderate*). Bikes are provided for guests' use, and the owners offer a range of other activities.

Villa Los Mapaches, by the beach west of town, **t** 875 2090, *www.losmapaches.com*. Comfortable *cabañas* and apartments (the largest in the *expensive* band); all have terraces and kitchens, and there's a mellow café for breakfast. Also free bikes for guests.

Posada Los Arcos, Av. Juárez, on the plaza, **t** 875 2043, *http://isla-holboxhotellosarcos.com*. The best budget option. To find the manage-ment, ask in Tienda Dinora, the store next door. Some of the big, light rooms, around a pleasant patio, have clanky a/c ($35–45), but you can be as comfortable with fan only ($25–35), prices varying by season.

Eating Out on Holbox

Of the hotel restaurants, those in **CasaSandra** and **Xaloc Resort** are the most refined, with subtle seafood and international dishes; the **Hotel**

Faro Viejo is the best mid-range choice, a great place to eat watching the waves and any other activity on the beach. And a Holbox 'institution' is **Maresa** home-made ice-cream, sold from a stand on the plaza and in island restaurants.

La Cueva del Pirata, on the plaza (*moderate*). Popular combination of Italian cooking, local seafood and Caribbean beach-hut style, overlooking the plaza.

Viva Zapata Grill, just off the plaza (*moderate*). Big place on a *palapa*-roofed balcony, with a nicely laid-back feel and classic Mexican fare.

Pizzeria Edelyn, on the plaza (*moderate–budget*). Given Holbox's quirkiness it's only fitting its biggest restaurant is a pizzeria. Pizzas are extra-generous, and a great range of seafood can be had too.

La Isla del Colibrí, on the plaza (*budget*). Very likeable little café catering for all needs with a range that includes fine breakfasts, irresistible juice combos, jumbo fruit salads and grilled steaks or seafood. *Open for breakfast and lunch, it closes early at night.*

Buena Vista Grill, Av. Juárez, behind Faro Viejo (*budget*). Backpackerish bar with (sometimes) surprisingly intricate fare at low prices.

Nightlife

Naturally enough, there isn't much, but every so often someone arranges a live music or DJ night in one of the restaurants.

Disco Carioca's, behind the beach east of the plaza. Holbox 'nightlife' revolves around this friendly combination bar, restaurant, beach disco and music venue. It's open intermittently, but there's usually something on every Sunday.

⭐ Pizzeria Edelyn
>>

⭐ La Isla del Colibrí >>

08 Cancún, the Islands and the Riviera Maya | Isla Holbox

Cozumel

 Cozumel

Mexico's largest island, **Cozumel** was an established holiday destination before there was a single hotel open in Cancún. However, the flows of tourist development are fickle, and the big money has long headed for the mainland, leaving many big Cozumel hotels with a certain '70s look to them. As an island it feels quiet and very safe, and is more family- and cruise-passenger-oriented than Cancún; it has its clubs and chain restaurants, but they're far less hectic. Cozumel's long dependence on tourism also means this is one place in Mexico where not only are prices posted in dollars but shop staff often don't seem to know the peso equivalents, and since the massive expansion of its cruise traffic still more of San Miguel (the only town) has been taken over by jewellery and souvenir stores. Away from its beaches and San Miguel, the island – despite many relics of Maya occupation – is a thinly populated slab of Yucatán brush.

The true riches of Cozumel lie not on the island but around it: it has the greatest concentration of inshore coral reefs in the whole Maya Reef system, and despite damaged cause by Hurricane Wilma the colour and vibrance of the undersea life just offshore is utterly spectacular. The way to get the most out of Cozumel is to spend as long in the water as possible.

History

Although there had been small fishing settlements on the island for centuries, large-scale Maya settlement of Cozumel did not begin until the Terminal Classic (about AD 700). Cozumel reached its greatest importance in the Postclassic, from about 1100 until the Conquest. It was the seat of an oracle and a shrine to the goddess Ixchel which, as Landa (*see* p.51) recorded, was with the great *cenote* at Chichén-Itzá one of the two most important places of pilgrimage in the Yucatán, 'held in as much veneration as Jerusalem and Rome are among ourselves'. Every inhabitant of the peninsula tried to visit it at least once in their lives, and lords and priests sought to go every year. Since Ixchel was the principal deity of fertility, a visit to the shrine was especially important for women before they had their first child.

This status, plus its role in coastal trade, made Cozumel a wealthy community. The layout of the island's capital, now known as **San Gervasio**, indicates Cozumel had a version of the *multepal* collective government seen at Mayapán, with authority shared between a *halach uinic* or 'first lord' and several subsidiary lords or *batabob*.

Cozumel was 'discovered' for the Spaniards by Grijalva's expedition in 1518, but was conquered in the following year by Cortés himself. Its people offered no resistance, fleeing into the woods. Cortés saw how many ceremonies were held on the island,

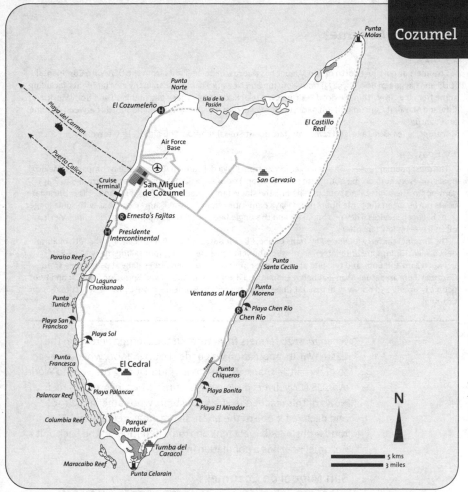

and, as his chronicler Bernal Díaz relates, he called together the lords of Cozumel to tell them, 'making himself understood as best he could', that their idols were evil, and that they had to abandon them. He ordered his men to smash all the idols they could, leaving in their place an image of the Virgin and a wooden cross. This may not have had such an immediate effect as Cortés expected, since pilgrimages to Cozumel were still being recorded by Landa 30 years later, but as Catholicism and Spanish rule imposed themselves more rigorously they and Cozumel's other sources of wealth were gradually eliminated. By 1600 the island was virtually deserted.

Over the next 200 years Cozumel, like Isla Mujeres, was used as a bolthole by pirates, from Henry Morgan in the 1660s to the Lafittes (*see* p.143) in the 1820s. In 1842, when Stephens and Catherwood came here, the only settlement was a small *rancho* built by an escaped pirate called Molas. Cozumel was only resettled after 1848,

Getting to Cozumel

By Air

Cozumel's airport, just north of San Miguel, has direct scheduled flights from the USA, with **Continental** (**t** US and Canada 01 800 523 5273) from Houston and Newark. There are also many charter flights, including some from the UK. Within Mexico, **MexicanaClick** (**t** 01 800 112 5425) has daily flights to and from Mexico City, and **Mayair** (**t** Cancún 998 881 9400, *www.mayair.com.mx*) runs a light-plane shuttle between Cozumel and Cancún.

Transporte Terrestre taxis and *colectivos* (fare about $9–12) run from the airport into town.

By Boat

The most popular route is on **passenger ferries** from **Playa del Carmen**. There are two companies. **Mexico** boats run every hour on the hour (with some 2hr gaps) from Playa 6am–11pm, and from Cozumel to Playa 5am–10pm. The boats take about 30mins, and the single fare is about $8. The big blue and yellow **Ultramar** boats run between the same hours (from Playa 6am–11pm, from Cozumel 5am–10pm) but with some longer gaps between services. They're a bit faster and the single fare is $10, but competition is fierce, and Mexico often has extra low fare offers.

The Cozumel **car ferry** (operated by **Trans Caribe**, **t** 872 7688) runs from **Puerto Calica**, just south of Playa del Carmen. Timings are unreliable, but most of the year there are at least four sailings daily Mon–Sat between 4am and 6pm, and two Sun at 6am and 6pm, with up to seven ferries daily at peak times; from Cozumel there are ferries Mon–Sat between 6am and 8.30pm, Sun at 8am and 8pm. Fare for a car and two people is around $30 one-way. In general, unless you stay for some time it's more convenient just to rent on Cozumel.

when *mestizo* farmers from Yucatán took refuge here from the Caste War. Its population was under 1,000 in 1900, when it began to grow a little thanks to the *chicle* trade. During the Second World War, US Navy divers discovered Cozumel's beaches and its reefs. News of this reached Jacques Cousteau, who came in the 1960s and declared it one of the finest diving areas in the world. The tourist business largely took off from there, and on the back of it Cozumel now has a population in excess of 80,000.

San Miguel de Cozumel

The town of San Miguel is home to around 90 per cent of Cozumel's population. Its relative newness and tourist-town status give it a neatness atypical of Mexican towns, and Av. Melgar itself is being overpowered by jewellery stores, but for the most part it's a relaxed, pleasant and friendly place to stroll around, and what gloss there is fades away as you leave the main streets. There is a narrow beach along Av. Melgar (also known as the **Malecón**, the seafront), but the island's main beaches are outside the town to the south. The waterfront is best just for wandering along, and taking in spectacular sunsets. By Plaza Cozumel there's a navy monument and a giant Mexican flag, a rather desperate reaffirmation of national sovereignty in this tourist zone.

On Av. Melgar next to C. 4 Norte there is an attractive museum, the **Museo de la Isla de Cozumel**, with a bookshop and very nice café (*see* p.167). In a pretty building, it has interesting displays (in Spanish and English) on the island's ecology and history, from Mayan Cozumel to the frontier island of the *chicle* trade.

Museo de la Isla de Cozumel
open daily 9–5; adm

Getting around Cozumel

Cozumel is 53km long and just under 14km wide, with one town and one main road that does a circuit around the southern half of the island. Anywhere in San Miguel is within walking distance. The local **bus** service runs only between San Miguel and the Hotel Zone and Chankanaab lagoon south of the town, and is infrequent. **Taxis** are the main form of local transport (from town to the north Hotel Zone, around $5; to Chankanaab around $9; a full tour of the island around $45). Always agree the price before you get in the cab.

To see Cozumel with any freedom you need to **rent** a **bike, scooter, car** or **jeep**, and there are many rental agencies. Bikes cost $12–15 a day, scooters $25–45, cars from $30 ($25 off-peak), 4WDs from $60. If you want to explore the dirt roads in the north of the island, you must have a four-wheel-drive (check the insurance status for driving off normal roads). One thing: since traffic is light, Cozumel rental companies seem to think they can send their stock out endlessly with minimal servicing, with the result that the island has some of the ropiest hire cars in Mexico. Check for strange noises before you set off. If you take a scooter you should be given a helmet (officially obligatory). The accident rate for scooters on the island is sadly high – look out for potholes. If you hire a car or jeep, it is officially illegal to have more than four people on board.

There are only two **petrol/gas stations**, both in town on Av. Juárez, one on the corner of Av. 30 and the other at Av. 75.

CP Rentals, Av. Juárez 2, corner of Av. 10 Norte, t 878 4055. Friendly and cheap, but some cars are pretty battered, so check them over.

Isla Bicicleta, Av. 10 Sur, off C. Adolfo Rosado Salas, t 878 4919. The best bike-only shop.

Rentadora Aguila, Av. Rafael Melgar 685, between C. 3 and C. 5, t 872 0729. A big range of vehicles, scooters and bicycles.

Orientation

The Playa del Carmen ferry brings you on to the main square, **Plaza Cozumel**, the meeting point of the seafront boulevard, **Av. Rafael E.** Melgar (or just Melgar) and the main street **Av. Juárez**, which runs off to the east to become the cross-island road. Cozumel's big hotels are in two beach-side 'Hotel Zones' on continuations of Av. Melgar north and south of the town. San Miguel's layout is a straightforward grid, but it has one of those peculiarly Mexican street-naming systems: streets parallel to the seafront are Avenidas, numbered by fives (5, 10, 15, etc.), those running away from it are Calles. The same Avenida can be Av. 10 Norte or Av. 10 Sur according to whether it is north or south of Av. Juárez; Calles north of Juárez are even-numbered (C. 6 Norte), those to the south are odd (C. 5 Sur). Some streets have names, too.

In the opposite direction, south of the plaza along Melgar, the view is dominated by **Punta Langosta**, a gleaming cruise terminal opened in 2001, with the obligatory mall at its landward end. To celebrate this asset a new official town centre has been created just south of the mall, with a new plaza on Melgar between Calles 11 and 13 Sur and a new town hall. The old town hall, across the old plaza as you get off the Playa del Carmen ferry, has been left as a shopping mall, as was sort-of predictable.

Around the Island

As on Isla Mujeres, the sheltered beaches and reefs of Cozumel with their tranquil, clear waters are all on the western, landward side, particularly in the southwest corner. The eastern side is much more rugged, and the sea more ferocious. Outside San Miguel, Cozumel is often impressively empty. The one main road runs dead straight across the island from Av. Juárez, then makes a circuit around the southern coast. The northern half of Cozumel is only accessible by dirt track, and is mostly left to the birds. The name Cozumel comes from *Cuzmil*, Yucatec for 'island of swallows', and during the winter months places like San Gervasio welcome great flocks of them.

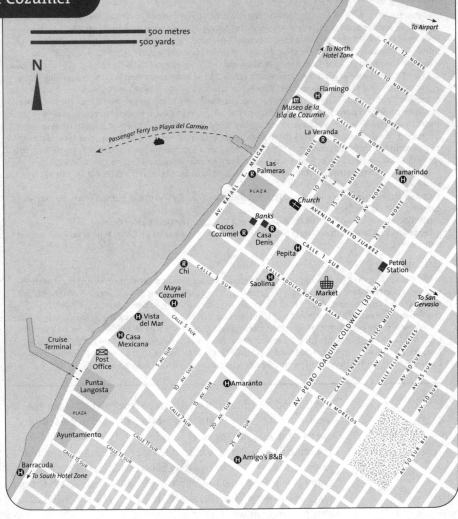

San Gervasio

San Gervasio
Open daily 7–4; adm.

There are over 30 Maya remains and ruins on Cozumel, most small shrines or navigational markers. The former capital, **San Gervasio**, is up a good road 6km north of the main road, from a turn halfway across the island. Its surviving buildings are all from the last centuries of Maya civilization, and crude compared to those of older Maya cities. San Gervasio's layout, though, is unique, and like El Rey in Cancún it is most interesting for the impression it gives of a Maya community as a whole.

At the entrance there's a visitor centre, with handicraft shops and fairly insistent local guides. The site is quite spread out, its sections connected by *sacbé* paths, so a visit can take one and a half hours or more. This dispersal reflects both Cozumel's role as a place of pilgrimage and its *multepal* government. San Gervasio has a number of residential complexes, with frontal porticos leading into interior rooms. Each of Cozumel's *batabs* would have maintained their own, outside the city's shared core.

Near the entrance is the **Manitas** building ('Little Hands', because red hand prints painted by the Maya as invocations to good health, now near-invisible, were found here), thought to have been the residence of the chief lord of Cozumel in about 1000; further on is the **Chichan Nah** complex, probably the seat of the *Halach Uinic* or first lord of the island from about 1200 until the Spaniards' arrival. To the west is a *sacbé* that was the main entry road for pilgrims from the mainland, with an **arch** with a small altar where arriving pilgrims left offerings to Ixchel. Towards the centre is the **Nohoch Nah**, a substantial temple with a Postclassic upper structure on a Late Classic base. Further on again are the **Casa de los Murciélagos** ('House of Bats'), a residential complex begun about 700, and the **Pet Nah** or 'Round House', unusual for a Maya building in being completely round. The **main plaza** is beyond that. With a little imagination it's easy to recreate this mentally as a Maya square, and some buildings still have traces of blue and red colouring. Some distance from the main site is the Postclassic **Casa Alta**, the largest pyramid, and possibly the principal shrine of Ixchel.

An added attraction of San Gervasio is the walk itself. The paths are lined with an enormous variety of plants, and there's often an exhilarating scent of wild spearmint. In the air, as well as swallows, you can see buntings, butterflies and red dragonflies.

Tourist Information and Services on Cozumel

In government buildings on east side of the plaza, facing the ferry landing (officially open Mon–Fri 9–2 and 6–8). Not much use unless you have a serious problem or complaint

t (987–)

The best free magazine is the little *Blue Guide*, distributed all around town. On the web, *www.islacozumel.com.mx* is the official island site, and *www.cozumel.net* is a useful general website. Cozumel's biggest public attractions (Chankanaab, Faro Celaraín, San Gervasio and the Museo de Cozumel) have a joint site, *www.cozumelparks.com*, and a **Cozumel All-Pass** is available that gives entry to all four for $35. It is on sale at each site.

Banks: several in the plaza or on Av. 5, all with ATMs. There are also several *cambio* offices.

Consulates: US Vice-Consul, Villa Mar Mall, Office 8, Av. Juárez 33, **t** 872 4574.

Health: Centro Médico de Cozumel, C. 1 Sur 101, corner of Av. 50, **t** 872 9400, is a comprehensive English-speaking medical centre, with an emergency service. There is a large **pharmacy** on the plaza.

Internet Access: Rx Internet Café, C. 7 Sur 14, off Av. Melgar; **Diamond Internet,** Av. 10 Norte, between C. 4 and C. 6 Norte.

Post Office: Corner of Av. Melgar and C. 7 Sur (*open Mon–Fri 9–6, Sat 9–noon*). Has a **Mexpost** desk.

Festivals

Cozumel hosts one of the biggest **Carnaval** celebrations in the Yucatán in late Jan or Feb, with a week of parades, concerts and parties including the 'Comparsas Ball', when different dance groups compete in wild displays. One of the most engaging traditional *fiestas* is **Santa Cruz** (3 May), held at El Cedral ever since the village was founded by Caste War refugees in 1848. Cedral is the island's centre of agriculture, and as well as music and dancing there's a horse and stock fair, and bullfights.

Shopping on Cozumel

As anyone can see just by looking along Av. Melgar, shopping is a major attraction. Cruise-liner traffic has fostered a boom in shops and malls selling souvenirs, glass, cameras, sunglasses and so on along the Malecón and around the Punta Langosta mall.

Craftwork comes from all over the country, and is often quite pricey. **Los Cinco Soles**, Av. Melgar, by C. 8 Norte, *www.loscincosoles.com*, has the biggest choice, and **Unicornio**, Av. 5 Sur, off the plaza, has a more varied range than most, with particularly good bags. **Almacenes Morales**, Av. Juárez 120, near Av. 15, is fun and colourful, with a huge stock of painted parrots, fish and baskets.

Jewellery has long been a speciality. Anyone into glitzy rocks can visit lush branches of **Van Cleef & Arpels** (Av. Melgar 54) and **Rachat & Romero** (Av. Melgar 101), or **Diamond Exchange** (Av. Melgar 111), for a cheaper, varied display.

For **general shopping** there is a market at the junction of Av. Adolfo Rosado Salas and Av. 20 Sur, and several central supermarkets.

Sports and Activities

Diving and Snorkelling

There are over 20 diving reefs round Cozumel, many close inshore. However, the inshore reefs closest to San Miguel such as **Paraíso** or **Chankanaab** have been badly damaged by Hurricane Wilma and subsequent shifts in the sea bed: they're still full of fish, but there is little surviving coral. Reefs further south, such as **San Francisco** or **Palancar**, are in far better condition, and still offer spectacular underwater scenery. Complete beginners and novice divers are still normally taken to the reefs near San Miguel, but some beginners' courses also go to the more intact reefs; since they are further from town, this may cost a little more. Intermediate-level divers can handle reefs such as **Santa Rosa** or **Cedral**, with wall dives, caverns, tunnels and coral pillars. For advanced divers there are spectacular dives such as the 'Devil's Throat' cave at **Punta Sur**, and there are other reefs (towards the north point or on the east coast) that most dive-masters warn anyone away from.

Local authorities' policy of favouring cruise ships does no favours for divers, but **safety** concerns are raised rather more by the amount of inadequately controlled small-boat traffic. When divers are in the water, their location should be clearly indicated by a buoy with a flag, and boats should stay with divers to warn off other craft; areas used for basic instruction should also be marked off and dive-masters must make clear to students that they should always look up and check what's above before surfacing. Cozumel has a state-of-the-art divers' emergency centre, at **t** 872 1430 (24hrs).

Many divers prefer **snorkelling** off Cozumel rather than bother with tanks. You can often see a lot of marine life just by putting your head in the water – although sadly, again, you now need to travel further from San Miguel to see much coral. Most dive shops offer snorkel tours, and there are snorkel-only operators who run tours for around $25–35.

Diving Courses and Operators

There are around 60 diving operators. Most offer a full range of courses and dives. The same considerations apply on Cozumel as anywhere else: your dive-master should have a PADI or NAUI certificate, and in beginners' 'resort courses' there should never be more than four people per dive-master. Prices begin at around $70 for a beginner's 'resort course' or for a two-tank dive, but there are many good price deals available: Cozumel has several specialized dive hotels (*see* below) and many dive shops offer good-value diving packages together with local hotels. For more dive operators and information on diving in Cozumel, check *www.cozumel-diving.net*.

Deep Blue, C. Adolfo Rosado Salas 200, corner of Av. 10 Norte, t 872 5653, *www.deepbluecozumel.com*. Long-running, friendly, very professional centre offering all kinds of diving: 'resort courses', certification, cavern diving, snorkelling trips, fishing, hotel packages and even post-dive massage.

Dive Cozumel, C. Adolfo Rosado Salas 85, between Av. Melgar and Av. 5 Norte, t 872 4567, *www.divecozumel. net*. One of the best-equipped operators, with special facilities for advanced and technical diving.

Kuzamll Snorkeling Center, Av. 50, off C. 5 Sur, and with a kiosk by the ferry dock, t 872 4637. Excellent-value snorkel-only tours.

Liquid Blue Divers, Av. 5, off C. Rosado Salas, t 869 7794, *http://liquidblue divers.com*. Popular operator using high-pressure tanks that allow more time underwater.

Fishing

The waters around Cozumel are known for marlin, sailfish, tuna, bonefish, snapper and billfish. Many dive shops also run fishing trips.

Aquarius Travel, C. 3 Sur 2, off Av. Melgar, t 896 1096, *www.aquariusflatsfishing.com*. Expert fly-fishing and deep sea-fishing guides.

Marathon Fishing Charters, t 872 1986, *www.haciendasanmiguel/marathon. htm*. Boats are available for full- or half-days.

Golf

Cozumel Country Club, t 872 9570, *www.cozumelcountryclub.com.mx*. Nicklaus-designed course with every luxury, near the north Hotel Zone. Packages are available with several hotels.

Horse Riding

Rancho Buenavista, Carretera Costera Oriente km 32.5, near Playa Bonita, t 872 1537, *www.buenavistaranch.com*. Very easy, guided pony treks, no experience necessary.

Sailing

Cozumel Sailing, Puerto de Abrigo, 1½km north of San Miguel, t 869 2312, *www.cozumelsailing.com*. Yachts for hire, or sailing and/or fishing tours.

Windsurfing, Water-Skiing and Others

The best places to find water-skis, wave runners, boards, parasailing and the like are **Playa San Francisco**, **Playa Sol** and the other 'beach parks' (**Playa Mía**, **Mr Sancho**) along Cozumel's southwest shore.

Where to Stay on Cozumel

Luxury–Expensive

Cozumel's big beach hotels are cheaper than those in Cancún, but they are still best booked as part of a package.

Casa Mexicana, Av. Melgar, between C. 5 and C. 7, t 872 9090, *www.casa mexicanacozumel.com*. A striking piece of architecture by the waterfront, with airy, stylish rooms, slightly Mexican-traditional décor and a fine terrace pool. Prices are very reasonable for this quality. The same company runs **Suites Bahia** (*www.suitesbahia.com*) and **Suites Colonial** (*www.suitescolonial.com*), both *moderate*, with simpler but still very comfortable suite-like rooms with kitchens.

Presidente Intercontinental, 6.5km south of San Miguel, t 872 9500, *www.intercontinental.com*. Cozumel's most opulent resort hotel, this 253-room complex has been regularly refurbished, and offers every comfort, plus private beaches, landing stages and marina, tennis, an in-house dive shop, snorkelling, fishing and a large pool.

Moderate

Amigo's Cozumel B&B, C. 7 Sur 571-A, between Av. 25 and Av. 30, **t** 872 3868, *www.cozumelbedandbreakfast.net*. Very pretty guest house run by Bob and Kathy Kopelman (who also have a house in Bacalar, *see* p.344), with three exceptionally well-equipped *cabaña*-style rooms (with a/c, kitchenettes, their own terraces) in a garden with a lovely pool. It's great for families, and breakfasts are served in a cosy *palapa*. Prices drop to *inexpensive* off-peak.

Baldwin's Guest House, Av. 55 Sur, between Av. Adolfo Rosado Salas and C. 1 Sur, **t** 872 1148, *www.moose pages.com*. Extremely popular B&B in a walled garden – with pool – in a quiet part of town. There are three rooms, and a *casita* with space for up to four (*expensive*). Breakfasts feature lashings of fresh fruit. A labour of love for its American owners, who take care of every detail.

Casita de Maya, Av. 65-bis, off Blvd Aeropuerto, **t** 869 2606, *www.casitademaya.com*. Unusual hotel in an unusual area, near the airport on the north side of San Miguel. Imaginatively designed, it has four rooms decorated with flair. There's an equally stylish little pool, and owner 'Island Dan' is especially hospitable.

Hotel Barracuda, Av. Melgar 628, **t** 872 0002, *www.cozumel-hotels. net/barracuda*. By the water at the southern end of the Malecón, this well-equipped specialist dive hotel is a long-established favourite, with bright rooms and great-value dive packages.

Hotel Flamingo, C. 6 Norte, off Av. Melgar, **t** 872 1264, *www.hotelflamingo.com*. Once a dive specialist, the Flamingo has been imaginatively renovated in contemporary 'boutique' style, with light, airy, very comfortable rooms, a sumptuous penthouse suite, the **Aroma** day spa and suitably chic **Aqua** Cuban restaurant, which hosts a live salsa band at weekends. Prices remain very decent, and good-value diving, fishing, spa and other packages are available.

Ventanas al Mar, Carretera Costera Oriente km 43.5, **t** 105 2684, *www.ventanasalmar.com.mx*. In romantic, windblown isolation, the one and only hotel on Cozumel's east coast. It's not brand new and a bit quirky, but its big suite-style rooms have plenty of atmosphere and limitless ocean views. Nearby there are a couple of restaurants, and a sheltered beach. 'Official' rates are high, but deals are often available.

Villa Las Anclas, Av. 5 Sur 325, between C. 3 and C. 5 Sur, **t** 872 5476, *www.lasanclas.com*. Stylish small hotel made up of 'suites' that are more like studio apartments, with double bedrooms that are very easy on the eye and very good small kitchens. It's great value, and the service is exceptional.

Vista del Mar, Av. Melgar 45, next to C. 5 Sur, **t** 872 0545, *www.hotelvista delmar.com*. Right on the Malecón, so rooms with front balconies are superbly placed for enjoying the sunsets. It's been attractively renovated, with rooms prettily decorated in natural colours. Dive packages are a speciality.

Inexpensive–Budget

Amaranto Bed & Breakfast, C. 5 Sur, between Av. 15 and Av. 20, **t** 872 3719, *www.tamarindoamaranto.com*. Brightly-decorated rooms in *palapa*-roofed bungalows or an original tower-house designed by the owner himself, with lots of extras including small kitchens.

Hostelito, Av. 10 Norte 42, between Av. Juárez and C. 2 Norte, **t** 869 8157, *www.hostelcozumel.com*. Clean and bright modern hostel, with dorms and private doubles with showers (*inexpensive*). Staff are friendly, and the atmosphere nicely relaxed.

Hotel Pepita, Av. 15 Sur 120, corner of C. 1 Sur, **t** 872 0098. Cozumel's best budget bargain; a big place with a/c, fridges and fans in all its rooms. Run by a very friendly family, it's very well looked-after. Popular, so call ahead.

Tamarindo Bed & Breakfast, C. 4 Norte 421, by Av. 20 Norte, **t** 872 6190, *www.tamarindocozumel.com*. An exceptional choice and exceptional value, with intimate suites and five a/c or fan-only (but still well-

★ **Hotel Flamingo** >

★ **Tamarindo B&B** >>

ventilated) rooms, in a pretty house and garden in a quiet street. House and rooms have colour and character, and French owner Eliane Godement serves delicious, generous fresh breakfasts. There's an open kitchen, and it feels enjoyably cosy.

Apartment and Villa Rentals

Longer stays are popular, and many hotels offer longer-term rates. Cozumel websites like *www.gocozumel.com* or *www.cozumel.net* have a range of information on rentals.

⭐ **Restaurante Chen Río** >>

Cozumel Vacation Rentals, t in US (512) 371 3062, *www.cozumel-vacation-rentals.com*. Condos or villas for weekly or longer rentals.

Eating Out on Cozumel

Expensive

El Capi Navegante, Av. 10 Sur, between C. 3 and C. 5 Sur. t 872 1730. Big, bright restaurant with fine catch-of-the-day fish and seafood.

Chi, Av. Melgar, corner of C. 3 Sur, t 869 8156, *www.chicozumel.com*. The island's most stylish option, a smart terrace above the waterfront – so great views – with a 'pan-Asian' menu including sushi, and a hip cocktail lounge.

La Veranda, C. 4 Norte, between Av. 5 and Av. 10, t 872 4132. Pretty bar-restaurant with tables in a lush garden, and an international menu of Caribbean seafood and more.

Las Palmeras, Av. Melgar, corner of Av. Juárez. A big, popular restaurant on the main square. Always buzzing, but service can be brusque.

Moderate

Casa Denis, C. 1 Sur 132, off the plaza by Av. 5 Sur, *www.casadenis.com*. A Cozumel institution, in a Caribbean wooden hut surviving from olden days on the island. It has outside tables, and serves Yucatecan dishes mixed in with burgers and other internationals. *Open all day.*

La Choza, C. Adolfo Rosado Salas 198, corner of Av. 10. Beneath a big *palapa* roof, this family-run restaurant is a Cozumel favourite for classic Mexican dishes and fresh fish.

Cocoanuts Bar & Grill, Carretera Costera km 44. Laid-back party restaurant on a bluff with fantastic views on the east coast, near the Ventanas al Mar (*see* p.166). Great margaritas and fajitas too.

Cocos Cozumel Café, Av. 5 Sur 180. A short walk from the plaza, this is one of the best places for a relaxing breakfast, with great juices. Choose either Mexican- or American-style, from breakfasts to other dishes.

Restaurante Chen Río, Carretera Costera, by Chen Río beach. A fabulous location, and huge platters of grilled seafood (enough for four, for $40), or more compact alternatives like refreshing *ceviches*.

Budget

As usual, the cheapest meals will be found at the *cocinas económicas* by the market, at C. Salas and Av. 20 Sur.

Café del Museo, Av. Melgar, by C. 4 Norte. On the rooftop terrace of the Cozumel museum, this makes a very attractive and good value place to eat or just spend time. It offers a great view, and good snacks and lunches, and you needn't go into the museum to use it.

Nightlife

Cozumel's nightlife is similar to that of Cancún, except that there's less of it and less hysteria, although lately some rather more hip venues have been opening up.

Havana Club, Av. Melgar between C. 6 and 8 Norte. Cuban rums and cigars, and live salsa bands to dance to.

Neptuno's, Av. Melgar by C. 11 Sur. A big, classic disco, with Latin and international music.

1.5 Tequila, Av. Melgar, corner of C. 11 Sur. Elegant cocktail bar with fine sunset views and ambient music.

Viva Mexico, Av. Rafael Melgar, by C. 3 Sur. Rooftop restaurant-club with Latin music, popular with locals and tourists.

The Coast Road

Returning to the main road, a left turn will take you to the east coast at **Punta Santa Cecilia**, as well known by the name of its lonely bar-restaurant, **Mezcalito's**. The east side of Cozumel is gaunt and windswept, with crashing surf, its gauntness further accentuated by the effects of hurricanes. There are beaches all along the coast, but swimming here can be dangerous, and it's advisable to be very careful, and swim, if at all, only in the more sheltered bays. From Mezcalito's a dirt track (4WD only) runs up for 20 kilometres to the lighthouse at the northern tip of the island, **Punta Molas**, past long, deserted beaches, and two Mayan temples at **El Castillo** and **Agua Grande**.

Turning south from Punta Santa Cecilia, the road rolls on past more windblown beaches and isolated restaurants. **Punta Morena** beach has the east coast's only hotel, **Ventanas al Mar** (*see* p.166), but there's a better beach at **Chen Río**, where a rocky headland gives extra shelter and creates a small lagoon for safe swimming. It also has one of Cozumel's most enjoyable beach restaurants. **Punta Chiqueros** also has a pretty, sheltered cove. A few kilometres further on, the main road turns abruptly towards the west side of the island. Beyond it, the whole southern tip of Cozumel has been made into **Faro Celarain Eco Park**, an ecological reserve accessible from the southeast corner of the coast road. From the car park, the old dirt track continues to the hurricane-battered Faro Celarain lighthouse, which you can climb up, on the southern point, **Punta Sur**. Look out for the extraordinary **Tumba del Caracol**, a miniature Maya temple with doors about half a metre high, from around 1200. Although it looks like a toy it is likely was built as a navigational aid or as a marker in rites involving the movements of the sun. Also in the park there is a turtle nesting beach, crocodile and flamingo lagoons, a snorkelling beach and areas full of birds, and 'exploration paths' have been laid out to enable visitors to get to see them.

Faro Celarain Eco Park
open daily 8–5; adm

The sea becomes calmer and the beaches more usable as soon as you round the point. The beaches of southwest Cozumel are well developed for tourism, with beach bar-restaurants that have facilities for scuba diving, snorkelling, kayaking and more. Among the most attractive are **Playa Palancar** and **Punta Francesa**. A turn inland leads to **El Cedral**, which hosts the island's most important festival in May (*see* p.164).

Chankanaab
open daily 7–5; adm

Nine kilometres south of San Miguel is the **Chankanaab** nature park, one of the most popular places on Cozumel. It's centred on a coastal lagoon, originally home to an enormous variety of fish and coral, surrounded by a lush botanical garden. Swimming is no longer allowed in the lagoon, and the reefs immediately offshore lost a great deal of their coral due to Wilma, but the sea off the beach is still full of fish and other marine life, making it a user-friendly introduction to snorkelling that's very good for kids. Scuba diving is also available. The road runs on past more beaches and hotels back to San Miguel, passing at Km 5.5 a newish attraction, **Discover Mexico**, a mini-theme park made up of all kinds of Mexican historic buildings and archeological sites in miniature.

Discover Mexico
open Mon–Sat 8–6; adm

The Riviera from Cancún to Xcaret

The first section of the Riviera corridor south of Cancún is the least interesting, as the road runs some way inland west of the Cancún lagoon through what is now the service centre for the whole area, lined with warehouses that keep the hotels going. Beyond the airport and the southern end of the Hotel Zone road, Highway 307 bends back toward the shore line, as mostly empty scrub and a few *ranchos* roll by alongside. The first attraction is at Km 30, the **Crococun** 'regional zoo'. This is primarily a crocodile and alligator farm, but despite the tacky name it's also a fairly well organized and cared-for collection of local wildlife that includes spider monkeys, Yucatán white-tailed deer and a range of birds and snakes, in a natural setting. Bus trips go to the park daily from Cancún (*information t 850 3719*).

Crococun
open daily 8.30–5.30; adm

Puerto Morelos

Puerto Morelos, 36km south of Cancún, has another staggering Riviera-fact to state for itself. In the era pre-Cancún this little place of one square and just three main streets was for a very long time the most substantial town anywhere on the coast north of Chetumal, the primary centre for shipping *chicle*, then Quintana Roo's main export. This trade had gone into decline by the 1960s, and Cancún's arrival only hastened the fading of the town's importance. It still has a working port, but don't let this fool you into expecting a bustling harbour. It has even lost the Cozumel car ferry route to Puerto Calica further south.

Despite its good beach and its proximity to Cancún, Puerto Morelos is radically different in atmosphere from the city or Playa del Carmen. It's actually one of the most low-key places on the Riviera, inhabited by real fishermen and frequented by divers, snorkellers and sport fishermen. It has a sizable international population of well-heeled bohemians who often say Puerto Morelos is like Playa del Carmen *used* to be, and fervently hope their retreat is not set for a similar fate. Many visitors come here for a couple of months at a time, or a whole winter. The town's attractions have not escaped the stare of hotel developers, and growing flocks of mega-resorts gathering around it have made its continuing tranquility even more unusual, and at times

Getting around the Riviera

Highway 307 runs south from Av. Tulum in Cancún down the length of the Riviera, 1–3km inland. From Cancún to Xcaret (72km), 307 is a four-lane divided highway; from there to Tulum (59km) it's a wide highway that's almost as fast, and then a more normal-sized road from Tulum to Chetumal. At Puerto Morelos a road turns inland that is paved to **Central Vallarta** (16km) and will soon be paved to Leona Vicario, on the Cancún–Mérida road. Otherwise there are no through roads inland off 307 between Cancún and the Cobá turn at Tulum, although the road from Playa del Carmen may be upgraded at some point. There are **petrol/gas stations**, by Cancún airport and at Puerto Morelos, Playa del Carmen, Puerto Aventuras, Xpu-Ha and Tulum.

Buses are plentiful. Shuttle buses run between Cancún and Playa, stopping at Puerto Morelos, every 10mins 4am–12.30am daily, and there are hourly first-class buses to Tulum and Chetumal, plus at least 13 Mayab *intermedio* buses daily that run the length of the Riviera to Tulum and Chetumal, stopping everywhere on route on request. There is also frequent *combi* and taxi traffic. At most places other than Playa and Tulum buses stop only on the main road, so you still have a walk, often of about 1km, down to the sea and the beach.

Taxis from Cancún, Puerto Morelos, Playa del Carmen and Tulum will take you anywhere on this coast, for a price (around $30, from Playa to Tulum). Be ready for some haggling.

---

make residents feel a little under siege. Inland, by the Highway, a new town is beginning to sprawl like so many along the coast. Nevertheless, the heart of Puerto Morelos is still there.

The Town

Belying its benign atmosphere today, Puerto Morelos has a hairy frontier past. It was founded in the 1890s, after the Díaz regime responded to US demand for chewing gum by granting exclusive rights to the *chicle* and anything they could find between Cabo Catoche and Tulum to a Mexican-British venture, the *Compañia Colonizadora de la Costa de Yucatán*. Puerto Morelos was its main base. The surrounding wilderness was still part-occupied by rebel Cruzob Maya, and in 1899 armed Maya appeared at the camp and warned its occupants not to move further into the forest. The company gave orders to tough it out, and eventually Maya rebelliousness faded away. Puerto Morelos contained around 1,000 workers – Mexicans, West Indians, Chinese, Spaniards driven out of Cuba – and had the wild, brutal life of a frontier camp.

All this has long been forgotten. The road into town from Highway 307 leads between peaceful marsh pools full of herons and stately white ibises to run out in the town **plaza**, facing the beach. Alongside it is Puerto Morelos' leaning tower, a **lighthouse** knocked out of true by Hurricane Beulah in 1966. It has been supplanted by a neat, white, upright tower next to it, but the old tower has been kept as a monument. Puerto Morelos' reef stands only 600 metres offshore, and is clearly visible from the beach. It is one of the richest coral environments on the mainland shore, rivalling Cozumel, and a protected marine park or *parque marítimo*.

On the beach, pelicans perch on mooring posts while fishermen land their catch, reinforcing the impression of an easy-going tranquility long lost by Playa del Carmen. Nightlife here consists largely of sitting in cafés watching the waves.

Getting to Puerto Morelos

Buses between Cancún and Playa del Carmen drop passengers for Puerto Morelos at the turn-off on Highway 307, 2km from town. If you don't want to walk, **taxis** run to the town plaza (about $1.50); sharing cuts costs. The **gas station** is by the Highway crossing.

Yaax Che-Jardín Botánico Dr Alfredo Barrera
open Nov–April daily 8–4, Oct–Mar Mon–Sat 9–5; adm

Back on the highway, a kilometre south of the Puerto Morelos turning is the **Yaax Che-Jardín Botánico Dr Alfredo Barrera**, containing an exuberant variety of bromeliads, palms and other Yucatán plant life; on the nature trail you can also see spider monkeys and birds. To the west of the Highway inland from Puerto Morelos there are a great many *cenote* pools, which until very recently were a secret more or less kept to locals and guides properly in the know. However, since the road towards **Central Vallarta** (16km from the Highway) began to be paved in 2006 they have very rapidly become the area's latest attraction, as the *Ruta de los Cenotes*. Several are already 'adventure parks' (*see* p.172), and Puerto Morelos dive shops offer good tours, but you can also find beauties such as the **Tres Bocas** ('three mouths') *cenote* and snorkel in them by yourself.

Tourist Information and Services in Puerto Morelos

t (998–)
The best websites for local information are those of Alma Libre (*see* below) and *www.vivapuertomorelos.com*.

Banks: no banks but **ATMs** on the plaza and by the Highway, and an **exchange office** nearby, by the supermarket.

Health: There's a **pharmacy** next to the church.

Internet Access: Computips, on the plaza near the church, and others around town.

Other Services

Alma Libre Bookstore, on the plaza, t 871 0713, *www.almalibrebooks.com*. A beacon for English-readers, run by Canadians Rob and Joanne Birce. Its also a good place to meet people and find out about new trips or activities, and the website has lots of information. They also exchange 'used' books. *Open daily Oct–May only.*

Marand Travel, beside the church, t 871 0332, *www.puertomorelos.com.mx*. Travel services, money exchange, car and bike hire and tours.

Sports and Activities

Diving, Snorkelling and Fishing

Diving facilities are more low-key here than in larger centres. The reef off Puerto Morelos is wonderful for snorkelling, and note that, since it's a marine park, parts of the reef can **only** be visited with a snorkel guide (a park entry fee is included in the tour price). There's also excellent fishing, as deep water and the Caribbean currents are close to the shore.

Almost Heaven Adventures, Av. Rojo Gómez, one block north of the plaza, t 871 0230, *www.almostheavenadventures.com*. Dive master Enrique Juárez and his team offer a flexible range of dives, courses and snorkel trips, including kids programmes, and are also experienced fishing guides.

Dive in Puerto Morelos, Av. Rojo Gómez 14, t 206 9084, *www.diveinpuertomorelos.com*. One-man operation of American Brett Nielsen: beginners' courses, reef, wreck and cave dives are all available.

Sociedad Cooperativa, on the plaza, t 206 9183. Based in a hut by the main pier, the local fishermen's co-op offers low-cost snorkel and fishing trips, with qualified guides.

The Cenote Route

Since the *cenotes* on the *Ruta de los Cenotes* through Central Vallarta are the closest to Cancún, they now feature in tours, and beside the road you can find a fast-multiplying crop of 'adventure parks' offering zip-lining, *ATV* tours and similar, as well as a polo field and a paintball park. With a car you can find some of the best swimmable *cenotes* such as **Mojarras** yourself *(adm on entry)*. Almost Heaven and other local guides also provide memorable *cenote* tours; these woods still contain hidden treasures.

Boca del Puma Eco Park, Central Vallarta road, km 16, **t** 886 9869, *www.bocadelpuma.com*. Created in a former *chicle*-tappers' camp around a *cenote*, this adventure park's big draw is zip-lining through the forest, but you can also cycle, walk, climb rocks and swim.

Where to Stay in Puerto Morelos

Long stays are popular here, and several hotels offer self-catering and long-stay rates. For house rentals, check local websites.

Moderate

Acamaya Reef Motel/Campsite, north end of the beach road, 2km from town, **t** 871 0131, *www.acamayareef.com*. Has a suitably beach-boho feel to it, pet monkey included. There are seven rooms with a/c (only just in the *moderate* band), or there's cheaper camping space ($15). You're soothingly isolated, but meals are available.

Amar Inn, on the beach, off Av. Rojo Gómez, **t** 871 0026, *amar_inn@ hotmail.com*. A delightfully beachcomberish house with a garden full of rusty anchors, a survivor of pre-'Riviera' days. There are four rooms with kitchenettes and three self-contained *cabañas*; all were well-restored after Wilma, but retain their quirky character, and waking up to the view from the upper rooms is bliss. Prices are *inexpensive* off-peak.

Cabañas Puerto Morelos, Av. Rojo Gómez, **t** 206 9064, *www.cancun cabanas.com*. Four blocks from the plaza, this lovely house in a garden – with a great pool – contains self-contained *cabaña*-style rooms for 2–3 people, each individually decorated and with plenty of home comforts. Top floor rooms have fine views. Popular, so book well ahead.

Posada El Moro, Av. Rojo Gómez 17, **t** 871 0159, *www.posadaelmoro.com*. Deceptively spacious guest house a short walk from the plaza. Around a garden, it has four well-kept rooms with fans or a/c, TV and other comforts, and two suites with kitchenettes. One fan-only room is *inexpensive* most of the year, others are just into *moderate*, and it's great value. There's a little pool in the garden, and the owners are charming.

Rancho Sak-Ol, by the beach, south end of town, **t** 871 0181, *www.rancho sakol.com*. This peaceful *cabaña* hotel is one of the most enjoyable in Puerto, and invites you to settle in for a while. Its *palapa*-roofed rooms are charming and comfortable, and several have great views. Ample fresh breakfasts and use of an open kitchen are included, and there's free WiFi and use of snorkels and bikes. The owners' quietly charming manner matches the house style perfectly.

Inexpensive

Hotel Inglaterra, Av. Niños Héroes 29, **t** 206 9081, *www.hotelinglaterra.com*. Curious little hotel with simple but well-kept rooms, ranging from mini-suites with fridges and a/c to dark fan-only rooms for around $35 (a bargain for the Riviera) off-peak. Not a 'boutique hotel' as the website now bizarrely claims, but a decent budget choice, with pluses such as a nice breakfast bar and lounge, free WiFi, a tiny pool and free coffee.

Hotel Ojo de Agua, Av. Rojo Gómez, **t** 871 0027, *www.ojo-de-agua.com*. Very good-value beach hotel at the north end of town with big, airy rooms (a/c or fan-only) of varying sizes – some with great views – a **restaurant** *(moderate)*, a pool and its own dive shop. The bar can get noisy, but if you don't mind that, it's a relaxing spot.

Posada Amor, just off the plaza, **t** 871 0033, *pos_amor@hotmail.com*. Long-running institution with plain rooms in varying sizes, some fan-only and

⭐ Rancho Sak-Ol
>>

some with a/c. The rooms are fairly elderly and don't offer any extras, but they have some of Puerto Morelos' lowest prices, and there's a funky, friendly atmosphere carried over from the ever-popular **restaurant**.

Villas Latinas, Av. Rojo Gómez, t 871 0118, *villaslatinas20@prodigy.net.com. mx*. Unusual hotel run by a very sweet family, with 22 big rooms, all with fridges and most with kitchenettes. Despite a blockhouse-ish look from the land side it's cosy, and the best rooms have nice sea views.

(★) **Los Pelícanos**

>>

Eating Out

John Gray's Kitchen, Av. Niños Héroes, t 871 0665 (*expensive*). It's a sign of Puerto Morelos' status that US chef John Gray set up this snug, tranquil restaurant here, offering refined dishes such as his signature crab cakes with chipotle mayonnaise. A gourmet land-mark on the Riviera; he also has a more laidback place on the beach just north of the plaza, **La Suegra de John Gray** *(moderate; open all day, closed Sun)* and other Gray restaurants are in

Cancún and Playa. *Open 6–10pm only, closed Sun.*

Hola Asia, on the plaza (*moderate*). Global fashion comes to Puerto Morelos with this 'pan-Asian' restaurant, happily mixing Thai, Chinese, Japanese and even more cuisines. The roof terrace has a great sea view.

L'Oazis, on the plaza (*moderate*). Original, laidback restaurant opened by a Québecois couple, with an attractive multinational menu. *Open 5–10pm only, closed Mon.*

Los Pelícanos, on the plaza by the beach (*moderate*). Impossible to miss, with a giant *palapa* roof and broad terrace; sitting over a conch ceviche and a beer while watching the pelicans go by is on of the Riviera's best experiences. Thankfully restored despite a battering by Wilma.

Posada Amor (*moderate*). A favourite stand-by, especially for breakfast.

El Pirata, on the plaza (*budget*). Very friendly little restaurant, *tortería* and *taco*-stand by the taxi rank, with fine breakfasts, juices and sandwiches.

Punta Maroma and Punta Bete

(21) **Punta Bete to Playa del Carmen**

South of Puerto Morelos are some of the most beautiful palm-lined beaches on the whole Riviera. Since the late 1990s more and more of the tracks leading off the Highway towards them have been staked out as entrances to resort complexes, each announcing its presence with a giant gatehouse like a set for a cheesy Arabian-Nights fantasy movie. In a diminishing number of places it's still possible to slip between the gateways to find a little unfenced beachside tranquillity that's open to all.

Rancho Loma Bonita
www.rancholomabonita. com,
t (998) 887 5423

Six kilometers from Puerto Morelos, **Rancho Loma Bonita** offers horse treks along the beach, or noisier trips in ATV quad bikes. A short way further down a road leads to **Playa del Secreto**, a beach development lined mostly with individual villas. The stunning beauty of the beaches nearby, combined with a little extra space between the coast and the Highway, has also made this the Riviera's prime stretch for really upscale, secluded luxury. At Km 51 (counting from Cancún) a small *palapa*-style hut announces the discreet entrance to the very luxurious **Maroma**. Beyond it are the two most opulent resort complexes on the coast, **Hacienda Tres Ríos** and the huge **Maya Koba**, with four separate resort hotels designed to different concepts, a PGA-rated golf course and more.

Hacienda Tres Ríos
www.haciendatresrios.com

Maya Koba
www.mayakoba.com

Where to Stay and Eat at Punta Maroma and Punta Bete

t (984–)

Luxury

Maroma, t (998) 872 8200, *www.maromahotel.com*. Peak of tasteful opulence on the Riviera, a secluded retreat in 80 hectares of exceptionally lush vegetation by the cape of Punta Maroma, with its own magnificent beach at the end of a near-endless driveway through thick palm groves. Most rooms have superb Caribbean views (some face the garden), terraces and all sorts of luxuries; every health treatment is offered, and there's a magnificent pool. The three fine **restaurants** (*expensive*) are open to non-residents.

The Tides Riviera Maya, t 877 3000, *www.tidesrivieramaya.com*. The most striking of the top-range hotels on Punta Bete itself, a bravura piece of tropical-fantasy design with elegant beach restaurant (*hotel guests only*), a sybaritic spa and every luxury – each suite even has its own pool. It's carefully pitched at couples, and honeymoons are a speciality. On the down side, the hotel doesn't have a huge plot, and is quite close to other hotels.

Moderate–Inexpensive

If you're not booked in at one of the upscale hotels, go to the road now signposted to the Tides Riviera Maya, and go left (north) past the Tides entrance. Mayab buses and *combis* stop at the road on request.

Coco's Cabañas, north fork of the Punta Bete road past the Tides, **t** 801 8076. It's not quite on the beach, and new building around it is relentlessly eroding this little place's seclusion, but it still has its attractions. The seven *cabañas* have good showers, pretty textiles and fittings and their own terraces, and there's a small pool and an enjoyable **restaurant** (*moderate*). Prices are *inexpensive* most of the year, *moderate* in winter.

Hotel-Restaurante Los Piños, north fork of the Punta Bete road past the Tides. A remarkable survivor, holding out amid the big-gun development around it. As well as a simple **restaurant** (*budget*), owner Fernando Rejón has 16 big rooms by the beach, all with showers (borderline *inexpensive*). There's also space to **camp**, and fishing and snorkelling trips are also available.

Great claims are made for the environmental standards at Maya Koba, but then, it is top of the range.

At Km 63, a road turns off to lead in 3km to **Punta Bete**, a series of gorgeous bays with perfectly curving beaches. This was once one of the spots where the usual accommodation was a basic palm-roofed *cabaña* on the sand, but it too has been targeted for development, and the name Punta Bete is less noticeable on signs than that of the Tides Riviera Maya hotel. However, it's in the nature of Riviera development than places get left behind, and if you carry on past the hotels you can still find a few of the original *cabaña* operations among the palms.

Playa del Carmen

Once upon a time (around 1985), there was this sleepy little fishing village on the Yucatán coast with one sand street, under 1,000 people, reefs offshore, a fabulous beach lined with coconut palms, a passenger ferry to Cozumel and not much else.

Today, Playa del Carmen is the fastest-growing town in the whole of Mexico. No one knows how many people live here, but it's over 100,000, with more arriving by the week to work in hotels or construction, or just see what they can find. The single street of yore, now known as the **Quinta Avenida**, is a pedestrian walkway lined end-to-end with restaurants, bars, mini-malls and jewellery, *artesanía* and dive shops. The transformation really took off with the Playacar development in 1991. Since then Playa has been through several identities: backpacker beach hang-out (1995); internationally hip mingling spot (1998); nowadays, with an all-new post-Wilma building boom, it's going full-throttle to become the Benidorm/Ibiza of the Caribbean. Local brochures still often suggest Playa is more sophisticated and has a more relaxed, small-town feel than Cancún. It's true it is still more of a recognizable town than the city up the road, but its concentrated size can make its main drags just feel more intense.

Playa del Carmen has its assets. It can be strolled around in a way the Cancún hotel strip can never be, and this gives it an intimate bar and beach life that makes it easy to run into people. The pace of its transformations has been such that traces of earlier eras have been left behind, from mellow backpackers' *cabañas* still gripping on to their prime beach spots to elegant small style hotels. Its range of hotels and easy-to-locate dive shops, markets and other services still makes it a convenient base for travelling round the region. And as a party town Playa is a lot hipper than Cancún, and far livelier than Cozumel; the beaches and the deep-turquoise sea are still fabulous, especially if you walk half an hour or so to the north. So long as you don't get sick of hearing 'boy, it wasn't like this when I was here 2/5/8/10 years ago...'

The Town

Contained within the plaza there's a testimony to Playa's former size that can't help but amaze: its original church, a tiny white chapel. Leading away from the square is the main people-watching drag of Quinta Avenida, with Italian restaurants and American-style coffee shops as well as *taco*-stands, and high-fashion beachwear stores amid the Mexican souvenir junk. All along it, streets run down to the beach.

From the main town beach by the plaza, the view is cut off by the bizarre bulk of the Hotel Porto Real, at the seaward end of Av. Constituyentes. The area behind the beach north of here is where hotel and condo construction proceeds at the most feverish pace. There is a hitch here in that, unless you just walk along from the town, the only places where you can easily get to the beach are 'beach clubs' such as Playa Tukan and Mamita's at the bottom of Calle 28, with bars, restaurants, loungers and so on. You must pay

Getting to and around Playa del Carmen

By Air

Buses to Playa from Cancún airport leave from outside domestic arrivals at Terminal 2, once or twice each hour (on the hour or at half-past the hour) 8.30am–10.15pm daily, and run to the old bus station in Playa (*see* below). The trip takes about 1hr and the fare is around $7. For more on arriving in Cancún, *see* p.125, and for buses from Playa to the airport, *see* below. A seat in a *colectivo* from the airport to Playa will cost about $16, a taxi around $30, and you can also book private transfers through *www.playa.info* for $60–70.

Playa has an **airstrip**, at the south end of Av. 20, mainly used by **Aerosaab, t** 873 0804, *www.aerosaab.com*, which offers sightseeing tours over the coast and to Chichén Itzá and Holbox (*see* p.154), and an air-taxi service around the region. The strip is also used by companies based in Cancún (*see* p.128).

By Bus

Note that Playa del Carmen has **two** bus stations, something local publications often do not explain clearly. **ADO** and its affiliates' first-class long-distance buses mainly use the station usually called the **ADO** or *Estación Alterna* on Av. 20, between Calles 12 and 14. Most buses along the **Riviera** (the Riviera shuttle to Cancún, Mayab services) and second-class services still use the 'old' **station** (recently rebuilt, and so entirely modern) on the main plaza, at Av. Juárez and Av. 5. You can buy tickets for all services at either station, and some buses still call at both, but the 'distribution' of bus routes changes, so **always** check which station your bus will leave from.

As well as those listed here, there are several more long-distance services to central Mexico.

Cancún (1¼hrs): Riviera shuttle from the old station every 10mins 5.15am–midnight, and over 20 Mayab *intermedio* services daily; fare $2–3. All stop at **Puerto Morelos**. Mayab buses stop anywhere on request, and there are frequent *combis*. Many first-class buses to Cancún also stop at Playa ADO station.

Cancún airport (1hr): once or twice each hour, from the old station, 6am–8.15pm daily; fare about $7. *Colectivos* run hourly 6am–6pm, from the old station ($16).

Chetumal (4½hrs) via Tulum (1–1½hrs): one ADO GL and 19 regular first-class daily from the ADO; 13 Mayab *intermedios* 1.15am–10pm and more second-class from the old station. Mayab and second-class call anywhere en route, such as **Akumal** and **Bacalar**. First-class fares to Tulum about $4, Chetumal $16.

Mérida (5–5½hrs): four ADO GL, 11–13 first-class daily from the ADO 6.30am–1.15am; fares $23–27. Also around five second-class daily from the old station via **Tulum, Felipe Carrillo Puerto, Peto** and **Ticul** ($19).

Palenque (10½–12hrs): three or more first-class daily from the ADO, via **Tulum, Chetumal** and **Escárcega**: with OCC (3.45pm, 5.15pm, 10pm, all daily, additional services less frequently) and ADO GL (7pm daily). All continue to **San Cristóbal de Las Casas** (16–17hrs) and OCC also stop at **Ocosingo**. The 3.45pm and 5.15pm and ADO GL go on to **Tuxtla Gutiérrez** (18hrs); 10pm bus goes on to **Comitán** and **Tapachula** (24hrs). Fares $39–46 Palenque, $50–59 San Cristóbal, $72 Tapachula.

Valladolid (2½–3hrs) via **Tulum**: seven to eight first-class daily from the ADO, two stopping at **Cobá** (7.30am, 8am) and some going on to **Mérida** via **Chichén Itzá**; also several *intermedios* daily from the old station. Fare about $9 Valladolid, $5 Cobá.

Xpuhil (6½hrs): three first-class daily from ADO (usually 3.45pm, 6.35pm, 7.30pm). Fare $21.

By Car or Bike

Playa has several **petrol/gas stations**, one on Av. Juárez one block in from Highway 307 and two on the Highway near Av. Constituyentes.

Car, Scooter and Bicycle Hire

Playa car rental rates are relatively high, but a wider range of offers is now available. There are also a number of shops offering scooters and bikes, and many hotels have bikes for guests' use. Machines are newer than on Isla Mujeres or Cozumel, but always check scooters and bikes over before renting, and get there early for the best choice.

Ace Rentacar, Highway 307, between C. 2 and C. 4, t 287 5100, *www.acerentacar.com*. Local franchise with very well-priced offers on standard cars and small jeeps.

CP Rentals, C. 1, between Av. 10 and 15, t 803 2907. Cars and scooters at low rates, fine for getting around locally.

Isis Rentacar, C. 4, between Av. 10 and 15, t 879 3111, *www.rentadoraisis.com.mx*. Reliable company with cars from $37 a day.

Universal Motors, Av. 10, between C. 12 and 14, t 879 3358. Bikes for hire from around $3 an hour, and scooters for around $38 a day.

By Taxi or *Combi*

The main taxi rank is opposite the old bus station on Av. Juárez. Playa taxi drivers will take passengers anywhere along the Riviera; they have long had a reputation for making up rates as they go along, but the official rates are now easy to check on *www.playa.info* and other local sites, as well as being posted up at cab ranks. Due to its growth Playa del Carmen has now been divided into zones with varying taxi rates – to add to the confusion – but in general, within Zone 1 (central Playa), taxis should cost about $1, from Zone 1 to Calle 38 (the Shangri-La) about $1.70, Playa to Cancún about $32, to Tulum about $30. As ever, **agree the price first**. *Combi*-sized taxi vans up and down the Riviera run from C. 2, between Av. 15 and Av. 20.

Ferries to Cozumel

The Cozumel ferry docks are in the southern corner of the plaza, on the opposite side from the 'old' bus station. *See* 'Cozumel', p.160

Orientation

The grid geography of Playa del Carmen is simple, despite its sprawling growth. **Av. Juárez**, the main street in from Highway 307, runs straight in to the old main **plaza**, next to the beach. North from the landward side of the plaza runs the **Quinta Avenida** (Av. 5), the main drag, pedestrianized for much of its length. Streets parallel to the Quinta are *Avenidas* and confusingly numbered by fives: Av. 10, 15, 20. Cross-streets (*Calles*) are even-numbered north of Juárez – C. 2, 4, 6 – and odd-numbered to the south. **Avenida 30** is the main cross-street between the Quinta and the highway; **Avenida Constituyentes**, parallel to Juárez, is the main street into north Playa.

---

to use their facilities, unless you stay at one of many hotels with deals with them. Recently, Playa Tukan and Mamita's have gone out to be cool and sophisticated (which has upped prices), and stay open at night for Balearic-style beach parties.

Continue on along the beach past the much more striking Shangri-La hotel and you'll reach the main topless beaches and Playa's favourite spot for snorkelling, **Chunzubul**, where the reef comes close inshore. More brilliant-white beaches stretch away to the north; the further you walk, the fewer people you'll have to share them with (but be wary of leaving things unattended on the beach, *see* p.179).

Back in town, along C. Juárez and Av. 30 you can find the *taco*-stands, *abarrote* stores and fruit shops of any Mexican town. Nearby the new city of Playa is being 'consolidated', after years of getting by: a new civic centre has been created at the junction of Av. 20 and Calle 8, with neo-Maya town hall and a family-size new church, and Playa now has two modern bus terminals. Eight blocks from Juárez, Av. 30 meets Av. Constituyentes, which in 1995 was the northern limit of Playa, but which now has over 50 blocks stretching away beyond it on the map. In these blocks a still-ragged new city is being created, as people build their own houses, badger authorities into laying on services, open up corner stores and carve out little corners of domestic comfort such as patios ringed with flowers.

Head south from the town plaza and you see a completely different side to Playa del Carmen. From the square the **Paseo del Carmen** mall leads into the eerily perfect avenues of **Playacar**, an enormous development of quiet, winding streets lined with

clipped hedges and neat flowerbeds, an alien world. Along its streets there are luxury villas and condominiums, and on the narrow beach there are some 15 resort hotels, while at its centre is a championship-standard golf course.

Aviario Xaman-Ha
open daily 9–5; adm

Playacar also contains the **Aviario Xaman-Ha** aviary, with the region's bird species (and a lot of mosquitoes) in a well-created natural setting. Scattered around the development there are also, rather bizarrely, the Maya ruins of **Xaman-Ha**, a series of small Postclassic temples of a similar style to those at El Rey or Tulum. They were some of the first Mayan buildings to be seen by the Spaniards, as Grijalva used them as a navigational marker in his exploration of the Yucatán coast in 1518. Today they have been landscaped into Playacar, so that access is free.

Tourist Information in Playa del Carmen

(i) **Playa del Carmen**
old town hall, Av. Juárez, corner of Av. 15 (open Mon–Sat 9–9, Sun 9–5). On Av. 5 there are many independent 'tourist offices', whose main aim is to sell tour tickets and/or timeshares.

t (984–)

Free multilingual or English-language information magazines can be picked up in Playa, some of which only last a few issues: among the stayers are a handy little booklet just called *Playa*, *Riviera* and the glossy *Quinta*. Of local websites, *www.playa.info* and *www.locogringo.com* are the most useful.

Services in Playa del Carmen

Banks: there are clusters of banks on Av. Juárez, between Av. 25 and Av. 20, and Av. 10, near C. 12. Many Playa banks do not change money on Saturdays, but all have ATMs. There are also plenty of *cambio* offices (*open daily*).

Health: Playamed, Highway 307, corner of C. 28, t 879 3114, is a fully-equipped hospital with a 24hr emergency service and English-speaking staff. There are plenty of **pharmacies**, especially near the plaza.

Internet Access: Playa as usual has plenty of internet shops, especially on Av. 10, between C. 2 and C. 10. Many double as **phone offices**.

Police: old town hall, Av. Juárez and Av. 15, t 873 0291. Playa has English-speaking 'Tourist Police' officers. The town's growth has encouraged petty crime: watch out for bag thefts and pickpockets, especially around the old bus station, and do not leave bags on the back of chairs or on the ground out of sight. Take care if you leave anything on the beach when swimming, especially on the north section of the beach past Porto Real hotel.

Post Office: Av. Juárez, between Av. 15 and Av. 20 (*open Mon–Fri 8–5, Sat 9–1*). Has a **Mexpost** desk (*open Mon–Fri 9–2 only*).

Shopping

Playa has plenty of places offering **Mexican handicrafts**, but many are not of a standard to justify the prices. **La Calaca**, on Av. 5 between Calles 12 and 14, has colourful original masks, ceramics and other craftwork. The Quinta has acquired a swathe of stores offering Mexican silver and amber jewellery, but there's little to choose between them.

Playa has a nice bookshop, **Qué Pequeño es el Mundo**, C. 1 between Av. 20 and Av. 25, which has new and second-hand English books. Also, Playa still has its share of cranky little shops around the back streets. One that's very handy is **Licorería El Campeón**, Av. 10 and C. 4, a supermarket and drinks store that seems to be open at any hour of the day or night.

Sports and Activities

Adventure Tours

Alltournative, Av. 5, between C. 2 and C. 4 and between C. 12 and C14, t 803 9999, from US and Canada 01 800 507 1092, *www.alltournative.com*. One of the 'big guns' in adventure trips on the Riviera, but also one that does most to combine its fun activities – cenote swimming, jungle bike rides, zip-lining – with concern for the environment and local communities. Day tours (from around $90) are very well-planned and varied, ensuring a memorable trip; all include visits to Maya villages, giving real contact with local people. They also have an office in Tulum (*see* p.198).

Diving, Snorkelling and Fishing

Playa is one of the best **diving** centres on the mainland, with high-standard operators who run trips to the local reefs and also usually offer cavern dives, night dives, and so on. Many also offer day trips to dive off **Holbox** (*see* p.155) during the whale shark season, but if you only want to snorkel with the beasts it's naturally more relaxing to stay on Holbox.

Diving costs in Playa are a bit higher than on the islands, but as usual there are good-value packages for several days' diving. Introductory 'resort courses' cost from about $80, two-tank dives from about $70. With a **snorkel**, you can just walk up to Chunzubul and launch into the water, but many operators offer snorkel trips to nearby reefs or cenotes (from $25 a day).

Fishing trips can be arranged through dive centres and specialist operators, for deep-sea or fly-fishing.

Cyan-Ha Dive Center, Shangri-La Caribe hotel, t 803 2517, *www.cyanha.com*. Longest-running dive operator in Playa (since 1983), with very personal service.

Phocea Riviera Maya, entrance to Hotel Colibrí, Av. 1 between C. 10 and C. 12, t 873 1210, *www.phocearivieramaya.com*. Highly recommended French-Mexican dive operation offering a complete range of courses and dives, with accommodation packages available.

Sealife Divers, Av. 10, by C. 34, t 151 9045, *www.sealifedivers.com*. Relaxed centre with very good prices for dives and snorkel tours.

Tank-Ha Divers, C. 10, between Av. 5 and 10, t 873 0302, *www.tankha.com*. One of the longest-running operations, very well-equipped and offering a full range of dives and instruction, in over seven languages. Good dive-hotel packages are available.

Yucatek Divers, Av. 15, between C. 2 and C. 4, t 803 2836, *www.yucatek-divers.com*. Very professional operator offering reef dives, courses, snorkel trips, Holbox tours in season and a programme for disabled divers. With **Casa Tucán** next door (*see* p.182), they offer dive-hotel packages.

Golf

Playa is at the heart of the Riviera's 'golf boom'. **Playacar** has the oldest course, but north of town is Mexico's first PGA Tour-rated course at **Maya Koba**, and there is another course at the Iberostar Playa Paraíso resort.

El Camaleón Maya Koba, t 206 3088, *http://mayakoba.com*. Green fees from $235.

Playacar Club de Golf, t 873 0624, *www.palace-resorts.com/playacar-golf-club*. Green fees begin at $180.

Skydiving

Sky Dive Playa, Plaza Marina (by the entrance to Playacar from the plaza), t 873 0192, *www.skydive.com.mx*. Plummet on to Playa from a great height; novices make a freefall 'tandem dive' on the back of an instructor.

Where to Stay in Playa del Carmen

As in most places on the Riviera, prices – especially for hotels in the *luxury* to *moderate* ranges – tend to go down a lot outside the mid-Dec–April and July–Aug high seasons. The big resort hotels are mostly run on an all-inclusive basis, and best booked as part of an agency package. Note also that, due to Playa's unstoppable growth as the beach dance-party capital of the Riviera, hotels near the hub of the scene (Avenidas 1 and 5 near the junction with Calle 12, near the Blue Parrot) can have background music late-night, especially in peak season.

Luxury–Expensive

Básico, Av. 5, by C. 10, t 879 4448, *www.hotelbasico.com*. The second venture into drop-dead stylishness in Playa by the Abita group, creators of **Deseo** (*see* below). The style here is post-industrial, so there's exposed pipes, 'distressed' metalwork, jokey use of retrieved materials; the rooftop pools are two big old gas tanks. As at Deseo, its rooms – especially by the bar – are for people who want to be in the picture and aren't looking for quiet or privacy, but they certainly have flair. The **bar-restaurant** (*moderate*) serves good seafood, in suitably cool style.

Blue Parrot, Av. 1, by C. 12, t 01 800 022 3206, *www.blueparrot.com*. One of Playa's permanent hubs, with its famed bar (*see* p.184), the Blue Parrot began life as a set of beach-bum *cabañas*, but has developed into an empire. The **Blue Parrot Hotel** near the bar has stylish rooms with balconies around a pool-courtyard on the beach (*expensive–moderate*, depending on season); the **Blue Parrot Suites** nearby have 22 studios with designer décor, Jacuzzis, kitchens and more (*luxury*), and **Blue Parrot 5th Ave** (*expensive–moderate*) on the Quinta has similar luxuries but without the beach, and **Playasia** global-fusion restaurant (*expensive*) in its patio. Great location, but the hotel can be noisy (from the bar).

Deseo, Av. 5, by C. 12, t 879 3620, *www.hoteldeseo.com*. A significant moment came in Playa history when Mexico City design hotel Abita created this 'branch', and so gave the town a real style hotel, much as you can find in London or New York, before following it up with **Básico** (above). The style (now a tad dated) is familiar – minimalism, hard surfaces, Japanese-ish dark woods – and some features are the kind that dazzle in magazines ahead of being practical (a stunning but shadeless pool deck, rooms facing the bar and pool with zero privacy), but if you seek post-2000 cool and can take the often snotty service it could be for you. It also has the hip **Deseo Lounge** pool bar (*see* p.184) and at street level hosts a smart Italian restaurant, **Di Vino** (*expensive*).

Las Palapas, C. 34, off Av. 5, t 873 4260, *www.laspalapas.com.mx*. By the beach at the north end of town are two 'hotel-villages' that blend the palm-roofed *palapa* idea with every luxury. They arrived years ahead of their neighbours, and so boast the best beachfront locations, and have a spaciousness the competition can't match. Rooms are in one- or two-storey villas. The beach bar and pool are lovely, and all the watersports are available. One glitch: nowadays, some rooms are affected by noise from the party venues at Mamita's Beach.

⭐ **Shangri-La Caribe >**

Shangri-La Caribe, C. 38, off Av. 5, t 873 2804, *www.shangrilacaribe.net*. Just north of Las Palapas, this too opened when there was still a kilometre between here and Playa, and offers the town's most stylish cabins on one of its best beaches. Its 70 *cabañas* are divided into 'Aventura', 'Caribe' and 'Pueblito' sections (Aventura and Caribe, nearest the beach, are best). They vary in size, view, and price: beachfront cabins are really lovely, the penthouses utterly seductive. Breakfast and dinner are included, and there's a lovely pool and on-site dive shop. It's also further from the party scene whenever you want some quiet.

Moderate–Inexpensive

Casa de las Flores, Av. 20, between C. 4 and 6, t 873 2898, *www.hotelcasadelas flores.com*. Charming small hotel in a quieter part of Playa with a friendly owner, a neat patio and pool, spacious, airy rooms with Mexican-rustic décor and a peaceful feel. Discounts may be available off-peak.

Hotel Cielo, C. 4, between Av. 5 and 10, t 873 1227, *www.hotelcielo.com*.

Exceptional-value 18-room hotel with a friendly style and imaginative Mexican-with-a-twist decor. Breakfast is included, and there's a hip rooftop bar, the **Cielo Lounge**.

Hotel Eclipse, Av. 1, between C. 12 and C. 14, t 879 4001, *www.hoteleclipse.com*. Pleasant, central small hotel with 18 rooms, suites and substantial apartments, all nicely decorated in Mexican style. There's a pretty garden patio at its centre, it's not too noisy, and prices are very reasonable.

Hotel Hul-Ku, Av. 20, between C. 4 and C. 6, t 873 0021, *www.hotelhulku.com*. Relaxing hotel run with slightly old-fashioned charm by the same family who run Cenote Kantun-Chi park (so guests get free entry, *see* p.186). It's bigger than it looks, with well-kept rooms and a pool. Prices are in the lower part of this band (around $80) and for some rooms go down to *inexpensive* off-peak.

Hotel Labnah, C. 6, by Av. 5, t 873 2099, *www.labnah.com*. A big white house with four well-sized rooms a short walk from the Quinta or the beach, with balconies that are ideal for lounging in a hammock by the sea. There's a little pool in the garden, and the owners are very welcoming and helpful. Prices for some rooms drop to *inexpensive* off-peak.

Luna Blue, C. 26, between Av 5 and 10, t 873 0990, *www.lunabluehotel.com*. The garden at this American-owned small hotel feels like a secluded hideaway, and staff go the extra mile to make guests feel welcome. Rooms are light, spacious and pretty, and there's a fun, friendly bar. Not on the beach, but guests have free entry to Mamita's a short walk away. Very popular, so it fills up.

Playa Palms, Av. 1, between C. 12 and C. 14, t 803 3966, *www.playapalms.com*. Spacious rooms and suites, all with balconies with sea views and small kitchens, curving round a pool right on the beach: this hotel has many of the attractions of the nearby Blue Parrot, but is more accessibly priced – a real bargain in low seasons – and much more peaceful if you want to get away from the partying.

Posada Freud, Av. 5, between C. 8 and C. 10, t 873 0601, *www.posadafreud.com*.

Very popular hotel on the Quinta, with Boho character to suit its great name. The 11 rooms in different sizes are in bright Mexican-ish colours, and between the *inexpensive* and *moderate* slots. Its *pièce de resistance* is Studio 192, the top-floor penthouse, sleeping up to four. The biggest drawback is the busy street outside.

Posada Mariposa, Av. 5, between C. 24 and 26, t 873 3886, *www.posada-mariposa.com*. Italian-owned inn in north Playa with rooms or suites, in a three-level building round a leafy patio. Rooms are attractive, but the best are the suites, with kitchenettes, balconies and at least a bit of a sea view.

Inexpensive–Budget

Cabañas La Ruina, C. 2, between Av. 5 and the beach, t/f 873 0405, *laruina@prodigy.net.mx*. Astonishingly holding on to its prime site not so much next to as actually *on* the beach amid all the new building, condo projects and the like. A cross between a *cabaña* hotel, campsite and collective sleeping space, this backpacker refuge offers several options: renovated and quite comfy *cabañas* with showers, and some even a/c (*inexpensive*); *cabañas* with shared bathrooms (*budget*), or camping or hammock space and a locker under gregarious *palapas* ($7 per person). Not great for privacy, but you couldn't be closer to the beach, and it has a funky beach **bar-restaurant** (*moderate*). What's more, it has its own little Maya ruin in the grounds.

Casa Santiago, C.10, off Av. 5, t 873 0492, *www.casasantiago.com.mx*. Bright modern hostel with well-kept, clean and colourful dorms – with a/c – and some bargain double rooms (all *budget*). Net access and simple breakfasts are included too.

Casa Tucán, C. 4, between Av. 10 and Av. 15, t 873 0283, *www.casatucan.de*. One of Playa's best bargains; rooms are bright, pretty and spacious, with extras such as free WiFi, and three are apartments with kitchenettes. Deceptively small-looking, inside it contains a lovely garden and pool, and hosts Spanish courses and other activities. It shares a building with **Yucatek Divers** (*see* p.180), and has excellent facilities for divers.

⭐ Casa Tucán >

Hotel Maya Bric, Av. 5, between C. 8 and C. 10, t 873 0011, *www.mayabric.com*. Popular, long-running, good-value hotel right on the Quinta, but nicely peaceful inside. It has light, airy rooms and a small pool in a garden, and all rooms have two beds and fans. Several rooms have a/c, and are in the *moderate* band in peak seasons.

Mom's Hotel, Av. 30, by C. 4, t 873 0315, *www.momshotel.com*. A home-from-home for many Playa regulars: as well as comfortable, characterful rooms (a/c or fan-only), it has a tiny pool and a terrace bar (which sometimes has food). Rates are a bargain (especially off-peak); plus Texan owner Ricco Merkle has added 15 condo apartments, available for longer stays. **Mom's bar** is a great place to meet people, where you may be able to arrange sailing, diving, snorkelling or other excursions.

Posada Las Iguanas, Av. Constituyentes, by Av. 1, t 873 2170, *www.posada lasiguanas.com*. A survivor of 'old Playa', with some devoted fans, identifiable by its jokey iguana mural up one wall. Las Iguanas has kept its mellow feel: the two-storey hotel stands in an unkempt garden full of trees, and rooms are simple but cosy, with hammock-space outside each (top-floor rooms are the best).

Apartment and Villa Rentals

With all the condo-building going on in Playa, there is an ever-expanding number of places available to rent. All the local websites advertise rentals, and check out too *www.villasplaya delcarmen.com*.

Condo Hotels Playa del Carmen, t 879 3918, *www.condohotelsplayadel carmen.com*. Agents for several upscale condo complexes in central, with self-contained apartments with maid service and other hotel comforts.

Eating Out

Playa's restaurants multiply as fast as its hotels, and offer a more international range of food than anywhere else on the coast. The Quinta is lined with cafés and restaurants, most with tables in front from where you can watch everyone go by, and as you go further from the plaza more of them are contained within deep-green gardens. Playa's hustling atmosphere, though, means that service along the main drag is sometimes irritatingly pushy.

Expensive

La Casa del Agua, Av. 5, by C. 2, t 803 0232. Rather incongruously placed near several fast-food outlets, this bistro-and-bar occupies a big, airy and elegant balcony up above (and so slightly removed from) the bustle of the Quinta, with a lovely roof terrace. With a German head chef, it offers refined, eclectic seafood-based cuisine.

Glass Bar, C. 10, between Av. 1 and 5, t 803 1676. Sleekly elegant restaurant and bar serving high-quality modern Italian food with Mexican and other touches, and one of the Riviera's best wine selections. The owners also run **Di Vino** in Deseo hotel (*see* above).

⊛100% Natural
>>

Ula Gula, Av. 5, between C. 10 and C. 12, t 879 3727. Hip roof terrace above the Quinta with food that's a creative mix of Italian, Asian and Mexican influences – for once, not just a case of chasing the 'fashionably global' tag, but prepared with skill, flair and enjoyment too. Service is excellent, and it's very popular. *Open daily 5.30– 11.30pm only*.

⊛Yaxche >

Yaxche, C. 8, between Av. 5 and 10, t 873 2502, *www.mayacuisine.com*. Best in Playa for refined Mexican – above all Yucatecan – food presented with care, in a comfortable setting. Alberto Lizaola has skilfully created original dishes based on Maya traditions, and the menus are always inviting, with adventurous combinations of citrus, seafood and spices.

Moderate

Café Andrade, Av. 20, by C. 8. Modern café with great Veracruz coffee and fine Mexican classics for breakfast, lunch or dinner. Popular with the local middle classes, so a place to go if you want to avoid the tourist crowds.

⊛Restaurante-
Coctelería Las
Brisas >>

⊛La Cueva del
Chango >

La Cueva del Chango, C. 38, off Av. 5 (near Shangri-La), t 147 0271, *www.lacuevadelchango.com*. A star among Playa's many restaurants, the 'monkey's cave' presents some of the best modern Mexican food you could

find, traditional-with-a-twist creations such as shrimp breaded with mild chili and cinnamon, and fabulous salad combinations. Service is friendly, the garden setting is lovely, and prices exceptional for the quality. Its location, away from the main Quinta drag, adds to the tranquillity as well.

La Diez Cantina-Bar, Av. 10, by C. 8. Smartened-up version of a traditional *cantina* (*see* p.79), but fun, and with enjoyable *botanas* (snacks).

Karen's Grill and Pizzas, Av. 5, between C. 2 and C. 4. Long-established pavement café on the Quinta with usually-friendly service and Mexican-Italian-American food.

Media Luna, Av. 5, between C. 12 and C. 14. Once hippyish, now trendy-looking terrace café with eclectic menus – light salads and pastas, larger dishes combining Mediterranean, Pacific and local flavours, vegetarian and health-food options.

100% Natural, Av. 5, between C. 10 and C. 12. Playa branch of the local health-food chain (*see* p.140), with great juices, sandwiches and light meals, and a lovely garden terrace that's a nice refuge from the Quinta crowds.

La Vagabunda, Av. 5, between C. 24 and C. 26. Relaxed place for breakfast, juices, lunch or dinner a block back from the beach, with some vegetarian options on the menu.

Budget

For a really good budget meal, head away from the tourist route; **Calle 4** between Avenidas 5 and 15, especially, contains several good-value small restaurants.

Cafetería Danae, Av. Juárez, between Av. 20 and Av. 25. Excellent breakfasts and great juices.

The Coffee Press C. 2, by Av. 5. American-style coffee house with some of the best coffee in town – espressos, lattes and so on – and tasty snacks. Very popular morning call-in.

Restaurant-Coctelería Las Brisas, C. 4, between Av. 5 and Av. 10. A great find; a big terrace-restaurant, plain and simple but with great fresh seafood – especially *ceviches* and cocktails – at non-Playa prices. Appreciated by locals and any foreigners who discover it.

Sofía Bar, C. 2, by the beach. Long-running and lively bar-café, good for bargain breakfasts, lobster and juices, and open late.

Tacos y Quesos el Sarape, Av. Juárez, between Av. 20 and Av. 25. Classic, hot terrace-*taqueria* with all the classic fiery Mexican snacks.

Nightlife

Cancún may get the biggest crowds, but Playa has staked its place as the hip nightlife hub on the Riviera. One essential feature of Playa style is that most venues are along or near the Quinta – the best-known, all together around the junction of Av. 5 and Av 1 with C. 12 – so you walk between them rather than taxi-hop. The Ibiza-style beach party scene has exploded in Playa too – to the chagrin of some local hotels who try to offer serenity to their guests – with another mini-hub at Mamita's and Kool at the bottom of C. 28. Also, while the headliners in Playa nightlife might be the sleek clubs with international DJs, there are still plenty of laid-back leftovers from the town's hippy days along the Quinta, with live bands chugging away at rock and reggae covers, and properly touristy places with *mariachis*.

Alux, Av. Juárez, between Av. 65 and 70, t 803 0713. Playa's 'cave bar' – in a real cave, a labyrinth of intimate spaces heading down into the ground. Sexy and romantic, but far from the rest of Playa nightlife (inland of Highway 307) so you need a cab to get there.

Blue Parrot, Av. 1, by C. 12. It was 1998 when *Newsweek* (apparently) lauded the Blue Parrot as one of 'the world's best beach bars'. Nowadays it has more competition, but the Parrot's ample bar-lounge and beach dance-space still hold their own, with hip-hop and pop on the beach, more ambient sounds in the lounge.

La Bodeguita del Miedo, Plaza Paseo del Carmen (near Cozumel ferry dock). A franchise of the famous bar in Havana, with Cuban rum and great mojitos, and some of the best live salsa bands in town for high-energy dancing in the hot, intimate space.

Coco Bongo, C. 12, by Av. 10, t 973 3189, *www.cocobongo.com.mx*. Another 'phase' may have begun in Playa when this Cancún mega-club (*see* p.142) opened here at the end of 2008. Playa fans say this isn't what their scene is about, but it may take off.

Coco Maya, Av. 1 bis, near C. 12. Big and loud beach club in bare-faced competition to the old Blue Parrot along the street: Mexican, US and European DJs, dancing under the stars and a cool raised chill-out deck.

Deseo Lounge, Deseo hotel, Av. 5, by C. 12. The summit of Playa cool, with ambient music, old movies projected onto a wall, and a hip crowd lounging on divans around the pool.

Fah Bar at Siesta Fiesta, Av. 5, between C. 8 and C. 10. Resolutely uncool, but this big hotel terrace restaurant is regularly packed with happy drinkers boogie-ing along to its trad rock and reggae bands.

Kartabar, Av. 1, by C. 12. Mellow cocktail bar, with a Middle-Eastern theme, Mediterranean snacks, seductive divans, hookahs and even belly dancers.

Kool by Playa Tukan, Playa Tukan, C. 28, *www.koolbeachclub.com*. This now-smart designer beach club hosts DJs, dancers and loungers far into the night.

Mambo Café, C. 6, between Av. 5 and Av. 10. Exuberant club that's a must-see for salsa and Latin fans, with high-quality live bands.

Mamita's Beach Club, Playa Tukan, C. 28, *www.mamitasbeachclub.com*. Another hip and sexy beach-party venue, with international DJs.

Om, C. 12, by Av. 1. Across from the Blue Parrot and Kartabar, this 'resto-lounge bar' mixes up Middle- and Far-East and (a little) Mexican to create a chic multi-area chill-out space.

La Santanera, C. 12, between Av. 5 and Av. 10. Often the wildest, wackiest club in Playa, with a baroque Mexican take on clubbing and an alternative feel. Gets going very late.

Site Information Xcaret

t (984–)

Bus transfers from Cancún are provided from the Xcaret office in the Hotel Zone, Blvd Kukulcán km 8.5, t (998) 883 3143. There are restaurants and cafés all around Xcaret, and riding, scuba and snorkelling trips are also available (though they're expensive).

Xcaret

Xcaret
t 984 879 3077,
www.xcaret.com.mx;
open daily April–Oct
8.30am–10pm;
Nov–Mar 8.30am–9pm;
adm exp, snorkel hire
extra.

Impossible to miss just south of Playa del Carmen is one of the Riviera's most visited attractions, the 'eco-archaeological' theme park of Xcaret. It is centred on one of the natural coastal lagoons, around which a large area has been landscaped into areas representing different elements of the local environment. Within the park there are also remains of the Maya port of **Polé**, once a main departure point for pilgrims to Cozumel. Some environmentalists detest Xcaret as a profanation of a natural beauty spot, but from the visitor's point of view its main sections are undeniably impressive, providing a unique, easy – and, on first experience, overwhelming – opportunity to see the sheer richness of a tropical environment. It's very well organized and well geared to families; prices are high, but it provides a complete day out, with lots to do.

Near the entrance is a small archaeological **museum**, but many people head straight for the part-underground **'snorkelling river'** that winds through the park to come out by the beach. It's one of the more controversial parts of Xcaret, as a natural underground river was blasted and remodelled to create the required effect. Equally controversial (and popular) is the **Delphinus dolphin pool** in the lagoon (see p.153).

Other parts of Xcaret include a fine **aviary**, a **botanical garden**, **jaguar** and **puma** 'islands' and an **aquarium** and **turtle-breeding farm**. There's loads of information in English, if you take time to read it. Perhaps most impressive of all is the *mariposario* (butterfly garden), claimed to be the world's largest. Among the kitschier features is a fake 'Mayan village'. Every evening except Sunday the day ends with a showbiz spectacular that begins with 'ancient Mayan' rites, moves on to a *charrería* cowboy show and ends in a (pretty long) tutti-frutti of Mexican folk dances and traditions.

The Southern Riviera

South of Playa del Carmen the road rolls on through the green scrub, lined by a palisade of giant billboards held up on poles in the sky, past more entrances to the beach. Not far from Xcaret is the turning for the Riviera's one and only industrial facility, the harbour of **Puerto Calica**, which now has car ferries to Cozumel (*see* p.160). About 17km from Playa another coastward sign indicates the track to **Paamul**, a small bay with a superb beach. Its main occupant is a *cabañas*, camping and RV site – the largest on the Riviera – but even the big RVs are fairly discreet, tucked away under *palapas*, and they don't dominate the view of palms and curving sand.

For a complete contrast, from there it's another couple of kilometres to one of the largest heavy-duty tourist developments in the area, **Puerto Aventuras**. Created from nothing, it's a collection of hotels, shops and condos in Mediterranean holiday-village style, centred around a purpose-built yachting marina with beaches on either side. It's never quite full, so there are always condos available to rent. Besides a lavish tennis centre and golf course, a wide range of activities is available, and in the marina there are some tame dolphins (*see* p.153), and even some manatees.

Xpu-Ha and Akumal

✪ Akumal

Anyone who travels independently nowadays can begin to feel distinctly unwelcome along stretches of the Riviera, as you pass one new bloated piece of theme-park architecture after another announcing another all-inclusive named El Dorado or Copacabana, each with a barrier across it to limit the inmates' visiting rights.

A case in point is **Xpu-Ha**, about 10km from Puerto Aventuras. With a line of fabulous beaches in small bays and some of the area's best reefs for diving and snorkelling, this is one of this coast's most beautiful places. However, of the seven entrances to the beach off Highway 307, each one strangely signed with an 'X', only three now remain even partly open to public access (X-4, X-6 and X-7), with a few small hotels and camping spaces by the beach. The others have been seized by resorts, some of which go further and try to keep 'their' beach to themselves too.

Cenote Kantun-Chi
open daily 9–5/6; adm

On the landward side of Highway 307 at Xpu-Ha there are three swimmable *cenotes*. The largest of these, **Cenote Kantun-Chi**, down a track a kilometre off the road, is run as a low-key private 'nature park'. The centrepiece is the broad and lovely *cenote* itself, with snorkel gear for hire (but no food facilities), but you can rent horses or bikes, and there's a mini-zoo of local wildlife. Two pools just to the south, the **Cenote Cristalino** and **Cenote Azul** (*adm*) have no extra facilities, but are still delicious for swimming,

Community Tourism near the Riviera

Big promoters tend to set the rules on the Riviera, but there are also smaller-scale operations that are run with and often by local communities, aiming, naturally, to share out the income from tourism more fairly. The Maya have survived since the Conquest in good part by being stubborn, and some villages – notably Punta Laguna – have a very firm idea of their rights. Publicity has always been a problem for village tourism schemes, but the Internet makes it far easier to find them.

Kanché (*www.kanche.org*, **t** 998 892 7767) is a Cancún-based association that arranges tours with several village tourism schemes, along a 'corridor' from Punta Laguna up the road to Chiquilá and Holbox. Options include wildlife tours, caving and snorkelling in village cenotes, dolphin- and whale-watching, and visits to the villages. Reactions are hugely appreciative. Of the larger organizations, Alltournative (*see* p.179) and CESiak (*see* p.204) work closely with local villages. Some schemes are part of the Red de Turismo Indígena (*www.rita.com.mx*), including one of the most fascinating, Xyaat in the 'rebel' village of Señor, near Felipe Carrillo Puerto (*see* p.334).

especially the Cristalino. The only drawback is the inescapable traffic noise from the Highway on the other side of the trees.

Akumal, 40km from Playa del Carmen, is another condo-land like Puerto Aventuras, with beachfront apartments along several beautiful bays. However, in contrast to the Puerto there was a small community here before building began, and it feels much less isolated and claustrophobic. Also, since more people live here throughout the year, it has a more consistent life to it. Based on self-catering more than hotels, it's a peaceful, relaxing place.

The northernmost entrance – looking deceptively like a private driveway to the Casitas Akumal resort – leads to the main Akumal 'village', with a very pretty beach. Akumal means 'place of the turtles', and turtles still breed on several of the beaches in the summer months: the **Centro Ecológico Akumal** seeks to ensure their survival and promote eco-respectful tourism. From the village's sand 'plaza', follow the road to the left for about a kilometre, around the arc of **Media Luna** bay, to reach the **Laguna Yal-Ku**, one of the most beautiful of the coastal coral lagoons, with sufficient marine life to make it wonderful for snorkelling.

Laguna Yal-Ku
open daily 8–5.30;
adm

South of Akumal village there are more condos and all-inclusives, among them the Hacienda Santa Isabel, sure winner of the Riviera all-time kitsch award, built to suggest a traditional *hacienda* but three times the size and in a riot of sugary colours. The Aventuras Akumal turn-off leads to another superb beach with condos and smallish hotels, facing one of the richest inshore reefs. On the landward side of the Highway 2km further south is **Aktun-Chen**, a private nature park around one of the Yucatán's biggest caves and cenote systems (*not suitable for swimming*). The guided tours (in English) are excellent, and as well as an array there's a collection of animal life, especially monkeys and wild boar.

Aktun-Chen
open daily Sept–May
9–5, June–Aug 9–6;
adm

A little beyond Akumal are **Chemuyil** and **Xcacel**, two places illustrative of the way in which Riviera develops. At the first there is for once a turning west, inland, to Ciudad Chemuyil, a 'new town' being built for Riviera workers. **Xcacel** meanwhile is the most important turtle-breeding beach in the whole region, a site of worldwide scientific importance. In 2001, in an unprecedented move, Mexican authorities actually blocked the plans of Spanish hotel conglomerate Meliá to build one more mega-resort on the beach here. Since then, though, Xcacel has been in a legal limbo as arguments go on. In the meantime, however, anyone can use it (except during the May–October turtle breeding season, when it is completely closed off) by going down the dirt track and paying a small charge (around 20 pesos) to the man at the gate.

Xel-Ha

Xel-Ha
Information
t (998) 884 7165;
www.xelha.com; open
daily 8.30–6; adm

After Akumal, signs promising 'Snorkel Heaven' announce you're nearing another of the most popular places on the Riviera at **Xel-Ha**, an 'ecopark' run by the same people as Xcaret. It was created around the largest of the coastal lagoons, a long inlet of turquoise-crystal water, coral and brilliantly coloured fish. It gets crowded, and the accusation is frequently made that overexploitation is killing the lagoon off, but if you swim away from the main landing stages it's still full of fish. It's a superb natural swimming pool and, like Xcaret, very user-friendly and child-safe. Snorkel hire is additional to admission. As well as the lagoon itself, the park contains swimmable *cenotes*, a beach, a forest trail, Maya remains and restaurants. Get there early.

It was from here that the Adelantado Montejo first tried to conquer the Yucatán in 1527, founding a settlement called Salamanca de Xel-Ha, of which nothing remains. Across Highway 307 from the park entrance, though, are the ruins of **Maya Xel-Ha**. This was once the largest of the Maya towns on the Quintana Roo coast, and has the longest record of continual settlement, from the Preclassic until the Conquest. It extended all the way out to the lagoon and the 'wharf group' of buildings, now within the park, from where traders and pilgrims set off along the coast or to Cozumel. Several areas have never been excavated.

Maya Xel-Ha
open daily 8–5; adm

It's a pleasant site among woods, and interesting even though most of its buildings are in a poor state. The largest set, **Group B**, formed the main plaza. The main parts of it were built in the Early Classic, around AD 300, but additions were made right up to the 1400s. A path on the left leads to the most fascinating building at Xel-Ha, the **Casa de los Pájaros** (Structure 8b or 'House of Birds'). It's only a small ruin, but on one side there are well-preserved mural panels in sienna and white of birds in flight, including very clearly drawn parrots. Dating from the Early Classic, they are among the oldest Maya murals in existence. On the other side of the building is a much fainter mural, with a checkerboard pattern around a man in an elaborate headdress. It shows strong central-Mexican influence, indicating that as early as AD 300–400 even a place as remote as Xel-Ha had contacts extending thousands of kilometres.

From the plaza itself, a path parallel to a Maya *sacbé* leads west through the woods to the much later **Jaguar Group**, mostly from the Late Postclassic after 1200. The most important temple, the **Casa del Jaguar**, has some faint murals in blue, black and red, especially of the Diving God seen at Tulum.

Punta Solimán and Tankah

Around 3km after Xel-Ha there is another turning off the Highway, signed to **Bahias de Punta Solimán**, where at the end of a dusty track there is a narrow but peacefully palm-lined beach (turn right at the end for the main path onto the sand). A little further on, the last accessible beach before Tulum at **Tankah** (difficult to turn into heading south) is indicated by signs for Casa Cenote and the Tankah Inn, and a small, scarcely excavated Maya temple by the roadside. It's another long, curving beach, which has been steadily acquiring more condos and hotels in the last few years, but retains a likeably relaxed atmosphere. By Casa Cenote restaurant there's a large, swimmable freshwater *cenote* just behind the beach.

Cenote-swimming and Cave Diving

The area just inland of the lower Riviera has the largest concentration of explored *cenote* pools, cave systems and underground rivers in the Yucatán, with over 100 known systems extending through 550km of water-filled caves. Naturally, this also makes it the region's – if not the world's – most important area for cave diving. *Cenotes* are among the Yucatán's most magical features (*see* p.66). Some of these are only accessible to divers, but others are easy to swim in or to explore with a snorkel. The further you go in, the more you'll see, but swimming in the deliciously fresh, crystal-clear water of the surface pools, with the sunlight filtered through towers of lush vegetation, is always a wonderful experience. *Cenotes* are mostly on the land of local *ejidos* (*see* p.61), and an entry fee of $1–2 is usually charged for swimming.

There is a clutch of small, easily swimmable *cenotes* further north at **Xpu-Ha** (*see* p.186), but the most spectacular of all the Yucatán caverns is about two kilometres south of Xel-Ha, the *cenote* of **Dos Ojos**. For a time it was considered the longest underwater cave system in the world, until the more recent discovery of caves like the **Ox Bel Ha** nearby that are even bigger. Large sections of Dos Ojos and the adjacent **Murciélagos** ('bat') *cenote* are close to the surface and can be visited independently (*adm*), but if this is your first time here you'll get more out of it if you take one of the tours provided by the Hidden Worlds facility (*see* p.190). Just behind the

Cave Diving and Snorkelling Specialists

You can enjoy the open pools at *cenotes* like Tankah or Aktun-Ha under your own steam, but to make the most of the experience and see less accessible caverns you need to go with a snorkel and a guide. An important difference is drawn between **cavern diving** (into the upper levels, still open to daylight) and **cave diving** (into underwater caves that are completely underground). Most local operators offer cavern snorkel tours – equipment provided, no experience necessary – and low-cost tours can be found at several places in Tulum. Many dive operators also offer cave-diving, but those listed here are the best cave specialists (which also offer snorkel tours). For any cave dives, divers must already have open-water certification.

Aquatech-Villas de Rosa, Aventuras Akumal, t 875 9020, *www.cenotes.com*. Best-equipped cave-diving specialist in the area. They offer a complete range of open-sea, reef, cavern and cave-diving courses and dives (cavern dives, from $85), snorkel tours, equipment rental and deep-sea fishing.

Cenote Dive Center, Av. Tulum, corner C. Osiris, opposite town hall, Tulum, t 871 2232, *www.cenotedive.com*. Per Dovland and his colleagues are highly qualified and well-equipped, and offer a range of cavern and cave dives (from $120) and cave-diving instruction – for British/European as well as US certification – as well as cavern snorkel tours, from $49.

Hidden Worlds, off Highway 307 south of Xel-Ha, t 120 1977, *www.hidden worlds.com.mx*. Based at Dos Ojos *cenote*, Hidden Worlds is run more like a big attraction than a dive operation, but for this reason offers some of the most accessible, good-value tours for newcomers to caves and caverns, particularly kids, which are now combined with other fun things to do such as zip-lining or the 'sky-cycle', which runs on wires through the forest at treetop height. Options include the 'Ultimate Adventure Package' ($89.95 adults, $29.95 under-12s, with big discounts for online bookings), starting with a 'junglemobile' ride through an exuberant stretch of forest and going on to take in all the activities including some easy cavern snorkelling, or partial tours that focus on just one or two activities (*cenote* snorkel discovery, $29.95 adults, $17.95 under-12s), while certified divers can try real cave diving in the 'stalactite forests' of the vast Bat and Dos Ojos caves (from $60). Hidden Worlds gets busy, and there's obviously a bit of razzmatazz, but staff are friendly and helpful too, and the caves and caverns are always stunning. *Open daily 9–5.*

beach at **Tankah** (by the Casa Cenote restaurant) there is a broad, open *cenote* that's great for easy swimming, with no problems of access. Three kilometres south of Tulum is the **Cenote Crista**l (which, though, can be dirtier and more bug-ridden than the best *cenotes*). There's a lovely *cenote* by the Sian Ka'an entrance lodge on the Tulum beach road (*see* p.203), but some of the best known accessible *cenotes* are beside the Tulum–Cobá road. About 3.5km north of Tulum is the **Gran Cenote** (*adm*), one of the best for casual swimmers and snorkellers, with an idyllically beautiful entrance, a wide open cavern with a collapsed roof surrounded by rock columns and exquisite flowers and plants. The large main pool runs into a wide, arching cavern where you can swim a long distance without need of scuba diving equipment, even as far as a second *cenote* entrance at the other end of the cave. Two more signposted *cenotes*, the **Cenote Sagrado** and the **Vaca-Ha**, are really only of interest to divers, but **Cenote Aktun-Ha** (*adm*), some 4km from the Gran Cenote, is another wonderfully tranquil, broad pool, with plenty of small fish, that leads into an extensive cave system. Divers often refer to it as the 'Carwash'. More *cenotes* are continually being opened up.

Tourist Information and Services in the Southern Riviera

Akumal t (984–)

Handy sources are *www.akumal council.com*, *www.akumaltips.com* and the free English-language paper *Sacbé* (*www.sac-be.com*). There is an **ATM** in Chomak Grocery in Akumal. More information on environmental questions in the area is available from SAVE (*www.saverivieramaya.org*).

Centro Ecológico Akumal, Akumal village, t 875 9095, *www.ceakumal.org*. Lively organization that monitors the Riviera's environment, and above all Akumal's turtles. They also run **turtle tours** of local beaches in April–Oct; check at the centre for details. Other activities such as snorkelling, cycle rides or bird-watching may be offered.

Travel Services of Akumal (TSA), Akumal village, t 875 9030, *www. akumaltravel.com*. Full-service travel agency (with **money exchange** desk) that also arranges rentals, a range of tours and transfers to Cancún airport.

Internet Access: Cyber Akumal, on the plaza in Akumal village.

Post Office: Next to the Centro Ecológico.

Sports and Activities

Diving, Snorkelling and Fishing

There are dive shops by nearly all the (open) beaches on this stretch of coast, and many hotels have their own scuba facilities or contacts. This is also the prime area for cave diving (*see* p.190).

Akumal Dive Shop, Akumal village, t 875 9032, *www.akumal.com*. High-quality dive centre offering a full range of ocean and cave dives, instruction and equipment rental, and also snorkelling, sailing and fishing.

Aquatech-Villas de Rosa hotel, Akumal (*see* p.190). The foremost cave diving specialist in the area, also offering open water diving.

Bahia Divers, La Playa (X-6 track), Xpu-Ha, t 116 4921, *www.bahiadivers.com*. Friendly, and offering diving or snorkelling at low prices.

Captain Rick's Sportfishing, Puerto Aventuras, t 873 5195, *www.fish yucatan.com*. Half- or full-day sport-fishing and/or sightseeing trips. User-friendly, but pricey.

ScubaMex Dive Shop, Paamul beach, t 875 1066, *www.scubamex.com*. Long-running dive operation which also has a house nearby with accommodation for clients.

Where to Stay and Eat on the Southern Riviera

Paamul t (984–)

Cabañas Paamul, t 875 1053, *www.paamul.com* (*moderate–inexpensive*). Prior to Hurricane Wilma, Paamul's permanent rooms were just large *cabañas*; it still has a few (with good facilities, fans and terraces) but also has rooms in a more conventional hotel, on a lovely bay, with a **bar-restaurant**, a pool and ScubaMex dive shop alongside (*see* above). Paamul is most known as the best-equipped **camping and RV park** between Cancún and Tulum, with every facility and good long-stay rates (but the RVs don't spoil the view).

Puerto Aventuras t (984–)

Puerto Rentals, t in USA (415) 513 5960, *www.puertoaventurasmexico.com*. Condos and villas, from around $250 a week.

Xpu-Ha t (984–)

Hotel Villas del Caribe, X-4, t 873 2194 (*inexpensive*). Individual beach hotel hanging in there in spite of the all-inclusives looming up nearby. The pleasant rooms are in beach cabins or a main block, all with sea view. It's run with charm, and also has the **Café del Mar** beach **restaurant** (*moderate*).

La Playa Beach Club, X-6 track, Xpu-Ha, no phone (*inexpensive*). Easygoing 'beach club' (so they charge admission, but it's refunded if you have more than a few drinks) with a nice restaurant, and Bahia Divers alongside.

Bonanza Xpu-Ha, X-7, no phone (*inexpensive*). Twelve simple rooms with showers – rather than *cabañas* – and RV or camping space for bargain rates. It's still right on a beautiful beach, despite the advance of all-inclusives.

Akumal t (984–)

There are more villas and condo complexes here than hotels, and many beach houses and self-contained apartments are available for holiday rentals. Prices are high for Christmas and New Year but drop away even more than the Riviera norm in off-seasons (April–Nov). Short-term rentals are widely advertised on the net: *www.bill-in-tulsa.com* and *www.akumal-villas.com* are two places to look.

Hacienda de la Tortuga, Media Luna bay, t 875 9068, *www.hacienda tortuga.com* (*expensive–moderate*). A 'suite-hotel' in a lovely beach location, with airy apartments combined with a pool and hotel services. Its **restaurant**, **La Lunita** (*expensive*) is one of Akumal's best for Mexican food.

Villas de Rosa, Aventuras Akumal, t 875 9020, *www.cenotes.com* (*expensive–moderate*). While she is a diving specialist at **Aquatech** (*see* p.191), Nancy de Rosa's hotel is also very enjoyable for families and non-divers, with a great pool, a gorgeous beach and birding, turtle-watching and great snorkelling. There's a choice of rooms, condo apartments or beach villas, all with exquisite views, and as an added plus a wonderful rooftop bar.

Vista del Mar, Media Luna bay, t 875 9060, *www.akumalinfo.com* (*expensive–moderate*). Offers a choice of spacious hotel rooms or pretty condo apartments with kitchens, all with great sea views. Off-peak it's wonderful value, especially for families.

Qué Onda, North Akumal road by Yal-Ku lagoon, t 875 9102, *www.queonda akumal.com* (*moderate*). Very relaxed little place with seven mellow rooms and two suites under palm roofs in a garden, and a **restaurant** (*moderate*) with an eclectic, mostly Italian menu. Not actually on the beach, but only a short walk away.

Imelda's Ecocina, Akumal village, next to the Centro Ecológico (*budget*). Fun wholefood café open for great breakfasts and lunches.

Punta Solimán t (984–)

Oscar y Lalo, Highway 307 km 238, t 804 4189 (*moderate*). An example of Mexican improvisation: this popular beach restaurant was knocked off its spot on Punta Solimán by Hurricane Dean in 2007, but has set up again in a garden by the Highway. No more sea views, but the Yucatecan food is still great.

Tankah t (984–)

For rentals, check *www.nahuxibal.com*.

Blue Sky Casitas, t 801 4004, *www.blueskymexico.com* (*expensive*). Small, secluded beach hotel on Tankah Tres Beach, with six rooms and suites with loads of extras. Its **restaurant** (*expensive*) has some of the best food on the coast, Italian-oriented and prepared with flair by chef/owner Tony.

Casa Cenote, t Cancún (998) 874 5170, *www.casacenote.com*. Right by two *cenotes* – Ojo de Agua and the Manatee – this place is best-known for its beachfront **restaurant** (*moderate*), but also has a smart beachfront villa to rent and boho *cabañas*, the **Last Resort** (*expensive–moderate*). Diving, snorkelling and kayaking are all available.

Tankah Inn, Tankah Beach, t 100 0703, *www.tankah.com* (*expensive–moderate*). Friendly, laid-back hotel, with five big rooms with comfort and character, and a restaurant and bar with hypnotic view. A fine place for relaxing or exploring all kinds of activities around the area – diving, kayaking, fishing and more

Tulum

⭐ Tulum
Open daily 8–5; adm.

The Riviera comes to a spectacular end at Tulum. This is both the furthest point reached by most tour buses from Cancún, and the beginning of a less well-trodden Yucatán. Architecturally Tulum is by no means a distinguished Maya ruin, but its location is magnificent, on a clifftop above a dazzling sea, the only Maya site with a beach. Below it, miles of shoreline stretch away to the south, lined with palms, dunes and beach *cabañas*, a magical place for counting the birds and watching the sunrise.

At the beginning of the 20th century, Tulum was under the control of followers of the Talking Cross (*see* p.54) and, when Professor Sylvanus Morley came to investigate the ruins in 1914, he did so by boat from the island of Cozumel with an armed guard, and concluded that work could only begin when there was 'no danger of attack'. To this day, behind the travellers' den façade, there are still people in Tulum who perform Cruzob rituals. Until recently, there was a pretty easy three-way split between the main centres along the Riviera: Cancún was the big-scale tour destination, Playa del Carmen was for people who preferred something a little smaller, and Tulum was the backpackers' capital. Today, Tulum has largely kept its beach-hangout character, but now also attracts the more well-heeled traveller, looking for a mellow tropical hideaway; it too has had its boom, not in hotels – although some recent projects are pushing severely at the boundaries – but in *cabañas*. Today there are *cabaña*-clusters virtually all the way along the 11 kilometres from the ruins to the Sian Ka'an reserve. The atmosphere is no longer as sleepily relaxed as it once was (and prices have rocketed). Nevertheless, if you pick your spot the old beach-breeze calm is still not hard to to track down.

We were amid the wildest scenery we had yet found in Yucatán; and, besides the deep and exciting interest of the ruins themselves, we had around us what we wanted at all the other places, the magnificence of nature.

John Lloyd Stephens
on Tulum

The Tulum Ruins

The name Tulum, from the Yucatec for 'wall', is fairly recent, and it is likely the city's original name was something like *Zama* or 'place of the dawn', an obvious reference to the cliff's dramatic outlook toward the east. The site was probably occupied from the Early Classic, as a carved stela found here, now in the British Museum, has a Long Count date from the year 564. It was in the Late Postclassic, though, that it developed into a prominent town, and its main buildings are the clearest example of the relatively crude, square 'East Coast' style of Mayan architecture also seen at El Rey and other Quintana Roo sites. Tulum was still a thriving trading community when the Spaniards arrived, and was occupied for several decades after the Conquest, longer than other places on the coast. Its ruins were partially uncovered by

...the next day toward sunset we saw a burg, or town, so large that Seville would not have appeared larger or better. We saw there a very high tower...

From the report of Juan de Grijalva's voyage to the Yucatán, 1518

08

Cancún, the Islands and the Riviera Maya | Tulum

Getting to and around Tulum

By Bus

The bus station is on the Avenida in Tulum Pueblo, one block south of the town hall between Calles Alfa and Jupiter. *Intermedio* and second-class buses and *combis* will let you off at the ruins or the crossroads (ask the driver for *Tulum ruinas* or *El Crucero*).

Cancún (*2–3hrs*) via **Playa del Carmen** and **Puerto Morelos**: 1 ADO GL and 13 ADO/OCC first-class daily, 4.10am–1.55am, and two or more Mayab *intermedio* services each hour 4.27am–2.28am, which stop at all points en route. Fares around $3–4 Playa, $5–7 Cancún. There are also frequent *combis*.

Chetumal (*3–4hrs*) via **Felipe Carrillo Puerto**: one ADO GL, 12 first-class 8.25am–1.41am daily, 13 Mayab *intermedios* 6.38am–2.53am (via *Bacalar*). Fares to Chetumal $9–16.

Cobá and **Valladolid** (*1½–2hrs*): seven first-class buses daily, two of which go on to **Mérida**, via **Chichén Itzá** ($10), plus eight Mayab *intermedios* that mostly terminate in Valladolid. Fares Cobá $2.50, Valladolid $5–7.

Mérida via **Felipe Carrillo Puerto**, **Peto** and **Ticul**: five second-class daily. Fare around $14.

Mexico City (*23½hrs*): one ADO first-class daily (1.40pm). Fare around $95.

Palenque (*10–11hrs*): three or more normal first-class via **Chetumal** and **Escárcega** with OCC (4.55pm, 6.25pm, 10.41pm, all daily, extra services less frequently) and one ADO GL (8.15pm daily). All continue to **San Cristóbal de Las Casas** (*15–16hrs*) and **Tuxtla Gutiérrez** (*17hrs*), and OCC also stop at **Ocosingo**. Fares $38–45 Palenque, $49–58 San Cristóbal.

Villahermosa: six first-class daily; fare $42.

Xpuhil (*5–6hrs*): three first-class daily 4.55–9.41pm, one *Intermedio*, 9pm. Fares $15–20.

By Car, Bike and Taxi

Tulum has plenty of **taxis**, which will take you between the Pueblo and anywhere on the beach for about 40 pesos, and to any point on the Riviera for an agreed price. There is no local *combi* service, so if you're staying by the beach without transport you're pretty dependent on the cabs. People often hitchhike between the village and the beach road, but this is not a way of getting anywhere fast.

Tucan-Kin, C. Acuario, Tulum, t 01 800 702 4111, *www.tucankin.com*. Airport transfers from $105 per vehicle.

Car, Scooter and Cycle Hire

Rental agencies have been multiplying in Tulum, but demand can still exceed supply at peak times. For getting back and forth from the beach, **scooters** or **bikes** can be as handy as a car. Scooter rental operations come and go, so ask around for current ones.

Alamo, Av. Tulum, corner C. Orion, t 01 800 849 8001, *www.alamo.com*. Wide choice and low-season offers.

Executive, Av. Tulum, near the ruins entrance, t 873 3433. A big stock of jeeps and a few standard cars, and good special offers.

Iguana Bike Rental, C. Satélite, off Av. Tulum, t 119 0836. Mountain bikes and *cenote* snorkelling tours.

Orientation

Tulum has two main parts, the beach and the town. Arriving from the north you first meet the landscaped entrance to the ruins, on the left. Just beyond it by the **petrol stations** there is a crossroads, called *El Crucero*. The road inland leads to Cobá, while a turn left (signposted Boca Paila) takes you to the **beach**, the *cabañas* and the Punta Allen road. The **town**, Tulum Pueblo, straggles along 2km of Highway 307 south of the *Crucero*. As the one main street, it is called Av. Tulum in town; cross-streets now have rather fancy names (planets, Greek letters), but it's often more practical to orient yourself by landmarks on the Avenida.

Stephens and Catherwood, but permanent excavations were begun by Morley in 1916. In the interim, in about 1890–1910, Tulum was occupied (or reoccupied) by a breakaway sect from the Talking Cross Maya, led very unusually by a woman 'high priestess', who held rituals in the temples of the Castillo and clashed many times with the *chicle*-tappers.

As you walk up the impressive approach it becomes very apparent that Tulum, like Mayapán, is one of the walled Maya

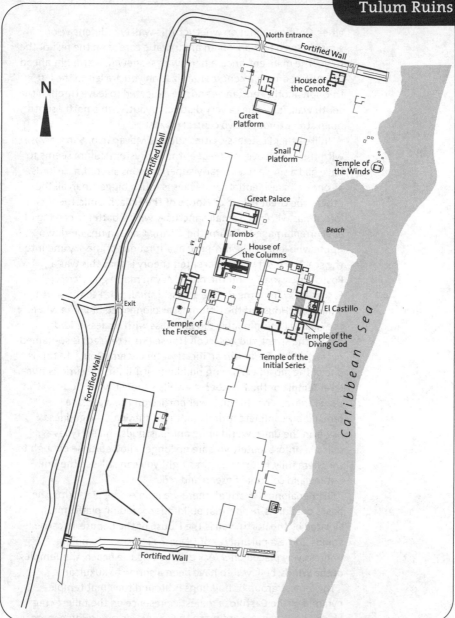

North Entrance

Fortified Wall

House of
the Cenote

Great
Platform

Snail
Platform

Temple of
the Winds

Great Palace

Beach

Tombs

House of
the Columns

Fortified Wall

Exit

El Castillo

Temple of
the Frescoes

Temple of the
Diving God

Fortified Wall

Temple of the
Initial Series

C a r i b b e a n   S e a

N

Fortified Wall

Visiting Tulum Ruins

Tulum is one of the most visited of Maya sites. By the entrance there is a visitor centre and souvenir shopping mall, and a tractor-driven 'train' is provided for those who don't want to walk the 800m or so to the ruins. Due to pressure of numbers many buildings are now roped off and can only be viewed from a distance. To avoid the crowds, get there early, and avoid Sundays, when most locals visit. **Night-time tours** of the ruins are now provided, nightly 7–10pm, for around $18. This is not a full 'sound and light' show, but visitors are given a recorded audio guide (45mins).

cities. Opinions differ on whether this wall was defensive or simply served to mark off an aristocratic core from the rest of the town. The main entrance, a narrow passageway, is straight ahead of you, but after a recent reorganization you are led to the left through another entrance, and are expected to leave through the south wall. Tulum has a very distinct layout, with a north–south main street through two central plazas.

Unlike other Postclassic cities such as Mayapán or San Gervasio, with their collective *multepal* authority system, Tulum seems to have had a single ruler clearly superior to his subordinate lords, as one of its residential complexes is much bigger than all the others, the **Great Palace** or **House of the Halach Uinic**, the first lord. It has within it a small sanctuary with a battered carving of a recurrent image at Tulum, the 'Diving God', an upside-down figure who looks to be jumping headfirst out of the sky and into the sea. The most widely accepted theory is that this was a Postclassic variation on the older Mayan maize god (*see* p.34). Facing away from the palace across a small plaza to the south stands the **House of the Columns**, a colonnaded building where the *Halach Uinic* probably did business with his lesser lords. Across the street, the **Reservoir House** (Structure 20) is so-named because it has a *chultún* artificial water cistern. Opposite this is one of the most fascinating buildings at Tulum, the curious two-level **Temple of the Frescoes**. As well as more Diving Gods on the upper frieze, it has in the lower portico on the west side remarkably complete mural paintings, showing the goddess Ixchel in the underworld amid animals, gods and everyday objects. Unfortunately you are no longer allowed close enough to see them fully, but if the light's right you can still see the fine outline and colours of green and red.

Further along the 'street' there are many more platforms, the bases of shrines, residential buildings or trading platforms. Isolated by the north wall is the **House of the Cenote**, because it stands above a natural *cenote*. Nearby is a small temple impressively placed on a rock overlooking the beach, the **Temple of the Winds**, believed to have been a shrine to Kukulcán.

The largest group of buildings is around the great temple-pyramid of the **Castillo**, a majestic presence on the tallest crag above the beach. According to the Spaniards, a flaming beacon was lit on the top of the temple, visible for miles along the coast. It faces inland, and Stephens, who took up residence in the temple, initially bemoaned the fact that its builders had not provided for a sea view, only to be grateful when night fell and he realized how strong the ocean winds could get here. It's no longer permitted to climb up the Castillo, but you can still see a Diving God on the upper temple frieze, and images of Chac on the corners. South of the Castillo is one of the oldest parts of Tulum, the **Temple of the Initial Series** (*Templo de la Estela*), where the British Museum stela was found; on the other side of the Castillo is the later **Temple of the Diving God**, with the clearest carving of the god at Tulum. Its walls are not straight due to the crude techniques of Postclassic builders; it's always been that way.

Tulum Pueblo

Virtually everything – the bus depot, chapels of Maya Protestant sects, backpacker services – is along the main road, called Avenida Tulum in town, with streets of concrete houses and a few *na* huts running off it. Despite a tentacular growth Tulum long remained a pretty ragged place – which was part of its charm – but the pace of 'urban improvement' picked up with the millennium, with solid kerbs and parking places, street name signs and, above all, a bank and a substantial town hall, in Tulum's growing 'civic centre', a block north of the bus station. It's starting to look tidy.

Tourist Information and Services in Tulum

t (984–)

Virtually all services are in the Pueblo, along Av. Tulum. The town hall, **police station** and HSBC bank are all in the block one north of the bus station. Along the beach, apart from *cabañas* and restaurants, there are two small **general stores**, at Punta Piedra and further down at Km 9, near Dos Ceibas hotel.

As usual there's a crop of free magazines distributed around town, of which the most useful is just *Tulum*. Of the local websites, *www.hotels tulum.com* has lots of hotel information, and *www.todotulum.com* offers a handy map of town and beach (downloadable online, and distributed free around Tulum).

Tulum's *cabañas*, especially the most basic ones nearer the ruins, have had a reputation for bag thefts and break-ins at times. The situation is currently better, but it's still advisable to be careful, especially in the cheap beach *cabañas*. If you are robbed, report it at

the police station for insurance purposes.

Banks: There are full-service banks with ATMs by the town hall and in the San Francisco mall by the Crucero, at least two more ATMs along Av. Tulum, and one at the ruins. The banks are often reluctant to change cash or cheques, so you may be obliged to use the ATM. There are also some **money exchange offices**, one by the Nohoch Tunich store on the beach, usually with poor rates.

Health: a **medical centre**, Av. Tulum, t 807 6666, and two large **pharmacies**, one next to the bus station.

Internet access and travellers' services: Cyberplanet, Av. Tulum, between C. Alfa and C. Jupiter. Cheap and friendly. Savana, Av. Tulum, between C. Orion and C. Beta, t 871 2081. A great resource: an internet centre, **phone office**, **travel agent** and courier.

The Weary Traveler, Av. Tulum, between C. Jupiter and C. Acuario (a block south of the bus station), t 871 2390, *www.wearytravelerhostel.com*. As well as being a hostel (*see* p.201) the 'Weary' acts as a backpackers' info centre: depending on which of the staff are around, it can be a good place to ask for advice if you ever have a problem.

Post Office: Av. Tulum, at the northernmost end of the village. Has a **Mexpost** desk.

Sports and Activities

Adventure Tours

For **Sian Ka'an tours** based in Tulum, see p.204.

Alltournative, Highway 307 by the Crucero, t 803 9999, from US and Canada 01 800 507 1092, www.alltournative.com. Branch of the Playa-based adventure company (see p.179).

Diving, Snorkelling, Kiteboarding

Tulum is a prime cave diving centre (see p.190). In the ocean, there's fine diving and snorkelling around the reefs just offshore and to the north and south. Lately, Tulum's giant beach has become something of a hub for a whole new fad, kiteboarding.

Abyss Dive Center, Av. Tulum, corner C. Osiris (by Cenote Dive Center), t 871 2068, www.abyssdivecenter.com. Very experienced Playa operator that has now opened up in Tulum, offering ocean diving in association with Cenote Dive Center (see p.190).

Acuatic Tulum, Cabañas Zazil-Kin, Tulum beach, t 100 7122, www.acuatictulum.com.mx. Tulum's oldest dive operator, with bargain courses, snorkel trips and cave dives.

Extreme Control, El Paraíso, Km 2, and Playa Azul, Km 7, Tulum beach, t 745 4555, www.extremecontrol.net. The latest thing on Tulum beach, whipping up into the sky on a kiteboard. Beginners' classes daily.

Halocline Diving, C. Andromeda, off C. Orion, t 120 6402, www.haloclinediving.com. Friendly operator with especially well-priced snorkel tours, which also has Tulum's only scuba equipment and rental shop

Health and Wellness

See also **Amansala**, p.200

Coqui Coqui Spa, Km 7.5, Tulum Beach, t 155 0201, www.coquicoquispa.com. A sybaritic little day spa half-hidden among palms and cabaña-clusters on the beach road.

Maya Spa, Km 3.5, Tulum Beach, t 01 800 123 3278, www.maya-spa.com. This very mellow centre, in gardens behind the beach, is part of the Copal, Azulik and Zahra hotels (see p.199), but open to non-guests. Options run from massage or shiatsu to local specialities like Maya sweat baths and healing.

Where to Stay in Tulum

Tulum's first cabañas were stick and palm huts, and spending time by the beach with the palms and the waves was a boho-backpacker preserve. But, they developed, and modern Tulum offers a whole range of comfort-levels on the beach. Prices have shot up as well, even for simple huts: the most basic cabaña now costs $25 or more a night, while at the other end there are plenty of beach houses over $200 in peak winter season. There's still a big range of prices, but in the winter season it's hard to find much on the beach for real budget rates. A few semi-resort-style hotels have begun to stick their claws into the beach too. However, so far most new places have stayed with the cabaña style, and one Tulum tradition that's generally been kept is the lack of permanent electricity. Many places now have 24hr generators or solar power, but others turn off their lights at 10–11pm, and a few still only have candles. Phone connections are still erratic, so many hotels use lines in Cancún (or even the US) or cellphones (so you may need to add 044 before the area code and number). Mosquitoes can be irritating at times, so take repellent.

As the beach has filled up, more places to stay have opened in Tulum Pueblo. Obviously, you can't get straight into the sea, but prices are lower, and there's a bigger choice of places to eat. Also, if you arrive late, you can always take a room in town the first night and try again at the beach the next morning.

The Beach Cabañas

From the Crucero the beach road runs seawards for nearly 2km before it meets a T-junction. The left arm runs north for 3km up to a back entrance (footpath only) to Tulum ruins, while to the right the road runs south for another 8km to the entrance to Sian Ka'an (paved for the first 3km, a fairly smooth dirt track after that). **Kilometre markers**, often used as address locators, are numbered for the 11km from the ruins, **not** from the T-junction. The *cabañas* are strung along the beach in either direction, and taxis are the only public transport, so getting between *cabañas* without your own transport can take time.

The T-junction may become a new building focus, following the arrival of the Azul Blue hotel, the biggest and most out-of-place hotel yet put up in Tulum. That aside, the first *cabaña* sites that opened, closest to the ruins left of the T, have some of the best spots, with a superb view of the Castillo, but curiously have mostly remained the most basic and the cheapest (these backpacker cabins are also the places where thefts are most often reported). There's a cluster of mellow, more upscale *cabañas* (Piedra Escondida, Zamas) a little south of the T, around Km 3.5, at **Punta Piedra**. Otherwise, the further south you go, the more beach you generally have to yourself.

Hotels and *cabañas* in each price band are listed here **from north to south** (with kilometres numbered from Tulum ruins). Nearly all Tulum hotels – above all on the beach – **change price slot according to season**: *cabañas* with *luxury* rates in winter peak seasons ($200+) may drop to *moderate* ($60–120) by late spring, and cabins that are *budget* most of the year may jump into *inexpensive* (over $30) Dec–Feb. Note too that many *cabaña* hotels have rooms at a big range of prices, depending on size and proximity to the beach, so it's worth checking what's available, even in the top-range places.

Luxury–Expensive

Mezzanine, Km 1.5, t 131 1596, *www.mezzanine.com.mx*. Nothing to do with the traditional Tulum *cabaña* – instead this represents the arrival of boutique-hotel style, with sharply designed rooms in emphatically contemporary colours. All have sea views and state-of-the-art electronics, and the pool deck is very sleek. As one of the hippest spots on the beach, Mezzanine also has a cool Thai-fusion **restaurant, Ph** (*expensive*), and a **bar-club** for beach parties (*see* p.201).

Azulik–Zahra–Cabañas Copal, Km 3.5, t 01 800 123 3278, *www.ecotulum.com*. Three related *cabaña* hotels in the same stretch of lush gardens-by-the-beach together with the **Maya Spa** (*see* p.198), and all made of natural materials. They cover an especially wide range, from top-scale to near-budget. Most opulent is **Azulik**, with 15 exquisite ultra-romantic villas on rocks above the beach, aimed at couples (*luxury*); **Zahra** is more family-oriented, with two-bedroom beach villas (*expensive–moderate*); while **Cabañas Copal** runs from large seafront cabins (*expensive*) to basic models with shared showers (*inexpensive*). Given this variety, make sure you know what you're getting, especially at Zahra and Copal. There are pleasant **restaurants** (*moderate*) in Copal and Zahra.

Piedra Escondida, Km 3.5, t 130 9932, *www.piedraescondida.com*. One of the most enjoyable Punta Piedra hotels, with eight pretty rooms in *palapa*-roofed buildings, each with its own terrace balcony and a superb outlook on a sheltered beach. Prices run from about $125 off-season to $245 for New Year, but for off-the-street bookings there are often deals off-peak. It's Italian-owned, and has a charming Italian-Mexican **restaurant** (*moderate*) with a beachside deck.

Maya Tulum, Km 4.3, t in US 1 888 515 4580, *www.mayatulum.com*. Just after the paved surface ends comes one of the longest-established of Yucatán's New Age hotels. It has very comfortable *cabaña* rooms with meditative 'hanging beds', and all kinds of treatments and workshops; most are for guests only, and all-inclusive health packages are offered. The **restaurant** (*expensive*) has a vegetarian menu, and fine seafood.

Posada Margherita, Km 4.5, t 100 3780, *www.posadamargherita.com*. Eight charming and spacious beachfront rooms in a very tranquil spot, with solar power. Prices go up to *luxury* at peak times. The Italian owners are

⭐ Piedra Escondida >>

friendly and thoughtful (it's perhaps Tulum's only beach hotel with disabled access), and have one of the best of Tulum's Italian **restaurants** (*moderate*).

Ana y José, Km 7, t Cancún (998) 880 5629, *www.anayjose.com*. One of Tulum's longest-established hotels. Its 15 rooms are still called *cabañas*, but are some of the plushest on the beach (albeit not all have a sea view). There are also bikes for hire, a lovely pool, a pretty, sand-floored **restaurant** (*moderate*), a spa and car-rental.

★ **La Zebra** >

La Zebra, Km 8.5, t 115 4276, *www.la zebratulum.com*. Another of the coolest spots on the beach, but one that stays closer to the Caribbean *cabaña* model and Latin style than Mezzanine (*see* p.199), with gorgeous cabins running back from a perfect beach, a cantina-restaurant-tequila bar (*moderate*) and a lounging deck, facing a beach dance floor for salsa lessons and Sunday Latin party nights.

★ **Hemingway** >>

Amansala, Km 8.7, t Cancún (998) 185 7428, *www.amansala.com*. Not quite a hotel, but one of Tulum's biggest successes – Melissa Perlman's 'bikini boot camp' six-day courses are a clever mix of fitness, beauty treatments, pampering and fun, with great meals at the beach restaurant. They're pitched at young women, but couples can also join some courses, and in between camps the attractive *cabañas* are often available on a hotel basis.

Milamores, Km 9.5, t 100 1209, *www.milarmorestulum.com*. Tulum's most spectacular option, a real bandits' lair – literally. Formerly known as the Casa Magna, these two giant beach villas were one of the hideaways of Colombian drug baron Pablo Escobar, seized by the Mexican government on his death in 1993. After falling into disrepair for years, they have been restored as a very opulent, if quirky, hotel – the manically overblown architecture gives the whole place a distinct operatic style, and suites have names like 'King Pin'. An experience, and it faces a superb beach.

Expensive–Moderate

Cabañas Diamante-K, Km 2.5, t 876 2115, *www.diamantek.com*. Attractive wooden cabins, some big with showers (*moderate*) and others with shared

bathrooms and *moderate* to *inexpensive* prices. There's a **bar-restaurant** (*moderate*) and massage facilities. Get a cabin near the bar, and you'll hear every drinker's thoughts. The owners have similar *cabañas* south of the T, at **Esmeralda-K**, Km 8, linked to the same website.

Zamas, Km 4, t in US (415) 387 9806, *www.zamas.com*. Hip in a laidback way, this *cabaña*-hotel at the south end of Punta Piedra gives a choice of beachfront cabins mixing Mexican-beach style with ample comforts, or, on the land side of the road, cabins and *cabañas* in a garden (*expensive–moderate*). One of the most popular *cabaña*-hotels, and its ¡Qué Fresco! restaurant is one of the best on the beach (*see* p.201).

Hemingway, Km 5.5, t 114 2321, *www.hemingwaytulum.com*. Twelve ultra-spacious beachfront villas – each has two double bedrooms and a broad terrace for lounging around a palm grove. Ample fresh-fruit breakfasts are included, and there's a bar and **restaurant** on the sands (*moderate*). A great beach retreat.

Tita Tulum, Km 8, t 877 8513, *www.titatulum.com*. Ten individual, spacious *cabañas*, with plenty of terrace space for relaxing. Those on the upper floors are especially well ventilated, and they're well-priced for Tulum nowadays, in the *moderate* slot for much of the year. Tasty seafood at the beach **bar-restaurant**.

Dos Ceibas, Km 9.5, t 877 6024, *www.dosceibas.com*. A *posada ecológica* on the crowd-free south end of the beach, with eight delightful rooms and solar power. As well as therapies and activities (meditation, massage), there's a **restaurant** (*moderate*) and snorkelling. The price range runs from $200 for rooms nearest the beach at peak times to $80 for garden rooms in low season.

Tierras del Sol, Km 10, t 807 9387, *www.tierrasdelsol.com*. Near the end of the road are these very beachcomber-ish, secluded *cabañas*. There's 24hr solar power, and the charming Argentinian owners can arrange snorkelling and other activities, and have a little **restaurant** (*moderate*).

Inexpensive–Budget

Cabañas Zazil-Kin, Km 0.5, t 871 2417. Once Don Armando's, this *cabaña* site on the north fork and its funky beach **bar-restaurant** has been a hangout for 'generations' of backpackers. Its *cabañas* are less basic than some – a few have their own showers – but you don't get a lot more for your money: prices nowadays can be a shock as *cabañas* with showers can cost $60 in winter, simple huts sharing showers $35–55. Service can also be infuriatingly offhand. **Acuatic Tulum** dive shop is based here (*see* p.198).

Mar Caribe, Km 0.7 (no phone). Simplest of the north road sites, with a superb beach and original-model sand-floored huts with plain beds or hammocks and no electricity at all, and still *inexpensive* rates (round $35 at peak time).

Tulum Pueblo

Rancho Tranquilo, Av. Tulum, southernmost end of the Pueblo, t 871 2839 . Pretty *cabañas* (*inexpensive*) and dorms (*budget*) in a fruit garden, with shared bathrooms and kitchen.

Villa Matisse, Av. Satélite 19, three blocks west of Av. Tulum, t 871 2636, *shuvinito@yahoo.com* (*inexpensive*). A stand-out among the Pueblo's low-cost options: owner Lourdes is exceptionally friendly and her 6 rooms are bright and well kept. An open kitchen and free-to-use bikes are among the extras, and rates are even lower for longer stays.

The Weary Traveler, Av. Tulum, between C. Jupiter and C. Acuario (a block south of the bus station), t 871 2390, *www. wearytravelerhostel.com* (*budget*). One of Tulum's best budget hostels, with rooms with shared showers (around $25) or dorm beds (around $9), breakfast included (though you get it yourself). There's a free daily beach shuttle.

Eating Out in Tulum

On the Beach

Most hotels along the beach road have restaurants. Also worth seeking out are those in **Zahra**, **Piedra**

Escondida and **Posada Margherita** (both Italian), **Ph at Mezzanine** for something different (global-Thai) and **La Zebra** for its seafood and setting.

El Paraíso, Km 1 (*moderate*). Spacious beach-terrace in one of the older hotels with fine seafood.

¡Qué Fresco!, Zamas *cabañas*, Km 4 (*moderate*). Enjoys one of the best locations, on a rocky bluff above the beach, and serves up great fish and seafood. Friendly service, too

Tulum Pueblo

Eateries are spread all along Av. Tulum.

Don Diego de la Selva, C. Palenque, off Av. Tulum at south end of the Pueblo, t 114 9744 (*moderate*). Distinctive restaurant with refined international cooking, beside a pool that also serves the great-value small hotel (*moderate*). *Open evenings only, closed Wed.*

Paris de Noche, Av. Tulum, between C. Beta and C. Osiris (*moderate*). French-Mexican combination offering local dishes or crêpes.

Don Cafeto, Av. Tulum, corner C. Orion (*moderate–budget*). Almost a landmark, with a big terrace, unpushy service and excellent Mexican standards.

El Mariachi, Av. Tulum, opposite Don Cafeto (*moderate–budget*). A huge, fun terrace, for some bargain Mexican authenticity.

Nightlife

Since electricity arrived on Tulum beach, it has become the focus for an Ibiza-style beach-dance scene. The **Fiesta en la Playa** night every Friday at **Mezzanine** is the main fixtures, with an international roster of DJs playing house and ambient music into the night. For something much more Latin, there are salsa parties most Sundays at **La Zebra**, usually with live bands. For other events, look out for flyers around town.

⭐ ¡Qué Fresco! >>

08 Cancún, the Islands and the Riviera Maya | Tulum

Muyil

About 25km south of Tulum on Highway 307 and just inside the limits of the Sian Ka'an reserve there is a little-known archaeological site, **Muyil** (some signs point, confusingly, to the *Zona Arqueológica Chunyaxché*, the name of the nearby village, but Muyil is the site's 'official' name). Despite its proximity to Tulum this Maya city had a very different history, as it rose to prominence in the Early Classic from about AD 300–600. Little is definitely established about Muyil, but it seems to have been closely associated with Cobá. When Cobá was overwhelmed by Chichén Itzá, Muyil slipped into decline with it, but revived in the Postclassic after 1200 to reach its greatest size. Consequently the ruins reveal a broad mix, from Classic-era buildings similar to those of Cobá to others in the plain, square East-Coast style of the Quintana Roo coastal settlements. A path beside the ruins leads to Lake Chunyaxché (*see* p.203).

Only a part of the Muyil site is fully open, so it is not possible to get a real impression of its size. On most days any visitors are likely to have it to themselves, except for the insects. The first group of buildings is right of the main gate, the **Entrance Plaza**, with the remains of three pyramids and several other structures around a small square. Most of these buildings are thought to be among the oldest at Muyil, from the Early Classic. The grandest structure is the steep, 17m-high pyramid known as the **Castillo** (*cannot be climbed*), which shows a strong Petén influence. It's also very distinctive, with a peculiarly complex temple at the top with a unique – and unexplained – circular inner core. A little north of this is a more conventional pyramid, **Temple 8**, with a squat Postclassic temple – similar to but larger than the Castillo at Tulum – on top of a base of several layers dating back to the Preclassic era. In the sanctuary of the temple it's still possible to see some of the original painted stucco in yellow, red, black and Maya blue.

Sian Ka'an and Punta Allen

✪ Sian Ka'an

The Riviera-strip of potential tourist development is effectively brought to an end by the **Sian Ka'an Biosphere Reserve**, the most comprehensively protected natural environment in Mexico. It extends over 530,000 hectares around the Bahía de la Ascensión, a huge area of all-but-uninhabited lagoon, reef, mangroves, lake, tropical forest and savanna. Somewhere within Sian Ka'an (Yucatec for 'where Heaven is born') there are examples of nearly every kind of the region's wildlife: jaguars, jaguarundis, howler monkeys and tapirs; crocodiles, turtles and manatees; and millions of birds. There's an extraordinary biological diversity, and the plant life is as fascinating as the elusive fauna. As you enter the reserve the road

Getting to Sian Ka'an

The Punta Allen track is a roller coaster of a dirt road, which sometimes – above all after rain – boasts somes of Mexico's champion potholes. More is now done to maintain it, and at its best – when it's been dry for a while – a standard car can get down there taking its time, but at times it's still 4WD only; ask about current conditions before you try it. In any vehicle, the 44km from the Sian Ka'an entry gate will take 2–3 hrs, with twists, jolts and bumps. **Fuel** is only available in Punta Allen from unofficial village sellers, so fill up in Tulum.

Even Punta Allen has a *colectivo*, a big 4WD van that normally leaves Tulum once a day, around 2pm from outside **Savana** and leaves Punta Allen on the return around 5pm. Times may vary, so check.

is surrounded by more and more of the giant fan palms called *chit* in Yucatec, one of the species peculiar to the Yucatán. Also common is the *chechen*, an apparently innocuous tree with a poisonous sap that can affect humans and animals even if they only stand near it. Close by, though, there will be a *chakah* bush, a natural antidote.

One particular feature of Sian Ka'an is that conservation has been given precedence over exploitation for tourism. There are very few roads, none of them paved: the main, gruelling track from Tulum to Punta Allen (*see* above), and two others that have only recently begun to be a little better known, from Felipe Carrillo Puerto to Vigía Chico on the coast, and from Mahahual to the south (*see* p.337). It's always best to visit the reserve with a **tour** (*see* p.204), as it's hard to find your way around by yourself.

There is also one small but beautiful part of the reserve that can be visited without need for any guide, right by the official entrance to Sian Ka'an. The reserve warden may ask you to sign a book, but there's no admission charge, and just behind his lodge there's a short nature walk to a deliciously clear and fresh *cenote* called **Ben-Ha**, which is great for swimming. Most 'proper' tours of Sian Ka'an continue on from there down to the *cabañas* at Boca Paila, with stops to look at the forest. You then take a boat through the mangrove lagoon and up a channel that separates it from the freshwater **Lake Chunyaxché**. This is one of the Yucatán lakes fed only by underground rivers, which can be seen bubbling up from the lake bed; a highlight of any tour is the chance to 'float' down the current between two lagoons, carried along with no effort at all. There is also usually time to visit one of the 27 scarcely explored Maya sites in the reserve, a tiny Postclassic temple on an island. Whether you will see any of the rarer Sian Ka'an animals is a matter of luck, but you will always see plenty of birds – orioles, ibises, blue and tricoloured herons, storks and many more.

The Punta Allen Road

If even the most distant Tulum *cabañas* feel too busy, much greater remoteness can be found by carrying on along the sand spit to the pirate village of Punta Allen, a wild, empty track that meanders through jungle to swing back again to meet the sea. It's completely deserted for miles, with nothing but windswept palms, wheeling

08 | Cancún, the Islands and the Riviera Maya | Sian Ka'an and Punta Allen

pelicans and empty dunes on the one side, and the deliciously still channels and islets of the coastal lagoons on the other. Along the way lie stretches of beach that are spectacularly beautiful.

One of the most accessible spots is three kilometres south of the reserve entrance, an open area behind the beach that's one of the (relatively) popular places to stop and camp. Fishermen, though, are the area's true devotees. The flats in the lagoons and Ascension Bay are considered the best bonefishing grounds in the world, while offshore there's good deep-sea fishing. Permits are required, which can be arranged by the fishing lodges. Eleven kilometres from the entrance is the longest-established at **Boca Paila**, from where many Sian Ka'an tours set off into Lake Chunyaxché, and where CeSiak also offers a fabulous place to stay. The next organized stopping-place is 20km further at **Rancho Sol Caribe**.

Punta Allen, 44km from the Sian Ka'an entrance, is a tiny collection of houses amid dunes and giant palms facing a huge open sea in variations of colour from turquoise to deep blue. It has a beach with a few landing stages where giggling kids play in the waves, a plaza, a school, a basketball court, four or five shops and a few very laid-back restaurants. One theory goes that it owes its non-Hispanic name to the *Allen*, the ship of Edward Teach, Blackbeard the Pirate, who in the 18th century used Ascension Bay as a bolt hole, and (some say) founded the village. Today its 450 or so inhabitants make a living from lobster fishing. In among them there's a sprinkling of international beachcombers. You can tell locals' houses from *gringo* homes: the former are Caribbean-style painted wooden huts or more modern Mexican concrete houses: the latter are put together from upturned boats and driftwood, with wind chimes and other junk out in front. A walk south out of the village will take you to the lighthouse at the tip of Punta Allen. Staying here, protected from the outside world by that dreadful road, is for those who want to sink into really deep tranquillity.

Tours and Activities

Punta Allen t (984–)

Cooperativa Los Gaytanes, Punta Allen, t 871 2001. As you come into the village on the beach road you pass the hut of this local guides' coop. Among their (flexible) options are flyfishing (from $150), tours of reefs and lagoons to see birds, dolphins and turtles, and snorkelling trips. You'll see signs around the village for other local tour operations.

Sian Ka'an

A growing number of agencies offer tours in the reserve, but not all do so with the same ecological awareness (i.e. jeep and ATV tours). Best by some way of the bigger operators is **Alltournative** (*see* p.179). Small-group tours that let you experience Sian Ka'an without snarling motors are more locally based. It's also possible to visit Sian Ka'an from the south side, via Felipe Carrillo Puerto or Mahahual (*see* p.339). For more on Sian Ka'an, check the site of **Amigos de Sian Ka'an**, *www.amigosdesiankaan.org*.

CESiak, Av. Tulum, next to the petrol station by the old ruins entrance, Tulum, t 871 2499, *www.cesiak.org*. The *Centro Ecológico Sian Ka'an*, which as well as providing the best accommodation in Sian Ka'an at **Boca Paila Camp** (*see* right), runs two main tours, with expert guides and in a range of languages: an all-day 'canal tour', leaving Tulum at 8am and returning around 4pm, including a forest walk, boat trip and a chance to float down an extraordinary current between lagoons (around $70 per person), and a shorter sunset birdwatching tour (Dec–May only, also $70). Fishing and kayaking trips and longer tours can be arranged, and in April–Oct there may be night turtle-watching trips. Proceeds help support CESiak's education and environment programmes in Tulum and Sian Ka'an.

⊛ **Boca Paila >> Camp**

Community Tours Sian Ka'an, Av. Tulum, between C. Orion and C. Centauro, **t** 114 0750, *www.sian kaantours.org*. An alliance of local guide operations and communities, with very friendly English-speaking guides who are especially knowledgeable of their area. Options include a 'forest and float' tour including Muyil ruins. Prices begin at $75 (birding).

U Yoochel Maya – Cooperativa de Chunyaxché, t 806 0860. Boatmen's cooperative in Chunyaxché, based at a hut opposite Muyil ruins, offering more basic tours. For about $45 a head you can spend a day in the lakes and mangroves, with a swim and ruins tour. Guides are less informed than on other tours, but some speak some English. Contact them at Muyil or try to phone a day or two ahead.

Where to Stay and Eat around Sian Ka'an

Outside of Punta Allen, there is just a scattering of places along this road, *cabaña*-hotels allowed within the reserve. Given Ascension Bay's importance for fishermen, most are specialist **fishing lodges** offering all-in packages, but rooms may be available to other visitors in low seasons. They are mostly quite expensive, and are best booked through *www.angler adventures.com* or other fishing websites. You can **camp** almost anywhere that isn't fenced off, but take everything you need.

In Punta Allen, as well as the places listed there are often signs offering rooms to rent, and if you ask at Posada Sirena or Serenidad Shardon they will try to search out a room for anyone who makes it down the road. There is **nowhere** to change money, nor can anyone handle **credit cards**, so take cash in pesos.

Boca Paila Camp, t 871 2499, *www.cesiak.org*. (*moderate*). Run by CESiak (*see* p.204), this fully low-impact ecohotel sits above the beach 11km south of the Sian Ka'an gate – an utterly magical spot that gives you a taste of this coast in pre-Riviera days. As well as a lovely and surprisingly sophisticated terrace **restaurant** (*moderate*) it has 'tent-cabins' around the forest, which for all their rustic style are very comfortable, all with balconies. Guests have discounts on tours, and it's a wonderful jumping-off point for exploring Sian Ka'an. The road this far down is a fairly easy drive.

Boca Paila Lodge, t 155 0012, *www. bocapailmexico.com* (*expensive*). Longest-established of the fishing lodges, 11km south of the Sian Ka'an entrance, with superior *cabañas*, its own boats and **restaurant**, and kiteboarding, tours and other activities as well as fishing. *Booking essential.*

Casa Blanca, Punta Pájaros, reservations via *www.angleradventures.com* (*luxury*). The ultimate destination for Ascension Bay fishermen, an extravagantly equipped fishing lodge on the private island of Punta Pájaros, south of Punta Allen across the bay. Access is by light plane transfer direct from Cancún, part of the all-included package.

Cuzan Guest House, Punta Allen, **t** (983) 834 0358, *www.flyfishmx.com* (*moderate*). Punta Allen's main hotel, with *cabañas* with bath and a **restaurant** (*moderate*) with sand floor and catch-of-the-day fish. It's mainly a bonefishing lodge, but rooms are open to anyone if not booked up, and it also arranges bird-watching, snorkelling, kayaking and other trips. The owners also have a ranch, **Rancho El Angel**, in a remote spot on the west side of the bay, amid real jungle.

Posada Sirena, Punta Allen, **t** 877 8521, *www.casasirena.com* (*moderate–*

inexpensive). Sirena runs her bohemian beach guest house with friendly verve: she has four cabins in the village, with kitchens, hammocks, good showers and all sorts of distinctive fittings. A fabulous bargain, and she can also arrange local excursions at low prices.

Rancho Sol Caribe, 35km south of Sian Ka'an entrance, t Cancún (998) 874 1858, *www.solcaribe-mexico.com* (*expensive*). Little *cabaña* hotel that with its beach bar appears bizarrely neat and tidy in the middle of emptiness. It's owned by Michael and Diane Severeign, who have four family-size beach cabins with 24hr solar power, and cook up great fresh fish.

One of the best places along the road for non-fishing obsessives, but, if you wish, fishing, snorkelling or diving trips and packages are on tap.

Serenidad Shardon, Punta Allen, t 876 1827, *www.shardon.com* (*expensive– budget*). Huge *palapa*-roofed residence in a fabulous location, offering a set of options: a whole 'beach house' with room for six people; two pretty beachfront *cabañas*, and a 'Penthouse Palapa' with dorm beds, which you can often have to yourself for $15 a head. **Muelle Viejo**, Punta Allen (*budget*). Friendly restaurant by the jetty, with great seafood.

Cobá

Cobá
open daily 8–5; adm

Despite its proximity to the coastal tourist areas, Cobá is far less well known than other great Maya cities, yet is one of the most intriguing. Its location and layout are different from any other, for it stands beside five lakes, the largest set of lakes in the Yucatán. Instead of the concentrated plaza-structure of cities like Chichén Itzá, Cobá, one of the oldest Maya centres, was made up of many separate groups of buildings spread over a huge area of some 70 square kilometres. Within this lie the remains of over 15,000 structures spread between 20 identifiable groups, only a part of which have been excavated. They were linked by the most complex network of *sacbés* or stone roads anywhere in the Maya world. Far enough from the coast to have lost the sea breezes and yet with the lakes alongside to raise the humidity, Cobá is also a powerfully hot and sticky site. It's also a great place to see birds and other wildlife.

History

As a source of water Cobá's lakes attracted Maya settlers from earliest times, but a city beside them first came to prominence in about AD 250. Cobá remained the largest city in the entire northern Yucatán throughout the Classic era, reaching its peak from about 650 onwards when it dominated the northeast of the peninsula. Compared to Dzibilchaltún, Uxmal and other northern cities, Cobá clearly had closer ties – cultural and economic – with the Classic Maya centres of the Petén to the south, reflected both in its architectural style and in the presence of many carved stelae. It is widely believed, but hard to substantiate, that as representatives of the Classic Maya tradition, the lords of Cobá considered themselves superior to other, less literate peoples in the north.

The decipherment of Cobá's stelae is limited by their poor condition, and so it does not yet have as personalized a 'history' as

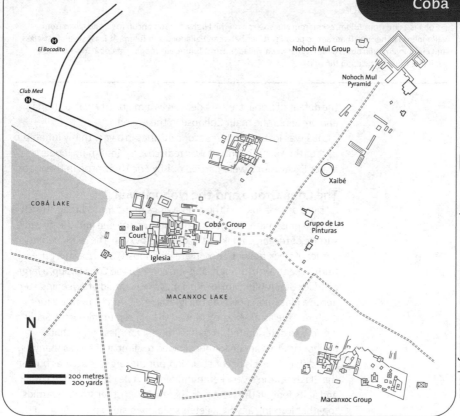

El Bocadito

Club Med

Nohoch Mul Group

Nohoch Mul Pyramid

Xaibé

COBÁ LAKE

Ball Court

Cobá Group

Grupo de Las Pinturas

Iglesia

MACANXOC LAKE

N

200 metres
200 yards

Macanxoc Group

the southern cities. Archaeological evidence indicates that by the 8th century it had as many as 50,000 people, living in clusters of house-enclosures between the *sacbeob* and building complexes, and with a sophisticated system of water management. Some of its *sacbé* causeways extended far beyond the limits of the city to link Cobá with cities such as Muyil and Polé (now Xcaret) and other settlements on the coast, and Yaxuná to the west. Examination of these causeways from Cobá has played an important part in demonstrating that Maya *sacbeob* had a military and trading role as well as being built for use in rituals or pilgrimages.

Cobá's downfall came with the rise of Chichén Itzá, and the long war between the two cities is one of the titanic confrontations of Maya history. In the early 9th century the longest of all Maya *sacbeob*, over 100km in length, was laid all the way from Cobá to its western stronghold at Yaxuná, an extraordinary operation that must have involved the mobilization of thousands of people. This reinforcement was only temporarily successful, however, and the destruction of Yaxuná by Chichén in about 860 was followed by

Getting to Cobá

Cobá is 45km from Tulum, 45km from Nuevo Xcan on the Highway 180 Cancún road, and 58km from Valladolid via Chemax. There are no petrol stations between Valladolid and Tulum. At least seven first-class and eight *intermedio* **buses** daily run between Valladolid and Tulum, all stopping at Cobá. Tours are also available from agencies on the coast.

the defeat of Cobá itself. Its decline as a major city was terminal and preceded the main Collapse in the region.

Cobá was lost in the forest for centuries in a very thinly inhabited part of the Yucatán, until it was rediscovered in 1891 by Teobert Maler. Excavations were carried out by Eric Thompson in the 1920s.

The Cobá Group and the Nohoch Mul

As you approach Cobá the road swings round into a broad stretch of open grass, with the site parking area at one end and the glazed surface of the largest lake, Lake Cobá, below you. The ruins, behind a barrier of trees, are not immediately obvious. Walk up a short rise from the entrance, though, and you come to the **Cobá Group**, a large complex of temples centred on a massive pyramid of sweeping steps above a plaza. It's known as the **Iglesia** (the Church), because for centuries the local Maya continued to hold ceremonies here. Sadly, it's now so deteriorated, in parts almost a formless cone, that ordinary visitors are no longer allowed to climb it. It has as many as nine different levels of construction, but the largest part was built in the Classic era, in a very Petén-influenced style with rounded corners, and at its foot on the west side there are two other small pyramids, together forming a typical Petén-style three-sided plaza. Around the Iglesia there are also several Mayan-arched passageways, and in the plaza there are several *stelae* in poor condition. On the north side of the Iglesia there is a Classic-era **Ball Court**, with some recently installed and rather obviously modern reconstructed scoring rings.

The main path continues past the Ball Court around the northern side of Lake Macanxoc, hidden behind the trees, although some of the paths leading off to the right will take you through to the lake shore. After about 500m a fork around the Pinturas group (*see* p.209) gives you a choice of places to visit first, the Nohoch Mul pyramid or the Macanxoc Group; to do the most strenuous part before it gets hotter, follow the left fork for a walk of around one kilometre to the Nohoch Mul. The density of Cobá's forest is such that even excavated areas can seem almost reclaimed by the brush, and makes it doubly hard to imagine thousands of people living here. Temples appear through the woods as if they've only just been discovered, and as a natural landscape, with soaring *ceiba* trees filtering luminous patches of dappled sunlight, it's fascinating.

Partway along this path is another ball court, and a very unusual pyramid known as the **Xaibé** or 'Crossroads' because it stood at the

Visiting Cobá

Cobá is one of the most dispersed of the big Maya sites, with walks of over a kilometre between the groups of structures. Only a few of the most important make up the main site that is normally visited, but even so a visit involves a healthy hike (or bike ride) over forest paths. **Guides** (at the entrance) take you round the main areas in about two hours (around $30), but it's best to allow at least a whole morning. You can also rent bicycles (around $2.50) or tricycle carts with 'driver' ($8) to get around Cobá. They can be found just inside the site, by the first ball court.

junction of several *sacbeob*. Almost like a massive, conical drum, it has only recently been excavated, and is believed to have been of special importance in the life of Cobá. Easier to see coming is the huge **Nohoch Mul** ('Big Mound') itself, by far the tallest pyramid in the northern Yucatán, 42m high, in seven levels of diminishing width. Again, it is in a Petén-like, rounded style, and begs comparison with the giant pyramids of Tikal. This one you can climb up, and those who do so are rewarded with a really fabulous view over the lakes, the Iglesia and the sea of forest. Having made the gruelling scramble up there, most people stay to take it in for a while, and at the very top there's a late addition, a small Postclassic temple with a Diving God carving. Near the foot of the Nohoch Mul is a small platform, **Structure 10**, with fairly well-preserved stelae. One, **Stela 20**, has a particularly fine carving of an unidentified *ahau* standing over two captives, and the latest Long Count date yet found at Cobá, corresponding to 30 November 780.

The Grupo de Pinturas and Macanxoc

If you retrace this path you can cut across to the Macanxoc track through the **Grupo de Pinturas**, which stands between the two sides of the fork. The last large group of buildings erected at Cobá, from the Late Postclassic around 1200, it was built in the East-Coast style of Tulum, partly by 'recycling' the stones of older temples, such as Classic-era stelae. Some of its buildings, especially the largest (**Structure 1**), have sections of the murals that gave the group its name, but you're not allowed close enough to see much.

Another 500m or so will take you to the **Macanxoc** cluster itself. There are several small buildings and temples, but the centrepiece is an area with over 20 stelae scattered among trees, each on its own small platform and sheltered by a *palapa*. Some appear lost in the woods, and take some clambering to get to. The concentration of so many stelae in such a small space suggests this was a place of great ceremonial importance, almost a collective 'archive' of Cobá. Some of them are very worn and hard to distinguish, but in others the carving is quite clear. One as yet unexplained feature of them is that they depict an unusually large number of women, as if Cobá had several women rulers. The most spectacular of all is **Stela 1**, which has an account of the Mayan creation myth with a time-cycle that corresponds to 41 thousand, million, million, million, million years,

08 Cancún, the Islands and the Riviera Maya | Cobá

Where to Stay and Eat

Cobá village is tiny, but it has two good places to stay that let you see the site at its best, first thing in the morning. For real tranquillity you can also **camp** or stay in hammocks nearby at **Punta Laguna** (*see* below).

Villas Arqueológicas Cobá, t (984) 206 7000, *www.villasarqueologicas.com.mx* (*moderate*). Upscale accommodation at lower-range prices, and a great place for a still-modest splurge. Right by the lake, it has pretty, colonial-style rooms, an attractive **restaurant** and bar, and a pool in a tropical garden.

Posada El Bocadito, by bus stop, no phone (*budget*). Also a good deal with basic rooms with showers and fans, and a terrace **restaurant**.

There are several more *moderate–budget* places to eat around the ruins car park, and in the village there's **Restaurant-Bar La Pirámide** (*moderate*), with enjoyable Yucatecan snacks served on a relaxing terrace.

the longest Long Count date ever written, and one of the largest finite numbers ever conceived by a human being.

If you still want to see more of Cobá, there are many more semi-excavated building clusters that can be found by wandering on down the forest paths. The official guides at the gate, on request and if you strike a deal, will also take you to lesser-known parts of the site. Continuing on past Macanxoc for about one and a half kilometres will eventually take you to the **Zacakal** group, and there's another good track that leads off south from the path between Macanxoc and Las Pinturas. You could easily explore for a whole day without exhausting the possibilities, amid the unearthly giant *ceibas* and the birds. Just don't get totally lost.

Punta Laguna

About 20km north of Cobá on the road toward Nuevo Xcan is the village of Punta Laguna. There is another small Maya site just outside it, one of the tributaries of Classic-era Cobá, with buildings in a similar style. The village is of more interest to most visitors today, though, for its **Reserva del Mono Araña** or spider monkey reserve. It's run as a community tourism scheme, and villagers guide visitors to the best spots to see wildlife, and rent out kayaks on the lake. In the middle of dense forest and with a beautiful lake, Punta Laguna is one of the best places to see wildlife in northern Yucatán. In the surrounding area there are alligators, deer, peccaries, and howler as well as spider monkeys. There are even quite a few jaguars, although they don't like to show themselves to humans.

Punta Laguna Tours

Villagers will guide you around the reserve and ruins for around $15; the best times to see monkeys are 6–8am and 2–4pm. You can also rent canoes on the lake for around $5–6.

Where to Stay and Eat

Punta Laguna has a lakeside **campsite**, where you can camp or sleep in a hammock beneath a big *palapa*, for around $4. Simple meals are also available. It's a pocket of complete, rural tranquillity.

Yucatán State

Glimpsed flashing by from a bus window, the Yucatán can appear like one continuous expanse of flat green scrub, each stretch the same as the last: all those kilometres with not a single river, not a single hill. The Yucatán does have rivers, huge ones, but they flow under the ground not over it, passing through giant caverns as at Loltún or Balankanché, and into cathedral-like subterranean pools such as Dzitnup near Valladolid. It has hills too, but they're the man-made, massive temple-platforms of the Maya, whether they're now overgrown contours in the countryside, or the stages beneath spectacular monuments like the great temples of Chichén Itzá and Uxmal. These are only some of the parts that make up the Yucatecan heartland's very particular character. Compared to the newly minted world of Cancún and the coast, it has a very solid sense of its own historic culture, and of a way of life with its own special colours and flavours.

09

Don't miss

⭐ **Cathedral-like cave pool**
Cenote Dzitnup **p.221**

⭐ **Mysterious, monumental Mayan city**
Chichén Itzá **p.224**

⭐ **The morning whistle of the zanate bird**
The gardens of Izamal **p.246**

⭐ **Pervasive charm and urban streetlife**
Mérida **p.253**

⭐ **Refined Mayan architecture**
Uxmal **p.299**

See map overleaf

50 kms
25 miles

N

Gulf of Mexico

Dzilar Brav

Puerto de Progreso
Progreso
Chicxulub
Uaymitún
Telchac Puerto
Chabihau

Chuburná
Chelem
Xcambó
Dzidzantún
Dz

San Diego

Sisal
Dzemul
Telchac Pueblo

Chablekal
Cansahcab

Parque Natural Ría Celestún
Hunucmá
Dzibilchaltún
Conkal
Motul
Teka

Xixim
Tixkokob
Tekantó

Kinchil
MÉRIDA
Tixpehual
Cacalchén
Aké
Izamal

Celestún
Kanasín
Katanchel

Uman
X'matkuil
Hoctún
Sudzal

Poxilá
Sotuta de Peón
Acanceh
Kantunil

Chocholá
Yaxcopoil
Tecoh
Cuzamá

Chunchucmil
Santa Rosa
Ochil
Temozón Sur
Telchaquillo

Uayalceh

Maxcanú
Calcehtok
Opichén
Yunkú
Mayapán
Sotuta
Yax

Oxkintok
Calcehtok
Muna
Sacalúm
Mama
Tekit

Tipikal
Chumayel

Dzan
Teabo

Ticul
Maní

Oxkutzcab

Uxmal
Santa Elena
Loltún

Kabah
Yaaxhom
Tekax

Sayil
Labná
Chacmultún

Xlapak

Tzucacab

Tenabo

To Hopelchén

pp.376–7

Don't miss

1. Cenote Dzitnup **p.221**
2. Chichén Itzá **p.224**
3. Izamal **p.246**
4. Mérida **p.253**
5. Uxmal **p.299**

YUCATÁN

BELIZE

GUATEMALA
HONDURAS

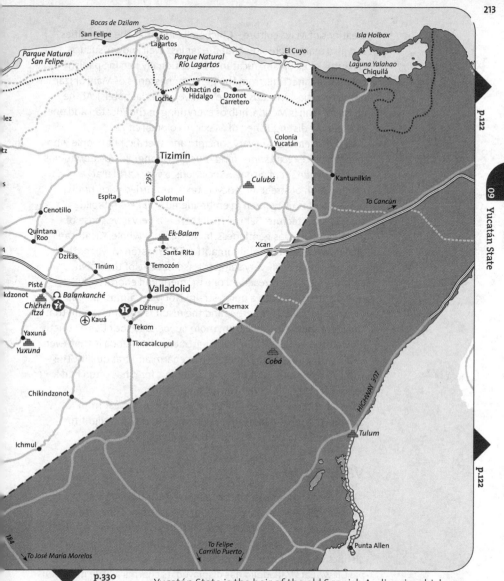

p.330

Anyone who can leave Yucatán with indifference, has never been an artist and will never be a scholar.

Desiré Charnay

Yucatán State is the heir of the old Spanish Audiencia which once governed the whole peninsula, until the Mexican government separated off Campeche and Quintana Roo, a 'truncation' that still rankles with some Yucatecans. Yucatán did not even have proper land communications with the rest of Mexico until the 1940s; contacts were carried on by ship or, lately, air. Self-contained, it developed its own history, its own food, its own music, becoming one of the most distinctive parts of Mexico.

The presence of the Maya is fundamental to the Yucatán, as alive today as in the past. The state contains many of the greatest

creations of Maya culture – Chichén Itzá, Uxmal, the Puuc cities –
but also many more sites that are far less well known, such as
Oxkintok or Ek-Balam. Yucatán is exceptionally rich in Spanish
colonial architecture, from the great monasteries of Maní or Izamal
to aristocratic *haciendas* (some now very special hotels). At the
centre of it all is Mérida, hub of everything in the Yucatán and one
of the most distinguished of Mexican colonial cities.

All these features are very concrete and specific, but people who
love the place recall something much less tangible. Yucatán towns
have a unique set of visual associations, a very particular
combination of street life, tricycle taxis, unhurried pace, bright
flowers and fruit, women in embroidered *huípiles* and solid
colonial architecture. Behind it all there is a pervasive sense of
amiable, courteous gentleness. In Mexico as a whole, Yucatecans
are known as sentimental romantics. The Yucatán Maya for their
part are very special, very self-possessed, aware of their own
culture, impassively reserved one moment and enormously
friendly the next, with a quiet, straightforward, almost palpable
decency. Put all this together and the result is an atmosphere that
can leave the new arrival from more nervy, edgy societies distinctly
disoriented. Perhaps the greatest attraction of Mérida is that, even
as a city, it manages to maintain this charm and tranquillity. The
Yucatán really has no right to be so benign, for it has often had a
terrible history. This is the Yucatecan paradox.

This chapter is ordered as if you are continuing west from
Cancún, though it can be just as practical to travel straight to
Mérida and tour outwards from there.

Valladolid

If you enter the Yucatán through Cancún and head west, the
town of Valladolid comes as a sudden blast of local life after the
multi-national, Pan-Mexican world of the coast. It's the first real
Yucatecan town you come to, a first encounter with the region's
distinctive way of being. Tourists come through here, and in the
past few years Valladolid has displayed its charms a little more self-
consciously, but the town's main business is still to fulfil, for the
villages around it, the role that Mérida carries out for the whole
state: that of place to buy and sell, meet up, catch a bus, hear
what's going on, sort out any official business and pick up
anything they can't find at home.

Experiencing this way of life is an attraction in itself, but the
town also has one of the finest easily swimmable *cenotes* nearby.
Valladolid also makes a good (and economical) base for visiting
Chichén Itzá, or Ek-Balam and Río Lagartos to the north.

Getting to and around Valladolid

By Bus

Valladolid's not-so-'new' **bus station** is at the junction of Calles 37 and 54, six blocks from the centre; some services, especially second-class, also call at the 'old' station at Calles 39 and 44. Valladolid is a good jumping-off point to northern Yucatán: there are second-class buses hourly to **Tizimín**, many of which carry on to **Río Lagartos**, and the Mérida bus to **Chiquilá** (for **Holbox**, see p.154) passes through Valladolid at 2.30am. Valladolid is also a hub of *colectivo* traffic to all the surrounding villages and further afield. Most leave from Calle 44, west of the plaza. Some run all the way to Cancún.

Other main services are:

Cancún (*3hrs*): seven first-class buses daily, and *intermedios* more or less hourly 6am–10.30pm, plus three during the night. Fares $6–10. Five first-class and two *intermedios* go on to **Playa del Carmen**.

Chetumal (*5–6hrs*) via **Felipe Carrilo Puerto**: five or six second-class daily.

Mérida (*2¼hrs*): along Highway 180, first-class buses about every hour 6.45am–9pm (plus two during the night) and many second-class daily. First-class fare about $10. Second-class Oriente buses run to Mérida about every two hours via **Dzitas** and **Izamal**.

Pisté, for **Chichén Itzá** (*45mins*): three first-class daily (four, Sat and Sun) and *intermedio* buses at least hourly 6am–10.30pm, plus a few during the night. Fares $1.50–$3.50.

Tulum (*1½–2hrs*), via Cobá: five first-class, two *intermedios* and more second-class buses daily. Fares Cobá $2.50, Tulum $5–7.

By Bicycle

Valladolid is particularly easy to cycle around, with dedicated cycle tracks beside the main roads into town, and out to Dzitnup.

Antonio 'Negro' Aguilar, C. 44 no. 195, x 39 & 41, t 856 2125, one block from the plaza. El Negro (Antonio's baseball nickname) is a character: formerly police chief of Valladolid, and prior to that a pro baseball player. Today he has a sports shop and rents bikes, for about $1 an hour or $5 a day. He also has rooms (see p.220), and provides any information he can to passing visitors in booming, self-created English.

By Car

Driving in and out of Valladolid is very easy, as Highway 180 west from Cancún becomes C. 39 in the town and runs straight to the main square, the Parque Principal, forming its north side between Calles 40 and 42; eastbound traffic runs along C. 41, the plaza's south side. For the 295 road to Río Lagartos, take C. 40 north from the same square. Parking is easy, even on the plaza. The most central *gasolinera* is on C. 41 between C. 46 and 48.

Orientation

Valladolid has a straightforward grid layout centred on the **Parque Principal**, between Calles 39, 40, 41 and 42 (even numbers run north–south, odd numbers east–west). Cross-streets are indicated with addresses, i.e., C. 46, x 39 & 41 (between 39 and 41).

History

As often in the Yucatán, Valladolid's current likeable calm belies a bitter history. It stands on the site of *Zací*, capital of the Maya lordship of the Cupules, although next to nothing remains of the pre-Hispanic settlement. A new 'city' of Valladolid was first founded in 1542 by Montejo el Sobrino in a place called Chauacá, closer to the coast, but its colonists found it unhealthy, and in 1545 it was decided they should take over the old Maya town. For its first 300 years Valladolid was a colonial frontier town, a white island amid a sea of Maya villages. Scarcely a year after it was established, in 1546, Valladolid was besieged in the first great Maya revolt of the colonial era.

Its distance from Mérida meant that Valladolid developed into a regional centre of its own, with fine colonial architecture. It was a place where little changed after the first decades of the Conquest, and its leading families were known for extreme conservatism. In the same way that the élites of Mérida or Campeche rejected interference from central Mexico, the *ladinos* of Valladolid resented control from Mérida. At the same time, the 'old wealth' on which they based their social pretensions was really very meagre. When Stephens arrived in 1841 he found a town semi-paralyzed in time, which bore 'the marks of ancient grandeur, but is now going to decay', with streets overgrown and roofless, and collapsing houses even in the main square.

It was only fitting that this symbol of old Spanish rule should see the outbreak of the great upheaval of the Caste War. It was in nearby Tizimín that, in 1838, Captain Santiago Imán began his anti-Mexican revolt and, against all previous practice, hit upon the secret weapon of recruiting the Maya for his revolutionary army. In January 1847 Valladolid was attacked and taken in yet another white-led, anti-centralist rising, but this time Indian troops got out of control, unleashing their anger in a brief orgy of looting and destruction. In July a local Maya leader, Manuel Antonio Ay, was executed, but this only spurred other village *batabob* into action. Once the revolt began Valladolid was cut off from Mérida and besieged, until in March 1848 the order was given to evacuate the 10,000 people left in the town up the road north to Espita. Once on the road they were easy prey to Maya guerrillas, and the withdrawal from Valladolid was the greatest catastrophe suffered by *ladino* Yucatán in the entire war.

After the Mayas' inexplicable failure to achieve final victory Valladolid, deserted, stripped and looted, was reoccupied in 1849. The Yucatán state legislature awarded it the title of *Ciudad Heroica*, which the town crest retains to this day, despite the fact that much of the current population is as likely to be descended from besiegers as besieged. In 1910 a last glimmer of the belligerent past surfaced when 1,500 Maya peasants briefly took over Valladolid, in a revolt locals often proudly describe as 'the first spark of the Mexican Revolution'. Since the Revolution, events in Valladolid have been less spectacular, and today it seems one of the best organized of Yucatán towns.

The Plaza and Cenote Zací

Everything in Valladolid homes in on the plaza or **Parque Principal**, a classic Yucatán colonial square with its *confidenciales* love-seats, laurel trees, several *taco*-stands and a Franciscan cathedral, tall and plain on the south side. In 1999 the then-governor of the Yucatán Víctor Cervera Pacheco decided the historic old town wasn't quite historic-looking enough and gave the square and streets around it a Campeche-style refurbishment, with façades in pastel colours instead of the traditional whitewash, gothicky lettering on shop signs and so on. But, much of this 'makeover' has since become comfortably faded, and for the most part Valladolid is happy enough being itself rather than dressing up for tourists. The main **market** is east of the plaza (Calles 32 and 37); the busiest shopping time, unusually, is Sunday morning. The Parque Principal has been colonized by souvenir stores, but C. 39 either side of the square is much more local, alive with crowds, bikes, buses and shops. One block west at the corner of C. 44 is the semi-official **Mercado de Artesanías** (craft market).

The plaza's railings are lined with *huípiles* and other embroidery that Mayan women from surrounding villages hope to sell to occupants of the tourist buses that turn up each morning from Cancún. Valladolid is a centre for *huípil* embroidery; there's even a rather cute statue of a lady in a *huípil* emerging from the fountain in the middle of the plaza. On the square's north side is another small handicrafts centre, the **Bazar**, but the goods on show are less interesting than the cheap restaurants in its patio.

Valladolid has some of the finest colonial church architecture in the Yucatán. The Cathedral of **San Servacio**, begun in the 17th century and finished in the 18th, is tall and white, with delicate twin towers. Beside it, the sides of the square are sheltered by deep, whitewashed colonnaded porticoes. On the east side is the colonial-style **Ayuntamiento** or town hall, which has a pretty patio; above it, one can see the plain 19th-century council chamber, while on the stairs there is a monument to the original Spanish settlers of the city in 1545. Behind the Ayuntamiento on the same block, a short walk along C. 41, the church of San Roque now houses the

Museo de San Roque
open daily 9–9; contributions requested

Museo de San Roque, an engaging local museum that makes the most of its setting. Highlights of its displays are fine ceramics and other artefacts from Ek-Balam; from later eras there are fascinating documents on the *conquistador* founders of Valladolid and 17th-century pirate raids, as well as thorough exhibits on colonial rural society and Maya folk traditions. However, it's only labelled in Spanish.

Cenote Zací
open daily 8–6; adm; swimming not permitted

In the middle of town, occupying the block between Calles 37, 39, 34 and 36, is an extraordinary natural attraction, the **Cenote Zací**. This was the original water source of Maya Zací and the early settlement of Valladolid. It's now a park, and steps lead down into the cavern mouth, at the top of which is a bar/restaurant and an underused crafts market. It's a huge, dramatic sinkhole, with fascinating patterns of light, even if the water is now grubby with algae.

San Bernardino Sisal

San Bernardino Sisal
Officially open Wed–Mon 8–12 and 5–7; outside service times a small adm fee may be charged; alternatively, the church may simply be left open.

Two blocks west of the plaza on C. 41, a narrow street unusually cuts off to the left diagonally across the grid. Officially C. 41-A, when Valladolid was repainted it was given the rather fake-old name *Calzada de los Frailes*, 'Friars' Pathway'. It is, though, one of the most charming old colonial streets in the town, and leads to the *barrio* of Sisal and the finest of Valladolid's colonial monuments, the monastery and church of San Bernardino de Siena. Begun in 1552, San Bernardino is the oldest permanent church – rather than a *capilla de indios* – in the Yucatán. As in the monasteries at Maní and Izamal, the work was supervised by the Franciscans' ever-energetic architect Friar Juan de Mérida. The location of the massive, fortress-like convent outside the town was due in part to the presence of a good *cenote*, but also to the fact that it had two functions: catering to the Spanish population of Valladolid, and acting as a missionary convent for the Maya villages around them. This was reflected in a unique feature of Sisal, that the open altar of the *capilla de indios*, rather than being placed alongside the monastery chapel as at Maní, was built on to the side of the church, facing south, so that the two groups could worship without coming into contact (the remains of the Indian chapel can be seen if you walk round to the right, from the main entrance).

The monastery was closed, and San Bernardino made into a simple parish church, as long ago as 1755. It has been extensively restored and, in line with other changes in Valladolid, the blockhouse-like façade has been unhistorically part-painted in white and yellow. It's an unusual, slab-fronted building, with the giant limestone columns of the frontal gallery giving it a distinctly medieval appearance. Inside, the highlight is a giant altarpiece in polychrome wood, a combination of high Baroque and a Mexican sense of colour. On the left-hand side a door leads to a two-storey cloister of massive stone colonnades, housing a beautiful garden full of giant palms. There is also a four-square 'well' dating from 1613, which was built over the mouth of the natural *cenote*.

East of San Bernardino, at Calles 40 and 49, is another fine 17th-century church, **San Juan**, with a twin-spired façade and a bougainvillaea-filled garden. A fuller tour of Valladolid's colonial churches includes the **Candelaria**, on a lovely square at Calles 44 and 35, **Santa Ana** – a missionary chapel – at 34 and 41, and **Santa Lucía**, at 42 and 27.

(i) **Ayuntamiento** *(town hall), in the arcades on the east side of Parque Principal, corner of C. 40 and C. 41 (open Mon–Sat 9–8.30, Sun 9–12 noon). A useful website is www.valladolidyucatan. com.*

Services in Valladolid

t (985–)

Banks: Two on the plaza with ATMs.

Internet Access and Phone Offices: Several internet shops around the square or on C. 39.

Police Station: In the town hall; the post office is alongside.

Shopping

Coqui Coqui Perfumes, Residence & Spa, Calzada de los Frailes (C. 41A) no. 207, t 856 5129,*www.coquicoquispa. com.* International chic comes to Valladolid: Argentinian model Nicolas Malleville first set up here to make and sell rare handmade perfumes, but has gradually added a day spa, a cool tea room nearby (the **Café de los Frailes**) and very seductive **guest rooms** *(luxury).*

Yalat Galería de Arte Mexicano, C. 39, corner C. 40 (on the Parque Principal), t 856 1969. Irrestistible, must-see little shop on the plaza with a brilliantly colorful display of Day-of-the-Dead materials, jewellery and other fine Mexican craftwork. It has the same owners as **Maruja** café *(see p.220).*

Where to Stay in Valladolid

Valladolid is one of the best places to find good value rooms in central Yucatán, as well as a handy base for visiting Chichén Itzá .

Moderate

Casa Hamaca, C. 49 no. 202, x 40, t 856 5287, *www.casahamaca.com.* Very charming B&B opened by American Denis Larsen, with eight beautiful rooms and suites including one with full disabled access. Massages and other spa treatments are available, and help is given to guests to make the most of their stay. Or, you can just enjoy the garden and the small pool.

Casa Quetzal, C. 51 no. 218, x 50 & 52, t 856 4796, *www.casa-quetzal.com.* A gem of a small hotel with seven rooms around a garden-patio, with a pool, in a quiet street near San Bernardino Sisal. Rooms are well-equipped and charmingly decorated, and a range of

(★) **Casa Quetzal** >

spa services are available. Prices are only in this band in the December–April peak season; at other times they go down to *inexpensive.*

Ecotel Quinta Regia, C. 40 no. 160-A, x 27 & 29, t 856 3472, *www.ecotel quintaregia.com.mx.* Valladolid's smartest hotel, with 112 rooms and suites, six blocks north of the Parque Principal. Though only a few years old it was built in neo-colonial style, combining traditional décor with modern comforts. The 'eco' tag means mainly that it's rustic-looking, but it does have exuberant gardens, with orchards that supply all fruit and herbs used in the hotel. There's also a pretty pool and tennis courts, and **El Mexicano** restaurant *(see p.220).*

Hacienda San Miguel, 8km west of Valladolid on the Dzitas–Izamal road, t 858 1539, *sanmiguel@hotmail.com.* A distinctive alternative. Similaritics between this venerable place and luxury *haciendas* are mainly architectural: until recently it was purely a farm, and it still has the feel of a working ranch, with plenty of cattle. There are eight big *cabañas,* each sleeping up to four, with roof fans and shady porches, and two plainer rooms in the main house with a/c. It has a pool, verandahs and a lovely terrace for breakfast and other meals, and you can rent horses or bikes for exploring the estate.

El Mesón del Marqués, C. 39 no. 203, x 40 & 42, t 856 2073, *www.meson delmarques.com.* Not as spick and span as the Quinta Regia, but the town's most historic hotel has much more charm (and lower prices). It's in an old colonial house on the plaza, with **restaurant** *(see p.220)* and lounge areas spread through flower-decked patios, and a pool in a garden. Rooms all have a/c, fans and cable TV, and are all quite bright; some have balconies overlooking the garden.

Hotel María de la Luz, C. 42 no. 193, x 39 & 41, t 856 1181, *www.mariadela luzhotel.com.* Hard to miss on one side of the Parque Principal, this hotel scores best for its ample patio, attractive **restaurant** *(see p.220)* and nice pool. The rooms are less striking, and some are a bit dark, but all have decent bathrooms, a/c and TV, and it's good value.

Hotel San Clemente, C. 42 no. 206, x 41 & 43, t 856 2208, *www.hotelsan clemente.com.mx*. On a corner just off the plaza, this is one of Valladolid's best-known hotels, with a pool, a restaurant, and TV and now a/c in all rooms. Some of its rooms could be better cared for, but the upper-floor ones get lots of light.

Hotel Zací, C. 44 no. 191, x 37 & 39, t 856 2167. A popular option at the bottom of this price bracket, a block west of the plaza, with pool, TV, a/c in some rooms and parking. Choose upper floors for more light and views of the cathedral, lower floors for a/c.

Budget

Albergue La Candelaria, C. 35, no. 201-F, x 42 & 44, t 856 2267, *candelaria_ hostel@hotmail.com*. A very well-run modern hostel, a lot brighter than many budget hotels, with dorm beds for around $7 or double rooms, sharing showers. Breakfast and locker use are included, and there's an attractive patio and lounge area, with TV, free water and coffee, and internet access. It's on a lovely little square, Parque de La Candelaria, two blocks north of the plaza.

'Negro' Aguilar, C. 44 no. 195, x 39 & 41, t 856 2125. As well as renting bikes (*see* p.215), El Negro has basic rooms, with fans and showers, in a former school a few blocks from the centre (go to the shop to make contact). Double rooms are around $10, or less for longer stays; they're simple but big, and some even have a/c. Amazingly, they also have access to a pool, a basketball court and a patio for hammock-lounging and cooking up barbecues. Your host and his family are ultra-helpful, and will drive guests to the bus station or set up their own 'tours'.

Eating Out in Valladolid

Valladolid has its own prized specialities within Yucatecan cuisine, above all *pollo oriental de Valladolid* (roast chicken with a sauce of chillies, garlic and bitter oranges) and *lomitos de Valladolid* (diced pork with chilli, garlic and tomatoes).

Moderate

Las Campanas, C. 41, corner of 42. Attractively atmospheric restaurant on a corner of the plaza, with a full range of local specialities, and (occasional) live music.

Hotel María de la Luz, C. 42 no. 193, x 37 & 39. Not as traditionally pretty as the Mesón del Marqués, but its patio is still a very pleasant place to eat, with enjoyable Yucatecan and local dishes, and good seafood.

El Mesón del Marqués, C. 39 no. 203, x 40 & 42. This very pretty hotel patio-restaurant is the classic place to eat in town, and home to a highly regarded version of *pollo oriental*.

El Mexicano, Ecotel Quinta Regia, C. 40 no. 160-A, x 27 & 29. Less atmospheric than the places right on the plaza, but pretty, and with a varied menu of Mexican, Yucatecan and international (Italian-oriented) food.

Yepez II, C. 41 no. 148. Off the plaza opposite the Museo de San Roque, with high-quality *tacos*, steaks and other Mexican, rather than Yucatecan, dishes served out in a garden.

Budget

Best for a cheap meal are the 20 or so open-air *cocinas económicas* around a kind of food court in the Bazar handicrafts market on the plaza, next to the Mesón del Marqués. They offer everything from Yucatecan traditional dishes to *burritos* and *enchiladas*.

La Casa del Café, C. 44, x 35 (Parque de la Candelaria). Laid-back little café opposite Albergue La Candelaria, with terrace tables and a good choice of coffees, juices, snacks and sandwiches.

Maruja, C. 41, by C. 40 (on the Parque Principal). Pretty little café on the Parque, under the same ownership as Yalat craft shop nearby (*see* p.219), which sells coffee, jams and other products made in nearby villages.

La de Michoacán, C. 41, x 42 & 44. An ice-cream stand, bakery and restaurant that's a backpackers' favourite, with bargain set meals.

Los Portales, C. 41, corner of 40. Atmospheric place from which to survey the plaza, with a terrace across the street from the tourist office, fine for breakfast or substantial Yucatecan dishes.

Entertainment

Some of the best local entertainment is free, at weekends. On Sunday evenings the plaza fills up with families, couples and bunches of kids, and at 7.30pm every week the Banda del Ayuntamiento gives a free concert, playing Latin American favourites – rumbas, stately Mexican *danzón*, Yucatecan *boleros*, cha-cha-cha – and sometimes even big-band jazz.

Cenote Dzitnup and Cenote Samula

⭐ Cenote Dzitnup
open daily 8–5; adm

One of the most spectacular of Yucatán *cenotes* lies only 7km west of Valladolid. It's most widely known as **Cenote Dzitnup**, although Yucatec *dzitnup* is the word that gave rise to the Spanish *cenote*, so this means nothing more than 'Cenote-Cenote'; in Maya it's ungraciously called the *Cenote Xkeken* or 'Pig Cenote'.

At the entrance, you can begin to wonder where the *cenote* has gone, as the way in is down a narrow ramp and still narrower passageway with room for one crouching person at a time (but steps and path are well kept, and easy to negotiate). Then, below, the passage suddenly opens up into a dramatic vision of the underworld, a cave of basilica-like proportions with a huge, arching roof filled with turquoise water; the thought occurs that, despite the Franciscans' best efforts, the *cenotes* and caverns are the true cathedrals of the Yucatán. A hole in the roof casts a shaft of light dead into the centre of the pool, creating a wonderful contrast of light and shade. A small stepped area leads down to a muddy 'beach', or you can swim directly from the rocks. The water is clear, clean and deliciously cool; few can resist swimming into the shaft of light, while all around strange forms of rock hang into and rise out of the pool.

Cenote Samula
open daily 8–5; adm

When the main *cenote* is crowded, there is another sinkhole on the other side of the road into Dzitnup, **Cenote Samula**. Though not quite as dramatic, it's still spectacular, with the roots of a huge *ceiba* tree stretching straight down from the surface some 40ft to the precious water below, a vivid image of the mystical powers that the Maya attributed to these trees. There's also a little landing stage, for easy swimming.

09

Yucatán State | Cenote Dzitnup and Cenote Samula

Visiting Dzitnup and Samula

Cenote Dzitnup is easy to find down a turn 5km from Valladolid off the Mérida road, just before Dzitnup village. *Colectivos* run there from C. 44, x 39 & 41. Alternatively, take an eastbound second-class bus to the Dzitnup turn and walk the last 2km, or hire a bike (*see* p.215). It's an easy 20 minute ride to the *cenote* along Valladolid's cycle tracks. At the entrance, there's a car park, a restaurant and a few handicrafts stalls. Dzitnup gets busy on Sundays, when it serves as Valladolid's swimming hole, and around 11am to noon daily tours from Cancún pass through (though they're not usually allowed time to swim). Cenote Samula, on the other side of the same entry road, is ignored by most coach parties, so you're more likely to have it to yourself.

If you swim, your feet get muddy when you get out, so bear this in mind when choosing footwear.

Ek-Balam

A little-known jewel of the Maya world, Ek-Balam is one of the ruined cities where recent excavations – begun only in 1998 – have produced extraordinary results, in the shape of some of the finest of all Maya sculpture. It's also one of the most unusual, with an architectural and sculptural style that seem entirely of its own.

Ek-Balam has one of the longest records of occupation in the northern Yucatán, from the Preclassic, about 100 BC, right up until the Conquest. The name means 'black jaguar', and a Spanish land grant of 1579 relates that the settlement was founded by a 'great lord' also called Ek-Balam, a story that must have come from the local Maya. It appears to have grown into a significant city above all in the Terminal Classic, around 700–950. Many of its most impressive structures were built very late, after 800, in or around the time of a powerful ruler called Ukit-Kan-Lek-Tok, whose tomb has been the most dramatic discovery of all. The grandeur of Ek-Balam's buildings indicate that it was a powerful, wealthy community, and there is much speculation as to how much of this wealth came from the control of salt beds near Río Lagartos. Like other northern cities it 'collapsed' politically around 950, but seems to have been partly inhabited throughout the Postclassic and pre-Conquest eras. In modern times it was first explored by Desiré Charnay in 1886, but was scarcely excavated until the 1990s.

The excavated site covers only the ceremonial core of Ek-Balam. The whole city covered a much wider area, and in 1987 *sacbé* roads were discovered stretching out 2km in every direction. One feature of central Ek-Balam is apparent as you approach: its compactness, contained within a perimeter wall. It is not clear whether this was purely to mark off the 'official' area or whether it was also for defence. Superficially it can seem similar to the wall at Becán (*see* p.362), but Ek-Balam's internal layout is different again. Within the wall are massive, rectangular temple-platforms around quadrangle-like plazas, giving a more inward-looking feel than most Maya squares.

You enter the ruins along an impressively ramp-like *sacbé*, facing north. Unmissable as you go through the gap in the wall are two of Ek-Balam's most enigmatic structures. The first is a unique **four-sided arch** that looks as if it served as a kind of ceremonial entrance over the *sacbé*. To the right of it is the **Palacio Oval** ('Oval Palace', also known as *La Redonda*), a semi-spiral-shaped round tower that from this angle looks more Middle Eastern than Maya. In place of the square symmetries of Maya platforms it seems made up of a series of round drums of different sizes and even at different angles, an almost abstract combination of interlocking shapes and spaces. Why it was built this way is a mystery. Relics of

Visiting Ek-Balam

Ek-Balam is reached via a right turn off the Highway 295 Tizimín road, about 18km north of Valladolid. From there, a narrow road leads 10km to the site, and the village of Ek-Balam. *Colectivos* run to Ek-Balam from Valladolid, and it's included in a growing number of tours from Mérida and the Riviera.

wealthy burials, including one of a child, have been found here, and it may have been used in astronomical ceremonies. From the *Redonda* or the arch you get a good view of the layout of Ek-Balam's squares, with the smallest below you. Beyond it to the left, sideways-on, is the first of the three huge platforms that form the main plaza, **Structure 2**, in one corner of which a large temple is being excavated. Forming a boundary between the squares is a **Ball Court**. A date found here indicates it was completed in 841, and other discoveries have included some stone balls (now in the Mérida museum) possibly used in the game.

Dominating the view, though, and filling the whole north side of the main plaza is the looming mountain known as **Structure 1** or the **Acropolis**, the part of Ek-Balam most dramatically transformed by recent excavations. Until 1998 it was an indistinct mound; today it has been revealed to be a multi-level palace and temple complex, similar to the Five Storeys at Edzná. Climbing up the middle there is a typically awe-inspiring, steep stairway, either side of which are temples with long Puuc-style friezes with stucco inscriptions and doorways leading into unusually deep chambers. The unique discovery is the temple three-quarters of the way up on the left, now sheltered beneath an equally huge *palapa* roof, and called **El Trono** ('The Throne'). It is believed to have contained the tomb of Ukit-Kan-Lek-Tok, clearly a major figure in Ek-Balam's history. Astonishingly complete, this is the largest, best-restored and most theatrical of Maya monster-mouth temple entrances, but one that stands on its own since, while in the more common Chenes style monster-elements run all around the entrance, here a giant-toothed jaw actually forms the floor of the doorway. Around it there are superbly modelled, unidentifed figures that rate among the finest Maya carving, and, either side of the 'mouth', traces of painted decoration are just visible. The seated figure above the doorway, who has lost his head, is believed to be Ukit-Kan-Lek-Tok himself. Beyond the *Trono* there is a large raised plaza, which filled the western end of the Acropolis.

From the top of the Acropolis you also get the usual fabulous view, and can pick out more *sacbés* and unexcavated platforms on the surrounding plain. You also get a good view of the Puuc-like residential buildings on top of Structure 2, and **Structure 3** on the east side of the main plaza. Another small plaza is beyond Structure 3. Back at ground level, **Structure 17**, which forms one side of this

Where to Stay and Eat at Ek-Balam

t (985–)

Dolce...mente Ek-Balam, t 103 6073, *www.dolcementeekbalam.com* (*inexpensive*). The Yucatán is full of surprises, and one of them is that the owners of an Italian restaurant in Cancún have decided to set up here in Ek-Balam village, opening a pleasant modern hotel with spacious, light rooms with excellent modern facilities. The restaurant offers Italian food of a rare quality in a Maya village.

Genesis Ek-Balam, t 852 7980, *www. genesisretreat.com* (*inexpensive*). A very enterprising 'ecocultural' and sustainable tourism project a short walk from the ruins at Ek-Balam village. Within an ultra-mellow garden there are comfortable *cabañas* and cabin-sized tents; additional comforts include solar-powered showers and a chemical-free pool. You can easily just laze in the garden and watch the tame parrots, but Genesis also encourages cultural exchange with locals, and activities on offer include informal introductions to Maya culture, language, cooking, medicine or local plant life, with 'guides' from the village; also available are massage and *temazcal* sweat baths, bikes to rent and an individual range of tours, including nature and bird-watching trips. A variety of special sessions and retreats is organized through the year. There is also a mellow, palm-shaded **restaurant**, with a healthy mix of vegetarian and local fare, in snacks or larger meals (*restaurant open daily 8–6; budget*).

plaza by the Ball Court, is known as **Las Gemelas**, 'The Twins', because of its pair of near-identical small temples. **Structure 10** on the east flank of this square is a wide platform with a raised plaza. The base dates from the Late Classic, but the structures on top were built much later, after 1200. On a platform in the middle of the plaza is an impressively clear carved stela – rare in northern Yucatán – believed to show King Ukit-Kan-Lek-Tok. One last square, the southwest plaza, sits below Structure 2. It seems far older than most of the city, with a simple, rounded style reminiscent of Classic cities further south.

Chichén Itzá

✪ Chichén Itzá
Open daily 8–5; adm

Chichén Itzá is the most famous of all the great Maya cities. This is a little ironic, for its most imposing buildings are not at all typical of Classic Maya architecture, and show strong influences from non-Maya central Mexico (just how much is one of the great debates). It is also the most visited site, by some way; in 2007, after a global online poll (in which every patriotic Mexican was urged to vote for their candidate) it was made one of the 'New Seven Wonders of the World', which may contribute to still more tour buses arriving every day. Because of the visitor numbers, there is less and less of Chichén that you're actually allowed to climb on or examine close-up, which used to be one of the best parts of any visit. Ruins fans have much more fun at more open sites, that you can actually explore. This does not mean, though, that Chichén Itzá is no longer worth visiting; other Maya sites may have more subtle architecture, but the combination of giant scale, monumentality and mysterious, precise astronomical calculation in the buildings of Chichén make it truly awe-inspiring.

History

Nothing has sparked off more argument among archaeologists and investigators of the Maya than Chichén Itzá. Until around 1980 it was widely stated with confidence that there had been three successive 'occupations' of Chichén: one that was purely Maya, in the Terminal Classic; one by an illiterate non-Mayan people called the Toltecs, who migrated to the Yucatán from central Mexico in about 1000 and built the largest part of the city (often called 'Toltec-Maya'); and another by the still less cultured Itzá in about 1200. Links between them were never clear, and it was sometimes suggested they were entirely separate, and even that the city had been abandoned in the interim. It is clear that Chichén at its peak was far less publicly 'literate' than the Classic cities of the south, and in particular did not erect stelae or many glyph-inscribed monuments (one reason why unravelling its history has been particularly difficult). Architecturally the most spectacular buildings at Chichén have a style of their own that is definitely related to those of central Mexico, and distinct from older Maya styles. However, recent research has shown that the great 'Toltec' structures at Chichén, such as the pyramid known as the High Priest's Grave, were built in the mid-9th century, within a few years of clearly 'Maya' buildings nearby like the Casa Colorada. At the same time, Maya glyphs have been found on Toltec buildings. Few now believe it possible to draw a line in time or space between the different occupiers of Chichén. Instead, it appears that Chichén Itzá – in contrast to its great rival, purely Maya Cobá – was always a hybrid, 'cosmopolitan' community, inhabited simultaneously by a mix of peoples from different parts of Mesoamerica.

Discussion is ongoing, and even the 'Toltec-Maya' theory still has its defenders, but in the most widely shared current view Chichén Itzá emerged as a significant city around 700, as a result of the convergence of several groups in northern Yucatán, driven there by a series of crises in other parts of Mesoamerica. In about 650 the giant central-Mexican capital of Teotihuacán had disintegrated, and it is likely some 'refugees' from this collapse migrated towards the Yucatán. With them, according to another theory, came the Putún Maya of Tabasco, who had long been a link between the Maya world and central Mexico. In Yucatecan chronicles recorded after the Spanish Conquest the founders of Chichén Itzá (meaning 'well of the Itzá') were always identified as a group of 'foreigners', the Itzá. Some say the Putún and the Itzá were one and the same, but it has also been argued that the new arrivals came north from the other region associated with this name, around Lake Petén-Itzá in Guatemala, and may have been refugees from Tikal and its ally-cities who had lost out in the 7th-century Petén wars with Calakmul.

Getting to Chichén Itzá

Chichén Itzá is just south of the Highway 180 Mérida–Cancún road, 120km from Mérida, 42km from Valladolid, and 200km from Cancún. **Pisté**, which has a **petrol/gas station**, is 1½km (an easy walk before the sun gets high) to the west of the ruins.

Pisté's little **bus** station is on the main street, near the Pirámide Inn. There are three direct **first-class** buses daily to/from **Mérida** (1½hrs; fare $7) and one to/from **Cancún** (3¼hrs; $12). Routes generally run to Pisté from morning to midday, from Pisté in the afternoons. There are also one or two first-class buses daily to **Cobá, Tulum** and **Playa del Carmen**.

Second-class services are far more numerous, with buses in each direction along Highway 180 every 30mins 7am–5.30pm (towards Mérida) and 8.30am–6.30pm (to Valladolid and Cancún). There's also a daily bus to Cobá, Tulum and Playa. One way to cut journey times is to take a first-class bus to Valladolid, and then second-class on to Pisté. Second-class buses drop passengers at the Chichén ruins entrance, as well as in Pisté. Plenty of local **taxis** and *combis* also run up and down between Pisté and the ruins.

There is a fully fledged Chichén Itzá **airport** at Kauá, 10km towards Valladolid. However, this flight of fancy is now only used for pricey day trips from Cozumel or Playa del Carmen.

At the same time, the founders of Chichén also included people who were clearly fully situated within more traditional Yucatán Maya culture. As well as the square-cut 'Toltec' pyramids there are many entirely Maya buildings in the city, and carved inscriptions with Long Count dates, confined to a relatively short time from 832 to 909. Over time, Chichén Itzá moved further away from Classic Maya culture, leaving behind the Long Count calendar as well as other earlier traditions. However, it retained others, and instead of the city being 'illiterate' throughout the Postclassic period, Maya glyphs seem to have still been used in bark manuscripts. Rather than an entirely foreign body, Chichén appears as an adaptation within Maya civilization.

Chichén Itzá, though, differed from Classic Maya cities in other ways besides its heterogeneity. Nowhere in the city is there a single image glorifying an *ahau* ruler and his lineage, the primary theme of carvings at Palenque or Yaxchilán. Instead, Chichén has representations of large groups of people of the same size and so, presumably, the same status: lines of seated lords on the Temple of the Chac-Mool, hundreds of carved figures in the Temple of the Warriors. The few deciphered inscriptions refer to several lineages, with no clear sense of precedence. This fits in with the image of Chichén as a 'new' city created by diverse groups, none of their leaders willing to grant any of the others superiority. Instead of being ruled by a hereditary *ahau*, Chichén had a complex system of government called a *multepal*, in which authority was shared between the heads of several lineages. This emphasis on the collective is also seen in the giant scale of Chichén's public spaces, as ceremonies must have involved huge numbers of people. Another consequence of Chichén's collective orientation was its style of sacrifice. Early idealizers of the Maya believed it was the Toltecs who introduced human sacrifice into pacific Maya cities, but this has been shown to be thoroughly mistaken. What there

Visiting Chichén Itzá

Many people visit Chichén on coach trips from Cancún, with a standard 1½hrs at the ruins, and it can be taken in as a stop-off along the road. However, it's far better to stay overnight. Get to the ruins early, to avoid the crowds and the heat. To see them at all well requires at least a whole morning (buy water in Pisté; facilities at the site are expensive). Most tour groups arrive around 11am, and are less noticeable after 2pm. Due to increasing visitor numbers many sections, sadly, are now closed off for conservation reasons.

The **admission ticket** now obligatorily includes the evening **Sound and Light Show**, which is why Chichén (and Uxmal) are more expensive than other Mayan sites (around $8.50 per person, plus $1 per car for parking).

At the main (western) entrance there is a **visitor centre** with **restaurant, shops**, and the **museum**; by the big hotels is another entrance with limited facilities. Handicraft-sellers are all over the site, and there is a handicrafts mall in the visitor centre. The centre stays open for the Sound and Light show to 9–10pm (*see* p.238). At the entrances official **guides** can be hired, who give 1½–2hr tours for about $35.

does appear to have been is a difference in scale: whereas in cities under one *ahau* the sacrifice of a few noble captives was often sufficient, ceremonies at Chichén seem to have demanded the killing of large numbers.

Chichén Itzá's period of glory was relatively short – about 800 to 1000 – but the *multepal* system gave it great collective strength, and in that time it was pre-eminent across northern Yucatán. Much has been learnt about Chichén from excavations at Yaxuná, 20km to the south. This was the main western vassal of Cobá, and was massively reinforced in around 800 to resist the expansion of the new city (*see* p.207). The conquest of Yaxuná around 860 was the prelude to a decisive victory for Chichén over Cobá, leaving it with few rivals. Like other Mayan cities it was a sprawling place, extending over 30 square km. It traded widely, and precious materials – turquoise, gold – have been found here from as far afield as modern New Mexico and Colombia. On the coast at Isla Cerritos, near Río Lagartos, the rulers of Chichén built the most sophisticated harbour in the Maya world, from where they controlled the salt trade.

Nevertheless the effects of the Collapse still reached Chichén, around 950. Unlike other cities such as Uxmal it never seems to have undergone a clear 'collapse', but no major buildings were erected after 1000, and its size and wealth evidently dwindled. According to the Yucatecan chronicles some kind of Chichén state survived until the 1190s, when a ruler called Chak-Xib-Chak was expelled from Chichén by a lord of Mayapán. Nor was it ever completely abandoned, for Bishop Landa wrote that at the time of the Conquest the great *cenote* of Chichén, with Cozumel, was still one of the great pilgrimage centres of the Yucatán. In 1532 Montejo el Mozo briefly occupied the ruins, and tried to make them a Spanish fortress. Due to its size and location Chichén was never

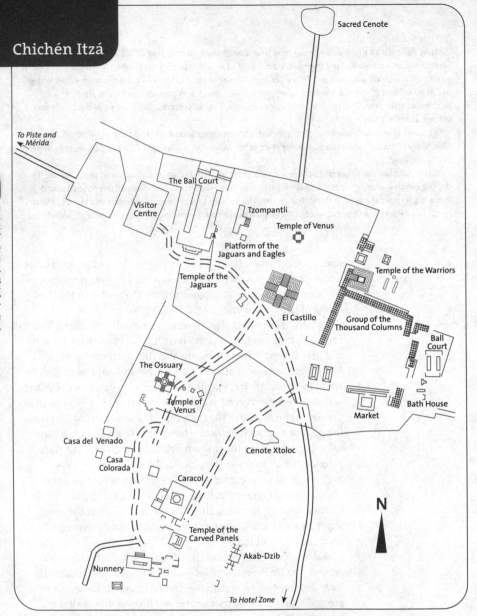

Sacred Cenote

To Piste and Mérida

The Ball Court

Visitor Centre

Tzompantli

Temple of Venus

Platform of the Jaguars and Eagles

Temple of the Jaguars

Temple of the Warriors

El Castillo

Group of the Thousand Columns

Ball Court

The Ossuary

Temple of Venus

Bath House

Market

Casa del Venado

Casa Colorada

Cenote Xtoloc

Caracol

Temple of the Carved Panels

Akab-Dzib

Nunnery

To Hotel Zone

N

entirely forgotten, and did not need to be 'discovered'. Stephens and Catherwood made the first serious examination of the site in 1842. In the early 1900s the US Consul in Mérida, Edward Thompson, bought the estate around the ruins for $100 and began excavations by trying to dredge the Sacred Cenote, an operation for which he has since been sorely criticized. Chichén Itzá was the first Maya city to be systematically excavated, by Morley and the Carnegie Institution, beginning in 1923.

The Castillo and the Ball Court

As you enter the site from the visitor centre you come over a slight rise, the remains of a wall that ran around the centre of Chichén. Given its small size it does not appear to have had any defensive purpose, but formed the boundary of the ceremonial core of the city. Straight ahead of you is the great plaza, and just to the right the giant bulk of the great pyramid, **El Castillo**, also known as the Pyramid of Kukulcán. This is now established as a standard image of a Maya pyramid – and a symbol of the Yucatán – but its severe geometry is, in fact, very central-Mexican. Its square, symmetrical plan, with steps on all four sides rather than the one giant stairway of most Maya pyramids, is reminiscent of buildings at the original Toltec city of Tula, or Teotihuacán.

The pyramid is actually a giant representation in stone of the *haab* calendar. It is made up of nine flat, square levels. Each side is divided by a massive staircase, making the number of terraces visible on each side 18, the number of months in the *haab* year. Worked into the slab sides of the terraces are lines of flat panels – all originally painted, like the rest of the pyramid – which add up to 52, the number of years in the Calendar Round. The number of steps in each staircase is 91, which with the one step to the temple at the top totals 365, the number of days in the year. Most extraordinary of all is the famous phenomenon known as the 'Descent of Kukulcán' (*see* 'The Descent of Kukulcán', p.232).

Nowadays, you have to observe the Castillo from behind a wire at the bottom, rather than climbing up between the two serpent-tails that flank the majestic north stairway. This makes it harder to appreciate the pervasive cosmological layout – easily apparent from the top – that Chichén Itzá shares with all Mayan cities, with a sacred mountain (the Castillo) facing sacred space (the plaza) leading to power points and entrances to the underworld (the Sacred Cenote, the Ball Court).

On the top of the Castillo – still just possible to see from below – there is a squat, square temple, with a portico on the north side leading to an inner sanctum. The two columns of the main entrance are more plumed serpents, with heads at the bottom and hook-shaped rattle-tails at the top. Like much of 'Toltec' Chichén, this temple is an ingenious combination of different architectural traditions. Central-Mexican peoples made great use of multiple square columns, but the only roofs they used had been timber frames supporting flat stones or palms; the Maya, meanwhile, had developed their characteristic V-shaped arch, but only used it directly on top of walls, producing distinctive narrow rooms. In the Chichén Itzá synthesis, Maya pointed vaults were placed on top of square columns and wooden beams, a combination that made possible much larger spaces, even though it was not ultimately

09

Yucatán State | Chichén Itzá

stable (which is why so few of the roofs from Chichén's columned buildings have survived).

The Castillo of Kukulcán was probably given its final form in the late 9th century, and appears massively solid. It is, though, really a casing, for inside it, in the common Maya pattern, a smaller pyramid was discovered. This has usually been dated to a century earlier, but one theory is that the new pyramid was built precisely 52 years after the first one, to mark the ending of a Calendar Round. The temple of the first pyramid, reached via an extremely steamy staircase from the top, is another part of Chichén that usually can no longer be visited. It contains, however, one of the most famous of the city's sculptures, a large Chac-mool, the characteristic Chichén reclining figure with its head looking fixedly sideways towards anyone approaching, and its hands apparently forming a flat space on its belly where offerings – the hearts and heads of sacrificial victims, and jewels and rich feathers – were placed. The posture of the Chac-mool, like that of the dying Pakal depicted on his tomb-lid in Palenque, represents a figure descending into the underworld. Also in the temple is an altar called the **Throne of the Red Jaguar**, a red-painted stone jaguar inlaid with jade roundels, sacred mirrors and bone teeth.

Across the plaza from the Castillo is the equally monumental great **Ball Court**. Formally 'dedicated' in rituals held in 864, this is the largest ball court anywhere in Mesoamerica, and radically different from the smaller, sloping-sided courts of Classic Maya sites or even the seven other ball courts at Chichén. It has great, vertical slab walls 160m long, on top of low, slope-sided base platforms and with two huge stone rings halfway along each side that formed the 'goals' of the game. From the carved reliefs on the lower platforms it appears that in this central-Mexican-influenced form of the game there were seven players on each side. The giant size of the court is an indication of the extra importance given to the Ball Court at Chichén, as a portal to *Xibalba*. Built onto the court's southeast corner are two temples on top of each other, one facing the plaza and the one above it looking into the court, the Lower and Upper **Temples of the Jaguars**. They are some of the most densely carved buildings in the city, covered in elaborate images that place the founders of Chichén within the Maya creation myth, so that the city gains its energies from the first makers of men, First Father and First Mother. The door columns of the **lower temple** have intricate panels showing a series of still-unidentified men together with gods such as Sak Ixik, the mother of the Hero Twins, while inside there is an astonishing carved mural of the foundation of the city in semi-mythological form. The **upper Temple** – also usually closed off – once contained an extraordinary series of painted murals on the history and triumphs of Chichén, which included some of the most vivid Mayan depictions of warfare. However, these murals, recorded in drawings in the 1900s, gradually became all-but invisible during the 20th century.

Inside the Ball Court, the carvings along the base are also of exceptional quality, many with monstrous images. Around each corner are sinuous feathered serpents, winding intricately for several metres, within which are extravagantly dressed figures of warriors, discs with mythical images and scenes of the ball game. It's a prime illustration of the Maya love of repetition, of the use of recurring motifs to create an unremitting visual rhythm. In each of the six panels one of the ball players is being beheaded, and of the seven snake-like spurts of blood from his neck one is being transformed into a flowering vine, a vivid image of the Maya idea of death (and so sacrifice) as an essential stage in the cycle of rebirth and new life. This beheading could also be, more directly, an illustration of the possible fate of losers in the game. One other feature of the ball court is its remarkable acoustics: echoes resound like a gunshot, and it's possible to hear a normal voice quite clearly from one end of the court to the other. This is just as enigmatic as the Descent of Kukulcán, for it must have been achieved deliberately, and presumably for a specific purpose.

The Tzompantli, Temple of Venus and the Sacred Cenote

Around the plaza there are several smaller structures. Alongside the Ball Court is the **Tzompantli**, a Nahua word meaning 'Wall of Skulls', one of the most gruesome shrines of Chichén's sacrificial cult. It's a low, T-shaped platform, 60m long, covered on all sides by rows of carved skulls, four deep, lightened by scenes of eagles devouring human hearts. Similar platforms are found in central Mexico. The heads of sacrificial victims were displayed here, as well as those of losers in the ball game. Next to it is the **Platform of the Jaguars and Eagles**, a small altar-platform with steps on each side and carved, as the name suggests, with images of these animals tearing open the chests of human victims to eat their hearts. This platform was probably associated with the military 'orders' of the Jaguars and Eagles, a tradition brought from central Mexico. Almost in the middle of the plaza is a similar but slightly bigger platform, the **Temple of Venus**. All these platforms probably served as 'stages' for ritual dances.

From the north side of the plaza a recently-widened white *sacbé*-style path leads through a gap in the perimeter wall for 300 metres to the great **Sacred Cenote** of Chichén. This is one of the essential stops on tours of the city, for this awesome well, 60m in diameter and 24m deep from the top to the level of the water, is one of the most spectacular natural phenomena in the Yucatán. The siting of Chichén, called 'the well of the Itzá', was almost certainly due to the

The Descent of Kukulcán

The main, north, staircase of the Castillo is lined by carved plumed serpents – an obsessive image in Chichén – leading down to giant serpent-heads at the bottom. On the spring and autumn equinoxes (21 Mar and 21 Sept) the afternoon sun coming round the corner of the pyramid exactly picks out the snake, which 'comes alive' – descending to finish at the head in March (when the effect is clearest), climbing up from it in September. The feathered serpents of Chichén are commonly associated with the mythical god-king Kukulcán, the Yucatecan form of the Teotihuacán god Quetzalcoatl, who was introduced from central Mexico some time around 900–1000 and had become a cult in the Yucatán by the time of the Spanish Conquest. However, they are just as likely to represent the vision serpents that in Mayan mythology had always formed the most direct conduit to the Otherworld. The descent of the sun represented as graphically as possible the community's contact with the heavens.

On the equinoxes the phenomenon begins around 4pm, and lasts about an hour. It's an astonishing demonstration of Maya astronomical, mathematical and building skills, and the lengths to which they were prepared to go in combining them. It's also very famous, and around 100,000 people go to Chichén for the spring equinox each year; admission is free for the day, and the authorities put on a programme of music, folkloric shows and so on to go with the event. For anyone who complains Chichén is now a Maya theme park, this is a day to avoid. The effect can also be seen for a shorter time and with smaller crowds in the weeks around the equinoxes, and is reproduced artificially every night of the year in the 'Sound and Light' show (see p.238).

presence of two large *cenotes*: one, the Xtoloc Cenote to the south, provided its main water supply, while the great *cenote* seems to have been used only for sacred ceremonies, as an opening into the underworld and the home of the rain god Chac.

On the south side of the great pit there is a small Toltec-style platform jutting over the water, and one of the eternal legends of the Sacred Cenote is that of the young virgins thrown off here as sacrificial victims. When Edward Thompson acquired Chichén in the 1900s one of the first things he did was to try to find the bottom of the *cenote* (it was reputed not to have one) and to dredge it. The bottom was reached (at about 13m, with a thick layer of mud beneath), and his and later explorations have produced some 4,000 objects that had been thrown into the *cenote* as ritual offerings, mostly in dry seasons to hasten the return of Chac. Among them were several human skeletons, both male and female, but these were outnumbered by a mass of other artefacts: jade and amber jewellery, ceramic pots and figurines, bells, animal bones, mirrors, and sculptures in alabaster and turquoise. Landa wrote that human sacrifices were thrown into the *cenote* only occasionally (with the belief that they did not die, but would be resurrected after three days), and a high proportion of small children suggests that some may have fallen in by accident. Among the relics there were pieces in gold and copper, which must have been imported from Mexico, Costa Rica or Panama. Few can be seen at Chichén; most of the objects found by Thompson and other early investigators were taken off to the Peabody Museum in Harvard or private collections, long before Mexican authorities got organized to stop it. Other finds are in the National Museum in Mexico City or in Mérida.

The Temple of the Warriors and the Thousand Columns

Heading back into the plaza from the Sacred Cenote, on the left stands the greatest creation of Chichén's 'Toltec-Maya' style, the **Temple of the Warriors** and the huge building complex alongside. This was one of the first major structures that was closed off to visitors, because at the top of the steps is another of the symbols of Chichén Itzá (reproduced in a million souvenirs), the figure of a Chac-mool between two columns, where tourists used to have their picture taken, placing their head on the spot where sacrificial victims were once laid. Sadly, no more. Many features of the temple at the top can, however, still be seen: it's a large, squat building with a Chichén-style vaulted roof that collapsed centuries ago.

The Temple of the Warriors takes its name from the dense rows of columns in front of it, each carved on all four sides with images of over 200 warriors and other figures. They are the foremost example of Chichén's preference for group, collective monuments, arranged in ceremonial groups as if in an eternally frozen procession. They do not simply depict generic images of warriors, for each carving is different, seeming to be a real, individual portrait. Most are warriors, some showing their wounds, but some are captives with bound wrists (to the right of the steps, looking towards them), while near the corner of the colonnade into the Thousand Columns is a line of priests, carrying offerings. Together they form a unique picture gallery that has been a vital source in reconstructing the history of Chichén Itzá.

At the south corner the warriors' pillars meet with still more long rows of columns, forming one side of the giant quadrangle called the **Group of the Thousand Columns**. As you wander past this forest of pillars – which like the Warriors once supported stone roof-vaults, in a huge colonnaded hall – you are not immediately aware of just how rambling it is. In place of the narrow, dark rooms of Classic Maya cities, the arch and column roof allowed the builders of Chichén Itzá to create spaces of a completely different size. These colonnade-halls (125m long on the north side of the Columns Group, 50m long by the Temple of the Warriors) fulfilled many other purposes as well as that of giant ceremonial spaces: public business, the settlement of disputes and buying and selling all went on between their well-shaded arcades.

When first constructed, like most buildings at Chichén they would have been painted in bright colours, predominantly red and blue, a very few faint traces of which can still be seen. There are also examples of fine carving. On the east side (furthest from the Temple of the Warriors) is the **Temple of the Sculptured Columns**, made up of individually carved square pillars like those of the Warriors', only in far worse condition. Forming the south side of the courtyard is the colonnade-fronted building known as the **Market**

(*El Mercado*), although no one has been able to demonstrate that this is really what it was. Next to it, in the far southeast corner of the courtyard, are the remains of a Maya **bathhouse**, built in a semi-Puuc style. These sweat-baths were regularly used in purification rituals before religious ceremonies. From the north side of the Columns quadrangle, a Maya-arched passageway leads to another small group of buildings outside the main colonnaded hall, one of them a small ball court.

The High Priest's Grave, the Casa Colorada and the Caracol

By the southwest corner of the Thousand Columns, near yet another ball court, you meet up again with the main path through the middle of Chichén Itzá, between the two entrances. By the rear of the Castillo a path runs off it to the south. On the right about 300m down this track is another pyramid, the **High Priest's Grave**, also known as the **Ossuary**. It is a smaller version of the Castillo, almost a prototype of the larger model. This building has been of major importance in forcing a reconsideration of the 'three stage' idea of Chichén's history, since despite being 'Toltec-Maya' in style it has a Long Count inscription dated 20 June 842, clearly within what had been seen as the 'Maya' period at Chichén. From the top there is a near-vertical shaft down to a natural cave at the base of the pyramid (*not open to visitors*), in which human remains were found with funeral offerings of jade, crystal and copper. It was clearly a tomb-chamber for high-ranking lords and priests of Chichén, hence its name.

The area south of the High Priest's Grave is what used to be thought of as 'Maya Chichén', separate from the Toltec city, but this division is no longer seen as valid (*see* above), and the buildings here now appear as one more element in an eclectic architectural mix. Most, however, are in a recognizably more Maya style than the Castillo and the buildings on the plaza.

The first substantial building you come to after the High Priest's Grave, right of the path, is the **Casa del Venado** ('Deer House'), so called because until the 1920s it was possible to see in one room a painted mural of a deer, now sadly lost. Just past it is the almost Puuc-style **Casa Colorada** ('Red House'), where it's still possible to see traces of the original red wall paint. Inside there is an antechamber and three small rooms and, though they're now very hard to see, some of the most extensive glyph inscriptions found at Chichén. They record that on 15 September 869 several lords of Chichén, among them two important figures named Kakupakal and Hun-Pik-Tok, took part in bloodletting rituals, presumably around the time the 'house' was built. Next to it there is another ball court, which may also have been connected with the building.

Across the path from here rises up the **Caracol** (the Snail) or **Observatory**, one of the most fascinating buildings of all at Chichén. It is a round drum-tower, on top of a large, low, two-level platform with side-temple attached. The whole structure was altered and added to over many centuries, and against all appearances large parts of the platforms were actually built after and around the main tower, not vice versa. It's now fairly well established that its first sections were built by 800. The lower stages of the tower are in a typically Maya style, with Puuc-style *atadura* mouldings between different levels topped by Chac masks. One other feature of the whole structure is that, in contrast with the symmetrical precision so common in Maya buildings, none of its parts – the approach staircases, the angles of the platforms – is aligned with each other, nor are they quite square.

The Caracol tower – which again you can only look at from outside – is one of those Maya buildings that seems incorrigibly obscure. Though often referred to as a spiral, it is really a series of concentric circles. The first 'room' is a very narrow outer corridor, with the remains of a vaulted roof; this connects through four entrances to a similar inner ring, from which another four entrances, not in line with the previous set, lead to the inner core. From here, a spiral staircase (the 'Snail') leads up to the upper level. Much of the small top-tower has collapsed, but in its sides there remain three window-slots. Sylvanus Morley showed that one points due south, a second towards the setting of the moon at the spring equinox (21 March), and a third, slightly wider slot points due west toward the setting of the sun on the spring and autumn equinoxes or, according to which side of it you stand to look from, the setting of the sun on the summer solstice (21 June). These astronomical observations were made with the naked eye alone, for the only equipment Mayan astronomers had to use was the cross-stick, to check the movements of stars against each other at specific times.

By the south side of the Caracol platform there are the remains of another steam-bath. The path up the east side of the Caracol runs back to the Group of the Thousand Columns, passing the **Xtoloc Cenote**, the source of water for practical purposes in Chichén, together with some *chultun* artificial cisterns dotted around the site.

The Nunnery and the Iglesia

From the Caracol platform there is a great view of the grandest buildings in this part of Chichén, **Las Monjas** or the Nunnery Complex (as with the 'Nunnery' in Uxmal, this Spanish name has no relation to the buildings' real function). This is a group of connected buildings, all with spectacular Terminal Classic carvings, around a platform 60m long. Between it and the Caracol stands the very different **Temple of the Carved Panels**. Its name is due to the carved

The Nunnery, from Désiré Charnay's book, Les Anciennes Villes du Nouveau Monde (1885)

reliefs in its northern chambers, now very faint, showing birds, gods, serpents and three figures in a hut among jaguars and warriors.

The 'Nunnery' is believed to have been the main palace and administrative area in the early years of Chichén. Much of it is in a relatively restrained style similar to that of the Puuc region – plain lower walls separated by *atadura*-type mouldings from upper friezes of geometric patterns and Chac-masks – but several parts of it have far more extravagant, Chenes-like carving, with a mass of intricate decoration that seems ready to overwhelm the buildings to which it is applied.

Inside there is what seems an enormous number of very small rooms, with benches around the sides. The most impressive parts of the Nunnery are the two smaller sections on the east side (on the left, coming from the Caracol). The addition to the main building, known simply as the **Annexe**, has adjacent façades in very different styles. The face that you see first as you walk towards it is a continuation of the same, Puuc-like style of the main block; walk around to the east end, though, and you are confronted by the most remarkable Chenes-style carving in Chichén Itzá. The wall is covered top to bottom in Chacs and other carvings that seem almost mobile, and the doorway, as in all Chenes building, is the mouth of a beast-god, with a row of hook-like stones to represent the teeth. Above the door sits a god-king, with a fabulous feather headdress. Around the lintel are glyphs, dating the façade to the year 880.

Forming a corner with the Annex, but entirely separate, is the strange structure the Spaniards called **La Iglesia** (The Church), because it had only one chamber inside. It is one of the oldest parts of Las Monjas, probably from the early 8th century. The lower walls are completely plain, and seem about to be crushed by the towering frieze and roof comb above. Massive Chac-masks form the corners, and appear in the middle of the longer walls. Between them there are images of the four *Bacabs* that sustained the sky at the cardinal points, represented by a snail, an armadillo, a turtle and a crab.

This is as much as you can see at Chichén Itzá on an ordinary visit. A little to the east of the Nunnery Platform there is a large 18-room complex that probably served as a lordly residence, known as the **Akab-Dzib**, with a date from 870. And to the right of the Nunnery– looking from the great plaza – a path leads into the woods towards **Chichén Viejo** or 'Old Chichén', an area with several temples in differing styles with dates from the 870s and 880s that have never been completely excavated. One, the **Temple of the Phalli**, has rare phallic sculptures, another has massive figures of warriors. However, both these areas are now gated off.

Where to Stay at Chichén Itzá

t (985–)

Chichén's three large upscale hotels – two of them much pricier than the other – are all on the eastern approach road to the ruins (the first turn, from Cancún). One other hotel, the Dolores Alba, is 3km east of Chichén Itzá, while all other hotels are in Pisté, 1½km west of the ruins (about a 20-min walk). They are spread along the main road, which forms the village's main street (officially C. 15). Despite its 'souvenir-ization' Pisté still has the laid-back charm of a normal Yucatán village.

Hotel prices in Chichén and Pisté are relatively high. An alternative is to stay in Valladolid (45mins by bus). It isn't usually hard to find a room at Chichén except around the equinoxes, when places are booked up everywhere, including Valladolid.

Luxury–Expensive

Hacienda Chichén, t (999) 925 3952, *www.haciendachichen.com*. Has the most character among the Chichén hotels, and has been given an attractive relaunch. Its heart is the old *hacienda* of Chichén, where the Carnegie archaeologists stayed when excavating Chichén in the 1920s. The rooms are in *cabañas* mostly built then, which have been beautifully redecorated in *hacienda* style. There's also a lovely spa and gorgeous garden pool, and the *hacienda* makes a serious effort to follow 'green' sustainable practice, and offers tours with **Yucatán Adventure** (see p.106), which has developed an imaginative range of trips and ecotours with Maya communities.

Hotel Mayaland, t 01 800 719 5465/ (998) 887 2495, *www.mayaland.com*. Biggest of the luxury hotels, the closest to the ruins, the traditional VIP first choice, and also the most expensive. It's a great barn of a resort hotel, with a slightly neo-colonial look, and rooms with a wonderful view of the ruins on one side, or over a patio and pool on the other. Next to it there is now the **Lodge at Chichén Itzá**, with a slightly more intimate 'boutique' style (no tour groups) and similar prices.

Moderate

Villas Arqueológicas Chichén Itzá, t 856 6000,*www.villasarqueológicas. com.mx*. The third of the big hotels by the eastern ruins entrance (like its sister-hotels at Cobá and Uxmal, no longer owned by Club Med) has prices far lower than its neighbours, but its rooms, **restaurants**, pool and beautiful gardens are of a comparable standard, making this a wonderful bargain. All three Villas hotels have the same *hacienda* charm, with rooms in *cabañas* or a main building.

Inexpensive

⭐ **Hotel Dolores Alba >**

Hotel Dolores Alba, Highway 180 3km east of Chichén (4½km from Pisté) near Balankanché, t 858 1555, *www.doloresalba.com*. Best-value hotel at Chichén, with very pretty rooms. All with a/c, they're bright, comfortable and in better condition than many in Pisté. There are two lovely pools, a bar and a restaurant. It's a bit isolated, but free transport is provided to the ruins every morning, so you only need a taxi back (about $3). Second-class buses also stop outside. The owners have a sister hotel in Mérida (see p.279). Very popular, so book.

Pirámide Inn, C. 15, Pisté, t 851 0115, *www.piramideinn.com*. Impossible to miss, this pastel-green travellers' institution is big and motel-like, with its own photo gallery of Maya excavations, a garden and daffy details like a fake Maya pyramid by its relaxing pool. There's a pleasant **restaurant**, and the 43 rooms (all with a/c) are brightly decorated. Camping space is also available.

Budget

Hotel Stardust, C. 15, Pisté, t 851 0089. Battered motel-style hotel next to the Pirámide Inn. It now does most

business renting out space at the back to RVs and campers, but still has plain, elderly rooms with showers too, and there's a surprisingly large pool.

Posada El Paso, C. 15 no. 48-F, Pisté (no phone). A real budget option, with very basic rooms with fans and showers. Those on the upper floor, around a courtyard, have decent light.

Eating Out at Chichén Itzá

Restaurants in the hotels (all *expensive–moderate*) are open to non-residents. Those at Hacienda Chichén and the Villas Arqueológicas are the most attractive. Piste's long main street is lined with similar restaurants, some of which have mushroomed into giant Maya-theme eateries to cater for the daily tour groups. For really cheap food there are several decent *loncherías* on the small plaza, towards the western end of town.

Las Mestizas, C. 15, Pisté (*moderate*). Most attractive of Piste's restaurants, with good local dishes – great *sopa de lima* – and charming waitresses in regulation *huipiles* who go about their work with a Yucatecan hush.

La Palapa, beside the main ruins entrance road from Pisté (*moderate*). Best place to eat near the ruins: a pretty restaurant with decent local fare at only slightly inflated prices.

El Carrousel, C. 15, Pisté (*moderate–cheap*). A reliable stand-by for enjoyable local fare.

Entertainment

Chichén Itzá's **Sound and Light** spectacular is presented nightly, at 7pm (Nov–Mar) and 8pm (April–Oct). Commentary is in Spanish, but headphones commentary are offered in other languages (an extra $2). Despite its high kitsch-quotient, the show is visually effective, and for most of the year this is your only opportunity to see the Descent of Kukulcán (electrically induced) down the Castillo. And since you're obliged to pay for it with the ruins, you might as well go...

Around Chichén Itzá

Ikkil Cenote

Ikkil Cenote
*Information, t (985)
851 0039; open daily
8–6; adm; restaurant-
buffet, moderate*

Some 3km east of Chichén, opposite the Hotel Dolores Alba, is a giant *cenote* that is now the centrepiece of an 'ecological park'. The *cenote* itself is spectacular: a giant, circular pit with creepers hanging down, crystalline water 13m below ground level and shafts of brilliant sunlight illuminating it from holes in the *cenote* roof. However, the park development around it is aimed squarely at coach tours from Cancún. The *cenote* itself is not open to being expanded, and access to it is by a path that only allows a few people to pass at a time, so if you actually want to swim rather than just catch a glimpse it's best to avoid midday and weekends. Around the *cenote* there are also 25 hectares of forest that you are free to explore (though most coach visitors only have time to see the *cenote* and have lunch).

The Balankanché Caves

Balankanché
*Museum open daily
9–5; adm*

This is one of the great Yucatán cave systems, but one that was entirely forgotten until it was discovered by accident by a local guide in 1959. Subsequent searches revealed that offerings had been left here throughout the Classic and Postclassic eras, suggesting that, like Loltún, it was seen as an important point through which to make contact with and invoke the lords of the Underworld. There is a botanical garden of local flora, a small museum and a café by the entrance.

The Balankanché caves are a little less extensive than the giant catacombs at Loltún (*see* p.316). Apart from turning on the 'Sound and Light' recorded commentary the guides tend to leave you to your own devices within the cave, so that a visit here is generally less informative than tours of Loltún. These limitations, though, cannot detract overly from the fascination of the cavern, a labyrinthine series of chambers leading dramatically into each other. One of the most remarkable is the 'sanctuary', where the stalactites and stalagmites meet to form a giant central tree. It was surrounded by over 100 Postclassic ceramic incense burners – many of which have been left exactly as they were found – of which the larger, hourglass-shaped pieces all have the face of Tlaloc, the central-Mexican equivalent of the rain god Chac. The most magical part of Balankanché is the very end of the cave, a

Visiting Balankanché

Balankanché is 5km east of Chichén on Highway 180 (signed *Grutas de Balankanché*). If you don't have your own transport, second-class buses stop at the entrance (usually twice an hour), and the caves are included in many Chichén tours. The museum is open all day but the caves can be visited only with an obligatory tour (about 1hr) and Sound and Light show at 11am, 1pm and 3pm (English); at 9am, 12 noon, 2pm and 4pm (Spanish), and at 10am (French); adm is about $4.

09

Yucatán State | Around Chichén Itzá

Getting to Yokdzonot and Yaxuná

Yokdzonot is easy to find on Highway 180. Second-class buses and *combis* will stop at the *cenote* entrance. A paved road off Highway 180 leads in about 25km from Pisté to Yaxuná. *Combis* run there frequently from Pisté to Yaxuná. Direct buses also run (infrequently) to Yaxuná from Terminal del Noreste in Mérida.

chamber with a pool of extraordinarily still, crystalline water, in which the cave bottom seen through the water appears almost a perfect mirror image of the cavern roof.

One thing should be mentioned: if you have a metabolism that's responsive to heat and/or humidity, don't go in if you're not prepared to come out like a wet sponge.

Cenote Yokdzonot, more *cenotes* and Yaxuná

In the opposite direction, towards Mérida, 18km from Chichén Itzá is an impressive – and very enjoyable – community project in the Maya village of **Yokdzonot**. In 2005 a group of local women looked around for new ways in which the community could make some money, and realized that one of their biggest potential assets was the village's huge *cenote*. This is one of the biggest in the area, a magnificent deep, round open pool, but was then completely unknown to outsiders and sadly neglected, surrounded by thick scrub. They formed a cooperative and worked for over a year, with some help from Yucatán Adventure at Hacienda Chichén (*see* p.237), to clean the *cenote* up, open up access, build a stairway down to the water and even add toilets to ensure high standards of ecological management. The resulting *parador turístico* of

Cenote Yokdzonot
open daily 9–5; adm

Cenote Yokdzonot is charming and very well-run, with snorkels to rent, and the water is beautifully clean and delightful for swimming. At the top there's also a little restaurant, with real Yucatecan home cooking, and local men offer forest tours. The *cenote* is easy to find from Highway 180, only 300m from the road.

Cenote explorers can also find many more pools in this area. **Cenotillo**, deep in the countryside north of Chichén and best reached by turning north from Pisté, has some 150 *cenotes* around it, large

Where to Stay and Eat

By the *cenote* at **Yokdzonot** the women's co-op has a simple restaurant offering great local favorites like *salbutes* and *sopa de lima* (*budget*).

Yaxuná has a village ecotourism scheme that makes use of eight simple *cabañas* that were built for archaeologists working at the nearby ruins, with beds, hammocks and showers. For around $30 a day you get accommodation, all meals, and the help of local guides to explore the area: Yaxuná

ruins, other Maya remains, abandoned *haciendas*, *cenotes*, woods full of wildlife and the village beehives. Immersion in modern Maya life is guaranteed, and your hosts have a very amiable charm; sometimes the village hosts special events, like a festival of traditional medicine.

It's advisable to make contact in advance, but they will try to fit in any arrivals. Bookings are best made through **Ecoturismo Yucatán** in Mérida (*see* p.274). For an introduction, see *www.ecoyuc.com/yaxuna*.

Getting to Tizimín

Tizimín **bus station** is on C. 47, between Calles 46 and 48, two blocks from the plaza. There are 5 *intermedio* and hourly second-class daily between Tizimín and Mérida (Terminal del Noreste) via Izamal, 12 *intermedios* or second-class to/from Cancún (one goes on to Playa del Carmen and Tulum), and hourly buses to/from Valladolid. There are many local services: 10 daily to Río Lagartos, 5 to San Felipe and 5 to El Cuyo. *Combis* run to all the coastal villages from the bus station area.

and small. A few are signposted, and local guides will take you to others. On Highway 180, another 20km west of Yokdzonot in **Holca** is another, much more cave-like *cenote*, **Chihuan**. Look out for signs.

South of Pisté lies **Yaxuná**, site of the bastion-city of Cobá and the most important battle in the war between Chichén and Cobá. Major excavations were undertaken in the 1990s, and several large pyramids uncovered that show clear similarities with Cobá. The site has never been open on a regular basis, but Yaxuná village has a community tourism scheme offering personal tours of the ruins.

Northern Yucatán and Río Lagartos

North of Valladolid is the cattle country of Yucatán, a sultry landscape of wide, flat, open fields of scrub grass with single palm trees marking the horizon like beacons, and where cowboys on horseback clop along the roads. For a visitor, its main attractions are the flamingo colonies of Río Lagartos, and the remote coastal villages.

Tizimín

The dead-straight road north from Valladolid, Highway 295, is surprisingly one of the best in the Yucatán, rolling on from the Ek-Balam turn-off through broad, hot fields. Some 20km further on is **Calotmul**, as slow-moving as so many villages round about, with a wide, slightly ragged plaza, and another big, plain Franciscan church. From there it's a short distance to the capital of the cattle country, Tizimín.

The name Tizimín supposedly comes from a Yucatec word for a type of devil, *tsimin*, apparently used to describe the Spaniards when the Maya first saw them on horseback. As the main centre of the cattle region Tizimín has an occasional bustle that can be quite surprising in rural Yucatán. The central **plaza** is particularly attractive, with plenty of room for strolling and people-watching; unusually it's divided into two, between the main Parque Principal and the smaller Parque Juárez. Dividing them are two huge colonial edifices, both Franciscan monasteries, the **Convento de los Tres Reyes** and **Convento de San Francisco**. They seem very medieval, and give the centre of the town a curiously Mediterranean look. Weekday mornings see the market packed with country people buying and selling.

Orientation and Services

t (986–)

Tizimín is a sprawling town, with the usual colonial grid (even numbers north–south, odd numbers east–west), although some streets have sub-sections (ie. 'C. 49-A'). The northbound road from Valladolid runs along C. 50, southbound on C. 52; they run into the main plaza between Calles 51 and 53.

The main **petrol/gas station** is three blocks east of the plaza on C. 49, between 44 and 46. There are several **banks** on the central plazas.

Festivals

Tizimín's spectacular main *fiesta*, the **Feria de los Tres Reyes** (Three Kings), runs for a month from 15 Dec. It includes a stock fair as well as the more usual celebrations.

Where to Stay and Eat in Tizimín

Hotel San Carlos, C. 54 no. 407, x 51 & 53, t 863 2094 (*budget*). Tizimín is not geared to tourists, but the most pleasant place to stay is a block west of the plaza. It has 25 modern rooms around a pretty patio, some with a/c.

Hotel San Jorge, C. 53 no. 412, t 863 2037 (*budget*). Easier to find than the San Carlos, on the plaza by the bank. All rooms have bathrooms and TVs, and most have a/c.

Tres Reyes, C. 52, corner of C. 53, t 863 2106 (*moderate*). A great restaurant to find in a small town, on the Parque Principal and run with amiable energy by *sr* Willy Canto. His menus cater for all needs, from snacks to ample daily specials at very decent prices. Mexican-style steaks are outstanding.

Amid miles of scrub and tiny villages some 35km southeast of Tizimín are the very little-visited Maya ruins of **Culubá**, a Terminal Classic-period city with a few large buildings that show strong Puuc influences, the easternmost limit of the style.

Río Lagartos and San Felipe

From about 40km north of Tizimín the savanna grasslands and tall palms are interspersed with more and more patches of reeds and marsh, and then mangrove lagoons and ghostly 'petrified forests' of dead mangroves, before the road runs out in **Río Lagartos**. This fishing village and its spectacular colonies of flamingos and migratory birds are mentioned in every book and brochure on the Yucatán, but because of their remoteness not so many people actually make it up here, and while facilities are expanding, it still rates low on the scale as a tourist town.

Río Lagartos really is the end of the road, for Highway 295 comes to a stop when it runs into the waterfront, along which the town stretches out on either side facing lines of tethered fishing launches. In front of you there's only the opal-coloured lagoon, with a long strip of sand and mangrove brush on the far side, and more pelicans and terns than people to be seen. This area was badly hit by Hurricane Isidore (*Isidoro*) in 2002, but the villages have bounced back with Yucatecan insouciance (and a little state aid). Seeing flamingos here is not nearly as 'packaged' an experience as at Celestún, but is more organized since the area was made a biosphere reserve (**Reserva de la Biósfera Ría Lagartos**). You can now get in touch with local guides online, but even if you

Getting to Río Lagartos and San Felipe

Frequent buses run to **Río Lagartos** and **San Felipe** from Tizimín (*1hr*), but there are also direct services from Mérida (Terminal del Noreste) and Valladolid. Many agencies in Mérida, Cancún and the Riviera offer flamingo tours to see the flamingos (*see* p.105).
Río Lagartos has a *gasolinera*, on the way in to the village beside the main road.

have a booking, since the best time for most lagoon trips is first thing in the morning, the best way to visit is get here a day ahead and stay the night in Río Lagartos or **San Felipe**, 12km west, to be ready for an early start. Those who plan on getting to the *ría* and back from Mérida in a day trip generally find the experience exhausting, and disappointing. If you arrive without a booking, both villages have waterfront information huts to help you find *lanchas*, and good guides are never hard to find. Their natural attractions aside, both are among the most deliciously relaxing places to spend some time anywhere in the Yucatán.

The flamingo colonies are to the east, along the 'river' (actually a lagoon between the mainland and the sandbar). The name Río Lagartos ('Lizard River') was given to it by the Spaniards because of crocodiles they saw here, and there are still a few about, though you're unlikely to see them by day. On the way, you travel at times across broad open water, at others through narrow mangrove creeks. After a while you approach the mud-flats that in the summer breeding season host a pink expanse of 20,000 flamingos, and large flocks all year. Local boatmen are more careful than those at Celestún not to disturb them (*see* 'Celestún', pp.285-6, for more on flamingos). Less celebrated is the lagoon's enormous variety of other birds: herons, ibis, ducks, egrets, birds of prey, still more pelicans. A few kilometres east there are natural salt beds at **Las Coloradas**, which were used by the Maya, and are now mined commercially. Boatmen will let you off to see these strange deposits, which tint the lagoon weird colours.

Río Lagartos itself doesn't have a beach, but there is one across the lagoon on the sand spit, and the same boatmen will take you there and pick you up, for about $15. You can also swim in a nearby *cenote*, **Chiquilá**. San Felipe, a beautifully tranquil village with wonderful sunsets, has a ragged beach beside it and a better one across on the sand bar, also accessible with local boats. Again, the bird life is abundant.

In the last few years, perhaps due to the effects of hurricanes and salt mining, many flamingos have been moving west from their breeding grounds in Río Lagartos lagoon to a still-more remote area from San Felipe west to Dzilam Bravo, the **Bocas de Dzilam**. This is now also protected. Trips can be arranged from San Felipe or Río Lagartos, and local boatmen in Dzilam Bravo have begun to offer them too (*see* p.294).

09 **Yucatán State | Northern Yucatán and Río Lagartos**

Flamingo and other tours

The flamingo lagoons cover an area over 20km long, and getting to them involves travelling over open water, so hats, sun block, water and bug repellent are all advisable. Routes vary depending on conditions, and guides will always adapt tours to what you want, but the usual main 'route' is to the first big flamingo lagoon, through the mangroves and to Las Coloradas; a tour takes around 2hrs and prices start around $60 per boat, though at slack times you can often strike a deal. Longer trips to more lagoons (3–4hrs) can also be arranged. As the water is shallow, boats hold from four to six people: for individuals it's best to go at a weekend, as you're more likely to run into people trying to make up a boat. The best times to see birds are mornings or late afternoon, and the best flamingo season is July to August; the busiest times for the boatmen are Easter week and weekends in December, January, July or August.

The same guides will also take you on **night trips** (looking for crocodiles), **birding** tours to look for other birds apart from flamingos, and some of the Yucatán's best **fishing** trips. There are now several local guides who are set up with websites, but if you just arrive in Río Lagartos the fishermen's co-op has a kiosk on the waterfront, and the San Felipe cooperative has one there too. Río Lagartos also has a local website, *www.riolagartos.com*.

Río Lagartos Adventures, Las Palapas de la Torreja restaurant, Malécon, t 862 0202, *www.riolagartosadventures.com*. Diego Núñez, an expert, authorized guide.

Río Lagartos Eco Tours, Restaurante Isla Contoy, t 862 0000, *www.rio lagartos-ecotours.com*. The family that runs Río Lagartos' most popular restaurant are also professional tour guides.

Where to Stay and Eat

The (still modest) growth in visitor number at Río Lagartos and San Felipe has led to the appearance of some pleasant small hotels. Finding good places to eat is never a problem.

Río Lagartos t (986-)

Hotel Punta Pontó, C. 7 no. 140, t 862 0509, *puntaponto@hotmail.com* (*inexpensive*). Pleasant hotel with rooms with balconies above the waterfront with great views. Very well kept, it's run by a charming, helpful family, and breakfast is included. Fan-only, but a/c is rarely ever need in Río Lagartos, thanks to the sea breezes.

Hotel Villa de Pescadores, C. 14 no. 93, t 862 0020 (*inexpensive*). On the waterfront near the lighthouse, with spacious, fan-only rooms with balconies and views over the lagoon.

Isla Contoy, C. 19 no. 134 (*moderate–budget*). Great local restaurant under a big *palapa* on a jetty over the sea, with moreish cocktails of seafood, limes and fresh coriander. To find it, go on around the waterfront to the left, facing the lagoon. The owners are also lagoon guides (*see* above).

San Felipe t (986-)

Hotel San Felipe, C. 9, x 14 & 16, t 862 2027, *hotelsf@hotmail.com* (*inexpensive*). Another very enjoyable place, with rooms in different sizes: some are quite basic, others are bigger, with a/c and/or waterfront balconies. Prices vary by size and the views, often fabulous at sunset. The **restaurant** (*moderate*) looks out over boats and the lagoon, and the owners are also fishing guides.

Restaurant Vaselina (*budget*). A big place by the village quay; utterly relaxing, with exceptional local seafood at very low prices.

El Cuyo

Around 60km east of Río Lagartos is the lost-looking and idiosyncratic village of El Cuyo, on a dead-straight beach with a jetty in the middle. You approach it after a long run through the savanna and cattle ranches of northern Yucatán, and then a narrow causeway across Río Lagartos lagoon and miles of sand and salt flats, which give it a feel of complete isolation. Most of the men of El Cuyo live by fishing. They go out before dawn and are

Getting to El Cuyo

Some maps show a coast road to El Cuyo from Río Lagartos via Las Coloradas, but even locals say this is barely passable even by 4WD. The main route **by car** from Valladolid (130km) is to take the road east to Colonia Yucatán from Tizimín, and turn north in Colonia. From Río Lagartos, a turning east in Loché, 25km south on the 295, leads onto a potholed but decent road that runs for 70km through lonely villages to join the El Cuyo–Colonia road.

Five or more **buses** run daily each way between Tizimín and El Cuyo. *Colectivos* are frequent, from Tizimín or Colonia Yucatán.

often back by noon, when they make for Conchita's bar. They're still a little surprised to see foreigners turn up, and are very friendly.

El Cuyo is one of the best places to appreciate the natural wealth of Yucatán's north coast. The bird life is spectacular, and the eastern end of the Río Lagartos lagoon nearby contains one of the richest flamingo breeding grounds. Also not far away is a breeding beach for hawksbill turtles, which appear every year in July and August. Up to now, El Cuyo has been best known for the quality of its fishing, both deep-sea and inshore, and the village is full of able fishing guides. El Cuyo has some of the feel of Holbox, an easy boat-trip away in Quintana Roo (*see* p.152). It also has its surprises – given the time it takes to get there – namely a few holiday homes along the beach, most only used by Mérida families from June to August. More foreigners are finding their way here too, and buying up beach houses – which has made more available for short-term rents – and golf carts have arrived as a way of getting up and down. Even so, El Cuyo is still well enough away from madding crowds to make a fine beach refuge for anyone looking to lose themselves in empty horizons. Beaches stretch away for miles on either side, lined with clumps of palms. There are no secluded bays as on the Caribbean coast, but if you want a beach to yourself, this could be the place.

09 Yucatán State | Northern Yucatán and Río Lagartos

Tourist Information and Services

t (986–)

Several websites deal in El Cuyo beach rentals, but *www.elcuyoyucatan. net* is a useful information source and also takes bookings by phone (t 853 4015), which given the shakiness of other local phones can be handy.

El Cuyo has a **petrol/gas station**, on the west side of the village, and a **pharmacy**. The village is easy to walk around, but there is a **golf cart** hire shop, on the main street. The nearest **bank** or ATM is in **Tizimín**, so be prepared.

Where to Stay and Eat in El Cuyo

Several El Cuyo beach houses are available to rent. Some can be rented through *www.elcuyoyucatan.net*, but to find others it's best just to check *El Cuyo Yucatán rentals* on the internet. **Puerto del Cuyo** (*www.puertodel cuyo.com*) is a joint site for five frankly astonishingly smart villas along El Cuyo beach, available to rent for a week or more, from $340 a week.

Flamingo's Cabins, *www.flamingos cabins.com* (*inexpensive*). Three pretty beachfront *cabañas*, with double beds, good bathrooms and terraces, and one with a kitchen. Prices are lower for longer stays, and the friendly owners can provide bikes or kayaks or take you out fishing, birdwatching, on visits to Holbox or other trips.

Cabañas Mar y Sol/Restaurante La Conchita, contact via *www.elcuyoyucatan.net* (*inexpensive*). El Cuyo's longest-running 'facility', left of the main street behind the beach. The great **restaurant** serves generous platters of fish and seafood; it closes around 7pm. Behind it are eight

family-size, cosy *cabañas* with beds and bathrooms, right on the beach.

Posada El Faro, contact via *www.elcuyoyucatan.net* (*inexpensive*). Pretty double rooms with good modern facilities – including a/c – in a charming house with terrace in the middle of the village.

Restaurante Tiburón (*budget*). El Cuyo's second real restaurant, on the main street four blocks back from the sea;. closes early, around 6pm.

Izamal to Mérida

In central Yucatán, from about 50km west of Chichén Itzá, the villages become thicker on the ground as you enter the core of the state. East of Mérida there are two major attractions: **Izamal**, one of the most fascinating of colonial towns and an ancient Maya city, and – far less well-known – the unique Maya site of **Aké**.

Between Izamal and the state capital lies one of the most populated areas of the Yucatán, a stream of villages and towns with plazas, palm huts, Cristal water ads, children, dogs and flashes of bougainvillaea. The most interesting route to take from Izamal is the back-country road through Tixkokob, a friendly little place with a market.

Izamal

 Izamal

Izamal is the most complete and most attractive of the Yucatán's Spanish colonial towns. If Mérida is the 'White City', Izamal is the *Ciudad Amarilla* or *Ciudad Dorada*, the yellow or golden city. Its elegant houses and arcades are painted a uniform yellow-ochre wash that gives it a unique feel and charm, while tricycle carts or horse-drawn victorias clip-clop along wide, quiet streets, all helping to maintain an old-world tranquillity. Still dominating the town is the grandest of all the Franciscan buildings in the peninsula, the monastery of **San Antonio de Padua**. Izamal has another label, as the 'City of the Three Cultures' – Maya, Spanish and the Yucatecan-Mexican synthesis. Here more than anywhere else in the Yucatán the superimposition of Catholicism and Spanish culture on top of Maya tradition is visible in stone, for the pyramids of ancient Izamal are still very intact, incorporated into the streets of the town.

History

Because modern Izamal stands on top of the Maya city, archaeological excavations have been limited. Nevertheless, it is clear that this was one of the oldest of Maya settlements,

Getting to and around Izamal

Izamal is north of Highway 180, 72km from Mérida, 270km from Cancún. To **drive** there from the east, turn right off 180 in Kantunil, where the 180 *Cuota* motorway ends (from the 180 *Libre*, this involves turning east on the *Cuota*, and then immediately left to get into the westbound lane for the Izamal turn). From Mérida, take the road via Tixkokob, or follow 180 as far as Hoctún (48km) and turn left. The main Mérida road becomes C. 31 in Izamal; Av. Zamná is a kind of bypass that runs around the south of the central area. The most central **gasolinera** is at the corner of Calles 31 and 34.

The **bus station** is on C. 32, a block from the monastery. *Intermedio* and second-class buses run frequently from Terminal del Centro and Terminal del Noreste in Mérida. Some 17 buses daily run to Izamal from Cancún via Valladolid.

Izamal is very walkable, but one of its traditions is its **Victorias**, the horse-drawn carriages that in Mérida are called *calesas*. A tour from the main plazas costs from $9.

---

09 Yucatán State | Izamal

> *There is here in Izamal one building among the others, of such height and beauty that it is frightening... I climbed to the top of this chapel and, since Yucatán is a flat land, one can see from there as much land as the eye could reach, and can see the sea...*
>
> Father Diego de Landa, Relación de las Cosas de Yucatán

occupied continually from about 300 BC till the Spanish Conquest. It developed powerfully as a city-state from around AD 600. In the Classic era Izamal was allied with Aké, and a long *sacbé* was built between them, although this alliance was subsequently broken for reasons unknown. By the time of the Spaniards' arrival it was politically less significant, as the seat of *Akinchel*, one of the weaker Maya lordships. However, it remained an important pilgrimage centre. The great pyramid of Izamal, the Kinich Kak Mo, is the largest pyramid-platform in northern Yucatán, and was a major shrine of Itzamná, the paramount god among the Yucatán Maya.

The arrival of Catholicism and the Franciscans in Izamal is inseparably associated with Bishop Diego de Landa (*see* p.51). According to his *Relación*, the friars first came here in 1549 at the invitation of local Maya chieftains, who urged them to build a monastery amid the old shrines. With its 12 large pyramids, like so many mountains, Izamal made a deep impression on the missionary brothers. A Franciscan chronicler relates that the precise site of the new monastery, one of the largest platforms and known as the *Paphol'chac* or 'Home of Chac', was chosen by Landa himself, in order that 'a place that had been one of abomination and idolatry, could become one of sanctity'. Intended as a symbol of the triumph of Christianity, the monastery was far the most ambitious of the Franciscan projects in the Yucatán, and its majestic *atrio* (courtyard) is the largest such church square anywhere in Mexico. Between the desire of the Maya lords that a centre of the new religion should be on the same site as the shrines of Itzamná, however, and Landa's belief he was 'sanctifying' a pagan place, the potential for confusion and ambiguity of motive and imagery was spectacular.

Not long after the completion of the monastery in 1561 an image of the Virgin, almost certainly painted in Guatemala, was brought to Izamal by Landa. As the first 'official' Catholic focus of pilgrimage in the Yucatán, **Nuestra Señora de Izamal** ('Our Lady of Izamal') played an important part in the Christianization of the peninsula, and was credited with several miracles. In 1829 the original image was destroyed in a fire, and substituted by another that had supposedly been brought from Guatemala at the same time and then preserved in a private home in Mérida. Its authenticity has often been questioned, but it is this image that is in the monastery today. On the *fiesta* of the Virgin, the Immaculate Conception (8 Dec), *Izamaleños* traditionally visit her at the monastery and then take a walk up the Kinich Kak Mo, a neat example of having it both ways (also known as 'syncretic religion').

In modern times the Virgin of Izamal has been rather displaced by the Mexican cult of Guadalupe, but remains the Yucatán's official patron. In 1993, Pope John Paul II came to Izamal for an 'encounter with the indigenous peoples of the Americas'. Such events aside Izamal is generally content to wear its historic status fairly lightly, as one of the most laidback of country towns. It holds on to its traditions in a friendly way, and holds another big *fiesta* around the day of the **Cristo Negro**, 18 October.

The Monastery of San Antonio de Padua

Whether you come into Izamal by bus or by car along C. 31 – which more or less follows the line of the old *sacbé* from Aké – you automatically come up against the great focus of the town, Bishop Landa's monastery, now in beautiful condition after extensive restoration work. Its great atrium stands squarely across the old platform of Chac, flanked on three sides by squares with shady arcades, in the same yellow and white colours, that mirror the colonnades of the quadrangle and give the town centre a particular sense of harmony and spaciousness. On the south side is the smallest square, with Izamal's lively little market; to the west is the town hall (with bus station behind it), and to the north is the largest square, the **Parque Itzamná**.

Massive ramps of steps lead up to the grass-covered *atrio*, measuring 520m by 420m. On some Sundays and *fiesta* days open-air Masses are held on the quadrangle, but on other days it's a huge, atmospherically empty space where the only noise will be from giggling kids who offer to show you around. The church on the eastern side is the finest work of the Franciscans' architect Friar Juan de Mérida. Only a section of the atrium arches, directly in front of the church, was built by him, the rest being added later and completed by 1618. They effectively block off the original *capilla de indios*, to the right of the main façade. On the walls of the quadrangle arcades are the remains of 18th-century frescoes, and carved inscriptions commemorating miracles performed by the Virgin of Izamal. More interesting are the frescoes in the passage from the atrium to the cloister, some of them from 1554, showing monks purging another monk with sticks, or friars adoring the

Virgin. Elsewhere, the decoration shows a combination of Spanish techniques with very pre-Hispanic colours and floral imagery.

The lines of arches give Izamal a lightness that is not found in many early colonial churches in the Yucatán, but inside it's still a plain, simple Franciscan building. The massive, two-level **cloister**, on the north side of the church, has a very pretty garden courtyard on one side. Also off the cloister is a room with a small exhibit on the visit of the Pope in 1993, and nearby there's a portrait of Bishop Landa, although it's not believed to be contemporary. Our Lady of Izamal currently resides in a small sanctuary to the right of the main church. At the very back of the church is another separate chamber, the **Camarín**, built as a sanctuary for the Virgin in 1650–56 and reached by a romantic-looking set of stairs from which there's a great view over the town.

The Centro Cultural and Izamal's Pyramids

Returning to the atrium, in the little plaza below the south side there's a statue of Landa himself in all his dourness. On the north side, in the wall below facing Parque Itzamná is a small local museum, the **Museo Comunitario Itzamal-Kauil** In the last few years Izamal has received a lot of attention and investment from the Fomento Banamex, promoters among other things of the Plan Group *hacienda* hotels (*see* pp.272-3) and of Mexican folk art, which has supported the renovation of many old buildings. One of their most striking projects is the lavish restoration of a historic house opposite the monastery on Parque Itzamná as the **Centro Cultural y Artesanal**. It hosts a superb collection of folk art from around Mexico, and a charming shop with exceptional craftwork; the centre also acts as a local information office, with a free map, and has an imaginative programme to support local craftspeople by publicizing their work and encouraging workshop visits.

At the back of the centre there's a stunning patio, with stylish café, which actually incorporates the **Kabul**, one of Izamal's surviving pyramids (you can also get a view of the same pyramid from the monastery atrium, across the Parque). When Stephens and Catherwood visited Izamal in 1842, the Kabul pyramid had on one side a huge stucco mask, shown in one of Catherwood's most impressive drawings, but when Desiré Charnay looked for it 40 years later in 1886 he found that it had already been destroyed, possibly in the Caste War.

From Parque Itzamná, take C. 28 (the right-hand corner, from the monastery) a couple of blocks to meet C. 27. A little to the right are some steps and an alley forming the entrance to the great pyramid, the **Kinich Kak Mo**. Getting to the top involves a stiff but gradual climb over several levels, since it consists of one pyramid base with another whole pyramid on top. The oldest parts are from the Early Classic and the latest from the Postclassic, a difference of

Museo Comunitario Itzamal-Kauil
open daily 8–1 and 6–9

Centro Cultural y Artesanal
C. 31 no. 201,
t 954 1012, open Mon–Sat 10–8, Thur, Sat until 10pm, Sun 10–5;
free

Kinich Kak Mo
open daily 8–5; adm

nearly 1,000 years. In Mayan times the entire space between it and the *Paphol'chac*, where the monastery now stands, was just one great square, which must have been one of the largest of Maya plazas. According to one legend the Kinich Kak Mo is the burial place of the head of Itzamná, while his right hand was buried on the Kabul pyramid and his heart on Itzamatul. Another explains the name Kinich Kak Mo, which means 'Fire Macaw – Face of the Sun': supposedly, Itzamná came down in the form of a fiery macaw to collect offerings left on the pyramid. Nowadays, most of the pyramid's masonry is in a fairly poor state. Once you get up there, though, you still have the same view that so impressed Landa.

Itzamatul
open daily 8–5; adm

Returning to Parque Itzamná, a turn left on C. 31, through the arch, will take you to the entrance to another pyramid, the Itzamatul, on C. 26. It's a smaller version of the Kinich Kak Mo, similarly built in stages in 400–600, 700–850 and 950–1150. The final platform at the top is quite overgrown, a strangely wild and beautiful place within the town, with a very good view back to the larger pyramid. These three are the only intact survivors of the 12 pyramids of Izamal counted by Landa. However, the remains of others are all around the town (the market is on one).

Tourist Information and Services in Izamal

t (988–)

The official **tourist office** in the town hall, on the plaza opposite the monastery, supplies maps and other information and has a (Spanish-only) website, *www.izamal.travel*. A more useful source of information is often the **Centro Cultural y Artesanal**, which produces a very informative free map, with directions to local craftspeople.

Bank: C. 31, x 28 (off Parque Itzamná).

Internet Access: Net Café, C. 31 no. 308, in the same building as Hecho a Mano (*see* below).

Shopping

Izamal is one of the Yucatán's foremost handicrafts centres, and this can now be better appreciated due to the **Centro Cultural y Artesanal**, which works with local craftspeople and showcases beautiful work – superb silver jewellery, delicate embroidery – in its charming shop. The Centro's free map also has details of many Izamal craftworkers, to encourage visitors to see them at work and buy direct – a very personal, engaging way to visit

the town. They include makers of hammocks. wonderfully colourful ornamental butterflies, metal toys and other surprises as well as jewellers and embroiderers.

Hecho a Mano, C. 31–A no. 308, **t** 954 0344. Texan-Yucatecan Hector Garza was an 'institution' in Izamal, always keen to talk about the folk art and handicrafts piled high in his shop. After his death, his partner has kept the shop going in the same style.

Where to Stay in Izamal

Not far from Izamal are two contrasting **hacienda hotels**. Only 8km south of the town near Sudzal is the moderately priced **Hacienda San Antonio Chalanté**, while about 40km west on the road towards Mérida is the luxurious **Hacienda San José Cholul**. *See* p.272-3.

Due to Izamal being so well-established as a day-trip destination, it has been oddly short on hotels, but attractive options have opened recently. **Hotel Itzamaltún**, C. 31 no. 251, x 22 & 24, **t** 954 0023, *www.itzamaltun.com* (*inexpensive*). Smart little hotel in a converted Izamal town house, with airy rooms around a patio-garden, with a well-sized pool, terrace restaurant and spa. Prices are around the top of the *inexpensive* band.

Hotel Rinconada del Convento, C. 33 no. 294 (behind the monastery), t 954 0151, *www.hotelizamal.com* (*inexpensive*). Likeable small hotel in a recently-converted old house right beside the monastery, with quietly charming owners. Rooms are well-equipped but conventional; what's special about it is the garden at the back, which actually climbs up the side of one of Izamal's old Maya pyramids to the small pool and the breakfast bar, from where there's a fantastic view of the monastery and the town.

Macan Ché, C. 22 no. 305, x 33 & 35, t 954 0287, *www.macanche.com* (*inexpensive*). The best place to stay in Izamal, a lovely B&B that's a little garden of Yucatecan tranquillity in an already-tranquil town. The 18 rooms are in bungalows spread around a secluded garden, a few blocks from the centre. US owners Emily and Alfred are extremely hospitable, and have thoroughly renovated (or built) every room in the last few years; individually decorated, they're very comfortable (with a/c), and there are also two fully self-contained cottages with kitchens. Plus there's a small swimming pool, and a palm-shaded space where breakfast is served and evening meals can be ordered. Macan Ché also hosts occasional retreats and yoga courses.

Green River, Av. Zamná 342, t 954 0337, *www.hotelgreenriver.com* (*inexpensive –budget*). Slightly eccentric motel-style

⭐ **Kinich** >>

⭐ **Macan Ché** >

hotel with large rooms in bungalows in a garden, with a/c and TV, two pools, two bars and a **restaurant**. However, it's a 20min walk from the centre.

Eating Out in Izamal

There are several cheap, open-air *loncherías* just off the main square, around the market.

Kinich, C. 27 no. 299, t 954 0489 (*moderate*). One of the best in the Yucatán for classic traditional dishes, presented in all their variety. Located just to the left of the entrance to Kinich Kak Mo pyramid, it's also very pretty, with tables in a shaded garden. *Open noon–6 only, exc Tues, Thurs, Fri, Sat also open eves (after Show below).*

Restaurante Tumben-Lol, C. 22 no. 302, x 31 & 33 (*moderate*). Attractive restaurant a few blocks from the centre (near the Macan Ché), with tables around a garden patio.

Restaurante El Toro, Plazuela 2 de Abril (*budget*). Pleasant little place with enjoyable local classics, below the monastery.

Entertainment

Izamal has an impressive **Sound and Light Show**, in the atrium of the monastery every Tues, Thurs, Fri and Sat at 8.30pm. It evokes the history of Maya and Catholic Izamal, and is more sophisticated, and more spectacularly effective, than the shows at Chichén and Uxmal. Tickets (about $5) can be bought on the spot.

Aké

Aké

Open daily 8–5; adm

Aké is one of the strangest and most enigmatic of Maya ruins, for its location and its unique architectural style. One of its most remarkable features is that ruins and the current village are all within a 19th-century *henequen* estate. The great main estate factory, a giant neo-French construction, survived with its extraordinary machinery up until 2002, when Hurricane Isidoro turned it into a ruin as atmospheric as those of any Maya city. Aké, moreover, is still a working *hacienda* today, for the few remaining workers moved operations into a more functional modern shed, where clattering machinery still processes *henequen* into sisal twine (available for sale).

Visiting Aké

The best route to Aké from Izamal is to head west through Citilcum and Cacalchén to Tixkokob. From Mérida, the Tixkokob road is well signposted off the *Periférico* ring road.

On the eastern side of Tixkokob, a turn off the main road to the south (hard to see if you're coming from Izamal) leads to Ekmul and Aké. After passing through Ekmul and several bumpy patches you eventually reach Aké. Note that the road to Aké from Highway 180 shown on some maps is still a dirt track, and rougher than the Tixkokob road. Without a car, there are several buses daily from Terminal del Centro in Mérida, and *colectivos* from Tixkokob.

The ruins begin beyond the *hacienda*. The largest, the **Templo de las Pilastras** ('Temple of the Columns'), is ahead and to the left. It is only one of several massively monumental buildings at Aké unlike anything else in the Yucatán. Most Maya temple platforms were built steeply upward, with many narrow steps; the great ramp of the Temple of the Columns is instead a gradual climb of huge, flat stone slabs, leading up to strangely crude drum columns, which probably held up a palm roof. It seems built to a different scale. While unlike Maya styles, it is similar to some central-Mexican temples, which has led to theories about Toltec-Mexican influence. However, it has also been shown this is a very old site, inhabited from around AD 100, and it has not been made clear if, when and how Toltec influence was exerted here, or even whether the Aké platforms do not pre-date 'Mexican' presence at Chichén Itzá.

The Temple of the Columns formed the north side of the **Great Plaza** of Aké, the centre of a city that covered 4 square km. Aké was an important link between Ti'ho (Mérida) and Izamal, and in about 600–700 a *sacbé* was built covering all the 32km from Aké to Izamal (still visible on the east side, the left looking from the Columns). Later this alliance must have broken down, for at some point a rough wall was built around the centre of Aké, crossing and so closing off the *sacbé*.

To the west of the Temple of the Columns two more large buildings were excavated only recently, in 2003: **Structure 2**, a looming pyramid with a strange, round stone tank on one side, and **Structure 3**, opposite the *hacienda*, another platform of massive stone slabs, with a superb view of the village from the top. Some of the most unusual buildings at Aké are outside the main site. Reached from a separate entrance off the village square is a pyramid, **Structure 14**, which astonishingly has the local church built on top, neat and whitewashed in its pagan setting. Many other remains are scattered around the village, combining with remains of the *hacienda*.

Mérida

 Mérida

Mérida, capital of Yucatán state and, in former times, of the entire peninsula, is a city of immense charm imbued with a pervasive romanticism. Beneath the arching palms and laurel trees of its squares there are always *confidenciales*, the S-shaped love-seats in which couples sit whispering and giggling in the cool of the night, and the city's favourite music is the lilting *bolero* of the Yucatán trios, wistful, unashamedly nostalgic songs in which lost loves and dark eyes are serenaded time and time again. *La Ciudad Blanca*, the 'White City', is the colonial city *par excellence* of the Yucatán, with grand stone portals opening on to patios of lush plants and deep shadows that recall Moorish towns of Andalucía. This is only part of Mérida's languid theatricality.

The colonial heritage is everywhere in Mérida – in the giant cathedral, in countless smaller churches, in carvings above gateways and faded inscriptions recalling long-forgotten governors – but the modern culture of the city always seeps through between the stones. It still fulfils very visibly the original role of a city, as market and commercial hub of its region, and every day people from villages and small towns flood into Mérida to buy and sell (the cause of its sometimes overwhelming bus traffic). Come into Mérida from the quiet of the surrounding villages and its urban tone comes as quite a shock. Walk around a little more, though, after the crowds have gone home, and a gentle, much more small-town feel asserts itself.

An essential way to appreciate the atmosphere of *la Ciudad Blanca* is to wander around it at night, when it is at its most mysterious. Churches loom white out of the darkness, the details on 18th-century houses are sharply etched, couples chat in their *confidenciales* with whole squares to themselves, drivers murmur at taxi stands. This exploration involves very little risk, for along with the romanticism for which Yucatecos are known is a gentleness apparent in every area of life here, making for one of the least threatening cities you're ever likely to see. Mérida is a city that invites you to drop your guard, and experience a type of urban life that's near lost elsewhere.

History

Mayan Ti'ho

When the Spaniards arrived in 1540 the city known as *Ichcansiho* or *Ti'ho* was already partially abandoned, with a population much smaller than fitted its imposing ruined pyramids and buildings. These ruins have long since been obliterated and their remains incorporated into the later city. Recent investigations, though,

09 Yucatán State | Mérida

suggest that there had been a settlement here since the Preclassic era, around 300 BC.

As a city Ti'ho reached its apogee between about AD 700 and 900, when it had about 10,000 inhabitants. Politically, though, it was probably subordinate to Dzibilchaltún, to the north. Like other cities in the northern Yucatán it was not completely abandoned in the centuries after the great Collapse like Maya cities in the south, but by the time of the Conquest it was only a tributary settlement of *Chakán*, one of the 19 Maya chieftancies into which the Yucatán was divided. It did, however, retain a giant square, surrounded by some of the region's largest pyramid-platforms.

The City of the *Conquistadores*

In 1540 Francisco de Montejo el Sobrino, youngest of the three identically named conquerors of the Yucatán, arrived in Ti'ho with under 50 men after a bloody, waterless march from Campeche. Its population was too small to offer resistance, while its massive ruins provided an ideal place for a fortified camp. He was shortly joined by his cousin Montejo el Mozo, with reinforcements. Still with only 200 men, they were besieged for months by a force brought together in a rare moment of cooperation by the Yucatán lordships, until in June 1541 the Mayan chiefs launched a frontal assault.

In the bloodiest battle of the conquest in Yucatán the Spaniards held back attack after attack, until one climactic day when Maya morale collapsed. They never again came together for joint resistance, and at the beginning of 1542 Tutul Xiú of Maní was the first of a string of Maya chieftains to come to Ti'ho to accept Spanish rule.

On 6 January 1542 the city of Mérida was formally founded as capital of the new colony. The name was chosen by Montejo el Mozo because its ruins reminded him of the ruins of Roman Mérida in Extremadura, near his home in Salamanca. He immediately began drawing up the city's grid, centred on its Plaza Mayor or Plaza de Armas. The plot on its east side was set aside for a future cathedral. The first Spanish stone building in Mérida, however, was the residence built for El Mozo and his descendants, the Casa de Montejo, completed in 1549.

As the colony was pacified, the conquerors settled down into reproducing the aristocratic way of life they had seen at home in Spain. Yucatán was a down-at-heel colony, which unlike central Mexico or Peru gave its new lords no El Dorado of precious metals. Mérida's leading citizens, though, did not let this blunt their ambitions. Like so much in the *conquistador* saga, this bordered on dreamland. Early colonial Mérida was a very peculiar settlement. Across it there were still plenty of Maya pyramids, especially the glowering *Xbaklumchaan*, a huge platform that filled the west side

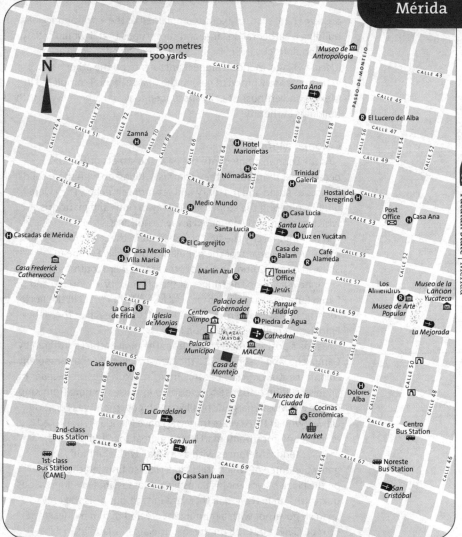

of the Plaza, where the Palacio Municipal is today. Around them most of the 'city' consisted of stick huts with palm roofs, between which there stuck out a growing collection of solid, stone buildings more or less in line with European styles of the late Middle Ages and Renaissance – the Casa de Montejo, the Hospital of San Juan de Dios, the Franciscans' Monastery of the Assumption – virtually all built by Mayan hands under the system of one day's compulsory unpaid labour each week.

Greatest among them was the towering mass of the cathedral. Juan Izquierdo, Bishop of Yucatán at the time of its consecration in 1599, reported to his king in Spain that in 30 years of service in the Americas he had 'never seen anything like it, or close to it'. An austere Franciscan, Izquierdo complained of the extravagance of building a cathedral 'so large and sumptuous that it would satisfy any populous city in Spain' in a settlement he referred to as an *aldea*, a village. Mérida's pioneer aristocrats, on the other hand, were immensely proud of having the first cathedral completed in Mexico, and enthusiastically subscribed to it and other new church buildings in the city.

Colonial Mérida

As the conquest faded into the past, the streets of Mérida became less dramatic in their contrasts, filling up with more solid houses of stone and masonry, and yet more churches. They were built by pilfering the stones of the Mayan ruins and platforms, which consequently dwindled away to nothing.

In the original city the first streets built in the grid, around the plaza, were reserved for the population of wholly European, Spanish origin. Communities of other races were confined to separate *barrios* on the fringes of the official city – Santiago and Santa Catarina to the west for local Maya, Santa Lucía in the north for African slaves and mixed-race mulattos. For each of them the Franciscans built separate churches.

Mérida's position protected it from the pirate attacks suffered by Campeche, and it settled into the slow-moving life of a somnolent colonial centre. Officials became more active in the last decades of Spanish rule, in response to reforming impulses coming from King Charles III. Most energetic of all Spanish governors was Lucás de Gálvez, who in three years from 1789 gave Mérida an unprecedented set of improvements. He was a great road builder, and rebuilt Mérida's defences with a city wall with eight lofty gateways, three of which still stand. He also finished the arcades on the Plaza Mayor. For his pains he was assassinated – for reasons unknown – in his *calesa* in the plaza in 1792, but he is the only Spanish governor with a monument erected to him by locals, the Cruz de Gálvez by C. 28 on the road towards Valladolid.

Independence and Caste War

At the end of the 18th century Mérida in its modest way also acquired a greater cultural life. Erudite gentlemen wrote and studied local traditions, and like others in more prominent Spanish American colonies founded discussion clubs. They had little effect on city life until Napoleon's invasion of Spain threw the empire into turmoil, and local liberals called (relatively mildly) for reform. After the restoration of King Ferdinand VII in 1814, leading liberals were imprisoned, but this only radicalized opinion. In February 1821 the governor marshal Echéverri carried out the last important measure of Spanish rule in the Yucatán, dissolving most houses of the

Getting to Mérida

By Air

Manuel Crescencio Rejón airport is 4km from the city centre on the southwest road to Umán and Campeche, Highway 180, called at this point Av. Aviación. There is a tourist information desk at the airport. Mérida has direct international flights with **Continental (t** 01 800 900 5000)to/from **Houston** and with **Aeroméxico (t** 01 800 021 4000) to/from **Miami**. Within Mexico, **MexicanaClick, t** 01 800 112 5425, and **Aviacsa, t** 01 800 284 2272, both have frequent daily connections with Mexico City, and **Aeroméxico Connect, t** 01 800 800 2376, flies to the capital and Guadalajara, Villahermosa and other cities in northern Mexico. There are also charter flights from the USA, Canada and Europe. **General airport information: t** 946 1530.

Getting to and from the Airport

Only official *Transporte Terrestre* taxis can take incoming passengers into town. A taxi to yourself is about $10, a place in a *colectivo* $5. On departure, any city cab can take you to the airport (about $6–7).

If you walk from the terminal out onto Av. Aviación (about a 5min walk), you can catch any Umán–Mérida local bus into central Mérida for about 50c. This will leave you in Parque San Juan, from where buses towards Umán past the airport also depart.

By Bus

Mérida is the hub of an extraordinarily intricate bus network with services to cities throughout Mexico, and to just about every town and village in the Yucatán. There is a bewildering variety of services running to major destinations, from various termini.

CAME First-Class Bus Station

C. 70, between Calles 69 and 71. The primary terminus for first-class buses, used by ADO and several other companies, and so the main depot for long trips. Many luxury services also pick up and drop off at a depot beside the **Fiesta Americana** hotel (*see* p.277).

For information call **CAME, t** 924 8391, or the **Fiesta Americana, t** 920 4444. Main services from the CAME are as follows. All timetables can change at short notice:

Campeche (*2½hrs*): three ADO GL daily, normal first-class one or two each hour 6am–11.50pm, and three during the night. Fares $10–12.

Cancún (*4¼hrs*): 16 ADO GL or UNO luxury services daily, normal first-class once or twice an hour 2.10am–11.59pm. Fares $19–31.

Chetumal (*6½hrs*) via **Felipe Carrillo Puerto**: four buses daily 7.30am–11pm. Fare $23.

Mexico City (*19–21hrs*): two ADO GL and three normal ADO buses daily. Fares $80–96.

Oaxaca (*21½hrs*): two ADO first-class daily, at 9.50am and 7.10pm. Fare $65.

Palenque (*7–8hrs*): via **Campeche** and **Escárcega**, four ADO or OCC buses daily, at 8.30am, 7.15pm, 10pm and 11.50pm. The 7.15pm OCC bus goes on to **San Cristóbal de Las Casas** (*12¾hrs*) and **Tuxtla Gutiérrez** (*13½hrs*). One ADO GL bus at 11.15pm goes to Tuxtla via Villahermosa. Fares around $28 Palenque, $38 San Cristóbal, $42–58 Tuxtla.

Playa del Carmen (*5–5½hrs*): three ADO GL buses and 12 normal first-class daily, via Valladolid, 6.05am–3.30am. Fare $21–26.

Tulum (*4–4½hrs*) via Valladolid: four first-class daily 6.30am–5.45pm. Fare $15.

Valladolid (*2¼hrs*) via **Chichén Itzá** (*1½hrs*): 15 buses daily 5am–7.30pm; three stop at **Pisté** (for Chichén), at 6.30am, 9.15am, 12.40pm. Fares $7 to Chichén, $10 to Valladolid.

Villahermosa (*8½hrs*): seven ADO GL or UNO, 14 normal first-class daily. Fare $32–49.

Terminal de Autobuses (Second-Class)

C. 69, between Calles 68 and 70 (around the corner from the CAME). The base for a great many routes run by many companies; some of the most useful are below. Many are now *intermedio* services rather than 'traditional' second-class, with a comfort level not far behind first-class. All second-class buses on the main road to Cancún and Playa del Carmen stop at **Chichén Itzá** and **Valladolid**.

Campeche: Autotransportes del Sur, buses every half-hour 4am–10.30pm, on Highway 180. Some are *semi-directos* and don't stop everywhere en route. Five buses daily serve the 'Slow Route' via **Uxmal** and **Hopelchén**.

Cancún: Buses hourly, 6am–midnight; nine or more daily continue on to **Playa del Carmen**. Also there are around six buses daily to Cancún that do not take Highway 180 but go via Tixkokob, Izamal, Tinúm and Valladolid. Average fare around $15.

Chetumal: via **Muna, Ticul, Felipe Carrillo Puerto** and **Bacalar**, seven or more buses daily, 7am–midnight.

Chiquilá/Isla Holbox: via **Valladolid**, one bus nightly at 11.30pm. Fare around $12.

Puuc Route: An ATS/Mayab bus leaves daily at 8am and returns at 2.30pm, stopping at **Uxmal** and the main sites on the route (but not Loltún), with time for each visit. Tickets are around $11. For **Uxmal** and **Kabah** there are eight buses a day along Highway 261 to **Hopelchén**, from where most go on to **Campeche** on the 'Slow Route', but one carries on to **Dzibalchén**. A second-class return to Uxmal only will cost around $6–7.

Autoprogreso Depot

C. 62 no. 524, between Calles 65 and 67. Buses to **Progreso** every 10mins 5am–10pm. *Colectivos* to Progreso can be found one street over, on C. 60, also between 65 and 67.

Terminal del Centro

C. 65, between Calles 48 and 50. The base for Autobuses del Centro second-class services to **Progreso** and along the north coast to **Dzilam Bravo**; also frequent buses to **Izamal**, including some that continue via Dzitas to **Valladolid** and **Cancún**; and many more village services in central Yucatán, with a few direct to **Aké**.

Terminal del Noreste

C. 67, corner of Calle 50. Used by several second-class companies operating local services, mostly within Yucatán State. Among the main destinations served are **Celestún** (Occidente, at least 10 buses daily roughly 5am–8.30pm); the north coast to **Dzilam Bravo**; **Tizimín, Río Lagartos, Colonia Yucatán** and **El Cuyo**; **Izamal** (Oriente, frequent buses); **Chichén Itzá** and **Valladolid** via **Izamal**, including some buses that go on to **Cancún** and **Playa del Carmen**; and **Mayapán, Maní, Oxcutzcab, Yaxuná** and other destinations in the eastern Puuc and central Yucatán.

Combis and Colectivos

Mérida's authorities have for some time hoped to rationalize the sometimes chaotic overkill of public transport in many parts of the city by providing garages for the *colectivos* and *combis* that run to and from villages all around Yucatán state. But, for the time being, most *combi* collecting-points are still in the street, often in squares and mostly not too far from the market. The **Parque San Juan** is used by *combis* to many locations south and west of Mérida, especially Umán, Muna and other places near the Puuc Hills such as Ticul, but also by some that run to the north, notably to Dzibilchaltún and Chablekal. **C. 69 between 56 and 54** and **C. 67 between 50 and 48** are main *combi*-points for Tixkokob, Izamal, Sotuta and other points to the east.

By Car

If you are **driving into Mérida** from Cancún and Valladolid on Highway 180 you will first meet the *Anillo Periférico*, the city's outer ring road. Cross straight over it to get on to C. 65, which will take you fairly directly (if in doubt, follow signs for *Mérida-Centro* or just *Centro*) into the centre of the city. Alternatively, turn left at the *Periférico* for Campeche and the south, or right for Progreso and the coast.

On C. 65 you reach an inner ring road, the *Círcuito Colonias*. Continue across it and you enter Mérida's central grid (*see* below). To get to the centre turn right at C. 52, then up two blocks before turning left on C. 61 for the Plaza Mayor.

Coming in from Campeche, Uxmal and the south on Highway 180-west, you will join Av. Aviación, a long, busy road that runs past the airport until it becomes the Av. Itzaes. Follow this till you see a sign to the right for *Mérida-Centro* on to C. 59 (a surprisingly abrupt turn).

Driving out of Mérida can be more complex. To get on to the Cancún road east from the city centre, the best way is to get on to C. 59 to the *Círcuito Colonias*, turn right, and then look for signs (often small) to the left for Cancún. For Campeche and Uxmal, take C. 65 west as far as Av. Itzaes, turn left, and follow signs for Umán and Campeche. For Progreso and the north coast, get on to C. 60 or Paseo Montejo and follow them straight out of town.

Getting around Mérida

A classic Spanish colonial grid, central Mérida has an easy-to-grasp layout of long, straight streets anchored on the **Plaza Mayor** or Zócalo, and the main street, **Calle 60**, that runs across it. Even-numbered streets run north–south, odd numbers east–west. This grid is interrupted to the north by the Paseo Montejo, and other larger streets with names rather than numbers. Away from the centre the grid breaks down, streets divide (31-A, 31-B, etc.), and some *colonias* and *fraccionamientos* have their own numbering systems.

Since the streets of the grid are so long, in addresses it's usual to indicate the block as well as the house number, as in C. 57 no. 436, x 56 & 58 (between Calles 56 and 58).

The compactness of central Mérida means the easiest way to get about is to walk, but if you need to get anywhere fast, a staggering range of transport is on hand to take you.

By Bus

It can seem that every street in the city has its own bus or *combi* route. Stops and destinations are written on the windscreen, so to find a bus to any part of town requires some knowledge of local geography. However, the only area most visitors use a bus to get to is just north of the centre, the Paseo Montejo and the Anthropology Museum, and it's fairly easy to find a bus marked 'Paseo Montejo' or 'Gran Plaza' (a big mall at the top of the route). For the return journey, look for any bus marked 'Centro'. Many routes to north Mérida begin and end on C. 59 between Calles 58 and 54. Most buses for Montejo run up C. 60, C. 56 or C. 52. Many buses to the west of the city run along C. 61, or from C. 65 south of the Plaza Mayor.

Away from route termini buses stop at street corners: in a few places there are blue and white bus stop (*parada*) signs, but otherwise, stand at a corner and flag a bus down. There is one set fare for each route, normally 3–5 pesos in buses, about 3 pesos in *combis*.

By Car and Bicycle

Parking in central Mérida is very restricted, and if you have a car it's best to find a hotel with off-street parking. Where parking is not allowed the kerb is painted yellow, and restrictions are strongly enforced. The most central **petrol/gas station** is on C. 59, x 62 & 64.

Angeles Verdes roadside assistance: t 983 1184.

Cycling in central Mérida can be nerve-wracking at peak times, but just a few blocks from the main drags and at weekends things are much quieter. Also, on Sunday mornings the whole of Calle 60 (from Parque San Juan) and Paseo Montejo are now closed to other traffic as a **Bici-ruta** to encourage cycling, with bikes to rent from a stand on the Paseo (near the Fiesta Americana).

Car and Bicycle Hire

Rental rates in Mérida are still, overall, lower than around Cancún, and this is always the best place to hire a car for driving around the Yucatán. Below is only a selection of the local agencies. Note: 'rentacar touts' may approach you around C. 60, offering to take you to a cheap rental agency; their 'commission' will be reflected in the price you are charged, which will scarcely ever be as low as the one they promised. It's best to go to an agency direct.

Easyway, C. 60 no. 484, x 55 & 57, t 930 9500, *www.easywayrentacar-yucatan.com*. A big choice and special offers.

Ecorent, C. 3 no. 235, x 32-A &34, Colonia Pensiones, t 920 2772, *www.ecoyuc.com*. Part of the Ecoturismo Yucatán agency, with cars, and mountain bikes ($10 a day) for rent.

Mexico Rent a Car, C. 57-A (Callejón del Congreso) Depto 12, x 58 & 60, and C. 62 no. 483 A, x 57 & 59, t 923 3637, *mexicorentacar@hotmail.com*. Highly recommended local company: personal friendly service and rates are the best in the region, beginning at around $30 a day for a small car with unlimited mileage; other models, with a/c, are also available. Costs are lower for longer-period hire, and drop-off can be arranged in Cancún. The main office is in the Callejón del Congreso pedestrian alleyway beside the Teatro Peón Contreras, just north of the Iglesia de Jesús.

Veloz Rent a Car, C. 60 no. 486, x 55 & 57, t 928 0373, *www.velozrentacar.com.mx*. Various models from around $35 a day ($45 in peak seasons)

By Taxi

Mérida's city authorities have taken the radical step of abolishing the single-union local taxi monopoly traditional in Mexico, with its fixed rates per area, and introducing taxis with meters (*taxímetros*). There are now several competing companies, and most (but not all) taxis now have meters. Fares are more expensive than in most Mexican cities, at around 30 pesos for journeys within central Mérida, but metered taxis are nearly always cheaper than those that still use set rates. Companies below have only metered taxis.

EconoTaxi, t 945 0000.

Radio Taxis Mérida, t 923 1317.

Taxímetro, t 982 2250.

Taxi Seguro, t 922 7575.

By *Calesa* (Horse-drawn Carriage)

A favourite way of seeing Mérida is from a *calesa*, one of the traditional horse-drawn carriages that ply for trade in the Plaza Mayor, by the junction of Calles 60 and 61. The most popular trip, the *tradicional* from the square up C. 60 and Paseo Montejo and back again, costs around $15 (per *calesa*), the longer *doble* $22. Some drivers speak English and are full of anecdotes on the city's history and its buildings, and the ride is especially enjoyable at night. Neither is it a purely touristy affair; on Sundays *calesas* are full of local families and couples.

religious orders. In September of the same year, the governor himself made his departure.

As capital of a semi-independent Yucatán, Mérida was the focus of all the factional intrigues of the new state, but its social life changed little. It was this city, small, remote and with a life still revolving around religious festivals, that John Lloyd Stephens visited in 1840. Falling in love apparently on a daily basis with 'charming young ladies', he wrote after an afternoon watching the *paseo* on the Alameda – a colonial-era promenade swallowed up by the modern market area – that, 'as the sun sank behind the ruins of the *castillo*, we thought that there were few places in the world where it went down upon a prettier or happier scene'.

This city was accustomed to treating the Maya villages around it at arm's length, and the upheaval of the Caste War came as an utter shock. In May 1848, as town after town fell to the Maya bands, refugees flooded into the capital, camping out in the Plaza Mayor and anywhere they could find. Gálvez' city gates were shut up against attackers for the first (and last) time, although to the north the road to Sisal was full of an endless line of escapees from the city, desperate to find a boat. At the end of the month the bishop left, and military leaders declared further defence unsustainable.

Then, when the Maya inexplicably turned back from the brink of victory and went home (*see* p.55), the jubilation was naturally immense. Bells rang, fireworks were set off and, as the hostile Maya were pushed back into the remote east Mérida received a shot of brio. In the years following the siege the Plaza Mayor was relaid, the Palacio Municipal was rebuilt and an 'Academy of Science and Literature' was founded.

The Boom Town of the Porfiriato

In 1865 Mérida welcomed Empress María Carlota, the Belgian wife of Maximilian, with 11 days of lavish celebrations, balls, concerts and *fiestas*. After the upheavals of the previous 40 years many of the city's good families liked the idea of having a monarchy under a real European royal house again, and María Carlota remembered Mérida as the most genuinely loyal place in Mexico. What's more, this loyalty was put to the test in 1867 as the Empire crumbled, when a force advanced from Republican Tabasco. The imperial commander, Colonel Traconis, somewhat quixotically decided to carry out his duty at all costs, and fought on even after Maximilian himself had been taken prisoner. The Republican army subjected Mérida to a 55-day siege.

After this imperial interlude there would be no more battles in Mérida. Under the Díaz regime after 1876, its great transformation was not political but economic. Railways and the new port at Progreso facilitated exports of sisal rope from Yucatán's *henequen* plantations, the 'green gold' for which the world had an insatiable demand. Money and people poured into sleepy Mérida, which doubled in size, from around 30,000 people in 1870 to over 60,000 by 1910, including 'exotic' communities from China and the Lebanon. A great part of the wealth of Yucatán's 'Gilded Age' also went straight to the *henequen* barons themselves. Yucatecan magnates became familiar figures in European resorts, while at home they picked up imported luxuries at stores with names like *Au Petit Paris* and *La Ciudad de Londres*.

Led by Governor Olegario Molina – the greatest *henequenero* of them all, and the Díaz regime's favourite figure in the Yucatán – the *henequen* oligarchs also set about improving their town to suit their new tastes. Mérida was the first Mexican provincial city to have fully paved streets, tramways were laid, and a new business area was created on C. 65, with multistorey buildings. Molina and his fellow modernizers also resolved to break out of the old colonial grid and give their city a modern, elegant avenue on a par with those of the great cities of Europe. Paris was the benchmark in sophistication for the élite of the *Porfiriato*, and their new boulevard, the Paseo de Montejo, was to resemble the Champs-Elysées. Begun in 1904, it gave a new centre to elegant society. The *henequen* boom saw the greatest transformation of Mérida since its foundation, the stamp of which can still be seen all over the city.

Revolution and the Modern Era

Thanks to Yucatán's confused internal politics – and the entrenched power of Mérida's *henequen* barons – much of local life carried on surprisingly unchanged through the first five years of the Mexican Revolution. Consequently, when General Salvador Alvarado was sent to bring the Revolution to the state in 1915, he sought to change things very visibly. In September 1915 he closed all churches in response to the anti-revolutionary activities of Catholic priests. On 15 September a revolutionary mob invaded Mérida cathedral, burning images and leaving it as bare as it is today.

Alvarado also introduced immediate improvements in the conditions of workers on *henequen* estates. In the 1920s, Yucatán's short-lived Socialist government under Felipe Carrillo Puerto brought in educational reforms and urban improvements. He also introduced an ultra-liberal divorce law that for a time made Mérida the divorce capital of the western hemisphere. The last major violence of the Revolutionary era came in January 1924, when right-wing soldiers in Mérida executed Carrillo Puerto. A popular hero, he is commemorated in street names throughout the peninsula.

Since then Mérida life has been far less eventful. The main change over the next decades was the decline in the *henequen* trade, which was only counterbalanced when the creation of Cancún brought tourism and a whole new source of wealth. In Mexico's new era of open politics since the mid-1990s, Mérida has sought a reputation as 'the best-run city in Mexico', with a reforming city administration that has made it something of a showcase for the PAN, producing a raft of urban initiatives including a formerly unheard-of range of cultural and arts programmes.

The Plaza Mayor

A near-automatic starting point is the grand main square, most commonly known as the Plaza Mayor but also referred to as the Plaza Grande, Zócalo, Plaza de la Independencia and, historically, Plaza de Armas. This was the centre of Mayan Ti'ho, surrounded by pyramids, and so the point that Montejo el Mozo took as the hub of the city's grid when he founded Christian Mérida in 1542. On each side of the square, in accordance with Spanish colonial practice, he and the first mayor Gaspar Pacheco founded major buildings: a cathedral on the east side, the *Casas Reales* (centre of government for the whole of the Yucatán) to the north, and the *Casas Consistoriales* (municipal government) to the west, while on the south side the *conquistador* built himself the most distinguished private residence in the city, the Casa de Montejo.

Dominating the vista is the giant, perpendicular mass of the **Cathedral of San Ildefonso**, begun in 1562 and completed in 1598. It is the oldest cathedral on the American mainland, and only Santo Domingo (in the Dominican Republic) is older in the whole continent. Its most important architect was Juan Manuel de Agüero, from Cantabria in northern Spain, who worked on it from 1585 to 1590, but the cathedral was the work of many minds and hundreds of Maya labourers. Its completion was often delayed, especially by the practice of successive governors of appointing their own protégés (and children) to the post of *Veedor* or supervisor of the works.

Like many smaller Yucatán churches it is a severe work of plain stone, in an austere Spanish Renaissance style with limestone walls lightened by elaborately carved Plateresque details. Although its builders were in touch with architectural ideas in Europe they had their eccentricities, such as the fact that the cathedral's two towers, despite appearances, are not actually identical. Between them are three portals, with an imposing main entrance flanked by figures representing St Peter and St Paul, and smaller doors on either side. Above the entrance the façade used to be dominated by a giant Spanish Habsburg crest but, in 1822, during Mexico's ephemeral 'First Empire', this was replaced by a Mexican eagle, still with crown, that remains there today.

The cathedral is still plainer inside than out, with whitewashed walls, having lost most of its images in Mérida's many revolutions, especially in 1915. At the end of the nave on the left is one of the most revered shrines it does retain, *El Cristo de las Ampollas* (Christ of the Blisters), a statue of Christ on the cross in blackened wood. The legend goes that it was made in Ichmul, deep in central Yucatán, from a tree struck by lightning that had burnt for a whole night without being destroyed. Then, after the statue survived a second fire that destroyed the church of Ichmul – albeit with a little blistering in the wood – it was attributed miraculous powers, and brought to Mérida in 1645. A third conflagration, that of 1915, saw the figure remade again. At the back of the cathedral on C. 61 there is a separate chapel, the **Capilla de los Apóstoles**, with bizarre life-sized painted figures of Christ and the apostles at the Last Supper.

Palacio del Gobernador
open daily 8–8

Forming a right angle with the cathedral on the plaza is the **Palacio del Gobernador**, seat of the state government of Yucatán, built in 1892 to replace an earlier colonial governors' palace. It is open to anyone to wander around its main patio and public rooms. Apart from the airy, neo-colonial patio, its main attraction is the series of intensely dramatic murals and paintings carried out by the Yucatecan artist Fernando Castro Pacheco in the 1970s, giving a fiercely felt synthesis of Maya and *mestizo* history. Particularly impressive is the mural on the main staircase, representing the Maya creation myth whereby man arose out of maize (*hombre de maíz*).

Palacio Municipal
open daily 8–8

The western side of the plaza, running down from C. 62, is dominated by the **Palacio Municipal**, the town hall. Only its main doorway, slightly lost beneath its later portico, remains from the original 16th-century *Casas Consistoriales*. The façade is now dominated by an elegant ten-arched colonnade, with matching loggia above, begun in 1735 and one of the finest creations of late-colonial Spanish architecture in the Yucatán. The Palace has been rebuilt several times, and its patios are plain, but on the second floor next to the loggia there is the *Sala de Historia* or old council chamber, a dark, wood-panelled room full of relics of local citizens and great events in the saga of Mexican independence.

Complementing the Palace, alongside it toward C. 61, is the **Centro Cultural Olimpo**, built in 1999 but in the style of a 19th-century theatre and indoor circus that stood here until it was knocked down in the 1960s. It contains exhibition spaces, a café and a bookshop, and from the upper floor you get a great head-on view of the Cathedral. Look up the next block on C. 62 and your eye is caught by the **Teatro Mérida**, an Art Deco jukebox of a cinema restored in 2000. As well as hosting music and theatre it is Mérida's official film theatre, showing an international range of movies.

The south side of the square is mainly taken up by 19th-century buildings, but the eye is drawn to the much older portico of the **Casa de Montejo**, built in 1549 as the residence of the *Adelantado* and his descendants, and retained by the Montejo family until the

09 Yucatán State | Mérida

time of independence. Very little of the present building is original, since it has been almost entirely rebuilt over the years, and now houses a Banamex bank. Still intact, however – despite the inevitable crumbling of limestone – is the extraordinary portico, one of the finest examples in Mexico of the Spanish Plateresque style. The lower section, around the main gateway, has a Renaissance elegance: above it, though, is a giant frieze, around a balconied window, which gives the whole façade its character. At the centre is the Montejo coat of arms; on either side are giant bearded warriors, in suits of armour, each of whose feet bears down on a screaming head. Beside them, there are two much smaller bearded figures with strange, scaled skin. The two warriors have long been believed to represent the Montejos, father and son, and the screaming heads the Yucatán Indians, making the façade a portrayal of the Conquest in the most brutally graphic manner possible, although it's conceivable they have a more mythological significance. In either case, the façade is still a remarkable combination of the Renaissance and Gothic imagination, transplanted to the Americas and almost certainly carried out in some part by Maya craftsmen.

The plaza also has other attractions. Big as the cathedral is, it was once even larger, for until the 20th century it occupied the entire block between the plaza and Calles 61, 63 and 58. The southern half of the block contained the Bishop's Palace, which was rebuilt during the Revolution to become the **Ateneo Peninsular**, a cultural centre for the new era. The pedestrian alleyway of **Pasaje de la Revolución**, between the Cathedral and the Ateneo, is used as an exhibition space for large-scale sculpture by the Museo de Arte Contemporáneo de Yucatán. Better known as **MACAY**, this now occupies most of the old Ateneo. Mérida is a lively contemporary art centre, and the MACAY provides a fine showcase. As well as hosting temporary shows, the museum has permanent exhibits. There are more works by Fernando Castro Pacheco, not as dramatic as his murals in the Palacio del Gobernador but similarly reflecting on the relation between the Indian past and the Mexican present; in complete contrast are the works of two other Yucatecan artists, Gabriel Ramírez Aznar and Fernando García Ponce, abstract and international in style. There is also *El Bordado Yucateco*, a display of Yucatán embroidery, and a patio which hosts a café with tables shaded by giant *huaya*, *caymito* and laurel trees.

In the streets around the Plaza Mayor there are plenty of other reminiscences of the colonial city, often in small details. Walk around to the back of the MACAY on C. 58 and you can admire the neoclassical portico of the **Seminary of San Ildefonso**, built in the 1750s. Usually ignored by the crowds below, it is topped by two engaging statues of the Virgin and Child and the Bishop-Saint Ildefonso. On C. 61, opposite the cathedral, stands one of the very

MACAY
entrance on Pasaje Revolución, t 928 3236, www.macay.org; open Wed–Mon 10–6, Fri, Sat until 8pm, closed Tues; free.

Moonlight Serenades

Sit under the colonnades of the Plaza Mayor at weekends, as it gets dark, and you may notice groups of men gathering on the pavements in the centre of the square and by the Palacio Municipal, carrying guitars, always in threes and dressed in white *guayaberas* and black trousers. These are members of the Yucatecan trios, available for hire, as they have been for over a century, to play *serenatas* (serenades). As you watch, cars drive up, kerb-crawling for musicians; a deal is agreed, and the three men get in the car and drive off to their booking for the night. Sometimes, the couple may only want one song, and the trio performs there and then at the car window.

Each trio has its spot around the plaza, and turns up with no idea whether they might be facing five performances or none. This unpredictability is met with typical Yucatecan disregard. The music they play – some international intrusions aside – is the languid, dreamy, nostalgic, Cuban-influenced boleros and similar rhythms of the Yucatán. There is a huge repertoire of Yucatecan songs, nearly all with utterly romantic lyrics in which a whole soul is given in a kiss and the light of the stars is reflected in flashing eyes. Tourists hear this music in hotels or at Thursday *serenatas* in Parque Santa Lucía, but few seem to contact trios off the street in the traditional way. The clientele that keeps them going is overwhelmingly local, and of all ages. It's traditional to have a trio for weddings, christenings, and family parties, but couples also go down to the plaza on their own to pick a trio on anniversaries or birthdays. If you wish to hire one yourselves, normal rates begin at about 300 pesos a *serenata*.

earliest colonial buildings in Mérida, the **Capilla del Hospital de San Juan de Dios**. Begun just after the cathedral but finished much earlier, in 1579, the chapel was built in a remarkably archaic, almost Romanesque style that makes it one of the most authentically medieval European buildings anywhere in the Americas.

Calle 60

After a circuit of the Plaza Mayor, a natural first step in getting to know Mérida is a stroll up Calle 60, off the square to the north between the Governor's Palace and the cathedral. The city's main thoroughfare since its foundation, it is still the site of theatres, hotels, restaurants and the best places for people-watching. There's also a big concentration of shops selling *artesanía*, hats, hammocks and other knick-knacks, and as you cross to enter C. 60 you will almost inevitably be approached by someone proffering a card. They're rarely persistent if you say you've bought enough junk already. From the same corner, horse-drawn *calesas* depart on tours around town.

At the end of the first block on the right by C. 59 is the **Parque Hidalgo**, Mérida's second most important square and one of the best places to take in the local scene. Full of exuberant fan palms that give it a delicious lushness, it has on a plinth at its centre a statue of General Manuel Cepeda Pereza, a major player in Yucatán and Mexico's 19th-century wars. Around him there are benches and *confidenciales*, newspaper sellers, tourists, young couples, old men spinning out conversations, taxi drivers waiting for fares, students, and men collecting their thoughts. A (sadly diminishing) number of cafés and bars provide suitable vantage points.

Across C. 59 from the square stands the **Iglesia de Jesús**. Built as the local seat of the Jesuits, relative latecomers to Yucatán, and consecrated in 1618, it is also known as the *Iglesia de la Tercera Orden*, after the Third Order of Franciscans to whom the church passed after the expulsion of the Jesuits from all Spanish dominions in 1767. As befits its Jesuit origins it is more ornate than its Franciscan neighbours. Like other colonial churches, the Jesús was built out of the stones of Maya temples. The Spaniards made every effort to ensure no trace of their former use remained visible, destroying carved surfaces or placing them inside the wall. Here, however, in the massive wall facing Parque Hidalgo (opposite the taxi stand), two stones bearing recognizable Maya carvings are clearly visible. Regarded as the prettiest of the city's churches, the Jesús usually has the most beautiful flower displays, and is a favourite place for weddings. The most popular time for them is Saturday evenings, taking advantage of the evening cool, when the church's spectacular decorations – from altar flowers to garlands in the aisles – are brilliantly illuminated against the night.

Alongside the Jesús is another small square, forming a pair with Parque Hidalgo, the **Parque de la Madre**. A pedestrian alleyway, the Callejón del Congreso or C. 57-A, separates this square and the Jesús from the giant bulk of the **Teatro Peón Contreras**, which takes up the rest of the block facing C. 60. By the time of the *henequen* boom, Yucatán's magnates decided that the city's humble theatre, built on this site in 1831, was no longer adequate, and in the 1890s the vastly expanded building you see today was commissioned from two of their favourite architects, the Italians Pio Piacentini and Enrico Deserti. Deserti's grand style won him many clients in Mérida at that time, and he was also responsible for the Palacio Cantón, now the Museo de Antropología. No expense was spared in building the theatre, inaugurated in 1908.

Restored in the 1990s, it has recently gained a new lease of life thanks to the city's new arts programmes, particularly as the home of Yucatán's symphony orchestra. Outside performance times visitors are free to wander around to examine its opulent fittings, especially the grand loggia overlooking C. 60. On the ground floor there's a tourist office. Outside at the far end of C. 57-A, forming a trio with the theatre and the Jesús, is the 1970s-modern **Yucatán State Congress** building. Across C. 60, the Peón Contreras faces another cultural institution: the main building of the **Universidad de Yucatán**. Its patio hosts folkdance displays every Friday.

Continue on up C. 60 and you will see, on the left at C. 55, one of Mérida's prettiest squares, the **Parque de Santa Lucía**. Parts of it date from 1575, and, lined on two sides with a low colonnade, it has a deliciously romantic ambience that sums up the essence of colonial Mérida. In the opposite corner from the street junction is a small stage, surrounded by busts of the great figures in *la Trova Yucateca*, Yucatecan song. Every Thursday this is the venue for the

Serenatas Yucatecas, free performances of traditional songs and dances, for which Santa Lucía is ideally suited.

Facing the square is the 17th-century church of **Santa Lucía,** slightly hidden by trees. In colonial Mérida, the surrounding *barrio* was reserved for black slaves and mulattos, and the church was first built to serve them. One of the simpler colonial churches, it's also one of the prettiest, and rivals the Jesús as a Saturday-evening wedding venue.

Beyond Santa Lucía C. 60 becomes more functional, but further along at C. 47 is another engaging square, **Parque de Santa Ana,** with a small food market and great cheap *loncherías* and cafés. On one side of the square is the **Iglesia de Santa Ana,** a pink-painted church with 1730 on its façade and two squat spires that can look like a pair of crude rockets or salt cellars by moon- and street-light. On the façade a stone commemorates the burial here in 1734 of Don Antonio de Figueroa, Governor and Captain-General of Yucatán, who died in August the previous year on his way back from Bacalar, where he had undertaken the 'extermination of the English', the Belize pirates who plagued Yucatán's colonial masters. The Santa Ana district has also become one of the city's hubs for contemporary **art galleries.** La Luz Galería and Casa de los Artistas both show striking, contrasting work.

La Luz Galería
C. 60 no. 415, x 45 & 47,
t 924 5952,
www.laluzgaleria.com

Casa de los Artistas
C. 60 no. 405, x 43 & 45,
t 928 6566,
www.artistsinmexico.com

East of the Plaza Mayor

Traffic becomes thinner and the atmosphere more placid as soon as you move away from the central area. To the east of C. 60, C. 59 runs for five long blocks to **Parque de la Mejorada,** another shady square, laid out in 1745. It contains one of the most imposing colonial churches, **La Mejorada.** A stone inside the portico commemorates its consecration in 1640, in the reign of King Philip IV, when it was built as part of a monastery of the same name. This was the only one of the Franciscan houses in Mérida that was allowed to remain after the dissolution of religious houses in the Spanish Empire in 1821, but it too was closed by the Juárez *Reforma* in 1857. Later a hospital, most of its buildings have stayed intact, if repeatedly used for new purposes.

Behind the church on the north side of the block is one of the city's most charming museums, spaciously housed in a former school. The **Museo de la Canción Yucateca,** C. 57 no 464, x 48 & 50, the 'museum of Yucatecan song', is a vivid indication of Yucatecans' devotion to their own music. The region's many composers and performers are all lovingly recorded, and the music can be heard on videos or through headphones; it also hosts live concerts. On the opposite side of the plaza, the foundation behind the Centro Cultural in Izamal (*see* p.249) has renovated the **Casa Molina,** a grand 1900s mansion built for the daughter of *henequen* baron

Museo de la Canción Yucateca
t 928 3660, open Tues–Fri 9–5, Sat, Sun 9–3; adm

Museo de Arte Popular de Yucatán
C. 50 no. 487, x 57 & 59; t 930 4700; open Tues–Sat 9.30–4.30, Sun 9–2; adm, free Sun.

Galería Mérida
C. 59 no 452A, x 52 & 54, t 924 0117, www.galeriamerida.com

Olegario Molina, as the **Museo de Arte Popular de Yucatán**. Apart from the attraction of the house itself, it's a must for anyone at all interested in Mexican folk art, with a fabulous collection and pretty shop. A block away is another gallery, **Galería Mérida**

South of the Mejorada on C. 50 there are two very solid relics of old Mérida, a pair of the eight huge gateways in the 18th-century city wall. Most imposing is the **Arco de Dragones** across C. 61, so called because next to it there was a barracks for Mérida's garrison of Spanish dragoons. The **Arco del Puente** on C. 63 has on either side two small doorways, built to allow people to pass through on foot when the main gate was closed. They are scarcely 1.2m tall, not to fit the average height of the local Maya population, but to make it difficult for interlopers to force an entry. Along Calles 61 and 63, the arches can be seen towering above the streets and easily give the impression that you still are within a walled city.

West of the Plaza Mayor

On C. 63, at the junction with C. 64, stands the **Iglesia de las Monjas** (Church of the Nuns), so called because it was built as the chapel of a closed Convent of the Order of the Conception. Most of the building still exists behind the church. The ex-soldiers and officials who made up Yucatán's 16th-century aristocracy sought to give their rudimentary town all the institutions of a Spanish city of the Golden Age, and this convent was founded in the 1590s on the initiative of one old *conquistador*, Francisco de San Martín. Like aristocratic families back home, he and other important citizens had pious daughters who wished to enter nunneries, and until then had been obliged to send them all the way to Mexico City. The church's most unusual feature is the watchtower or *mirador* above the apse, visible from C. 63, with a pillared loggia built to allow the nuns to take some air without leaving their enclosed world. Inside, Las Monjas, now only a parish church, still has in place the impressive metal grilles, the oldest in Mexico, that separated the nuns from visiting lay worshippers.

The other surviving convent buildings of Las Monjas were converted in the 1970s into a cultural centre, the **Casa de Cultura del Mayab**, which among other institutions houses the **Casa de las Artesanías**, the state handicrafts store (*see* p.276).

Northwest of Las Monjas at Calles 59 and 72, the solid walls of the cityscape give way to another unfussily charming square, **Parque de Santiago**, with a local market, and a 17th-century church, Santiago. The placid streets around it are a popular location for small hotels. Just off the square is **Casa Frederick Catherwood**. A remarkable piece of old Mérida, this early-1900s house has been carefully restored, as a labour of love. Its prime exhibit is a beautiful complete set – the only one in Mexico – of the original

Casa Frederick Catherwood
C. 59 no 573, x 72 & 74, www.casa-catherwood.com; open Mon–Sat 9–2 and 5–9; free

The *Jarana*

The music that accompanies the *jarana*, best-known of Yucatecan folk dances, can almost represent the distinctiveness of the region in itself. Played by a band with plenty of trombone, cornets and drums, it has some of the bouncy regularity of Mexican traditional music, but with an obvious touch of the more sensuous rhythms of the Spanish Caribbean. Its recurrent rhythms, meanwhile, give it a flavour that is different again from either.

The dance developed on the *haciendas* of Yucatán, as part of the annual vaquerías or country *fiestas*. Like so many Mexican traditional dances it is a flirtation dance, but one with an extra delicacy. The man courts rather than teases the woman, and at times the flirtation element is lost within the movement of the dance. Men and women enter in separate ranks, break up into couples and then re-form, in a great variety of set patterns. Also popular are the different 'prowess' dances: one involves threading and unthreading ribbons around a kind of maypole, while another (always shown to tourists) includes dancing with bottles on a tray on the head.

Groups dance *jaranas* every week in the Plaza Mayor, Santa Lucía and other venues. All the dancers must wear the same uniform: high-collared *guayabera*, plain trousers and panama hat, all in white, for the boys; magnificently embroidered *ternos* for the girls, with plenty of traditional jewellery and their hair up in a bun, held by a silk band adorned with roses, carnations and daisies, bunched on one side of the head.

09 Yucatán State | Mérida

Galería Tataya
*C. 72 no. 478, x 53 &
55, t 928 2962,
www.tataya.com.mx*

Parque del Centenario
open daily 6–6
zoo
open daily 8–5

1844 lithographs of Frederick Catherwood's famous drawings from his Yucatán travels, but it also acts as an unusual cultural centre, with a café and a little fair-trade shop. Nearby there's another art gallery, **Galería Tataya**, with original craftwork as well as fine art.

Another seven blocks west is **Parque del Centenario**, at the junction of C. 59 and Av. Itzaes, Mérida's largest park, which contains its **zoo**

South: the Market District

The streets south and immediately east of the Plaza Mayor form the commercial heart of Mérida, on which, every weekday, what seems like half the entire population of Yucatán converge to buy, sell, do any other business and look for anything else they might need (as a result, this is also the area with the most bus congestion). They will almost certainly find what they're after, for it's difficult to think of anything you *can't* buy here. On C. 56, between C. 59 and C. 61, you can find car parts, cheap trainers and lots of watches, and buy and sell gold; continue on down between C. 61 and C. 63, and there are ranks of fridges, cookers and other electricals, sewing machines, yet more shoes, and toys. Since people here still expect to repair rather than replace things when they go wrong, there are plenty of repairers and shops selling spares for every kind of item, from radio parts to sewer pipes and bags of cement.

Busiest of all is C. 65 between C. 60 and C. 64, although for a change, just east next to C. 56, the street is largely given over to multicoloured shops selling jokes, *piñatas* and anything else you might fancy for a *fiesta*. The greatest hub of activity is the junction of Calles 65 and 56, an open space developed slightly by accident. It's given a focus by the imposing 1908 former post office, which

**Museo de la
Ciudad**
*t 923 6869; open
Tues–Fri 8–8, Sat and
Sun 8–2; free*

now stands out even more in the area as it contains the **Museo de la Ciudad**, the city museum. It's a mine of information on the city's past, with artefacts from Mayan Ti'ho and carvings, paintings, prints and photographs from the colonial and Díaz eras, all attractively presented. Also of interest is the upper floor, which hosts often very dynamics shows by young Yucatecan artists.

Outside, on this part of C. 65 and calles 65-A and 63-A you'll find the best hammock shops (*see* p.276). The market proper is behind the museum. In 2006 a huge new market building opened, **Mercado de San Benito**, but many traders refused to leave the historic **Mercado Lucás de Gálvez**, so that instead of being relocated the market just got even bigger. Theoretically between Calles 65, 69, 54 and 58, it actually sprawls over several more blocks. On C. 56 is a battered but elegant colonnade, in terracotta and white, which is the oldest part of the market, the 18th-century **Portal de Granos** ('Grain Gate'). Beneath its columns Maya women sit amid selections of fruit or fresh chillies, and stalls selling T-shirts, bags or cutlery; this is only a taster, though, for the truly extraordinary variety inside.

Some of the market's crisscrossing lanes are quite broad, while others are narrow alleys that barely allow two people to pass at a time, with stalls held up by ropes that catch taller wanderers unawares. In some lanes there are dazzling displays of fresh flowers, or bright fruit – mangoes, oranges, pineapples – and fierce red chillies. Elsewhere there are lanes full of nothing but leather sandals, every possible size of metal pot, religious images or hundreds of varieties of bags. Above the main market, reached by a ramp from C. 56 with C. 67, is the handicrafts market, the **Bazar de Artesanías** (*see* p.276), on the same level as the *cocinas económicas*.

This area has its monuments. At the corner of Calles 50 and 67 is the church of **San Cristóbal**, another limestone blockhouse. By contrast, eight blocks west along C. 67 by C. 64 – and unfortunately often locked – is **La Candelaria**, a beautiful early Franciscan chapel with a Baroque altarpiece. This is near the other focus of south-central Mérida, the **bus stations** at Calles 69 and 70. A block south of the Candelaria at C. 69 and 64 is another square, **Parque de San Juan**. Today its most noticeable feature can be the mass of *combis* that set off from here, but look around and you see 18th-century houses and another church, **San Juan**, in a neo-Moorish style. This has been an entry point into Mérida for centuries, as demonstrated by another of the 1790 city gates, **Arco de San Juan** above C. 64, once the *Camino Real* or 'Royal Road' to Campeche.

If you continue through this gate, cross over to C. 66 and carry on down to C. 77, you will come to one of the most atmospheric relics of colonial Mérida, the little **Ermita de Santa Isabel**. A plain rustic chapel, it was built, as an inscription states on the façade, in 1748, and a similarly simple cloister was added in 1762. It was established as a stopping point outside Mérida on the Camino Real, where those arriving could give thanks for a safe deliverance, and those leaving could pray for an equally trouble-free arrival at their destination. The gardens behind the cloister are now a secluded park.

The Paseo de Montejo and North Mérida

North Mérida has a very different atmosphere. In place of the narrow pavements and stucco-walled houses of the old city, there are long, tree-lined, very quiet streets with broad pavements. In some, there are striking residences with wide driveways. At the heart of the district is a broad, elegant avenue, the **Paseo de Montejo**, beginning at C. 47 two blocks east of C. 60. This was where Mérida's leading citizens decided to create their own Champs-Elysées. It's nowhere near as long as its Parisian model, but is vaguely similar with its wide green lawns and promenades.

Paris provided the Yucatán magnates not only with a model of urban elegance but a suitably opulent style of architecture for the mansions they built around the new avenue, a tropical adaptation of the Beaux-Arts style of the French Second Empire. European architects were brought in to provide a final touch of refinement. The most extravagant of all these buildings, the great wedding cake of the Palacio Cantón at the corner of the Paseo and C. 43, now houses the **Museo de Antropología e Historia**, one of the most important collections of pre-Hispanic artefacts in Mexico after the national museum in Mexico City.

Museo de Antropología e Historia
open Tues–Sat 8–8, Sun 8–2; adm

The house was built between 1909 and 1911 for General Francisco Cantón, former servant of Emperor Maximilian and leading figure of the Díaz era. The design, by Enrico Deserti, is typically Frenchified, and Italian marble and other fine materials were imported to give it its finer touches. By the time it was finished, though, the Díaz regime had fallen, and Cantón died six years later. The museum collection includes artefacts from Maya sites in Campeche and Quintana Roo as well as Yucatán state. From the caves at Loltún there are Preclassic carvings, and from Chichén Itzá there are dramatic sculptures and sacrificial items from the great *cenote*, including three cases of fine jade. The ceramics collection covers all the eras of Maya culture: highlights include delicately coloured pottery from Mayapán, and figurines that show clearly and in colour, Maya styles in textiles and clothing. Mérida's museum is a particularly good place to fill out impressions of Maya society gleaned from visiting sites. Displays deal with agriculture, hunting, war, architecture and cooking, and an exhibit demonstrates vividly the apparently bizarre practices associated with beauty that can make the Maya appear very alien: the filing of teeth into sharp points, or the deliberate deformation of the heads of babies to produce a flat, elongated forehead.

Yucatán Specialities: *Hacienda* Hotels

Haciendas, plantation houses with broad colonnaded terraces amid extensive grounds, are emblems of the Yucatán. Many date back to the 17th century, others were extended or rebuilt during the *henequen* boom of the 1900s. Most were long neglected, but since the 1990s many have been restored and reborn as the Yucatán's most distinctive hotels. The most prominent are seductively luxurious, an indulgent blend of aristocratic colonial architecture, lush tropical gardens and stylish modern comforts, but there are also more modest *haciendas* that offer an equally memorable experience of the Yucatán countryside (one of the simplest is **Hacienda San Miguel**, near Valladolid, *see* p.219).

Haciendas are usually quite isolated, and once inside their gardens there's an obvious temptation not to leave, but most offer transport and a range of tours. They make great bases for exploring the countryside, and several are within an hour's drive of Mérida.

The best-known have been restored by the Grupo Plan, with a common style and website (*www.thehaciendas.com*). They are also marketed by the Starwood Group in their 'Luxury Collection'. Others are independent (another, the long-running **Hacienda Chichén** at Chichén Itzá, has 'remade' itself in *hacienda* style after years of neglecting its historic assets, *see* p.381). There are also *haciendas* in Campeche: the more rustic **Blanca Flor** (*see* p.237) and Grupo Plan's **Hacienda Uayamón** and **Hacienda Puerta Campeche** in Campeche city (*see* p.390). All the Plan *haciendas* have beautiful **restaurants** open to non-residents. Plan's **Hacienda Ochil**, near Uxmal, is just a restaurant (*see* p.319).

Hacienda San Antonio Chalanté, 8km south of Izamal via a turn east in Sudzal, t (988) 103 3367, *www.haciendachalante.com* (*moderate*). A fine way to experience the charm of a *hacienda* at non-luxury prices. This atmospheric 17th-century manor has 10 individual rooms, a pool and a Maya sweat lodge; breakfast is included, and meals can be provided. Nature trails are marked out around the estate, and horse riding, ruins tours and *cenote* and bird-watching tours are all specialities. It also makes a very enjoyable, peaceful base for exploring the Yucatán countryside. Don't go expecting standard hotel service – much of the time, guests are left to themselves – but if you like tranquil seclusion, this is it.

Hacienda San José Cholul, 30km east of Mérida on Tixkokob–Tekantó road, t (999) 924 1333, *www.haciendasmexico.com* (*luxury*). A intimate Plan Group *hacienda*, in a very peaceful part of the countryside between Mérida and Izamal. The 17th-century main house has been imaginatively restored, the gardens are gorgeous, and there's a terrace **restaurant** and spectacular pool. The 15 rooms are spread around the gardens, in four sizes from large to very large; all have terraces and giant bathrooms, and the master suite has a pool to itself.

Hacienda Petac, 20km south of Mérida, *www.haciendapetac.com*. The ultimate in neo-colonial luxury must be a whole *hacienda* to yourself. This lavishly restored estate has five bedrooms sleeping up to 10, lounges, terrace and dining room, a pool, games room and huge gardens. It can only be rented complete, usually for at least a week (shorter stays can be arranged on request). This is no self-catering operation though, the house comes with hotel staff and services (maids, cooks, gardeners, a driver and a manager to greet you) and fine meals, airport transfers and a big choice of activities (tours, sports) are all included. The downside: rates begin at US $8,400 per week. One for a serious party.

Hacienda San Pedro Nohpat, about 3km east of Mérida, t (999) 988 0542, *www.haciendaholidays.com* (*expensive–moderate*). The closest *hacienda*-hotel to Mérida, by the Acanceh road, San Pedro nevertheless still feels lost in the countryside. It's not as opulent as grander *haciendas*, but house and gardens are still very pretty, and the Canadian owners' hospitality has won them many friends: ask, and they'll arrange all kinds of activities to make the most of your stay in the Yucatán – ruins tours, bird-watching, riding and more. Rooms vary in size, and include family-sized suites. There's a great garden pool, and delicious meals are provided.

Hacienda Santa Cruz Palomeque, 14km south of Mérida, t (999) 254 0541, *www.haciendasantacruz.com* (*expensive*). Another low-key *hacienda* just a short way from Mérida, beside a tranquil village. The house and its 6 hectares of grounds have been carefully and very attractively restored. There's a choice of rooms and suites, a spa, and a lovely restaurant, the **Casa de Máquinas** (*expensive*), with superior French and Creole cuisine. The pool and gardens are especially delightful.

Hacienda Santa Rosa, off the road off Highway 180 towards Chunchucmil, near Maxcanú, t (999) 910 0174, *www.thehaciendas.com* (*luxury*). The countryside off the Camino Real west of the Puuc region is not an area where people have traditionally lingered – there are no conventional hotels – but among its villages there is this seductive retreat, one of the Plan Group *haciendas*. Very secluded, it has only 11 rooms, all with very high, wood-beamed ceilings, traditional furniture, hammocks, opulent bathrooms (a *hacienda* essential) and, in several, their very own gardens. Moreover, there are two bars – one in the former chapel – and a very pretty pool and **restaurant**.

Hacienda Temozón Sur, 8km east of the 261 road, 43km south of Mérida, t (999) 923 8089, *www.the haciendas.com*. Flagship of the Plan Group *haciendas* and the first to open, Temozón provides the most luxurious accommodation near to the Puuc region. The 17th-century main house, gardens, pool and terrace **restaurant** are especially ravishing. 'Superior' (aka standard) rooms and four sizes of suite all have giant bathrooms, lofty ceilings, old-plantation décor and opulent comforts. Many excursions are offered, and there's 36ha of grounds; hard to resist.

Hacienda Xcanatún, Xcanatún, 12km north of Mérida off the Progreso road, t (999) 930 2140, *www.xcanatun.com* (*luxury*). This 18th-century house and gardens were converted in 1999; the lovely **Casa de Piedra** restaurant is one of Mérida's best (*see* p.281). Shielded from the diners are 18 spacious suites, in three sizes but each with a terrace with Jacuzzi (honeymoons are a speciality). There are also two pools, a terrace bar and a spa, but those expecting total seclusion should note that the *hacienda* is surrounded by the village of Xcanatún.

Hacienda Yunkú, Yunkú, 50km south of Mérida, t (999) 943 7762, *www.haciendayunku.com*. A special opportunity to have a *hacienda* to yourself, deep in the Yucatán countryside. The restored 17th-century estate has four bedrooms, sleeping up to 10 people. It's only rented to one client at a time, but renters can choose between just the *Casa Principal*, with two grand bedrooms, huge dining room, games room, kitchen and magnificent terrace (from $350 a day), or for around $450 a day can add the Guest House, with two more rooms. There's also a lovely spring-water pool and rambling, bird-filled gardens, with the *hacienda*'s own swimmable *cenote*. Outside, Yunkú village is a charming place, a real immersion in Yucatecan rural life.

Outside, the shady pavements of Paseo de Montejo make a fine place for strolling, and are now lined by an impressive open-air gallery of modern sculpture by Mexican and international artists, another product of the city's arts programme. Also along the Paseo and in the streets around it are more examples of Yucatecan-Beaux Arts architecture, such as the **Cámara house** at Paseo de Montejo 495, a block south of the museum, not so much in Beaux-Arts style as a faithful reproduction of an 18th-century Parisian *hôtel* of the *ancien régime*, even though it was built in 1906.

Beyond C. 35 the Paseo opens up into one of its grandest junctions, a Parisian-style meeting point of several wide streets presided over by a statue of Justo Sierra, a 19th-century intellectual and one-time ambassador to Washington of an independent Yucatán. This part of town is especially atmospheric to walk around at night, with its houses all shuttered up as you go past. Its peculiar tropical neoclassicism then becomes most apparent and most ghostly, while the bats twittering above you remind you that you can't actually be in 16th-*arrondissement* Paris.

Alternatively, if you continue north on Paseo Montejo, you cannot miss the giant mass of the **Altar de la Patria**, Mérida's contribution to large-scale patriotic sculpture. Designed by sculptor Rómulo Roza – originally, in fact, from Colombia – and built from 1945 to 1956, it typifies the nationalistic 'Neo-Aztec' style favoured by the authorities of the Mexican Revolution at their most confident. Beyond this traffic circle the Paseo becomes **Prolongación de Montejo**, along which can be found many more offices, malls, middle-class residential areas, restaurants and international-style clubs.

(i) **Mérida**

Official tourist information offices are in the Palacio Municipal, in the Teatro Peón Contreras on the corner of Calles 60 and 57, at the corner of Calles 59 and 62, and on the Paseo de Montejo, corner of C. 39 (all open daily 8–8). They provide basic maps and leaflets on various attractions, but the most useful thing they always have is the free magazine Yucatán Today. *Also informative and interesting is the expat website* www.yucatanliving.com

Tourist Information and Services in Mérida

t (999-)

Travel and Tour Agencies

For more on Mérida-based tour agencies, *see* p.106. For tours to nearby *cenotes, see* p.297.

Ecoturismo Yucatán, C. 3 no. 235, x 32-A & 34, t 920 2772, *www.ecoyuc.com*. Leading local specialists in wildlife tours and ecotourism, offering an enormous range of options, and car hire. *See also* p.106.

Iluminado Tours, t 924 3176, *www.iluminadotours.com*. Trudy Woodcock and her team provide a special range of trips giving a real insight into Yucatán and Maya culture – villages, markets, nature, beliefs and more – from custom-made one-day tours to longer trips and workshops. From around $65 per person.

Yucatán Connection, t 163 8224, *www.yucatan-connection.com*. Enterprising local operator with day tours focusing on less obvious Maya sites – Mayapán – and the Puuc region, and other trips on request.

Yucatán Discovery, C. 54 no. 476, x 55, t 923 4711, *www.yucatandiscovery.com*. Tours of Mérida and all around the region, based at the Alma Mexicana store (*see* below).

Yucatán Trails, C. 62 no. 482, x 57 & 59, t 928 2582, *yucatantrails@hotmail.com*. Especially handy to know, an agency run by Canadian long-term resident Denis Lafoy. As well as providing varied tours, he has a wealth of local information, luggage lockers and a free English book-exchange service. With the Mérida English Library (*see* right) he also organizes international community parties on the first Friday of each month that are a good opportunity to meet a wide range of people.

Services in Mérida

Banks: Mainly around Plaza Mayor and on C. 65, between 60 and 62. All have ATMs. Of the exchange offices, **Cambiaria del Sureste** in Pasaje Picheta on the Plaza Mayor, has competitive rates. **American Express** is at Paseo Montejo no. 492 (t 923 4974), corner of C. 43, opposite the Museo de Antropología.

Consulates: US Consulate, Paseo Montejo no. 453, near corner of Av. Colón, t 942 5700, *http://merida. usconsulate.gov*; **Cuban Consulate**, C. 42 no. 200, Colonia Campestre, t 944 4215. Local travel agencies selling flights to Cuba can provide visas.

Health and Emergencies: Mérida has a 24hr emergency line (t 066), but it is often best to call individual services (**police**, t 942 0060; **fire**, t 924 9242; Red Cross **ambulances**, t 924 9813). Mérida has **tourist police**, in cream shirts and brown trousers; ask for *Policía Turística* (ext. 462) on the central number. If you need a **doctor**, the **Clínica de Mérida**, Av. Itzaes 242, x 27 & 29, t 920 0411, in Colonia García Gineres west of Paseo Montejo, is a well-established private clinic with English-speaking staff. A highly regarded **dentist** is Dr Javier Cámara Patrón, C. 17 no. 170, x 8 & 10, t 925 3399. **Pharmacies** are abundant, and Farmacia YZA (Plaza Mayor) is open 24 hrs.

Internet Access: Internet cafés are abundant all around the city centre. **Cibercafé Santa Lucía**, C. 62 no. 467, corner of C. 55, is cheap, popular, open late, and has good a/c. Also, Mérida's forward-looking authorities have placed free WiFi hotspots in several city plazas, including the Plaza Mayor.

Library: Mérida English Library: C. 53 no. 524, x 66 & 68, t 924 8401, *www.meridaenglishlibrary.com*. Excellent place to find books, check the press/internet and meet the local English-speaking community. The collection includes a fine stock on Yucatán and Maya culture, and it hosts international community parties.

Phone Offices: Many phone/fax offices are on or near C. 60. **Telworld**, C. 60 no. 486, x 55 & 57 has decent rates.

Post Office: C. 53, x 52 & 54 (*open Mon–Sat 8–6*). Has a **Mexpost** desk.

Religious Services: Catholic Mass in English – Santa Lucía church, Sat 6pm.

City Tours

Guided Walks: Free 1hr guided walking tours begin Mon–Sat at 9.30am, from the tourist office in the Palacio Municipal. The 'route' is fairly limited, around the main buildings of the Plaza Mayor, but tour is informative.

Mérida City Tour: the longest-running introduction to Mérida's sights, a 2hr tour with bilingual guide in an open-sided bus from Parque Santa Lucía, C. 60 x 55, Mon–Sat at 10am, 1pm, 4pm, 7pm, Sun at 10am, 1pm ($7, $4 children 6–10, free under-6s). You can book on t 927 6119, but it's not usually necessary.

Mérida House and Garden Tour (www.meridaenglishlibrary.com/tours). Mérida's often-hidden patios are among its most fascinating secrets, and this walking tour run by Mérida English Library (see p.274) lets you into a selection of them. Tours begin at the library, from Oct–Mar Wed only at 9.45am, and last about 2hrs; the fee, to aid the library, is around $15.

Turibus: modern-style sights-and-shopping tour ,with headphone commentary, in open-top buses, which run up and down the same set route daily, from Plaza Mayor up to the Gran Plaza shopping mall, with several stops en route. With a ticket (1-day $7.50, $4 under-12s; higher fares at weekends; 2- or 3-day tickets also available) you can get on and off the bus as many times as you want the same day. Buses run about every 30mins daily, 9am–9pm.

Festivals

Festival Internacional de las Artes (Jan): A two-week programme covering all the arts.

Carnaval (Jan or Feb): One of Mexico's biggest, climaxing in several days of parades, events and revels up to Shrove Tuesday. Check dates on www.merida.gob.mx/carnaval.

Easter Week: Low-key, with few celebrations other than that everyone goes to the beach.

Cristo de las Ampollas (Oct): Culminates on 13 Oct, when the blackened image of Christ is carried in procession through the streets.

Otoño Cultural (Oct–Nov): A very varied arts programme, in venues in Mérida and throughout Yucatán state.

Feria Yucatán X'matkuil (Nov-Dec): Yucatán's State Fair, on a permanent site that has taken over the village of X'matkuil south of Mérida. Four weeks of concerts, discos, cattle shows and the state's biggest fairground.

Courses

Cookery Classes: Los Dos, C. 68 no. 517, x 65 & 67, t 928 1116, www.los-dos.com. American chef David Sterling is a huge enthusiast for Yucatecan cuisine, and in his finely restored house gives a personal, convivial introduction to its riches – including trips to the market – in half- or one-day classes (around $100), or longer courses with accommodation in Los Dos's guest rooms.

Spanish Classes: Centro de Idiomas del Sureste (CIS), C. 52 no. 455, x 49 & 51, t 923 0083, www.cisyucatan.com.mx. Well-established school with three centres in Mérida and a full range of courses, with or without homestay accommodation with local families. Fees begin around $350 for two weeks.

Shopping

Mérida is far the best place in the Yucatán to pick up traditional local products: embroidery, panama hats, ceramics, guayabera shirts and, most of all, hammocks. As the great market of the peninsula, Mérida is in fact the best place to shop for anything, ancient or modern. For more conventional shopping, head for **Prolongación de Montejo** (beyond the Paseo itself), where there are several malls.

Books and Maps

Mérida has the best bookshops in the peninsula, so this is the place to look for background reading in English on the Maya.

Amate Books, C. 60 no. 453A, x 49 & 51, t 924 2222, www.amatebooks.com. Mellow shop with books in English on every aspect of Mexico – art, food, history and, particularly, Maya history and culture.

Librería Dante, Centro Cultural Olimpo, C. 61 no. 502. The Dante branch in the Plaza Mayor has the largest English-language stock; there are others on Parque Hidalgo and on C. 59, and four more in other parts of the city.

Librería-Papelería Burrel, C. 59 no. 502, x 60 & 62. Best for maps: if you expect to drive in the region, stock up here while you can.

Chocolate

Ki-Xocolatl, C. 55 no. 513, x 60 & 62, t 920 5869, *www.ki-xocolatl.com*. Mérida has expats doing all kinds of things – including Belgian chocolate-makers who have gone back to the roots of chocolate, working only with Mexican organic cacao.

Crafts and Markets

Should you take up the invitation of any of the men proffering cards advertising *artesanía* at the corner of C. 60 and the Plaza Mayor and follow them to their shop, you will almost certainly find some quality items mixed in with a lot of dross, and goods from all over Mexico as well as strictly local embroidery and hammocks. A better place to look for craftwork is in and around the market area, although even here quality is very variable.

Alma Mexicana, C. 54 no. 476, x 55 & 57, t 923 4711, *www.folkart-mexico.com*. A dazzlingly colourful display of fine folk art from all over Mexico, irresistible for browsing. Part of the house is also a lovely two-room B&B, **Casa Esperanza** (*www.casaesperanza.com*).

Bazar de Artesanías, above the main market building, reached by a ramp from C. 67 at the junction with C. 56. The most organized outlet for local handicrafts, aimed directly at tourists. It's interesting to look around to get an idea of the range of goods on offer: you'll find fine work and engaging curios such as the *maquech*, live scarab beetles decorated as costume jewellery (a Maya tradition) alongside near-production-line items. Stallholders are often prepared to haggle.

Casa de las Artesanías, C. 63 no. 503, x 64 & 66. A place to see and buy local handicrafts in more tranquil surroundings is this official Yucatán state handicrafts store, next to the Iglesia de las Monjas. Not as high-quality as it could be, but it has some attractive, often usable pieces, in textiles and other media.

Hammock-buying

The Yucatecan hammock is one of the most cherished local institutions, and the state of contented contemplation it induces has been celebrated by local poets in verse. A mystique may be attached to it, but buying one is a logical process. Most hammocks today are made of nylon, light but often sweaty, cotton, the most popular material, or mixes of the two; you also find hammocks of traditional sisal, which is strong but scratchy. They come in three basic sizes, single (*sencillo*), *matrimonial* and *familiar*. For each size, the basic determinant of quality is the number of pairs of end-loops used to produce a given width: 50 is the minimum number for a single hammock, and anything under that will lack strength. The more strands that are used of finer material over the same area, the softer and more comfortable it will be. This affects the weight, and a single hammock should weigh at least 1kg. You should also check the end loops, which should be large, tightly bound and well-finished. Another thing to look out for is the length, as many hammocks are made for Yucatecan height. Hold one end of the hammock up with one arm until the far end of the body of the hammock (i.e. without the end strings) is by your feet. The body of the hammock should be at least as long as you, and as wide as you can afford.

It's a good idea to ask for a demonstration on how to repack your hammock. Local lore states the two ends of a hammock should never touch, not so much a matter of avoiding bad luck as of preventing infuriating tangles.

Hammock Specialists

There are some good hammock stalls in the Bazar, but the best places to buy are the specialist hammock shops, which are also in the market area, especially near the crossing of Calles 65 and 56. The quality of hammocks varies a lot, so it pays to buy with care. Sadly, the vendors with bags of hammocks in the streets rarely have much that's worth buying.

Hamacas Mérida, C. 65 no. 510, x 62 & 64. A more modern-than-usual hammock shop.

La Poblana, C 65 no. 492, x 58 & 60. Huge choice of quality hammocks in all sizes. Once you're past his bluff exterior, owner *sr* Razu gives very helpful, knowledgeable service (partly in English). Satisfied customers are spread around the world: adult-size cotton hammocks go from about $12–15.

Hats

Panama hats can be bought in all C. 60 craft stores and the Bazar, but you generally find a better choice at lower prices if you seek out the panama-specialist stalls in the main market and the neighbouring streets.

El Sombrero Popular, C. 65 Depto 18, x 58 & 60. Half-shop, half-stall outside the market, with a very friendly owner and fine panamas.

Textiles and Clothing

Mérida's market and the shops around it naturally contain many other things as well as hammocks and ornaments: *huarache* sandals, embroidered *huipiles*, rows of *guayaberas* for men. The best places for *guayaberas*, though, are the factory outlets run by manufacturers themselves. The same consideration applies to traditional embroidery and *huípil* dresses as with hammocks and hats: there are very good examples in the Bazar, but a wider range and better prices in the stalls in the main market.

Códice, C. 59 no. 501-A, x 60 & 62. Attractive modern and traditional crafts and clothing.

Guayaberas Jack, C. 59 no. 507, x 60 & 62. Highly regarded *guayabera* manufacturer.

Mexicanísimo, C. 60 no. 496, x 59 & 61. Not traditional, for once, but an attractive shop on Parque Hidalgo with stylish lightweight clothes made with Mexican cottons and traditional techniques, that make for great hot-weather clothing.

Sports and Activities

Club de Golf de Yucatán, La Ceiba, 14½km north of Mérida, t 922 0071, *www.golfyucatan.com*. An 18-hole course, tennis, a gym, a pool and activities for kids. Some hotels have guest memberships.

Where to Stay in Mérida

Mérida's hotels are among its great attractions: many are in buildings – some genuinely colonial, some more recent – with deliciously peaceful interior patios, many of which, even in the cheaper ranges, also contain swimming pools. Mérida hotel pools tend to be small, but are still wonderfully refreshing after a day's tramp. In the last few years Mérida has enjoyed something of a hotel boom, and the range has been broadened with luxury *haciendas* at the top, and some very charming, individually run guest houses that make the most of the local architecture lower down.

Luxury

The region's most seductive top-flight accommodation is in the colonial *haciendas* around the Yucatán countryside that have been turned into hotels. Two, **Hacienda Xcanatún** and the more modest **San Pedro Nohpat**, are only just outside the city limits, and several others are close enough to make day-trips into Mérida easy. For details of all hotel *haciendas*, see p.272.

The Villa@Mérida, C. 59 no. 615-A, x 80 & 82, t 01 305 538 9697, *www.the villasgroup.com*. Upping the ante for hotels in Mérida itself, an attempt to bring *hacienda* style (and prices, at around $240 a night) within the city, mixed with the chic exclusivity of an international boutique hotel. It occupies a stately colonial mansion, with gardens, restored with suitable magnificence. The design seeks to maintain a feel of stylish intimacy: there are just 7 suites, with every possible comfort. There's no regular restaurant, but breakfast is naturally included and an eclectic 'tapas-style' restaurant is available all day. Two things: gardens and pool are lovely, but can't compare with those of a true *hacienda*; also, the location is out of the way, 12 long blocks west of C. 60.

Expensive

Mérida's traditional-style big hotels, the Fiesta Americana, Hyatt and InterContinental, are oddly but conveniently near each other on Av. Colón, by Paseo Montejo.

Fiesta Americana, Paseo de Montejo 451, t 942 1111, *www.fiestaamericana. com*. Most impressive to look at of the big Mérida hotels, a giant mansion with grand-hotel style. A luxurious feel is sustained inside with a spectacular atrium topped by a stained-glass roof; the traditionally styled rooms are also very attractive. Special and low season offers are in the *moderate* slot.

InterContinental Presidente Mérida, Av. Colón 500, x C. 60, t 942 9000, *www.ichotelsgroup.com*. The 1900s mansion at the base of this hotel has been rebuilt and expanded many times, most recently in 2005 when it was given an opulent makeover by InterContinental. Rooms mix old-world luxury with high-tech services.

Villa María, C. 59 no. 553, x 68, t 923 3357, *www.villamariamerida.com*. An opulent hotel in a 17th-century Mérida town mansion that has been expensively restored to make the most of its spectacular Hispano-Moorish patio architecture. The 11 bedrooms and suites have an unusual semi-duplex layout and are lavishly appointed; however, the patio layout of the house also means that they get no natural light. The pool, in an inside patio, is also small. In low season prices drop down to the upper-*moderate* band. The Villa María also has a high-standard, European-based **restaurant** (*see* p.281).

Moderate

Angeles de Mérida, C. 74A no. 494, x 57 & 59, t 923 8163, *www.angelesdemerida. com*. Intimate B&B in a classic old Mérida house, with, suitably hidden from the street, a sumptuous little pool in a palm-lined patio. The four guest rooms, sitting rooms and dining room are all in similar but individual style, decorated with craftwork and antiques. A place with great character, in a very peaceful area near Parque de Santiago, and a near-neighbour to Cascadas (*see* below).

Casa del Balam, C. 60 no. 488, x 57, t 924 2150, *www.hotelcasadelbalam.com*. Charming, long-established, very central hotel, with an atmospheric 19th-century patio skilfully blended into a modern addition. Bedrooms are attractive and well-equipped, and the suites in the old building are truly lush. Rates are near the top of this price band. The same owners also have the **Hacienda Chichén** at Chichén Itzá (*see* p.237).

⭐ **Hotel Marionetas >>**

⭐ **Cascadas de Mérida >**

Cascadas de Mérida, C. 57 no. 593-C, x 74A & 76, t 923 8484, *www.cascadas demerida.com*. One on its own among Mérida's guest houses. When long-time New York resident Chucho Basto and his wife Ellyne returned to Mérida to the plot of land where he was born, he set out to build an all-new hotel, with four entirely original guest rooms. Plentiful imagination is on show: instead of the old-colonial feel common in Mérida B&Bs, there's a stylishly contemporary – but very comfortable – look, with special features such as bathrooms with a 'waterfall' effect around the shower. Outside, there's a lovely, sheltered garden with a pool. Guests are made to feel right at home, and generous breakfasts are enjoyed around one convivial table.

Casa Mexilio, C. 68 no. 495, x 57 & 59, t 928 2505, *www.casamexilio.com*. Almost a museum or art exhibit as much as a guest house, this grand old mansion has nine rooms, each distinctively decorated with a spectacular array of traditional furniture, artwork and antiques. The way each space has been created to sustain the nostalgically romantic atmosphere is remarkable: rooms lead into each other in labyrinthine fashion, and there's a delightful, grotto-like pool, a lush fruit-filled patio garden and a bar on the roof. Several rooms have balconies, but there's a common breakfast room. Rooms vary in size and so price, and one is a self-contained cottage. Service can be as quirky as the house itself.

Hotel Julamis, C. 53 no. 475-B, x 54, t 924 1818, *www.hoteljulamis.com*. Charming patio hotel with seven bright rooms and suites, well renovated but still full of old-house charm. The suites are beautiful: two smaller – but still very pleasant and airy – rooms are in the *inexpensive* band. The owners are very obliging, and provide plenty of extras. The only drawback is that it has only a plunge pool, on an upper terrace.

Hotel Marionetas, C. 49 no. 516, x 62 & 64, t 928 3377, *www.hotelmarionetas. com*. A very popular guesthouse-style small hotel in an imaginatively renovated Mérida house. The rooms, around a charming patio with a pool, combine lofty ceilings and old timbers with fine modern bathrooms, imaginative colour schemes and beautiful tiled floors. Owners Sofi and Daniel Bosco – she from Macedonia, he originally from Argentina – came to Mérida hotelkeeping after varied careers on different continents, and run their hotel with individual verve. Nothing is too much trouble, from providing different breakfast options every day, served in the patio, to giving guests every kind of tip to help them make the most of their stay.

Hotel MedioMundo, C. 55 no. 533, x 64 & 66, t 924 5472, *www.hotelmedio mundo.com*. A very attractive small hotel created in an old Mérida house by Uruguayan-Lebanese owners Nelson and Nicole, who arrived here after living in many parts of the world. Spacious rooms are decorated in warm, tropical colours, and there's a small patio pool with café-bar alongside, where delicious fresh breakfasts (*extra*) are served. A warmly individual welcome also marks it out from many more routine hotels.

Hotel Zamná, C. 53 no. 547, x 70 & 72, t 924 0103, *www.hotelzamna. blogspot.com*. An attractive guest house run with character by British expats Linda and Keith Newell – so you can have a full English breakfast if it tickles your fancy. As usual in Mérida B&Bs, there's a pool in the patio; the five very comfortable guest rooms, though, have a style of their own, with ornate touches.

Piedra de Agua, C. 60 no. 498, x 59 & 61, t 924 2300, *www.piedradeagua. com*. A striking step in Mérida's progress on the path of stylishness, a chic 'boutique hotel' in a grand old building just off the Plaza Mayor. Rooms, in tastefully understated colours, are very state-of-the-art, but some are cramped, and the location is not just ultra-central but also noisy. An elegant patio **restaurant** leads to the sleek bar and tiny pool.

Inexpensive

Las Arecas, C. 59 no. 541, x 66 & 68, t 928 3626, *www.lasarecas.com*. Bargain B&B in an old patio house with five attractively decorated rooms, two suite-style with their own terraces, and all with good fittings. One is fan-only, the others all have a/c.

Rooms are shaded from direct light, but bright, folk-art influenced colours make up for it, and owners Mauro and Raúl are very helpful.

Casa Ana, C. 52 no. 469, x 51 & 53, t 924 0005, *www.casaana.com*. A few blocks' walk from Mérida's main drags, this little guest house is great value, with five delightfully airy rooms and even a pool in the tranquil garden of a charming old house. All rooms have new facilities (including a/c, for an extra charge), and upper rooms even have a fine view. English-speaking Cuban owners Ana and Mariana are very friendly, there's an open kitchen, and breakfasts (included) with fresh fruit are served in the garden.

Hotel Caribe, C. 59 no. 500, x 60, t 924 9022, *www.hotelcaribe.com.mx*. Popular traditional hotel on Parque Hidalgo, in a 19th-century building with rooms on three levels around a stone-columned patio, which contains the restaurant. The biggest plus is its rooftop pool, with a view of the cathedral. Rooms vary in standard and price, and some are fan-only; the best ones are around the pool.

Hotel Dolores Alba, C. 63 no. 464, x 52 & 54, t 928 5650, *www.dolores alba.com*. A 4-block walk from the Plaza Mayor, but one of the most popular Mérida hotels. A large leafy patio and a pool are some of its attractions; another is the relaxed atmosphere. The best rooms are in the new annexe around the pool at the back, and are plain in style but have very good a/c, TV and other facilities; rooms in the old building have more character and are cheaper, but are also darker and more time-battered. Breakfast is extra ($4–5); the hotel also has its own off-street car park. The owners' other hotel with the same name is one of the best at Chichén Itzá, and can be booked here (*see* p.238). Both fill up, so always book or call ahead.

Hotel del Peregrino, C. 51 no. 488, x 54 & 56, t 924 5491, *http://hoteldel peregrino.com*. Good-value guest house in a quiet area between the centre and Paseo Montejo. Double, twin or family rooms are pretty, airy and comfortable. Upper floor rooms are especially attractive. Breakfast and

WiFi are included, and there's an open kitchen for guests' use, plus a roof terrace with a bar.

Hotel San Juan, C. 55 no. 497-A, x 58 & 60, t 924 1742, www.hotelsanjuan.com. mx. Good-value little hotel with light, bright and comfortable rooms with good facilities (TV, phone, fans and a/c), a neat little pool with a bar, and rates near the *budget* slot. Under the same ownership is **Hotel Santa Lucía**, C. 55 no. 508, x 60 & 62, t 928 2672, www.hotelsantalucia.com.mx, across C. 60 on Parque Santa Lucía, very similar in style.

Hotel Trinidad Galería, C. 60 no. 456, x 51, t 923 2463, www.hotelestrinidad. com. Mérida's most eccentric/funky (or just cranky) hotel, as seen in films and photo shoots. In the lobby you're greeted by a riot of vegetation, dolls, inflatable superheroes and paintings; inside, there's more eclectic art in a maze of interlocking patios. Rooms are more basic (most fan-only, some with a/c). They vary a lot (rooms without a/c are in the *budget* band), and if you don't like one you're shown just ask to see another, maybe with more light. The palm-shrouded pool has a wonderful hidden-glade quality – a magical place from which to take in starscapes. The same owners also have the **Hotel Trinidad**, C. 62 no. 464, x 55 & 57, t 923 2033, an old house two blocks away with a García Márquez-ish charm. Guests can use the Galería's pool.

★ **Luz en Yucatán >**   **Luz en Yucatán**, C. 55 no. 499, x 58 & 60, t 924 0035, www.luzenyucatan .com. One of the most enjoyable places to stay in town, a true urban oasis in a city not short of them. In the 1990s part of the 17th-century convent behind the church of Santa Lucía was transformed into an art gallery, but was then acquired by American Madeline Parmet, who made into a guesthouse 'urban retreat' with a unique approach. She took off in 2006, but new owners Tom and Donard aim to maintain the easy-going style that has won it fans far and wide. The beautifully shady old house is huge, and within it there are fully equipped apartments with kitchens; in the garden at the back there's also a pool. Changes since the handover have included complete renovation of all fittings, and the

addition of several new rooms above the garden. A real home from home, Luz is ideal for settling in for a completely hassle-free stay: guests have the run of a very large kitchen, and free beers in the fridge on arrival is another nice touch.

Budget

Mérida's cheapest hotels rarely have pools, but most offer showers in rooms.

Aventura Hotel, C. 61 no. 580, x 74 & 76, t 923 4801, www.aventuramerida.com. Fresh and friendly modern budget hotel near Parque de Santiago with some of the best rooms you'll find for under $25, compact but clean and comfortable, all with fans and good bathrooms. An excellent bargain.

Casa Bowen, C. 66 no. 521-B, x 65 & 67, t 928 6109. A cheapo favourite near the bus stations, with a pleasant patio, and a little café alongside. Rooms are plain, big and airy, some with a/c.

Hotel Mucuy, C. 57 no. 481, x 56 & 58, t 928 5193, www.mucuy.com. A long-term favourite with budget travellers. The 24 rooms, with showers and fans (a/c is available for an extra charge), are straightforward but well kept. There's no pool, but a leafy patio.

Nómadas, C. 62 no. 433, x 51, t 924 5223, www.nomadastravel.com. With 'backpackers' on the façade this hostel couldn't be more clearly targeted. Beds in 8-bunk dorms cost around $9; some are mixed, but there's a spacious women-only area. There are also double rooms with or without bath-rooms (from $23), and camping or hammock space. It's bright, well-kept and very clean, and newer and airier than many budget hotels; breakfast is included, and there's free Internet access, an open kitchen and a pretty patio. The enthusiastic owners also provide a raft of other services and information, and a low-cost travel agency (open to non-residents).

Eating Out in Mérida

The classics of Yucatecan cuisine – *cochinita pibil*, *sopa de lima*, *poc-chuc* – are everywhere, but the city also offers other cuisines: central-Mexican, Italian, Middle-Eastern (from the Lebanese community), Chinese. The experience to be had in Mérida restaurants, though, is peculiarly erratic – still more than in most Mexican cities, price differences don't always reflect quality, and better meals are often found by seeking out special places rather than paying more. Try venturing into areas favoured by locals, such as Paseo de Montejo. Most restaurants are not expensive.

One peculiarity of the most traditional Yucatecan restaurants, here and in country towns, is that they usually only open for long, extended lunches (usually 11–6), not in the evenings. This is incomprehensible to outsiders, but is changing very slowly.

Hacienda Restaurants

In the same way that several of Yucatán's *haciendas* have been converted into upscale hotels, others are now restaurants where you can sample local cuisine on an arcaded terrace, and see a little of the gardens and ambience. All are expensive and booking is always advisable; some – such as **San Antonio Cucul**, the only *hacienda* within Mérida's *periférico* (*www.sanantoniocucul.com.mx*) – only take group bookings, and so are best visited with a hotel or tour agency. The best and most beautiful *hacienda* restaurants, in any case, are in the hotels; for details, *see* p.272.

Hacienda Teya, Ctra Mérida–Cancún (Highway 180) Km 12.5, **t** 988 0800, *www.haciendateya.com*. One of the first *haciendas* to open to visitors. It's often busy with tour groups, but its classic Yucatecan dishes are well regarded by locals. *Open 12–6pm only.*

Casa de Piedra, Hacienda Xcanatún, 12km north of Mérida off the Progreso road, **t** 941 0213, *www.xcanatun.com*. Only just beyond the Mérida *periférico*, this *hacienda* has a deliciously pretty restaurant, with cuisine combining Yucatecan, Caribbean and French traditions, and a superior wine selection. A fine choice for a special meal. *See also* p.273.

Expensive

See also hotels such as the **Fiesta Americana** and **InterContinental** (*see* pp.277-8).

Alberto's Continental, C. 64 no. 482, x 57, **t** 928 5367. Quirky place in a classic Mérida house from 1727, which owner Alberto Salum has filled with a huge collection of religious images, mirrors and Baroque bric-a-brac. The family are Mérida-Lebanese, so the menu includes things like tabbouleh and unusual salads alongside Yucatecan standards, served with home-baked Lebanese bread.

Los Almendros, C. 50 no. 493, x 57, **t** 928 5459. Mérida's best-known restaurant, on Parque de la Mejorada, a branch of a 'chain' that began in Ticul (*see* p.322). Traditionally the foremost showcase for Yucatecan cuisine, the Almendros claim to have invented *poc-chuc* (pork marinated in garlic and bitter oranges), now a standard all over the peninsula. Their approach, with dance shows and waitresses in embroidered *ternos*, is very tourist-kitsch, and standards often slip, but if you catch it on a good day this is still a memorable place to sample local dishes. There is also an Almendros in the Fiesta Americana hotel (*see* p.277).

Néctar Food & Wine, C. 21 no. 412, x 6 & 8, Colonia Díaz Ordaz, **t** 938 0838. Mérida is clearly no backwater, and here's a demonstration: chef Roberto Solis has trained around the world, including a time under Heston Blumenthal at the renowned Fat Duck in England, and at Néctar presents exquisite, inventive, global food, served by charming, very professional staff. Note that prices are well above the local norm too. It's hard to find in a smart part of town, so take a cab. Open daily, for lunch and dinner.

Trotter's, Circuito Colonias, x C. 60, **t** 927 2320, *www.trottersmerida.com*. The most eye-catching place to eat in town, a spectacular dome sheltering a lovely garden. The Canadian Trotter family have been in Mérida over 30 years, and also own Pancho's (see p.283). Their flagship restaurant offers an imaginative mix of Mexican and international dishes, and great wines.

Villa María, C. 59 no. 553, x 68, **t** 923 3357, *www.villamariamerida.com*. This hotel (*see* p.278) has brought an elegant style to dining in Mérida with its French- and Mediterranean-oriented restaurant. It might seem odd to come to the Yucatán to eat European cuisine, but the subtle dishes are nicely done, especially meats, and the grand patio makes an exquisite setting.

Moderate

Mérida has a number of new-style *cantinas*, specializing in snacks or *botanas* (*see* p.79), which are more mixed, and more comfortable, than the men-only *cantinas* of yore. However, they are closed in the evenings.

Amaro's, C. 59 no. 507, x 60 & 62. Good for vegetarians, set in the house where Andrés Quintana Roo, Yucatán's most important participant in Mexican independence, was born in 1787, with a patio dominated by a giant orchid tree that explodes into flower in winter. As well as Yucatecan meat dishes, it has vegetarian specialities such as *crêpes de chaya*, made with the spinach-like *chaya*, pizzas and Mexican standards.

⭐ **La Casa de Frida**, C. 61 no. 526-A, x 66 & 68, t 928 2311. Frida Kahlo-inspired décor can be a bit overdone in Mexico these days, but this 'restaurant-gallery' carries it off with style. The central Mexican (rather than Yucatecan) cuisine is subtly delicious, especially the classic *chile en nogada* (green chilli stuffed with beef and herbs, with a walnut and pomegranate sauce). *Open Mon–Sat 6–10pm, closed Sun.*

⭐ **Eladio's**, C. 59 no. 425, x 44, *www. eladios.com.mx*. Most central branch of a hugely popular chain of *cantina*-restaurants with five outlets in Mérida and one in Progreso. They're very big, and family- and women-friendly, but have a cantina-style food range, so you choose between a full menu or *botanas* (snacks), which are complementary with drinks. The *botanas* are delicious, enormously varied, and very generous, so a visit here is a great way to try out the whole range of Yucatecan specialities for a modest outlay. Hugely enjoyable, Eladio's are never short on atmosphere, as dance bands play most days (there is also a – relatively – quiet area). *Open noon–8pm only.*

El Lucero del Alba, C. 56, x 47. Quite smart, comfortable, air-conditioned modern *cantina*, still with a whole range of delicious *botanas* just for the price of a drink.

Pane e Vino, C. 62 no. 496, x 59 & 61. Popular place off the Plaza Mayor offers high-quality fresh pasta (with vegetarian choices) and Mediterranean favourites.

La Vía Olimpo, Centro Cultural Olimpo, Plaza Mayor. The café in the Olimpo centre next to the Palacio Municipal is a bit bright and modern, but has charming service, pavement tables, effective a/c inside and an all-purpose menu, from Mexican classics to crêpes, burgers and salads. *Open 24hrs.*

Budget

In line with the local 'rule' that quality food has nothing to do with price, some of the best local restaurants are actually in the budget or street-food sector. Several of the *cocinas económicas* attached to the market are very good as well as extremely cheap. All in a row, at the top of the ramp facing C. 67 that leads to the crafts market, they offer *tacos*, *salbutes* and other specialities such as *mole con arroz, mondongo* or *cochinita pibil*. Order at one of the stands, then find a space at the nearest table, lined with salads, fierce *salsa verde* and other things you may or may not wish to add to your food. There are also plenty of food stands in the main market on the floor below.

There's no alcohol at market *cocinas*, but stands offer fresh juice *licuados*. Opening early every day, they close, like the market, by mid-afternoon. More enjoyable budget *loncherías* can be found around the smaller local markets in **Parque Santa Ana** and **Parque de Santiago**, with pavement tables and longer hours.

Café Alameda, C. 58 no. 474, x 55 & 57. Very friendly old Mérida-Lebanese café with a lofty interior and Arab specialities (superb fresh bread) as well as local standards. A tranquil place to collect your thoughts.

El Cangrejito, C. 57 no. 523, x 64 & 66. Final proof that in Mérida price and quality can be strangely disconnected: the traditional seafood dishes – especially the *tacos* of fresh octopus, *camarones* or lobster – prepared by Don Felipe Santos Ché and his crew at this cranky little café have a high reputation, but it's still cheap and unpretentious. Staff can be brusque, and hours are more than usually erratic. *Open daily, usually until 5pm.*

Marlín Azul, C. 62 no. 488, x 57 & 59. Another great bargain: a simple, street-side bar, but its Yucatecan seafood dishes – especially the *ceviche mixto*, with prawns, octopus and conch – are among the best you'll find.

Pizzeria Vito Corleone, C. 59 no. 508, x 60 & 62. This basic little place looks like a standard Mexican snack-house, except for the bicycles above the entrance, its flame-fired pizza oven and the name. As well as fine standard pizzas, you can try *pizza mexicana* with *jalapeño* peppers and refried beans.

Restaurante Café-Club, C. 55 no. 496-A, x 58 & 60. Laid-back café by Santa Lucía with an Iranian owner and a 50%-vegetarian bill of fare that includes Mexican standards and classic breakfasts. *Closed eves and Sun.*

Drinks, Cafés and Juices

Dulcería-Sorbetería Colón, C. 61. Branch of Mérida's leading ice-cream makers, with terrace tables on the north side of the plaza.

Jugos California, C. 63-A (the pedestrian alley parallel to C. 63), x C. 58. The local best-juicer award has to go to this company, with several branches. Behind the counter is every possible local fruit, ready to be juiced.

La Michoacana, C. 61, x 56. A wonderful classic ice-cream, juice and *agua* shop in the busy area north of the market.

Entertainment and Nightlife

The Yucatán state government's support for the arts is reflected in a festival in January and other programmes, above all the **Otoño Cultural** (see p.275). A monthly leaflet of upcoming events is available from tourist offices and other outlets.

Teatro Peón Contreras on C. 60 is the main concert venue, particularly for the **Orquesta Sinfónica de Yucatán**, which has a growing reputation.

Much of Mérida's best entertainment, though, is open to all on the streets, with free events nightly. This is the standard programme, but there are also one-offs.

Monday: Vaquería Regional, *jarana* music and dance, in the Plaza Mayor, from 9pm.

Tuesday: Remembranzas Musicales, nostalgic big band music, Parque de Santiago, 9pm.

Wednesday: varied events in the Centro Olimpo, Plaza Mayor, from 9pm.

Thursday: Serenatas Yucatecas, Parque de Santa Lucía. Held every Thursday for over 40 years, the *serenatas* feature an ever-changing programme of all the classic elements of Yucatecan music: *jaranas*, folk dancing, trios, even poetry recitals. An essential date. And it's free.

Friday: Serenata Universitaria, Patio of the Universidad A. de Yucatán, C. 60, traditional dances from around Mexico, from 9pm.

Saturday: Corazón de Mérida, when the city centre (Calles 60, 62) is closed to traffic from 8.30pm and taken over by salsa bands, cafés and so on; meanwhile the **Noche Mexicana** showcases classic Mexican music at the bottom of Paseo Montejo from 7pm.

Sunday: Mérida en Domingo (Mérida on Sunday). The Plaza Mayor and C. 60 as far as Santa Lucía are closed to traffic to make way for an all-day *fiesta*. There are *jarana* displays in the Plaza Mayor and other shows, and opportunities to dance yourself in the Plaza, Parque Hidalgo and Santa Lucía.

Bars and Clubs

¡Ay Caray!, C. 60, x 55 & 57. One building with four night-spots that draw a noisy local crowd: ¡Ay Caray! itself, a big *cantina*-dance bar (with food), **El Nuevo Tucho**, a glitzy cabaret with live salsa, **Azul Picante**, a salsa bar, and **Xtabay**, a dive-like disco-bar.

El Cielo, Prolongación de Montejo, x C. 25, t 944 5127. Sleek, all-white, mostly open-air bar much liked by Mérida's wealthiest youth, in much the best part of town. Look cool.

Jazzin' Mérida, C, 56 no. 465, x 53 & 55, t 924 5628. Mérida's first-ever jazz club, with a cool mix of music. *Open Wed–Sat from 7pm.*

Pancho's, C. 59 no. 509, x 60 & 62. Mexican-theme bar-restaurant, lined with pictures of Pancho Villa and Zapata, that's an ever-popular hangout in the heart of town. Two big bars open to the stars, one of the world's tiniest dance floors, and on-the-ball staff.

09 Yucatán State | Mérida

Around Mérida

Mérida may have the feel of a big city by Yucatán standards, but go beyond the *Periférico* and everything becomes very rural. Within a short range of the city there are examples of all the state's prime attractions: the Maya ruins of **Dzibilchaltún**, the flamingo breeding grounds at **Celestún** and the **beaches** of the Gulf coast.

The Yucatán coast west and north of Mérida is made up of a long, thin strip of sand, originally covered in coconut palms, virtually unbroken for over 150km and separated from the mainland by a mangrove lagoon. This sand bar and the shallow sea beyond it has been a problem for all the region's modern rulers, since they make it exceptionally difficult to establish ports on the Yucatán coast, but the lagoon provides breeding grounds for an enormous range of water birds, above all flamingos. The flamingo lagoons west of Mérida around Celestún are now a national park.

The fishing towns along the sand bar, apart from Mérida's port of Progreso, are small, dusty and feel apart from the world, with no harbours but lines of fishing launches pulled up on the shore. Their beaches fill up with Mérida families every weekend and in summer, and in the last few years efforts have been made to lure some of the international beach-seeking masses across from Cancún. The sandy seas of the Gulf coast will never really be as big a draw as as the clear turquoise waters and coral reefs of the Caribbean, and this coast is prone to high winds, especially the *Nortes* from November to April, but either side of the towns there are miles of empty sand, while in the lagoons you can get an immediate sense of wild, remote nature.

Sisal and Celestún

Calle 59 from central Mérida becomes Av. Jacinto Canek, the road for Celestún. After an imposing beginning this dwindles into a quiet country road, running on through villages and small towns. Biggest of them is **Hunucmá** (29km from Mérida), where the road divides. One fork runs 25km northwest to **Sisal**, once the main port of the Yucatán. In 1800 one of the last Spanish governors resolved to provide Mérida with its own port here; previously there was no harbour at any point along the sand bar, and all traffic had to go via Campeche. It was never a great success as a harbour, as ships had to wait offshore, bobbing against the *Nortes*, to unload on to launches, but it entered the English language, as the first ship-ments of *henequen* rope were exported through here in bales marked with the word *sisal*, which became the international term for the rope itself. However, the inadequacies of Sisal were such that once a new port was opened at Progreso in 1872 its brief

Getting to Celestún

Buses to Celestún and Sisal leave from the Terminal del Noreste at C. 67, x 50. There are 10 daily to Celestún, 5am–8.30pm, and returns to Mérida 6am–7pm. Most are stopping buses (*2hrs*), but some are more direct (*1½hrs*).
Drivers from Mérida should take C. 65 or 57 west to Av. Itzaes and turn right, to the north, before a left turn onto the Celestún road.

---

prominence came to an abrupt end. Today it is a windblown, dusty little place that seems well forgotten by history.

Back on the main road west from Hunucmá, the landscape is more lush. About 40km from Hunucmá there is a turn south on to a dirt road that's an interesting short cut (a relative term) to the Campeche and Puuc roads (*see* p.294), through **Chunchucmil**, lost in birch woods around one of the grandest of decaying *haciendas*.

As you approach the coast the trees become thicker, so that when you emerge on to the long bridge across the lagoon to **Celestún** it catches you almost by surprise. A sharp left turn after the bridge leads to the official **Embarcadero** for boat trips to the flamingo grounds. Since this facility was built visiting the Celestún flamingos has become fairly 'processed', and if you want to see flamingos in a more relaxed way, it's worth making the trip to Río Lagartos (*see* p.242). Once you have joined your *lancha* it will hare off, driven by a noisy outboard, into the lagoon. The lagoon is very shallow in places, so hair-raising twists and turns are part of the trip (accidents and groundings, though, are virtually unknown). Along the way you glimpse fishermen's huts amid the mangroves, egrets, ibises, herons and many other birds. The flamingos first become visible as a pink streak on the horizon. They are at their densest from June to August, but hundreds can be seen all year round. The best time to see them is in the morning.

Flamingos are shy, nervous creatures, and Celestún's *lancheros* have come in for a lot of criticism for their working practices. Since this is a national park they are under instructions not to disturb the birds unnecessarily, especially when breeding. Some responsibility, however, lies with the tourist, for the boatmen provide a service, and you get what you ask for. If you make it clear you do not want to disturb the birds or go too fast (try, '*No queremos molestar a los pájaros, OK?*' and '*Queremos ir tranquilamente*'), the *lanchero* will comply, and if you ask '*¿Se puede parar el motor?*' ('Can you stop the motor?') you may be able to sit in relative silence for a while (this takes more time, and deserves a tip). If, though, you ask for the boat to get closer, they do that too. On weekends you may find that whatever deal you make with your *lanchero*, someone else will have their boat roar in to get a flock of flamingos in flight on their video.

Most people come to Celestún just to see flamingos and leave, but it's also a likeable beach village. Its long, white beach, with a

09 | Yucatán State | Sisal and Celestún

string of little restaurants, is a popular weekend target for locals. It's getting better known, as reflected in the appearance of a few new hotels and the buying-up of some village properties by foreigners. Stay here overnight or mid-week, though, and you can still feel you have the place to yourself. As well as flamingos there are other birds out to sea, especially pelicans and frigate birds, the fishing is excellent, and the white sands are great for beach-combing. Also, since Celestún faces west, those who do stay here are often rewarded with superb sunsets, followed by astonishing starscapes after dark.

There is a dirt road, passable in a 4WD or with difficulty in an ordinary car, that runs north from Celestún behind the beach to Sisal, through miles of deserted dunes, more pristine beaches and coconut groves that house a huge variety of birds. It's possible to stay in this wilderness at **Xixim**, or camp for free at **El Palmar** (*see* below), where there is a giant lighthouse, a bird reserve and little else.

Flamingo Tours

Lanchas to the lagoon leave from the **Embarcadero** (*open daily 6am–5pm*) by the bridge into Celestún village. The service is very organized, with two set routes, of one or two hours, and set fares. One-hour trips take you round the main flamingo grounds and mangroves; two-hour trips go on to the sea entrance to the lagoon. Boats take a maximum of six, and if full cost about $60 for one hour, around $80 for two; for two people only, the fare is around $40 for one hour, $55 for two. The boats have canopies to give some shade, but exposure to sun and wind is inevitable, so take sun block and a hat.

All-in **tours** to Celestún, including bus, *lanchas* to the flamingos and a meal, can be booked through most Mérida travel agencies. The cost is around $30 per person.

Where to Stay in Celestún
t (988–)

It's possible to **camp** for free at **El Palmar**, between Celestún and Sisal, but you must take water, food and other supplies with you.

Eco-Paraíso Xixim, t 916 2100, *www.ecoparaiso.com* (*luxury–expensive*). You might expect rooms in this area to be basic, but 9km north of Celestún is this 'ecoretreat' hotel, reached by a very rugged dirt track. It has 15 palm-roofed cabins by a huge Gulf beach, each with a terrace facing out to sea, and utterly comfortable; there's a nice pool, and the restaurant has a full vegetarian menu as well as great fish and home-made bread. Guests have the benefit of a whole range of tours: flamingos, other birds, night lagoon tours, *cenotes*, fishing and more. Low-impact technologies are used as much as possible, but electricity is available 24hrs. Turtles breed on the beach, and it feels utterly remote.

Hotel Manglares, C. 12 no. 63, t 916 2156, *www.hotelmanglares.com.mx* (*moderate*). Modern hotel right on the beach with 15 comfortable rooms and four smart little *cabañas* with kitchens, and a nice pool. Rooms and cabins all have great views, and flamingo tours are available.

Ecohotel Flamingo Playa, C. 12, x 3 & 5, t 916 2133 (*inexpensive*). Nothing especially 'eco', but still a likeable hotel on Celestún beach with a big pool and 12 large, airy rooms, with fans and air conditioning. Four of them have the same great sea views as the nearby Manglares, but at a much lower price.

Hotel María del Carmen, C. 12, x 15, t 916 2043 (*inexpensive*). Pleasant beach hotel in Celestún village with friendly owners and clean, white, bright rooms, all with balconies with fine sea views (some also have a/c).

Eating Out in Celestún

Celestún has several more good-value seafood *loncherías*, spread along the beach.

La Palapa, C. 12, x 11 (*moderate*). Celestún's most prominent eating-spot, with a bar and beach terrace beneath a *palapa*-palm roof. As it has expanded to fit in tour groups, the atmosphere has got more impersonal, but the fish and seafood – *ceviches*, *camarones*, mixed platters – are still high-quality.

Restaurante Celestún, C. 12, x 9 (*budget*). A big beachfront restaurant with bargain *ceviches* and other local fish and seafood.

Dzibilchaltún

The Maya centre of Dzibilchaltún, 20km north of Mérida, doesn't have the giant pyramids of the best-known sites, but has other special features: a Franciscan chapel blending in with the older ruins, a superb *cenote* where you can swim, and one of the cosmological tricks that fascinate in Maya architecture, the Temple of the Seven Dolls, through which the sun appears at dawn on the spring and autumn equinoxes.

History

Dzibilchaltún – translatable as 'the place where there is writing on the stones', a modern Maya name that, as so often, has no relation to what it was called in its heyday – has one of the longest histories of unbroken occupation of any Maya site, extending over 2,000 years from around 500 BC to shortly before the Conquest. Its growth well preceded that of Uxmal and the Puuc centres further south, and Dzibilchaltún was the most powerful city-state in the northwest Yucatán through most of the Classic era. It was also a wealthy port and centre of coastal trade, controlling salt beds in the lagoons, and had a population as big as 20,000 around the year 800. Like others Dzibilchaltún declined from about 950, but the site continued to be occupied on a smaller scale.

Dzibilchaltún was very widely dispersed, and the full site covers around 30 square km, although the nucleus is more concentrated.

The Museo del Pueblo Maya

Dzibilchaltún Museum
open daily 8–4; adm

In a spacious semi-open-air building, this is one of the best site museums, with artefacts from sites all over Yucatán State as well as Dzibilchaltún itself and from the colonial era as well as pre-Conquest Maya culture, giving an imaginative view of the region's past that places this and other sites in context. The display begins with some of the largest objects – carved columns from Dzibilchaltún and Uxmal, relics from Chichén Itzá and an impress-ively powerful figure of a warrior from Oxkintok – but there are also less common items that show how Maya artisans could handle the small-scale as well as the massive. Ceramic vases are

Getting to Dzibilchaltún

Dzibilchaltún is an easy short trip from Mérida, but it seems pretty much expected that you get there with your own transport or a tour. It is easy to find **by car**, on the right-hand side of the Progreso road just outside the Mérida *Periférico*. From there it's about 5km to the turn-off to the ruins, clearly indicated on the right after Dzibilchaltún village.

There are two ways to get there **by bus**. One is to take the frequent Autoprogreso buses for Progreso (*see* p.291), get off at Dzibilchaltún turning and get a passing taxi or *colectivo* (this can be quick or slow). It's also possible to go direct: *colectivos* to Dzibilchaltún village and Chablekal leave from or near Parque San Juan (look for *combis* marked Chablekal, or ask around). They leave you at the site entry outside Dzibilchaltún village, from where it's under 1km to the ruins. Leaving the ruins, walk back to the road and flag down a bus or *combi* (last return about 7pm). *Combis* are frequent Mon–Sat, but are less numerous on Sun.

Virtually all Mérida travel agencies offer **tours** to Dzibilchaltún, which usually include a visit to Progreso and a *hacienda* as well.

---

finely decorated with flowers, a reminder of the colour that has now been lost from virtually all Mayan sites.

Artefacts from Dzibilchaltún itself have a room to themselves. Most important is a fine stela of Chac, Stela 19, dated to 716. Perhaps most intriguing are the 'Seven Dolls', seven crudely modelled little figures that look very much like gingerbread men. The Temple of the Seven Dolls, where they were found, owes its name to them, and it is believed they were placed there as offerings. Later rooms feature the colonial and later eras – from *conquistador* armour to a first edition of a Yucatec-Spanish vocabulary, and carriages, prints and weapons from the 19th-century Caste War.

The Ruins and the *Cenote*

Dzibilchaltún Ruins
open daily 8–5; adm

Leaving the museum, you emerge into the Yucatán brush. There are two paths, one that takes you fairly directly to the ruins, the other a *sendero ecológico* that meanders through the woods and gives you the opportunity to see and hear a wide range of birds. On the direct path, you emerge after 400 metres on to the main *sacbé*, the long path that linked the two key centres of Dzibilchaltún, stretching away on either side and looking exactly like what it is, a road abandoned in the middle of the woods.

The *sacbé* runs almost exactly east–west. Away to the left, the east, at the end of an impressive approach is the smaller of the two centres, around the **Temple of the Seven Dolls**. A small altar and the remains of four other buildings block the path, and behind them is the temple atop a low square platform. Because of its long history of occupation, at Dzibilchaltún still more than at most Maya sites buildings were superimposed on top of each other, and the base-platform here dates from the Early Classic, prior to 600. The temple on top is in a different style reminiscent of Chichén Itzá, and dated around 700. This temple was in turn submerged beneath a larger temple platform in the last years of the city, and it was here that the 'Seven Dolls' themselves – dated to about 1200 – were found. This last structure has been dismantled to reveal the 8th century temple.

Visiting Dzibilchaltún

The same ticket admits you to the site and the museum. The site is arranged so you pass first through the **museum** before meeting the path to the ruins, but you can easily do the tour in reverse. There's also a **café** and a **shop**.

At dawn on the spring and autumn equinoxes (20 and 21 March, 20 and 21 September), the rising sun strikes directly through its east and west doors and along the line of the *sacbé*. This effect was known but could not be fully appreciated until the 1994 restoration. The site opens at 5.30am on these days for visitors to see the sunrise, best appreciated at 6–6.15am. Still more mysterious is the phenomenon at full moon in March and April, when the light of the moon similarly strikes through the doors (*check dates with tourist offices*).

From the temple platform the other main section of Dzibilchaltún can just be seen, about 1km away at the western end of the *sacbé*. This path of stones, sand and gravel was laid in about the year 600; in addition, 11 other *sacbés* run through Dzibilchaltún. On one side of the path there are the badly deteriorated remains of a simple platform, which you pass before you reach the larger western group of buildings around the broad **Plaza Central**. Again, they are of many different eras, mixed up and on top of each other. On the right as you enter the plaza is one of the largest, a Classic pyramid (**Structure 36**), near which Stela 19 was found. Nearby there are cruder buildings from about 1200, while beyond the pyramid is the residential complex known as **Structure 38**, from about 600. The south side of the plaza is filled by one of the longest of Mayan buildings, a 130m bank of steps topped by the remains of columns that once formed three large chambers. Officially **Structure 44**, this is often called the **Palacio**, and probably was a residential complex for the city's rulers.

Most curious of all the plaza's buildings and impossible to miss, is the remains of a Catholic **chapel**, built for Franciscan missionaries in the 1590s. This was a *Capilla Abierta* ('open chapel'); in contrast to

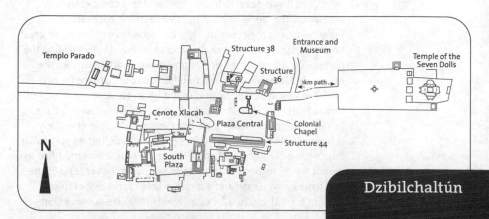

Templo Parado
Structure 38
Entrance and Museum
Structure 36
1km path
Temple of the Seven Dolls
Cenote Xlacah
Plaza Central
Colonial Chapel
Structure 44
N
South Plaza

Dzibilchaltún

09 Yucatán State | Dzibilchaltún

the *capillas de indios* attached to missionary monasteries it was free-standing, but similarly consisted only of a round stone apse around the altar, attached to a rough nave of wood and palm leaves. The apse was decorated with rare murals of saints, but in the last fifty years these have decayed into invisibility. Beside it, it's still possible to see the remains of the meagre friars' house, as well as some walls from a 17th-century ranch.

Just west of the Plaza Central is the main attraction of Dzibilchaltún for most locals, the **Cenote Xlacah**, the giant sinkhole that was the city's water supply. It was explored in the 1950s by divers from Tulane University, who found it to be 44m deep. This *cenote* can truly be called bottomless, for at that level it bends round into a large chamber that extends away beneath the Yucatán rock. They also found thousands of offerings thrown into the waters, mostly ceramics but also more precious pieces, though no traces were found of human sacrifices. On one side it is obvious from its intense blue just how deep the water is, but on the other it's shallower and more inviting for gentle basking. On Sundays the rocks around it are taken over by family outings and kids doing bomb-dives, but on other days it has a wonderful tranquillity.

Like other sites, Dzibilchaltún tails off into the woods. Almost hidden in the brush west of the *cenote* is Structure 57, known as the **Templo Parado** or 'Stopped Temple' because only half of its arched roof is still intact, and built about 800–850.

Progreso and the North Coast

Progreso

Progreso, the modern port of Mérida, was created by the reforming followers of Juárez who governed Mexico in the years after the overthrow of Maximilian. The inadequacies of Sisal as a port had been obvious for years, and as *henequen* exports multiplied it was decided to give the Yucatán a completely new gateway to the world. The *Juaristas* were strong believers in progress, and so the new town got its name. They got over the great problem of this coast, the shallowness of the water, by building the harbour out to sea, at the end of an extraordinarily long pier, the **Muelle de Altura**, which now stretches into the distance for over 6km. The view from the far end might be an attraction in itself, but unfortunately you're not usually allowed to visit unless you have business there. As a trading harbour Progreso had never entirely recovered from the decline in the *henequen* trade, but its port-town bustle has picked up significantly since the *muelle* was modified to permit the occasional arrival of cruise ships. At the very end of the pier there's now a mall and a range of other services for cruise passengers, but you're still not allowed in if you're not on a ship.

Getting to Progreso

Getting to Progreso **by car** from Mérida is easy: follow C. 60 to Prolongación de Montejo, and keep going (33km). There is a **petrol/gas station** by the entrance to the town.

Buses to Progreso go from the Autoprogreso depot at C. 62 no. 524, x 65 & 67, every 10mins, 5am–10pm daily, and *colectivos* can be found on C. 60, x 65 & 67. The bus terminus in Progreso is at the corner of C. 29 and C. 82. Returns to Mérida run till about 11pm.

Taxis, *micros* and *combis* run from Progreso to outlying villages like Chicxulub or Chelem.

Orientation

Progreso has a straightforward grid running back from the seafront, the **Malecón**. Odd numbers run parallel to the Malecón, even numbers run down to it. Finding addresses in Progreso was long given extra spice by the fact that the town had two parallel street-numbering systems, so the same street could be called C. 78 or C. 28. It has now been pretty much accepted that lower numbers are used for the 'odd' streets, higher numbers for the north-south 'even' ones, but the older numbers still turn up on street signs. Also, in order not to be too logical, the Malecón, which of course is the first street back from the sea, is officially, inexplicably, Calle 19.

This occasional foreign traffic, however, has still not made much difference to Progreso's prime role for most people in Mérida, as the city's favourite piece of seaside. Since the harbour is effectively over the horizon it doesn't interfere with the beach at all. At the height of the heat in July and August and on many Sundays the rest of the year, half the city decamps up the road to Progreso to flop on its sands and eat in its seafood restaurants. Large parts of Progreso and the villages alongside it are taken up by beach-houses owned by *Meridanos*, which are only really used during those two months of the year. The rest of the time most are shuttered up, and on weekdays in January or February, especially, Progreso is peculiarly quiet and empty.

Any image of Progreso as a 'resort' is limited by its pleasantly Yucatecan raggedness, an utter failure to be sleek or glossy. The beach has little shade but fine, white sand (and wheelchair-access ramps) and the water stays shallow for a huge distance, so that it's a great beach for splashing around or easy swimming, especially for kids. Going to the beach on a Sunday in Progreso is a different experience from beach-squatting on the multi-national Riviera. Instead, it's as near as most foreigners are likely to get to being invited to a Mexican family party. All along the Malecón there are vendors pushing *triciclo*-carts selling ice creams, fruit, *aguas*, fresh coconuts and little cakes. In the seafront restaurants tables are taken over by huge family groups.

On the west side of Progreso a gap in the sand bar forms the entrance to a broad, open section of lagoon, **Laguna Yucalpetén**. The road to its western side is reached by heading back out of Progreso on the Mérida road, then taking a right turn to rejoin the coast. The villages here, **Yucalpetén** and **Chelem**, have more attractive beaches than Progreso itself. Windsurfing boards can be hired in Chelem. After 20km the road reaches a village in the dunes, **Chuburna**, and dwindles into a rough track to Sisal.

09 Yucatán State | Progreso and the North Coast

Where to Stay in Progreso

t (969–)

Sand Castle Inn, Chelem, t 935 4275, *www.sandcastleinnmexico.org (moderate)*. Laid-back American-owned B&B on the beach in ever-tranquil Chelem, just west of Progreso. Rooms overlook the beach or pool; they're pretty and very well-equipped, with fridges, WiFi and other extras.

Casa Isidora, C. 21 no. 116, x 58 & 60, t 935 4595, *www.casaisidora.com (inexpensive)*. Friendly Canadian-owned small hotel a block from the beach. Its **Cheers** bar and grill is a social centre for local English-speakers, resident or passing through. The six rooms, all with a/c, are very good value: breakfast and internet access are included, and there's a nice patio and pool. Special rates are available for longer stays. Also a **language school**, with residential Spanish courses, teacher-training courses and English for Progreso locals.

⭐ **Flamingos** >>

Hotel Real del Mar, Malecón, x C. 70, t 935 0798 *(inexpensive–budget)*. On the seafront, with a certain faded grandeur. Rooms (fan-only or a/c) are well kept and bright; the best have immense sea views.

Tropical Suites, Malecón, x C. 70, t 935 1263 *(inexpensive–budget)*. Next to the Real but ahead in the character stakes, this wonderfully-named place has a touch of Graham Greene-ish decadence, but rooms are pleasant, and some have sea views.

House Rentals

Houses and apartments in Progreso and on the Gulf Coast can often be rented very cheaply. Many can be found by looking around vacation rental websites, but local agencies include:

Progreso Vacation Rentals, C.21 no. 84, x 16 & 18, Mérida, t (999) 949 0861, *www.progresovacationrentals.com*.

Tierra Yucatán, t (999) 923 7615, *www.jensyucatan.com*.

Vacations Yucatán, t (305) 767 2097, *www.vacationsyucatan.com*.

Eating Out in Progreso

Progreso's Malecón has a line of restaurants with big terraces specializing in fresh fish and seafood, which are among the town's essential attractions. There is also an **Eladio's** (see p.xxx) near the pier. On the road through Yucalpetén there are more shaded terrace fish restaurants, such as **El Varadero** and **La Terracita**.

Flamingos, Malecón, x C. 72 *(moderate)*. An especially attractive terrace, with a fine view, friendly service and deliciously fresh ceviches and grilled fish platters.

Los Pelícanos, Malecón, x C. 70 *(moderate)*. One of the best on the Malecón, in front of the Real del Mar hotel. A friendly terrace packed with Meridanos at weekends, it has great brochettes of *camarones*, conch or meat, and huge platters of grilled fish.

East Along the Coast to Dzilam Bravo

East of Progreso the coast road continues for over 80km, lined by beach-houses that gradually fade away to leave windblown fishing villages, between clusters of coconut palms. On the landward side of the road there are more silent, bird-filled wetlands. Around 30km from Progreso a road leads just inland to a small Maya site, **Xcambó**.

First along is **Chicxulub**, a relaxed beach town. The lagoon behind it is another that hosts large flamingo colonies. At **Uaymitún**, 5km further east, there is a watchtower or *mirador* (*binoculars free, but tips appreciated*), built to allow people to see birds easily. The air is wonderfully fresh and clear, and as your eyes adapt to the light you

Getting around the North Coast

Buses run along the coast road from Terminal del Noreste in Mérida, and there are *colectivos* from Progreso. The only **petrol/gas station** past Progreso is in Telchac Puerto.

can pick out whole flocks of flamingos and other birds spreading across the lagoons.

After **San Benito** the road becomes more empty. About 15km further east a road turns inland, signposted to Dzemul, which leads in 1.5km to the Maya ruins of **Xcambó**. This seems to be the preferred INAH spelling, although you may see 'Cerros de Xtampu' on signs. Its central area consists of a large pyramid-platform facing a broad plaza, surrounded by smaller buildings. They mostly date from the Late Classic, and Xcambó was probably a salt-trading settlement, perhaps a subsidiary community of Dzibilchaltún. Its most fascinating feature, though, is the rustic Catholic chapel built alongside the main platform. It was used for years long before excavations began, and is the focus of a *fiesta* for the local villages on 19–20 May, an event of some solemnity.

If you continue inland past Xcambó on the same road, you'll eventually reach the site intended for **Flamingo Lakes**, a 'golf and country club resort' planned by international investors. As with many such projects, its construction has overshot its initial dates. Back on the coast road, just before **Telchac Puerto**, there is one of its stranger sights, the not entirely successful all-inclusive 'tourist complex' of **Nuevo Yucatán**, one of local promoters' efforts to achieve takeoff along this coast. **Telchac** itself is a more attractive, low-key place, with a fishing harbour, good beaches and more restaurants.

Between **Chabihau** and **Santa Clara** the road twists away from the beach to run along the landward side of the lagoon. On the far side of it is a long, wooded island, **El Bajo**, with utterly secluded beaches. Boatmen from Santa Clara or Dzilam Bravo will take you across and bring you back (take everything you need). **Dzilam Bravo** is where the coast road ends. It has a certain fame as the supposed last resting place of one of the Louisiana pirate brothers Lafitte. In 1821, after they were attacked by the Spanish Navy on Isla Mujeres (*see* p.143), the two Lafittes, both wounded, escaped in an open boat and made their way along the coast. According to local folklore they stopped at Dzilam Bravo, where one of them died. It has always been said that it was the most dashing Lafitte, Jean, but it seems likely it was his less active brother Pierre.

Dzilam Bravo is also the closest point to one of the wildest, most remote areas of the Yucatán, the expanse of mangrove and lagoon known as the **Bocas de Dzilam**. Local fishermen have recently set up a guides cooperative (*see* p.294).

Xcambó
open daily 8–5; adm

09 | **Yucatán State** | Progreso and the North Coast

Tours

Visits to the Bocas de Dzilam can also be arranged with **Ecoturismo Yucatán** (*see* p.274) and some other Mérida agencies.

Dzayachuleb, Dzilam de Bravo, t (991) 912 2520, *www.ecoturyucatan.com.mx*. Recently-set-up cooperative in Dzilam that offers a fascinating range of trips in this remote area: mangroves, *cenotes*, lonely beaches...

Where to Stay and Eat

There are few places to stay on this coast, so it retains an out-of-the-way feel. There are cheap fresh-fish restaurants in every village.

Libros y Sueños, Telchac Puerto, t (991) 917 4125, *www.l-y-s.net* (*budget*). Canadians Dave and Mary Jungquist have set up here with this relaxed little hotel, with seven cosy rooms, a café, Net access, a gift shop, an English-language bookstore and bikes to rent. A real bargain hideaway.

Uxmal, the Puuc Cities and Southern Yucatán

Directly south of Mérida are the Puuc hills, also known as the *Sierrita* or 'little sierra' of Yucatán, modest rolls in the ground that are the more noticeable (*Puuc* itself means hill) because of the contrast they make with the absolute flatness of northern Yucatán. This is one of the richest of all regions in Maya sites: from some of the oldest (the caves at Loltún), to the grandest (Uxmal). It was also an important area throughout the Conquest and colonial eras. More than this, though, its towns and villages full of bicycles, dogs and *huípil*-clad women are also some of the most engaging places to get a feel of life in Maya Yucatán today.

From Mérida a busy highway leads 17km southwest to **Umán**, beyond which the roads divide. Highway 180 follows the old Spanish Camino Real southwest to Campeche, while Highway 261, well signposted for Uxmal, turns off left, due south (also called .the *Via Larga*, 'long route', to Campeche). The established 'Puuc Route' (**La Ruta Puuc**) consists of Uxmal and the sites along the 60km between there and the town of Oxcutzcab (Kabah, Sayil, Xlapak, Labná and the caves at Loltún), and can be reached quickly on the 261 road, or, in the opposite direction, with the newer Highway 18 via Mayapán (*see* p.322). Archaeological work in the 1990s, though, extended the 'route' with the opening up of two more sites, at Oxkintok, reached via the Campeche road, and Chacmultún to the east. The shape of the Puuc area has also been 'distorted' by excavations having been concentrated in Yucatán state, and across the line in Campeche there are more ruins – Chunhuhub (*see* p.400) and Xcalumkín (*see* p.380) – which in Maya terms fall within the Puuc.

The Camino Real to Campeche and Oxkintok

From Umán the roads south run through an area known as *Zona de Cenotes* for its high number of sinkholes (for trips *see* p.297). A little before Maxcanú you enter the **Sierrita**, a welcome change in the landscape. One feature of the Yucatán becomes very noticeable: the smaller a settlement is, the more solidly Maya it is likely to be.

Oxkintok

Oxkintok
Open daily 8–5; adm.

Oxkintok has been regularly open for some years now, but still does not get many visitors, and on most days you can have the place to yourself apart from the caretaker and some huge iguanas. These ruins are not a recent discovery – Stephens came here in 1841 – but only since 1990 have extensive excavations been undertaken.

The main structures are at the top of a gentle rise, built on crests to give a more commanding view of the surrounding hills. Across on the north side of the road are more pyramids, unexcavated but clearly recognizable. As in many sites, the name Oxkintok ('three flint sun-stones') is an archaeologists' invention, and no one knows what it was really called, but it is believed that in its prime this may have been one of the largest communities in the region, with 20,000 inhabitants.

It is of exceptional interest to Mayanists because of the very long time it was occupied, and because Oxkintok exhibits a unique mixture of styles that reveals a great deal about the pattern of communications and trade in the Maya world. Buildings have been discovered here from the Preclassic as far back as 300 BC, and from the very end of the Postclassic, on the verge of the Conquest. It has the oldest inscribed date this far north in the Long Count calendar (from 475), and one of the latest (859). It is believed that Oxkintok was a major city throughout the Classic era, from 300 to around 950, and so for much longer than the more famous Puuc sites to the east. Architecturally it was once considered an offshoot of the Puuc, but after more recent excavations it has been attributed an eclectic 'Oxkintok' or 'Pre-Puuc' style of its own.

The excavated structures at Oxkintok mainly consist of three building complexes, around plazas and sub-plazas in usual Maya style. Largest is the **May Group**, centred on the slab-sided main **Pyramid**. The most complete buildings are in the **Canul Group** to the left, with several residential complexes of which the most impressive is the Puuc-like **Palacio Ch'ich** (Structure 7), with well-preserved bedchambers with raised sleeping platforms and niches for lamps. It fronts on to a small plaza, in which three column-like statues of warriors still stand; leading into this square from the

Getting to Oxkintok and Calcehtok

If you're driving, shortly before Maxcanú on the main Highway 180 to Campeche (55km from Mérida) a left turn, signposted to Muna and Calcehtok, leads to Oxkintok. In Calcehtok, take a turn right signed to *Grutas de Calcehtok–Oxkintok* for Calcehtok caves and the ruins. After a sharp climb uphill and 2km, there is a turn right to Oxkintok.

There are second-class **buses** every half-hour on the Mérida–Campeche road which stop at **Maxcanú**. From there you can get a *colectivo* to **Calcehtok** village, from where you can have a stiff hike or take a taxi to Oxkintok ruins. Returning, *colectivos* run from Calcehtok to Muna and the main Puuc road.

main plaza there is a long building (Structure 6, or the **Palacio de la Serie Inicial**) in which the date inscription of AD 475 was found (on a lintel now in the Mérida museum). A stela of a warrior (**Stela 21**) with the last Long Count date at Oxkintok (859), now in the Dzibilchaltún museum, was also found near here.

The most famous building at Oxkintok, however, is the **Satunsat** or **Labyrinth** (also written *Tzat Tun Tzat*), a small squat pyramid built into the hill on the west side of the main plaza. It is entered from the other side, facing on to a large plaza leading to the little excavated **Dzib Group**. Once inside the very small doorway explorers must turn left or right, into pitch-dark, narrow passages that circle round each other and up and down steep inclines and even narrower stairways; if you're lucky, you can find your way up to a second level and out again through semi-ruined entrances near the top of the building. Stephens came here in 1841, and, after hearing that local Indians believed it to be a bottomless pit and that no one in living memory had dared enter it, set out to investigate by going in with a ball of string to keep track of his movements. He spent a day scrambling about the tunnels, only to conclude it was just a series of blind alleys. Current opinion is that the Labyrinth was a power point, part of one of the theatrical gestures central to Maya kingship. It has openings on the west, north and south, but none to the east, the origin of the sun: the tunnels were perhaps an entrance to the Otherworld, into which only the *ahau* of Oxkintok could enter.

If you wish to enter now, it's eerie but not dangerous; take a powerful torch (flashlight) and expect lots of bats and a few bees. You may also wish to be aware, though, that local folklore holds that the Satunsat is a haunt of *aluxes*, Mayan goblins (*see* p.300), left there by the old gods and kings to guard the site.

The Caves of Calcehtok

Returning from Oxkintok, at the junction with the road back to Calcehtok village, a right turn will take you up steep hills to the **Grutas de Calcehtok**, one of the least-known of the Yucatán cave systems, and perhaps more awe-inspiring for that reason. The cavern is a vast basilica; whole trees are contained within it, along with flocks of birds whose shrieks echo off the cave walls. A rickety

Exploring *Cenotes* in Yucatán State

Until recently they were less well-known than the divable *cenotes* near the coast around Tulum (*see* p.190), but Yucatán state actually has more *cenote* sinkholes and underwater caverns than Quintana Roo, above all in the areas south and south-east of Mérida towards Uxmal and Mayapán. Traditionally, most have been known only to local villagers, but with the growing emphasis on ecotourism, communities are becoming aware of the interest in their *cenotes* and are opening them up to visitors, as at Yokdzonot (*see* p.240) and Cuzamá (*see* p.328). More signs announcing that village *cenotes* are open for visits appear beside major roads all the time. Some village schemes are also affiliated to the Red de Ecoturismo de Yucatán.

There are many other beautiful *cenotes*, though, off the main routes. It's possible to seek them out by yourself through the back roads and villages of the Yucatán, as long as you speak a little Spanish and take time, but as a short cut *cenote* snorkel tours are available. They can be booked from agencies such as Ecoturismo Yucatán (*see* p.274), but some of the best are run by *cenote* specialists.

Adventure Tours, Calle 28 no. 345, x 29 & 31, Mérida, t (999) 944 4157, *www.adventuretours.com.mx*. Highly experienced cave-diving specialists, but who also offer kayaking and other trips.

Mayan Ecotours, Calle 80 no. 561, x 13, Colonia Pensiones, Mérida, t (999) 987 3710, *www.mayaneco tours.com*. Connie Leal and her team are *cenote* experts – even when they have no tours booked, they often spend their time exploring caves – and their passion is infectious. The most usual route for one-day snorkelling trips (around $50) is to visit two *cenotes* south of Mérida near Abalá, Yaax-Ha and Kankiriché, with lunch in a smart *hacienda* or a Maya village. Cave diving, kayaking in mangroves near Telchac and other trips can also be arranged. A real experience of the Yucatán countryside.

metal ladder helps you into the first part of the cave, from where a dirt path leads down as far as most casual visitors want to go, though the caves extend for another 2km. Sudden changes in temperature and humidity are felt immediately on the skin, and the plants have an unearthly look, from banana plants in the upper levels to giant ferns and moss lower down. Insect repellent is essential, and the strange air currents and gases in the deeper caverns – some produced by concentrated bat-droppings – can actually be dangerous (if you wish to explore beyond the main cavern, ask the caretaker at Oxkintok; **do not** enter the caves on your own). Back in the fresh air, as this is one of the highest points in the area, there is a wonderful view south over the Yucatán plain.

After leaving Oxkintok and the caves, a right turn in Calcehtok village will take you in about 22km to Muna, to join the main Uxmal and Ticul roads.

Uxmal and the Puuc Route

Yaxcopoil
www.yaxcopoil.com;
open Mon–Sat 8–6, Sun
9–1; adm

The 261 road south from Umán runs more or less straight across flat brush. A place worth stopping at is **Yaxcopoil**, 33km from Mérida, where a rambling 19th-century *henequen hacienda* has been turned into a museum. As you arrive it's impossible to see where village and *hacienda* divide, as the big square is entirely made up of former estate buildings, including the shop, formerly the *tienda de raya* or company store. Of all the *haciendas* open to view in the Yucatán, this best conveys how life functioned on these estates when 'green gold' dominated the life of the region. The tour begins with the big house, built in the 1860s, with its crumbling rooms with imported French tiles, 1920s swimming pool and fine gardens. There's a tiny chapel, and a room of Maya ceramics discovered nearby. Also fascinating are the working buildings: Yaxcopoil produced *henequen* until 1984, and the giant machinery, built in Germany in 1911, is still in place. The *hacienda* also has a **guest house**, with kitchen, available for rent.

A few kilometres further south on either side of the main road are two classic *haciendas*, the hotel at **Temozón Sur** and the restaurant at **Ochil**. A detour past Temozón can also take you to the 'museum hacienda' at **Sotuta de Peón** (*see* p. 328). Although no one

The Puuc Cities

The Mayan cities of the Puuc Hills and their 'capital' Uxmal long represented an archaeological enigma. At one time this was one of the most densely populated of all the Mayan regions, and produced the most refined style of architecture. And yet the area seems unfit for human habitation. In the hills, the water problems of the Yucatán are multiplied 100 times: the water table is far below the surface and there are none of the *cenotes* that supported the Maya in other parts of the peninsula. The Puuc settlements had to create their own water supply by building *chultunes*, underground ceramic-lined cisterns, and *aguadas*, natural dips in the ground that were reinforced to form reservoirs. To found cities in these conditions seems perverse.

This is one of the regions where knowledge has been most extended by modern archaeological techniques such as soil surveys and radar mapping. It appears that because of lack of water the Puuc remained very thinly inhabited until AD 600 or even later. The Maya were highly aware of differences in soil quality. While the hills are very dry, their soils are exceptionally rich in minerals and, if watered, provide very productive land. It seems that the Puuc Hills were first 'colonized' at the end of the 7th century thanks to a combination of factors – overpopulation in lowland areas, the migration of Maya groups from the Gulf Coast or maybe of 'exiles' from wars in the Petén (*see* p.38) – but the Puuc cities only really 'took off' around 750 as the system of *chultunes* was refined. An unprecedented number of settlements existed in a small area, surrounded by intensively cultivated fields maintained with a high degree of land and water management. It has been calculated that towards the end of the Terminal Classic around 900, the populations in the Puuc – 10,000 in Kabah, 9,000 in Sayil – had reached the very limit the land could support. In this fragile environment, it seems likely they fell victim to an acute version of the general 'Collapse', intensified by severe drought. Their agricultural and social systems imploded, and in the century after 950 the cities disintegrated. The Puuc has scarcely been inhabited ever since.

Hence the Puuc cities flourished for only 200 years, with the result that they are unusually homogeneous in style. Characteristic of Puuc style are an emphatic sense of design and geometry, particularly in contrasting plain and decorated surfaces; recurring motifs such as drum columns and *atadura* roof friezes (representing the roof of a thatched hut); as well as constant interplay between apparently abstract shapes and natural and everyday objects. An obsessive image in all the Puuc sites is a god-mask with a long, curling nose. This is commonly identified with the rain god Chac, but may also represent other supernatural figures such as Itzam-Ye, the animal manifestation of Itzamná that sits atop the World Tree at the centre of creation.

The short era of glory enjoyed by Uxmal and the Puuc cities formed part of an extraordinary late flowering in the northern half of the Maya world, the same period that saw the rise of Chichén Itzá and the peak years of the cities in the Chenes and Río Bec. These areas were all in close contact with the Puuc, and 'exchanged' features of their architectural styles. One peculiarity of the Puuc cities is that they seem to have been the Maya communities least devoted to the ball game: there is only one ball court at Uxmal, and none at some smaller sites.

Getting to Uxmal and the Puuc Route

This is one area where a **car** is a big advantage. Roads are easy to follow and in good condition; Mérida to Uxmal takes about 1½hrs. After Umán there are **petrol/gas stations** on the 261 and 184 roads in Muna, Ticul, Oxcutzcab and Tekax. If you are driving up and down the Puuc Route it's advisable to have a full tank.

Buses here follow the needs of local people, not tourists, and as the Puuc is little populated there are relatively few buses and *colectivos*. Around eight second-class buses daily run from **Mérida** (from Terminal de Autobuses, C. 69), five to Campeche and one to Dzibalchén, all passing Uxmal (*2hrs*), Santa Elena and Kabah, from 6am. The cheapest way to do the full 'route' is on the Mayab **Puuc Route bus** that leaves Mérida (also C. 69) at 8am daily, passes Uxmal and goes to Labná before turning back to stop for 30mins at each of the four route sites, and 1½hrs at Uxmal (a bit tight). It gets you back to Mérida by 2.30–3.30pm and costs about $11 (not including site adm). In peak seasons and at weekends, book 2–3 days ahead. In **Santa Elena** you can find *colectivos* and taxis to **Ticul** and its abundant bus traffic (*see* p.321).

would be aware of it from the highway, the surrounding area has one of the densest concentrations of *cenote* sinkholes anywhere in the Yucatán. Some of the most beautiful, such as **Kankiriché**, are near **Abala**, just to the south. They can be visited with Mayan Ecotours and some other agencies.

The 261 road stays pretty flat as you roll down towards **Muna**, where most local traffic takes Highway 184 towards Ticul, while most foreign travellers stay on 261 to Uxmal. Muna is the first of a string of engaging small towns across southern Yucatán, with a market, restaurants, a big plaza and a 17th-century church. From there the road winds up a steep ridge as you enter the Puuc Hills for the 16km to Uxmal.

Uxmal

⊕ Uxmal
Open daily 8–5; adm

Palenque may be richer in inscriptions and known history, and Chichén Itzá may triumph in awesome monumentality, but architecturally and aesthetically it is hard to challenge Uxmal as the most majestic of all the great Maya cities. Its buildings have a special subtlety and sense of proportion: their powerful geometry could not be more emphatic, and they encapsulate the central strengths of Maya architecture just as the Parthenon in Athens or the Pantheon in Rome do for Greek or Roman styles. The clear sense of design demonstrated by their unknown builders also makes them appear strangely modern.

Visiting Uxmal

The site is more compact than Chichén, but two hours is still a minimum time to see it reasonably. Uxmal (like Chichén) is more expensive to visit than most Mayan sites, at around $8.50 (plus $1 per vehicle for parking), because the evening Sound and Light show is inescapably included in the ticket.

In the **visitor centre** at the site entrance there is a **museum**, a **café**, a **souvenir market**, an **ATM** and a better-than-usual **bookshop** (at other sites similar facilities are very limited). The visitor centre stays open for the Sound and Light show until 9–10pm (*see* p.319). By the entrance there are official guides, who charge in the region of $35 for a 1½–2hr tour, in English or several other languages.

History

The name Uxmal means 'three times built' and, unusually, is probably the original name of the city, since it was told to the Spaniards at the time of the Conquest. Its origins are cloaked in legend (*see* story box, below), and exactly how many times it was 'built' is not entirely clear. It is known, however, that this was one of the first large settlements in the Puuc, founded around 700. It is quite possible that a smaller community existed before then, and the oldest part of the Pyramid of the Magician has been carbon-dated to 560, but this date is very questionable. Uxmal is in one of the lowest parts of the Puuc hills, and its 'hilliness' was artificially accentuated, as most of the major buildings stand on man-made platforms. A difference is drawn in its architecture between 'Early Puuc', from 700–800, and refined 'Late Puuc' buildings such as the Nunnery Quadrangle, from around 900. This was not the only Mayan city where some of the finest buildings were created on the verge of its collapse.

Uxmal has several glyph inscriptions and stelae. It maintained literate Maya culture, and has the second-latest date yet found anywhere in the Long Count calendar, in the Nunnery Quadrangle and from 907 (only Toniná in Chiapas has one later, from 909). These inscriptions, though, have not provided anything like as complete a history as has been built up at Palenque or Yaxchilán. In

The Aluxes and the Dwarf of Uxmal

An *alux* (pronounced al-oosh) is a Maya leprechaun, a little spirit with the body of a baby and the face of an old man, born out of an egg. Always mischievous, they can be benign or malevolent. To this day, many Maya farmers leave offerings in their fields as they plant their corn, to win the cooperation of the *aluxob*. According to one story, some *aluxes* are spirits of the old gods, driven from their temple-homes by the Spaniards, and have been taking revenge on *dzulob* (non-Maya, in Yucatec) ever since.

The most famous *alux* of all is the Enano de Uxmal, the Dwarf of Uxmal. His story, which crops up in different versions throughout the Yucatán, was told by local Maya to Stephens. When the story begins Uxmal was a humble place, with nothing like the grandeur it later attained. It was ruled over by an old king, who lived in fear of a prophecy that he would be dethroned by a new lord, who was to announce his arrival by beating on a drum. Meanwhile, an old woman who lived alone in the woods, and cast spells, decided she wanted a child before she died. She spoke to some crows who gave her an egg. From it there duly emerged a baby with an old man's face, who already spoke and was 'as bright as a squirrel'; obviously he was an *alux*, the Dwarf. One day, he found a drum in his mother's *na*, and began to play it. Hearing it, the old king was thrown into a panic, and sent all his men out to find the source of the noise.

The Dwarf was brought before the king, sitting beneath a sacred *ceiba* tree, and told him that he would be the new king of Uxmal. The king demanded that he prove it in tests of wit and strength, to which the Dwarf replied that he would, on the condition that the king matched every test himself.

The king was first confounded in a string of riddles, and left looking stupid. Then, the Dwarf said he would build a path to Uxmal from his house, suitable for a king and his mother; the *sacbé* from Nohpat and Sayil duly appeared. When the king challenged the Dwarf to build a house higher than any other in Uxmal, in one night he created the Pyramid of the Magician, worthy for a king. Finally, a crucial test saw both of them hit over the head with giant hammers. The Dwarf's mother placed a special tortilla over her son's head, and he survived; the king, of course, did not. The Dwarf ruled over Uxmal for centuries, transforming it into a great and wealthy city.

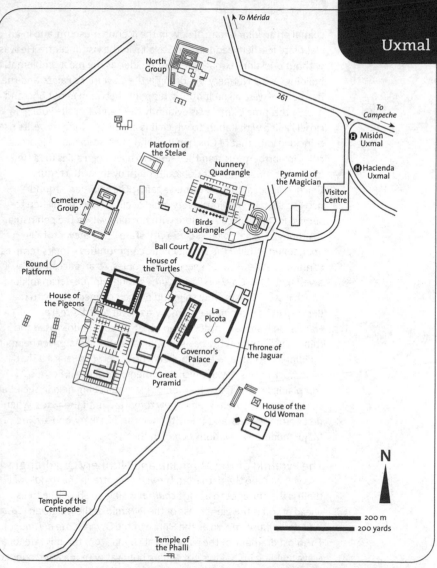

the Yucatecan chronicles written down after the Spanish Conquest the rulers of Uxmal, like the Itzá of Chichén Itzá, were described as a group of 'foreigners', called the Tutul Xiu, and the Xiu clan of Maní proudly told the Spaniards that they were the descendants of the lords of Uxmal. This story has often been questioned, but it now seems very likely that the dominant group among Uxmal's founders were migrants from other Maya regions further south, and could have included the Xiu. Unlike the similarly 'new' Chichén Itzá, Uxmal did not have a collective *multepal* leadership, as monuments to individual rulers have been found. The one prominent lord of Uxmal who has clearly emerged is Chan-Chak-Kaknal-Ahaw, better known as Lord Chak, who is shown as *ahau* of

Uxmal on an altar (altar 10) now in the Mérida museum, and in an elaborate feather headdress on Stela 14, in the visitor centre. He was without question Uxmal's greatest builder, as the most emblematic buildings – the Nunnery Quadrangle, the Governor's Palace and the Ball Court – were all built during his reign, between about 890 and 910. By this time Uxmal was evidently the 'capital' of the Puuc, closely allied with Kabah, to which it is linked by a long *sacbé*. Its rise coincided with that of Chichén Itzá, and as the two most vigorous cities in northern Yucatán they seem to have been allies for a time in Chichén's wars against Cobá, although by the 10th century Chichén appears to have turned against Uxmal. Then, around 920–50 Uxmal went into a very rapid decline, leaving Chichén to survive for a few decades more with no real rivals in the peninsula.

Although Uxmal collapsed as a city-state it was never totally abandoned – unlike the smaller Puuc communities – for its temples continued to be used for special ceremonies. As an ancestral city of awe, Uxmal, like Chichén Itzá, figures strongly in Yucatecan folklore, which is why the Xiu were so proud of their connections with it. Because of its prominence Uxmal was never a 'lost' site. The Franciscan historian Father Diego López de Cogolludo visited the ruins in 1658 and, on the basis of Spanish equivalents, gave the main buildings the names – the Nunnery, the Governor's Palace – that have stuck to this day. Spanish documents from the 1680s also complained that pagan ceremonies were still being held in secret at Uxmal. The ruins were then largely forgotten until the 1830s, when first Count Waldeck and then Stephens and Catherwood arrived. Major modern excavations began in the 1930s.

The Pyramid of the Magician and Nunnery Quadrangle

As you walk up the path from the visitor centre, in the middle of it there is the entrance to a huge *chultún*. Rising up above the trees ahead of you is the giant mass of the **Pyramid of the Magician** (*Casa del Adivino*), also known as the House of the Dwarf (*Casa del Enano*). The most dramatic of the pyramids at Uxmal, 39m tall, it is rare for a Maya building in that it is not square but oval, with massive rounded ends to the north and south. The east side, facing you, is dominated by a great ramp of steep steps reaching almost to the top. Uxmal may mean 'built three times', but the Pyramid of the Magician in fact contains five stages of building. Partway up the east side an opening has been made in the steps to give access to the confined rear chamber of Temple II, previously buried under later building work.

Sadly, due to pressure of visitor numbers you're no longer allowed to climb up the steps to the top of the Pyramid of the Magician. There's no option but to make the best of things and admire the giant tower by walking around it at ground level. The temples of the pyramid all face west, and from the side it is clear that the east face is very much its back, 'projecting' the whole structure towards the ceremonial centre of the city. At the very top is the last part to be added, Temple V, from around 900, with a façade of Puuc-style stone latticework panels. The platform in front of it is actually the roof of the older Temples II and IV – the same temples that run through to the opening on the east side. Temple IV (from about 850) has a monster-mouth entrance in the Chenes style, with the whole façade and doorway covered in carved decoration to form one giant image of Chac. This monster-temple is in local legend the House of the Dwarf himself. More curl-snout heads line the steps down. At the bottom on the west face there is a gap between the pyramid and the steps, buttressed with a Maya arch, beneath which are the remains of Temple I, the very oldest part of the pyramid.

At the foot of the west face of the Pyramid is the heavily restored **Birds Quadrangle** (*Cuadrángulo de los Pájaros*), or Antequadrangle. In Late Puuc style, it is believed to date, like the Nunnery, from around 900. In front of you there is a perfectly formed Mayan arch, and on the façade to the left there are beautifully modelled carvings of birds amid feather patterns, a fine example of the naturalism of Puuc decoration.

Leave the Antequadrangle through the far-left corner from the Pyramid to walk around to the entrance of the **Nunnery Quadrangle** (*Cuadrángulo de las Monjas*). This is the most complete complex of buildings at Uxmal: each of its parts is impressive, but it is the complete ensemble that is extraordinary. Against the verticality of the pyramid, its geometry is decidedly horizontal, with long single-storey buildings, topped by friezes, that seem to parallel the flatness of the Yucatán countryside. It has 88 rooms, and was named by Cogolludo because it reminded him of a convent, but there is no evidence that anything like nuns existed in Maya society.

The four parts of the Quadrangle are all separate (and do not form an exact square), but this doesn't mean the complex is not a very integrated whole. Dates have been found indicating that the various sections were built simultaneously – over several years – and completed in fairly rapid succession: the South Building was dedicated in April 906, the East side in October the same year and one of the two temples in front of the great North Building in April

The East Building of the Nunnery at Uxmal, drawn by Frederick Catherwood

907. The main entrance is the arch in the **South Building**. Entering through it you immediately appreciate that the East and West Buildings on either side are at a higher level, with their platforms parallel with the South Building Frieze, and that the North Building facing you is higher again, giving the complex the authoritative quality that is a keynote in Mayan building. The vistas from the West Building across to the Pyramid of the Magician and from the North Platform to the Governor's Palace also seem to have been planned.

The carving on every one of the buildings is stunning, its effect heightened by the Puuc contrast between carved upper friezes and plain lower walls. The stone-mosaic friezes feature intricate imagery with which Lord Chak's sculptors evoked the great Maya creation myths and connected Uxmal's rulers with them, in a complex that served as an administrative and ritual centre for the city.

Especially striking is the very original Puuc combination of dynamic, apparently highly geometrical design and symbolism drawn from everyday Maya life. The South Building is the only 'double-sided' part of the Quadrangle, and the simplest of the four sections. In its inner and outer friezes there are repeated lattice-pattern panels, reminiscent of the wooden latticework seen in Maya houses, while above each doorway there is a realistic depiction of a *na* wood-and-palm hut, scarcely different from those seen in any Yucatán village today. Along the moulding at the top of the frieze there are small flowers, symbols of magic, while above each *na* hut a spirit-monster-head sprouts bunches of flowering maize. This identifies the building as a magical one and links it with the place where the Maize God was reborn, and the house where the First Mother and First Father made the first men out of maize (*see* p.33). In the entry arch there are also two red handprints, left by the first builders as invocations to Itzamná, the paramount god known as 'Divine Hand'. The **East Building**, meanwhile, is the most spectacular as pure design – almost a piece of Art Deco – although even here the frieze is based on a homely latticework pattern. Again there are references to magic: the six grid-like, inverted triangles are made up of double-headed vision serpents, the conduit between men and the Otherworld, and in the middle of the frieze and in each corner there are stacks of Itzam-Ye masks.

The **West Building** opposite is the one that had to be most extensively restored, and has the most elaborate of all the friezes. Intertwined with great intricacy along its whole length are two giant feathered vision serpents (with rattler tails), which are believed to represent the War Serpent, bringing the power to make war from the Gods to the Lords of Uxmal. Only one snake still has its head, at the north end, but out of its mouth a human head is emerging, probably an ancestor of the Uxmal dynasty come via the serpent to advise the living. The background is a very complex lattice-pattern, with flower-symbols in each diamond-shape. This 'flower-lattice' pattern (also seen on the North Building), as well as invoking magic, is thought to indicate a *popol na* ('meeting house'), where important gatherings were held and decisions taken. Between and inside the loops of the snakes there are *nas*, stacks of God-masks, and squared-off, spiral-like panels that represent the Maya glyph for *muyal* ('cloud'), another symbol of contact with the heavens. Above the three central doors there are niches with carved awnings representing the canopies of feathers held above Maya lords, and in the middle niche there is a curious little king-like figure with the body of a turtle, one of the five *Pahauhtuns* or 'sustainer gods' who held up the sky at the moment of Creation, also related to the Cosmic Turtle from whose back the Maize Gods emerged in the same process. The **North Building** has similar imagery to the West, including repeated masks of Tlaloc, the central-Mexican war god, and flower-lattice panels indicating that this was also a 'meeting house', although given their position as the focus of the whole Nunnery Complex it is pretty clear that the North Building and the platform in front of it were much the more important section. Unlike the East and West sides it is also decorated at the back, with latticework panels and sculptures of naked, bound figures: war captives taken by Uxmal. On either side at the foot of the steps up to the North Building there are small temples, called the **Temples of Venus** because early investigators mistakenly interpreted their carvings as symbols of the planet Venus. In the very middle of the steps there is a very badly eroded stela which seems to have recounted events in the life of Lord Chak.

This remarkable combination of buildings and sculpture was intended to create a grand space for Lord Chak to hold court, celebrate rituals and summon up supernatural forces, things never separated in Maya tradition. In the centre of the quadrangle there was also an altar and a column, representing the *wakah-kan* (world-tree) at the centre of Creation. Early travellers also recorded a phallic monument in the quadrangle, but this was removed to avoid embarrassment to the first VIP visitor brought to Uxmal, Maximilian's Empress Carlota in 1865, and has not been seen since.

The Governor's Palace and House of the Turtles

From the arch in the south side of the Nunnery Quadrangle a path leads south, past some recently restored – and strangely artificial-looking – colonnaded buildings, through the middle of the **Ball Court**. In style it is midway between the Chichén Itzá-style ball court and the smaller ones of older Maya cities: smaller than the one at Chichén, but with similar stone rings for scoring on

There is no rudeness or barbarity in the design or proportions; on the contrary, the whole wears an air of architectural symmetry and grandeur... If it stood at this day on its grand artificial terrace in Hyde Park or the Garden of the Tuileries, it would form a new order. I do not say equalling, but not unworthy to stand side by side with the remains of Egyptian, Grecian and Roman art...

John Lloyd Stephens reporting on the Governor's Palace at Uxmal

either side. One of the rings, now in the Mérida museum, has an inscription mentioning Lord Chak and the dedication of the court, with a date from 901 (the rings now at Uxmal are replicas). The path continues towards the giant rock-and-earth platform on which the Governor's Palace and House of the Turtles stand. The building of this platform, extending over 180m by 154m and 17m high, involved transporting as much as a billion kilos of material.

As you walk up to the platform, in front of you is the great sweep of the **Governor's Palace** (*Casa del Gobernador*), for many the pinnacle of Mayan architecture. It stands atop a second platform of its own, another 7m high. The palace is 100m long and made up of three parts, connected by exceptionally tall, false Maya arches which once allowed access from one side to the other but were blocked off only a short time after the palace was built. As in the Nunnery buildings, there is a clear vision in the design that is emphatically horizontal. It may appear dead straight, but the two ends are in fact slightly lower than the middle. Mayan builders, like the Greeks, were aware of the optical principle that a truly straight and level building of this length actually looks as if it sags in the middle, and calculated their effects to compensate.

For once the Spanish name is fairly valid, for while there is no record of a specific 'Governor' at Uxmal it is near certain this was the main palace and residence of Lord Chak. It has 20 rooms, mostly small and arranged in two long rows, so those at the back are entered from those in front. In the middle there is an unusually long chamber with three entrances, which though by no means huge is actually the largest single space built by the Maya using their traditional arch technique. This was also the chamber in which Stephens, Catherwood and their ornithologist companion Dr Cabot camped out during their second visit to Uxmal in 1841, after first lighting fires inside for all of a day to clear out bats, bugs and the damp. Frederick Catherwood spent long periods alone here working on his drawings, while the others went off to explore. At that time a large section of the façade had collapsed, but this has since been restored, and with it most of the palace's frieze.

Like those of the Nunnery the frieze is an extraordinarily complex mixture of lattice patterns, *muyal* cloud images, masks of Chac, Itzam-Ye, Tlaloc and other gods, and human figures. In the centre a kingly figure, believed to be Lord Chak of Uxmal himself, sits surrounded by vision serpents as proof of his divine status. Over 20,000 individual pieces were used to create the frieze, an operation that involved a staggering degree of organization. It originally included precisely 260 god-masks, equalling the number of days in a *tzolkin* year, and it appears likely that the whole frieze symbolized the course of the year and the alternation of rain and sun.

Sharing the platform with the Governor's Palace is the small, rectangular **House of the Turtles** (*Casa de las Tortugas*), which with its delicate proportions has often been compared to classical Greek architecture. It is the archetype of the pure Puuc style: above the usual plain, lower storey there is a frieze of Puuc drum columns, topped by an *atadura* frieze decorated with a string of very simple carved turtles. The turtle is another recurrent symbol at Uxmal. Its relation to the Cosmic Turtle aside, this is believed to be because turtles, like the people of the Puuc Hills, always relied desperately on the coming of the rains.

Around the platform there are a few more structures, most in fairly poor condition. Most apparent, in front of the palace steps, is a very worn monolith lying almost on its side, called **La Picota** ('the Whipping-Post'). It has on it some inscriptions that have long been completely indecipherable and is one of several clearly phallic monuments to have been found at Uxmal. It still leans at almost exactly the same angle as is shown in Catherwood's engravings. On the far side of the Picota from the palace there is an impressive altar, known as the **Throne of the Jaguar**.

From the east side of the platform, looking away from the palace, you can see amid the woods on the other side of a track a large pyramid called the **House of the Old Woman** (*Casa de la Vieja*), supposedly home to the Dwarf's mother. It is believed to be one of the oldest structures at Uxmal, from 680–750. It's in poor condition, but recent clearing work has made it easier to get to, with a scramble through the brush.

The Great Pyramid and House of the Pigeons

Forming a corner with the southwest angle of the palace platform is the **Great Pyramid** of Uxmal, a vast ascending pile of steps in a more conventional Maya style than the Pyramid of the Magician. It is older than the palace buildings, probably from about 750–850, as is shown by the fact that part of the palace platform is built over the pyramid base; of the same age is a small temple with Chenes-style square pillars near the northwest corner of the platform, also partly covered by later building. At the top there is a temple with some fine carvings – especially of parrots and other birds, giving it the name **House of the Macaws** (*Casa de los Guacamayas*) – and in the centre an imposingly large, throne-like Chac-head. It is partially buried, almost certainly because in the 10th century they began to build a new temple on top of the existing one. For reasons unknown, this later temple was never completed.

09 Yucatán State | Uxmal

From the Great Pyramid there is a good view west over the **House of the Pigeons** (*Casa de las Palomas*), so called because its most distinctive feature, a long roof-comb of nine triangular crests perforated by square holes, looked like dovecotes to early travellers. It was the largest complex in the city, with several sections: to the north was a three-sided quadrangle, open on the north side into the central area of Uxmal. This led to the main, four-sided quadrangle of the House of the Pigeons, beneath the roof-comb. Like similar Maya complexes elsewhere the Pigeons group was probably a combination of religious building and lordly residence (in the main quadrangle).

Other Buildings at Uxmal

Like most Mayan cities Uxmal had a considerable spread, and there are many other structures in the woods. From the House of the Old Woman a track leads about 500 metres to a simple building known as the **Temple of the Phalli**. One part of the Puuc obsession with fertility in all its forms seems to have been a phallic cult. It is reflected here in penis-shaped tubes sticking out of the roof, which acted as drains to take off water, presumably into recipients to preserve the precious liquid. On the opposite, right side of the main track a path leads to the **Temple of the Centipede** (*Templo del Chimez*), which is of more architectural interest as one of few 'multi-storey' buildings at Uxmal. Its name comes from its step-pattern frieze, a little like a centipede.

Another 400 metres south along the main track, nearly a kilometre from the central buildings, stands an imposing, isolated Maya **Arch**. It has long been put forward that this arch stood at the beginning of a *sacbé* running to the very similar arch at Kabah (*see facing page*). It may also have marked the southern boundary of Uxmal.

Returning to the central area, on the west side of the main open space opposite the Nunnery and the Ball Court there is another complex, called the **Cemetery Group** (*El Cementerio*) because of its many death's-head carvings. Another quadrangle, it has in its courtyard four altars, dated to about 880, covered in carved skulls-and-crossbones. To the south of the Cemetery a path leads from the Ball Court to the strange **Round Building** (*Estructura Redonda*), which is just that, a round drum platform. This was one of the last structures built at Uxmal, from the 10th century, and may have been partly inspired by Chichén Itzá's famous Caracol observatory.

North of the Cemetery Group is the **Platform of the Stelae**, a low artificial mound with 15 monument-stones, on their sides. Most are in very poor condition. Lastly, a short walk from here is the **North Group**, another sizable complex, probably from the early years of the city, centred on a pyramid. Excavations here have been limited.

The Puuc Road

From Uxmal it's 15km to **Santa Elena**, only village on the Puuc Route, which also has some of the area's best places to stay (*see* pp.318–9). It has a village church from the 1770s, with a sacristy near-unchanged since it was built, and which has been effectively restored. Attached is a village museum which offers the rather ghoulish remains of colonial-era burials found beneath the church floor – and you can climb up to the church roof for a wonderful view.

The ruins of Kabah are another 8km south. While Uxmal had never been entirely lost from view, the existence of this and the other Puuc sites was unknown to the outside world – including the rest of Yucatán – before Stephens and Catherwood came here in 1841, and their discovery, achieved by following the directions of village priests and local Maya, came as a revelation. As well as the four main Puuc sites there are more ruins in the area (such as **Nohpat**, also visited by Stephens), scarcely excavated at all and accessible only by 4WD or on foot. Small hotels in the area (see pp.318–9) can often put you in touch with local guides.

Kabah

Kabah
8km south of Santa Elena; open daily 8–5; adm

The ruins of **Kabah** straddle the Campeche road, with the main buildings on the east side. Their feel of remoteness has diminished with the building of modern facilities, but even this site, between the times when buses arrive, can still feel far away from the world. From about 750 to 950 Kabah was the most important community in the Puuc after Uxmal, its political significance demonstrated by its being linked to the regional 'capital' by a finely constructed *sacbé*.

As you enter the main, eastern area of Kabah past the caretaker's hut, straight ahead at the top of a rise stands the long, low **Palacio**. It has a façade of multiple entrances supported by elegant columns, forming porticos to the usual small, dark inner chambers. If you look back from in front of the palace, you can have a first view of the Great Temple pyramid across the road, looming among trees and still almost entirely covered in brush. To the left of the Palacio, a path leads through woods to the **Temple of Columns** (called the 'Tercera Casa' by Stephens), a classic of the Puuc style. Before you reach it, just to the right of the path there are two well-preserved *chultunes* among the trees. To the north of the Temple of Columns there are some more unexcavated structures, believed to be **tombs**.

Each of the Puuc sites has its 'star attraction', and this leaves till last on this side of the road the extraordinary **Codz-Poop** or 'Palace of Masks', to the right of the Palacio as you come up from the road. The normal Puuc style is for the lower walls to be entirely plain and topped by a frieze, with a noticeable sense of restraint, but here every inch is covered in decoration. The west façade, facing the road, is an absolute riot of Chacs, so that the whole building appears like one giant altar to the rain god. Its current name means 'rolled blanket' and is only a post-Conquest Maya reference to the 250 curling god-snouts that protrude from it. In front of this façade there is an impressive courtyard, containing rows of column bases, a *chultún* and an altar densely carved with glyphs (still scarcely deciphered). The Codz-Poop was almost certainly a residential complex, and has an unusually large number of rooms, 27 in all. The east façade, away from the road, has undergone extensive restoration that has revealed superb carving. Halfway up, impressive king-like figures extend along the wall; on the sides of the entrance into the main chamber carved panels show warriors in battle. The giant figures are unlike anything in any other Puuc cities, and a similar bust-like head of a man with a headdress, known as the 'King of Kabah' and now in the Mérida museum, was also found in the courtyard in front of the Codz-Poop.

From the Codz-Poop a bank of steps leads back to the entrance. Across the road, a broad path leads through a gate into the woods, past, on the right, the pile of rubble that is the **Great Temple**. Amid the brush to the left of the path there are the remains of another whole building complex, known as the **Western Quadrangle**, still almost entirely covered up. Further away again in the woods to the west – and very hard to find, off the main paths – there are the ruins of two more large buildings, where Stephens found intricately carved wooden lintels that would be priceless if they still existed today. He had them shipped to New York 'in order to preserve them', but they were then destroyed in a fire. Today, the

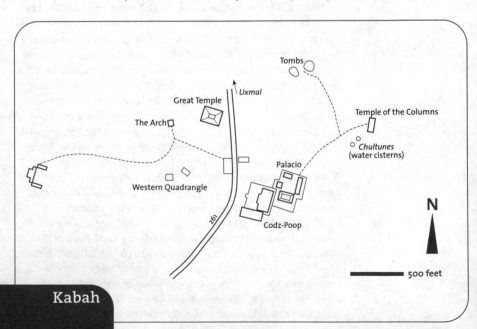

Kabah

Detail of the Codz-Poop, drawn by Frederick Catherwood, 1842

most attractive monument on this side of the road is the **Arch**, standing alone across the track around a bend in the path.

After Kabah the Puuc Hills justify their name a little more, as the road runs gently up and down. Five kilometres further south, a sign indicates the left turn east on to the *Ruta Puuc* road. If you stay on Highway 261 here you continue down to **Bolonchén** and **Hopelchén** in Campeche, passing, in the first few kilometres, a much less-known continuation of the Puuc region (*see* p.366).

Sayil

Sayil
4km from the turn, on the south side of the Puuc road. Open daily 8–5; adm.

Sayil is quite an extensive site with buildings dispersed along thickly wooded paths. It was clearly one of the richest Puuc settlements but, like those around it, is almost entirely the product of one relatively short period. A lintel from its Palacio has been carbon-dated to about 730, while a stela inscription has a date from 810. The ceramics found here are all of the same era, from about 750 to 950. At around this time the population of Sayil and its satellite communities may have reached around 17,000.

From the site entrance the main path swings round in a wide arc through the woods. To the left, concealed by trees so that it comes up almost by surprise, is the greatest glory of Sayil, the magnificent **Palacio**, facing south. All of 85m long, it is a sweeping, three-level palace complex with similarities to the Five Storeys at Edzná (*see* p.394); as there, the 'floors' are not real storeys built on top of each other but tiers in a pyramid-like structure. Thought to have been built in several stages through the 8th and 9th centuries, it had over 90 rooms and could have housed over 350 people, served by eight water *chultunes* for their exclusive use, some of which can be seen by the northwest corner. The palace's drum facings and friezes, and the entrance columns, give it an elegance that has been compared to classical Greek architecture. Among the drum columns, as well as the usual Puuc god-masks, there are some carvings of a Diving God like those at Tulum (*see* p.197). Apparently inexplicable so far from the sea, this has given rise to endless speculation.

The Palacio steps lead directly down to an impressive *sacbé* that formed the main axis of the city, connecting its main areas along a north–south line. After 400 metres you see, to the left, the **Mirador** ('Watchtower'). Thought to be older than most of the Palacio (from about 750), it occupies a small pyramid-platform, with a plain, five-room building supporting a massive roof-comb. What you see now is mostly only the rubble core, pierced by holes to reduce its weight; purely decorative, it must once have been covered with stone and stucco carvings in livid colours. Remains found nearby indicate that next to the Mirador was the main market area.

Around the Mirador there are the remains of more *chultunes*, and amid the trees on the right (west) side of the path is the partly excavated **Temple of the Hieroglyphic Lintel**, with some quite well preserved inscriptions around the doorways. Back across on the other, left side of the path is the phallic **Stela 9**, a carving of a naked warrior with an erection that was probably part of a Puuc fertility cult. From here, back on the main path, it's a pleasant walk of 400 metres to the **Palacio Sur**, last of the main excavated complexes at Sayil. It had 18 rooms, several unusually spacious. Behind the Palacio Sur, to the west (right of the path), is a **Ball Court**. On the way to it you pass the **Stela Platform**, where the stone dated 810

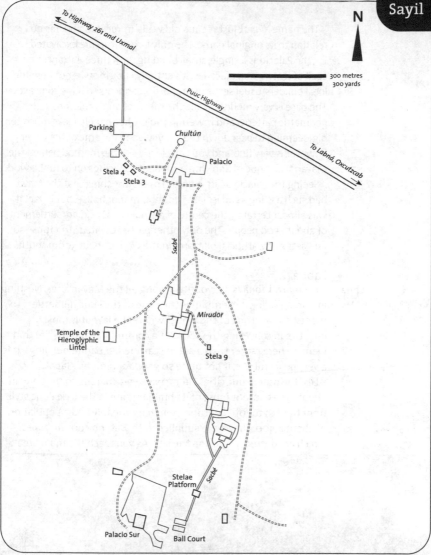

Map labels:

To Highway 261 and Uxmal

Puuc Highway

300 metres
300 yards

To Labná, Oxcutzcab

Parking

Chultún

Palacio

Stela 4

Stela 3

Sacbé

Mirador

Temple of the Hieroglyphic Lintel

Stela 9

Stelae Platform

Sacbe

Palacio Sur

Ball Court

was found. For a Puuc city Sayil has an unusually high number of stelae, more typical of 'classic' Maya cities like Cobá.

Xlapak

Xlapak

*5km on from Sayil.
Open daily 8–5; adm*

Xlapak is the smallest of the main Puuc sites. For this reason it's often missed out by tours, but it has plenty of attractions. New excavations are planned at the site, but for the moment its thick woods and undisturbed quietness make it the best of all the Puuc sites in which to see birds and even small mammals, worth visiting as much for a nature walk as for its ruins. First thing in the morning, especially, the range of bird song is quite wonderful.

The name *Xlapak* just means 'old walls' in Yucatec, and has no relation to its original name. The only large structure excavated so far, the **Palacio**, is a single, small building with three entrances on each of its two main façades. It's entirely Puuc in style, but here the local builders' usual sense of proportion appears to have gone astray. The base is very modest, while the frieze, of drum columns, geometric patterns and towering triple-Chac panels, looks much too big, seeming to bear down too heavily upon it. Some of the carving, however, is very fine, and you can clearly see the method behind the Mayan technique of applying ornament as facings on to rubblework.

Seeing the Palacio on its own can make one think that the Maya had such a thing as an isolated country manor house, but in fact it was almost certainly the centre of a smallish, subsidiary settlement of about 1,500 people. The only other part-excavated structure – so far – is a stony, artificial platform in the woods about 300m south.

Labná

Labná

*3km from Xlapak.
Open daily 8–5; adm*

For many **Labná** is a favourite among all the Mayan sites. Nestling in a small valley, it exemplifies the style of the Puuc hill settlements; it is also one of the places where the layout is most effective in conveying the sense of a community and the life that went on here rather than a set of scattered, separate buildings. It is a very peaceful site, if not quite so good for birds as Xlapak.

*The Arch at Labná,
drawn by Frederick
Catherwood, 1841*

Like the other Puuc cities Labná was a prosperous community in about 750–950, but most of its buildings are in the Late Puuc style from the 9th to 10th centuries, when it probably had a population of about 4,500. They were supplied with water by 60 *chultunes*, which are dotted all around the site. As you reach the main area of

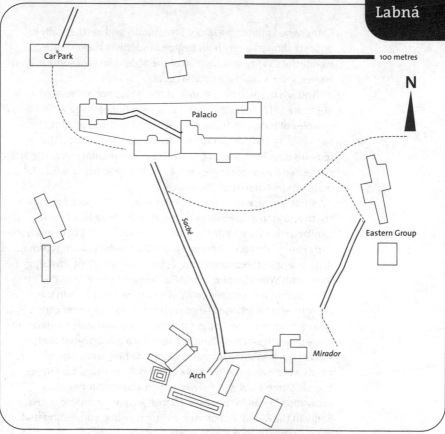

Car Park

100 metres

N

Palacio

Sacbé

Eastern Group

Mirador

Arch

Labná from the entrance you come up alongside the first of its major buildings, the grand **Palacio**, facing south. It has many similarities with the palace at Sayil, with two main levels built up pyramid-style and a bank of steps in the centre connecting with a *sacbé*. It had 67 rooms – fewer than at Sayil – but they were distributed over seven patios, and other levels as well as the main two. Above each level there is a frieze with the customary Chac masks, and on the southeast corner a sculpture of a human face emerging from a serpent's jaws, similar to those at Uxmal. On the northern side of the Palacio one of the Chac masks has an inscription on its nose with the date 862. Excavations suggest that the central patio was the palace's principal court and receiving space, while in the east patio (to the right, looking at the façade), *metates*, stones for grinding corn, have been found, indicating that cooking went on here and that this was probably the preserve of the servants. The west patio to the left formed the living quarters of the lordly family of Labná.

From the Palacio a well-restored *sacbé* runs to the south group of buildings. To the right, at an angle to the *sacbé*, is the greatest of all Mayan arches, the **Arch of Labná**, subject of several of

Catherwood's finest drawings. Structurally and aesthetically its builders showed a very high degree of sophistication, creating a wonderful solidity, and, instead of the abrupt lines of some Mayan arches, a finely crafted elliptical curve.

Although the arch now stands alone, it was not an isolated arch like those of Uxmal and Kabah but an interior passage within a complex of buildings that combined the functions of administrative building and aristocratic residence. On the east side, the remains have been traced of a sizable quadrangular plaza. The arch connected this quadrangle with a smaller patio to the west, the main residential part of the palace.

A short distance from the arch, to the left of the *sacbé* going south and atop a very rubbly pyramid, is the **Mirador** of Labná. Similar to the Mirador at Sayil, and likewise thought to be from the Early Puuc period and therefore older than most buildings around it, it's a simple, three-room temple supporting a giant towering roof-comb. When Stephens and Catherwood saw it in 1841 – 'the most curious and extraordinary structure we had seen in the country' – it still retained large sections of its high-relief carvings, and even some of their original colour. They were able to make out a line of death's-heads along the top and a giant, seated central figure with two smaller figures alongside him, while above their heads were two dynamic figures with balls, perhaps a reference to the ball game. However, between then and the time serious excavation began in the 1950s all this decoration disintegrated. Beneath the Mirador another building is visible, suggesting that the pyramid was built up in stages.

As usual, there are more buildings and structures around the woods that have only been excavated to a very limited extent. The most important are the **Eastern Group**, down a path to the right of the Mirador, looking towards the roof-comb.

The Loltún Caves

Loltún
guided tours at 9.30am, 11am, 12.30pm, 2pm, 3pm and 4pm; adm

In some ways, the caves at **Loltún** are the most fascinating of all the sites on the Puuc Route. They are both the most awe-inspiring of the great Yucatán cave systems, and also the oldest and most mysterious of the peninsula's Maya sites, used and occupied by local people from remote prehistory up until the 19th century.

The Loltún caves were 'discovered' for the outside world by the American consul Edward Thompson in the 1890s, and fully investigated in the 1950s. The local Maya seem to have been aware of them for ever. Remains found here have been dated to about 5000 BC, and are the earliest evidence of human occupation in the Yucatán; Preclassic carvings from Loltún from about AD 100 are among the region's oldest identifiably Maya relics. There are also carvings in the caves from the Classic period, contemporary with

Visiting Loltún

The caves, 12km east of Labná, are quite easy to miss. From Labná, take a short cut to the left signposted to Yaaxhom for about 4km, or stay on the main road till Emiliano Zapata and turn left; either way you come upon the Loltún **visitor centre** fairly abruptly, round a left-hand bend. In the other direction, from Oxcutzcab, the entrance is more visible. Leaving Loltún, it is 8km to the left and downhill to Oxcutzcab.

You can visit the caves only with **guided tours** (around $4, plus $1 to park a car), but times can be imprecise; they officially include a Sound and Light show, which here does not feature any sound but only quite subtle lighting. The local guides are knowledgeable – but are paid only through tips, so generosity is in order. Several speak some English, and if possible it's worth checking when a tour in English will be leaving. Each tour lasts about 1–1½hrs and covers nearly 2km of caves; a further 2km of pathways are closed to visitors, and beyond that the caverns extend for more semi-explored kilometres into the ground.

There is a **restaurant** at Loltún, by the exit. Its open-air tables are very welcome, since one other thing to note is that inside the caves the extraordinary variations in temperature and humidity can be overpowering.

the Puuc cities on the surface, and others from the Postclassic. The caverns were important as a venue for rituals involving contacting or placating the subterranean gods – in many caves there are painted red hands, an invocation to the gods for good health. They also played a part in virtually every other area of life. The rich clay of the cavern floor was greatly valued in making ceramics, and many of the stalactites have had their ends cut off, for use as weapons, or ground down for use in potions. The caverns were still of use to local Maya during the Caste War of the 1840s, as a refuge in which they hid from white armies.

And the caves themselves are staggering. Different minerals make rich patterns in the rock, and all through the caves there are inexplicable draughts and cold air currents, while only a few steps away you can walk into a steam bath that can stop your breath. Sylvanus Morley thought this was not a natural phenomenon but another product of Mayan ingenuity, refining the air-flows for their own purposes. The name *Lol-tun* means 'stone flower', and may refer to the caves' magical productivity – though in another theory it evokes only the echo made by hitting a stone on the stalactites. There is evidence of occupation throughout: of fires having been lit, god-heads, or rubble trenches from the time of the Caste War.

Chacmultún

Chacmultún
Open daily 8–5; adm

The ruins of **Chacmultún** are one of the least-known Puuc sites, and little visited. Its buildings are in the now-familiar Puuc style, and it can best be recommended to Maya completists and those who like their ruins with a sense of discovery and remoteness. Its greatest distinction is that it is the only visitable Puuc site to retain some painted murals, although these are now in very poor condition.

It is often the case with Maya sites that their fame and state of preservation does not reflect what has been discovered about their original importance, and this is so with Chacmultún. The most important city of the eastern Puuc, it covers a wide area, and was larger than Labná. It was occupied for longer than many Puuc

Visiting Chacmultún

Chacmultún is quite hard to find: from Loltún, instead of heading for Oxcutzcab take the right turn south towards Xul. After about 6km there is a left turn signed to Tekax, which rolls for several kilomtres through deep-Mayan villages until you reach Kancab, where there's a right turn for Chacmultún. It's easier to find coming the other way, from Tekax (10km). From the turn the road winds further uphill through Chacmultún, until, just when you think you're really lost, you hit the site.

communities, with settlement from the Early Classic, about AD 300, and into the Postclassic.

One of its most distinctive features is that, whereas at other Puuc sites the 'hills' often seem only incidental elements, Chacmultún is built on some of the tallest hills in the whole region, with commanding views over the surrounding landscape. The largest group of buildings is up the hill behind the caretaker's hut. The **Edificio de las Pinturas** is the first (*ask the caretaker for 'los murales'*). Only three of its eleven rooms survive, of which one has the remains of the murals. They are very faint, but can just be seen to show men in headdresses and rich jewellery, in a procession. Above this building is the **Palacio of Chacmultún**, with some fine Puuc *na*-carving, and nearby, past the opening to a *chultún*, is the small **Structure 10** which also has some remains of painted decoration inside. Other groups of buildings, the **Cabalpak** group and the **Xethpol** group – the tallest building on the tallest hill in Chacmultún – are only partly excavated out of the woods.

Where to Stay at Uxmal and on the Puuc Route
t (997–)

It's possible to visit Uxmal and some smaller sites and return to Mérida the same day, but to see anything well you have to stay in the area at least one night, preferably two. There's no village at Uxmal, so prices are quite high. One cheaper alternative is to carry on to Ticul or Oxcutzcab (*see* p.321). The most luxurious accommodation near the region is without question at **Hacienda Santa Rosa** and **Hacienda Temozón**, and you can also have a whole *hacienda* as a base at **Hacienda Yunkú**.

⭐ The Flycatcher Inn B&B >>

Luxury-Expensive
Hacienda Uxmal, t 01 800 719 5465/(998) 887 2450, *www.mayaland. com*. Owned by the Mayaland Group like the largest Chichén hotel, this is modern-ish (1950s) but colonial-style; it

has airy rooms with traditional furniture and every comfort, bars on shady verandahs, a lovely pool and gardens, tennis courts and fine **restaurants**. Peak prices sometimes go into the *luxury* band.

The Lodge at Uxmal, Uxmal entrance road, **t** 01 800 719 5465/(998) 887 2450, *www.mayaland.com*. Owned by Mayaland like Hacienda Uxmal, the Lodge is even closer to the ruins and aims to provide a more intimate experience, with rooms in palm-roofed villas. They don't really justify the prices (it's mostly booked by tours), but it has two pools and a pretty **restaurant**.

Moderate–Inexpensive
The Flycatcher Inn B&B, C. 20 no. 223, Santa Elena (off Highway 261, opposite Chac-Mool restaurant) **t** 102 0865, *www.flycatcherinn.com*. American Kristine Ellingson and her husband Santiago Domínguez have spacious rooms, an ample suite and a whole

cottage (the 'Owl House') with space for four people around their modern house and garden in the village of Santa Elena. All are comfortable and very spacious, with pretty décor, modern facilities and distinctive furniture made by Santiago, a skilled craftsman. Great breakfasts are included, and there's a well-marked nature trail into the woods at the back of the house. Guests also benefit from the owners' vast local knowledge, with a fascinating variety of visits and excursions that can make a trip special.

Misión Uxmal, t 976 2022, *www. hotelesmision.com*. A little blander than its neighbour the Hacienda – and now a good deal cheaper – but still very comfortable. All the balconied rooms in the arc-shaped building, plus the restaurant terrace and lovely pool, are oriented to get a magnificent view of the Uxmal ruins. Some great price deals are available in low seasons, down to the *inexpensive* band.

Villas Arqueológicas Uxmal, by the entrance road to Uxmal ruins, **t** 974 6020, *www.villasarqueológicas.com.mx*. Like the similar Villas Arqueológicas at Cobá and Chichén Itzá, this is an amazing bargain. Prices remain around $70, but the rooms, restaurant, gardens and especially pretty pool are all lovely, and the hotel has a quiet charm. Note that all three Villas are no longer part of Club Med.

Budget

Hotel Sacbé, just south of Santa Elena, 16km from Uxmal, **t** 978 5158, www. sacbebungalows.com.mx. The only really good budget accommodation near Uxmal, and a great place to find. Edgar and Annette Portillo (he Mexican, she French) are very friendly and calmly hospitable. They have seven very pleasant double rooms in cabins around a peaceful wooded garden, for around $18–26, and a little house available, with a kitchen. There's solar electricity, and all rooms have good showers. Bargain breakfasts are available ($3). Sacbé is on the west side of the road (the right, from Uxmal); if you're on a bus, get off not in Santa Elena but beyond it, by the baseball field (*Campo de Beisbol*). Look out for the 'Hotel Sacbé' sign.

⭐ **Hotel Sacbé >**

Eating Out at Uxmal and on the Puuc Route

At **Uxmal** the **visitor centre** restaurant has straightforward, mid-price food. Better options are the restaurants in the big hotels – less pricey than the rooms – or the small *moderate–budget* restaurants beside the road north of Uxmal, especially the **Hal-Tun** and **Papp-Hol-Chac**. There are two other pleasant restaurants in Santa Elena, **La Central** on the village plaza and the **Chac-Mool** on the main Uxmal–Kabah road.

Hacienda San Pedro Ochil, Highway 261 km 176, **t** (999) 924 7465, *www.haciendaochil.com* (*expensive*). The group that runs Temozún has opened this smaller 17th-century *hacienda* as a restaurant and park alone. The restaurant, on a terrace by a lush garden, has finely prepared Yucatecan dishes with modern touches, and inventive salads. After a relaxing lunch you can also explore craft workshops, a high-quality crafts shop and two museums, one on *hacienda* history and the other of folk art. *Open daily 10–6.*

The Pickled Onion, just south of Santa Elena, 16km from Uxmal, **t** 111 7922 (*moderate–budget*). Food options on the Ruta Puuc have been greatly expanded by Briton Valerie Pickles with her café on a hill outside Santa Elena, almost opposite the Sacbé. The menu mostly features Yucatecan dishes, with a few international favourites made with local ingredients. Diners can rest up around a swimming pool and check the internet, and there's even a laundry service. She also offers box lunches and sandwiches.

Entertainment

Uxmal stays open nightly for its **Sound and Light Spectacular**, at 7pm (Nov–Mar) and 8pm (April–Oct), for which you pay with your entry ticket whether you fancy seeing it or not. The commentary has the usual kitsch element, but it does show up the buildings to dramatic effect. Commentary is in Spanish but non-Spanish speakers are offered cassette commentary (an extra $2).

Ticul and the Southern Yucatán Towns

The village of Ticul, to which we were thus accidentally driven, was worthy of the visit, once in his life, of a citizen of New York.

John Lloyd Stephens

When you emerge from the Puuc–Loltún road into Oxcutzcab, you leave the world of ruins behind to re-enter the land of the living. On a weekend, especially, there will be a slow but steady stream of traffic along the 184 road, much of it bicycles, and whole families bunched up in the front of tricycle-carts propelled at a beautifully calm rhythm by the father or eldest son. The towns along the foot of the Puuc hills represent something of a Yucatecan heartland. A rich mineral content makes the land lush when water is applied to it, and this is one of the best fruit-growing areas of the state, with mango, papaya, lemons and sugar cane appearing between the more usual maize patches and brushwood. It is also a major centre for handicrafts. This does not mean that the pace hots up. Probably nowhere else in the Yucatán will you see so many tricycle carts: they seem ideally suited to the locals, for if they tried to ride regular, two-wheeled bikes quite so slowly they would almost certainly fall over.

The main southern towns are all Spanish foundations, established around Franciscan monasteries and churches. **Oxcutzcab** itself is known for the largest fruit and produce   markets in the state, which take over its plaza on most days with succulent piles of oranges, pineapples, *mamey* and watermelons. Presiding over the scene is the whitewashed façade of the church of San Francisco, completed in 1645, one of three similar basilica-style churches in the area (the others are at Tekax and Teabo).

Seventeen kilometres to the northwest along Highway 184 is **Ticul**, the principal town in the district. Ticul has banks, a post office, enjoyable restaurants and a few hotels that make it a good base for looking around the Puuc area. When John Stephens first saw the town's plaza, he wrote, 'it struck me as the perfect picture of stillness and repose'. He and Catherwood were given essential aid in finding Puuc ruins by the local priest, Padre Carrillo, and convalesced here from some of their bouts of fever. So taken was Stephens by Ticul that he declared that 'altogether, for appearance, society and conveniences of living, it is perhaps the best village in Yucatán', and in one memorable episode broke off from scrabbling among the ancient stones to ride through the day to catch the local *fiesta*, of which he wrote 'it was something entirely new, and remains engraven on my mind as the best of village balls'.

That was in 1841, and things change. One has to guard against romanticizing too much, but looking at Ticul it's easy to think some of the same air of benign contentment is around today. Nothing much happens in the town square, but it has an atmosphere that's enjoyable in itself, the very opposite of hassle and hussle. Ticul reveals the curious mixtures of Yucatán towns –

Getting to Ticul and Oxcutzcab

As this area is well populated there are lots of **buses** and *colectivos*. From Mérida's Second-Class Terminal (C. 69) there are at least 10 *intermedio* or second-class buses daily along Highway 184 to Chetumal via Muna, Ticul, Oxcutzcab and Peto. From Oxcutzcab market, it's possible to find a *colectivo* or taxi to just about anywhere in the region.

There are **petrol/gas stations** along the 184 road in Muna, Ticul, Oxcutzcab, Tekax and Peto.

palm *nas* stand alongside candy-coloured houses with a Nissan in the driveway, and while some local women wear traditional *huípiles*, others are in ankle-threatening heels. It has its (slightly) busy side, and produces huge quantities of shoes, embroidery and ceramics.

From Ticul it's 22km to Muna and the 261 road back to Mérida. In the opposite direction, southeast from Oxcutzcab, Highway 184 runs on through more Maya towns and villages. Largest of them is **Tekax** (18km from Oxcutzcab), which has one of the grandest of Franciscan basilicas, completed in 1692. Near the town there is a clutch of *cenotes* (*ask at the town hall for directions*). The next significant town is another 42km on, at **Peto**, from where those seeking strange, lost atmospheres can follow a narrow road another 37km east to **Ichmul**. The original home of the 'Christ of the Blisters' in Mérida Cathedral, the village has been partly abandoned ever since the Caste War.

From Peto and Tzucacab the road – recently upgraded – continues through little-populated backwoods to Felipe Carrillo Puerto (*see* p.332). For drivers it's advisable to have fuel for the whole 130km, so fill up in Peto.

Sidebar: 09 Yucatán State | Ticul and the Southern Yucatán Towns

Services

There are **banks** with ATMs in both towns, on the main plazas. Both also have several **internet centres**, again mostly around the plazas.

Shopping

Ticul has many shops with locally produced **shoes**, but most are versions of international styles (though they are cheap). There are also any number of outlets for local **earthenware pots** and **ceramics**. A good deal of what's on offer is tacky, but a place with quality higher than the norm is **Arte Maya**, C. 23 no. 301, on the Muna road on the western edge of town.

Where to Stay and Eat

Around **Ticul** plaza there is the usual line of *loncherías* and *taco*-stands offering cheap meals and soft drinks, and in **Oxcutzcab**, **Tekax** and **Peto** there are plenty of *loncherías* around the markets.

Oxcutzcab t (997–)

Hotel Puuc, C. 55 no. 80, x 44, t 975 0103 (*budget*). Bright little hotel with 24 light, spacious rooms, all with fans and a/c, and good modern fittings. A very good-value base for visiting the Puuc ruins.

Restaurante El Peregrino, C. 51 no. 80 bis, x 44 & 46 (*moderate*). This charming little restaurant is owned by the same family as the Hotel Puuc.

They're exceptionally friendly, and give any lost-looking foreigners a special welcome. The menu is more flexible than usual, ranging from light snacks and *tablitas* (platters of mixed meats) through seafood to real feasts of Yucatecan specialities. Open for breakfast, too.

Ticul t (997–)

Hotel Plaza, C. 23 no. 202, t 972 0484, *www.hotelplazayucatan.com* (*budget*). Best in Ticul by a long way. It's fittingly right on the plaza, and has large, functional, airy and comfortable rooms with good facilities such as bathrooms, fans, a/c and TVs, making them exceptional value.

Los Almendros, C. 23 (Tekax road) no. 207, t 972 0021 (*moderate*). Ticul's celebrated restaurant, parent of flashier branches in Mérida and Cancún. When the first Almendros opened in 1963 it was credited with being the first place ever to present Yucatecan country cooking '*para los dzules*', for non-Maya, and even with inventing dishes such as *poc-chuc* that are now seen as utterly 'traditional'. This has also been a fine place to try unquestionably traditional dishes such as *pavo en relleno negro* (turkey in a savoury black *chilmole* sauce with hard-boiled eggs). So successful is it that it has abandoned its original building in the middle of Ticul for a new, larger one nearby, with more room for tour groups. Overall, though, Los Almendros is still worth checking out on a visit to the Puuc. *Open daily 11am–7pm*.

The Maní Road to Mayapán and Acanceh

The 'back country' route from the Puuc back to Mérida, north from Oxcutzcab and Ticul, was once one of the most meandering of remote Yucatán roads, but has been fully upgraded by the state authorities as Highway 18, with bypasses around most towns, and can now be as fast as the 261 Muna road. Take it more slowly and wander off the Highway, though, and this remains one of the most characterful stretches of Yucatán countryside, a landscape of quiet Maya towns, *henequen* fields and long stretches of green scrub. This road has been labelled the **Ruta de los Conventos** ('Convent Route'), as a showcase for Yucatán's colonial church architecture. This is a little arbitrary, since there are Spanish churches in every part of the state. It is, though, truly steeped in history, for it contains some of the oldest, most impressive Franciscan foundations in the region, and the remains of the last great Maya city, Mayapán.

Maní

Only 10km north of Oxcutzcab is Maní, oldest of all the Spanish missionary monasteries in the Yucatán and scene of one of the most dramatic episodes of the Conquest, Father Landa's *auto-da-fé* and bonfire of Mayan treasures in 1562 (*see* p.51). Maní was the seat of the Xiu, whose leader Tutul Xiu was the first of the Maya lords to accept the authority of the Spanish crown in 1542. It was because of the loyalty of the Xiu that the Franciscans sent their first missionary expedition to this area in 1547, two years after the order had arrived in Yucatán. The friars originally established themselves in Oxcutzcab, but after hearing rumours of a plot to murder them they accepted the suggestion of Tutul Xiu to move closer to his centre of power in Maní.

Getting around the Maní Road

Highway 18 has bypasses around most small towns, and meets Highway 184 just east of Oxcutzcab; to get to Maní, follow signs to the old road north. There are few **petrol/gas stations**, so it's best to fill up for the 100km between Mérida and Oxcutzcab or Ticul. There are also no official fuel stations on the 122km road between Oxcutzcab and Chichén Itzá via Sotuta. Note too that village churches all close for lunch, from about 1pm to 4pm.

Buses along this road run from Terminal del Noreste in Mérida, with several daily. There's also fairly steady *colectivo* traffic between all the towns during the morning, but this tends to thin out in the afternoons.

The Monastery of Saint Michael the Archangel was dedicated in 1549. A major effort was made to build it as quickly as possible: the Franciscans' architect Friar Juan de Mérida oversaw the work, and a large part of it was built in six months in 1550. The friars established a school to teach Christian doctrine in Yucatec using Latin script, and even a choir school, where Mayan boys were taught to sing polyphonic Masses. The Franciscans, as Landa declared, sought to recruit into the school 'the young sons of the lords and principal people', in the expectation that when they returned to Maya society they would carry back a full knowledge of the new religion.

It was some of these very children who in May 1562 informed the friars that their Maya elders were celebrating old rituals in secret, and showed them a cave full of idols and offerings. Investigations revealed a large-scale relapse into 'idolatry'. It appears likely that many Maya lords simply had the wrong end of the stick: used as they were to having many gods, who were flexible enough to admit others, it seems they had not quite understood how exclusive the new Christian god was intended to be. When the news was relayed to Landa, however, he was appalled. He resolved to root out the devil's work with no half measures, organizing a solemn *auto-da-fé* in the great square in front of the monastery of Maní. None of the 'idolators' was actually executed or burnt at the stake, but some died in the course of their tortures.

In later decades the monastery was supplanted as a missionary centre, and Maní was left as one more rural town. The great mass of the monastery still stands almost completely intact over the grass expanse of the town square, which is now very quiet. The square is so big because it was once the ceremonial plaza of the Xiu capital. On the left of the monastery façade, looking at it, is the great open arch of the *capilla de indios*. The façade and bell towers of the church were added in the 18th century.

Behind the Indian chapel and alongside the church is the two-storey cloister. It's a monument of Franciscan austerity, crude and powerful, with walls so thick they're almost cavern-like. Exuberant giant ferns soften the lines a little, and in one corner the remains are visible of a mural of the Visitation of the Virgin, probably from the 1580s. Contrary to some leaflets there is no museum here, only a very austere retreat house; the garden, still with its original well and water wheel, is full of flowers, and in spring the crumbling upper arches are full of swooping swallows.

About 6km further along the road is **Tipikal**, from where it's 6km again to **Teabo**, with one of the most elegant Franciscan churches, from 1650–95. Ask the sacristan if you can see the wood-beamed sacristy, which has extraordinary mural paintings of saints. They were long covered in whitewash, and only discovered by accident in the 1980s. At Teabo you can get onto Highway 18 towards Mérida, or onto a long, slow road that runs northeast to the main 180 Cancún road and Chichén Itzá, via **Sotuta**, once seat of the Cocom, enemies of the Xiu and dogged opponents of the Spaniards.

The main 18 road from Teabo next runs past **Chumayel** (5km), place of origin of the *Book of Chilam Balam of Chumayel*, one of the Maya chronicles that were written down in Yucatec in Latin script in the 16th century. From there it's 9km to **Mama**, which has a fine church with a particularly grand bell tower and a roofed-over 16th-century well (no longer in operation). Next town up is the slightly busier **Tekit**, from where it's another 20km through fairly empty country to the ruins of Mayapán.

Mayapán

Mayapán
Open daily 8–5; adm.

At **Mayapán** the Mayan past leaves the realm of archaeology and crosses into conventional history. The city collapsed as capital of northwest Yucatán in the 1440s, only 80 years before the arrival of the Spaniards, and one of Landa's chief sources on Mayan ways, baptized as Juan Cocom, was the grandson of the last ruler of Mayapán.

There is evidence the site had been occupied since the Early Classic, but scarcely anything remains from any time before the 12th century. Mayapán rose to prominence around 1200, the most vigorous product of the modest Postclassic revival in the northern

Eating Out

All the towns on this road have cheap *loncherías* that are good places for sitting to admire church façades and watch vultures go by, but **Maní** has its only full-scale restaurants.

 Tutul-Xiu >

El Príncipe Tutul-Xiu, C. 26, x 25 & 27, Maní, t 978 4076 (*moderate*). Despite its remote location this charming restaurant is one of the region's very

best for Yucatecan cooking, especially classics like *poc-chuc*, and in fact its food is now often much better than that of the more celebrated Almendros in Ticul, and served in a prettier setting. *Open 11–7.*

Restaurant Los Frailes, C. 27, x 28 & 30, Maní (*moderate*). Pretty restaurant with all the Yucatecan standards. *Open 11–6 only.*

Yucatán, and it seems that its growth triggered the final collapse of Chichén Itzá. At its peak the city had a population of around 12,000. In Yucatecan chronicles it was sometimes described as the seat of the 'League of Mayapán', and one legend maintains that the other members of this 'League' were Chichén Itzá and Uxmal, but this has now been discounted since it is clear these cities had both declined before most of Mayapán was built. Instead, it was the joint capital of a loose confederacy of small lordships – Maní, Chakan (around Dzibilchaltún-Ti'ho), Kin-Pech (Campeche) – into which the Yucatán had divided. The 'rulers' of Mayapán, the Cocom lineage, were not strictly kings but only the first among several lords in a *multepal* collective leadership, able to take decisions only with some consensus behind them.

This system involved a degree of bureaucracy. According to Landa, each of the local princes maintained their own establishment in Mayapán, headed by a *mayordomo* (*caluac*), responsible for communications with the home domain. This type of government was also inclined to instability. The authority of the Cocom was fairly effective for many years, but in the late 14th century the Xiu of Maní emerged as a centre of disaffection, accusing the Cocom of acting tyrannically. A 'coup' was staged in which leading Cocom princes were murdered, except for one who escaped to lead resistance. Civil wars went on for years, until in 1441 the Cocom withdrew to their own base at Sotuta, and Mayapán was abandoned. This Xiu-Cocom feud was still flaring up when the Spaniards arrived, and was enormously useful to them in the Conquest.

Mayapán is another place where major new excavation and restoration work has been carried out just in recent years: important finds include several rare and richly coloured painted frescoes, and many fine ceramic pieces, most of which are now in Mérida's museum. Large parts of the site, though, remain scarcely excavated.

Mayapán's status as a confederal capital gave it a particular structure. The area that has been excavated is inside a rough perimeter wall, which swings round in a kidney shape. It seems clear that an etiquette designed to avoid flash points was a feature of relations between the lords of the League, so that the walled centre of Mayapán was a kind of collective 'no man's land' shared by all but belonging to no one in particular. According to Landa, each lord had the right to keep a residence within the wall, but kept most of their followers in separate areas outside, where there are enough semi-buried structures in the woods to intrigue any amateur archaeologist.

Looking at Mayapán it soon becomes clear that by the time the city was built many of the most sophisticated Maya skills in carving and stoneworking had been lost. In their finish the buildings are much cruder than those at older sites. On the right, going in, is **Structure Q-62**, a residential area of stone walls making up three rooms; behind it are three pyramid-like temple platforms, the **Cemetery Group**, while to the left of the main path there is a large platform and pyramid complex, the **Templo del Pescador** ('Temple of the Fisherman'). Fully excavated only since 2002, this has at its top a stucco altar painted with a monstrous god-like figure, the 'fisherman' of its name (although the protective fence around him makes it hard to get a good look). Beyond it is the 'mini-pyramid' known as the **Templo de Nichos Pintados** ('Painted Niches'), which has the best-preserved, most strongly coloured frescoes at Mayapán – including powerful images of vision serpents – and the **Templo de los Guerreros** ('the Warriors'), with another stucco altar. These two almost form an entrance to the main plaza of Mayapán, centred on the city's largest structure, the great pyramid or **Castillo de Kukulcán**, a cruder, smaller copy of the Castillo at Chichén Itzá. Recent restoration has made it much easier to appreciate that, however much Mayapán's builders may have lacked in carving ability, in the structure of its plaza the city had a curiously distinctive elegance, one more Maya surprise. Forming the sides of the square around the pyramid are several almost Grecian colonnades, and lines of columns lead up to the steps on the Castillo's east and west sides, especially from the **Temple of Venus** platform to the west. The main fresco fragments are around the lower levels of the pyramid, protected by *palapa* roofs. Those in the northeast corner, facing into the plaza, show warriors, some of them decapitated; fragments of skulls have also been found here, suggesting this was a place of sacrifice. Larger and more impressive are the scenes on the south side, outside the square, showing richly adorned figures carrying standards, surrounded by animals, stranger creatures and the inevitable death figure, in a style extraordinarily similar to modern Day-of-the-Dead souvenirs and the images of the great 19th-century Mexican folk artist Posada.

Just south of the Castillo is the main *cenote*, which had a temple platform at its mouth. On the east side of the plaza are the palace/temple buildings known as the **Chac complex** or 'Hall of Masks', which this time seem to imitate the Puuc style, with a Chac mask in the centre. Beside them is the intriguing circular **Caracol** or **Observatory**, again very like the great Caracol tower at Chichén, although oddly it has none of the slots in its walls that would have been used for astronomical observations. Whether these round

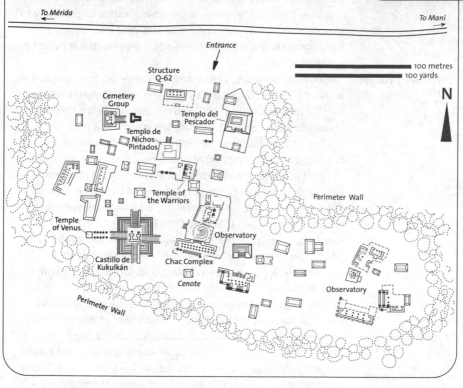

To Mérida

To Maní

Entrance

Structure
Q-62

Cemetery
Group

Templo del
Pescador

Templo de
Nichos
Pintados

100 metres
100 yards

N

Temple of
the Warriors

Perimeter Wall

Temple
of Venus

Observatory

Castillo de
Kukulkán

Chac Complex

Cenote

Observatory

Perimeter Wall

buildings were observatories is still not certain, but there were four such towers at Mayapán. The area outside the plaza to the east can be recommended to anyone who wants to see Maya ruins in their 'natural' state, with many more platforms and pyramids scattered around the woods.

Tecoh to Acanceh

Only 3km from Mayapán is the next village, **Telchaquillo**, which has the entrance to a *cenote* in its main plaza. Eleven kilometres further on is **Tecoh**, another delightfully somnolescent town. Its twin-belfried church, from 1751, stands on another Maya platform. It has a rival in the *Palacio Municipal*, a piece of peach-coloured Victoriana from 1904–6 which local jokers say was copied from Chicago City Hall.

The last stop on this road (8km from Tecoh) is the most extraordinary, **Acanceh**. Like Izamal, this is one of the places where the pre- and post-Conquest worlds exist side by side. As you enter the dusty village square, on the right is an 18th-century colonial church, while forming a corner with it is a Maya pyramid, still substantially intact despite having been plundered to build the church and many other parts of the town. Despite its proximity to Mayapán it is much older, and one of the most intriguing buildings in the Yucatán for the insight it gives on the links within the Maya world.

Acaneh pyramid
Open daily 8–5; adm

Acanceh pyramid dates from the Early Classic, AD 300–600, and so is one of the oldest large structures in the north. There is evidence too that the site had been occupied for centuries before then, from about 300 BC. Moreover, stylistically the pyramid has great similarities to buildings in the Petén, far to the south in Guatemala or Campeche, indicating that Maya from southern cities may have travelled to northern Yucatán even at this time. Most of Acanceh has been covered over by the later village, but two blocks south of the plaza there are two more survivors, the **Palacio de los Estucos** and the plainly named **El Edificio** ('The Building'). All three structures have stucco friezes that, again, are unusual for the Yucatán and more typical of areas further south such as Río Bec. Those on the 'Building' show rich decoration of animals, birds and astronomical signs, still with traces of bright colours.

Ruins aside, two detours either side of this road can show you two different sides of rural Yucatán. A turn west in Tecoh will lead you very shortly to **Hacienda Sotuta de Peón**. This is one of the last *haciendas* in the Yucatán that actually works *henequen*, but is now run pretty squarely as a tourist attraction. Tours are lively, including a ride on one of the 'truck' railways used around the estate and a *cenote* swim as well as seeing how *henequen* is worked and explanations of *hacienda* life, and there's an attractive terrace restaurant. Alternatively, a turn east in Acanceh will take you through 16km of countryside to **Cuzamá**, known for its three fine swimming *cenotes*. The village is very well organized, and as you arrive signs point you to local guides, who will take you to the *cenotes* on another horse-drawn truck railway. The *cenotes* are deliciously refreshing, but be aware that at two of the three the only access is down narrow metal ladders. Also, since Cuzamá is increasingly widely known the pools can be crowded.

Hacienda Sotuta de Peón
t 999 941 8639,
www.haciendatour.com;
tours Tues–Sat at 10am
and 1pm; adm

Otherwise, from Acanceh a country road runs 12km straight north to Ticopo to meet Highway 180, the Mérida–Cancún road going east, while to the west an all-new, widened road takes you quickly back along 19km to Kanasín and Mérida.

Southern Quintana Roo and the Río Bec

South of Tulum along the Caribbean coast traffic slims down and the world of beach bars, eco-theme parks and resort hotels comes, for the moment, to a pretty abrupt end. Highway 307 is pushed away from the coast by the great expanse of the Sian Ka'an reserve; the population thins out drastically. Inland, roads span huge distances through uninterrupted forest between tiny Maya villages, the domain of birds and butterflies. On the coast, despite the momentum toward development, there are still long miles of empty beaches and palm groves, between far-away cabaña hotels and villages that once gave refuge to pirates. This region contains an extraordinary wealth of Maya ruins, which are now being energetically publicized, and the coast has been earmarked as a new tourist prospect, but so far most new constructions are of a scale that would barely register on the Riviera Maya. It remains a place best appreciated by travellers who are prepared to explore and lose themselves unhurriedly, amid a still intact atmosphere of beachcomber isolation.

10

Don't miss

① Remote beaches and reefs
Xcalak p.338

② Fabulous lake of seven colours
Bacalar p.341

③ Eating *tacos* on the Bay Boulevard
Chetumal p.345

④ Superb Maya ruins, shrouded in giant fan palms
Kohunlich p.356

⑤ A moated and walled city
Becán p.362

See map overleaf

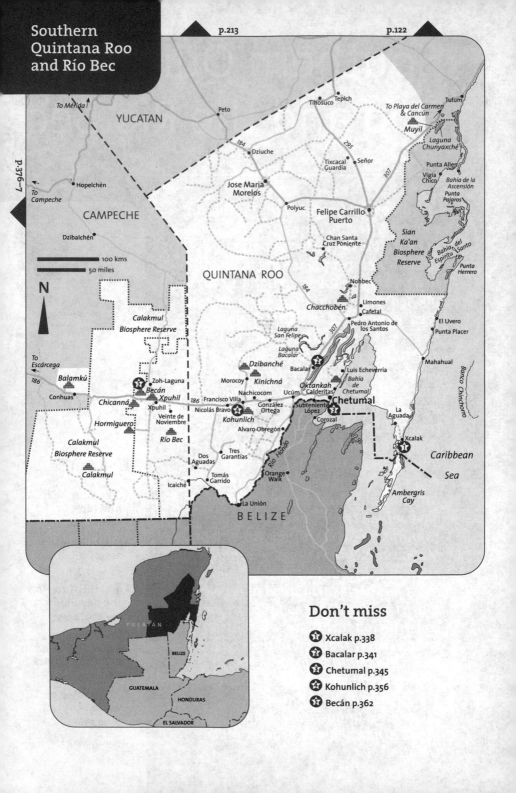

Southern Quintana Roo and Río Bec

p.213

p.122

p.376-7

To Merida

YUCATAN

Peto

Tihosuco

Tepich

Tulum

To Playa del Carmen & Cancún

Muyil

Laguna Chunyaxché

Dziuche

Tixcacal Guardia

Señor

Punta Allen

Vigia Chico

Bahia de la Ascensión

Punta Pajaros

Hopelchén

To Campeche

CAMPECHE

Jose Maria Morelos

Polyuc

Felipe Carrillo Puerto

Chan Santa Cruz Poniente

Sian Ka'an Biosphere Reserve

Bahia del Espíritu Santo

Punta Herrero

Dzibalchén

QUINTANA ROO

Nohbec

100 kms

50 miles

N

Calakmul Biosphere Reserve

Chacchobén

Limones

Cafetal

El Uvero

Punta Placer

Laguna San Felipe

Pedro Antonio de los Santos

To Escárcega

Laguna Bacalar

Dzibanché

Bacalar

Luis Echeverria

Mahahual

Balamkú

Zoh-Laguna

Becán

Morocoy

Kinichná

Nachicocom

Ucúm

Oktankah Calderitas

Bahia de Chetumal

Banco Chinchorro

Conhuas

Chicanná

Xpuhil

186

Francisco Villa

González Ortega

Subteniente López

Chetumal

La Aguada

Xpuhil

Nicolás Bravo

Kohunlich

Corozal

Xcalak

Hormiguero

Veinte de Noviembre

Alvaro Obregón

Río Hondo

Caribbean Sea

Calakmul Biosphere Reserve

Río Bec

Dos Aguadas

Tres Garantias

Orange Walk

Ambergris Cay

Calakmul

Icaiché

Tomás Garrido

La Unión

BELIZE

YUCATÁN

BELIZE

GUATEMALA

HONDURAS

EL SALVADOR

Don't miss

⭐ Xcalak p.338

⭐ Bacalar p.341

⭐ Chetumal p.345

⭐ Kohunlich p.356

⭐ Becán p.362

The southern part of Quintana Roo was once one of the least-visited regions in the whole of Mexico. And yet, belying its isolation in modern times, in the Classic era of Mesoamerica this area was one of the major centres of Maya culture. Not far from Chetumal there are the remains of major Maya cities, such as Kohunlich. Further west they connect with the string of distinctive sites in the Río Bec area and Calakmul, one of the 'superpowers' of the Classic Maya world. Until the late 1990s the Maya sites of this area were known only to archaeologists, and its stunning coast only to dedicated fishermen. People came to find what was in short supply further north: towns unaffected by tourism, unknown beach villages and intact rainforest; Calakmul is the largest rainforest reserve in the Americas outside the Amazon. The coast, now dubbed the 'Costa Maya', is being opened up, with paved roads, and a cruise-ship dock to attract the attention of tourism's big batallions. For the moment, though, big projects are more often heard about here than seen.

The Land of the Talking Cross

Three roads lead into southern Quintana Roo from the north: Highway 307 from Tulum, the 295 south from Valladolid and the recently upgraded 184 from Mérida via Ticul and Peto. All three meet at Felipe Carrillo Puerto. Signs by the roadside warn drivers '*Cuida su vida, no se distraiga*' ('Look after your own life, don't get distracted'), and they're not kidding: the empty forest becomes a great green blur, and the combination of tree after tree, dead-straight road and sweaty heat is hypnotic. If you travel these roads between March and June, you may be prodded out of your torpor by thousands of tiny white butterflies, splattering against windscreens like bullets.

If the country around Carrillo Puerto was where the rebel Maya carved out a place for themselves at the end of the Caste War, the region south of Valladolid is where the great conflagration actually began. Thirty-nine kilometres from Valladolid is **Tepich**, where the Caste War 'officially' started on 30 July 1847, while 15km beyond is the extraordinary village of **Tihosuco**. Towering up on one side of its baking plaza is the half-ruined shell of a Franciscan church. Beside it, a street of Spanish colonial houses show the remains of grille windows and stucco mouldings. It looks like 20th-century bomb damage, but this destruction was carried out during the Caste War, between 1849 and 1865. Until very recently, the church and other ruins in Tihosuco were still fire-blackened.

Tihosuco was a substantial town under Spanish rule and in the first years of independence, with wealthy *ladino* planters. It was also the home of Jacinto Pat, *batab* of the local Maya and greatest of the leaders of the Caste War. Once the revolt began the town was taken quickly by the Maya; then, as the Maya retreated, it was reoccupied by the Yucatán army at the end of 1848. Tihosuco became the main base of the *ladino* armies in their efforts to advance against the followers of the Cross, and just as important a target for Maya raids out of the forest. It was fought over time and again until, after a ferocious siege by the Cruzob in 1865, it was decided in Mérida that Tihosuco was not worth keeping, and the town was left deserted. It was only resettled after 1930. The 'new' village is completely Maya, and something of a memorial to Jacinto Pat: a statue of him, machete in hand, stands in the plaza.

Museo de la Guerra de las Castas
Tues–Sun 10–6; adm

The village also contains the **Museo de la Guerra de las Castas** the only museum dedicated to the conflict, off the plaza. Set up under state auspices, it's also a community project; if it's not open when you arrive, ask a passer-by and great efforts will be made to find the key. The museum is also part of informative tours around Tihosuco run by **Xiimbal** from Felipe Carrillo Puerto (*see* p.335).

Felipe Carrillo Puerto

Eighty kilometres from Tihosuco is Felipe Carrillo Puerto. Official centre of the 'Zona Maya' of Quintana Roo, it is for the most part a nondescript town, with recent concrete buildings taking up most of the centre, fading into *na* huts like any Mayan village. For many travellers it's just a fuel stop, but it is unique, for as Chan Santa Cruz this town was 'capital' of the last independent Maya semi-state in Mexico, called the ***Cruzob*** or Followers of the Cross.

History

José María Barrera, renegade *mestizo* leader of one of the Maya bands wandering in the forest after the main Caste War, first announced that he had found a Cross by a *cenote* that spoke and offered leadership to the Maya in late 1850. He was then at Xoccén, not far from Valladolid. Pursued by *ladino* troops, he retreated south to a still more remote place in the forest, and by May 1851 the 'Sanctuary of the Cross' was established next to the small *cenote* where it is today, in Chan Santa Cruz ('Little Holy Cross'). The Cross spoke only through its Maya 'secretaries', the most important of whom was Juan de la Cruz Puc. The cross is of course a Christian symbol, but to the Maya it could equally represent the *wakah-kan*, the world tree, and Cruzob crosses, painted bright colours and surrounded by flowers, are very Mayan.

The Cross was first kept in a hut called the *Gloria*. Its messages told the Maya that their cause was righteous, and that if they followed the instructions of the Cross and kept themselves ready for war they would one day be victorious. Yucatecan troops who marched down to Chan Santa Cruz delighted in uncovering the chamber at the back

Getting to Felipe Carrillo Puerto

Highway 307 runs through Felipe Carrillo Puerto. Even-numbered streets go north–south, odd east–west. The town is a **fuel stop**, with the only real petrol/gas stations on the Highways between Valladolid or Tulum and Bacalar: one north of town, another in the centre a block south of the junction with the Valladolid road. The **bus station** is on the plaza, by the town hall. Ten first-class buses each way between Cancún and Chetumal stop here daily, and more second-class. Four first-class and seven second-class stop on the route to Mérida via Peto and Ticul, and there are five or six second-class daily to Valladolid via Tihosuco.

of the *Gloria* from which the 'secretaries' supposedly performed their ventriloquist act. But this did nothing to stop the growth in the cult's popularity among the Maya, for hundreds of rebel bands converged on Chan Santa Cruz, and in 1852 the Cruzob launched an offensive that sent a wave of fear through Yucatán.

In Chan Santa Cruz the Cruzob established their own system of religious and political authority, mixing Catholicism, the village hierarchies of colonial Yucatán and older Maya traditions. The most important figure was the 'Patron of the Cross', also known as the *Tatich* or *Nohoch Tata* ('Great Father'), originally Barrera, followed by the *Tata Polin* or 'Interpreter of the Cross', through whom the Cross spoke. Holders of these posts seem to have been chosen by community leaders, a little as in the old Maya *multepal*. Another element was military organization, for Cruzob society was permanently on a war footing, and all men had to take turn in 'standing guard' over the Cross. Chief in the military hierarchy were the *Tata Chikiuc*, or General, and the *Tata Nohoch Zul* or 'Great Father Spy', who gathered information for raids into pacified Yucatán. These won the Cruzob booty and prisoners, to be used as slaves; they grew most of their own food, and could trade with British Honduras for anything else they needed. In 1857 they took Bacalar, only remaining *ladino* outpost south of Tihosuco. They built a town around the Sanctuary of the Cross, and in 1857 added a solid, church-like temple, the *Balam Na*. The Cross was moved to it as the focus of Cruzob rituals.

After the abandonment of Tihosuco by the Mexican army in 1866 the Cruzob were left virtually undisturbed in control of a huge area almost from Valladolid to the Belize border. Over time, though, epidemics, crop crises, internal feuds and the non-appearance of the long-promised final victory led to a crisis in morale and numbers. In 1887 Tatich Aniceto Dzul tried to secure the community's future by asking to be admitted to the British Empire, but didn't get a reply. The death knell for the Cruzob came with the Spencer-Mariscal treaty between Britain and Mexico of 1895. The British Honduras frontier was closed to them by 1898, and in 1901 General Ignacio Bravo took Chan Santa Cruz. The Maya fled into the forest – fortunately for them, as Bravo had intended to 'extinguish' them completely. In 1915 the Revolutionary General Salvador Alvarado ordered that the Maya should again be left to themselves, but few returned to Chan Santa Cruz, which they considered 'defiled'. In the 1920s problems arose between the remaining Cruzob and incoming

Visiting the Zona Maya: Señor

Señor (or Xyaat in Yucatec Maya) is one of a few former Cruz Maya rebel villages that continued to reject Mexican authority after the peace agreement in 1930. This 'resistance' has become largely an anecdote, but these villages have stayed apart, and until very recently were the Maya communities most averse to tourism. They still reject commercial tours, but like every Maya village need more sources of income, and younger Señor residents have led the way in setting up an imaginative village cooperative, Xyaat, to receive small-groups, on the basis that they come as guests, not just clients.

There are two main day-tour routes, which can be combined: a 'nature tour' with bird-watching, a forest walk and a swim in Señor's *laguna* (a beautiful, broad *cenote*), and a fascinating 'culture tour' of the village, to see its Maya beehives, how *henequen* is worked, traditional medicine, and hear stories of the Caste War and other aspects of local life from local elders – in Maya, with translation into Spanish and then English, or directly into English, for a side of the tours the Señor group is very keen on is that foreigners should be able to hear their language, rather than it be forever hidden under Spanish. Each tour also includes a delicious, very friendly lunch. They also have a campsite by the laguna. Day tours cost around $30–38; get in touch a while in advance, as they need time to get a group together. Visits can be arranged direct, or through Xiimbal in Felipe Carrillo Puerto (*see* p.335).

Xyaat, Marcos Canté (Presidente), C. 12 no. 114, Señor, **t** (983) 118 9129, *www.xyaat.com*

chicle tappers, which led some to feel they would be better protected by reaching a settlement with the Mexican state. This finally came about in 1930. The town was renamed after the Yucatecan socialist leader Carrillo Puerto, as a new beginning.

This was not the end of the Cruzob, though, for some did not accept the agreement, and north of Felipe Carrillo Puerto there are villages – especially **Señor** and **Tixcacal Guardia** – still inhabited by followers of the Cross who have never formally accepted Mexican authority. In Tixcacal Guardia, the most traditional village, men still 'mount guard' over their shrines. These communities long dismissed point-blank any attempt to make their odd customs into tourist attractions, but in Señor a local group has now decided to develop sustainable tourism – always under their own control (*see* p.335).

The Balam Na and the Sanctuary

Modern Felipe Carrillo Puerto is a ramshackle little place. Its busiest centre is a road junction, the meeting of Highway 307 (Av. Juárez, or C. 70, in town) and the Valladolid and Peto roads (C. 71). Along 307 there is the vital *gasolinera* and a scattering of hotels, restaurants, *taco*-stands and rough-and-ready little shops.

One block west of the highway along C. 67 is the main plaza, laid out by the Cruzob in the 1850s. Today it's surrounded by a complete range of buildings. Look east and the view is dominated by the **Balam Na** ('Jaguar House'), the last pre-Hispanic pagan temple built in the Americas. As soon as you see it, it's clear that by the time they built it the Maya had lost all contact with their own architectural traditions after long domination by those of the Catholic church. It bears no relation to any pre-Columbian Maya building, but instead is a massive, upright, round-roofed single-nave temple, as solid as an early Franciscan monastery, but without towers or belfry. Abandoned for years, the Balam Na was taken over as an official

Plumridge and Twigge meet the Cross

The Cruzob 'state' enjoyed a special, up-and-down relationship with Belize, then British Honduras. The British colony was an essential source of weapons, bought from traders and planters along the frontier and paid for with loot plundered from Yucatecan towns. The colonial governors in Belize City did not take part in this trade but did very little to stop it, thus convincing white Yucatecans of how truly perfidious Albion could be. The Cruzob, though, often made difficult neighbours. In 1861, after the Maya had been stealing cattle in British Honduras, the colony's Superintendent sent two army lieutenants, with the marvellous names Plumridge and Twigge, into the lion's den with a letter warning the Cruzob they were pushing the British Empire too far. They were also instructed not to put up with any nonsense about talking crosses, but to find the Indians' chief and talk to him. Once across the Río Hondo, and not knowing any Yucatec, they hired an interpreter, a *ladino* gun-runner called José María Trejo. The intrepid pair then presented themselves to the nearest Maya chief, but were abused and obstructed at every turn, and took a week to get from Bacalar to Chan Santa Cruz. Taken before the current *Tatich*, the fearsome Venancio Puc, they presented their letter. Puc said he couldn't decide anything as they would have to talk to God. Plumridge and Twigge were stripped of their swords, and locked up.

At midnight they were led out through a huge crowd to the Balam Na, packed with Maya chanting in prayer. They were forced to their knees, until 'a rather weak voice', as Plumridge described it, was heard from nowhere, the Cross. It told them the letter was insulting, and that if the English wanted a fight with the Cross they could have it, and the first victims would be Plumridge and Twigge. The pair attempted to negotiate. Trejo, in fear of his life and clearly thinking his employers were missing something, decided to ignore what they were saying and told the Cross the letter meant nothing and they had really come to arrange trade. In that case, replied the Cross, the Cruzob wanted 1,000 barrels of gunpowder. Certainly, said Trejo.

The lieutenants were not at all grateful for his initiative. Moreover, they were not able to leave immediately, for Tatich Puc announced that he wanted to celebrate the 'deal' with a *fiesta*. When he saw that his guests weren't joining in the party spirit, he told Trejo that if they insulted his hospitality they were dead men. They were obliged to drink and eat until they vomited, and the three-day binge ended with Plumridge and Twigge hugging the *Tatich* and joining in drunken singing and dancing, sending their hosts into hysterics. When the two ragged lieutenants got back to Belize City, the Superintendent was not impressed, and their humiliation was recorded in detail by a board of enquiry. The Cruzob never got their barrels of gunpowder, but neither did they ever reply to demands for an apology for having mistreated British officers.

Catholic church in 1948, but only by an American/Irish order, because the local Maya would not accept Mexican priests.

Next to it a cloister-like building is now the **Centro de Cultura**, with an excellent bookshop. Little else of the Cruzob town survives. The modern town hall occupies the site of the *Chikinik*, residence of the *Tatich*, once an impressive building with arcades.

Go north up C. 66, turn left and walk four blocks on C. 69 and you will reach the **Sanctuario de la Cruz Parlante**, the sacred *cenote* where the Cross was first kept. It's in a small, shady park, with a few huts housing a small museum on the town's unique history. The Quintana Roo state government now likes to show its sympathy for the people of the Zona Maya, and in 2004 a very white, church-like building was put up around the Sanctuary, which originally was very like a missionary *capilla abierta*, a massive open-air altar with a round niche to contain the Cross. People still place flowers there, and the stones are blackened by the burning of recent offerings. Ceremonies are held particularly on 3 May, day of the Holy Cross.

Tourist Information and Services

t (983–)

Banks: HSBC bank with ATM on Highway 307 next to the petrol station, and another ATM by the bus station.

Internet Access: Balam-Na Computación, C. 65, x 66 & 68, on the plaza.

Post Office: North of the plaza on C. 69.

Xiimbal, inside Balam-Na Computación, C. 65, x 66 & 68, t 834 1073, *www.xiimbal.com*. Very enthusiastic young local ecotourism agency. They can set up trips with Xyaat cooperative in Señor (*see* p.334), and other tours in association with nearby villages: adventure tours to spectacular bat caves and forest at Kantemó, near José María Morelos and Tihosuco. Also a helpful source of local info.

Where to Stay and Eat in Felipe Carrillo Puerto

Next to the old petrol station, there is a line of *loncherías* and *taco*-stands, for very cheap meals and fresh juices.

Casa Regina, Av. Lázaro Cárdenas, x C. 68, t 267 1229 (*inexpensive*). The best in town, with all the essentials – spacious rooms, a/c, and even WiFi.

Hotel Chan Santa Cruz, C. 68 no. 782, t 834 0021 (*inexpensive–budget*). Modern hotel with spacious rooms around a garden.

Hotel-Restaurante El Faisán y el Venado, Av. Juárez 781, t 834 0702 (*budget*). Not a great hotel, but an enjoyable **restaurant** (*moderate*), with good breakfasts and a big choice of Yucatecan and Mexican dishes.

The Costa Maya

From Felipe Carrillo, Puerto Highway 307 runs on south through trees and more trees, and villages with big *topes* where women and kids wait patiently for someone to buy their peeled fruit. At 70km from Felipe Carrillo Puerto you reach a larger village, **Limones**, and 6km south of there, a sign points east to Mahahual, 56km away on the coast. Until recently the coast either side of it was known only to adventurous souls who were willing to bounce for hours on dirt tracks or, better still, came upon it by boat. Those in the know prized it as one of the undiscovered paradises of the Caribbean. Offshore is the fabulous reef of **Banco Chinchorro**. On land, there are bonefish lagoons, mangrove creeks full of ibis and blue heron and miles of white beach rimmed by lush, dense palms.

Undiscovered paradises, of course, are no longer undiscovered once they appear in guidebooks, nor are they once investors and state authorities notice that white-sand Caribbean beaches extend south of Sian Ka'an as well as north of it. The label 'Costa Maya' was thought up around 1996, and since then more effort has been put into improving communications than at any time in history. The road was paved, first, and then a pier was built at Mahahual to bring in cruise ships, with the essential souvenir shops.

Things were coming along, and Mahahual was slowly taking shape as a new tourist centre, until August 2007 and Hurricane Dean, which knocked it flat, even destroying the cruise dock. For a while everything stopped. But the catastrophe was then the spur to a new burst of energy, grand schemes and building. Dean, it was announced, would not hold things back, and actually gave an

Getting to and around the Costa Maya

The turn east off Highway 307 for the Costa Maya is 6km south of Limones at Cafetal, about 70km from Felipe Carrillo Puerto and 45km north of Bacalar. From there it's 56km to Mahahual. The Cafetal–Mahahual –Xcalak road is paved all the way, and has been fully repaired after Hurricane Dean, so it's possible to get all the way from Chetumal to Xcalak in about 3hrs. Outside Mahahual there is a fork northwards to El Uvero (28km) and Punta Herrero (70km), while a larger road turns south, running inland, to Xcalak (59km).

There is a **petrol/gas station** at Mahahual; apart from that, the nearest ones are at Felipe Carrillo Puerto and Bacalar. In Xcalak there is an unofficial gas-seller, with irregular supplies.

Mahahual is now included in the **ADO first-class bus** network: there are two buses daily from **Cancún** (5½hrs) via **Playa del Carmen** and **Tulum** (7am, 11.30pm; returns from Mahahual 8.30am, 5.30pm); three daily from **Chetumal** (2½hrs) via **Bacalar** (5am, 2.30pm, 7.30pm; from Mahahual 7.30am, 1pm, 6.30pm); and one a day at 11.30pm Fri, Sat, Sun only from **Mérida** (6hrs; from Mahahual, same days at 7pm). Note that these routes are not shown on ADO websites. Xcalak can still only be reached direct by **second-class bus** (4hrs), with two each way daily, from **Chetumal** at 6am and 4pm, and from Xcalak at 5.30am and 2pm.

Colectivos run between Mahahual/Xcalak, and **taxis** from Mahahual will take you anywhere on the coast. Mahahual and Xcalak both have **airstrips**, mainly used by air-taxi companies like AeroCosta (*see* p.128) or Aerosaab (*see* p.176).

opportunity, to rebuild Mahahual as a proper modern town, with a bigger, better cruise dock and mall. Reconstruction has gone at a fast pace, and the new expanded cruise pier, the **Puerto Costa Maya**, duly opened in October 2008.

The Costa Maya is now much more widely known, so hotels fill up at peak holiday times. Fortunately it is not yet overdeveloped. The big deterrent for developers is still the lack of mainstream services, outside of Mahahual. Some of the loveliest places are still only accessible by bumpy sand track, and the only places to stay are beautiful small hotels with acres of beach (often built by foreigners prepared to bring in solar power, composting toilets and so on themselves). Several meet the highest green tourism standards, out of necessity and conviction. In between, long stretches of the 130km of coast still feel very remote, its peace and beauty impenetrable.

Mahahual and Placer

The road from the highway traverses another empty stretch of scrub, to finally reach the coast at **Mahahual** (also spelt Majahual), now the hub of the 'Costa Maya'. A tiny, sand-street village a short time ago, post-Dean Mahahual is taking more solid shape in the untidy way of new Mexican tourist towns. Before the road in meets the sea, a turn north (left) leads to the **Puerto Costa Maya** and its mall, and a new part of town called **Nuevo Mahahual**. The arrival of the cruise ships, before and after Dean, prompted the emergence of a range of new businesses, but their effects are intermittent. A number of cruises call in from November to March, but far fewer in the rest of the year. When there's a ship in town, shops open, tours are run, souvenir-sellers arrive from around the region, and (minor) crowds appear in the streets; when there isn't, the Puerto itself is closed up, and things are much more quiet.

Along the new waterfront Malecón south of the road junction, there are small, unfancy restaurants, shops, hotels, backpacker services and laid-back beach bars. Aside from its status as a cruise stop, Mahahual has been getting a reputation as the 'new Tulum', especially since prices have rocketed so much in the original Tulum. The budget beach *cabaña* operations south of town have found it particularly hard to pick up after Dean, and many have been replaced by more solid accommodation, but there are still a few. Prices overall remain modest by Riviera standards, and the atmosphere is easy going. Further south again are the prettier small hotels. The beach is not as beautiful as Tulum's, but it's great for easy swimming.

North of Mahahual, the road skirts around the Puerto to cut back towards the coast and head up to Sian Ka'an. It is paved as far as **Punta Placer**, where there are a few hotels, and **El Uvero**, 28km up. Beyond there a dirt track continues on through wild forest, lagoon and beach to the southern entrance to Sian Ka'an at Tampalam and a tiny settlement at **Punta Herrero**, 70km from Mahahual. Once you get there, there's one shop, one little restaurant and a sleepy fishermen's co-op for tours (*see* p.339), but anyone who makes it up there is likely to feel they have a whole world to themselves.

South of Mahahual the old Xcalak sand road continues behind the shore, swerving occasionally to avoid palm trees. Along it there are more beach hotels and bars, widely spaced out so they make no impact on each other's mellow isolation. Potholes aside, it's no longer possible to carry on down this road all the way to Xcalak (59km), so after about 10km take one of the turnings back to the new, paved road. About 30km from Mahahual at **Xahuaxol** another stretch of beach is now being opened up.

Xcalak and Banco Chinchorro

It was the reefs of **Banco Chinchorro**, 20–40km offshore, that first drew foreigners to Xcalak. Chinchorro is a great ring of coral, 50km from north to south, with a few uninhabited sand and scrub islands. The difficulties of getting there have made them most attractive to experienced divers, but there are shallow-water reefs accessible to novices or snorkellers as well. The great attraction of Chinchorro is the range of dives it offers: tunnels, wall dives, dazzling coral. It also has an extraordinary range of wrecks, from Spanish galleons and pirate ships to modern hulks, numbering over 100.

The paved road into Xcalak comes into the back of the village. From the beach the old road turns up through the sand and palms back toward Mahahual. Along the lower 15km or so of this road are some of the coast's most enjoyable small hotels; for those looking for an empty Caribbean beach in Mexico, this is one of *the* places to go.

🟠 **Xcalak**   **Xcalak** itself consists of a collection of small houses, a plaza, palm trees, sand streets, a beach, a dazzling sea and one of the best anchorages in a long distance, where many a Caribbean yachtsman has taken refuge from storms. It has a sizable number of resident *gringos*, to go with its Maya and *mestizo* population. A while ago

Xcalak was expected to be the real big thing on this coast, but with the cruise dock the focus has shifted to the more accessible Mahahual. As well as Chinchorro, around Xcalak there is fabulous snorkelling and inshore diving, deep-sea fishing and inshore bonefishing, and the nearby mangrove islands are alive with birds.

Tourist Information and Services

t (983–)

Most phones here are cellphones, so you will often need to use 044 rather than 01 before the area code. Even these connections are often shaky, so email is the best way to make bookings. The *Sacbe* free English-language magazine is useful, and a big range of local information can be found on *www.xcalak-info*, *www.bill-in-tulsa.com* and *www.mayanbeach garden. com* (including the annual cruise-ship schedule).

There are military checkpoints at the entrance to Mahahual, and just north of Xcalak. However, they are laid-back and are rarely interested in tourists.

There is a *cambio* office on the waterfront in Mahahual, and an **ATM**, but it often runs out of money, and so is not entirely to be relied on. Otherwise, the nearest ATMs or banks are in Bacalar and Felipe Carrillo Puerto. If staying in Xcalak, especially, plan to bring sufficient cash, in **pesos**, for the length of your stay.

Internet Access: Internet Público, on the waterfront (south end) in Mahahual; there is also a local Net centre in Xcalak village.

The Native Choice, Chacchoben, t 103 5955, *www.thenativechoice.com*. Two young local guides who offer an imaginative range of tours, to Chacchobén ruins, villages, Kohunlich and further afield; their personal tours have won enormous praise. They will collect customers from most places in the area, and in Mahahual can also be contacted through the Costa Maya Inn.

Sian Ka'an by the Southern Route

The road north from Mahahual is the southern entry to Sian Ka'an (*see* p.202). It is unpaved from El Uvero and inside the reserve, so the 70km from

Mahahual to **Punta Herrero** can take 3hrs (and is driven more easily in a 4x4). At Punta Herrero a local cooperative now offers fishing, birding, snorkelling and kayak tours, but it's easy to get there and not locate them, or find you can't take a tour till the next day (and there's nowhere to stay). Some hotels – notably **Mayan Beach Garden** (*see* p.340) – are in contact with the co op and can set up tours in advance.

Sports and Activities

Scuba Diving, Snorkelling and Fishing

Local fishermen offer snorkelling and fishing trips along the beach in Mahahual, and in Xcalak boats and fishing guides can be found by asking around. From Xcalak trips can also be arranged to San Pedro on **Ambergris** in Belize, a short boat ride away. Several hotels along the coast also offer dive packages, of which **Casa Carolina** in Xcalak is one of the best. North of Mahahual, **El Placer del Caribe** is a small, individual dive operator which can often most easily be contacted via Mayan Beach Gardens hotel.

Diving on Banco Chincorro, with any operator, should be arranged in advance.

Bahia Blanca Tours, Xcalak, *www.xcalak-ecotours.com*. Cooperative formed by Xcalak fishermen offering fishing trips, diving, snorkel tours and bird- and manatee-watching tours, with guides.

Dreamtime Dive Resort, Ctra Mahahual–Xcalak Km 2.5, Mahahual, t 834 5818, *www.dreamtimediving.com*. Well-equipped centre with very high ecological standards. A full range of dives is on offer, and comfy *cabañas* on the beach for longer dive packages.

XTC Dive Center, by the beach road, north side of Xcalak village, *www.xtc divecenter.com*. Fully equipped dive centre run by young Americans with expert knowledge of the area. They offer good-value scuba training, a range of dives, snorkelling, fishing, bird-watching tours and trips to San Pedro, and have the best boat in the area for diving at Banco Chinchorro.

Where to Stay and Eat on the Costa Maya

Most hotel owners here have had to bring their own services such as solar electricity. Power may only be available part of the day. Rates of hotels normally in the *moderate* band may go into *expensive* in the peak season.

North of Mahahual

There are also some basic *cabaña* sites at Río Indio, 9km north of Mahahual, but these have had trouble picking up after Hurricane Dean, and may soon be replaced by more solid developments.

Mayan Beach Garden, El Placer, 20km north of Mahahual, *www.mayan beachgarden.com* (*moderate*). A lovely small hotel on the beach, enjoying complete seclusion. Americans Kim and Marcia Bates have pretty, spacious rooms and a suite in intimate beachside *cabañas*, all with solar power and low-impact services, and also handle rentals for nearby villas. There's a mellow terrace **restaurant**, and breakfast is included. Kayaks, boogie boards, snorkels and similar are provided for guests' use, diving can be arranged with El Placer (*see* p.339) and other operators, and the Bates can set up trips and other activities. Their website is also a source of local info.

Chac-Chi Cabañas, 5km north of Mahahual, t 111 7703, *www.costamaya-chacchi.com* (*inexpensive*). Twelve pleasant beach *cabañas*, and a *palapa*-roofed **restaurant**. Very tranquil.

Mahahual

Balamku Inn on the Beach, Ctra Mahahual–Xcalak Km 5.7, t 839 5532, *www.balamku.com* (*moderate*). Ideally relaxed eco-hotel opened by Canadians Carol Tumber and Alan Knight, with nine very pretty, comfortable rooms in *palapa*-style villas or two-storey buildings, and an equally relaxing terrace restaurant. Services are low-impact (solar and wind power) giving it a full inter-

national green rating. Generous breakfasts, kayak use and internet access are included, and diving, fishing and other activities can be arranged.

Hotel Maya Luna, Ctra Mahahual–Xcalak Km 5.2, t 836 0905, *www. hotelmayaluna.com* (*moderate*). Seductive hotel in an exquisite location. It has four spacious 'studios' and one family-sized room in individual villas, each with its own beach terrace and, as a special plus, a roof terrace, ideal for counting stars. The **restaurant** offers lots of fruit, seafood and vegetarian choices, and breakfast is included. Dutch owners Jan and Caroline are very friendly, and kayaks or snorkels are available, as are diving, horse riding and much more.

Maya Palms, Ctra Mahahual–Xcalak Km 10, t in USA (314) 843 3483, *www.mayapalms.com* (*moderate*). One of the biggest hotels south of Mahahual, with neo-Maya architecture – a mini-Tulum castillo – a fine pool, a good **bar-restaurant** and plenty of beach. It's mainly a **dive resort**, so a range of all-in packages is offered, but rooms are easily available to non-divers. As well as scuba trips there are snorkel excursions and other activities.

La Posada de los 40 Cañones, Ctra Mahahual–Xcalak Km 1.5, t 123 8591, *www.40canones.com* (*moderate*). Large, attractive rooms, some with a/c, overlooking the beach at the south end of Mahahual waterfront. The **restaurant** offers Mexican and Italian.

Luna de Plata, Ctra Mahahual–Xcalak Km 2, t 125 3999, *www.lunadeplata. info* (*moderate–inexpensive*). Italian-run small beach hotel with ten pretty rooms and suites that are excellent value, and a mellow Italian **restaurant** (*moderate*). Various tours available.

Kohunbeach Cabañas, Ctra Mahahual–Xcalak Km 7, no phone, *www.kohun beach.o-f.com* (*inexpensive*). Likeable beachfront *cabaña* operation in a secluded spot with plenty of sea to itself, and three *palapa*-roofed cabins, all with showers.

Travel'In, Ctra Mahahual–Xcalak Km 6, (*budget*). Roadside beachbum-style restaurant and bar. The owners are Dutch and English, so the fare is less Mexican than an eclectic mix. They also rent bikes and kayaks.

Xcalak

Playa Sonrisa, 10km north of Xcalak, t in USA (719) 966 4309, *www.playa sonrisa.com* (*expensive–moderate*). 'Clothing optional' beach hotel with comfortable villa-style rooms with fridges and (solar-powered) a/c, and a **bar-restaurant** for guests only. Tours, bikes and kayaks are all available.

★ **Casa Carolina** >

Casa Carolina, 4km north of Xcalak, t 831 0444, *www.casacarolina.net* (*moderate*). Very likeable place, ideal for relaxation, with four big, pretty rooms, all with full kitchens, balconies and the sea right outside. Owners Bob Villier and Caroline Wexler are extremely hospitable, and Bob is NAUI **dive master**. A full range of dive training/trips is avail-able, including to Chinchorro. Snorkelling or fishing, boat trips can also be arranged to San Pedro in Belize.

★ **The Leaky Palapa** >>

Costa de Cocos, 3km north of Xcalak, t 831 0110, *www.costudecocos.com* (*moderate*). Rustically decorated *cabañas* with every comfort, a pretty **bar-restaurant** and a fine beach. Diving on inshore reefs, snorkelling and bone- and fly-fishing are specialities. Internet access available.

AC Sin Duda, 10.9km north of Xcalak, t in USA (415) 868 9925, *www.sinduda villas.com* (*moderate*). The most individual choice on this coast, a labour of love created by Robert Schneider and Margo Reheis. He designed the place himself, and the striking rooms are full of interesting touches; all are different, and run from spacious doubles to apartments and a *casita* with full kitchens. Robert and Margo are also hugely hospitable, and there's a beautifully sheltered beach. Diving, snorkelling, fishing, ruins visits and bird- and animal-seeking trips can all be arranged. Gorgeous, and very reasonably priced.

Tierra Maya, 3.5km north of Xcalak, t in USA 1 800 216 1902, *www.tierramaya.net* (*moderate*). Relaxing hotel with six very large suite-style rooms, with pretty Mexican furnishings and superb sea views. Three have fridges, and two full kitchens; there's also a **restaurant** open to non-guests, a great beach terrace, and a full range of diving, snorkelling or fishing.

The Leaky Palapa, north side of Xcalak village, *leakypalapa@yahoo.com* (*moderate*). A star find. In 2004 Canadians Linda and Maria took over this little place and brought to Xcalak imaginative cooking that's quite amazingly sophisticated for this remote spot, without losing their hut's bar-on-a-lost-island feel. Prices are low, too. It's usually open Nov–July only, evenings only every day except Wed. Email reservations are advisable.

Toby's Brisas del Mar, Xcalak village (*budget*). Tiny local restaurant where *sra* Luz Maria cooks up excellent fish.

Around Laguna Bacalar

Along the Highway south of the Mahahual turn, the forest scrub gives way a little to broader, more open spaces. After a while you glimpse flashes of water through the trees to the left, the Laguna Bacalar. Mexico's second-largest lake, 80km long, it is wholly fed by underground rivers. Its postcard name is *Laguna de Siete Colores*, the Lake of Seven Colours; whether that's the right number is up to you, but it can easily run from Prussian blue and deep grey to sandy blue, opal and bright turquoise.

About 15km south of the Mahahual road is the straggling roadside village of **Pedro Antonio de los Santos**, near which there is a little 'ecopark' by the lake, **Uchben Kah** This was set up with the participation of the people of San Antonio to provide an attraction for cruise-ship passengers from Mahahual. There's a nature walk through the forest, kayaks, a mountain bike tour and even ATVs, but

Uchben Kah
www.uchbenkahtours .com; usually open daily

it's charmingly low-key by the standards of Riviera ecoparks. Further down at **Buenavista**, more roads lead off to lakeside *balnearios* with simple restaurants. Between them Highway 307 meets the 283 road from Mérida and Peto, recently upgraded like so many others. A 9km detour up this road will take you to a Maya site at **Chacchobén** This is a very old site, its main structures all from the Early Classic, before AD 600. There are two massive pyramid platforms and an unusual long, thin plaza known as **Las Vasijas**, all in a plain, rounded Petén style, giving a powerful demonstration of the emphatic Maya sense of geometry and scale. On one side of the biggest pyramid, the enormous **Temple I**, a stucco frieze is being uncovered. Chacchobén is also a lovely, peaceful site, with plenty of wildlife. Some energetic young guides from nearby Chacchobén village have set up their own company, **The Native Choice** (*see* p.339), and an illuminating website, *www.chacchobenruins.com*.

Chacchobén
open daily 8–5; adm

Bacalar

🐚 Bacalar

From Buenavista, it's 35km to **Bacalar** itself, one of the most atmospherically tranquil small towns in the Yucatán, and with the only real castle in the peninsula. 'Salamanca de Bacalar' was founded in 1544 by 28 Spaniards led by Gaspar Pacheco, the first mayor of Mérida, who had marched south from Valladolid to subdue the Maya lordship of Chetumal. As a colonial town, however, Bacalar failed to develop, and was gradually abandoned. Spanish interest in the area revived after British pirates established themselves in modern Belize in the 1670s. In 1725 an unusually energetic governor of Yucatán, Antonio de Figueroa, ordered Bacalar's reoccupation as a bastion of Spanish power. He died of disease in the same campaign, but not before he had ordered the building of Bacalar castle, and brought 700 migrants from the Canary Islands to form a real colony. In spite of appearances there are channels that make it possible to sail from Lake Bacalar to Chetumal Bay, along an intricate route known as *El Recorrido de los Piratas* ('The Pirate Run'). Spanish boats could get from the lake out to sea, and the pirates could get in to attack, so the castle saw plenty of action.

After independence Bacalar, still the only *ladino* town in the whole of southern Quintana Roo, led a quiet life until the Caste War, when it was fought over several times. After the Cruzob established themselves in Chan Santa Cruz, Bacalar survived for a while, but in 1857 the Cross ordered a mass attack and the town fell to the Maya, with a massacre of *ladino* soldiers and civilians. Bacalar was not reoccupied until 1901.

Modern Bacalar doesn't feel at all like a military strongpost, but seems to gain an extra placidity from the lake, despite the widening of Highway 307 and increase in truck traffic. The town is long and thin, strung along a ridge between the highway and the water with one long main street, **Avenida 7,** leading to the necessary plaza,

Getting to Bacalar

Highway 307 skirts Bacalar town to the west; there are big turn-offs to the centre and the lake at the north and south ends. This road was upgraded and widened in 2007–8. There are two *gasolineras* along the Highway. *Intermedio* and second-class **buses** on the Chetumal–Cancún route all stop here, as do three **first-class** buses from Chetumal (*1hr;* fare $2). There are frequent *combis* from Chetumal.

where more cafés and restaurants are appearing now Bacalar has finally been (slightly) discovered by tourism. Along the lake shore below there is a positively genteel boulevard, the Costera Bacalar, from which some distinguished houses look out across the water, and at the north end there are traditional *balnearios*, lakeside areas where Mexican families go to swim. Several things make swimming here a blissful experience: the cavern-fed water is crystal-clear and wonderfully refreshing, the shallowness of the lake keeps it at a balmy temperature, and the absence of current makes the waters very gentle. The view is exquisite.

The castle, the **Fuerte de San Felipe de Bacalar**, is on the ridge above the lake-shore drive. It's an impressively squat and solid piece of 18th-century military engineering, with four massive bastions called, in Spanish fashion, after saints: San José, San Antonio, Santa Ana and San Joaquín. Around the walls there are several old cannon, once used against the pirates. Inside the castle is a local **museum**, with informative exhibits (in Spanish) and charming staff.

museum
open Tues–Sun 9–7; adm

To the south, the Costera ends at the **Cenote Azul**. This is one of the very largest Yucatán *cenotes*, a giant green pit with water 90m deep, overlooked by an enjoyable *palapa* restaurant. On weekdays there's rarely anyone around, but at weekends it's crowded with people from Chetumal out for the day, and teenage boys jumping into the water from the cliff-like edges. The *cenote* is also a growing attraction for cave divers. Another 12km or so further south is **Xul-Ha**, not long before Highway 307 meets the 186 road from Escárcega, where there's one last turn-off to the lake, down a bumpy road that ends on a bluff above the water, with a small restaurant.

Tourist Information and Services

t (983–)

There is no regular bank in Bacalar, but three **ATMs** on or near the main plaza. The nearest banks are in Chetumal. Handy sources of local information are *www.bacalarmosaico. com* and *http://bacalarhotels.com*. There are a few **internet cafés** near the town plaza, and **Sr Café** (*see* below) also acts as an informal info centre.

Where to Stay in Bacalar

Along the Costera in Bacalar signs often announce rooms to rent, and rentals can also be found through *www.bacalarmosaico.com*.

Rancho Encantado, off Highway 307 3km north of Bacalar, **t** 101 3358, **t** USA/Canada 1 800 505 6292, *www.encantado.com* (*expensive*). The longest running in Bacalar, with upscale *cabañas*, one a family -size villa, in a lakeside garden that's sadly no longer as peaceful as it was before the upgrading of the Highway. The **restaurant** (*moderate*) sits beneath a huge *palapa*. Retreat groups and yoga are specialities, as are trips to Maya sites. Prices are high for the area.

★ **Villas Ecotucan** >>

Amigo's B&B, Costera Bacalar, t in Cozumel (987) 872 3868, *www.bacalar.net* (*inexpensive*). With the same owners as Amigo's on Cozumel (*see* p.166), this guest house has a lovely location on the lake shore, about ½km south of the castle, and five attractive rooms with double beds, a/c and balconies with lake views. Breakfast and use of a lounge-TV room are included. It has its own landing-stage and free kayaks for guests, and can arrange boat tours of the lake. Also **kayak rental** for non-guests.

Casita Carolina, Costera Bacalar, t 834 2334, *www.casitacarolina.com* (*inexpensive*). Original lakeside guest house run with friendly enthusiasm by American Carolyn Niemeyer, with the feel of a home-from-home. She has three rooms in separate *casitas* and three in a main house, all pretty and with loads of extra comforts. Breakfast is not provided, but there's free coffee and an open kitchen. Carolyn is a painter, and hosts art weekends; there are kayaks for guests' use, and she provides all sorts of information.

★ **Hotel Laguna Bacalar** >

Hotel Laguna Bacalar, Costera Bacalar, t 834 2205, *www.hotellagunabacalar. com* (*inexpensive*). One of the great hotels of the Yucatán – at least in potential – the Laguna sums up the off-track appeal of Bacalar. It's also slighty nuts, in a very Mexican sort of way. On the lakeshore road by the south turn off Highway 307, it's hard to miss. In white and pastel Art Deco, it is arranged up a bluff between flower beds; then, by the pool there's a chapel with an image of Christ, and lots of coloured glass. There are rooms and bungalows of different sizes, with kitchenettes. The Laguna has sadly got a bit run down (especially the bungalows), and the widening of the Highway has intruded on its tranquill-ity, but it still has many pluses. The **restaurant** (*moderate*) has good local classics, and from all the rooms you get fabulous sunrises.

K'iin Yeetel Ha, Highway 307, 1km north of Bacalar, t 836 0257, *rarceos@ hotmail.com* (*inexpensive*). Charming little place just outside town with four roomy, well-ventilated *cabaña*-suites above the lake. Each has a fridge, and there's an open kitchen.

Villas Ecotucan, off Highway 307 5km north of Bacalar, t 834 2516, *www. villasecotucan.info* (*inexpensive*). A lovely, very peaceful 'ecohotel' by the lake, 1.5km down a track off the highway. For once it's genuinely 'eco', well thought-out and with five low-impact but comfortable *cabañas*, solar power and a botanical garden. There are very good facilities for children, and a little **restaurant** (*moderate*), under a *palapa*, and breakfast is included. Owners Arturo (Mexican) and Sophie (Canadian) are very charming and helpful, and provide kayaks, bikes and a big range of other activities. The forest around the villas teems with birds.

Laguna Azul, Pedro Antonio de los Santos, t 114 7002 (*budget*). Not far south of Pedro Antonio village a sign for Laguna Azul indicates a dirt track. After a bumpy 3.5km this leads to a lakeside *cabañas* and camping site set up by Swiss traveller Fritz Vatter. There's a choice of *cabañas* (astonish-ingly cosy, given the location), RV hook-ups or camping space. Solar power provides good showers. It's a very tranquil spot amidst forest and the lake, and you can rent kayaks or canoes. Take bug repellent. Allow time if you try to get in touch in advance.

El Paraíso-Botadero El Pastor, about 10km south of Bacalar (*budget*). Between the Km 11 and Km 10 markers on Highway 307 (which number from the south), a rough stone gateway on the lake-side of the road has signs for El Paraíso and/or Botadero El Pastor. This track leads in 1km to a magical spot on the lake, where a local family has turned an old *chicle*-tappers camp into a campsite. You can sleep in one of their tents or hammocks, under *palapas*, or bring your own; toilets and showers are basic, but there's a kitchen. There's also an orchid garden, and free kayaks, and it's possible to arrange kayak tours such as a trip through the *Recorrido de los Piratas*, the pirate route to Chetumal Bay.

Eating Out in Bacalar

Restaurants are now multiplying in Bacalar. The long-running lakeside *balnearios* are still great for lunch, offering mostly grilled fish or seafood: best is the big **Balneario Bacalar Mágico** (*moderate–budget*), with wonderful *ceviches* and a fine place from which to watch everyone swimming. **Hotel Laguna Bacalar** has lake views and good Yucatecan food (*moderate*), and at Cenote Azul, **Restaurante Cenote Azul** (*moderate*) is a big, traditional place under a *palapa*. **Los Aluxes**, Costera Bacalar, (*moderate*). Laid-back restaurant with a big Yucatecan menu in an irresistible location under a *palapa* right by the water's edge, ideal for watching moonlight over the lake. It also now has pretty *cabañas* (*inexpensive*). **Señor Café**, Av. 5, on the main plaza (*budget*). Attractive modern café with good coffee and snacks.

Chetumal

 Chetumal

Chetumal, state capital of Quintana Roo, sits beneath fan palms and giant laurel trees on the banks of the Río Hondo, northernmost river on this side of the Yucatán peninsula and the frontier with Belize. It is still the capital even though Cancún is now a great deal bigger and busier. Long isolated from the rest of the country, it is a very Caribbean town, with clapboard houses with painted wooden porches and tin roofs, wide streets, open skies and a very Caribbean pace.

The frontier-town location is an essential aspect of Chetumal. This is where most of Belize comes to shop, and on most days there will be some Belizeans along the main street, from black families talking *patois*-English to very white Mennonites talking old German. To aid border areas in the 1940s the Mexican government gave them a variety of duty-free concessions, and this became the best place in the whole of southern Mexico to find foreign goods at bargain prices: Japanese electronics, American sunglasses, Dutch cheeses. This trading attracted people from many parts of the world, which with the Belizean influence means that this is one of the most ethnically mixed towns in Mexico. It also attracted a cast of eccentrics fit for a lost town by a hot river, from the adventurer-archaeologist Thomas Gann in the 1930s to an aristocratic English lady who befriended everybody in town. Modern Chetumal has a very good museum of Maya culture, but its greatest attraction is its amiable atmosphere, its ultra-laid-back air. It makes a great base for visiting the whole region.

History

Chetumal is one of the nicest towns founded on a drunken afternoon. In 1898 the Mexican navy, aided by the newly co-operative authorities of British Honduras, towed an armoured barge, the *Chetumal*, into the Río Hondo. Commanded by Commandant Othon P. Blanco, its mission was to re-establish Mexican sovereignty on the border. After making a few forays onto land and not finding much resistance, his men built a small stockade. Corozal in northern Belize was full of Yucatecan Caste War refugees, who had lived there for years. Part of Blanco's brief was to begin the repopulation of the north bank with Mexican citizens, and for the patriotic holiday of 5 May he invited prominent members of the Corozal Yucatecan community and several British officers to lunch aboard the *Chetumal*. The party were so inspired by Blanco's rhetoric that it was decided that they should head for land, the British included, and found a town at the stockade. First called **Payo Obispo** (Bishop's Point), its earliest residents included Mexicans, Belizeans and German and English wanderers.

Blanco tried to deal with the Cruz Maya peacefully, unlike his genocidal successor General Bravo. Following Bravo's conquest of the Cruzob in 1901 the centre of administration moved to Chan Santa Cruz, but in 1915 it returned to Payo Obispo. In 1936, at the height of Mexico's nationalist 'cultural revolution', its name was changed to Chetumal, like the barge. Both recall the Maya lordship of *Chetumal* or *Chectemal*, which, aided by Gonzalo Guerrero (*see* p.48), fiercely resisted the Spaniards in the 1530s. However, Maya Chetumal was probably located at Oxtankah (*see* p.353), or even south of the Río Hondo near Corozal in Belize, rather than on the site of today's town.

Major events in Chetumal's recent history have been hurricanes, most of all Janet, *La Juanita*, in 1955, compared to which 2007's Dean was a minor blast. It was also struck by a hurricane of another sort in the NAFTA agreement, which cut back its duty-free status. This hit Chetumal hard, and tourism is pushed as a possible solution.

Héroes and the Malecón

The most impressive thing about Avenida de los Héroes, Chetumal's prime thoroughfare, is its range of shops with gaudily painted signs, the number of them selling exactly the same thing, and their still more extraordinary amount of stock. Chetumal caters for all human needs, and does so in bulk. The centre of activity is the **old market**, at Héroes and Av. E. Aguilar, a marvellous bazaar of dense alleyways.

As you walk down Héroes towards the bay there's a distinguished building on the right, by Av. Héroes de Chapultepec, the Belisario Domínguez school from 1936–8, a fine example of Revolution-era architecture with a frieze bravely identifying it as an *Escuela Socialista*. This is now the **Centro Cultural de las Bellas Artes**, which contains exhibition spaces, a **bookshop** and the **Museo de la Ciudad**, an entertaining display on the city's brief but eventful history.

Museo de la Ciudad
open Tues–Sun 9–7; adm

Most of the rest of Héroes, rebuilt after different hurricanes, is made up of concrete, but in the streets alongside, especially Av. 5 de Mayo, there are still many of the old clapboard, porched houses that make parts of Chetumal look very un-Mexican. Héroes ends in

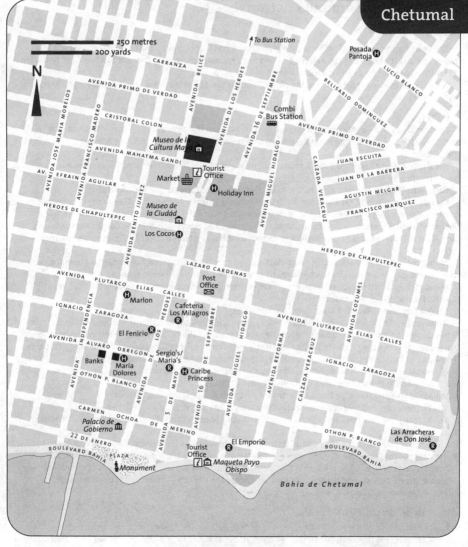

a wide plaza, shaded by massive laurel trees, at the **Malecón** or Bay Boulevard, the waterfront. In front of you there's a tall clocktower, and beyond that a view across the broad, green Río Hondo to Belize, an unbroken line of trees in the distance. The largest presence here is the **Palacio de Gobierno**, the Quintana Roo state government, an attractive 1950s building with Caribbean-style arcades.

At dusk, a welcome breeze comes in off the river, and a large part of the town comes down to meet up and enjoy it in the evening *paseo*. This is also the time to experience not a sight, but one of the sounds of Chetumal, as hundreds of birds roost in the laurels, producing a tropical cacophony that's truly astonishing. A block to

Getting to and around Chetumal

By Air

The small airport is just west of town off Av. Obregón. It has flights only to and from Mexico City, with **MexicanaClick, t** 01 800 112 5425, **Aviacsa, t** 01 800 284 2272, and **Aeroméxico Connect, t** 01 800 800 2376, each of which has one flight daily in each direction.

Only **airport cabs** may take you from the airport into Chetumal, but they're as cheap as ordinary taxis in many towns.

By Bus

Chetumal bus station (ADO first- or second-class) is far from the centre, on Av. Insurgentes near the junction with Av. Héroes. From there, take a taxi into town (they're very cheap). There are luggage lockers at the station.

Bacalar (*1hr*): three first-class daily (8.30am, 2.30pm, 11.45pm), and frequent *intermedios* and second-class. First-class fare $2.

Campeche (*6¼hrs*): one first-class, two second-class daily via **Escárcega**. First-class fare $20.

Cancún (*5–6hrs*): two ADO GL and regular first-class buses at least once an hour daily; many long-distance buses to Cancún pass through Chetumal during the night. During the day, there are also at least 13 Mayab *intermedio* and more second-class buses. Most first-class and all others stop at **Felipe Carrillo Puerto, Tulum** and **Playa del Carmen**, and all *intermedio* and second-class buses stop at **Bacalar**. First-class fares to Cancún $17–21.

Mahahual (*2½hrs*) via **Bacalar**: three first-class daily, at 5am, 2.30pm, 7.30pm; fare about $6. There are also two second-class buses daily (6am, 4pm) which carry on to **Xcalak** (*4hrs*). Fare is about $7.

Mérida (*6½hrs*): four first-class, seven or more *intermedios* and seven second-class daily, via **Ticul, Peto, Carrillo Puerto**. First-class fare $22.

Mexico City (*20hrs*): two first-class daily. Fare about $74.

Palenque (*6–7hrs*): three standard OCC first-class daily (8.20pm, 9.50pm, 2.20am) and one ADO GL (11.50pm) via **Escárcega**. All continue on to **San Cristóbal de Las Casas** (*12hrs*), the OCC buses via a stop in Ocosingo. The three evening buses then go on to **Tuxtla Gutiérrez** (*13hrs*); the 2.20am OCC bus goes on from San Cristóbal to **Comitán** and **Tapachula** (*20hrs*). Fares around $23–27 Palenque, $33–40 San Cristóbal, $37–44 Tuxtla.

Río Hondo: one second-class daily to **Unión**; also three daily to **Tomás Garrido** and **Tres Garantías**. *Colectivos* run more often to all these destinations, from the *combi* station.

Valladolid (*5–6hrs*) via **Felipe Carrillo Puerto** and **Tihosuco**: five or six second-class daily.

Villahermosa (*8–9hrs*): five first-class daily via **Escárcega**. Fare about $27.

Xpuhil (*2hrs*): 3–8 first-class and several second-class daily. Some second-class buses go on to **Zoh-Laguna**. First-class fare $6.

Chetumal is unusual in having a *Combi* station (corner of Avenidas Primo de Verdad and Miguel Hidalgo), two blocks east of Av. Héroes. *Combis* run to virtually every village in the region, especially Bacalar, Luís Echeverría and Chetumal Bay, the Tomás Garrido–Tres Garantías road, and the Río Hondo. *Combis* also leave from the streets outside, and some buses to villages near the city run from behind the market, at Av. Juárez/Av. Mahatma Gandhi.

Buses to Belize and Guatemala

Plenty of buses run to Belize from Chetumal, operated by various Belizean companies. From the main bus station, **Premier Line** (the best, but still not as comfortable as Mexican first-class buses) has three buses daily usually at 10.45am, 1.45am, 4.45pm to **Corozal** (*1hr*), **Orange Walk** (*2½hrs*) and **Belize City** (*3hrs*). The fare to Belize City is about $9. **NTSL's** more basic, a/c-free buses run five times daily on the same route, from the main station, for around $5–6.50, and clanky old buses run about every half-hour across the border to **Corozal** from the **Mercado Nuevo** (Mercado Lázaro Cárdenas) at the corner of Calzada Veracruz and Av. Confederación Nacional Campesina, north of the centre.

Two Guatemalan companies, **Linea Dorada** (*www.tikalmayanworld.com*) and **San Juan**, have two or three buses daily between them to **Flores** (for **Tikal**, *8hrs*) via **Belize**, from the main bus station. The fare on Linea Dorada (the most comfortable) is about $35–40.

By Car and Taxi

Chetumal streets are wide enough to make driving easy, and parking is less restricted than in most Mexican cities. There are several *gasolineras* on the main road from the west. Taxis are the main form of local transport: any ride within Chetumal costs around 12 pesos. Cab drivers seem very honest here.

Car Hire

There are only a few car hire companies, and rates are relatively high. It's better to hire a car in Mérida, Cancún or Playa. There is another car rental desk at **Hotel Los Cocos**, and **Perico's Tours** (*see* p.351) has rental cars. **Continental**, Holiday Inn Lobby, t 832 2411, *www.continentalcar.com.mx*. A good choice of cars, from $42 a day. **Frontier Rentacar**, Av. Juárez 298, corner Av. Justo Sierra, t 129 2488, *www.rentacarfrontier.com*. Local agency with cars, jeeps and vans, from $40 a day. Also tours, to Bacalar and Maya ruins.

Orientation

Chetumal is a sprawling town of broad avenues. Highway 307 meets Highway 186 from Escárcega south of Lake Bacalar 19km from the city, and enters Chetumal from the west. It becomes a broad boulevard, **Av. Insurgentes**, which runs around the north side of town. On this road, just as you enter the city, there's a big junction with an exit right marked *Centro*. This becomes **Av. Alvaro Obregón**, which runs to the town centre. The main street is **Av. de los Héroes**, which runs back from the river, and crosses Obregón. Héroes also meets the **Malecón** or Boulevard de la Bahía, the attractive drive that skirts the river eastwards.

Maqueta Payo Obispo
open daily 9–6

the east by Av. 16 de Septiembre a large sign announces the Maqueta Payo Obispo. In a curious clapboard pavilion, this is a scale model of Payo Obispo in the 1920s, all made by one elderly local citizen with the very Chetumal name of Luis Reinhardt McLiberty. Further on round the boulevard there are restaurants, with terraces ideally placed to make the most of the view and the evening air.

The Museo de la Cultura Maya

Museo de la Cultura Maya
Open Tues–Sun 9–7, until 8pm Fri, Sat; adm

Chetumal's museum of Maya culture is an impressive, slab-like modern building in the next block from the market on Av. Héroes. It differs from other museums in the region in that it has few original Maya artefacts. Instead, it seeks to present and explain Maya civilization through imaginative modern displays. The layout itself represents the three-level Maya conception of the universe – the heavens, the physical world and *Xibalba* – and cosmology, agriculture and glyph writing are all covered. It's a very enlightening overview of the Maya world, well labelled in Spanish and English. The museum also hosts exhibitions on Maya and local themes.

Excursions from Chetumal

As a small city Chetumal can still seem dominated by the lush nature around it, the reverse of what happens in most cities. Nearby there are still swathes of primary rainforest and untouched wetlands, some parts of which are at least partly accessible.

The Manatee Reserve

Chetumal bay contains one of the world's largest surviving populations of the manatee, a mangrove-dwelling aquatic mammal, like a slow-moving seal, which is one of only three related species in the world, collectively known as sea cows. The all-but-uninhabited northern end of the bay has been made into a manatee reserve.

Getting to the Manatee Reserve and Río Hondo

The Manatee Reserve

There are surprisingly few regular manatee-watching trips. **Villa Manatí** (*see* p.351) currently has the most regular tours, for about $10 per person, and Chetumal's tourist offices are places to ask if any more are around, even though their information may be incomplete. Manatee tours can sometimes be arranged through Uchben Kah park near Bacalar (*see* p.341). Independently, you can enquire at the **Club Naútico**, by the Terminal Marítima on the Malecón, if fishing or manatee-seeking trips can be arranged, or if you get to the village of Luís Echeverría, up the bay north of Calderitas, you may find fishermen willing to take visitors to the manatee grounds. Prices are a matter of negotiation.

The Río Hondo

'Tourist infrastructure' here is virtually nonexistent, for there are no hotels, nor even many *loncherías*, but if you make your way to **La Unión** you can ask around for local guides (second-class buses and *combis* run from Chetumal). Easier alternatives are offered by **Villa Manatí** and sometimes other agencies (*see* p.351). Trips can be tailored to your requirements, and can include kayaking on the river, *cenotes*, forest treks with village guides, horse riding and camping in the jungle. Tours are not usually run in the rainy season (*late June–Oct*).

Tres Garantías

Campamento La Pirámide. The 'camp' is in the forest some way from the village, and consists of simple but decent *cabañas*, with showers. Guests can take walks with local guides, and meals are cooked by women who come out from Tres Garantías village. English-speaking biologists who work with the *ejido* may also be around to translate. It's now difficult to get in touch with the village directly, so it's best to ask around first with Villa Manatí, other tour offices and at Chetumal tourist office (but be prepared to be told they know nothing about it). Second-class buses and frequent *combis* run to Tres Garantías. Plenty of bug repellent is a must.

Manatees are notoriously timid and dislike any disturbance; the best chance of seeing them is during a flat calm; if there's any swell, they'll be totally invisible. The best season is from October to January, and it's best to set out in the early morning.

The Río Hondo and Tres Garantías

About 10km west of the crossing into Belize (*see* below) at **Subteniente López**, the Río Hondo, still the frontier but increasingly narrow, swings due southwest. A paved road runs with it from Ucum on Highway 186 for 90km down to **La Unión**, last village on the Mexican side. Near the top of this road villages extend along the river, but as you go on you enter scarcely touched rainforest. Toucans, parrots and monkeys are common, and even the elusive jaguar sighting is possible. The river is fast-flowing, with some dramatic rapids, and there are spectacular jungle *cenotes*, especially the **Cenote Encantado**. Kayaking, hiking and camping trips on and around the Río Hondo are becoming more accessible, through agencies like **Villa Manatí** (*see* p.351).

Further west is one of the region's oldest ecotourism schemes at **Tres Garantías**, an *ejido* village 45km south of Highway 186 from a turning 70km west of Chetumal. In the 1980s the villagers took the brave decision, advised by local ecologists, not to cut down the forest on their land but to try to manage it to ensure its conservation. As part of this they built some *cabañas* out in the rainforest itself. It's now difficult to contact the village direct, but it is still functioning. Tapirs, monkeys, ocelots and jaguars are found nearby, and there's a fabulous range of birds.

Tourist Information in Chetumal

t (983–)

Tourist offices: Chetumal has quite helpful (if erratically open) tourist offices, one on Av. Héroes in front of the Museo de la Cultura Maya, and one by the river on Boulevard de la Bahía, next to the Maqueta Payo Obispo. They have a good range of information on local tours, and can help with bookings for some. Both are officially open Mon–Fri and Sun 9–8, Sat 9–2, but these hours seem a little theoretical, and they often close for lunch on weekdays and open late on Sat. Information in English is available on *www.chetumalmosaico.com*.

Tours and tour agencies

If you don't want to hire a car, tours are the easiest way to get to the more distant Maya sites and other attractions, and many local travel agencies offer tours to ruins such as Kohunlich. Less obvious, more adventurous routes are often harder to locate: visitor numbers here are still relatively small and intermittent, so adventure and ecotour companies find it hard to do consistent business, and often fold not long after setting up. However, others are always giving it a try, and it's worth checking on what's currently available. The tourist office itself sometimes organizes trips such as boat cruises on the Río Hondo, and should have information on any other adventure tours currently available.

Perico's Tours, C. Manuel Acuña 109, **t** 839 1100, *www.lagunabacalarweb. com/pericos*. Tours of the Costa Maya and Maya ruins, car rental and vehicle transfers all around the region.

Villa Manatí, Blvd de la Bahia 301, **t** 129 3204, *rruiza@grupodomos.com.mx*. Enterprising group with an exciting catalogue of options, as one-day or longer tours: ruins tours, inshore and deep-sea fishing, kayaking, Bacalar by boat on the 'pirate route' creeks and – particular specialities – boat trips, jungle hikes and camping on the Río Hondo, or boat tours of Chetumal Bay, with the possibility of seeing manatees. Can also be found through *www.chetumalmosaico.com*.

Services in Chetumal

Banks: Several near the junction of Av. Héroes and Av. Obregón, with ATMs. Many Chetumal banks do not change travellers' cheques, or are very slow in doing so. There are many *cambios* along Av. Héroes, which specialize in changing Belizean dollars, and there is also an exchange desk at the bus station. If you come in from Belize it's a good idea to change any leftover currency in Chetumal.

Consulates: Guatemalan Consulate, Av. Héroes de Chapultepec (not the same as Av. Héroes) 356, **t** 832 3045; **Belizean Consulate,** Av. Armada de México 91, **t** 832 1803.

Internet Access: Ciber-Net, Av. Héroes, next to the Holiday Inn; **Cyber Coatl,** Av. 5 de Mayo between Obregón and Othon P. Blanco.

Phone Office: there is a long-distance phone office on Av. I Zaragoza, corner of Av. Héroes.

Post Office: Av. Plutarco Elías Calles, corner of Av. 5 de Mayo (*open Mon–Fri 8–7, Sat 9–1*). The **Mexpost** office is beside the main one.

Shopping

Shopping in Chetumal is a way of life for the people of Belize, and this could be a place to stock up on cheap goods from shoes to leather goods, cooking pots, bright things in plastic and other Mexicana. If you're planning a picnic, the **food market** is inside the market on Av. Héroes. The bookshop in the **Centro de Bellas Artes** is good for books on the Maya.

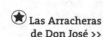

Las Arracheras
de Don José >>

Where to Stay in Chetumal

A luxury option in this area is the **Explorean** 'adventure hotel' near Kohunlich (*see* p.358).

Moderate

Holiday Inn Chetumal Puerta Maya, Av. Héroes 171-A, t 835 0400, *www.holiday-inn.com/chetumalmex*. Opposite the museum, this has the reliable if conventional standards usual in Holiday Inns, which makes it stand out in Chetumal. Prices are very reasonable, and as it caters mainly to business guests there are often even better weekend offers. Plus the staff are friendly and helpful, the **restaurant** is impressive, and the creature comforts are great.

Hotel Los Cocos, Av. Héroes 134, t 835 0430, *www.hotelloscocos.com.mx*. Two blocks from the Holiday Inn, Chetumal's 'other' main hotel is more individual. Successive renovations have actually made it less attractive – reducing the size of garden and pool to add more rooms, and enclosing most of the very popular terrace **restaurant** in an air-conditioned box – but in return the rooms are comfortable and well-equipped, and very good value

Inexpensive

Hotel Caribe Princess, Av. Obregón 168, t 832 0900, *caribe_princess@hotmail.com*. Very popular hotel, centrally located on Obregón. Its now rather-dazzling lobby has been made over more recently than the pastel-coloured rooms, but they're big, airy, light, comfortable and well looked-after, and all have phones, cable TV and good a/c.

Hotel Marlon, Av. Juárez 87, t 832 1065, *hotel_marlon@hotmail.com*. Large-ish (40 rooms, 10 suites), pink-and-pastel modern hotel that's very central. Facilities aren't as shiny-new as they seem at first sight, but among its comforts are a small pool, a bar and a **restaurant**, and it has a nicely friendly feel. The owners also have two other hotels, the **Grand Marlon**, Av. Juárez 88, and **Marlon Héroes**, Av. Héroes 368, which similarly are not as grand as they look, but still pleasant.

Budget

Hotel María Dolores, Av. Alvaro Obregón 206, t 832 0508. Backpacker's stand-by and the best budget choice in the centre, with plain, fan-only rooms that have plenty of mileage on the clock but are well looked-after. It also has a likeable **restaurant** for breakfast.

Posada Pantoja, C. Lucio Blanco 95, t 832 1781. The most comfortable budget hotel, with very clean, neat rooms with fans or a/c, good bathrooms and (in some) TVs. The owners are very obliging. It's some way from the centre (corner of Av. General H. Lara), but this means it's peaceful.

Eating Out in Chetumal

Moderate

Las Arracheras de Don José, Blvd de la Bahía, corner of Av. OP Blanco. One of several places on the bay boulevard where you can sit out to enjoy the breeze, with fabulous *fajitas* and Mexican classics, so you can eat a lot or a little, and pay more or very little, as you wish. Popular, and very enjoyable.

El Cocal, Hotel Los Héroes, Av. Héroes 134. Los Cocos's terrace restaurant is a centre of local life, even though its new mostly-enclosed design makes it less good for people watching. Rich Yucatecan dishes are also an attraction.

El Emporio, Av. Carmen Ochoa de Merino 106. A novelty in Chetumal – an Uruguayan steakhouse, ideal for real meat-eaters. It's housed in an old wooden house, with a porch, that's a charming reminder of the old town from before several hurricanes.

Mahahuana, Blvd de la Bahía, corner of Av. PE Calles. A rather hip, buzzing terrace bar and restaurant on the bay boulevard, very popular with young *chetumaleños*, with enjoyable *arrachera* steaks, *gringas* and other Mexican classics, and DJs and sometimes live bands.

AC Sergio's, Av. Obregón 182, t 832 2355. Food is a bargain in Chetumal, and Sergio's Pizzas is its foremost restaurant (also, inexplicably, known as María's). It's a neat, cosy and rather eccentrically smart little haven, with stained-glass windows, dark woodwork, charming service and a/c, still at *moderate* prices. You can have pizzas, steaks, or a refined range of Mexican and Yucatecan dishes – especially good seafood with tropical seasonings. Excellent for breakfast.

Budget

Cafetería Los Milagros, Av. I. Zaragoza, just east of Av. Héroes. A coffee-specialist with a big shady terrace, where many local gents go to play cards and dominoes. Also a great place for bargain breakfasts.

El Fenicio Super & Restaurante, Av. Héroes, corner of Av. I. Zaragoza. Travellers' stand-by, serving Mexican and Yucatecan standards (including sizable breakfasts) around the clock, and with a 24hr **supermarket**. Its food is more satisfying than interesting.

Into Belize

The international bridge across the Río Hondo into Belize is in **Subteniente López**, 8km west of Chetumal, well indicated off the highway. This is one of the world's more humble border crossings, with a big, old iron bridge, although the customs buildings on the Mexican side look more impressive than those in Belize. For their part, the Belize authorities have set up a duty-free 'free zone' south of the bridge, with a shopping mall and a **casino**. Such a thing is still illegal in Mexico, but it's much visited by Chetumal locals, and travel agents offer tours. Note that Mexican rental cars cannot usually be taken into Belize. For immigration requirements, *see* p.101.

Maya Sites in Southern Quintana Roo

In the most widely known accounts of Maya civilization, southern Quintana Roo scarcely figured. Its most important Maya city, Kohunlich, was only discovered in 1967, and then by accident. In the 1990s, excavations multiplied, and more has been discovered since then than in all the region's earlier archaeological history.

Oxtankah

Oxtankah
Open daily 8–5; adm.

The road north of Chetumal through Calderitas along the bay shore (not the wider road that veers inland) eventually becomes a winding lane through a landscape of explosive vegetation, with fan palms, fields of horses and zebu cattle, and the milky-green waters of the bay off to the right. It then becomes an (easily passable) dirt track, which leads in 5km to the ruins of **Oxtankah**. The site was discovered in 1913, but only extensively excavated in the 1990s. It is of special interest because it was occupied for a very long time. Its largest structures are from the Early and Late Classic, but were built, Maya-fashion, over much older buildings; abandoned after 800, it was resettled in the 14th–15th centuries, attracting the attention of the Spaniards, who tried to found a settlement of their own here at the time of the Conquest.

Oxtankah is laid out to combine a ruins visit with a nature walk, and you approach the site along a delightful path through the woods. The largest excavated structure is the first you come to, **Plaza de las Abejas** (Plaza of the Bees), an impressive Petén-influenced plaza with a pyramid, **Structure IV**, facing the sunrise, and smaller platforms on two other sides. Beside the plaza there is also the unique **Structure I**, with steps only in one corner. To the south, a well-cleared path leads to the **Plaza de las Columnas**, another large Classic-era plaza; down a branch off the same path is the site's small *cenote*, still almost lost in the jungle. On the way back, to the north of Las Abejas, there is a very different structure, the ruins of an abandoned **Franciscan chapel**. This was not recorded in church archives and has given rise to a great deal of mystery, but it is now believed it was built by the expedition of Alonso Dávila, one of the Montejos' lieutenants, who tried to establish a settlement somewhere near Chetumal in 1531. It was abandoned after two years of struggling against the surrounding Maya, and was not reoccupied even when the Spaniards conquered this area 15 years later.

Dzibanché and Kinichná

Dzibanché and Kinichná

Both open 8–5; adm. Same ticket admits you to both sites.

Dzibanché and Kinichná are two more sites, far grander than Oxtankah, that were only opened up in the late 1990s. Dzibanché was first explored in 1927 by Thomas Gann, who gave it this name, Yucatec for 'written on the walls', owing to its remarkable wooden lintels, some of the oldest and best-preserved Maya woodcarvings. The smaller Kinichná is about 2km away, but it is now thought that with other unexcavated complexes nearby they both formed part of one dispersed community, rather like Cobá. The imposing size of their pyramids indicate that this was a powerful state throughout the Classic era, from about 300 until the 8th century. Southern Quintana Roo, like the Río Bec further west, was an important channel in the flow of contact and trade between the Classic Maya heartland in the south and northern Yucatán. Dzibanché's massive architecture, like that of Kohunlich, suggests that from the Early Classic (AD 250–600) these cities had many links with the Petén, and there is strong inscription evidence that Dzibanché was particularly closely connected to Calakmul. Like other cities in the region, Dzibanché (a name now often used for the whole city) entered into a decline later than cities further south, around 850.

Just beyond the hut on the Dzibanché road a whole separate, slightly Río Bec-style temple-platform has been excavated, an indication of the complexity and richness of the whole site. As you arrive at **Dzibanché** itself you initially see nothing but vegetation, but the ruins take shape as you walk up through the trees. This is one of the most beautiful of Maya sites, and one of the best places to see tropical birds.

Getting to Oxtankah, Dzibanché-Kinichná and Kohunlich

Getting around these sites is easy **by car**: Oxtankah is 6km up a continuation of the road through Calderitas; Dzibanché, Kinichná and Kohunlich are all easy to find off Highway 186, the road west from Chetumal into Campeche. About 50km west of Chetumal, not far beyond the village of Nachi Cocom, a paved road, well-signposted for **Dzibanché** and **Kinichná**, turns north through fields of maize and sugar cane to Morocoy (15km). Another 5km beyond this village the road divides: the main track continues 2km to Dzibanché, while Kinichná is up a fork to the right. You have to stop at the junction, as this is where you'll find the warden's hut for the two sites, with cold drinks on sale.

Back on the Highway, the turn south for **Kohunlich** is another 10km west near Francisco Villa, and the ruins are 9km south.

It is impossible, though, to get to them directly **by bus**: buses toward Oxtankah only go as far as Calderitas, and buses west only stop on the highway; there are *combis* to Morocoy, but this is still several km from Dzibanché. One possibility is to take a *combi* to the nearest villages (Morocoy, Francisco Villa) and then a village taxi to the ruins.

The last petrol/gas station going west before Xpuhil is in Ucúm, 26km from Chetumal.

The core area of Dzibanché is made up of three giant connecting **plazas**, each at a different level. This is one of the truly monumental Maya cities, a theatrical complex of massive, glowering pyramids built with an extraordinary sense of scale, their size now magnified by the towering trees. As you walk up the hill, the first large building you come to on the left in the first plaza, is the towering pyramid-platform known as **Structure VI** or the **Building of the Lintels**. Astoundingly it still contains its original wooden lintels found by Gann, including one dated 618. The base of the platform dates from the Early Classic, while upper levels were added between 600 and 800. In this case the Maya skill in adding layer on layer seems to have wavered, as at the back it can be seen that extra buttresses had to be added to keep the upper levels stable. Fresh excavations have been carried out recently at Structure VI (which you can no longer climb up), exposing some tunnels and a temple with stucco panels. Forming another side of the square is **Structure XVI**, with a battered monster-mask in its façade. It is dual-fronted, with a second façade on the Main Plaza.

Dzibanché's **Main Plaza**, reached by a climb from the first square, is one of the largest of all Maya squares, and standing on it is the tallest of all the city's buildings, the huge pyramid of **Structure II**, another with a dual façade. At the top of its steps there are two levels of galleried chambers. The top one has carved stone lintels, while the bottom one has three Maya-arched chambers. In one a man's tomb was found, with rich adornments and offerings. He has been dubbed the 'Lord of Dzibanché' and was almost certainly one of its *ahauob*. Opposite across the plaza is **Structure XIII** or the **Building of the Captives**, an Early Classic platform with a stucco 'mask' of a spirit-monster on one side of its main stairway, and glyph inscriptions on the steps. One of these panels, which gave the structure its name, has a carving of a captive taken by a lord identified by the *Kaan* or 'snake' glyph associated with the lords of Calakmul, but is dated no later than 518, over a century before the earliest record of it at Calakmul. This has led to a theory that Calakmul's ruling dynasty may originally have been from Dzibanché. Behind Structure II, the third, smaller plaza is less excavated and more of a scramble, but has another awe-inspiring pyramid, **Structure I** or **Pirámide del Buho** ('Pyramid of the Owl'), a giant tower with an extremely steep staircase.

Kinichná really consists of just one building, the **Acropolis**, facing a plaza. This building, though, is huge. Effectively three structures in one, it's a vast temple platform, made up of three complete levels from different eras, and climbing up it in the sweaty heat makes you think the Maya were a very masochistic culture.

The massive, squat base (**Level A**) was built fairly crudely in the Preclassic, and is in poor condition. More sophisticated masonry and recognizable temples begin at **Level B**, above it. It has all the sense of geometry and symmetry of Maya architecture, with a dramatic central staircase facing a 'plaza' on the top of Level A, and flanked by twin temples with monster-masks, in poor condition. This staircase in turn leads to **Level C**, another complete pyramid (and giant staircase) on top of B, probably built around 600. At its top there is a temple that contained the tomb of two people who were buried with some of the richest Maya jade offerings ever found. There was also an effigy of the sun god, the origin of the name *Kinichná*, or 'House of the Sun'.

Kohunlich

☻ Kohunlich
Open daily 8–5; adm

Kohunlich ruins were discovered in 1967 by a local Maya, Ignacio Ek, whose family were for years the site caretakers. Kohunlich is one of the grandest of the lesser-known Maya cities, and one of the sites where most has been revealed by ongoing excavations, adding continually to its fascination. Like Dzibanché it was a major centre for a long time, from around AD 300 to 900. It's also one of the sites that gives most food for the imagination, with a strong feel of having been a real community, and made all the more impressive by an astonishing location. As you reach the end of the entry road you are enclosed by huge palms, an extraordinary jungle vision.

A path has been created that takes you in a circuit around the site. As you come in you have a choice, between going left into the great main square, the **Plaza de las Estelas**, or beginning the circuit anti-clockwise to the right. Immediately to your left is a small raised plaza, ringed by buildings with many small rooms. Known as the **North-West Residential Complex** and a focus of recent excavations, this gives you first sight of one of the intriguing 'enigmas' of Kohunlich (also, but less visibly, seen at Dzibanché). In most Maya cities it has been assumed that only royal and élite lineages lived in stone buildings, while the mass of the population lived in wood-and-palm *nas*. Dzibanché, Kohunlich and some Río Bec sites, on the other hand, have a high number of solid, stone

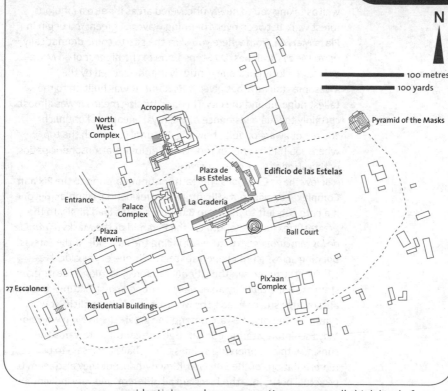

N

100 metres
100 yards

Acropolis

North West Complex

Pyramid of the Masks

Plaza de las Estelas

Edificio de las Estelas

Entrance

Palace Complex

La Gradería

Plaza Merwin

Ball Court

27 Escalones

Pix'aan Complex

Residential Buildings

residential complexes, suggesting an unusually high level of prosperity, or even a more 'democratic' distribution of wealth. There is even evidence that this North-West Complex was lived in by artisans, perhaps master potters.

At the paths' junction is the giant agglomeration of the **Palace Complex** (Structure B2), the temple-residence that forms the western side of the main square. Filling the north side of the plaza is Kohunlich's main pyramid, the **Acropolis** (B1). It's an untidy structure that was built over many times, and although mainly a temple platform it too has a residential complex on the top, which would have been invisible from the square below, in a vivid contrast between private intimacy and public grandeur. Part of the pyramid had an impossibly steep 'false staircase' in Río Bec style, but this was buried under later additions. Across the plaza is the structure known as the **Gradería** (B3) or grandstand, a 100m-long ramp of steps. The Plaza de las Estelas takes its name from the stelae on a small platform near the building on its east side, the **Edificio de las Estelas** (B4). The stelae at Kohunlich are in poor condition, so it has not yet been given a dynastic history. The Edificio de las Estelas is one more Maya hodge-podge, assembled over centuries, with a second façade facing the Masks pyramid.

Turn back through the plaza to take the path around the site. As well as taking you to newly uncovered areas it's also a fabulous forest walk, between overwhelming waves of green. You begin in **Plaza Merwin**, from where you skirt the site to come dramatically up to the **27 Escalones** ('27 Steps'), one of the biggest of all Maya palaces. Its location alone is hugely grand: reached by the awesome stairway that gives it its name, it was built on to the tallest ridge around the city. This, and its size, means it was almost certainly the main residence of the royal lineage of Kohunlich. You're not aware of quite how big it is until you reach the top, where you find a series of rooms and intimate, atmospheric patios, with a strong sense of exclusivity.

Below the 27 Escalones the path continues around to the **Pix'aan Complex**, a smaller but still impressive residential complex. Beyond it a path cuts left to the main **Ball Court**. Paths lead finally to the greatest treasure at Kohunlich, the **Pyramid of the Masks** (*Pirámide de los Mascarones*, Structure A1), facing the east side of the Estelas building across a broad open space. This is one of the oldest surviving structures in the city, built before 500. Alongside its giant staircase – sheltered by an equally giant *palapa*-structure – there are six huge stucco heads, the **Mascarones de Kohunlich**. Now a symbol of the city, they are among the greatest surviving works of Maya sculpture, staring out through the centuries towards the sunset, with an unnerving stillness. They have been said to be representations of the Sun God, Kinich Ahau, but they also seem to be actual portraits – the faces are all different, and very individual – of the ruling lineage of Kohunlich. Astonishingly, the heads were partly covered by a later stage of building in the Late Classic, stripped away in modern excavations.

North of the Masks Pyramid a path leads to the largest of Kohunlich's *aguadas*, or reservoirs. Rainfall is heavier here than further north, but the Maya of Kohunlich had the same problems as the rest of the Yucatán in retaining water in dry seasons, and as in the Petén cities they reinforced natural depressions to catch water in *aguadas*. There are still more structures to be excavated at Kohunlich, away in the woods.

Where to Stay at Kohunlich

The Explorean, t 01 800 504 5000, *www.theexplorean.com* (*luxury*). This area is an easy day-trip from Chetumal, but staying over is a possibility with this surprising luxury resort, built by Posadas hotel group on the Kohunlich access road. Its opulent *cabañas*, pool and **restaurant** have been designed to make the most of a superb location, with a jungle-fantasy look; its slogan is 'soft adventure', and activities include kayaking, ruins tours, jungle walks and health treatments. It operates on an all-inclusive basis, with meals and activities all in the price.

The Río Bec

Highway 186 runs on west past Kohunlich across the bottom of the Yucatán peninsula towards Campeche and the rest of Mexico. In modern times, until this road was built in the 1970s this area was near-uninhabited, a forgotten space on the map. During the Classic era of Mesoamerica, by contrast, this was one of the most heavily populated parts of the Maya world, a string of cities with a very distinctive architectural style of their own, called Río Bec after one of the largest sites. Not really part of the Río Bec as such, but reached from the same road, is the most exciting of all recent discoveries in the Maya world, the huge city of Calakmul. It stands within the largest and most wildlife-rich area of untouched rainforest in Mexico, the Calakmul reserve, which has survived precisely because of its remoteness.

Getting to see these sites used to be pretty arduous. When the road was cut across the peninsula, the forest either side was laid open to be settled by landless farmers. 'Villages' of knocked-together huts grew up like squatter camps, and the road had a tough reputation for robberies. This is one more part of Mexico, though, that has changed very fast. Highway 186 itself has been repeatedly upgraded, turning it into a main artery between the Riviera Maya and central Mexico (sadly, this also means that the jungle seclusion of hotels along the road can be interrupted at night by the rumble of buses and trucks). The villages, especially Xpuhil, may still have a feel of the frontier about them but get more solid by the week, with proper permanent buildings. Crime (other than a tendency to short-change foreigners) has fallen drastically. Most of the Maya sites have rough but paved access roads.

Above all, the number of visitors has increased as the area's archaeological and natural riches have become more widely known, and so too has the range of facilities. In the early days of Río Bec tourism the only sleeping options were basic *cabañas*, but a much wider mix has appeared. Anyone who suspects this might make the Río Bec disappointingly ordinary, though, can console themselves with the thought that visiting here is still a different experience from the on-tap world of the Riviera. Tourism and 'service' are recent inventions: many locals are still unused to foreigners, and visiting is a learning experience for both parties.

The Río Bec is in Campeche, but is included here as it is closer to Chetumal. Xpuhil and Calakmul are increasingly popular as stop-offs on the 'Yucatán Loop' around the peninsula, and/or between the Riviera and Palenque. Many people plan to stop just one night here, drop in on Calakmul and be in Tulum by nightfall. If so, be aware that Calakmul and back from Xpuhil will already take five to six hours out of your day.

Getting to and around the Río Bec

The easiest way to get to the sites is by **car**, and those normally open to the public have paved or mostly-paved access roads. The main highway is good, but **watch your fuel**: there are only three *gasolineras* along this road. Going west from Chetumal, the last one is in Ucúm (26km); from there it's 95km to Xpuhil, and then 145km to Escárcega. The boys who run the Xpuhil station are famed for trying to run scams on foreigners, so be wary. From Xpuhil a road runs north through Zoh-Laguna to Hopelchén (about 150km), to reach Campeche (230km) or Uxmal and Mérida. There is no fuel on this road between Xpuhil and Hopelchén.

Several first-class **buses** along Highway 186 (from Cancún and Chetumal going west, from Palenque, Villahermosa and other towns going east) now stop at **Xpuhil**. However, not all do, and timetables change, so check. Second-class buses along this road are fairly frequent, and all stop here. Three second-class buses a day turn north to **Zoh-Laguna**, one of which goes on to **Hopelchén** and **Campeche**.

In Xpuhil there are the usual *combis* and **taxis**, which serve the whole area. Getting to the ruins sites near the road – Xpuhil, Becán, Chicanná and Balamkú – is easy by bus: second-class buses and *combis* drop you there on request. For others, you need to make a deal with an Xpuhil cab-driver; for **Calakmul**, you need a taxi for the whole trip (from $45).

History

The Río Bec area was occupied very early, at least from about 300 BC, and there is evidence from Becán that the site was inhabited by 600 BC, before a defined Mayan culture had taken shape. The Río Bec communities reached their peak, though, from about AD 600 onwards. They have many peculiarities, within the usual pattern of Maya culture. Becán was the dominant centre, but one striking feature of the Río Bec is the concentration of sites so close to each other. Another is their apparent illiteracy: glyph writing normally stands out as one of the most refined achievements of the Maya, but there are scarcely any inscriptions at Río Bec sites, making them more than usually enigmatic. They were, though, wealthy communities which, like the Quintana Roo cities played an important role in the flow of contacts across the peninsula and up to Cobá. Like Dzibanché or Kohunlich, the Río Bec cities seem to have resisted 'Collapse' until after 900, and Becán itself was only finally abandoned after 1300, making it one of the Maya sites with the longest histories of continued occupation.

The Río Bec is known for the most extravagantly operatic of all Maya architectural styles. A typical Río Bec temple complex consists of three tall towers in a line, the middle one lower than the ends or vice versa, with a single-storey building linking them. On the tower façades there are 'false staircases', impossibly steep, and created entirely for visual effect (access to the temples at the top was usually via easier sets of steps at the back). Many Río Bec buildings also feature elements of the Chenes style from further north, like monster-mouth temple entrances.

Standing apart from the Río Bec is Calakmul, 60km to the south. Deep in the forest, it is the largest Maya site to have been only recently explored, and since the 1990s each excavation has upgraded its importance, identifying it as a 'superpower' of the Classic Maya world. Elsewhere in the forest more ruins are continually being explored; ask in Xpuhil or at Río Bec Dreams (see p.367) on how to get to them.

Xpuhil and Zoh-Laguna

Xpuhil (Xpujil) is the region's 'town' and centre, with shops and restaurants, a phone office and pharmacies. From the road junction, combis and cabs come and go to all the surrounding villages. Once most definitely a part of backwoods Mexico, it has been the main focus of official efforts to give the Highway 186 settlements a less 'provisional' look, and now boasts a market, a shiny bus depot and even proper kerbs. Appearances aside, though, it still has a raggedy feel, helped by its role as a rest stop for truckers who leave their monster vehicles all along the road.

Xpuhil
open daily 8–5; adm

The Maya site of **Xpuhil** is on the north side of 186 just west of the village. A small site, it was probably a subordinate of Becán. Most of its structures were put up between 500 and 750, but some building went on after 1000; it was rediscovered in the 1930s. Small though it is it contains one of the most extraordinary Río Bec temples, **Structure I**, with three giant towers, the middle one much bigger than the others, with façades at an angle of 70°. In this case, there was no easier way up at the back, so unless the local priest-lords were especially athletic the temples on top of the towers were entirely for show, and ceremonies went on at a lower level. There are still many traces of deep-red stucco. Other large buildings (**Structures II–IV**) were aristocratic residences, some with intricate decoration. There are 17 more unexcavated structures, and, like all Río Bec sites, it's great for seeing birds.

Zoh-Laguna is just 10km north of Xpuhil, but feels quite different. It's more orderly-looking, with a big grass plaza, and although smaller it is an older village than Xpuhil, and has a calmer, friendlier atmosphere, with a likeable feel of rural quiet.

Hormiguero

Hormiguero
open daily 8–5

This is another community that was at its peak in the Late Classic (650–850), but was part-occupied until around 1200. Only a few of its 84 known structures have been excavated. Getting here is made difficult by the erratic state of the road, but it's very atmospheric, approached through dense brush, ceibas and flowering plants.

Straight ahead of you at the end of the entry path is **Structure II**, the most complete excavated building at the site and one of the most wildly theatrical of all Río Bec buildings. It's a rectangular platform, with two soaring, false-staircase towers either side of a massive Chenes monster-portal. Inside this are several outsize chambers, for this is one of many Río Bec-Chenes buildings that

Visiting Hormiguero and Río Bec

The ruins of Hormiguero are in the savannah 22km south of Xpuhil, down the road south from the main crossroads in Xpuhil village. After 14km, turn right on to a track for the final stretch. This road is very badly maintained and needs a 4WD, or at the very least a high-clearance vehicle. From the car park there's a sizable walk to the ruins.

The site of Río Bec (*not regularly open to visitors*) is 15km east of Xpuhil and 20km south down a very bad dirt road (4WD only) through the village of 20 de Noviembre. These sites are especially inaccessible in the rainy season.

seems peculiarly out of scale. Forming a small plaza along with Structure II is the much less excavated platform of **Structure I**, but because so little of the site has been cleared it is difficult to appreciate the layout of Hormiguero, and ruined buildings loom up at you by surprise out of the undergrowth. A path to the right of Structure II leads to the **Central Group**, a complex of large buildings, most of which are unexcavated. In front of you is **Structure V**, a towering, part-excavated pyramid with an awesome Chenes-style temple at its peak.

The site that gave its name to the whole region, **Río Bec** itself, is southeast of Xpuhil, beyond the village of **20 de Noviembre**. It's even more difficult to get to; enthusiastic ruins-seekers should check on the current state of the road at Río Bec Dreams.

Becán

❂ Becán
7km west of Xpuhil;
open daily 8–5; adm

Becán is a Maya centre unlike any other. The name means 'ditch of water', and it is the only Maya site ringed by a very recognizable moat. It runs around a very solid wall. Within this tight perimeter, looming Río Bec-style towers around plazas form spaces with a feel of enclosure that adds to their monumental power.

The oldest permanent structures at Becán are dated to about 550 BC, the latest to about 1200. Excavations here have shown that the fortified wall was first built around AD 150–250, even before the Classic Era had begun, forcing a reconsideration of many aspects of Maya history. From around AD 650 to 900 Becán was the dominant centre of the whole Río Bec region, and it is believed other communities nearby were its offshoots or vassals. The site was discovered by archaeologist Karl Ruppert in 1934, but was only really uncovered in the 1980s, and major excavations are ongoing.

The main entrance is now through a gap in the east side of the wall, beyond which you enter a small space that gives you a choice of routes into Becán's maze. To your left steep steps lead up beside the giant **Structure IV** into the smallest but most dramatic of the city's squares, the raised **East Plaza**. Forming its north side, Structure IV is a huge residential platform, with rooms over several levels and in an 'annexe' at the back, some with fine geometrical decoration. From its top levels you get a fine overview of the

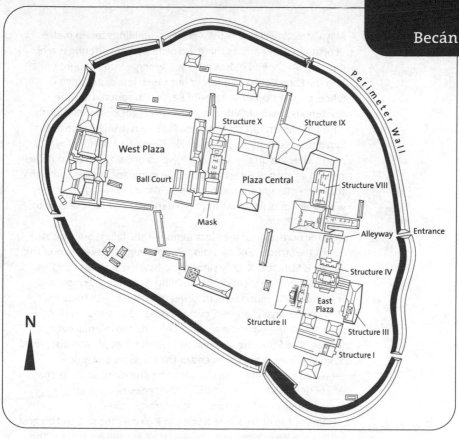

Structure X

Structure IX

West Plaza

Ball Court

Plaza Central

Structure VIII

Mask

Alleyway

Entrance

Structure IV

East Plaza

Structure II

Structure III

Structure I

N

square, and can appreciate that despite its size this was very much a residential plaza for Becán's élite, for all its buildings have multi-room complexes above their temple-façades. Several bear traces of red stucco and checkerboard-pattern facings. **Structure II** on the west side has the most intact façade; **Structure III** facing it has the best-preserved rooms, including a *temazcal* or steam bath. Outdoing Structure IV in size is the vast pile of **Structure I**, with two of the steepest-ever Río Bec staircases on its giant towers. From their positioning it is likely the temples on top were astronomical observatories. Structure I is dual-fronted, and its main façade actually faced south, outside the plaza. In one corner of Structure I is an intriguing internal staircase, connecting the East Plaza with lower levels and the outer plaza.

One of the most distinctive features of Becán is the way in which it combines immensity with a sense of being a contained whole, a series of interlocking, interconnecting spaces. This also helps give the ancient city its remarkable feel of human habitation. Instead of continuing in a circuit from the East Plaza, walk back to the entrance square. To the right is a unique intact

Maya 'street', which runs between two buildings for 60 metres. Beneath its Maya arches there are niches where offerings were once left. At the end of this alley you emerge into the light right into the **Plaza Central**, far larger but much less of an ordered whole than the other squares of Becán. On your right is the mysterious **Structure VIII**, a massively vertical Río Bec platform with temples on top. Its strangest feature is inside it, a series of labyrinthine chambers (usually closed up); very tall for Maya rooms, they are utterly dark and have no openings to the outside beyond an entrance passageway. One mundane suggestion is that they were storage spaces, but a more common view is that they were built for rituals that required darkness and seclusion, or to represent *Xibalba*.

On the north side of the Plaza Central is the tallest building at Becán, the **Structure IX** pyramid, while forming the west side of the square is **Structure X**. Only since 2000 have excavations revealed the full dramatic extent of this building, a combined temple and residence with a spectacular Chenes monster-mouth frieze facing the Plaza, 12 large chambers over two levels, and an astonishingly intricate complex of more rooms, platforms and internal patios on its west side. Structure X's greatest treasure, though, was discovered at ground level at the south end of the platform, and is now protected behind glass: an extraordinary stucco **mask** of – perhaps – one of the lords of Becán, still with vivid colours, a powerfully serene, handsome face staring into eternity.

From the top of Structure X you can look over the last and biggest square, the **West Plaza**, most of which awaits full excavation. The density of large buildings in the city is extraordinary. The West Plaza also has Becán's main **Ball Court**. The buildings within walled Becán were obviously used by the city's élite, and around the walled city there was an extensive network of *sacbés*, humbler residential areas and fields.

Chicanná

Chicanná
*2km west of Becán;
open daily 8–5; adm.*

Only slightly west of Becán, **Chicanná** was almost certainly an offshoot of the larger city, but is very different. It is the most striking example in the region of the mixing of styles: Río Bec, Chenes, even the Puuc styles from the north. It does not have giant pyramids, but relatively small buildings with an ornateness and quality of decoration that suggest this was a centre only for the region's élite. Relics of jade, obsidian and other fine materials have been found here, imported from Guatemala, Honduras and further south. It was occupied almost as long as Becán, from about 100 BC to around AD 1000, and as with other sites seems to have been part-inhabited until about 1100.

The main path now takes you in an anti-clockwise circuit from the entrance. The first major building is the tallest at Chicanná, **Structure XX**. A large two-tier building, facing south, it's one of the latest at the site, from around 850. The main entrance is an impressive Chenes monster-mask, while above, on the second tier, are 'towers' of Chac-heads. Some rooms have benches with fascinating stucco decoration, such as rosettes around little human faces. A detour right leads to **Structure XI**, which by contrast is one of the oldest and simplest buildings here, from about AD 300.

From there it's 100m to the central plaza. To the right is **Structure I**, which goes back to Río Bec style with two near-vertical towers at either end of a six-room building. Interrupting the 'staircases' of the towers are Chac-faces, but these and the traces of red stucco are in bad condition. **Structure III**, the north side, is another Maya structure built up over centuries; **Structure IV**, opposite, is a residential-temple platform that once had rooms on a now-destroyed upper level.

The most famous building at Chicanná is **Structure II**, the east side of the square. Built around 700, it's relatively small, with eight rooms reached from many doorways, but its awesome main entrance is one of the greatest of all Chenes monster-portals. Above and around the doorway, formed by the gaping mouth of the beast-like god, are its teeth; further above are its eyes with

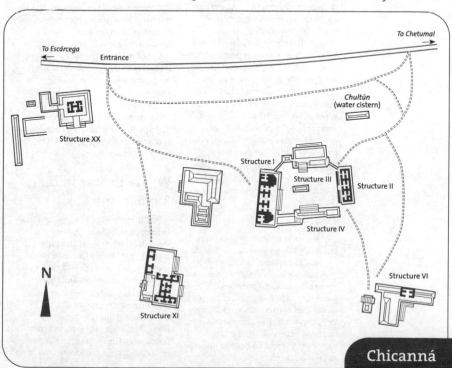

Chicanná

hook-like pupils, while its ears, alongside, are adorned with jewellery. Winding away either side of the mouth are more diagrammatic shapes, perhaps indicating the flow and breath of the spirit. These Chenes portals were representations of an 'Earth Monster', one of the spirits of the Earth of which Itzamná was the most prominent manifestation (though referred to as 'monsters', like most Maya gods their fearfulness was very ambivalent). Between the eyes above the doorway there's a niche that probably held an image of one of the lordly lineage who lived here, making clear his divine status. Elsewhere there are carved animals, looking unusually cute amid the terrorific style of Chenes sculpture.

From the southeast corner of the square a path leads to another isolated building, **Structure VI**. The main section is from around 650, and has a restrained Chenes portal and a large roof-comb; on the east side are two rooms with Puuc columns added around 900. From there, the path continues through the woods back to the entrance, passing remains of one of the *chultún* reservoirs that supplied Chicanná with water.

Tourist Information and Services in the Río Bec

t (983–)

There is a tourist information desk in Xpuhil bus depot that usually has very little information but may sell tickets (also available from Hotel Calakmul) for tours to Calakmul and Balamkú (about $40 per person). There is **no ATM** in Xpuhil, and **nowhere** that regularly changes **money**, nor can many places handle credit cards. Take sufficient cash with you for your stay, in **pesos**. **Río Bec Dreams** (*see* p.367) is also a mine of local information.

At **site entrances** there may be drinks for sale, but little else. Take water.

Internet Access: Selva Internet Café, Av. Calakmul (main street). Xpuhil does, though, have communications.

Tours

At the more accessible sites there are nearly always a few men offering to guide you around, but how much they actually know varies a great deal. **Río Bec Dreams** also provides a full guide service to every part of the area, sometimes with archaeologists, and including Maya sites and remote locations not regularly open to visitors. They must be booked ahead, as far in advance as you can.

Servicios Turísticos Calakmul, Xpuhil, t 871 6064, *serviciosturisticos@yahoo. com*. Based in the hut with información Turística prominently written on it at the eastern end of Xpuhil, on the south side of the Highway, this is the main local guides cooperative, led by Leticia Santiago and Fernando Sastre. They provide a fascinating range of ruins visits and forest trips, including Calakmul ruins, rainforest walks and bike and even horse rides. They also have the only authorized camp site in Calakmul reserve, though this may be closed under current plans. To arrange trips they need to be contacted preferably at least two weeks in advance.

Where to Stay in the Río Bec

Due to the cost of bringing services in from Campeche or Chetumal, prices in Xpuhil can be higher than some might expect in such an out-of-the-way spot. Staying in Zoh-Laguna can be both more pleasant and cheaper.

Chicanná Ecovillage, Highway 186, Km 144, near Chicanná ruins, t (Campeche) (981) 811 9192, *www.chicannaecovillageresort.com* (*moderate*). The most comfortable upscale option in the Río Bec, made up

★ Cabañas Mercedes >>

★ Río Bec Dreams >

of 42 pretty rooms with terraces in villas with *palapa* roofs around a garden, with a nice pool and attractive **restaurant**. As an 'ecovillage' it's frankly confused: some electricity is solar-powered, and rooms have a/c, but much of the food has come a great distance. But it is very comfortable.

Río Bec Dreams, Highway 186, Km 142, near Chicanná ruins, *www.riobecdreams.com*. Created in a true spirit of adventure by Canadians Ric Bertram and Diane Lalonde, this jungle hotel and eating spot provides some of the Río Bec's best and friendliest accommodation. They have amply sized *cabañas*, all with big bedroom, sitting room, terrace and bathrooms that look much too good to be in a jungle (top of the *inexpensive* band), and smaller 'jungalows', some with showers, others sharing bathrooms (*inexpensive–budget*). All are made from local materials, and there's solar power. They also have a great **bar-restaurant**, with an international menu, and a **gift shop**. Huge Maya enthusiasts, they arrange tours and provide information and orientation regardless of whether you are a guest.

Hotel-Restaurant Calakmul, Xpuhil, t 871 6029 (*inexpensive*). Xpuhil's main and best hotel, with a choice between simple, airy double rooms with a/c, TV and bathrooms, and basic but clean *cabañas* with shared showers (*budget*).

Hotel Mirador Maya, at the top of the hill, Xpuhil, t 871 6005 (*inexpensive–budget*). *Cabaña*-style huts that have been redecorated in the last few years: several have good bathrooms, and are quite comfortable, but they can be very stuffy in hot weather.

Cabañas Mercedes, Zoh-Laguna, t (village *caseta*) 871 6054 (*budget*). Just off the grassy plaza in Zoh-Laguna, one of the area's most enjoyable places to stay, and exceptional value. There are six pleasant *cabañas*, with showers and fans, around a yard behind Sra. Mercedes' restaurant, where she cooks up bargain Yucatecan meals. She and her husband are also very friendly, and it's a beautifully peaceful place to stay.

El Viajero, Zoh-Laguna, t (village *caseta*) 871 6054 (*budget*). Another very friendly *cabaña* operation, with three bright cabins with showers and TVs, and one that even has a/c.

Eating Out

Of the two best restaurants, the one at **Chicanná Ecovillage** (*moderate*) is pretty, and has often-good, sometimes hit-or-miss refined Mexican fare; **Río Bec Dreams'** big neat terrace is more fun and more consistent (*moderate*).

Xpuhil is the only place with a choice of eating: **Hotel-Restaurant Calakmul** is the best, but the **Mirador Maya**, and the **Templo Maya** opposite all offer similar, decent Mexican-Yucatecan food (all *moderate*). There are also ultra-cheap *loncherías*, and shops for water or picnic food.

In **Zoh-Laguna**, *Cabañas* **Mercedes** has great bargain local fare (*budget*). Further west the only real restaurant is at the Puerta Calakmul (see p.372), but every village has a few very basic roadside *loncherías*.

The Calakmul Biosphere Reserve

The largest forest reserve in Mexico, Calakmul covers an area of 7,230 square km. It extends both north and south of Highway 186, but there are few entry routes into the northern area. The main changes in vegetation are from Yucatán scrub in the north to dense rainforest in the south, but within the whole area there is a prodigious range of plant life, including 85 species of orchid. Animal life includes tapirs, monkeys, rodents, armadillos, over 230 species of bird and every one of the region's types of big cat. Animals you can come across in the early morning are grey foxes, *tepezcuintles*, white-tailed deer and margays (a medium-sized cat, here called *tigrillo*). Jaguars are, as ever, an outside bet. Among those birds that aren't too hard to see are ocellated turkeys, curassows, *chachalacas*, cardinals, Yucatán jays, orioles, humming-birds, toucans and hawks, while yellow-headed parrots are positively plentiful.

The first 20km south of the highway is a 'buffer zone', where some farming is still permitted, before you reach the reserve proper at an old warden's hut. About 7km further on a small parking area has been cleared to the right of the road, which should have a sign saying *sendero*. This indicates a specially cut nature path, leading in about 200m to a natural *aguada*, a dip in the ground that fills with water during the rains (June–Sept) and retains it for several months. All the forest animals come here to drink, and this is one of the places where, even in the dry season, you have most chance of seeing rarities such as the jaguar (or, with no great effort, a band of monkeys arguing with a coati over some fruit). It is accessible during the rains, but you will get bitten a lot by bugs and ticks, and need to be careful of scorpions and snakes. Also in the reserve is the celebrated **bat cenote**, one of the largest bat caves in the world and home to some 10–20 million of them. You need a guide to get there, and lately it is often closed by the reserve; ask in Xpuhil or at Río Bec Dreams on current possibilities.

There are other good places along the road to find birds and animals that a guide will be able to show you. From the *sendero* it's a tiring 33km to the ruins.

The Calakmul Ruins

Calakmul Ruins
Open daily 8–5; adm.

The great city of **Calakmul** is the most important recent revelation in American archaeology. It was actually discovered in 1931, but mapping was only begun in 1985. Within an area of over 25 square km, over 600 structures have been identified, and more are still being found. Its population at its peak has been estimated at over 60,000. Over 115 carved stelae have been uncovered, and the dates deciphered range from the 4th century AD to 810. Superb artefacts have also emerged – such as ceramics and the fabulous jade funeral masks known as the *Máscaras de Calakmul* – the finest of which are in **Fuerte San Miguel** museum in Campeche (*see* p.389).

History

Ever since the first Maya name-glyphs were deciphered in the 1950s one of the great questions for Mayanists was the identity of a place known as the *Kaan* or Snake Kingdom, references to which were found in inscriptions all over the Maya lands, indicating a city-state of enormous power and prestige. As excavations have gone on it has become clear that the Snake Kingdom was Calakmul.

Visiting Calakmul

The entrance to the Calakmul reserve is a turn south 52km west of Xpuhil. From there, it's another 60km, or a bit over an hour's drive, along a paved but bumpy road to the ruins of Calakmul. As the ruins are in the heart of the reserve, it's best to do both in one day trip. The main Calakmul ruins are now well-cleared and a guide is not really necessary, but if you want to see more, especially wildlife, it's a good idea to have a guide such as those from **Servicios Turísticos** in Xpuhil or **Río Bec Dreams** (see p.367). Birds and animals are most active at dawn, so it's best to start from Xpuhil around 5.30–6am to see as much as possible.

At the Calakmul turn off the highway there is a check-in hut, where the warden lives. Cars are currently admitted to the reserve daily 7am–6pm (with no last-exit time), and there is an adm charge of around $4 per vehicle plus $2 per person; the ruins are open normal **INAH hours** (8–5), and have a separate adm. An official proposal has been made that cars will have to park at a point 20km down the road, from where there will be a shuttle-bus service to the ruins. How this will work in practice is a mystery, given that on many days Calakmul has only a few visitors spread through the day, and for the moment it's only a project, but it may be implemented. It seems groups with guides will be allowed all the way to the ruins.

With the aid of inscriptions from other cities – given the poor state of its own carvings – the position of Calakmul as one of the 'great powers' of the Classic Maya world has emerged.

Calakmul was occupied very early, from around 600 BC, and the first layers of most of its large structures were already in place before AD 100. It is believed that its enmity with other cities further south also originated in this era, in particular its rivalry with Tikal. Calakmul's rise to major power status, though, seems to date from the early 6th century, when Tikal had been the dominant force in the Petén for over 100 years. From the 520s to the 550s Calakmul's rulers forged a series of alliances with cities in the southeast Petén (in modern-day Belize and Guatemala), such as Naranjo and Caracol. This culminated in the great defeat of Tikal by Calakmul and Caracol in 562, after which Tikal's ruler was sacrificed and his city fell into a long crisis. For the next 140 years Calakmul was the foremost power in the whole Petén, with a web of alliances and vassal relationships that ran from Yaxchilán to Dzibanché. One indication of its wealth and size is its extraordinary water management system, with five huge reservoirs to retain water in dry seasons, including one, 2km north of the main site, that is 51,000 square km in area and the largest aguada in any Maya city.

Calakmul's greatest ruler was Yuknoom 'the Great' (636–86), a contemporary and enemy of Pakal of Palenque. The struggle against a resurgent Tikal and its ally Palenque was a constant feature of his reign; in 657 he attacked Tikal and forced its ruler to take refuge in Palenque (see p.439), so that Calakmul's pre-eminence was kept up for another 30 years. Yuknoom is not as well known as his son Yuknoom Yich'ak Kak or Jaguar-Paw (Garra de Jaguar), the first Calakmul ruler to be identified. He reigned for only eight years (686–95), but was easily identified because in 695 he led Calakmul into a disastrous defeat at the hands of Hasaw-Chan-Kawil of Tikal, which turned the scales again and brought the city's 'golden age' to a fairly abrupt end.

It was believed that Jaguar-Paw was captured and sacrificed at Tikal, but the recent discovery of his tomb indicates that he at least survived the actual battle, and one of his successors Yuknoom Took (702–31) fought back against decline by cultivating an alliance with Yaxchilán. However, Calakmul's prestige and power never fully recovered from the 695 defeat. The vigour of Becán and the Río Bec cities in the next century is probably related to the decline of Calakmul, since Maya cities often gained energy when they came out from 'under the shadow' of larger states. In the later 8th century Calakmul's main contacts, as reflected in ceramics and architecture, seem to have been with the Río Bec, the Chenes and other cities further north, in place of its earlier interaction with the Petén to the south. From about 790 it appears to have 'collapsed' more rapidly than other cities nearby: the last dated inscription at the city is from 810, although there is evidence that people still inhabited the site into the 13th century.

The Great Plaza and Structure II

From the entrance gate and parking area you have a forest walk of about a kilometre to the ruins. At the end of the path you come into the north side of Calakmul's giant main square, the **Great Plaza** (Plaza Central). This is one of the great, immense Maya ceremonial spaces. Around it there are many stelae (mostly pretty indistinct), some of which were excavated in other parts of the site and then brought together here. Immediately to their right is the small **Structure VIII**, probably an astronomical observatory, beyond which is the much larger **Structure VII**. At the top of it a tomb was found which contained the most beautiful of the jade *máscaras* now in the Campeche museum. The largest building in this part of the plaza is the residence-platform to your left, **Structure IV**. Its base is extremely ancient, perhaps older than 100 BC, but the last rooms were added above it around 750. In front of it are over a dozen stelae, all referring to events between 750 and 810. **Structure VI**, facing it across the plaza, was one of the ceremonial hearts of the city, an astronomical platform incorporating a Mayan cosmological trick. On the shortest and longest days of the year the sun shines directly through the building to land on the small altar in front.

Around the small platform of **Structure V** are some of the best-preserved stelae. The most prominent on the north side, facing the main square and dated to 623, unusually tell the story of a marriage, between the daughter of an *ahau* of Calakmul and a prince from Yaxchilán. In the stela on the right the prince is shown making offerings of friendship; to the left the princess is shown in a

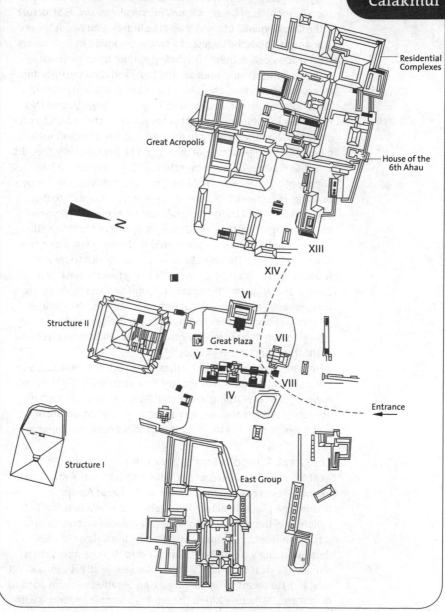

Residential
Complexes

Great Acropolis

House of the
6th Ahau

N

XIII

XIV

VI

Structure II

Great Plaza

VII

V

VIII

IV

Entrance

Structure I

East Group

more belligerent posture above an earth monster, and trampling on a prisoner. On the south side are eight stelae erected by Yuknoom the Great around 660–70, one of which, **Stela 33**, shows his predecessor (and probably father) Scroll-Serpent, who twice attacked Palenque, in 599 and 611.

Beyond here in the south section of the Great Plaza you come to the true monster of Calakmul, now prosaically known as **Structure II**, the **Great Pyramid** of the city and the hub around which the rest is arranged. This is the largest of all Maya pyramids. Its base covers several acres; above, there are whole pyramids upon pyramids – from the bottom you cannot see the top – and climbing up is an awesome progression. The role of Maya architecture in creating a power centre – symbolically and literally – was never clearer. This pyramid is the ultimate product of the Maya practice whereby each *ahau* had to add something to the city's buildings to continue the glory of his lineage: it just got bigger and bigger. Curiously, they did so not so much by covering over the existing structure – it had already nearly reached its final height in the Preclassic era – as by building up successive façades, so it 'grew' northwards into the plaza. Either side of the central stairway are enormous monster-mask carvings from the Early Classic, built over in the 7th or 8th centuries and only recently uncovered. In the main temple on the first large flat level (**Temple 2B**) an exceptionally rich tomb was found in 1997, containing a man with a jade funeral mask, and surrounded by lavish offerings of jade, obsidian and more. This is very probably the tomb of Jaguar-Paw. He was lying on a unique painted wooden bier, which disastrously disintegrated very shortly after air entered the tomb; the other objects (and a reconstruction of the tomb) are now in Campeche.

From this temple there's a further climb up three more levels to the plain, small platform at the top. Your great reward is the view, towering over everything in the endless green forest. From here, you have a view of another, very vertical pyramid, **Structure III**, which would count as huge itself were it not seen in comparison.

The Great Acropolis and the Muralla

Off to your left as you come down Structure II is the other main excavated area of Calakmul, known as the **Great Acropolis**. Nearest the plaza, **Structure XIV**, is one of the few dual-fronted buildings in the city, dated to 740. The Acropolis is structured around another large square, within which is Calakmul's main (but surprisingly small) **Ball Court**. Next to this is a stela with a remarkably clear carving of a ball player (above all his sandals and toenails). He seems to be holding a kind of tablet, perhaps used to keep scores. **Structure XIII** to the right is a temple-residence with a stela of a woman.

Much of the Great Acropolis is still overgrown and scarcely excavated, but a path to the right of Structure XIII leads to one of the most atmospheric parts of the site, a line of residential complexes, on different levels reached by scrambling down steep steps. Their size is another testimony to the wealth of Calakmul,

Where to Stay at Calakmul

There is a campsite in the reserve, not far from the ruins, run by **Servicios Turísticos Calakmul** (*see* p.369), although it may be closed under current official plans (*see* above).

Puerta Calakmul, t (998) 884 3278, *www.puertacalakmul.com.mx* (*expensive–moderate*). It's hard to be closer to the forest and the ruins and yet still enjoy comforts like this. This *cabaña*-hotel is in the forest off the Calakmul road just after it turns south off Highway 186 (1km down a track that turns left behind the warden's house). There are 15 colourful cabins with an astonishing level of jungle luxury – terraces, good solar-powered showers. There's also a little pool, and an attractive **restaurant** – very necessary, as there's nowhere else to eat nearby. A variety of tours can be arranged. Prices are quite high, due to high costs.

but they're also very varied. The one known as the **House of the 6th Ahau** (*Casa del 6 Ahau*) has a particularly secluded feel. At the far, western end of the Acropolis they are built against a part of the giant **Muralla** or defensive wall that ringed the core of Calakmul. This too seems on a different scale from most Maya cities, thick enough to be from a European castle.

Beyond the walls there are of course more structures still in the woods. Not far away but hard to find without a guide is a round slab often called the **Piedra de los Cautivos** ('Stone of the Captives'). On its flat surface there are four huge, apparently tormented carved figures, and it is suggested prisoners were tortured here. Another school of thought calls it the **Piedra de la Fertilidad**, suggesting people came here if they wanted a child, on the basis that one of the figures seems to have an erection.

Balamkú

A long way from the main Río Bec area, this small site was only discovered in 1990, but is one of the most fascinating. It has one of the largest surviving stucco friezes in the Mayan world, and nowhere else will you see so much original Mayan colour.

Balamkú

5km west of the turn off to Calakmul; open daily 8–5; adm.

Balamkú is another site that was occupied from about 300 BC, and its most important buildings are from AD 300–600. There are three groups of interlocking plazas, only two of which have been excavated. You first reach the **Grupo Sur**, with two broad squares divided by a near-Río-Bec-style semi-vertical pyramid. From there, you carry on along the wooded path to the larger **Grupo Central**, announced by a medium-sized square with a platform with a residential patio, and a monster-mask façade.

Beyond that is the largest of the plazas and the great star of Balamkú, the **Templo de los Frisos** ('Temple of the Friezes'). During excavations the removal of a later layer of building uncovered an intact, 20m-long painted stucco frieze from 550–650, a mass of

Southern Quintana Roo and the Río Bec | Balamkú

10

mythological images and animal figures. This is now sheltered within a strange concrete structure to preserve it, guarded by one of the site warden's children, who lets you in (*for a tip*). Inside, the 'shed' generates a temperature of around 45°C, but the visit is worth it. Along the bottom level of the frieze there are earth monsters, representing the basic level of existence, the border between this world and the underworld, from which all other things spring. Above them are various animals, such as finely modelled monkeys. The most prominent creatures at Balamkú are toads, companions and helpers of the earth spirits. The largest toad's mouth is thrown right open, and a king-like figure, an *ahau*, is shown emerging from it. The frieze thus reaffirms the *ahau*'s sacred origin and his connection to the spirits of the earth.

A little way back from Balamkú, near the Calakmul turn, is the village of **Conhuas**, where a dirt track leads 15km (with a 2km walk at the end) to yet another Maya site at **Nadzcaan**. Only 'officially' opened very recently, this is potentially a very large site, with another massive central pyramid. Otherwise, if you don't have to go back to Xpuhil, it's 88km west from Balamkú to **Escárcega**, from where there are roads to the north and south (*see* p.404). Around 40km along the road at Centenario is **Laguna Silvituc**, a big jungle lake with a waterside restaurant where locals (and the odd intrepid foreigner) go to cool off.

Nadzcaan
open daily 8–5; ad, though the warden may not be around to collect it.

Campeche State

*The old city of Campeche sits inside a
ring of stone walls and massive
baluartes or bastions, built to keep out
pirates in the days when this was one of
the foremost cities of the Spanish Main.
Within the walls, the delicate green,
blue, yellow and terracotta façades of
the old colonial houses add to
Campeche's touch of romance, their
colours picked out in light that seems to
gain an extra clarity when reflected in
the opal waters of the Gulf alongside.
When you stop to eat, there is a
distinctive cuisine to be discovered,
inventively combining tropical fruit, fish
and seafood. Campeche state itself has
more archaeological ruins than any
other state in Mexico – though most are
still remote and only partially
excavated. This striking region receives
far fewer visitors than the east side of
the Yucatán and travelling here has an
enjoyable tang of exploration.*

11

Don't miss

🌑 **The old colonial city**
Campeche p.380

🌑 **Superb Maya jade funeral masks**
Museo Regional de Campeche p.388

🌑 **A soaring Five Storey palace**
Edzná p.393

🌑 **Opal waters, empty space and quiet fishing villages**
The Gulf coast p.402

See map overleaf

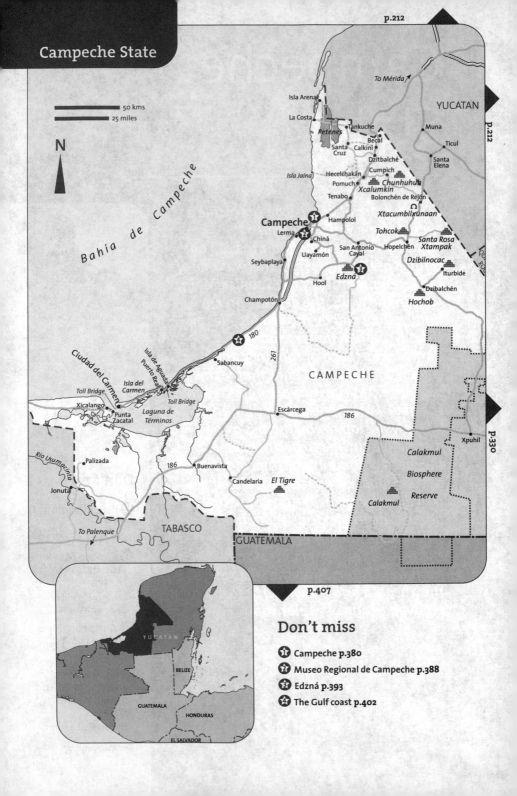

Campeche State

50 kms
25 miles

N

To Mérida

YUCATAN

Isla Arenas

La Costa
Tankuche
Muna

Petenes
Becal
Ticul

Santa
Cruz
Calkiní

Dzitbalché
Santa
Elena

Cumpich

Isla Jaina
Hecelchakán

Pomuch
Chunhuhub

Xcalumkin

Tenabo
Bolonchén de Rejón

Campeche
Hampolol
Xtacumbilxunaan

Lerma
Tohcok

Chiná
Santa Rosa
Xtampak

San Antonio
Cayal
Hopelchén

Seybaplaya
Uayamón
Dzibilnocac

Iturbide

Hool
Edzná

Dzibalchén

Champotón
Hochob

180

261

Sabancuy

CAMPECHE

Ciudad del Carmen

Isla de Aguada

Puerto Real

Isla del
Carmen

Toll Bridge

Xicalango
Toll Bridge
Escárcega
186

Punta
Zacatal
Laguna de
Términos

Río Usumacinta
Xpuhil

Palizada
Calakmul

186
Buenavista
Biosphere

Jonuta
Candelaria
El Tigre
Reserve

Calakmul

To Palenque
TABASCO

GUATEMALA

p.407

YUCATAN

BELIZE

GUATEMALA
HONDURAS

EL SALVADOR

Don't miss

1 Campeche p.380

2 Museo Regional de Campeche p.388

3 Edzná p.393

4 The Gulf coast p.402

The state of Campeche feels hard done by. Until quite recently, of the thousands who visit Mérida and Yucatán state each year, let alone Cancún, only a handful took even a look at the third state of the peninsula.

Campeche, though, has plenty of attractions. The state capital is the most complete Spanish colonial fortified city in the whole of Mexico, still ringed by its 17th-century bastions. The city has perhaps the most striking archaeological museum in the whole region – a 'must' for anyone interested in the ancient Maya – with, as its centrepiece, the superb treasures excavated at Calakmul. There are rare and fascinating landscapes, and a remarkable range of wildlife. Campeche has Gulf-coast beaches, and the most varied and subtle food in the Yucatán. Inland there is the great city of Edzná, one of the most enigmatic of Maya sites.

Campeche was the first city founded by the Spaniards in the Yucatán and, until virtually the end of the colonial era, was the only port of the peninsula and one of the most important cities of Spain's American empire, one of the few allowed to carry on foreign trade. After independence it squabbled endlessly with Mérida in the semi-independent Yucatán, refusing to accept second-city status, until Campeche finally got its wish with the granting of separate statehood by Juárez in 1863. It's true to say, though, that left to itself Campeche has scarcely ever taken off. The ending of the imperial trading monopoly, and the diversion of Yucatán trade through Sisal and then Progreso, were the beginnings of a prolonged decline. Since the 1970s oil, discovered around the Laguna de Términos, has pumped new wealth into parts of the state, but Campeche is still thinly populated, and compared to Yucatán state there's noticeably less activity, a more remote feel and a pervasive sense of quietness.

Travelling in rural Campeche therefore has its eccentricities. Since there have been few visitors, there have been few facilities. Things have begun to change a little, and the state government has made great efforts to attract more outside attention, polishing up the old city of Campeche and improving access to Maya sites. The range of places to stay has expanded, from luxury *haciendas* to Río Bec *cabañas*. In many areas, though, hotels, signposts and organized tours remain thin on the ground. To appreciate the place you have to be prepared to meet it halfway, and explore.

11

Campeche State

The Camino Real and the Campeche Petenes

The northern part of the state grew up around the *Camino Real*, the old Spanish road from Mérida that is now Highway 180, and all its main towns lie along it. Just inside Campeche is the famous little town of **Becal**, long dedicated to the making of *jipis*, panama hats, woven from the local *jipijapa* palm. Becal hats are found all over the Yucatán (Mérida market is their biggest outlet), but in Becal itself surprisingly little is done to push them at the passing tourist. Around the plaza there are shops (*often closed*) with local *artesanía* inside, and on the north side of town there are a few small workshops. Traditionally hats are made in caves in the limestone to keep the palm supple, and some workshops near the Mérida road have backyard caves that customers can visit. A shop that's usually open and has hats, bags and other items is **Artesanía Becaleña** (C. 30), off the plaza. Be sure to get the price clear when buying.

Calkiní, 8km further on, is the largest town on the road, with a big market and one of the most venerated of Yucatán country churches, **San Luís Obispo**. Built in the 18th century, it has a fine neobaroque façade, but is known above all for its carving, especially the painted altarpiece. In a chapel left of the altar is the *Cristo de Calkiní*, a powerfully carved figure of Christ surrounded by flowers and clad in a vivid purple apron. The chapel also retains some of its original wall painting, in a European neoclassical style, but in Mexican pinks and blues with plenty of flowers.

The Petenes

Calkiní is the point of access into the Petenes region of coastal Campeche. The northern coastal strip of the state consists of a dense network of mangroves, lagoons and *petenes*, a word of Mayan origin for 'islands' of solid land and jungle vegetation that appear within the swamp. Because of their isolation the *petenes* form microclimates, and are peculiarly rich and fragile ecosystems. The whole area contains a wealth of fish, crustacea, and birds and animals such as flamingos, dwarf falcons, armadillos, deer and (they say) pumas. Many of its water birds such as ibis and blue herons are unused to being disturbed by humans and therefore easy to spot.

Since 1996 this scarcely inhabited region has been a protected area. From Calkiní a seemingly endless road winds 70km west across the *petenes* to **Isla Arena**, one of very few communities on this coast. This island fishing village used to be a *campechano* secret, but in 1999 a causeway from the mainland made getting to

Getting to and around the Petenes

Isla Arena

Second-class **buses** run daily from Calkiní to **Isla Arena**, usually at 8am and 11am. *Combis* run more frequently, especially before noon. **Taxis** also run along the whole route.

---

it easier, and recently the wealth of its fishing grounds, especially for tarpon, has made it a new target for fly-fishing fans, who are catered for by several specialist agencies based in Campeche and an attractive fishing lodge near the village. Many less expensive trips are also possible with the aid of local fishermen: into the *petenes* and mangroves, up to the flamingo grounds and Celestún, or to 'lost beaches' nearby. On the way to Isla Arena, in incomprehensible isolation about halfway along the road from Calkiní at **El Remate**, there is a surprisingly neat and pretty little nature park around a natural *cenote*.

El Remate
official adm charge, but there may be nobody around to collect it

Lancheros from Isla Arena can also take you to see and just *possibly* visit the mysterious **Isla Jaina**, 40km south along the coast, one of the most remarkable but least seen of Maya sites. For centuries Maya lords were brought here to be buried, often with exceptionally fine offerings: ceramic pots, jade jewellery and above all superbly modelled clay figurines, made in a unique style. Often in the form of whistles, each one was a completely individual portrait, of the lord, his family and retinue; they are some of the greatest creations of Maya art, and are among those artefacts that most bring the culture to life before the modern eye.

Jaina figurines can be seen in many museums, but there are very few people who have visited the island itself. So in demand are Jaina figures among collectors that there has been heavy looting of the site, and to prevent this the island is protected by the Mexican navy. Because of its 'closed' status Jaina has a special fascination for Maya enthusiasts, and it is often rumoured that the island is about to be opened to properly organized visits. Some of these rumours are sparked by statements from the state's own tourism authorities, and occasionally some Campeche travel agencies even advertise tours. However, they never seem to clear their ideas with the archaeological authorities of the INAH, who continue to insist that everyone who sets foot on Jaina must have a special permit issued by the INAH alone. There is very little record of any non-archaeologist ever having obtained one, and agencies who try to set up tours generally give up shortly afterwards. Hacienda Uayamón (*see* p.390) advertised Jaina visits at one time, but perhaps they have extra clout. Those interested can still apply for a permit themselves at the INAH office in Campeche (in the Casa del Teniente del Rey, *see* p.387), but don't hold your breath.

11 Campeche State | The Petenes

Tours and Fishing

t (996–)

Campeche Fly Fishing Tarpon Bay, Campeche t (981) 100 8512, *www. campecheflyfishingtarponbay.com.mx*; **Campeche Tarpon Bay**, Campeche t (981) 819 3077, *www.campechetarponbay. com.mx*. Both these agencies arrange all-inclusive fishing trips, with superior accommodation at Carey Lodge (from about $400 a day).

Sociedad Ojo de Agua, t 963 8801. For much lower prices this village co-operative provides boat trips to the Petenes, flamingo lagoons, beaches and any other part of the area with local guides, including birding/fishing trips. Costs are per boat (max. six people).

Where to Stay and Eat

At the luxury end of the scale, **Hacienda Santa Rosa** near Maxcanú (*see* p.272) is not far from this area. In **Isla Arena**, the **Ojo de Agua** co-op (see left) has a few basic *cabañas* and homely beachside restaurant with good fish (both *budget*). There are also now upscale *cabañas* at **Carey Lodge**, but these are currently only available for all-inclusive fishing trips.

Hecelchakán

Hacienda Blanca Flor, Highway 180 Km 88, t 827 0266, *www.blancaflor. com* (*expensive*). An 18th-century *hacienda* by the Camino Real north of Hecelchakán, converted not into a luxury *hacienda*-hotel but something a bit more modest. Very peaceful with rambling gardens, terrace restaurant, pool, horse riding and other activities

Museo Arqueológico del Camino Real

open Tues–Sat 10–1 and 4–7, Sun 9–12)

Xcalumkin

open daily 8–4.30; adm

Hampolol wildlife reserve

often closed; officially open Mon–Sat 9–noon; adm

Back on the Camino Real, from Calkiní it's 24km to **Hecelchakán**, the last sizable stop before Campeche. Beside its plaza there is a small museum, the **Museo Arqueológico del Camino Real**. Its main attraction is its display of Jaina figurines, but it has ceramics and stone stelae, all unlabelled. Just to the north a road cuts east across to Bolonchén (*see* p.399) and the Puuc hills. A detour of 12km up this road leads to a Maya site at **Xcalumkin**. It's down a dirt track about a kilometre from the road on the south side, indicated by a small blue INAH sign. This is really one of the Puuc sites, but is little known due mainly to its out-of-the-way location in Campeche. It is of notable significance as one of the oldest 'pre-Puuc' communities, established in the early 7th century. Several small pyramids and temple-platforms, with Puuc-style mouldings, are visible, but the site's greatest attraction is its atmospheric location, nestling in a snug valley.

Returning again to the Camino Real, 20km north of Campeche is **Hampolol wildlife reserve**. It's mainly a study centre, but has a small collection of local wildlife (and a tame, greedy spider monkey).

Campeche

🟊 **Campeche**

Old Campeche sits within a ring of walls and seven *baluartes* or bastions, overlooked by fortresses on hills to the north and south, which make it impossible to forget its one-time status as a citadel of the Spanish Main. Within the old walls, there is as great a density of churches as in many a European city, and streets of elegant colonial houses with tropical patios glimpsed behind sober façades and windows faced with very Spanish-looking iron grilles.

In the last few years the houses of old Campeche have been beautifully restored and repainted in their original delicate colours of blues, greens and ochre, with details picked out in white.

Campeche's old city is one of the gems of the Yucatán, and thanks in good part to the model way in which its charms have been restored it was declared a UNESCO world heritage site in 1999. This has played its part in putting it more 'on the map', and more foreigners are now visible on its streets. There is, though, something a tad odd about Campeche. To add to its fine architecture it has a romantic history, of pirates, seafarers and sieges. It has a seafront location, and some of the best restaurants and one of the best museums in the Yucatán. Parts of the city are quite prosperous, and there's less visible poverty than in many Mexican towns. The oddness is that the constant street life that's so much a feature of colonial cities like Mérida or San Cristóbal just isn't there in Campeche. It is visibly a city, but on most days seems to have the movement of a small town. Even the market is relatively quiet, and the excitement of pirate days seems long forgotten. Essential to its charm is an airy, seafront tranquility.

History

There is no real evidence Campeche was an ancient Maya settlement, but by the end of the Postclassic, about 1500, it was a prosperous small city on the trading route around the Yucatán, the capital of a lordship known as Kin Pech or Ah Kin Pech (translatable as 'Lord Sun Tick', as in cattle tick). Its ruler was a redoubtable leader called Moch-Cuouh. Its people got their first sight of Europeans on 22 March 1517, when the ships of Hernández de Córdoba hove into view. It was the day of Saint Lazarus, and so the Spaniards first called the town San Lázaro. They were desperate for water, having found nowhere to put in all the way round the peninsula. Moch-Cuouh gave them some, but made it clear he wouldn't allow them to stay. Hernández sailed on to the mouth of the river at Champotón, still within the lands of Kin Pech. When they landed Moch-Cuouh attacked the Spaniards, and nearly destroyed the whole expedition.

Grijalva was also driven off in 1518, and although the *Adelantado* Montejo took Campeche in 1531 he was forced to abandon it three years later. It was not until 1540, by which time Moch-Cuouh was dead – almost certainly from disease – that Montejo el Mozo, marching up from Champotón, managed definitively to take Campeche. On 4 October that year he made it the first properly established Spanish 'city' in the Yucatán, this time with the name San Francisco de Campeche.

As the essential point of communication between the Yucatán and both the home country and New Spain to the west, Spanish Campeche grew and prospered. In 1545 the Franciscans arrived and

Getting to and around Campeche

By Air

Campeche's little **airport**, 5½km southeast of the city along Av. Central or Av. Gobernadores, has flights to **Mexico City** daily with **Aeroméxico Connect**, t 01 800 800 2376. A cab into town costs about $8.

By Bus

Campeche's modern **first-class bus station** is some way from the centre on the corner of Av. Casa de Justicia and Av. Patricio Trueba, a continuation of Av. Central, the long avenue that runs south from the Puerta de Tierra. It is also used by the main local **second-class** bus company (**Sur-ATS**), but some services still run from the old **second-class station** on the corner of Av. Gobernadores and Av. Chile. To get to the centre from either station, take a cab or any local bus marked *Centro*. There is a **Ticketbus** outlet on Av. Miguel Alemán, just outside the old city near Baluarte de Santiago.

Main routes are these; many first-class and all second-class buses south stop at **Champotón**:

Ciudad del Carmen (*3hrs*): 1–2 first-class each hour, 1am–10.30pm, and more *intermedios* and second-class. First-class fare about $11.

Chetumal (*6½hrs*): one first-class daily (12 noon) via **Escárcega** and **Xpuhil**. Fare $20.

Cancún (*7hrs*): via **Mérida**, five ordinary first-class, two ADO GL daily; one first-class (11.50pm) goes on to **Playa del Carmen** (*8½hrs*). Fares (Cancún) $26–32.

Hopelchén: at least 12 second-class daily, from the main bus station; six continue to **Dzibalchén** and **Iturbide** (from where one goes on to **Xpuhil**), and five go on the 'slow route' to **Mérida**, passing **Kabah** and **Uxmal**.

Mérida (*2½hrs*): Three ADO GL daily, 1–2 first-class each hour, 1.10am–11.50pm daily; fare $9.50–11. From the main station there are also second-class buses every half-hour, 3.45am–11.30pm, and five second-class daily on the 'slow route' inland (*see* above).

Mexico City (*16–18hrs*): one ADO GL, three ordinary first-class daily. Fare $70–80.

Palenque (*5–6½hrs*): via **Escárcega**, three ADO and one OCC ordinary first-class daily. The OCC bus (9.45pm) goes on to **San Cristóbal de Las Casas** (*11hrs*) and **Tuxtla Gutiérrez** (*12½hrs*). These buses originate in Mérida so timings at Campeche can vary. Fares $17 to Palenque, $25 to San Cristóbal, $32 to Tuxtla.

Villahermosa (*6–7hrs*): two ADO GL, seven ordinary first-class, several second-class (via **Carmen** or **Escárcega**) daily, all from the main station. One ADO GL (9.35pm) goes on to **Tuxtla Gutiérrez** (*12hrs*). First-class fare to Villahermosa about $20.

Xpuhil: one first-class (12 noon Chetumal bus, *4½hrs*) and two second-class daily via **Escárcega**; one second-class via **Hopelchén** and **Zoh-Laguna** (*7hrs*). First-class fare $14.

Combis, many second-class routes to nearby villages (including Edzná) and local buses to the fortresses and other points nearly all leave from or pass the **market**, on Circuito Baluartes.

By Car, Bike and Taxi

Campeche's lack of traffic means it's easy to drive around, and there's even unrestricted parking in many streets. There are big *gasolineras* on Av. Ruíz Cortines north and south of the old city. Campeche is the one Mexican city where you actually have to look for a **taxi**, or call for one (t 815 5555). However, they're still cheap. Cycling is also quite easy, as the city is fairly flat and traffic relatively calm.

Car and Cycle Hire

There are only a few rental agencies, with relatively high rates (around $50 a day); others can be booked through hotels. If you can carry on to Mérida, you will usually get a better deal by renting there.

Aventura Bicycle Rental, C. 59, x Av. 16 de Septiembre, t 811 9191. Near the Malecón, by the Hotel del Mar, with bikes to rent for about $7 a day; opening times are erratic.

Campeche Car Rental, Lobby of Hotel Alhambra, Av. Resurgimiento 85, t 811 4769, *campechecar_rental@yahoo.com.mx*. Also via Xtampak Tours (*see* below).

Localiza, Desks in Hotel Baluartes and Hotel Castelmar, t 811 3187, *pirata_rentacar@yahoo.com.mx*.

Orientation

The main north–south highway forms a loop inland around Campeche, allowing through traffic to bypass the city. The road south into town meets the shoreline and becomes Av. Ruíz Cortines along the waterfront, the **Malecón**. Most of Campeche's hotels and attractions – except for the two fortress museums – are within the old city, inside the Spanish walls, the **Circuito Baluartes**. Streets parallel to the sea have even numbers, those running away from it have odd ones.

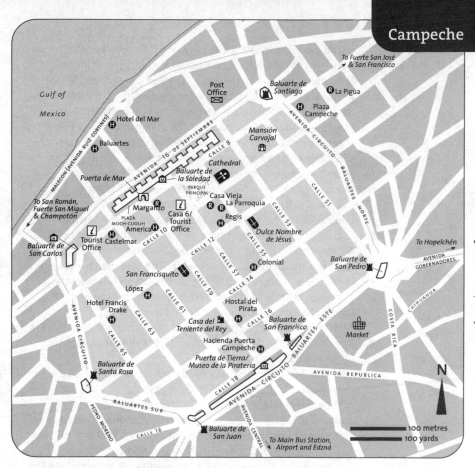

began to build the first permanent church in the peninsula, San Francisco. While the Yucatán produced no precious metals, Campeche developed a trade that was almost as valuable in salt and tropical dyewoods, *palo de tinte*, found around the Laguna de Términos and in great demand throughout Europe.

It was the dyewood trade and its profits that attracted the attention of the one group who would have most impact on the history of Campeche – pirates. In the 1550s a band of French maritime roughnecks established a stronghold on the Isla de Tris at the mouth of the Laguna de Términos (now the Isla del Carmen), and the first attack on Campeche followed in 1561. The city was rich, and yet its relative isolation made it a far safer target than a better defended city like Veracruz. For over a century, battered Campeche was one of the places most raided by Caribbean buccaneers. Time and again, the Spanish population had to take refuge from pirate bands in the convent of San Francisco, closer to God and the most solid building in Campeche.

One of the greatest attacks was in 1635, when 500 men led by Diego *el Mulato* and a Dutchman known as *Pie de Palo*, 'Peg-leg', seized the town and held it to ransom, with a message sent to San Francisco that they would only leave for a hefty payoff in gold. Determined not to pay, the locals launched a break-out. The pirates went back to their ships, but took nearly everything movable in Campeche with them. Spanish governors seemed incapable of eliminating the anarchic haunt of Tris, or holding on to pirates if they captured them. In 1669 'Rock Brasiliano' (another Dutchman) was caught off Campeche, but had a letter sent threatening an assault by another (nonexistent) pirate band if he was not released. The governor was suitably duped, and let him go.

When in 1684 another large-scale attack was made on Campeche, led by the Flemish pirate Laurent Graff (known to all as *Lorencillo*), the governors finally decided something must be done. A special tax was levied, and work began on building a ring of ramparts and bastions around the city. The city's merchants were able to sleep more peacefully in their beds, especially once the pirate den of Tris was at last overwhelmed in 1718. The walls of Campeche were further supplemented throughout the 18th century, above all with the building of the forts of San José and San Miguel north and south of the town, this time against possible attacks by the British Navy.

As a trading city in contact with the outside world Campeche had great hopes of independence. However, as soon as it lost the commercial privileges of the Spanish imperial system its trade – and with it shipbuilding and many other occupations – fell by almost mathematical progression. The dyewood trade faded away too, Campeche's forests having been overexploited. Nor were Campeche's politicians ever able to sort out their relationship with Mérida in the new state of Yucatán. The two were briefly able to come together in 1842, when Santa Anna (*see* pp.53–4) tried to reincorporate the Yucatán into Mexico by force, and landed an army which besieged Campeche, using the Fuerte San Miguel as his headquarters. To the surprise of all concerned, the Yucatecan army was victorious, and the 'Mexicans' were beaten back. The shock of the Caste War, though, undermined the idea of a united Yucatán and made easier the division into two states in 1863. From then on the role played by city and state in Mexican affairs has been discreet. Since the 1960s, revenues from oil – discovered in southern Campeche – have been the main element in the state capital's fortunes.

Around the Old City

At the core of old Campeche there is naturally a plaza, the **Parque Principal**, which long ago opened directly onto the shore and landing-stages for ships. At its centre there is a very Victorian-looking bandstand between magnificently spreading trees, and the inland side is lined by attractive, shady arcades; the seaward side is now filled by a **library** in a similar style that harmonizes neatly with the rest of the square. It was actually completed only in 2001, but as far as its exterior goes is a fairly close recreation of Campeche's old city hall, which was built on this same spot in 1779 but carelessly demolished in the 1960s. On the left-hand side of the Parque, looking towards the sea, is the **Casa Seis**, a more than usually gracious old Campeche house which has been carefully restored. As well as housing the main tourist information desk, exhibitions and cultural events, it contains several fascinating rooms where antiques from around the city have been charmingly used to recreate Campeche interiors of the 19th century. Guided tours are sometimes available. The Casa Seis patios and the square's bandstand are also the hub of the city's free music and entertainment programme.

Casa Seis
open daily 9am–9pm

The view across the Parque Principal is dominated by the giant towers of Campeche's **Cathedral**. It was built over a very long time, mostly from the 16th to the 18th centuries, and so is a mixture of several different elements. The central section of the façade is one of the older parts of the building, from the early 17th century, and in a plain Spanish Renaissance style reminiscent of the Escorial near Madrid or other buildings of the reign of Philip II; the towers either side of it were added over the following century, and not entirely finished until after independence.

Behind the library on the seaward side of the square is one of the largest Spanish bastions, the **Baluarte de la Soledad**, and one of the longest remaining sections of rampart. Walled Campeche had two main entrances. Curiously, the **Puerta de Mar** ('Sea Gate') is not on the plaza itself but just to the south of the Soledad at the end of C. 59, which runs straight through to the other main gate, the Puerta de Tierra. If you walk through the Puerta de Mar you come into another broad plaza, renamed **Plaza del Patrimonio Mundial** to commemorate Campeche's new global status. Here you will find illuminated fountains that dance to music each night, cannons and other relics of old Campeche, and a great view of the Soledad.

For years Campeche made surprisingly little of its seafront. In the 1960s, when 'modernization' rather than tourism was seen as the way ahead, the city was the target of a prestige programme called the *Resurgimiento* (Resurgence) *de Campeche*, which included sweeping away several surviving stretches of the walls and rebuilding the waterfront. However, the very different policy adopted in the 1990s of restoring historic Campeche – to the extent of rebuilding whole parts of the walls, and historic buildings such as the library – has also led to the **Malecón** or waterfront being rebuilt again. It's now a much more attractive waterside promenade that's popular with locals for evening strolling (it could still do with some cafés, especially for watching the wonderful sunsets). Just south of Puerta de Mar is the **Plaza Moch-Cuouh**, built during the *Resurgimiento* as a new, 'modern' town centre for official Campeche. Here are the tower-block **Palacio del Gobierno** and the **Palacio del Congreso**, the state Congress. The latter must have looked the height of new-wave modernity back in 1962, and is known as the *platillo volante* ('flying saucer').

A good way to see the old city is to walk around the *baluartes*, following the line of the walls. Most of its bastions now contain museums and cultural institutions. The full circuit is about 2km, but can be shortened by cutting corners.

Campeche's walls were major products of the military technology of their time. The initial work, planned by the Spanish engineer Martín de la Torre, was refined and extended by French military engineers after the arrival on the Spanish throne of the Bourbon dynasty under Louis XIV's grandson, Philip V, in 1700. The bastions are massive hexagons, with pepper-pot watchtowers at the corners. The **Baluarte de la Soledad**, designed to protect the Puerta de Mar and the sea approach to the city, is a classic example. Inside it there

Museo de la Arquitectura Maya
open daily 8–8

is the **Museo de la Arquitectura Maya**, with a collection mainly of carved stelae from Maya sites throughout Campeche state. Some of these stelae had been looted, but have since been recovered.

Taking the circuit in an anticlockwise direction, the next bastion, past Puerta de Mar and Plaza Moch-Cuouh, is the **Baluarte de San Carlos**. One of the oldest, begun in 1686, this hosts the **Museo de la Ciudad**, an entertaining, old-fashioned but detailed collection (mostly in Spanish only) on *conquistadores*, Franciscan church-building, pirates and much else. As well as climbing up to the ramparts, visitors can look into the dungeons down below. On the south side of the city there was once another gate, now demolished, which led to the *barrio* of San Román. Near where it stood there remains the **Baluarte de Santa Rosa**, now an exhibition space. It has an impressive ramp used to take cannons up to the battlements, and solid rooms for storing shot and gunpowder. Next is **Baluarte de San Juan**, the beginning of the longest surviving unbroken stretch of wall, which runs 500m to the **Puerta de Tierra** ('Land Gate'), built in 1732, and alongside it the **Baluarte de San Francisco**, now an INAH library. In the bastion beside the Puerta de Tierra is Campeche's most fun museum, the **Museo de la Piratería**, which trades shamelessly on all the most adventure-story sides of pirate history. Recently redone, it has audio guides for non-Spanish speakers, and videos. As part of the visit you can go up to the ramparts to enjoy fine views, and walk back along the wall to San Juan. On top of the gate there is still a bell, which warned travellers that the city gates were about to be shut for the night. The Puerta de Tierra is also the centre of the *Lugar del Sol* sound and light show (*see* p.392).

Museo de la Ciudad
open Tues–Sat 9–8, Sun 8–1

Museo de la Piratería
open daily 9–5; adm

Outside the walls by the Puerta de Tierra there is a shady but unkempt little park dating from the colonial era, the **Alameda**, with a curious bridge called **Puente de los Perros** because of the stone dogs guarding it. The next block along is the only place in Campeche where you are ever likely to see a real crowd, as it contains the **market**. Beyond it in the east corner of the old city is **Baluarte de San Pedro**, which was used as a prison by the Inquisition and so has a Vatican coat-of-arms above its gateway. Below its dramatic ramparts the lower floors now house the **Museo de Arte Popular**, a rather disappointing display of *campechano* handicrafts and textiles, with a souvenir shop. The last bastion in the northern corner, the **Baluarte de Santiago**, was partly torn down in the 1900s, then restored in the 1950s. It now contains a delightful little botanical garden, the **Jardín Botánico X'much Haltún**. Occasional free explanatory tours are given, in Spanish and English.

Museo de Arte Popular
open Tues–Sat 9–8, Sun 9–1

Jardín Botánico X'much Haltún
open daily 9–9

Within the 'walls', the streets of old Campeche have a special, old-world atmosphere enhanced by their very quietness, especially at night. Some of the most distinguished buildings are on C. 59, between the two main gates. At number 36, between Calles 14 and 16, is the **Casa del Teniente del Rey**, former residence of the Spanish Lieutenant-Governor of Campeche, with plain ochre-walled patios behind a grander portico, and which now contains the local INAH offices. Old Campeche is also full of churches, more colourfully ornate than those of Mérida and Yucatán proper. On the corner of C. 59 and C. 12 is the 18th-century **San Francisquito**, a wonderfully lush piece of Mexican Baroque with an altarpiece restored in its full colours of red and gold. It also contains a 17th-century painting of the Sacred Heart, by an artist, probably Flemish, called Michael Budesino. Three blocks along C. 12 at C. 55 is the **Dulce Nombre de Jesús**, also 18th-century, with a white interior interrupted by huge gold-on-white side altars.

On the next block on C. 12 is the city's very grand neoclassical **theatre**, built in the 19th century. One block from there towards the sea is one of the finest post-colonial residences in Campeche, the **Mansión Carvajal** (*C. 10 no. 14, x 51 & 53*). It was built around 1900 for Ramón Carvajal y Estrada, a local *hacendado*, in a Hispano-Moorish fantasy-style with patios of blue and white columns vaguely inspired by Córdoba and Granada, and an extraordinary curving staircase built of a single piece of Italian marble. Today anyone is free to wander around, as it's an advice and health centre, usually full of families with small children. At the other end of C. 10, beyond the square by C. 63, stands one of Campeche's largest churches, **San José**. Built as a Jesuit church in 1756, it's used today as an exhibition space. It's often closed, but it's still possible to appreciate its tiled façade, in chequered patterns of blue, white and gold.

Outside the Walls

Early colonial Campeche, like other Spanish American cities, had separate *barrios* outside its walls for other racial groups who were not allowed to live within the purely white city. San Román, south of the Circuito Baluartes and reached by continuing a few blocks along C. 12, was originally the district for blacks and *mulatos*. At its centre there is a large, pretty and very tranquil plaza, dominated by the early Franciscan church of **San Román**. Inside it's similarly simple but pretty, with fine tiling, but its most distinctive feature is the figure of Christ above the altar, which is black.

North of the *baluartes*, a walk along Av. Miguel Alemán, the continuation of C. 8, takes you into the *barrio* of Guadalupe, past little houses painted in blues, greens, reds and more of the local ochre. Beyond it is the very oldest surviving building of Spanish Campeche, **San Francisco**. Founded in 1546, this was the first missionary convent and chapel built by the Franciscans anywhere in the Yucatán, and its massively simple walls provided a place for *campechanos* to shelter from pirate attacks. Beside the church is the **Pozo de la Conquista**, a well where the expeditions of Hernández de Córdoba and later the Montejos are said to have come for fresh water. The district between San Francisco and the sea is modern Campeche's new 'growth area', with a convention centre, shopping malls and multiplex movie houses. More attractively, at the north end of the Malecón the authorities have also provided for a *Parador Gastronómico*, with a line of rather neat little restaurants, serving up local seafood on pretty terraces close to the water's edge.

The Fortress Museums

❷ Museo Regional de Campeche

The **Museo Regional de Campeche** was once a modest affair, despite the wealth of archaeological sites in the state. It was transformed by the extraordinary discoveries made at Calakmul and the Río Bec sites (*see* p.368) in the 1990s, including such spectacular artefacts as the jade funeral masks known as the *Máscaras de Calakmul*. To accommodate its new size, the museum was split and relocated to the Spanish forts on hilltops either side of the town: the Maya collection in the **Fuerte San Miguel**, to the south, while post-Conquest and maritime history is in **Fuerte San José** to the north. Fuerte San Miguel was made into a striking modern space to show off Campeche's Maya treasures, and a visit is an essential complement to a trip to the Río Bec.

The two forts, built from 1779 to 1801 (San Miguel before San José), were as much at the forefront of military technology as the city's ramparts a century earlier, and are among the best examples in the Americas of the ideas of the French fortress-builder Montalembert. They squat deep into their hilltops, behind mounds of earth and moats, with sunken zigzag driveways to prevent any

Getting to the Fortress Museums

Fuerte San Miguel is easy to find by car: follow the coastal avenue south, and look for a sign left on to a winding road up the hill. **El Guapo** tourist bus runs there (*see* p.390), but otherwise take any normal bus marked 'Lerma' along Av. 16 de Septiembre or Av. Ruíz Cortines to the same road junction, and take on the steep (but not killing) walk up to the fort. If you take a **taxi**, it may be worthwhile to pay the driver to wait to take you back; check whether there are any other cabs waiting outside when you arrive.

Fuerte San José is harder to find: by car, follow Av. Miguel Alemán to San Francisco, turn right and look out for signs to the left for San José el Alto. The road takes many twists and turns. As well as *El Guapo* there is a fairly direct bus: from the market, take any marked José el Alto or Bellavista, and ask the driver for the Fuerte San José. Buses return by the same route. Taxis are not plentiful.

**Museo de
Cultura Maya**
*open Tues–Sun
9.30–7.30; adm*

attacker getting a clear shot at the gates. However, they were only ever used once, during Santa Anna's attack of 1842.

The **Museo de Cultura Maya** in Fuerte San Miguel stands atop a hill about 3km south of the Parque Principal. Despite its expensive renovation the museum still has its quirks, especially in labelling (Spanish only, with many items not fully identified), but is still a fascinating demonstration of the sheer range of Maya art. Most of its rooms are arranged by theme (Time, City Life) rather than location, which can be confusing, but the most impressive spaces deal with specific places, especially **Room V**, devoted to Calakmul, with the great stars of the museum, the *Máscaras*. With white stucco and black obsidian for their strange, staring eyes, and all with their accompanying necklaces and earrings, they have faces that range from monstrous to highly naturalistic; some have an extraordinarily lifelike beauty, an almost smiling stillness (*note: the masks are also in demand for exhibitions worldwide, so some may be absent at any one time; check ahead if you're hoping to see the full set*). There's also a replica of the tomb of Yich'ak Kak or Jaguar-Paw of Calakmul just as he was discovered in 1997 (*see* p.370). **Room IV** is given over to Isla Jaina, with a dazzling collection of the island's figurines, showing an enormous variety of posture and expression: big-bellied merchants, women quietly weaving, even a man having a very difficult shit, another example of the constant Maya ability to surprise. Spread through all the rooms are superb, intricate ceramics, such as a fabulous modern-looking alabaster vase believed to have been made in Honduras, macaw-design pots from Balamkú, and stucco reliefs from Xcalumkin. After you've been around the collection, go up to the fort's ramparts for a wonderful view. Down below, by the sea, there's another small fort, San Luís.

**Museo de Barcos
y Armas**
*open Tues–Sun
9.30–5.30; adm*

The collection at Fuerte San José, now the **Museo de Barcos y Armas**, is far less spectacular. There's a fair amount of information on early Campeche and pirates (*all in Spanish*), plus muskets, swords, plates, nautical relics, and a few oddities that seem to have got here by accident, like an Arab axe. From the top, though, there's an even better view. Not far from the fort, overlooking Campeche, there's an ugly 1940s statue of Juárez, a fine example of the similarities between Mexican Revolutionary and Stalinist art.

(i) Campeche

There are three city information offices close to each other around the Parque Principal: inside Casa Seis (daily 9–9); a kiosk on the land side of the plaza (daily 9–8.30); and left of the Cathedral (daily 9–9). All have maps and local information, and sell tickets for the Sound and Light show, city tours and other events (see p.392). At Casa Seis you can also rent an audio guide. The Campeche state office (open daily 8–9, www.campeche.travel) on Plaza Moch-Cuouh, south of Puerta de Mar, is usually much less useful.

Tours and Tour Agencies

t (981–)

Campeche has two open-sided tourist bus tours, both starting from the Parque Principal. Tickets are sold in tourist offices. The **Tranvía de la Ciudad** does a circuit of the old city taking in all the main sights, and normally runs hourly every day (*9am–1pm and 5–9pm*), and costs around $7 (children $1.50); the **El Guapo** has a longer route including San José fortress (*9am, 5pm*) or San Ramón and the fortress of San Miguel (*10am–1pm and 6–8pm*), for a similar price. English-speaking guides are on board. Schedules reduced in low season.

Several local agencies run city tours, one-day tours to Edzná and the Chenes, and longer trips to Calakmul and the Río Bec (*see* pp.334 and 342).

Campeche Tarpon, C. 57 no. 6, x 8 & 10, t 816 4450, *www.campechetarpon.com*. Expert fly-fishing guides. *See* also p.380.

Expediciones Ecoturísticas de Campeche, C. 12 no. 168-A, x 59 & 61, t 816 0197. Kayaking, mountain biking, caving and other adventure trips.

IMC-Intermar, entrance to Hotel Baluartes, Av. 16 de Septiembre 128, t 816 9006, *www.grupointermar.com*. Big mainstream agency with tours of Campeche and archeological sites. Also has car rental and sometimes offers more adventurous trips such as kayak tours in the Petenes (*see* p.378).

Xtampak Tours, C. 57 no. 14, x 10 & 12, t 812 8655, *www.xtampak.com*. Low-cost agency with tours of the city, to Edzná (around $13) and more adventurous longer trips.

Services in Campeche

Banks: Several near the Parque Principal.

Health: Farmacia Cantó, C. 10, x 59, is centrally located and open late.

Internet Access: Lots on C. 10 and C. 12.

Post Office: Av. 16 de Septiembre, x C. 53 (*open Mon–Fri 8–7, Sat 9–1*).

Festivals

Carnaval (*Jan or Feb*): Proudly claimed to be the oldest Carnaval celebrations in Mexico: days of parades and other fun things, including a flower festival and face-painting day (Shrove Tuesday).

Shopping in Campeche

There is an attractive handicrafts and book shop in **Casa Seis** on the Parque Principal, and along Calle 59 there are several good crafts shops. **Casa de Artesanías Tukulná**, C. 10 no. 333, x 59 & 61, *www.tukulna.com*. Campeche's semi-official state showcase for local handicrafts, with a wonderful array of ceramics, baskets, embroidery and less classifiable things such as handmade deckchairs. There are beautiful traditional Campeche blouses, a variation on the *huipil*, with black-on-white embroidery.

Where to Stay in Campeche

Luxury

Hacienda Uayamón, 35km south of Campeche, off the Edzná road, t 813 0530, *www.thehaciendas.com*. Top of the options around Campeche is this *hacienda* hotel, in the 19th-century buildings of a remote old *henequen* estate towards Edzná. There are 10 rooms and two very chic suites, with *de rigueur* grand bathrooms, in pavilions around the main house, which like all Luxury Collection *haciendas* has a lovely terrace and **restaurant** (*expensive*). The transformation was done with panache, and the pool, in a ruined building, is stunning (even if its sun deck can be a fearsome suntrap). The surrounding countryside is very empty, and it feels still more like a lost rural retreat than Yucatán *haciendas*, but a superior range of excursions is available.

Hacienda Puerta Campeche, C. 59 no. 71, x 18, t 816 7535, *www.thehaciendas.com*. A change for the 'Luxury Collection' group that runs Uayamón, not a true *hacienda* but a colonial town mansion in Campeche's old city (by the Puerta de Tierra), converted in similar style. The 15 rooms, pool, gardens and **La Guardia** restaurant (*expensive*) are naturally luxurious and stylish, with the essential wow-factor design touches. The feel, though, is tightly intimate – or a bit cramped, depending on your taste – in place of the baronial expansiveness of the country *haciendas*.

Expensive–Moderate

Best Western Hotel Del Mar, Av. Ruíz Cortines 51, t 811 9191, *www.bestwestern. com*. Campeche's 'top hotel' until the arrival of the *haciendas*, the Del Mar is a big white 1970s block, presiding over the Malecón. It has two **restaurants** (*expensive*) and a good pool. It doesn't deal in character, but the plus of front rooms is a panoramic sea view; rooms at the back are far less attractive. Rates are only just into the *expensive* band.

Hotel Baluartes, Av. 16 de Septiembre 128, t 816 3911, *www.baluartes.com.mx*. Alongside the Del Mar, with a similarly bland style, the Baluartes has been extensively refurbished. Rooms are big, light and airy; there's a nice pool and **restaurant** (*moderate*), and front rooms also get a geat sea view.

Hotel Castelmar, C. 61 no. 2A, x 8 & 10, t 811 1204, *www.castelmarhotel.com*. This historic hotel a few steps from the Parque – dating from the 1880s – was in a decrepit state, but has recently been fully restored to make the most of its colonial-style patios, with the addition of a snug little pool. Rooms are traditionally styled but with high-quality modern facilities and WiFi. Prices are at the low end of the *moderate* band.

Hotel Plaza Campeche, C. 10 no. 126, t 811 9900, *www.hotelplazacampeche. com*. A plush modern hotel in an imposing colonial-style building by the Baluarte de Santiago. The traditional décor is a bit hacienda-like but without the same style, so comes at a lower price. The sheltered patio has a pool, and there's a decent **restaurant** (*moderate*). Facilities (WiFi) and service are excellent.

Inexpensive

Hotel América, C. 10 no. 252, x 59 & 61, t 816 4588, *www.hotelamericacampeche. com*. A characterful hotel very near the main square, in a renovated colonial house with a big, light patio. Not all its rooms are as impressive as the exterior, but they're airily spacious. Service is charming; breakfast and internet access (WiFi) are included.

Hotel Sir Francis Drake, C. 12 no. 207, x 63 & 65, t 811 5626, *www.hotelfrancis drake.com*. With an excellent old-city location, this is one of Campeche's

most comfortable mid-range options (near the top of price band). The 24 rooms have good bathrooms, a/c, TVs and fittings, suites have WiFi, and the restaurant, **La Balandra** (*moderate*), is nice for breakfast. Popular, so should be booked well ahead.

Budget

Hotel Colonial, C. 14 no. 122, x 55 & 57, t 816 2630. One for lovers of oddities: Campeche's oldest hotel is in the one-time home of Miguel de Castro y Araoz, Lieutenant-Governor of Campeche and one of the last Spanish governors of the Yucatán, who died in 1820. Modern hotel trends have passed it by, but it certainly has atmosphere, and rooms are very clean.

Hostal San Carlos, C. 10 no. 255, t 816 5158, *www.hostelcampeche.com.mx*. Dorm-only hostel ($8.50 per bed) in a bright, clean and colourful old house with airy patios, three blocks east of the old city along Calle 10. Breakfast, internet access and bikes for rent.

Monkey Hostel, C. 57 no. 6, on Parque Principal, t 811 6605, *www.hostal campeche.com*. Well-kept backpacker hostel in an unrivalled location, right on the Parque facing the Cathedral. There are dorm beds ($6) and double rooms (about $13), breakfast included; dorms are basic, but some have balconies and views befitting a far grander establishment. There's also a nice lounging area, a great roof terrace and a internet café.

Eating Out

One major reason to stop off in Campeche is to eat. Apparently unexcited about so many things, this city cares about its food, and *cocina campechana*, highlighting fish and seafood, is very distinctive and has greater subtlety than many Mexican cuisines. Classic dishes are *pan de cazón*, young hammerhead shark (*cazón*) chopped up and baked between *tortillas* in a tomato sauce, *camarón al coco* (prawn/shrimp in coconut), *arroz con pulpo* (octopus and rice salad), *manitas de cangrejo* (crab claws, mixed with other seafood) and fish many different ways, especially shark, red and black snapper, pompano and prawns.

As in Mérida, some of the best restaurants open only for long lunches, not at night.

Expensive

(★) **Chac-Pel** >

Chac-Pel, Av. Lázaro Cárdenas 8, **t** 813 1071. Less well-known than the more sedate La Pigua, this bustling, friendly restaurant has a very high reputation among locals. Seafood is naturally the mainstay, but there are ample meat options too; you can stay on the menu for a cheaper meal, but for something more memorable (and still not pricey) go for the wonderful fish-of-the-day specials, cooked to order in one of several different ways. The Chac-Pel is well off Campeche's tourist trails – on one of the avenues on the south side of town – but cab drivers know it (if driving, follow Av. República to Santa Ana church, then head right). In line with tradition, it's lunch-only, but a fish feast here can happily fill a whole afternoon. *Open 11am–7pm only.*

(★) **Rincón Colonial**>>

La Pigua, Av. Miguel Alemán 179A, **t** 811 3365, *www.lapigua.com.mx*. The most prestigious address in town, this pretty but discreet seafood restaurant is just northeast of the *baluartes*. Its variations on traditional dishes are skilfully done – especially the great *camarones al coco* – with superb local ingredients, and it is extremely comfortable. By international standards it is also still very cheap. La Pigua also opens in the evenings (*daily 1–5.30 and 7.30–11*).

Moderate

Casa Vieja, C. 10 no. 319 (Parque Principal). This bar-restaurant with *campechano* favourites stands or falls by its great location, in the first-floor colonnade above the *portales* on the square, with views of the Cathedral.

La Iguana Azul, C. 55 no. 9, x 10 & 12. A vaguely youth-oriented modern restaurant, opposite the traditional Parroquia: food can be hit and miss, but there's a fun atmosphere.

La Parroquia, C. 55 no. 8, x 10 & 12. A great long-running family restaurant just off the main square, with the special plus of being open 24hrs a day. Unfussily friendly and fine value, it offers enjoyable *campechano* fish specialities as well as Mexican standards and excellent breakfasts.

Restaurante Marganzo, C. 8 no. 267, x 57 & 59, **t** 811 3898. With colourful semi-traditional décor, the Marganzo is just off the Parque Principal. Service is charming, and it's open at night, but its dishes are not quite at the same level as at the Pigua or the Chac-Pel.

Restaurant Miramar, C. 8 no. 291-A, x 61. Near the Marganzo, but simpler and cheaper with good seafood.

Budget

Restaurant Campeche, C. 57 no. 2 (Parque Principal). Right on the square, and a foreigners' favourite for breakfast, lunch and dinner. Recently done up with the addition of a/c, too.

Rincón Colonial, C. 59, x 18. Fabulous museum-piece of a classic wooden-doored, lofty-ceilinged *cantina*, opposite the chic Puerta Campeche (*see* p.380), with amazingly cheap but great *botanas* to go with beers, a few bigger dishes, and musicians playing most days. A lot of young women go there as well as men, and on Sundays everyone is exhorted to 'bring the family'. *Open daily 9–8.30.*

Entertainment

Like Mérida the city sponsors a varied programme. **Casa Seis** hosts free *Jueves de Música Campechana* sessions of traditional music every Thurs, and *Viernes Folclórico*, of folk music and dancing, every Fri, both at 8pm. The fountains near the **Puerta de Mar** are lit up to music every night, and there are free concerts and folklore shows in the **Parque Principal** every Sat from 6pm, and all day Sun from 9am–11pm. *El Lugar del Sol* ('The Place of the Sun',) a sound and light show evoking Campeche's pirate history, is presented at the **Puerta de Tierra** from 8pm every Tues, Fri and Sat. Tickets can be bought in the Museo de la Piratería or Casa Seis.

El Lorencillo, **t** 816 1990. This pretty unconvincing 'pirate ship' (it only has one mast) cruises up and down the coast twice a day, Tues–Sun (12 noon, 6pm), with entertainment on board. It leaves from **Lerma**, south of the city, so take a cab if you don't go with a tour. Cost: about $7 adults, $3.50 under-12s.

Edzná and the Chenes

If Campeche as a whole does not receive many visitors, the centre of the state sees even fewer. The Chenes style of architecture is referred to in every book on the Maya, yet the Chenes sites and even the nearby city of Edzná are little known, too far from the well-publicized Mérida–Cancún routes and at the end of too many winding forest roads to be an easy trip. This area, though, is not really hard to get to, and the very absence of other travellers can make a visit here an enjoyably personal experience.

Edzná

★ Edzná
Open daily 8–5; adm

Although Edzná is on the western edge of the Chenes region, it is really one of the great Maya cities that, like Chichén Itzá, stands on its own, with a unique mix of styles and features that reflects its position at a crossroads in the flow of trade and cultural influences. The site was occupied from around 600 BC, but as a city Edzná developed from about AD 300 and reached its greatest extent, like others in central Yucatán, in the Late Classic. The valley it occupies is slightly isolated from the main regions of Maya civilization, but this location gave it an influential position on the routes between the Puuc, the Chenes and northern Yucatán to the north and east, and the Río Bec, the Petén and the Usumacinta to the south.

It also brought Edzná into early contact with the Putún-Itzá traders of Tabasco. It used to be thought the name Edzná came from the Yucatec for 'House of Grimaces', a reference to its Temple of the Stone Masks, but a more recent theory is that it meant 'House of the Itzá', suggesting Edzná was influenced by the Itzá long before Chichén Itzá. A substantial number of dated stelae have been found here, with dates from the 4th century to 810, the same year as the last date at Calakmul. The great Maya crisis reached Edzná around 850–950, but the site was still occupied on a small scale until after 1300. Despite its closeness to Campeche, Edzná was lost in the forest until 1927, when it was found by a local ruins enthusiast, Nazario Quintana Bello. Even now you can still often have the site to yourself on weekdays. At the weekend there is a sound-and-light show (*see* p.396).

The Great Plaza and the Great Acropolis

A good deal has been opened up quite recently at Edzná. The area normally visited around the Great Plaza is only one part of the city, known as the 'Eastern Group'. To the west is another group of partly excavated buildings centred on a large pyramid known as the **Casa de la Vieja Hechicera** ('House of the Old Witch'). Edzná, in a very dry area, also had one of the most sophisticated Maya systems for channelling and retaining water, with over 13km of canals and ditches connecting more than 100 *chultunes* and *aguadas*.

Edzná's mixture of styles stands out immediately: the layout of the city – its recurrent 'trios' of pyramids on top of flat platforms – is reminiscent of the Classic cities of the Petén such as Tikal, but among the individual buildings there are several in Puuc, Chenes or Río Bec styles, and others that are entirely original. The path from the main entrance takes you to the northwest corner of the Great Plaza. To the left, forming the north side of the square, there is a long, low platform, the **Platform of the Knives**, so-called because flint ritual knives were discovered buried beneath it. This was a residence for some of the élite of Edzná, with seven large rooms and an **Annexe** at its western end. To the right of the path along the west side of the Great Plaza there is a giant 130m ramp of steps, the **Nohochná** or 'Big House', with four buildings along the top. These may have had some specific or administrative purpose, but it's likely, too, that the abnormally long steps of the Nohochná were used as 'grandstands' for spectators watching ceremonies in the Great Plaza.

This was only fitting, for the plaza and acropolis of Edzná form one of the most dramatic examples of the Maya conception of cities as theatrical ritual stages. As well as systematic geometry the whole ensemble has a cosmological design: a line from the steps of the Five Storeys, through the centre-stones of the acropolis steps and the Nohochná and across to the partly excavated Structure 501 (west of the plaza) corresponds to the line of the setting sun on 13 August, Maya creation day. The Great Plaza also has a distinctive echo, which was deliberately accentuated by the ramps on the back of the South Temple, at the south end of the Nohochná.

The **Great Acropolis** itself is a huge, low platform, measuring 170m by 96m, probably started about AD 400. It conforms closely to the Petén style of temple platform, with one large pyramid and several smaller ones forming a raised 'sanctuary-plaza', of a higher level of sacredness and exclusivity than the main square below it. The structure that dominates the view, though, is unique to Edzná, the extraordinary **Building of the Five Storeys** (*Edificio de los Cinco Pisos*). It was built in five different stages, and probably began as a simple pyramid in Petén style (the 'storeys' are built on to the pyramid sides, not on top of each other). Then, from about AD 600, five tiers of rooms were added to the side facing the plaza. This took a long time: an inscription near the bottom has a date from 652, but it was probably finished after 800. Inside are rows of rooms, which were probably both ritual spaces and residences for the *ahau*-lineage of Edzná. A steep ramp of steps runs straight up the middle to the fifth 'storey', a small temple with a Río Bec-like roof-comb. There is also an internal tunnel-staircase to all five levels, though unfortunately this cannot be visited. From the top there is a superb view, across to the 'Old Witch' pyramid to the west. This too aligned with the Five Storeys, along the line of the moon on certain nights of the year.

Getting to Edzná

There are two ways to **drive** to Edzná from Campeche. The shortest route (55km) is to take Av. Central south from Circuito Baluartes as far as the main highway around Campeche, turn left, and then look for a right turn signed to Chiná. From this village a country lane carries on 30km until it meets the Hopelchén– Champotón road, where you turn left (Edzná is 10km to the east). A longer route (61km) is to follow Av. Gobernadores until it becomes Highway 261 to Mérida, and then, after 40km, turn southwards in San Antonio Cayal.

The Edzná area is thinly populated and there are few **buses**. *Combis* from the market in Campeche and a few second-class buses to the villages of **Alfredo Bonfil** and **Pich** all pass the ruins, but check the times of the last buses back if if you want to return the same day (the last return may be around 3pm). Hence tours are handy, especially the shuttle-like service of **Xtampak Tours** (*see* p.390).

As you come down the steps you can better appreciate the features of the other buildings on the Acropolis. All face inwards, accentuating the separateness of the Acropolis-plaza. To the left is the **Temple of the Moon**, a large and very steep platform. Next to it in the corner of the Acropolis is a small pyramid, the **Southwest Temple**, which, it is believed, was only added to maintain the symmetry of the Acropolis after the **Northwest Temple** was begun on the other side. The latter was added to many times, from around 450 until the last days of the city, and has Puuc columns and Chenes carvings on its basic Petén structure. In around 800 a small platform

11   Campeche State | Edzná

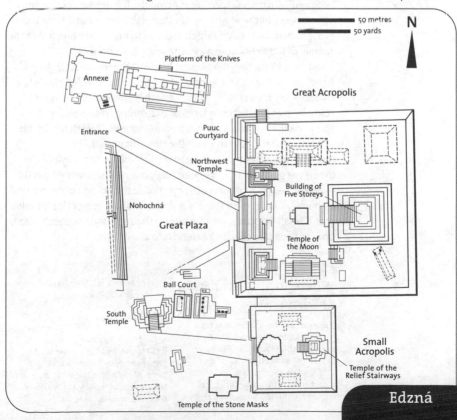

50 metres
50 yards
N

Platform of the Knives

Annexe

Great Acropolis

Entrance

Puuc Courtyard

Northwest Temple

Building of Five Storeys

Nohochná

Great Plaza

Temple of the Moon

Ball Court

South Temple

Small Acropolis

Temple of the Relief Stairways

Temple of the Stone Masks

Edzná

was added on its north side, which forms one side of the **Puuc Courtyard**. This and other buildings on the north side of the Acropolis were probably residential complexes, possibly for court servants or scribes. In one there was a *temazcal* or ritual steam-bath.

The Small Acropolis and the Stone Masks

On the south side of the Great Plaza is Edzná's main **Ball Court**, surrounded by annexe-buildings which must have had some function to do with the game and its ritual. Next to them is the **South Temple**, which you approach from the back: the main temple faces into another plaza to the south. The main body of this pyramid was built around 500 in a Petén style, but the final temple at the top was added after 700.

Filling the square to the left of the south plaza is the **Small Acropolis**. It is a temple platform very similar to the Great Acropolis, but its earliest buildings are probably some of the oldest at Edzná, from the Preclassic or Early Classic. In the same way that the Maya built pyramids on top of older ones, so the Petén cities built whole new temple platforms to supplant earlier, smaller ones, which may have been in use a relatively short time. Thus, this platform was 'replaced' by the far larger Great Acropolis. It was also considerably altered, since in the very Late Classic stelae from around Edzná were brought here and used fairly chaotically to make the staircase of the **Temple of the Relief Stairways**, the largest pyramid.

Just next to the Small Acropolis is one of the most fascinating structures at Edzná, the **Temple of the Stone Masks** (*Templo de los Mascarones*). It's a smallish temple with, either side of its main stairway, two giant stucco faces or *mascarones* representing the sun-god Kinich-Ahau: as dawn, a young face, on the left (east) side; as dusk, a wizened old man, on the right (the west). The mythological faces incorporate many features of the Maya of the time – the god's teeth have been filed, and he is shown fashionably cross-eyed – while other motifs symbolize the sky and other natural elements. It is believed there is a similar mask in one of the temples of the Small Acropolis, yet to be unearthed. Around the south plaza, unexcavated bits of Edzná extend into the woods.

Where to Stay and Eat at Edzná

Turístico San Pedro, Tixmucuy, t 812 7929. Facilities are minimal at the ruins, but this place near Tixmucuy, 5km from Edzná on the road from Chiná, offers a restaurant (*moderate*), a pool and a little 'adventure park' with horse-riding, cycles, quad bikes

for rent and more. There are also a few simple cabañas (*inexpensive*).

Entertainment

The *Luz de los Itzaes* ('Light of the Itzá') **sound-and-light show** is presented every Fri and Sat at 7pm (8pm, Mar–Oct), in the same style as the shows at Chichén Itzá or Uxmal. It's often included in tours.

Hopelchén and the Chenes Sites

Chen is Yucatec for 'well'. In the Chenes Hills of central Campeche, as in the Puuc Hills just to the north, the water table is a long way beneath the surface. To obtain water, the Maya – as well as using *chultunes, aguadas* and other ingenious techniques – had to search far underground, in 'wells' that were sometimes giant caverns. Nevertheless, in the Late Classic era this apparently unfavourable area contained a large number of small Maya cities, which flourished at the same time as the Puuc and Río Bec sites to north and south, and were an important conduit in the flow of communications in the Maya world. The Chenes cities developed a very original style of architecture, in which intricate decoration was used to make whole buildings in the form of gods and mythological creatures, around giant-mouth doorways, presenting more vividly than any other style the Maya concept of a building as a point of contact with the spirit world. These Chenes characteristics spread all over the Yucatán.

The original Chenes sites have been known about for years, but only very recently has much effort been put into making them properly accessible to visitors. They can be recommended to people who like a sense of solitude with their ruins, and enjoy exploring; one that at many times has been all but inaccessible, Santa Rosa Xtampak, counts among the most dramatic of Maya sites. The Maya villages along the roads, most with names ending in *-chen* because of their wells, are full of remote placidity.

While Edzná is close enough to Campeche to make an easy day trip, visiting the Chenes means staying at least one night in the area. **Hopelchén** is the region's town, road junction, bus stop, market and centre of everything else, and has the one hotel. It's also an enjoyably quirky piece of the Mexican countryside.

In the middle of Hopelchén there are two interconnecting plazas, a little market, a large, plain Franciscan church and, quite often, signs welcoming you in an old German dialect. This is because Hopelchén was 'chosen' to be the site of Campeche's largest colony of Mennonites, numbering over 4,000, who started coming here in the 1950s from the USA and Canada. The local Maya do good business driving them around, and comment only that they work very hard and have a lot of children, which coming from a Maya is saying something. Just west of the town there is a tiny Maya site, **Tohcok**, with one small, Puuc-style plaza.

The sites described here are those normally accessible to visitors. True ruins devotees can find many more that have never been opened up or scarcely excavated at all, and are reachable only by 4WD trek and/or a hike. At Hopelchén town hall they can help you find guides and maybe even a vehicle, but this will take a day or so to set up.

Santa Rosa Xtampak and Bolonchén

Santa Rosa Xtampak
open daily 8–5; adm

About 5km north of Hopelchén on the road toward Uxmal there is a turn-off east for **Santa Rosa Xtampak**. The sign says 36km, but the real distance is over 40km. The Maya site at the far end was visited by Stephens and Catherwood and many expeditions since then, but its distance from any road long kept it utterly remote. A paved road was laid in 1998, in an effort by the local administration to open up the area; however, it has not been consistently maintained, and is often in a bad state for months at a time. In a standard car you need to take your time, and you'll get there more comfortably with a 4WD vehicle.

Studies have indicated that, despite its apparent isolation, Xtampak was the dominant city in the whole Chenes region, enjoying its greatest prosperity in about 650–850. It had 67 *chultunes* for retaining water, which could have supported a population of about 12,000, and had more glyph inscriptions than any other Chenes site, with dates running from 750 to 889. Sadly, all these carvings were looted from the site between the 1920s and the 1980s. Another very intriguing aspect of Xtampak is the exceptional size of its surviving structures, some of which look as if they were made on a completely different scale from that normally seen in Maya buildings.

The well at Bolonchén, drawn by F. Catherwood (1842)

Xtampak stands on some of the tallest and steepest hills in the Yucatán, which were added to by the city's builders. They are still covered in forest and at first, as you trudge off up the very steep path from the caretaker's hut, you don't see any ruins except the remains of a few *chultunes*. After Stephens came to Xtampak, which he knew as Labphak, in 1841 he wrote that '...we saw peering through the trees the white front of a lofty building, which in the imperfect view we had of it, seemed the grandest we had seen in the country...'. You can have virtually the same experience today. As you emerge near the top of the hill into a broad area flattened off as a plaza, there ahead of you is the towering mass

Getting to and around the Chenes

Hopelchén and the Chenes are served by second-class **buses**. There are five daily each way on the 'slow route' between Mérida and Campeche via Uxmal, and one more between Mérida and Hopelchén and Dzibalchén only. From Campeche there are six more services every day to Hopelchén, Dzibalchén or Iturbide, one of which continues on the long drive to Xpuhil. These buses will take you to the villages, but not Mayan sites: to do that, negotiate with local taxi or *combi* drivers.

Hopelchén is on Highway 261, the 'slow route' from Mérida to Campeche via Uxmal, and can be visited easily **by car** from the Puuc Route. From Campeche, the 261 road is a continuation of Av. Gobernadores, often signposted *Mérida–Via Larga*. To get to Hopelchén from Edzná, turn right to join Highway 261 at San Antonio Cayal (19km), where you turn right again.

From Hopelchén a paved road also leads south to Xpuhil in the Río Bec (*see* p.360), through 150km of forest, swamps and lonely farmsteads. Hopelchén's **petrol/gas station** is the only one in a very wide area.

of the **Palacio**, rising through three levels. This is the most sophisticated of all Maya 'multi-storey' buildings, with over 40 rooms and intricate internal staircases; very unusually it must have been planned from the outset as one structure, rather than being built up through 'add-ons' over decades like most large Maya buildings. At its top is the **Casa del Rey**, a monster-mouth temple with a fabulous view. One of the most striking features of the Palacio is its un-Maya proportions: even the doorways seem made for a different race.

The Palacio formed the axis of two interconnecting plazas. Across the larger one there is a fine Chenes monster-mouth, and a temple with a **Diving God** carving like those at Tulum or Sayil, the presence of which is unexplained. A path from this plaza leads to a residential complex called the **Casa Colorada** ('Red House'), because when Teobert Maler came here in 1902 it retained some of its original colour. Further down the path is the extraordinary **Cuartel** ('Barracks'), so named for its severe appearance, a giant blockhouse that seems far too big to be Maya, and which once formed just one side of a huge quadrangle. In the woods are more quadrangles – the **Monjas** (Nunnery), the **Southeast Quadrangle** – all built on a similar scale. Along the way you pass relics of *chultunes*, a ball court and buildings part-covered by forest, and the foot of the **Pyramid of the Sun**, one of four pyramids at Xtampak, built on to a natural hill.

As you wander around the site you also find wonderful views, of forest stretching into infinity. Xtampak is also one of the sites with the widest variety of wildlife, such as some of the most exotic the Yucatán has to offer: jaguars supposedly appear quite frequently, and there are said to be snakes about, above all whenever it's wet.

Leaving the Xtampak access road, the road north toward Uxmal leads in 30km to **Bolonchén de Rejón** or 'Nine Wells', one of the most pleasant Chenes villages. About 3km south, a sign points to the

Grutas de Xtacumbilxunaan

open Tues–Sun 10–5; adm

Grutas de Xtacumbilxunaan, or Great Well of Bolonchén, the most spectacular of the Chenes cavern-wells and the subject of one of Catherwood's most famous drawings (*see* p.398). For centuries, this was the only source of water in the dry season for miles around.

When Stephens came here he described an extraordinary scene as long lines of Maya clambered down with water jars, in pitch darkness or by the light of torches, through passages hundreds of feet below ground to whichever level retained water. Once a year, he was told, a *fiesta* was held at the bottom of the great chamber.

The cavern also has its legends. *Xtacumbilxunaan* means 'the hidden maiden', and refers to Lolbé, a Maya princess who wished to marry a humble young man called Dzulan. Her father the local king, however, wouldn't hear of it, and in his rage hid Lolbé in the cave. The hero Dzulan, of course, found out and went in after her, and the two wander the caverns for ever after. The bottom of the cave leads into seven underground rivers. Today visits to the *Grutas* include a **sound and light show**, but you're only allowed as far as the first level, the top of the great pit. The huge wood-and-rope staircase Catherwood saw survived until a few years ago, and it has been promised it will be rebuilt, but this is a long time coming.

A little north of Bolonchén a lonely road leads west off the highway to the village of Xculoc. About 11km up this road is a Maya site,

Chunhuhub
open daily 8–5; adm

Chunhuhub. One of the early Puuc cities, it has been all-but ignored because it is (only just) in Campeche, but it was one of the sites explored by Stephens in 1841. It has an elegant **Palacio** with fine Puuc mouldings, recorded in a beautiful drawing by Catherwood.

South of Hopelchén

A narrow road winds south from Hopelchén for about 40km to the second-largest community in the Chenes, **Dzibalchén**. The road, shrouded in forest, is paved, but it's still useful to have a guide, as many roads and tracks are unsignposted. Also village *topes* are not indicated, so you need to watch out.

When you eventually bounce into the grass-patch plaza of Dzibalchén, there's a ramshackle hut grandly marked '*módulo de información turística*'. This can seem wildly optimistic but there are many places in this empty region that are impossible to find without local help. Eventually, someone will offer their services. Nearby at

Hochchob
open daily 8–5; adm

Hochchob, 4km away and reached by turning southwest from the

Tourist Information in Hopelchén

t (996–)

Hopelchén has a **bank** (with ATM), **post office**, **shops** and a **tourist information kiosk** (*Mon–Fri 8–2 and 5–8*), next to Hotel Los Arcos in the plaza. It's often unattended, but staff can find local guides for you. Just north of town there is a shop-workshop with local handicrafts, the **Centro Artesanal Los Chenes**.

Where to Stay and Eat in Hopelchén

Around the plaza there are many *loncherías* and taco-houses. Nowhere seems to serve alcohol with food.

Hotel Los Arcos, on the plaza, t 100 8782 (*budget*).This is the region's one and only hotel. It has two things going for it: a) it's there; b) it doesn't capitalize on its monopoly by pushing up prices. Be ready for minimal furniture, plain beds and cell-like walls. But it's clean and the showers work.

plaza, there is a small Chenes site of three steep platforms around a hilltop plaza, with intricate decoration using typical Chenes imagery.

Returning to Dzibalchén plaza, to the right is the road which after many hours will get you to **Xpuhil** (*see* p.361); alternatively, if you continue through the village to the northeast, you will in 20km come to **Iturbide**, a village marked forever by the Caste War, still with crude blockhouses built to defend against Mayan attacks. Around 2km east is another Chenes site, **Dzibilnocac**. This is potentially a large site, but only the central plaza has been fully excavated.

Dzibilnocac
open daily 8–5; adm

South from Campeche

There is only one route towards 'Mexico' from Campeche city. The avenue along the Malecón goes through several changes of name, until it runs south into **Lerma**, now Campeche's main port area and the base for most of its fishing fleet. Beyond Lerma is **Playa Bonita**, traditionally Campeche's favourite beach, although water and sand are often dirty. The coast road meets the *Periférico*, the ring road around Campeche, where drivers have a choice: for heavy-duty traffic there is a *cuota* motorway that runs inland to Champotón (toll), leaving the winding Highway 180 coast road more tranquil. First-class buses take the *cuota*, second-class the coast road.

The old 180 road also runs a little inland after Lerma, rolling through valleys just out of sight of the sea. It rejoins the coast 30km south at **Seybaplaya**, a windblown little town with a long beach lined with fishermen's launches. The Gulf Coast waters are sandy and opal-coloured rather than crystalline, but by this point are pretty clean, and the beaches here can be fine for a stop-off. A better place to stop than Seybaplaya is **Sihoplaya**, 10km further south, with just one, specially attractive upscale hotel.

The road continues on past more beaches, and a turning inland for Edzná and the Chenes. Sixteen kilometres on from this junction you reach **Champotón**, at the mouth of the Río Champotón, the most northerly river in the Yucatán. This was where Hernández de Córdoba made the first proper Spanish landfall on the Mexican mainland in 1517, and nearly died shortly afterwards at the hands of Moch-Cuouh and his men, in a struggle so desperate that the Spaniards remembered the place as the *Bahía de la Mala Pelea* or 'Bay of the Bad Battle'. To commemorate its place in history Champotón still has a crumbling Spanish bastion at the mouth of the river, built like the walls of Campeche in the 17th century to guard against the pirates of Tris. It's a friendly, straightforward little town, with a sizable fishing fleet. It also has another role as a no-frills beach town, mostly for day-trippers from Campeche.

Below Champotón the road divides. Heavy traffic takes Highway 201 straight south to Escárcega, the only direct road to Chiapas, but

Where to Stay and Eat

Hotel Tucan Sihoplaya >

Hotel Tucán Sihoplaya, Ctra Campeche –Champotón Km 35, **t** (982) 596 1817, *www.tucansihoplaya.com* (*moderate*). Distinctive hotel in a much-altered old *hacienda* atop a low cliff by the Gulf Coast. The modern rooms and **restaurant** could be more in style with the setting, but they're very comfortable, and its great assets are its superb setting, its beach all to itself (where turtles breed in spring) and a beautiful pool above the rocks.

an alternative is to follow the Gulf round to Villahermosa on Highway 180. A few kilometres south on the coast road the view is suddenly filled by a huge construction site. This is supposedly a key to raising Campeche's international profile, **Campeche Playa**. Planned by a Spanish developer and heavily boosted by the state government, it is due to include apartments, shops, a Jack Nicklaus-designed golf course and more. However, completion dates have been repeatedly postponed, and whether it will survive in the post-2008 economy is questionable (*see www.campecheplaya.com*).

The Gulf Coast Route

The Gulf coast

Campeche Playa apart, the coastal strip along which the 180 road runs is all but empty for 150km, with a continuous shell beach and opal sea on one side, and on the other mangroves and endless electricity pylons. There are superb sunsets here, from terracotta to deep purple blue. At distant intervals there are stopping-places – **Playa Varadero, Sabancuy** – with beach bars offering fried fish.

After Sabancuy the road runs along a peninsula called **El Palmar**, the Palm Grove, lined by coconut palms and lush banks of *ceibas*, and with an abundance of pelicans and terns. At 105km from Champotón you reach the north side of Laguna de Términos and the 3km **Puente de la Unidad** (*toll*) to Isla del Carmen. It's 40km to Ciudad del Carmen, with only beach bars along the way.

Ciudad del Carmen

Ciudad del Carmen is not on anyone's list of must-see Mexican cities today, but it has as romantic and dramatic a history as any in the country. The Isla del Carmen on which it stands was once none other than the Isla de Tris, a legendary pirate stronghold that for decades drove the region's Spanish governors to despair. In the last 30 years two giant bridges have clamped the island into Mexican territory, but in the 17th century its position at the mouth of the Laguna de Términos left it completely isolated, a perfect place to defend. French lowlifes were the first to gather here in 1558, to be joined by others from England, Holland and many other countries. It was from Tris that buccaneers like Diego the Mulatto, 'Peg-Leg' and *Lorencillo* launched their assaults on Campeche, while one Spanish expedition after another was sent against the island without much success. Finally, a more solid attack was mounted,

Getting to and around Ciudad del Carmen

Carmen's busy **airport** has more flights than Campeche. **MexicanaClick (t** 01 800 112 5425) and **Interjet (t** 01 800 011 2345) fly from Mexico City, and **AeroMexico Connect (t** 01 800 800 2376) to Mexico City, Veracruz and Tampico. It has **international** flights too, **Continental Express** from Houston (**t** US and Canada 01 800 5233273). The **bus station** is on Av. Periférica, outside the centre. There are first- and second-class buses at least once each hour to Villahermosa or Campeche and Mérida, five to Mexico City, nine to Cancún and Playa del Carmen via Mérida, and two to Chetumal via Xpuhil.

Arriving **by car** from the north, Highway 180 runs through the outskirts to become Av. Periférica. Follow this round to the right and look for signs for *Centro* on to C. 31, which leads to the main plaza. **Taxis** cost $2–3.

Car Hire

Agrisa, C. 40 no.101-B, x 31 & 31-C, **t** 382 7550, *www.agrisa.com.mx*. From around $40 a day.
Alamo, C. 31 no.45-A, x 34 & 36, **t** 382 9304. Good low-cost offers at weekends.

Orientation

Despite a disconcerting street numbering system (odd numbers east–west, evens roughly north–south, but each street is divided into sections, 42A, 42B, etc.), the town is easy to get around. Once off Av. Periférica, streets converge on the plaza, officially Parque Ignacio Zaragoza, by the waterfront on the western edge of the island. Carmen's two main commercial streets, 31 and 22, meet at the plaza.

---

and in 1717 the island was taken. Every last pirate was driven out, and in 1722 a new town was founded, with the suitably Catholic name of Ciudad del Carmen.

After the pirates, the town made its living from fishing and exporting dyewoods, but the biggest thing to hit it lately has been oil. Modern oil-town Carmen is a sprawling place, and noticeably busy: the oil business has brought in a flow of outsiders from Mexico City and around the world, to stir up the rhythms of local life. It's also a major fishing port, and known to Mexicans as a holiday town, with Gulf Coast beaches.

Down by the waterfront is **Parque Ignacio Zaragoza**, with restaurants and, around dusk, a stream of people meeting up, talking, looking, eating and just mingling. The slightly Gothic **Cathedral**, built in the 1850s, is plain and white from the outside, but inside its apse is a riot of colour, with pink and grey walls and chubby painted cherubs around a gold-clad *Virgen del Carmen*. Calle 20 leads to the tidied-up **Malecón**, with waterside bars and cafés. South of the plaza is the remaining part of the little 18th-century town, a few streets of grille-windowed colonial houses.

Museo de la Ciudad
open Wed–Sun 9–5; adm

Five blocks north on C. 22 from the plaza is Carmen's **Museo de la Ciudad**, an attractive collection that tells you a huge amount about the town and its island, from Maya settlement to pirates. Carmen has beaches on both sides of the island: **Playa Caracol** to the south and **Playa Norte** on the ocean side, a much bigger affair.

In the southwest corner of the town the Periférica runs on to the huge **Puente Zacatal**, across the mouth of the Laguna de Términos. A few kilometres beyond its western end is **Xicalango**, famous as the site of a landing by Cortés in 1519 and the place where he acquired *La Malinche* (*see* p.48). The 70km road to the Tabasco state line is thinly populated and very swampy, lined by lakes full of birds.

Tourist Information in Ciudad del Carmen

(i) **Ciudad del Carmen**
near the plaza, in the Casa de Cultura, C. 24, x 27 & 29 (open Mon–Fri 9–2 and 5–8). Has decent free town maps.

t (938–)
Banks: around the plaza or on C. 24.
Internet Access: CompuNet-Cyberclub, on C. 29 just off C. 24, is cheap.

Where to Stay in Ciudad del Carmen

Hotel Acuario, C. 51 no. 60, x 26 & 28, t 382 3947, *acuario@prodigy.net.mx* (*inexpensive*). On the north side of town towards the beach, but with pleasant rooms and good facilities, and a nice pool and garden.

Hotel del Parque, C. 33, x 20 & 22, t 382 3046 (*inexpensive*). Comfortable hotel on the plaza. Book early.

Eating Out in Ciudad del Carmen

The cheapest places are on the plaza, the two-level line of *loncherías* along the C. 33 side (all *budget*), which are great vantage points for watching the square's movements.

Los Pelícanos, C. 24 no. 46-A, x 29 (*moderate*). Pretty restaurant-bar in a garden, with Mexican standards and local seafood specialities. The bar is a local meeting point.

Cafetería La Fuente, C. 20 x 29 (*moderate–budget*). Café on the Malecón where local gentlemen play dominoes next to two pirate-era cannons. No alcohol, but great for breakfast and light meals.

Inland through Escárcega

The main route for all traffic out of Yucatán is Highway 201, south from Champotón. After a long while the Yucatán woods begin to fade away, to be replaced by cattle pastures and *ranchos* across southwest Campeche into Chiapas and Tabasco.

Escárcega, 150km from Campeche and 86km from Champotón at the junction of Highways 201 and 186, has the reputation of being the ugliest town in Mexico. A giant truck-stop, it's probably a town best seen in the rain. Just about every vehicle travelling into or out of the Yucatán peninsula has to stop in Escárcega, at the giant *gasolinera* that is the town's *raison d'être*, but few choose to stay much longer. Beyond Escárcega, the road, now Highway 186, continues southwest for over 140km of flat, featureless, almost hypnotically green tropical cowboy country to enter Tabasco. About 60km west is a turn off south to the shabby border town of **Candelaria,** beyond which a paved track leads in another 70km to the ruins of **El Tigre.** This is believed to be the site of **Itzamkanaak,** capital of one of the last of the Maya kingdoms, which resisted Cortés when he came through here in 1521. This is another ruin for Maya explorers and lovers of the remote; facilities at and near the site are minimal. As an alternative to the long bumpy drive, you can also get there by hiring a boat in Candelaria.

El Tigre
open daily 8–5; adm

Where to Stay and Eat in Escárcega

t (982–)

Both these worn but reasonable hotels in Escárcega are beside Highway 186, and also have straight-forward **restaurants** (*moderate*).

Hotel Escárcega, Av. Justo Sierra 86, t 824 0187 (*budget*). Plain but decent rooms, with fans only or a/c, with good light and lined up around a quite pretty patio.

Hotel María Isabel, Av. Justo Sierra 127, t 824 0045 (*budget*). Motel-style, with big rooms (fan or a/c) and TV.

Tabasco

In landscape, Tabasco offers a total contrast from the Yucatán. Whereas in the peninsula a great deal of life has been taken up with looking for water, in Tabasco there's too much of it. Criss-crossed by two giant rivers, the Grijalva and the Usumacinta, and innumerable tributaries, the state seems almost a series of islands between broad lagoons. Everything is a deep, lush green, simmering at near to 40° C. For some 60 years this sultry tropical delta has been a hub of Mexico's oil industry, the driving force behind the often crazy-looking urban tangle of the state capital, Villahermosa. Three thousand years earlier, the delta was also the unlikely location for the emergence of the first of the great Mesoamerican cultures – the Olmecs, who left a breathtaking legacy of massive, powerful sculptures. Later the Maya too arrived here, and built one of their strangest cities at Comalcalco.

12

Don't miss

⭐ Tropical vegetation and deserted beaches
Centla coast, p.411

⭐ Extraordinary Olmec sculptures
La Venta park, Villahermosa, p.417

⭐ Villahermosa's own Rio carnival
The *Feria de Tabasco*, Villahermosa, p.421

⭐ The Mayan city of brick
Comalcalco, p.424

⭐ Chocolate haciendas
Around Comalcalco, p.429

See map overleaf

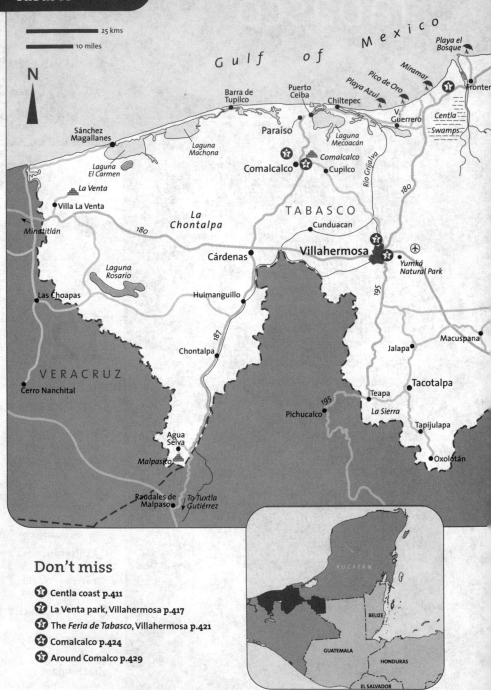

Tabasco

25 kms
10 miles

N

Gulf of Mexico

Playa el Bosque

Miramar

Pico de Oro

Playa Azul

Fronter

Barra de Tupilco

Puerto Ceiba

Chiltepec

V. Guerrero

Centla Swamps

Sánchez Magallanes

Laguna Machona

Paraíso

Laguna Mecoacán

Laguna El Carmen

Comalcalco

Cupilco

La Venta

Villa La Venta

Comalcalco

Rio Grijalva

180

Minatitlán

La Chontalpa

180

TABASCO

Cunduacan

Villahermosa

Yumká Natural Park

Cárdenas

Laguna Rosario

195

Las Choapas

Huimanguillo

187

Macuspana

Chontalpa

Jalapa

VERACRUZ

Tacotalpa

Cerro Nanchital

Teapa

La Sierra

Pichucalco

195

Tapijulapa

Agua Selva

Malpasito

Oxolotán

Raudales de Malpaso

To Tuxtla Gutiérrez

Don't miss

⚝ Centla coast **p.411**

⚝ La Venta park, Villahermosa **p.417**

⚝ The *Feria de Tabasco*, Villahermosa **p.421**

⚝ Comalcalco **p.424**

⚝ Around Comalco **p.429**

YUCATAN

BELIZE

GUATEMALA

HONDURAS

EL SALVADOR

To Campeche
Isla de Aguada

180

180

Ciudad del
Carmen

To Escárcega

P.376

Río Usumacinta

Palizada

CAMPECHE

186

Buenavista

Candelaria

ad Pemex

El
Triunfo

El Piche

Bridge Toll

Balancán

Reforma

Catazajá

Emiliano Zapata

Cascadas
de Reforma

186

Región
de los Ríos

ca

Palenque

Pomoná

Tenosique

HIAPAS

San
Claudio

Benito
Juárez

San Francisco

P.434

Tabasco has the merit of being the only Mexican state subjected
to sustained abuse by a major English writer. Graham Greene
visited in 1938 to investigate the persecution of the Catholic church,
on the trip that produced a travel book, *The Lawless Roads* (*Another
Country* in the USA), and *The Power and the Glory*. Greene loathed
Mexico, and he loathed Tabasco most of all. He made the place into
a metaphor, an image of heat, squalor, brutality and hopelessness.

That was then, and this is now. Today, if you're not a morose
English Catholic convert looking for things to disapprove of, Tabasco
has much to recommend it. Greene did get one thing right, in that it

is powerfully hot, a steamy tropical delta where the thermometer sits close to 40°C for much of the time. The state capital Villahermosa is, like Phoenix, Arizona, one of those cities where life has been transformed by the arrival of air conditioning. It is the least Mayan of Mexico's southern states, one where the culture of the modern Maya – and of the Zoque, a non-Maya people who inhabit south-western Tabasco – has largely retreated to villages and remote areas. During the colonial era Tabasco was all but ignored for decades at a time, an underpopulated wilderness of rivers, swamps and forest. It was gradually occupied by a variety of independent settlers: dirt farmers, coffee growers, loggers, even pirates. This diversity is reflected in the mixture of family names that is typical of Tabasco: English, French, Maya, Spanish and more.

Tabasco grew up as a rough-and-ready, frontier sort of place, with much less of a sense of tradition than other parts of Mexico. Since the 1950s the state has been completely transformed by the dis-covery of oil and a population boom that has made Villahermosa one of the busiest cities in the country. This rough-and-readiness must be partly responsible for a trait characteristic of Tabascans, a noticeable openness and friendliness. *Chocos*, as locals are known, have far less of the reserve so pronounced in much of Mexico, even a certain chippiness compared to the stillness of Yucatán.

This spikey, take-it-as-it-comes character seems well suited to the delta landscape, where green rivers wind through towns where it's often just too hot to put up with much formality. Until 30 or 40 years ago, between the channels and creeks you would also have seen dense forest. Alongside the oil business the other great modern transformation of Tabasco has been the cutting down of 90 per cent of its forest cover and the turning over of the state to agriculture: fruit, coffee, and vast cattle pastures. Along with oil, this has made some people in the state extremely wealthy.

Tabasco is also sexy. Foreigners may have heard of the Olmec relics of La Venta, but one oft-repeated part of modern Mexican folklore is that *Tabasqueñas* are the most beautiful women in Mexico. Tabascan traditional dress for women – rarely worn outside *fiestas* nowadays, unlike the *huípiles* of the Yucatán or Chiapas – consists of the kind of off-the-shoulder blouses and embroidered skirts once worn by Rita Hayworth in her sultry Latin-spitfire roles. The beauty of the local womenfolk is a big thing in Tabasco. It is celebrated above all in the election of the *Flor de Tabasco* at the State Fair, an annual *fiesta* of off-the-shoulder-blouses and big hair.

Tabasco has more conventional attractions. Its greatest treasures are relics not of the Maya but of the far older Olmec civilization, the extraordinary sculpted heads in Villahermosa's Parque La Venta. Elsewhere there is a unique Mayan city at Comalcalco, and deserted Gulf beaches. Villahermosa also has the busiest airport close to Palenque, a good jumping-off point for northern Chiapas. One thing that is not from the state is Tabasco sauce, which was invented in Louisiana, but it does have very good food, making great use of river fish unique to the Grijalva-Usumacinta delta.

History

Until the building of roads – in living memory – Tabasco's inhabitants have always been river people. It was the rivers, swamps and creeks around the base of the Gulf of Mexico in Tabasco and Veracruz that were home to the **Olmecs**, the first civilization of Mesoamerica, providing them with a food source and a means of communication. From there, Olmec influences spread across the region, from central Mexico down to Guatemala and Honduras. Later cultures avoided the deltas until, centuries later in the Classic era, eastern Tabasco and southern Campeche saw the emergence of the people known as the **Putún** or **Chontal Maya**, one of whose sub-groups – it is now widely believed – were the **Itzá**, who were among the rulers of Chichén Itzá.

The Putún are a mysterious people, the object of a great deal of speculation. Skilled sailors, they were an illiterate culture, which, given that the glyph writing system was one of the defining elements of Maya civilization, has led many to doubt whether they were Maya, although it is now generally accepted that in language and most other aspects they were. Though the more refined Maya of the cities to the east probably looked down on them, they were important to these Eastern Maya as fetchers, carriers, traders and intermediaries with the cultures of central Mexico. The delta swamps that were home to the Putún were also the origin of the finest cacao, an essential source of wealth in Mesoamerica. In the Late Classic, the Putún began to raid more aggressively up the Usumacinta and around the coast, taking over whole cities and founding some of their own. Nevertheless, many stayed in their home region, and the largest Maya group in Tabasco today, the Chontal of the Centla region north of Villahermosa, have their own language, believed to be descended from that of the Putún.

When the Spaniards appeared off the coast, the great river, that Grijalva named after himself, soon attracted their attention. In 1519, after landing at Xicalango on the Laguna de Términos, **Cortés** fought his first battle in Mexico at Centla in Tabasco, before moving on to Veracruz. He passed through Tabasco again in 1521, in pursuit of an unruly subordinate, **Cristóbal de Olid**, who was trying to carve out an independent governorship for himself. Cortés brought **Cuauhtémoc**, the last Aztec Emperor, with him as a prisoner, afraid to leave him in Mexico City. Believing, he claimed, that Cuauhtémoc was planning a revolt, Cortés had him executed somewhere near Tenosique. Even his own soldiers were shocked by his brutality.

12

Tabasco

When Graham Greene came to Tabasco it was shortly after the fall of Governor Tomás Garrido Canabal, who had attempted to eradicate Catholicism in the state. Garrido used to say this would not do anyone any harm since Tabascans had never been good Catholics anyway. He had a certain point, in that Tabasco was something of an anomaly within the very Catholic Spanish Empire. It was the object of an unbrotherly dispute between the Franciscans of Yucatán and the Dominicans of Chiapas as to who should evangelize the area, and consequently nobody quite took on the task. In the 'spiritual conquest', Tabasco fell through a bureaucratic loophole.

In the absence of friars, Tabasco was populated by seekers after dyewoods and cacao. Like Campeche, it was plagued by pirate attacks from the 16th to the 18th centuries. To escape them, people moved further up the rivers, to be joined later on by descendants of the pirates themselves.

After independence Tabasco was a centre of radical and anti-Church feeling, and strongly resisted the French and Maximilian. This was the background to the rise during the Revolution of the most famous figure in Tabasco's history, **Tomás Garrido Canabal**, absolute boss of the state for 16 years from 1920. With his Partido Socialista Radical and its youth wing, the *Camisas Rojas* ('Red Shirts'), he made Tabasco into a little republic of his own, launching 'anti-fanaticism campaigns' of antireligious propaganda, setting up co-ed schools and a feminist movement, and generally doing anything that wasn't Catholic. Greene presented the Garrido regime as a kind of totalitarian dictatorship, but he had a lot in common with a huckster politician like Huey Long of Louisiana, wheeling, dealing and using demagogic appeals to get the vote out. His fall came after he began to believe too much in his empire-building and tried to keep control of his party outside the official PNR. In 1936 Lázaro Cárdenas had him expelled from office and the country.

The 1950s saw the beginning of Tabasco's great transformation, with the arrival of **oil**, **deforestation** and **air conditioning**. The oil boom was at its loudest in the 1970s, when Villahermosa acquired its largest modern buildings. Tabasco has retained a tradition of argumentative politics, and spectacular corruption scandals, but the PRI has retained the state governorship.

The catastrophic floods of October–November 2007 left Villahermosa and much of the state under water for weeks. It is generally believed their impact was made far worse by deforestation and the blocking of delta channels caused by uncontrolled urbanization. Developing long-term solutions to these problems requires a level of decisiveness the political system is scarcely geared up to provide. However, ordinary Tabascans are immensely resourceful in the face of disasters; recovery has been hard, but the most apparent marks of the great flood are diminishing fast.

The Centla Coast

🟡 **Centla coast**

The main route into Tabasco from Yucatán is Highway 186 from Escárcega, which, after dipping into eastern Tabasco near Emiliano Zapata cuts across northern Chiapas to re-enter the state and cross pastures and fruit farms to Villahermosa. To the west, the same road, renumbered Highway 180, runs on towards Veracruz. If you have time and are looking for a relatively empty beach, there is another route through the coastal **Centla** region on the old 180 road from Ciudad del Carmen.

After crossing the Río San Pedro (the state line), this road runs on past swamps, ranches and a few oil wells to the capital of Centla, **Frontera**. This was where Greene arrived, when the only way to get from here to Villahermosa was by river boat. From the centre of town a road leads north to **El Bosque** at the mouth of the Grijalva, with a long beach, pelicans and a great view. If you stay on the main road, you quickly come to the bridge across the Grijalva.

The Centla world of lagoon, creek and causeway begins on the other side. Only theoretically a highway, the road is narrow, winding between exuberant clumps of coconut palms, banana plants, cacao plantations and tropical flowers, with a lushness that's absolutely overwhelming. About 20km west of the bridge, past Chontal Maya villages and smart ranch houses, a road north leads to **Miramar** (5km), with a curving beach stretching away for miles. On Sundays food stands are set up and the place may suddenly get noisy; on other days you can have it to yourself.

About 5km further on, the 180 road bends south toward Villahermosa, and in the tiny village of Santa Cruz a road turns right to continue along the coast. This is even narrower, with some alarming dips, but still passable in a standard car if you take your time (*combis* from Frontera or Paraíso negotiate it). In Vicente Guerrero there's a turn north to **Pico de Oro** (8km), one of the best Centla beaches, with a restaurant, **Las Huellas del Pescador** (*budget*), where you can camp or sling a hammock under a *palapa* for free, assuming you eat there (which, as there's nowhere else, you probably will). In Cuauhtémoc, 7km west, there is a turning to another fine beach, **Playa Azul**.

At around this point, the channels and lagoons become wider and more numerous, making it feel as if you're travelling more through water than land. From Chiltepec the road runs along the north edge of the huge **Laguna Mecoacán** to **Paraíso**, which has Villahermosa's favourite Sunday beach, with more solid *palapa*-bars and restaurants. From there it turns south for Villahermosa (75km) via Comalcalco (*see* p.424). On the west side of the lagoon is the area's most enjoyable spot at **Puerto Ceiba**, with laid-back restaurants and boat trips to see mangroves, birds and lagoon islands.

West of Paraíso a road runs straight for 150km along the sand bar beside the coastal lagoons, past beaches, palms, a few isolated fishing villages (only **Sánchez Magallanes** approaches town-size), thousands of birds and vast, watery horizons.

Villahermosa

To know how hot the world can be I had to wait for Villahermosa.

Graham Greene, The Lawless Roads

Tabasco's state capital is not one of Mexico's colonial cities, nor is it today the sweltering, languid tropical river town that Greene would recognize. As you approach the city you pass what appear to be endless miles of suburbs and *colonias*, and big highways that carry a near-incomprehensible quantity of traffic. Further in, many areas are taken over by a disorderly mixture of cars, offices, parking lots, billboards and brash shop fronts. Parts of Villahermosa look a bit like downtown Los Angeles (after all, everybody there speaks Spanish too); some still show the scars of flood damage. All this bustle and scrambled modernity (and the heat, which hasn't changed) has led some people who only come to Mexico looking for the traditional and picturesque to dismiss the place outright, and avoid it. But, like the state as a whole, Villahermosa has its positives.

First of all, there are the unique Olmec relics of Parque La Venta, alongside which is one of the best wildlife collections in the region. Villahermosa's Anthropology Museum, sadly still awaiting post-flood restoration, is one of Mexico's best. On a wider level, it's a lively city, with an urban edge in place of the tranquillity of Yucatán cities; you need to have your guard up more than you would in Mérida or Chetumal, but there's plenty of Tabascan friendliness too. One feature of Villahermosa is the continual presence of water, in creeks, rivers and entire lakes that turn up throughout the city, or the slow-moving River Grijalva itself. And the city has a living heart: in the centre, the streets of the 19th-century town Greene knew, renovated as the **Zona Luz**, are full of life, with cafés in which to sit out as the heat of the day fades a little, and watch everybody go by.

Villahermosa began life in another place and under another name. In 1519 Cortés founded a settlement at the mouth of the Grijalva, near present-day Frontera, called Santa María de la Victoria. After the pirates of Tris appeared off the coast in the 1550s, however, life for its inhabitants became increasingly impossible, and in 1596 it was decided to move the whole town upriver and take over a Chontal fishing village as the site of a new 'city', to be called Villahermosa de San Juan Bautista, the 'Beautiful City of

Saint John the Baptist', normally known simply as San Juan
Bautista. Over the next two centuries the city became the hub of
the Tabasco dyewood trade, surpassing in importance older towns
such as Tacotalpa. San Juan Bautista covered itself in glory in 1846
during the Mexican-American war, when American ships sailed up
the river in an attempt to take the town, and the *gringos* were
actually forced to withdraw in defeat. Since the Revolution the
city's name has been reduced to Villahermosa.

The Zona Luz

The streets of 'old' Villahermosa (which dates mostly from the
late 19th century) occupy a walkable area between Av. Gregorio
Méndez Magaña, the river, Paseo Tabasco and Av. Miguel Hidalgo.
At its heart is a clutch of pedestrianized streets, called the Zona
Remodelada or Zona Luz. Its hub is the little square of **Parque
Juárez**, with the busiest street, **Avenida Francisco Madero**,
alongside it and the main pedestrian *paseo*, **Calle Juárez**, running
south from it to Av. 27 de Febrero. The name 'Zone of Light' makes it
sound rather grand, but the area is really a more entertaining
combination of a slight elegance and a more basic, very tropical
take-it-as-you-find-it quality. Mixed up together on Madero, Juárez
and Aldama are cafés, cheap hotels, great ice-cream stands, the
kind of cheapo shops typical of Mexican city centres with names
like 'Liz Minelli', pile-'em-up-high stocks of shoes, bags or curtain
material, and an ever-increasing number of fast-food outlets.

Villahermosa is something of a centre for contemporary art,
much of it with a noticeable Tabascan sensuality. Opposite Parque
Juárez on Madero is the **Centro Cultural Villahermosa**, a sleek
modern arts centre designed with great panache by a trio of young
local architects. A few streets west, smaller galleries are clustered
around the charming **Calle Narciso Sáenz** (also just called C. Sáenz),
housed in well-restored old Villahermosa townhouses with bright
patios that make excellent showcases for the often vividly
colourful artwork. **Galería Casa Siempreviva** on Av. Lerdo de Tejada
just off C. Sáenz, occupies a lovely old house with beautiful stained
glass inside; among other galleries are **El Jaguar Despertado**, and
the recently-restructured **Colegio de Artes Tabasco**.

On the corner of C. Juárez and Av. 27 de Febrero is old Villahermosa's
most historic building, the **Casa de los Azulejos** ('House of Tiles'), so-
named for its façade of bright metal-blue tiles set between ornate
windows and white porticoes. It was built in 1889–1915 for the most
prosperous merchant in Villahermosa at that time, with the fine
Tabascan name of José María Graham McGregor; in style it mixes
Hispano-Moorish with French Beaux-Arts opulence. Restored in the

Centro Cultural Villahermosa
*t 314 5552; open
Tues–Sun 10–8*

Galería Casa Siempreviva
*open Mon–Fri 9–8,
Sat, Sun 9–5*

El Jaguar Despertado
*C. Sáenz 117; open
Mon–Sat 9–8, Sun 10–6*

Colegio de Artes Tabasco
*C. Sáenz 122; hours
variable*

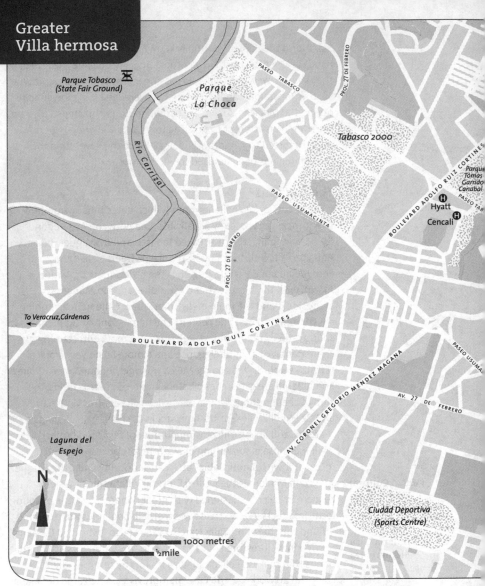

Parque Tobasco
(State Fair Ground)

Parque
La Choca

Rio Carizal

Tabasco 2000

PASEO TABASCO

PROL 27 DE FEBRERO

PASEO USUMACINTA

PROL. 27 DE FEBRERO

BOULEVARD ADOLFO RUIZ CORTINES

Parque
Tomás
Garrido
Canabal

PASEO TAB

Hyatt

Cencali

To Veracruz, Cárdenas

BOULEVARD ADOLFO RUIZ CORTINES

AV. CORONEL GREGORIO MENDEZ MAGAÑA

AV. 27 DE FEBRERO

PASEO USUMA

Laguna del
Espejo

N

Ciudad Deportiva
(Sports Centre)

1000 metres

½ mile

**Museo de Historia
de Tabasco**
*t 314 2175; open
Tues–Sun 9–5; adm*

1980s and again after the 2007 floods, it houses the **Museo de
Historia de Tabasco** The interesting collection (partly labelled in
English) covers every period of the state's past, with artefacts from
Comalcalco and the time of the Conquest, and plenty from the
Garrido Canabal era, including an *Himno Feminista Tabasqueña*.
There's also a good book and handicrafts shop. Just as interesting as
the collection is the house's part-restored interior. One strange
feature is that it has a corrugated iron roof, since in this climate the
first parts of a house to go are usually the roof timbers.

From the museum, cross Av. 27 de Febrero, walk a block to the right
and then go up steep Av. Aldama to come up beside the Porfirian-

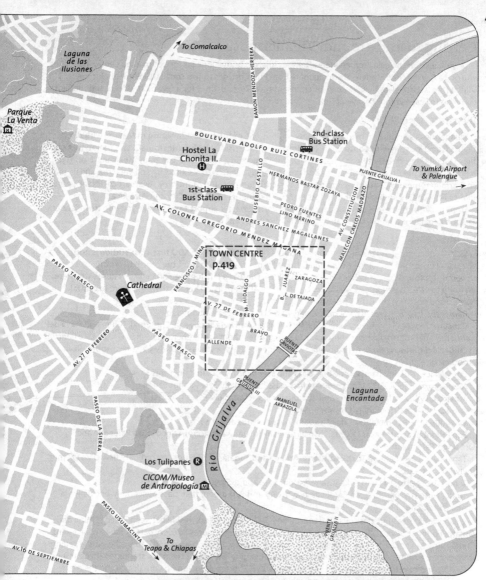

era **Palacio de Gobierno**, Tabasco's state house, into the **Plaza de Armas**, the 'official' main square of the old city, on a hilltop with a view over the river. At the south end of the square is Villahermosa's most historic church, La Concepción, better known as **La Conchita**. Like Tabascan Catholicism it has been through torrid times. Begun in 1800, it was burnt by the US Navy in 1847, rebuilt, demolished by Garrido Canabal in 1931 and rebuilt yet again in the 1940s, but in the same bizarrely ornate, neogothic wedding-cake style. One corner of the plaza leads to **Puente Gaviotas** footbridge over the Grijalva. Beside it, the long **Malecón** waterfront boulevard is still – for the moment – lined by a wall of cement bags put up during the floods,

Getting to and around Villahermosa

Driving in from the east, immediately after the **Grijalva I** bridge look for an exit marked *Centro*. This takes you on to Av. Francisco Madero, the main route from Ruíz Cortines to the **Zona Luz**, centre of old Villahermosa. First-class **buses** into Villahermosa stay on Ruíz Cortines for a few more streets and turn left down on to Paseo Francisco Javier Mina.

By Air

Villahermosa's airport, 13km east off Highway 186, is one of the busiest in southern Mexico, with direct flights from Houston with **Continental, t** 01 800 900 5000. Inside Mexico, **MexicanaClick, t** 01 800 112 5425, flies several times daily between Villahermosa and Mexico City, and parent company **Mexicana, t** 316 3132, has flights to Cancún. **Aeroméxico, t** 01 800 021 4000, has services to Mexico City and Veracruz, and its low-cost arm **Aeroméxico Connect** flies to Mérida, Veracruz, Tampico and Monterrey. **Aviacsa, t** 01 800 284 2272, flies to Mexico City and **Aeromar, t** 01 800 237 6627, has flights to Mexico City and Poza Rica.

From the airport, there is an abundance of *Transporte Terrestre* **airport taxis** to take you into town (about $10); on departure, a normal city cab to the airport will cost $8–9.

By Bus

First- and second-class bus stations are separate in Villahermosa. The **ADO first-class station** is north of the Zona Luz (corner of Paseo FJ Mina and C. Lino Merino), far enough from the centre to be an uncomfortable walk carrying bags (a taxi is about $2). There is a **left-luggage** office. Many buses stop here en route to other destinations. Main services from the ADO are listed below; there are more to central Mexico and north on the Gulf Coast.

Campeche (*6-7hrs*): two ADO GL, 14 ordinary first-class daily. Fare about $20.

Cancún (*12–13hrs*): five luxury, nine ordinary first-class daily, via **Escárcega, Chetumal, Tulum** and **Playa del Carmen**. Many ordinary first-class buses stop in **Xpuhil**. Fares about $25 to Chetumal, $38 to Playa, $42 to Cancún.

Ciudad del Carmen (*3hrs*): 10 luxury buses daily, and ordinary first-class hourly 5.30am–11.30pm, all via **Frontera**. Fare about $9.

Comalcalco (*1hr*) and **Paraíso**: one first-class and several *intermedio* daily. Fares $3–5.

Mérida (*9hrs*): six luxury and 13 ordinary first-class buses daily. Fares about $29–43.

Mexico City (*10–12hrs*): 10 luxury and 23 ordinary first-class daily. Fares from $50.

Oaxaca (*12-13hrs*): four daily. Fare about $32.

Palenque (*2½hrs*): nine buses daily 3.40am–9.15pm. Fares about $7.

San Cristóbal de Las Casas (*7½hrs*): two buses daily (usually at 9.30am, 12 noon), via **Palenque** and **Ocosingo**. Fare about $15.

Tapachula (*10–11hrs*): via **Tuxtla Gutiérrez, Arriaga** and **Tonalá**, one luxury, one ordinary first-class (7.15pm) daily. Fare $39–46.

Tenosique (*3–4hrs*): 13 buses daily 4am–7.50pm. Fare about $9.50.

Tuxtla Gutiérrez (*4–5hrs*): via **Cárdenas**, two luxury and 13 ordinary first-class buses daily; one daily via **Teapa** (*7hrs*). Fare about $16.

Villahermosa's **second-class bus station** is on Blvd Ruíz Cortines (north side between Paseo FJ Mina and Grijalva I bridge). Several different companies provide stopping services to every part of Tabasco (including Comalcalco, La Venta and Huimanguillo), and to Palenque, northern Chiapas and Campeche, plus gruelling long-distance routes. Some companies have their own depots alongside the main station, so check around.

Combis and *colectivos* to towns and villages around Villahermosa, including Comalcalco and the coast, mostly leave from the streets around (and behind) the second-class station.

Villahermosa's **city buses** and *combis* aren't hard to use. Any bus north up Paseo Tabasco marked 'Tabasco 2000' or 'La Choca' will take you to the Ruíz Cortines junction and Parque La Venta; from Av. Madero or Av. Constitución, buses south marked CICOM run down the Malecón. To get back, take any 'Centro' bus.

By Car

If you have a car try to stay in a hotel with its own parking provision, as parking space in the old centre is at a premium. There are plenty of *gasolineras* around the city.

Car Hire

Villahermosa has a sizable choice of rental agencies. Most also have desks at the airport.

Budget, Av. 27 de Febrero 712, **t** 314 3790, *www.budget.com.mx*. Decent and centrally placed local franchise. Check cars for lights, strange noises etc., before you drive off.

Ekorenta, Av. Vicente Guerrero 120, **t** 312 9890. Near Puente Gaviotas, south of Plaza de Armas. Low rates.

By Taxi

Taxis are abundant in Villahermosa, and cost around $1.50–$2 in the city. Be warned, though, that taxis here often operate *combi*-style along popular routes, picking up several passengers along the way (who all pay part of the fare). This is very inconvenient if you need to get to anywhere specific quickly (such as the bus station or airport). To get a direct cab in a hurry, it's best to phone for one, or better still have a hotel do it for you. Allow plenty of time – especially for airport runs – as phone cabs are in short supply at busy times.

Radio Taxis, t 315 1465, 314 3456

Orientation

Post-oil boom Villahermosa is built to car scale, with districts linked by broad avenues and freeways, and chiefly the main road from the airport, Palenque and the east, Highway 186 – **Blvd Adolfo Ruíz Cortines** inside the city – which rolls in over **Puente Grijalva I** bridge (toll), curving through the city to continue out the other side as Highway 180 to Veracruz. The three Grijalva bridges are numbered according to when they were built, so the next one south is Puente Grijalva III. In general, wider streets are *avenidas* or *paseos* and smaller ones *calles*.

The main visitor attractions are concentrated in three areas. The **Zona Luz** runs back from the riverside avenue of the Malecón. South of the old centre is Paseo Tabasco, which runs northwest from the river for 3km to cross Blvd Ruíz Cortines. This junction is the hub of the second major area of interest, with **Parque-Museo La Venta** and the zoo, the main upscale hotels and the Tabasco 2000 complex. A final focus of attraction is the **CICOM area**, south of the centre along the river, down the Malecón.

---

which with time have become as solid as rock. Through gaps in the barrier you reach the **Embarcadero**, a project intended to revitalize the riverfront with bright-and-noisy bars and restaurants, and the departure point for the **Capitán Beuló II** trip boat.

Museo de Cultura Popular
Av. Ignacio Zaragoza 810; t 312 1117; open Tues–Sat 10–7, Sun 10–4

A few blocks west of the Zona Luz is the **Museo de Cultura Popular**. In an old house, it's an engagingly simple collection of traditional dress, embroidery, ceramics, and musical instruments. Cutting south from there, a hot walk along Av. 27 de Febrero will lead to the junction with Paseo Tabasco and Villahermosa's **Cathedral**. The city's 19th-century cathedral was knocked down by Garrido Canabal in the 1920s, and building a new one did not begin until 1960; construction then fizzled out with it only part-finished in 1963, and one indication of the lack of religious fervour in Tabasco is that not much has been done since.

Parque La Venta, the Zoo and Tabasco 2000

⭐ La Venta park
Park open daily 8–5 (last entry 4pm), Sound and Light Show Tues–Sun 8pm, 9pm, 10pm; adm; Zoo (entered on park ticket) open Tues–Sun 8–5; Museo de Historia Natural open daily 8–5

Villahermosa's greatest cultural possessions are matchless, with no equivalent anywhere else. They consist of over 30 huge basalt heads and other sculptures from the Olmec city of La Venta, 130km west of Villahermosa, arranged as a unique open-air 'museum' in a jungle park between Boulevard Ruíz Cortines and the Laguna de las Ilusiones, the largest of the city's lakes. Like many other cultural institutions in Tabasco this arose out of an initiative from the poet and writer Carlos Pellicer Cámara. In the 1950s, when oil exploration was accelerating in the state, it seemed that the monuments of La Venta would be threatened, and Pellicer proposed that they be moved to Villahermosa for their protection. The result was the

12 Tabasco | Villahermosa

creation of **Parque-Museo La Venta** in 1957. Like everything else near water in Villahermosa it had to be restored after the 2007 flood. The main park has reopened, but there have been suggestions that the sculptures be moved to a conventional museum for their protection, which would be sad – and, given the many restoration projects needed in Tabasco, this is not likely to happen soon.

La Venta flourished from about 900 to 400 BC. As the 'mother culture' of Mesoamerica, the Olmecs are seen as precursors in many areas – the building of monumental symbolic cities, the calendar, the central cosmic vision of a 'live' universe divided into three levels of existence – in which their influence was inherited by many later cultures. Olmec sculpture, however, has a special quality that stands out across the centuries. The peculiarities of Olmec carvings – the emphasis on massiveness, the faces that at times seem African, at others vaguely European, only occasionally Native American – have given rise to a great deal of speculation, and fed theories of some kind of early transatlantic contact. However, it appears likely that the Olmec heads may have been given their 'strange' features in an effort to make them similar to the face of the jaguar, an animal with a central place in Olmec religion and mythology.

As well as the Olmec relics another essential draw of Parque La Venta is the **zoo** that is partially intertwined with the monuments. Within the limitations of a zoo, most of the animals, all native to southern Mexico, have a fair amount of space, and the enclosures are quite well landscaped. This part of La Venta has taken longer to recover from the floods than the sculpture park, but you can still spot dazzlingly colourful parrots and toucans, and an astonishing assortment of different kinds of forest cat. By the park entrance, a **Museo de Historia Natural** has more static displays.

Every one of the sculptures has its own dynamic character. Already striking at stop 3 is **Monument 5** – *la Abuela* (the Grandmother), a strange bug-like creature that seems different from any other Mesoamerican monument; similarly, while the giant Olmec heads can appear African, **Stela 3** or the 'Bearded Man', could almost be European or Middle-Eastern, although it has been shown that his un-Mesoamerican 'beard' could be a chin strap to a headdress. At stop 12 is **Altar 5**, the *Altar de los Niños* ('Altar of the Children'), one of several altars to show a male figure with a jaguar-skull headdress semi-seated in an alcove beneath a slab-like stone, also with a carved jaguar-face. They are believed to represent Olmec lords emerging from the Underworld, origin of gods and kings, a repeated image in Olmec carvings. Altar 5 is one of the most intriguing, since the figure has in his arms a child who appears dead, while either side of the altar are pairs of figures, each of which also carries a strange-looking child.

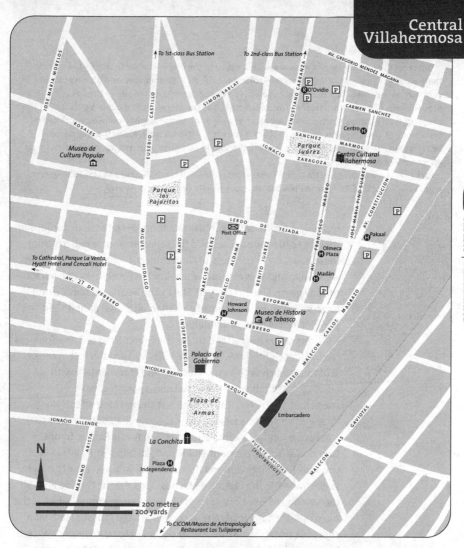

Central Villahermosa map showing streets including Jose Maria Morelos, Castillo, Simon Sarlat, Venustiano Carranza, Av. Gregorio Mendez Magana, Carmen Sanchez, and landmarks: Museo de Cultura Popular, Parque los Pajaritos, Parque Juárez, Centro Cultural Villahermosa, Post Office, Olmeca Plaza, Pakaal, Madán, Museo de Historia de Tabasco, Palacio del Gobierno, Plaza de Armas, La Conchita, Plaza Independencia, Embarcadero. Directions to 1st-class Bus Station, 2nd-class Bus Station, To Cathedral, Parque La Venta, Hyatt Hotel and Cencali Hotel, To CICOM/Museo de Antropología & Restaurant Los Tulipanes. Scale: 200 metres / 200 yards.

About halfway round (at stop 15) there is a refreshment stand and craftwork shop. In the second half there is a near-unbroken sequence of powerful sculptures. At 18 is **Monument 56**, the *mono mirando el cielo* ('Monkey looking at the sky'), an eerily modern carving of a remarkably strong monkey face. Stop 23 is **Altar 4**, the *Altar Triunfal*, the finest of all the Olmec altars showing priest-lords in the entrance to the Underworld. The lord, a tremendous figure of strength, has a rope in each hand attached to the wrists of submissive prisoner-figures on the sides of the altar, and appears to be dragging them towards the netherworld. Three stops further on you come upon the finest of the colossal Olmec heads and the best-known image of La Venta, **Monument 1** or the *Cabeza del Guerrero* ('Warrior's Head'). In spite of its having survived nearly three millennia, it can still seem

Site Information

You enter the park via a small **museum**, with a model of the original La Venta site. By the entrance there are always guides waiting (*tours $10–20*) but the park is well-organized and it's easy to find your way on your own. Past the museum you have a choice of paths, to the zoo or the Zona Arqueológica, although they later run into each other. The sculptures are laid out in a circuit of a little over 1km, with 33 'stops' (each monument also has a separate archaeologists' number, which can be confusing). At various points you can cut back if you want a shorter walk. Along the way, despite being within a city, you feel as if you're passing through a real jungle of dense, lush vegetation (*wear insect repellent*).

Park tickets are about $3; extra tickets (*around $7*) are needed for the **Sound and Light Show** (*every night except Monday*). They can be bought with park tickets, or entirely separately.

bizarrely modern in its near-abstract form. Despite the distortions in their faces (flattened noses and thickened lips) some experts think these heads were 'portraits' of Olmec rulers, filtered to appear more jaguar-like, and shown wearing a helmet believed to have been for the ball game. Finally, stop 33 is **Stela 1**, the 'Young Goddess', a rare large-scale Olmec sculpture of a woman, although at first sight she may not look especially feminine.

Visitors can return after dark for the *Espectáculo de Luz y Sonido*, a 'Sound and Light' show. The route takes you around just 13 major sculptures, each with its own display and commentary with readings from Tabascan poets. For non-Spanish speakers the translated poetry has less impact, but the lighting effects are imaginative and less kitschy than at some *Luz y Sonido* shows.

Between Parque La Venta and Paseo Tabasco is **Parque Tomás Garrido Canabal**, a pleasant, shady park, and if as you leave La Venta you walk to the right around the outer wall you will come to a lovely walkway beside the **Laguna de las Ilusiones**. Parque Garrido ends at the junction of Ruíz Cortines with Paseo Tabasco, around which is the main upscale hotel zone. A turn north up Paseo Tabasco leads via a short but sweaty walk (this road is designed to be driven, not walked) to a symbol of Villahermosa's oil-boom wealth, the **Tabasco 2000** complex, begun in the 1970s. Within it are the city hall, a convention centre, a shopping mall and the **tourist office**; further out, there's a smart residential area. On the side furthest from the city centre, where Paseo Tabasco meets Villahermosa's second river, the Carrizal, is **Parque La Choca**, another park, with a public swimming pool, while a dramatic bridge leads over the river to yet another, **Parque Tabasco**, the permanent site for the annual *Feria de Tabasco* (*see p.421*).

CICOM and the Museo de Antropología

South of the city centre is another group of modern buildings in a landscaped area beside the Grijalva, known as the CICOM. The **Centro de Investigación de las Culturas Olmeca y Maya** arose out of another initiative of Carlos Pellicer in the 1950s, and expanded to become a general cultural complex containing the state theatre, a public library, an art school, a gallery, a bookshop, and the excellent **Los Tulipanes** restaurant *(see p.423)*. But this was one of the parts of Villahermosa worst-hit by the floods. Most parts of the CICOM have now been put back into use – though still visibly battered – but one that has not, is its biggest attraction for visitors, the **Museo Regional de Antropología Carlos Pellicer Cámara**.

The great attraction of Villahermosa's museum has been that it covers all the many cultures of ancient Mesoamerica, from the Olmecs onwards, providing context to set beside purely Maya museums. Treasures include Maya stelae from Reforma, wonderful Totonac *cabezas sonrientes* ('smiling heads') from the Gulf Coast, and a 1,500-year-old toy of a jaguar on wheels, from Veracruz – a staggering demonstration that Mesoamerican cultures did know of the principle of the wheel, but didn't use it for anything practical.

Sadly, it's hard to see them. The museum has been the worst cultural victim of the floods, and its restoration has been set back behind other projects. Re-opening dates have been announced and then revised, and it is unlikely to reopen before late 2010, if then.

ⓘ **Tabasco State Tourist Office:**
Av. de los Rios, Tabasco 2000, t 316 3633, www.tabasco.gob.mx/turismo (open Mon–Fri 8–4 and 6–9, Sat 9–1). Helpful and quite well supplied with leaflets, but located in Tabasco 2000, near the big hotels, not the city centre. There are also information desks at the airport and Parque La Venta

✪ The *Feria de Tabasco*

Tours

t (993–)

Universo Maya, Hotel Maya Tabasco, Blvd Ruíz Cortines 907, t 314 3696, *www.universomaya.com.mx*. Villahermosa has relatively few guides or tour agencies, but this company provides a full range of trips in Tabasco and northern Chiapas.

Vámonos de Pesca, Blvd Ruíz Cortines 1420, t 317 7471, *www.vamonosdepesca.com.mx*. Fishing guide Paco Marroquín has become a Tabasco celebrity through his weekly spots on local TV. Fishing is his forte, but on the way you can explore many remote spots.

Services in Villahermosa

Banks: Central branches on or near Av. Madero, and around the Plaza de Armas.

Emergencies: Central number for police and all emergency services, **t** 066

Health: Clínica AIR Médica 2000, Paseo Tabasco 1114, t 913 1933, has a 24hr emergency medical service. There are several **pharmacies** along Av. Madero.

Internet Access: Several in the centre, especially around the corner of C. Aldama and Av. I. Zaragoza.

Post Office: C. Narciso Sáenz, corner of Av. Lerdo de Tejada (*open Mon–Fri 8–6, Sat 9–1*). Has a **Mexpost** desk.

Festivals

Feria de Tabasco: *late April–May*. Tabasco is a pagan state, so it's only fitting that its great celebration is the State Fair, with its own site in Parque Tabasco. It is preceded all through April by a pre-*feria* of parades, parties and competitions. The parades are the city's mini-Rio carnival, while the park is an amazing combination of amusement park, market, free concert, stock fair and rodeo. Here you can buy local produce, watch folk dancing or buy a prize bull, but the highlight is the election of the annual **Flor de Tabasco**, queen of the state's celebratedly pretty girls.

Shopping

Mis Blancas Mariposas, Casa de los Azulejos (Museo de Historia de Tabasco), C. Juárez, corner of Av. 27 de Febrero. Located inside Villahermosa's most engaging museum, this charming shop showcases Tabascan handicrafts.

Where to Stay in Villahermosa

As a business centre the city has a big range of hotels, but rates even for luxury rooms are far lower than in more touristy areas. Villahermosa's top-range hotels are in an upscale 'hotel zone' by the Ruíz Cortines-Paseo Tabasco junction, near Parque La Venta.

Moderate

Hyatt Regency Villahermosa, Av. Juárez 106, t 310 1234, *http://villahermosa. regency.hyatt.com*. Top of the line, this has every comfort, smart modern decor, two **restaurants**, a fine pool and a lovely garden. Note: this Av. Juárez is not the one in the Zona Luz.

Olmeca Plaza, Av. Madero 418, t 358 0102, *www.hotelolmecaplaza.com*. Centrally- located in the Zona Luz, and with good a/c, WiFi and other facilities. There's a functional **restaurant** and an oddly-located (streetside) pool. Rates are borderline-*inexpensive*, with regular discounts.

Quality Inn Villahermosa Cencali, Av. Juárez 105, corner of Paseo Tabasco, t 313 6611, *www.qualityinnvilla hermosa.com*. Pleasant, modern upscale hotel, with character and excellent-value rates. La Isla **restaurant** looks out onto a pretty garden and pool, and there's an impressive lobby with a Maya-inspired mural by local artist Daniel Montuy.

Inexpensive

Best Western Hotel Madán, Av. Madero 408, t 312 1650, *www.madan. com.mx*. A reliable choice in the Zona Luz, that's been well-renovated since affiliating to Best Western. Rooms are conventional but well-equipped (all now have free WiFi), and there's a pleasant **restaurant** and bar (*see* right).
Hotel Pakaal, C. Lerdo de Tejada 106, t 314 4648. Friendly little hotel near the river. Rooms are simple but quite comfortable, with a/c, and near *budget* prices make it good value.
Hotel Plaza Independencia, C. Independencia 123, t 312 1299, *www.hotelesplaza.com.mx*. Long-running, decent-value, with rooms that have seen plenty of use but are well-equipped, plus a breakfast buffet, parking and pool. Free WiFi in lobby.

Howard Johnson Villahermosa, C. Aldama 404, t 314 4645, *www. hjvillahermosa.com*. Reliable modern services (free WiFi) and a **bar-restaurant** (*moderate*) with good a/c.

Budget

Hostel La Chonita II, C. Abelardo Reyes Hernández 217, t 131 2053, *http:// hostelachonita.com*. Villahermosa's backpacker hostel, brightly painted to look a bit like a tropical forest, is a couple of streets north of the ADO bus station. Friendly and well run, it has double and quad rooms as well as dorms, and a pleasant patio, internet, breakfast room and other facilities.
Hotel del Centro, Av. Pino Suárez 209, t 312 5961. One of the best-kept of Villahermosa's many cheap hotels, north of Parque Juárez. Some rooms have a/c; exterior rooms are bright but noisy. Another part of the Hotel is at Av. Madero 411, t 312 2565, with big, plain, a/c rooms and studios.

Eating Out

Tabasco has a distinctive cuisine. Its big specialities use river fish, especially the pike-like *pejelagarto*. Sometimes called crocodile-fish, it's unique to the Grijalva-Usumacinta delta, and may have been a staple food of the Olmecs. It has a subtle, almost sweet flavour. Another favourite is *tortilla de camarón*, which is like a Spanish *tortilla* (an egg omelette, not Mexican corn tortillas), filled with prawns (shrimp), herbs and more goodies.

Moderate

Capitán Beuló II, Malecón Carlos A. Madrazo, t 314 4644, *www.olmeca express.com*. A local institution, a modern replacement for the first Capitán Beuló, this riverboat cruises up and down the Grijalva from the Embarcadero. On board, the menu features *pejelagarto* and other local specialities, and a dance band keeps things lively. Cruises last about 2hrs on Sundays, 1hr on other days; booking is essential. *Dinner cruises Wed–Fri; lunch and dinner cruises Sat, Sun.*

Restaurante Madán, Best Western Hotel Madán, Av. Madero 408. Simply decorated, and its fare is unexceptional – Mexican standards with a few Tabascan fish dishes – but the Madan's dining room has effective a/c and lots of animated sociability. Locals come to sit and chat in the cool.

Los Tulipanes, Av. Carlos Pellicer Cámara 511 (CICOM), **t** 314 3183. Beside the river near the anthropology museum, the Tulipanes has thankfully recovered from the floods, and is a lovely spot in which to sample local dishes. Enjoy the view with a/c from the comfortable dining room, or take on the heat of the terrace. *Open only for lunch, daily 11am–6pm.*

Budget

Villahermosa has any number of cheap eateries, particularly catering to the crowds in the Zona Luz and around the bus stations.

Cocktelería Rock & Roll, Av. Reforma 307, between Madero and Juárez. Big, boisterous and boozy bar-restaurant specializing in good quality *ceviches* and *cocteles*, which are also very cheap. Don't go seeking a quiet dinner, but local colour, and the *cantina* atmosphere that spills onto the street.

Cafés, Ice Creams and Coolers

As a hot city Villahermosa naturally has plenty of traditional juice and ice-cream shops or stands to help you cool down. Unusually, the favourite cooler in Tabasco is not juice but *horchata*, made from rice and cinnamon. Villahermosa has traditionally also had a good number of relaxed cafés, but many have lately been taken over by fast-food outlets.

Café La Cabaña, C. Juárez 303. Airy little café, opposite Casa de los Azulejos.

Café del Correo, C. Narciso Sáenz, corner C/Lerdo de Tejada. Relaxed modern café with snacks and organic coffee from Chiapas, ideal for sitting to plan your next move.

La Catedral del Sabor, Plaza de Armas, corner of C/Independencia. One of a little local chain of ice-cream and juice stands: try the *horchata de arroz* or *guanábana con leche*.

Horchatería La Catedral, Paseo Tabasco. As any Tabascan will tell you, the best *horchata* in Mexico is made at this street-corner booth, opposite the cathedral.

Entertainment and Nightlife

D'Ovidio, Av. Venustiano Carranza 132, north of Parque Juárez. Large bar-restaurant where, most days, from about 2-3pm, musicians gather to play the music of tropical Mexico: *boleros*, *danzón*, Yucatecan trios... Some have been playing for decades, some are able musicians, some are bawling drunks. Any foreigner who wanders in will be drawn into conversation; women without male companions should perhaps avoid it unless they have a very high banter-tolerance. Sessions usually break up by about 9pm.

Around Villahermosa

The delta country around Villahermosa is a maze of narrow lanes, between creeks, palms and banana leaves. Apart from sleepy towns with odd churches, its main attractions are Yumká park, cocoa estates and a unique Maya city at Comalcalco.

Yumká Nature Park

Yumká Nature Park
t *(993) 356 0107, www.yumka.org; open daily 9–5 (last adm 4pm); adm*

Yumká was a private estate, covering 101 hectares, taken over by Tabasco state in 1987. The most staggering fact about it is that, because its former owners did not develop it, it became, pretty much by accident, the sole remaining patch of original forest in central Tabasco, which 25 years before had been covered in trees.

Getting to Yumká

Yumka is 17km east of Villahermosa near the airport. There is no regular public transport to the park, but buses can be booked through the park. A **cab** will cost around $14.

Site Information: Yumká

Visits are by **guided tour**, every 45mins. A full tour lasts 2hrs, and is usually in Spanish, but can be given in English for groups by arrangement.

It's now managed as a park, seeking to preserve examples of the three characteristic natural landscapes of Tabasco: jungle, savanna and lagoon. One surprise is that as well as local wildlife it contains 'exotics', such as tigers, elephants, antelopes and zebras. Purely native animals were not thought sufficiently interesting for local visitors, though foreigners tend to be far more interested in the Mexican wildlife. Even so, it can be an enjoyable day out.

The Road to Comalcalco

The 'back' road to Comalcalco, winding through the Chontal town of **Nacajuca**, is of interest in itself. As soon as you leave Villahermosa you cross rivers and streams, as the road abruptly widens and narrows to cross small bridges, amid an impossible depth of green. After 40km there is an essential stop at **Cupilco**, which has the most spectacular of Tabascan churches. Tabasco's village churches were built very late, often after independence, so they are 100 per cent Mexican, and decorated in exuberant colours with only slight and/or oblique references to European styles. Closed up in the 1930s, Cupilco's church has been lovingly restored and recoloured.

Comalcalco

✪ Comalcalco
Open daily 10–5 (last entry 4pm); adm

Tabasco's great Maya site of Comalcalco lies northwest of Villahermosa amid a typical Tabascan landscape of water, drained fields and emerald-green vegetation. Conditions here were different from anywhere else in the Maya world; the rock that formed the base material of Maya architecture elsewhere was completely missing, and there was only thick, soft alluvial clay, sand and seashells from the coast. Comalcalco, however, is one of the great demonstrations of Maya ingenuity, for out of what they had to hand, its builders created the only Maya city made of brick.

Comalcalco was once considered remote within the Maya world, but recent surveys have revealed a large number of smaller settlements around the Grijalva-Usumacinta delta. The site was occupied from at least the Preclassic, but flourished in the Classic era and reached its greatest extent around 600–800. Though located near the area inhabited by the Putúns, Comalcalco seems to have been more refined than the small Putún settlements. Apart from its brick construction, another special feature was its burial customs: several bodies have been found here buried in a crouching position, with offerings inside large cone-shaped ceramic jars. Also distinctive was its complex system of drainage channels; if in the northern Yucatán Maya builders devoted their energies to conserving water, Comalcalco is a demonstration of what they could do when they had an excess of it. The city has fine mouldings in stucco, similar to many at Palenque, and one theory suggests that Comalcalco was an important point in trade between the Usumacinta valley and areas further west. However, because Maya inscriptions were usually carved in stone, there are few glyph inscriptions at Comalcalco to provide the city with a fuller history. After about 1100 it was completely abandoned.

The North Plaza

From the main entrance and museum (*see* below) you approach the site on a long straight path, with plenty of trees for shade, from which you see the largest group of buildings, the North Plaza, over to your left. Facing precisely east, toward the origin of the sun, is Comalcalco's great pyramid, **Temple I**. Its long rows of thin red bricks and angular lines make it look strangely as if it belongs to another time and place than Classic Mesoamerica, like a Mayan pyramid built as part of some English municipal architecture project of the 1970s. Bricks were, in fact, only used in the second phase of building at Comalcalco. In the first centuries temple platforms were created by massing together huge piles of earth, packing them down and letting them dry out, then cladding them in stucco to give them extra solidity, a method used by the Olmecs. The use of brick, built onto the earth base, developed around 600–700 as the city grew and larger structures were required. In several places, where the brickwork has worn away, the original base can be seen, giant, smooth ramps of stucco baked into a kind of concrete. Even the stucco is very special: instead of the powdered limestone that formed the main ingredient of Maya stucco further east, Comalcalco's people used ingredients from the coast, especially sand and powdered oyster shells.

Along the southeast corner of Temple I facing the plaza – the first corner you come to if you head straight into the square – there is a tremendous fragment of stucco relief, dated to *c.*700, of a reclining figure with smaller figures and animals. He has especially fine feet. Above him, the pyramid rises in 12 tiers to a flat platform, with a two-room east-facing temple, though the stucco steps have virtually

Getting to Comalcalco

Comalcalco is 60km northwest of Villahermosa off the road to Paraíso. To **drive** there, you can go across the delta through Jalpa and Cupilco – turn right off Blvd Ruíz Cortines up Av. Universidad, follow this road out of the city, and then look for signs to Paraíso or Comalcalco. The faster route is to follow Blvd Ruíz Cortines west out of the city (signed Cárdenas, Veracruz) and in Cárdenas turn right onto the main road signed to Paraíso and Comalcalco. Comalcalco town is 38km north of Cárdenas, and the ruins are off the Paraíso road 3km north of the town.

Several *intermedio* and second-class **buses** run to Comalcalco town daily from Villahermosa, and many continue to Paraíso. On a Paraíso bus, ask to get off by the access road (say *las ruinas de Comalcalco*). From there it's a 1km walk. Local **taxis** are cheap.

disintegrated so you cannot climb up. The bricks used at Comalcalco, on show at the site museum, are also unusual. Many have modelled shapes of animals (crocodiles), human figures, buildings or symbolic motifs baked into them; stranger still, the bricks were normally placed so that these designs faced inwards, never to be seen again.

Only two more of its structures have been fully excavated, **Temple II** on the north side and **Temple III** to the south. Both are smaller versions of Temple I, which adds to the impression of the plaza as a coordinated whole. Alongside Temple III two small pyramids have been partly uncovered, while the mounds on the north and east sides remain unexcavated. The square also has a strange echo which you can experience if you stand on the mound in front of Temple I and clap your hands.

The Acropolis and the Museum

From the southeast corner of the North Plaza a steep climb will take you to the great Acropolis of Comalcalco, atop a huge two-level platform. The only hill for miles in the flat delta, it is entirely man-made, a task that must have taken centuries, and was begun long before the North Plaza. Removed from the city below, the Acropolis and its Palacio contain unusually intimate spaces.

Exploring the Acropolis, in its semi-excavated state, involves a bit of scrambling and stumbling. Its structures were all built around a still-recognizable internal plaza that was almost certainly a space reserved for Comalcalco's élite. As you reach the first level there are two temples to your right, facing into this plaza. Immediately right, the **Temple of the Mask** (Temple VI) has, in the middle of its stairway, a stucco mask of the sun god *Kinich Ahau*, interesting to compare with the image of that god at Edzná. Next to it, the **Temple**

Site information: Comalcalco

Comalcalco is a competitor for the accolade of hottest of all Mayan sites, and one of the sweatiest; it's wise to get there early. Heat and humidity also lead to a high concentration of bugs (and butterflies). In the new visitor centre, as well as the museum, there's a café, where after scrambling round the Acropolis you can reward yourself with a cold drink. For a leisurely lunch, carry on 20km to Puerto Ceiba (*see* p.411).

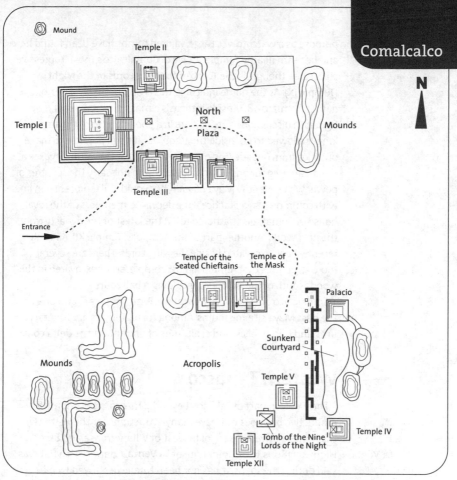

of the Seated Chieftains (Temple VII) has a more spectacular relief showing two tiers of seated figures in the elaborate regalia of Mayan lords, beneath a vision serpent. In a corner of Temple VII you can also inspect one of Comalcalco's 'crouching burial' funeral jars.

On two sides of the Acropolis, to the west and east, there are taller, later platforms. The eastern platform contains the **Palacio**, reached after another steep climb. This is one of the most intriguing of Mayan residential buildings, consisting mainly of two parallel rows of rooms. Several surround a sunken courtyard (*patio hundido*), a hub of the domestic life of the lords of Comalcalco. On one side it has a well-head, connected to a drain in the middle of the courtyard, with an intricate network of other drains. This seems to have been an early system of air conditioning: water collected in the patio ran through the building, moderating the heat. From the rear of the Palacio there is an endless view over the simmering delta.

Beside the Palacio there is a still higher pyramid with an even further view, topped by **Temple IV**, which must have had a dual purpose as a watchtower. Large, vaulted tombs have been found here and beneath nearby **Temple V**. One of Comalcalco's most impressive structures, though, is the **Tomb of the Nine Lords of the Night (Temple IX)**. As the name indicates, this is also probably a tomb, dating from 720-780; inside it there is a magnificent relief of nine figures in discussion. Parts of it are in a poor state, and you are no longer allowed to go inside the tomb, but it's still possible to make out a lot from outside. The modelling of two of the figures evokes a remarkable vigour and naturalness; they do not carry the sceptres of power which identify Maya *ahauob*, but could still represent – in line with common Maya practice – the deceased members of the royal house of Comalcalco, gathered to aid the latest of the dynasty from the next world. Another part of the Acropolis, **Temple XII**, has only recently been excavated beside the Nine Lords. There are several more structures that remain almost completely unexcavated in the woods south of the Acropolis, including a **ball court**.

Comalcalco also has a **visitor centre**, with shop, café and one of the best Maya site **museums**. Among its highlights are funerary urns and burial relics, and sculptures of animals of the delta coast.

Western Tabasco

The western part of Tabasco, beyond **Cárdenas**, is economically productive but does not have many attractions for the visitor. On the borders of Veracruz, 130km west of Villahermosa and 8km from Highway 180, is the original site of **La Venta**. Contrary to what was said during the 1950s, it has not been totally destroyed by oil exploration. Stripped of its main monuments, though, the site is a little denuded, but some remain and copies of others have been installed. The greatest attraction is the immense age of the Olmec city, parts of which, such as the glowering earth mound of the great pyramid and the ball court of **Complex C**, are 3,000 years old.

La Venta
open daily 10–5; adm

The area south of Cárdenas has become much more accessible, and so busier, since Highway 187 was widened. Beyond **Huimanguillo** the road climbs into a range of thickly forested hills, thinly inhabited with Zoque villages and crossed by fast-flowing rivers and streams. Now known as the **Agua Selva** reserve, the area

Where to Stay

There is nowhere to stay in **Villa la Venta**, so it's best visited on the way to somewhere else. The nearest facilities to Agua Selva and Malpasito are at Huimanguillo. Some rustic *cabañas* and restaurant have been built at Agua Selva, but they're only intermittently open, and the only way to find out about them is to go there (or to Malpasito) and ask.

Huimanguillo t (917–)

Hotel Guayacán, Av. Allende 124, t 375 0523 (*budget*). The best in town.

Getting to Western Tabasco

Frequent second-class **buses** run daily from Villahermosa to **Villa La Venta**, an oil town 3km from the ruins. Most first-class and all second-class buses from Villahermosa to Tuxtla Gutiérrez stop in **Huimanguillo**, and second-class also stop at Raudales de Malpaso, near Malpasito. To get to the ruins, the only easy way is naturally with your own car (and even then the track is hard to follow), but you may be able to find a *combi* or local taxi ready to take you there, and to villages and nearby waterfalls. There have been robberies on Highway 187 at night, so it's especially advisable to drive there only by day.

Malpasito
open daily 10–5; adm

west of the highway contains more than 100 waterfalls, including some over 100 metres high. In the southwest corner of Tabasco there are the little-known ruins of **Malpasito**, believed to have been built up by ancestors of the Zoque from around 300 to 800 AD. At the end of a dirt track, it's a dramatic, spectacular site, built as a series of terraces up a mountainside with a stunning view, and with a remarkably well-preserved steam bath. For a tip the site wardens or other locals can guide you to some of 38 waterfalls in the surrounding forest, many with exquisite swimmable pools.

The Sierra de Tabasco

 Around Comalco

South of Villahermosa the old road to Chiapas, Highway 195, runs straight down to become one of the most spectacular mountain roads in Mexico. It already starts to climb before it enters Chiapas, into the **Sierra de Tabasco**. Some of its valleys are home to one of Mexico's least-known indigenous peoples, the non-Maya Zoque.

The road south stays fairly flat, lined by banana plants, until you reach **Teapa**, after which it rises very quickly. The valleys of the Tabasco sierra are not high by the standards of Chiapas – under

12

Tabasco | The Sierra de Tabasco

The First Home of Chocolate

The Tabasco delta country is the home of the first, and some say the finest, cacao beans – it is likely they were first cultivated domestically here, by the Olmecs in about 1000 BC. Once the Spaniards developed a taste for chocolate they took Tabasco cacao to create plantations in other parts of their empire.

In modern times, Tabasco's cacao growers have found it hard to compete with big producers elsewhere, but recently, some cacao *haciendas* have set out to survive by producing high-quality, native chocolate with traditional, often organic methods. Several around Comalcalco are open to visitors, forming a homely *Ruta del Cacao* that makes an enjoyable 'extra' to a trip to the ruins. Each tour ends with a tasting and a chance to buy the *hacienda's* products: since it's so hot, it's hard to take them home, so you may just have to eat them on the day. While you can book visits ahead, it can be easiest just to turn up, even outside 'official' hours. All are quite well signposted.

Finca Cholula, 3km off Comalcalco–Paraíso road, **t** (933) 334 3815. This small traditional estate also contains monkeys and other wildlife. *Open Tues–Sun 9–4, adm.*

Hacienda Cacaotera Jesús María, off Cárdenas road just south of Comalcalco, **t** (933) 337 6176, *www.haciendacacaoterajesusmaria.com*. A lush *hacienda* producing fine-quality chocolate products under the Cacep brand. Informative tours include the house and a traditional Chontal kitchen, and guides are very charming. *Open Mon–Sat 8–3 or by arrangement, adm.*

Museo del Cacao y Chocolate – Hacienda La Luz, Calle Wade, Comalcalco, **t** (933) 334 1129. Founded by the German Wolter family in the 1950s, this estate has the added bonus of a museum of everything chocolate, and lush tropical gardens. *Open daily 10–4, adm.*

Getting to and around the Sierra

Teapa, main centre of the Sierra, is 59km south of Villahermosa. It has a *gasolinera* and banks, with ATMs. A road leads east from Teapa to **Tacotalpa**, near which is a turn south to **Tapijulapa** and **Oxolotán**. Parts of this road can be in poor condition after bad weather.

Only one first-class **bus** from Villahermosa to Tuxtla (at night) now takes the 'long route' via Teapa, but there are frequent second-class busses. Local *combis* run between the various towns.

Some Villahermosa travel agencies, such as **Universo Maya** (*see* p.421) occasionally offer adventure tours in the Sierra. Check state tourist websites for agency lists, and then check with each one directly for current offers.

1,000m – but enough to moderate the temperatures a little. Teapa is a pleasant little town, with an attractive plaza and three 18th-century churches. The hills around it are full of caves that were important focuses of pre-Hispanic settlement, and in nearby valleys there are beauty spots – among them **El Azufre** and **Puyacatengo** – that are visited by Tabascans for river swimming and their natural 'spas', some (pretty pungent) sulphur pools in the rocks.

East of Teapa is **Tacotalpa**, a quiet little town that until 1795 was the capital of the colony of Tabasco, long preferred by the Spaniards to anywhere down below. Not far south, 27 hectares of

Kolem Jaá
t (993) 314 3192;
wwwkolemjaa.com

mountain forest have been made into an ecoreserve, **Kolem Jaá**, which offers the opportunity to try 'adventure tourism' – nature trails, mountain biking, rafting, zip-lines, climbing – in an easy-to-handle setting. Further south again is **Tapijulapa**, largest of the Zoque villages of the Sierra. The Zoque, whose language is one of the Nahua group like the peoples to their west, were a reclusive people, who avoided major conflicts with the Aztecs or the Maya. They did not offer strong resistance to the Spaniards either, but retreated into their mountains. Their religion, even more than others in Mesoamerica, venerated mountains, rivers and natural features as centres of divine energy, and rather than build temples they held ceremonies in caves. Some are still held today.

Rather than the unobtrusive Zoque, you are first likely to notice the idyllic prettiness of Tapijulapa. It comes as a complete surprise: the houses are almost Mediterranean, with whitewashed walls and red-tile roofs, and climb up mountainsides along winding streets connected by narrow alleyways. Below are more sulphur springs and waterfalls at **Villa Luz**, the secluded hideaway where

Where to Stay and Eat

Teapa and Tapijulapa t (932–)

The main plazas of Teapa and Tapijulapa both have their crop of cheap restaurants.

Hacienda Los Azufres, t 322 2031/ Villahermosa (993) 354 5926 (*inexpensive*). In a beautiful location by the springs of El Azufre, this recently-rebuilt hotel and simple spa has natural hot and cool pools, a restaurant and comfortable *cabaña*-style rooms, with a/c.

Hotel Quintero, C. Eduardo R. Bastar 108, Teapa, t 322 0045 (*budget*). A block from the plaza, with pleasant rooms, low rates, and a **restaurant** (*moderate*).

Getting to the Rivers Region

Highway 203 turns south off the 186 Escárcega–Villahermosa road inside Chiapas, signposted for Emiliano Zapata (9km). From there it continues to Tenosique (66km). There are **petrol/gas stations** at Emiliano Zapata, Tenosique and Balancán.

Frequent first-class **buses** from Villahermosa run to Emiliano Zapata and Tenosique, and there are many more second-class. Local *combis* run mostly from Tenosique. With them or second-class buses you can get to Pomoná (3km walk from the main road), but Reforma is very hard to reach without a car.

Casa-Museo Tomás Garrido Canabal
open daily 8–5

Governor Garrido entertained his cronies, which is now the **Casa-Museo Tomás Garrido Canabal**

South of Tapijulapa the road winds, rises and falls, until finally you see below you a lush valley, with a village around the very medieval-looking monastery of **Oxolotán**.Built in the 1550s, it was intended as a way-station on a possible land route to the Yucatán. However, the friars found it very hard to sustain, and by the 1640s it had been abandoned. The chapel continued in use as the village church; built with rocks from the nearby river bed, it has a rough-hewn quality like a European early Christian church. Still cruder are the buildings

Museo de la Sierra
open daily 9–5; adm

that now house the **Museo de la Sierra**, a small collection of Baroque religious images and relics of the colonial era. The building and the sombre friars cells are the most remarkable artefacts.

The Rivers Region

On the map of Tabasco there is a separate region stretching to the Guatemalan border in the east, almost an 'annexe', which cannot be reached directly by road from the main part of the state. Known as the *Región de los Ríos* or Rivers Region, it is part of Tabasco because it was settled not by road but by river, up the Usumacinta and its tributaries. It's a classical tropical savanna landscape of vast, flat horizons that seem to simmer in the heat. It can make for an interesting detour between the Yucatán and Palenque.

Emiliano Zapata is very much a riverside town, almost on an island between the Usumacinta and a lake. From Zapata a road rolls south until after nearly 40km there is a sign to the Maya site

Pomoná
open daily 10–5; adm

of **Pomoná** Despite its remoteness this was one of the first Maya cities for which an 'emblem-glyph' was identified, allowing references to it to be traced in inscriptions. First occupied in the Preclassic, in the Classic era Pomoná fought many battles against Palenque and Piedras Negras. Its last Long Count date is from 790, suggesting the 'Collapse' reached here very early.

Pomoná was an unusually dispersed site, with six main areas spread over low hills, only one of which has been extensively excavated. Its builders faced similar problems to those at Comalcalco, a lack of local building stone, but instead of using brick they brought stone from mountains up to 20km away. Hence Pomoná's structures have a strangely rubble-like look. It gets few visitors, but has an attractive **museum**, with exceptional ceramics and reliefs.

Back on the main road, about 15km from the Pomoná turn the road crosses the Usumacinta at **Boca del Cerro**, where the river emerges dramatically from a gorge. From there it's a short distance to **Tenosique**. A rather ragged town along another long main street, it reveals its river-born origins in its waterside promenade where a few slow-moving launches still pull in.

Many ancient sites have been found in the Rivers Region, but it has been neglected in terms of excavations. A lonely road southeast from Tenosique towards Guatemala leads to a small, recently-opened Maya site at **San Claudio**. More satisfying is **Reforma**, best reached by making a 'loop' northeast from Tenosique towards El Triunfo. After 45km a sign left indicates the **Cascadas de Reforma**, rapids where Tenosique residents picnic and swim in big, cooling pools. Further north, just before the village of La Cuchilla, a signed turn leads to the Reforma site. Like Pomoná it is potentially rich; it was discovered by Teobert Maler in 1897, and later expeditions found many fine stelae. It was occupied from around AD 200. Between expeditions it was looted, and in 1961 a local initiative led to some stelae being removed to the museum in Balancán (*see* below). Excavations were undertaken in 1992-3 but have not been repeated, and only five of 25 major structures have been uncovered, the most intriguing an unusual, very steep 'stepped pyramid'.

From the ruins the road continues north to meet the dead-straight road that runs across the Rivers Region. Head west for 30km to the turn for **Balancán**. An archetypically sultry little town by a bend in the river, this has in its plaza the humble **Museo Dr José Gómez Panaco**, named after the local doctor who suggested the Reforma stelae be rescued. It has some fine exhibits, especially *Stela I*, dated 756 and known as the **Señor de Balancán**, a fearsome image of a king subduing a prisoner.

San Claudio
open daily 8–5; adm

Reforma
open daily 8–5; adm

Museo Dr José Gómez Panaco
open daily 9–8; adm

Festivals

Tenosique

Juego del Pochó 'Game of Pochó', *20 Jan–Ash Wednesday*. Tenosique is famous for a unique *fiesta*, which begins on St Sebastian's day and continues every Sunday until Lent. It's of pre-Conquest origin, but its history is unrecorded. Men dance through the streets in anonymous painted wooden masks or jaguar costumes, amid strange sounds made by a kind of drum called a *pochó*, while women dance gracefully and silently around them.

Where to Stay and Eat

Tenosique and E. Zapata t (934–)

Hotel Hacienda Tabasqueña, C. 26 no. 512, Tenosique, t 342 2731 (*budget*). Friendly small-town hotel with well-kept rooms, a/c in some rooms, free WiFi and a pleasant **restaurant** (*moderate*).

Chiapas

Chiapas feels almost like a continent by itself, with as much variation in landscape: tropical rainforest, near-alpine mountains, Pacific-coast beaches and valleys of desert-like aridity. The sheer diversity of animal, bird and plant life in the state is staggering, and most of Mexico's rarest species are found only here: quetzals, green macaws, obscure varieties of forest cat. Within Chiapas there are some of the most dramatic relics of the ancient Maya: Palenque, Yaxchilán or Toniná, and also the communities where Maya culture survives with most idiosyncrasies intact in Mexico today: in the Highland villages that surround the old Spanish city of San Cristóbal de las Casas. Travelling here is a different experience from exploring the flat, open Yucatán. Many ruins, waterfalls, sometimes even the nearest town can only be reached by long jolting drives along forest tracks or up and up through endless switchback curves. But once you get there, forest cabañas, lakeside villages and mountain-top retreats offer a wonderful feeling of remoteness.

13

Don't miss

⭐ **The pyramids of King Pakal rising up out of the forest**
Palenque p.436

⭐ **Swimming under a dazzling waterfall**
Misol-Ha p.453

⭐ **Ruins enveloped in a jungle full of howler monkeys**
Yaxchilán p.459

⭐ **Astonishing Maya murals**
Bonampak p.465

⭐ **Glimmering mountain lakes**
Lagunas de Montebello National Park p.510

See map overleaf

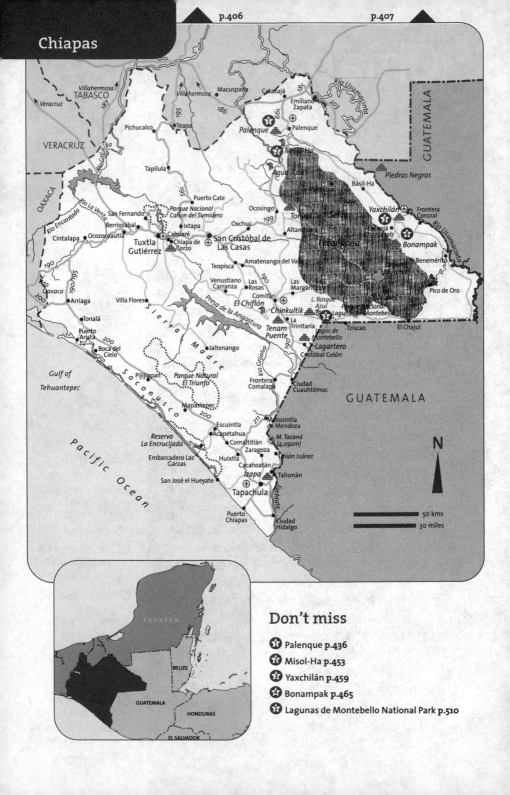

Chiapas

Villahermosa
TABASCO
Veracruz
187

Villahermosa   Macuspana   Catazajá
186   Emiliano Zapata
195   199
Pichucalco   Teapa   Palenque   Palenque

VERACRUZ

Río Grijalva
Tapilula

OAXACA

Puerto Cate
195   Ocosingo
Parque Nacional   Oxchuc
Cañón del Sumidero
San Fernando   Ixtapa   Altamirano
Berriozábal   Cahuaré
Cintalapa   Ocozocoautla   Chiapa de Corzo
Tuxtla   San Cristóbal de
Gutiérrez   Las Casas
Teopisca   Amatenango del Valle

Río La Venta
Río Encantada

Basil-Ha
Piedras Negras

Tonalá   Selva
La Selva
Yaxchilán   Frontera Corozal
Lacandona   Bonampak
Benemérito

Venustiano   Las   Las
Carranza   Rosas   Margaritas
Río Oaxaca
190/195
Comitán
Villa Flores   El Chiflón
Arriaga   Chinkultik
200

Tonalá   Tenam   La Trinitaria
Puente   Tziscao   El Chajul
Puerto   Lagos de
Arista   Boca del   Montebello
Cielo   Jaltenango   Lagartero
Cristóbal Colón

Gulf of   Pijijiapan
Tehuantepec   Parque Natural
El Triunfo   Frontera   Ciudad
Comalapa   Cuauhtémoc

GUATEMALA

Mapastepec
200   Motozintla
Escuintla   de Mendoza
Reserva   Acapetahua   M. Tacaná
La Encrucijada   Comaltitlán   (4,092m)
Zaragoza
Embarcadero Las   Huixtla   Unión Juárez
Garzas   Cacahoatán
San José el Hueyate   Izapa   Talismán
Tapachula

Pacific Ocean

Puerto   Ciudad
Chiapas   Hidalgo

Sierra Madre
Soconusco

L Bosque
Azul
Parque Nacional
Lagunas de Montebello

Presa de la Angostura
Río Grijalva

Misol-Ha
Agua Azul

Pico de Oro

Lacanjá Chansayab

N

50 kms
30 miles

YUCATÁN

BELIZE

GUATEMALA

HONDURAS

EL SALVADOR

Don't miss

1 Palenque p.436

2 Misol-Ha p.453

3 Yaxchilán p.459

4 Bonampak p.465

5 Lagunas de Montebello National Park p.510

Each of the four states that make up the north of Mayan Mexico has a certain uniformity: the flat, dry scrub and Yucatec Maya villages of Yucatán and most of Quintana Roo; the forested tranquility of Campeche; the sweltering delta of Tabasco. No such generalization can be applied to Chiapas.

As late as the 1960s the route from Palenque up to San Cristóbal de Las Casas was only a dirt track. Early explorers searching for Maya ruins in the 19th century often travelled in a *silla*, a 'chair' on the back of an Indian bearer, since the only paths were impassable even to mules. The different regions of the state developed in isolation from each other, and the state as a whole was almost as isolated from the rest of Mexico. Under Spain Chiapas was governed as part of Guatemala, and it was joined to Mexico in the 1820s more or less as a result of a political fix.

The many diversities of Chiapas can be divided into four main regions. For the last millennium the hot lowlands to the north and east along the Usumacinta river have been covered in forest and – until very recently – thinly populated, but 1,500 years ago this was one of the greatest areas of Maya civilization. It contains not only the great city of Palenque, but the just-as-spectacular sites of Bonampak and Yaxchilán. To the south and 2,000m up are the Highlands, centred around the Spanish mountain city of San Cristóbal de Las Casas, where the temperature, even the feel of the air, are utterly different. Along the valleys and ridges around San Cristóbal are the Tzotzil- and Tzeltal-speaking communities where living Maya culture survives most completely today. Still well above sea level but much lower than San Cristóbal is the Central Valley, stretching southeast from Tuxtla Gutiérrez and closed off to the north by the gorge of the Sumidero. This is the driest part of the state, and the dominant economic region of modern Chiapas. Along the south side of the valley is the massive barrier of the Sierra Madre, highest, least-populated mountains in Chiapas, home to its rarest wildlife. This separates off the last of the four regions, the hot Pacific plain of the Soconusco, with the city of Tapachula, the old coffee plantations climbing the mountains behind it and the oldest Maya remains in Mexico at Izapa.

The isolation of the state from the rest of Mexico and of its regions from each other has long been put forward as a main cause of the 'problem' of Chiapas. Economic development, political reform, always arrived here last. Chiapas was also a wild region, a byword for corruption and cronyism, and since the 1990s has been famous for its role in Mexico's political crises, with the Zapatista rebellion (*see* pp.472–7). However, this situation rarely ever creates special dangers for travellers (*see* 'Political Conflict and Military Checks', pp.110). Without dismissing these problems in any way, they need not detract from the immense fascination of Chiapas.

Palenque

 Palenque

There is no other Maya site about which so much is known as Palenque. It was the first Maya ruin to attract exploration in the 18th century, the primary target of Del Río, Waldeck and then Stephens and Catherwood when they made their way into the region. The grandeur and sophistication of the architecture of Palenque, the very model of a 'lost city', first brought the attention of the outside world to the existence of a refined ancient culture in the Maya region, even if its early explorers thought that it had been built by stray Greeks or Egyptians. Later, it was here again that the 'Palenque Round Table' meetings of the 1970s first succeeded in deciphering Maya glyphs. Palenque has the most magical location of all the major Maya cities, its pyramids and temples looming out of valleys between cascading vegetation and fast-flowing rivers. No other Maya city has such a density of sculpture and of glyph inscriptions, which have given it a vivid living history.

Palenque is also one of the largest of Maya sites, in its full extent spreading over a huge area well beyond the section normally open to visitors. And, despite all that's known about it, a vast amount remains unexcavated, so that for the non-archaeologist too, there are always new things to discover. Particularly spectacular finds have been made in the South Group since the 1990s, which represent a whole 'new' area of the site. More is being discovered about Palenque all the time, and what follows can only be a brief summary; more details and an overview of current knowledge can be found on *www.mesoweb.com/palenque*.

The town of Palenque is also the main centre for visiting anywhere in the forest lowlands of Chiapas, the jumping-off point for trips into the Lacandón rainforest and to the other great Maya sites in the Usumacinta valley, Yaxchilán and Bonampak.

History

'Palenque' is a Spanish word for a palisade or fence, and comes only from the name of the Spanish town, which was then extended to the ruins. The original name of the settlement was almost certainly *Lacam-ha* ('Big Water'), while the domain over which it ruled was often referred to in inscriptions as *Bak* or the 'Bone Kingdom'. The hills around it were probably sacred spaces long before any pyramids began to be built at the site. Palenque was a growing settlement through the Preclassic era, but is associated above all with the great flourishing of Classic Maya civilization in the Usumacinta region during the centuries from about AD 350 to 800.

The first *ahau* or ruler of Palenque whose name is known was K'uk-Balam ('Quetzal-Jaguar'), who ascended to the throne in March 431, at the age of 34. From then on we know the names and the

Getting to and around Palenque

By Air

Palenque's airport, 5km north of town, does not at the moment have any scheduled flights, but is used by private planes and air taxis. There is an official plan to extend Palenque airport to make it accessible to jets, but for now the most convenient 'real' airport for Palenque is **Villahermosa**, a 2hr drive away.

By Bus

Palenque's bus companies have not set up a joint station, but their depots are in the same place, in the lower stretch of Juárez. The **first-class** depot is used by the main companies (ADO, OCC). Principal first-class routes are listed below; there are many more services to northern Mexico via Villahermosa.

Cancún (13hrs): via **Escárcega, Chetumal, Tulum** and **Playa del Carmen**, five ordinary first-class buses daily, one luxury ADO GL. Fares $37–44.

Mérida (7–8hrs): via **Escárcega** and **Campeche**, four ordinary first-class daily. Fare about $24.

Mexico City (13hrs): two ordinary first-class daily. Fares around $50.

Oaxaca (15hrs): one ADO first-class daily at 5.30pm. Fare about $36.

San Cristóbal de Las Casas (5hrs) and **Tuxtla Gutiérrez** (6–7hrs), via **Ocosingo**: eight ordinary first-class, one ADO GL daily. Fares about $9–10 San Cristóbal, $11–14 Tuxtla.

Villahermosa (2–2½hrs): 10 ADO or OCC first-class daily 4am–9.30pm. Fares about $7.

Second-class companies are next to the first-class depot or across the street. All have frequent services on the Ocosingo–San Cristóbal–Tuxtla road (via Misol-Ha and Agua Azul) and to Villahermosa or Emiliano Zapata. Some are *intermedios*. Transportes Lacandonia usually has one bus daily to **Metzaboc** and **Naha**.

Combi companies are based in various locations. The main *colectivo*-corner is Av. 5 de Mayo and Av. Allende, here *combis* go to Palenque ruins, Catazajá and other local destinations, and Cooperativa Río Chancalá, which has services down the frontier road to **Lacanjá** (for Bonampak), **Frontera Corozal** (for Yaxchilán or Guatemala) and **Benemérito**. On Av. Hidalgo, just off Av. Allende, is the office of Transportes Chamoan, which has hourly *combis* to **Lacanjá**.

Opposite Chamoan on Av. Hidalgo is Colectivos Chambalú, with *combis* to the ruins, Misol-Ha and Agua Azul.

Getting to Palenque Ruins from Town

Frequent *combis* run along Av. Juárez out to the site (8km) from early morning until about 6pm. Look for any marked 'Ruinas'. Colectivos Chambalú run *combis* to the ruins from their office, but foreigners must buy a return ticket, which may be useless when you want to leave the site and there's no Chambalú vehicle in sight. It's better to flag down a *combi* on the street, or go to Av. 5 de Mayo. *Combis* drop you anywhere en route, such as the *cabaña* sites.

Getting to Guatemala

There is now a well-used route from Palenque across the Usumacinta river to Flores (for Tikal) in Guatemala, by bus to Frontera Corozal, then a boat across the river to Bethel (where there is a Guatemalan immigration post) and a Guatemalan bus for the last leg. You can do this independently by combi, but all-included trips are run by tour agencies (*see* p.450). For Guatemalan immigration requirements, *see* p.101.

By Car and Taxi

The **gas station** in Palenque is the last one south on Highway 199 until Ocosingo (103km); on the *Carretera Fronteriza* (Highway 307) there is one 42km south in Reforma. There are no car hire agencies; rent in Villahermosa, Mérida or Cancún. **Taxis** are plentiful (basic fare about $1.40); drivers will go anywhere in the area.

Orientation

The Palenque **ruins** are 8km from the town, down a right turn off Highway 199 south. The surrounding area is a national park; there is an entrance gate 4.5km down the same road, where everyone entering the reserve (at least, all foreigners) has to pay 20 pesos.

The modern town is an east–west grid. The *gasolinera* and bus stations are all in the 'dip' of Av. Juárez, near the **Cabeza Maya** monument (*see* p.441). From the bus stations, head uphill for the town centre. Most of the lanes of **La Cañada** (*see* p.441) do not connect with the streets of the main town, but there is a walkway between C. Merle Green and Av. Hidalgo. The main way in to La Cañada is from Highway 199, by the Maya Palenque hotel.

Despite Palenque having street names, a curious effort was made to introduce one of the intricate street-numbering systems found in most Chiapas towns. Hence you sometimes see odd signs like 'Av. Central Poniente (Av. B. Juárez)'. Most people just use the names.

birth, accession and death dates of ten generations of Palenque's rulers, from the 5th to the 8th centuries. This unique dynastic record is preserved above all in inscriptions on monuments erected by the city's greatest *ahauob*, **Pakal 'the Great'** (properly known as Janaab Pakal, 'Great Sun-Shield'), who ruled from 615 to 683, dying aged 80, and his son **Kan-Balam II** ('Snake-Jaguar', also known as Chan-Bahlum), who ruled officially from 684 to 702. Pakal's greatest work was the Temple of Inscriptions, with his extraordinary tomb; Kan-Balam II completed this giant pyramid and then matched or surpassed his father with the trio of temples called the 'Cross Group', the temples of the Cross, the Sun and the Foliated Cross.

These two recorded their 'family tree' in such detail – Pakal in great 'king-lists' of glyphs on the Temple of Inscriptions – for good reasons. Like all Maya cities Palenque had its long-running feuds – notably with Toniná and Piedras Negras, now on the Guatemalan side of the Usumacinta. It also became an ally of Tikal in its complex conflicts with the other Classic 'superpower', Calakmul. Another, separate issue was that the royal house of Palenque seems to have had a problem in maintaining an unbroken male line: on two occasions, with no male heir, the throne passed to daughters of a previous ruler, and it is clear from the inscriptions that these women were not just consorts or regents but rulers themselves. In 583 Lady Kanal-Ikal (also called Yohl Ik'nal) succeeded her father Kan-Balam I. She ruled for 22 years, but during this time, in 599, her kingdom suffered a ferocious attack from Calakmul, recorded as a disaster in the Palenque inscriptions. She was followed by her son Ah-Ne-Ol-Mat, but the city was sacked by Calakmul a second time, in 611. Ah-Ne-Ol-Mat's exact fate is not recorded, but when he died in 612 the only remaining heir to the royal line was Lady Sak-Kuk, the daughter of a brother (Pakal I) who had never actually ruled. Sak-Kuk and her husband Kan-Mo-Balam were the parents of the great Pakal, born in 603. By this point, however, not only had Palenque suffered two devastating defeats but the succession of the *ahau* contravened all the conventional rules of Mayan patriarchal lineage, since Pakal, in terms of the male line, was two removes away from the original ruling house. It seems certain there was a long period of instability in the early years of Pakal's reign while he was a child, which was dealt with by his mother.

Pakal's great monuments fulfilled two propaganda functions: 'confidence-building' as he restored Palenque's power, and legitimizing his own kingly status, by presenting very graphically his own connections with all previous rulers. On his tomb, for example, he is shown surrounded and aided by six preceding generations of the ruling house. These carvings also re-emphasized the divine nature of the *ahau* lineage as a conduit to the Otherworld, beyond mere male and female. On Pakal's tomb, his ancestors are shown emerging god-like from fruit trees in the earth, and far from hiding the shifts in his ancestry these monuments give pride of place to his mother and great-grandmother, associating Sak-Kuk with the First Mother, mother of gods and *ahauob* at the dawn of creation. In the face of any crisis of confidence, the dynasty's divine source and the ritual passing-on of power, as much as simple details of heredity, are shown as the basis of authority. Kan-Balam II in his temples went further, creating the greatest ever statement in inscriptions and sculpture of the shamanistic concept of Maya kingship and the *ahau*'s place in the divine order of the universe. In the Cross group temples his ancestry is traced further and further back in time to a supposed first king of Palenque who ruled from 967 BC, and was in turn descended from three gods known as the 'Palenque Triad', all born in 2360 BC to the First Mother herself.

This grandiose self-image was a reflection of real power, for Pakal rebuilt Palenque's strength and wealth and made it the major power in the northern Usumacinta. For many years Pakal, who officially became *ahau* at the age of 12, had to follow the directions of his mother – evidently not someone to trifle with – and did not begin to commission significant buildings himself until after 640, the year she died, when he was already 37. A significant event, given great importance in Pakal's inscriptions, came in 659 when Palenque welcomed the *ahau* Nun-Bak-Chak of Tikal after he had been driven into exile by Calakmul, and it is likely that Pakal and his son aided Tikal in later campaigns against their old enemy. At its height Palenque was one of the largest Maya kingdoms, with a population of as much as 70,000, and its tributary-settlements extended from Tortuguero, near Villahermosa, in the west – or possibly Comalcalco – well into the Petén to the east.

This grandeur, however, was always fragile. Kan-Balam II died childless and was succeeded by his brother, **Kan-Hok-Chitam II** (also called Kan-Xul), who was already 57. He was an energetic builder, notably in the Palacio, but in 711 he launched another war against Toniná. Against the odds, for Palenque was much the larger, Kan-Hok-Chitam II was defeated, captured, tortured and almost certainly sacrificed, as was gleefully recorded at Toniná (*see* p.477). Palenque was again in crisis. Knowledge of what happened next has been transformed by discoveries in Temples XIX and XX, built by the next ruler, **Kinich Ahkal Mo Naab III**. Probably a grandson of Pakal and so a nephew of the previous two *ahauob*, he did not formally take the throne until 721, ten years after the death of his predecessor, reigning until some time between 736–740. As in other Maya kingdoms where the ruling dynasty had been weakened he relied a great deal on a supposedly subordinate *sahal* or lord, a general called Chak Suutz, who though not a member of the royal house is treated with great respect in inscriptions. Between them these two succeeded in restoring some of Palenque's influence, and Kinich Ahkal Mo Naab III undertook a last great round of building in the South Group. Not much is known about his successors, but Palenque clearly had to struggle harder against outside threats as the 8th century progressed. The 'Collapse' encroached upon it less than a century after the death of Kan-Balam II, and Palenque's last dated inscription, on the accession of an *ahau* still called Pakal after his ancestor, is from 799. Despite the city's size – or perhaps because of it, given the possible extent of environmental degradation – it was abandoned quite quickly over the next 200 years.

By the time of the Spanish Conquest the site was completely overgrown, and was not even noticed when a village was established nearby in the 1560s. Some time in the 18th century local Indians came upon the ruins, and rumours about them began to reach their Spanish overlords. In 1773 Friar Ramón de Ordóñez y Aguiar, a canon of San Cristóbal cathedral with antiquarian interests, decided to follow them up. He returned with an enthusiastic account of what he had seen, and was the first to suggest the city must have been created by some alien civilization from across the Atlantic. His and subsequent local reports filtered up to Guatemala, and even to King Carlos III in Madrid, and in 1787 Captain del Río was duly sent to take a proper look. After visits by Waldeck, Stephens, Maudslay, Blom and many others, major excavations were undertaken by the INAH from 1946 under the great Cuban-Mexican archaeologist Alberto Ruz Lhuillier. His finest achievement was the discovery of the tomb of Pakal in 1952, and in recognition Ruz himself is buried here, just below the Temple of Inscriptions.

Palenque Town

Originally Santo Domingo de Palenque, the town now 'attached' to the ruins began life as a colonial way-station on the long trails between Tabasco, the Highlands and Guatemala, one of very few Spanish settlements in the region. Since Captain del Río arrived in the 1780s its inhabitants have grown used to the interest shown by the outside world in the nearby relics. When Stephens arrived here in 1840, 'the most dead-and-alive-place I ever saw', the local Prefect offered to sell him the ruins for $1,500. He was eager to go ahead, but came up against a hitch in the Mexican law – which even in this godforsaken spot had to be observed – that a foreigner could only buy land if he or she was married to a Mexican citizen. Stephens looked into it, but after noting that 'society in Palenque was small; the oldest young lady was not more than fourteen, and the prettiest woman, who already had contributed most to our happiness (she made our cigars), was already married', had to accept the deal was off.

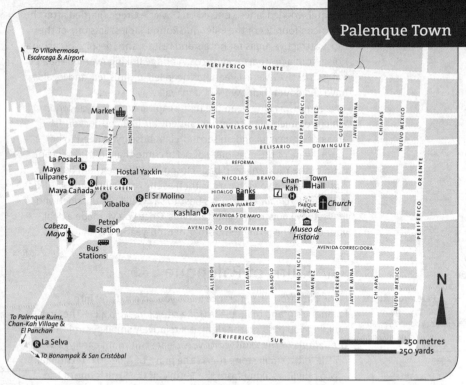

Since then, as the flow of visitors has increased, Palenque (having lost the 'Santo Domingo') has grown up as a town of hotels, restaurants and other services for archaeologists and tourists. More recently, as commercial farming has expanded in northern Chiapas, it has grown sizably as a regional centre in its own right.

As you enter modern Palenque from the north you come to its main monument, in the middle of a road junction, the **Cabeza Maya** ('Maya Head'), a giant bust based on a head of Pakal. Straight ahead, the road continues towards the ruins and San Cristóbal; to the left is the main street, **Avenida Juárez**, which curves down through a marked dip in the ground before winding left and climbing up again to the main square, the **Parque Principal**. Surrounded by snack-stands and box trees, the Parque is a likeable square, usually occupied by a mix of local teenagers, old men, backpackers and Highland women down from the hills to sell handicrafts. On the south side there is a modest little **Museo Etnográfico**, with a basic collection of traditional costumes, tools and other artefacts. The **Ayuntamiento** (town hall) on its north side is smartly painted in bright yellow.

North and west of Av. Juárez the 'dip' becomes a steep little ravine, dividing the main town from the area running west to Highway 199. Known as **La Cañada**, this is made up of unpaved,

Museo Etnográfico
officially open daily 10–4, but hours vary

tranquil wooded lanes, centred on C. Merle Green (named after the American founder of the Palenque Round Tables). It is one of the most attractive areas for hotels and restaurants, despite occasional noise from a few bars and discos. A bridge linking Avenida Hidalgo in town with C. Merle Green has been left unfinished, and locals have laid down their own wooden walkway instead.

Palenque has long been the hippy capital of the Maya world, which complements its rather raggedy air. In its busier tourist areas, at Agua Azul and on second-class buses, you need to be more aware of the possibility of petty crime than in the innocent calm of the Yucatán (keep bags closed, don't leave them out of sight in bars). If you have a car, then at the ruins and Agua Azul kids will offer to *cuidar el carro*. It's best to say you'll pay up when you leave; they know how to flatten tyres. Once you've made a deal, your car will be protected from other ten-year-olds.

The Ruins of Palenque

Palenque Ruins
Site open daily 8–5; museum open Tues–Sun 9–4.30; adm

The path from the entrance leads you up a hill and into Palenque's grand main plaza (for a site plan, *see* p.444). The first building you pass, on the right, is a relatively small pyramid, called the **Temple of the Skull** for its very clear skull-motif carvings, while on the left, a small stone marks the grave of Alberto Ruz Lhuillier.

Two buildings along from the Temple of the Skull is one of the most remarkable recent discoveries at Palenque, in **Temple XIII**. In 1994 an exceptionally rich tomb of a woman in her 40s was found here, with a green malachite funeral mask and over 1,000 pieces of jewellery and adornments of jade, oystershell and other precious materials (now in the Palenque museum), as well as the bodies of a younger woman and a boy, sacrificed to accompany the dead queen to the next world. Her body, her sarcophagus and even the tomb walls were covered with an unusual quantity of cinnabar, the red pigment often applied to bodies in Maya burials to symbolize rebirth, and so it has been labelled the **Tomb of the Red Queen** (*Tumba de la Reina Roja*). However, strangely, there are no inscriptions identifying who she was. There was much speculation that she was Lady Sak-Kuk, mother of the great Pakal whose own giant tomb rises up alongside, but more recent research has made it more likely that she was his queen, Lady Tz'akbu Ajaw.

The tomb is one of the most impressive of the more mysterious structures at Palenque that is still open to wander around freely. Inside it is one more of the strange Maya spaces-within-spaces. From bright sunlight an entrance leads into a horseshoe-shaped main chamber, within which there is what seems to be an entirely separate, 'house-like' structure. Facing the entrance is a central chamber flanked by two empty parallel ones. The Queen's red-lined

Visiting the Palenque Site

At Km 4.5 on the ruins road from the town there is an entrance gate to the national park, where everyone entering (including *combi* passengers, at least foreign ones) must pay 20 pesos, on top of the site ticket. The road then curls round the ruins to approach them from the west. On the way you pass the **museum**, with its reconstruction of Pakal's tomb (*adm incl. in site ticket*) which is best left until after visiting the ruins.

As at the major Yucatán sites there are who will give you a 1–2hr tour, for $40–45. They will take you through the main areas – and some are very knowledgeable – but Palenque is, more than most, a Maya site where you can choose between the best-known buildings or exploring along forest paths. It's naturally very hot and humid, and has some of the most exhausting climbs of any Maya temple-mountains.

The best way to experience Palenque is to give it a full day. Get there as it opens, when the pyramids are often shrouded in a ghostly mist, and take a break part way round. Take plenty of water and bug repellent. And avoid visiting on Sundays, when it's crowded, and Mondays, when the museum is closed.

sarcophagus is still in the middle chamber, and has traces of fine carving. From the sides of the outer chamber, more passages and stairways lead away mysteriously into the pyramid.

Once outside again you can't miss the giant mass of the **Temple of Inscriptions**, soaring up next to Temple XIII and dominating the square. Commissioned by Pakal as his tomb and monument, it is an awesome testimony to his importance in the life of the city. Built against a natural hill, it rises through nine levels, ascended by a narrow, very steep stairway. At the top is a temple with a characteristic feature of Palenque, a Mansard-style roof, which once supported a roof-comb. This type of roof was an innovation made by the city's builders. In place of the conventional Maya arch with sides of equal length, they developed a variation with two rows of rooms either side of a central wall, thicker than those at front and back, so that the outer sides of the arches 'leant' against the centre. This made it possible to create larger multi-room spaces.

The temple and top of the pyramid now look oddly white and clean because in 2001-2 much of the cement used in early restoration work was replaced by a reproduction of the original stucco, which has still not aged into the grey of the rest of the structure. Sadly, you are no longer normally allowed to climb to the top of the Temple of Inscriptions, but a lot can be seen from the square. The pyramid was begun years before Pakal's death. The upper temple has five entrances. Of the pillars between them, the outer ones are covered in inscriptions, while the stucco panels either side of the stairway were taken over by Kan-Balam II to glorify his own position by showing his presentation as heir as a baby in his father's arms, in the year 641. The pillar just right of the steps shows Pakal with the child, while that to the left shows Kan-Balam II with his mother; on the outer pillars are the founder of the dynasty Kuk-Balam (second from left) and the 6th-century *ahau* Kan-Balam I (second from the right), both looking favourably on the succession from the Otherworld. Kan-Balam II seems to have had six toes on each foot, making him easily recognizable. Inside the temple (so invisible from down below), two

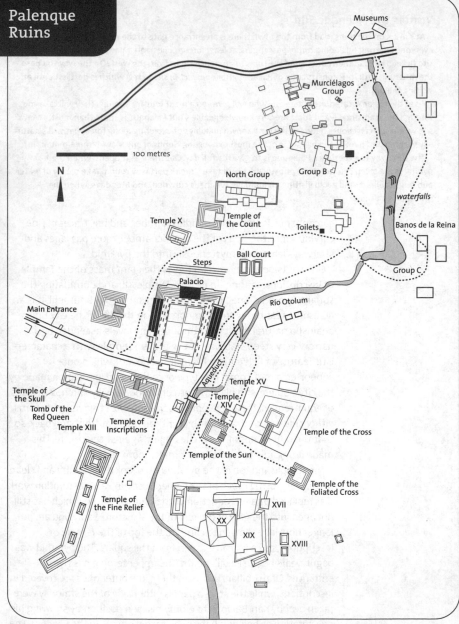

large panels and the whole back wall of the middle chamber contain Pakal's 'king lists', detailing his divine lineage. The length of Palenque's inscriptions is perhaps a reason for one of its peculiarities – that its rulers did not commission standing stelae, preferring to place their historical records directly on to buildings.

Also in the central chamber was a flagstone. In 1949, Alberto Ruz noticed some holes through which ropes could be passed, in order to move the stone. It was removed to expose a passageway, deliberately closed up with earth. After three years of digging this was found to lead to the most dramatic of all discoveries at Palenque, the **Tomb of Pakal**. Below, in a considerable feat of engineering, a remarkably steep staircase had been built as a succession of Maya-arched vaults, in order that the whole Inscriptions pyramid could not collapse on top of it. The tomb itself was at the same level as the very bottom of the pyramid. A triangular stone door sealed off the Maya-vault tomb after Pakal was interred. Beyond this door Ruz's team found five skeletons: four men and a woman, sacrificed to accompany Pakal to the Otherworld; past them, at right-angles to the antechamber, was the great sarcophagus containing the *ahau* himself, in jade jewellery and a jade and obsidian funeral mask. Most of these treasures are now in the national museum in Mexico City.

After years of argument over the possible damage caused to the tomb by crowds of tourists shuffling through, it is now definitively closed to visitors. However, as a substitute, there is now a full-size replica in the Palenque museum, the **Sala Tumba de Pakal** (*see* p.449).

The Palacio and the North Group

Opposite and below Pakal's massive pyramid is the **Palacio**, the most compact and well-defined 'royal court' of any Maya city. Palenque's palace is an astonishing maze of patios, corridors, chambers and – contrary to appearances – entirely separate buildings, interlocking on top of an 80m by 100m artificial platform and reached by two massive banks of steps. It has always been recognized as a palace, and its many spaces served the lords of Palenque probably both as residence and as a place for ceremonies, meetings and state functions. It was built and rebuilt over 400 years, but its surviving form is largely the work of Pakal, who from the 650s rebuilt the central sections, building on top of many earlier structures, including entire buried chambers. Within its disorderly structure it has three main patios, the largest, the East Court, in the northeast corner. The palace's most distinctive feature, its three-storey tower, with small Mansard-ish roof (which nowadays you're not allowed to climb up) was probably added in the mid-8th century, possibly as an astronomical observatory.

The use of Mansard-style arches enabled the Palacio's builders to create one of the most refined of Maya buildings, with a far greater feel of spaciousness and light than most Maya royal residences. It was once covered in fine stucco reliefs and carvings, and many survive (the most important have been replaced by replicas, but the originals can be seen in the museum). In **House E**, facing the Southeast Court, is a replica of the 'Oval Tablet', dated to 654, in which Pakal is shown receiving his royal status from his mother, in the costume of the Maize Goddess, emphasizing her divine status. From the time of Pakal this building and patio were the scene of the most intimate accession rituals of Palenque's *ahaoub*, and near the tablet there was once the throne where they sat during these ceremonies; part of it was removed by Del Río in 1787, and is now in the Museo de América in Madrid. The larger **West** and **East Courts** (also known as the *Patio de los Jefes Guerreros*, 'of the Warrior Chiefs', and *Patio de los Cautivos*, 'of the Captives') were more public spaces used to celebrate war victories; the East Court is lined by large stone reliefs of male figures, in a powerful style that seems strangely modern, representing captives taken by Pakal in the 660s. Pakal's second son Kan-Hok-Chitam II also took great interest in the Palacio and added the **North Gallery**, closing off the East and West Courts. In it he placed a 'Palace Tablet', showing him receiving symbols of authority from his father and mother (now in the museum).

From the Palacio a path leads across a grassy square to **Temple X**, a small, very old temple platform, and next to it the larger **Temple of the Count**, facing east. This was the second major project undertaken by Pakal at Palenque when he began building in the 640s, after the **Templo Olvidado** ('Forgotten Temple'), away in the woods to the west. It is so named because a hut at the foot of this pyramid was where mad Count Waldeck and his Indian mistress lived in 1832–3. Next to it is the **North Group**, a line of several temples atop a platform, some built by Pakal, facing back into the city. Some have fine stucco reliefs, especially the temple furthest right, looking from the square.

Between the North Group and the Palacio is a **Ball Court**. Not far from it, along the east side of the Palacio, there is one of the most ingenious constructions at Palenque. Called the **Aqueduct**, it is really a covered canal, a 100m diversion of the Otolum river through a corbel-vaulted, reinforced underground channel. The purpose of channelling the river in this way was to prevent the fast-flowing stream from flooding and undermining the Palacio platform when in full spate during the rainy season.

The Cross Group

A path leads across the Otolum to Kan-Balam II's group of temples, built at the end of the 7th century. This 'Cross Group' faces away from the main ceremonial core of Palenque, which seems strangely disorderly in a Maya city, but Kan-Balam would have had his reasons for building in this way. Having the group form a partial square open to the south echoed the earliest Maya plazas, and so emphasized the temples' strength as power points; the use of three temples also mirrored the three centring-stones in the Mayan creation story (*see* p.33), and the number three continually crops up in the group, in the number of entrances, chambers and so on. In building the Cross temples Kan-Balam II naturally wished to place himself and his lineage centre-stage, but at the same time he created the most comprehensive presentation ever made of Classic Maya beliefs, of cosmic order and the interconnected universe.

As in other parts of Palenque, access to the Cross temples is increasingly restricted, and visitors are often only allowed up to the Foliated Cross. If this is so, the replicas (or sometimes originals) of the carvings now in the site museum are as usual the best available substitute, and at least allow you to see everything clearly. The path from the river brings you round the back of the **Temple of the Sun** (from where a path to the right leads to the South Group). The Sun Temple is small, atop a four-level pyramid, with a still-intact roof-comb; also partly preserved is the entablature on the Mansard roof, with images of cosmic monsters that, like Chenes temple doorways, made clear the temple's role as portal to the Otherworld. The subject of the relief inside is warfare. Kan-Balam II, the large figure on the right, receives the power to wage war from his father Pakal. As in all the Cross Group reliefs, Pakal is shown as smaller than his son, as he was already dead and in *Xibalba*, and wrapped in thick clothing, perhaps his funeral robes. He is also standing on a kneeling god, and the great war-shield at the centre of the relief is bearing down on the two gods that support it, as if warfare was a burden for gods as much as men. Panels either side refer to the formal accession of Kan-Balam II as *ahau* in January 690.

Opposite is the **Temple of the Foliated Cross**, which thankfully you can usually climb up to, and which holds a more spectacular and better-preserved relief within. The theme here is more pacific, the sustaining of existence. The 'Foliated Cross' is a flowering variant of the world-tree, representing cultivation and agriculture, the cycle of growth essential for the community. It arises out of a 'water-lily monster', the Maya god of swamps and drained land, and at the end of the 'arms' of the cross human heads appear out of ears of corn, a reference to the Maya idea of humans as having been created out of maize. Beside the 'tree' Kan-Balam, this time on the left, waits to receive a blood-letting instrument that Pakal holds in his left hand, in order that he might fulfil his duty of sacrifice. At the top of the tree sits the Celestial Bird, spirit of nature, kept in order by cultivation and the performance of sacrifice by the king.

The **Temple of the Cross** itself still has its roof-comb, but the façade has deteriorated. The subject of its extraordinary relief is not any one aspect of existence but all of it. The 'cross' at its centre is the great world-tree itself, the axis of existence, topped again by the Celestial Bird; on either side, again, are Pakal and Kan-Balam, at the time of the latter's accession. The great scheme of the universe and the relationship to it of the lords of Palenque could not be clearer. At the point of his formal accession, the relief indicates, Kan-Balam through vision rituals descended to *Xibalba* to be reunited with his great father, and there receive from him the attributes of kingship. The side panel to the left again shows Kan-Balam II on his accession day, 20 January 690, in all his kingly regalia; in the right-hand panel there is the figure of 'God L', one of the wizened old gods of *Xibalba*, who has helped the new king return from the Otherworld to the land of the living. He is shown with a spectacular cigar. This is the oldest known image of anyone smoking in the world.

The gap between the Temples of the Cross and the Sun leads to the smaller **Temples XIV** and **XV**, on two sides of a separate pyramid-platform. Built for Kan-Balam's brother Kan-Hok-Chitam II not long after his accession, Temple XIV has a fine relief (now a reproduction) showing Kan-Balam dancing with his mother after his arrival in the Underworld, to secure the future of the city. Temple XV is actually older than any other part of the Cross Group, a complex structure inside which three élite tombs have recently been discovered, although they have not yet been identified.

The South Group

This remarkable extension to the 'known area' of Palenque south of the Cross Group has been extensively excavated only since the 1990s. Work is still in progress, and so it is often closed off. Its core is a large square, facing and 'complementing' the Cross plaza to its north. It was built in the 720s and 730s by Kinich Ahkal Mo Naab III, who in the traditional style of Maya rulers built massively as he sought to escape the crisis that followed defeat by Toniná, reassert the cosmic roots of the Palenque kingdom and demonstrate his own authority. In **Temple XIX** he created the largest single building yet found at Palenque, a long thin structure that served as a new palace-residence and ceremonial temple. The most dramatic discovery in Temple XIX has been a stone bench, which probably served as a 'throne', with exceptional carvings. On one side, Kinich Ahkal Mo Naab is shown seated between two men, probably early kings of Palenque, while on the other he is surrounded by six powerfully carved but still unidentified figures. In inscriptions on the bench Kinich Ahkal Mo Naab traces his ancestry back into mythological time, and to the divine source of the ruling house of Palenque. Other finds include a superb carved tablet showing Kinich Ahkal Mo Naab and a more delicate stucco relief of a young man, both now in the museum.

Other structures are yielding up discoveries of equal worth. In **Temple XVIII** on the east side, three still-unidentified tombs were found, along with inscriptions on the life of Kinich Ahkal Mo Naab, while **Temple XVII** has an altar with relief (in the museum) of a woman kneeling before a king, perhaps Kinich Ahkal Mo Naab and his queen. Most intriguing of all is the massive **Temple XX** pyramid the core of which is much older than the rest of the group. Rebuilding on top of this base was begun by Kinich Ahkal Mo Naab around 720, but for unknown reasons was never finished. In 1996 ground-penetrating radar discovered a space inside Temple XX: a camera was lowered into it, to reveal a chamber with mural paintings of figures in some kind of ceremony, which may be the most important Mayan wall paintings after Bonampak.

Other Buildings at Palenque

Near the North Group several paths lead down to the road and the museum, one of which is well marked as an *Andador Eco-arqueológico*. In a walk of about a kilometre, this takes you through some of the most magical jungle at Palenque, past delicious pools and waterfalls on the Río Otolum and its partner the Arroyo Murciélago ('Bat Creek') — signs now emphatically prohibit swimming, but you might get away with just cooling your feet. They also give you a feel for the sheer mysterious size of the city, with all kinds of still-unexcavated structures visible in the woods, often gripped by the roots of giant *ceiba* trees. Along the way there are some buildings that have been excavated, known as the **Murciélagos** ('Bats' Group), mostly consisting of intimate 8th-century residential complexes that were probably home to the élite families of Palenque. Most striking of all is **Group B**, for its fabulous location below the falls known as the **Baños de la Reina** ('Queen's Bath'), clearly chosen so that its wealthy inhabitants could make the most of the natural setting.

The buildings described so far make up the main 'public' area of Palenque, but anyone who enjoys exploring can find many more. Another path leads from behind the **Temple of Inscriptions** uphill to the tiny **Temple of the Fine Relief** (*bello relieve*). Perched on a forest slope, it has inscriptions and reliefs that are in a poor state, but once featured an image of a jaguar (it's now only possible to see one paw clearly). An alternative is to head out of the main site and take the path to the west from the car park, in which direction ruins extend for over a kilometre to Pakal's first building, the **Templo Olvidado**. Many of the professional site guides are willing to take visitors to the less 'usual' parts of the site, for a negotiable fee.

The Museum

Visiting the museum is a must. It can be reached by following the *andador* path past the waterfalls and out through the north site entrance. Since 2007 the museum's star attraction has been the **Sala Tumba de Pakal**, a carefully assembled replica of Pakal's Tomb. It's air-conditioned, so the experience can't really be compared to that of the asphixiatingly clammy tomb itself, and the state-of-the-art display is too glitzy for some, but it certainly gives a good idea of the tomb and the imagery around it. The centrepiece is a fine reproduction of the giant sarcophagus lid, one of the most extraordinary images in Maya sculpture, showing the dying Pakal sliding down the *wakah-kan*, the world-tree, into *Xibalba*, to join the gods and be reborn. Only 30 people are allowed into the *Sala* at a time, every 30 minutes from 9.30am–3pm.

In the rest of the museum is one of the most spectacular of all collections of Maya artefacts, nearly all from the city itself. Treasures from the Tomb of the Red Queen – her funeral mask, stunning jade necklaces – are superbly displayed. Other highlights include the stucco tablets from the Palacio, and intricately carved throne-benches from Kinich Ahkal Mo Naab's South Group temples. Ceramics and modelling in stucco are especially impressive, above all a wonderful female head and busts of Pakal and others of his line. As well as exquisite jade jewellery, there is the world's largest collection of Maya incense burners, an extraordinary menagerie from the Otherworld. Most represent the three levels of existence and other aspects of the Maya cosmos, with monsters of *Xibalba* at the bottom and the Celestial Bird appearing at the top. Alongside the museum there's also a café and shop.

Tours

ⓘ **Palenque**

By the Mercado de Artesanías, at the junction of Av. Juárez and Abasolo (open Mon–Sat 9–2 and 5–8).There is also a kiosk in the plaza, but it's rarely open.

t (916–)

Palenque has many agencies that run tours around the region. They can be a big help in getting to places (relatively) hard to reach without your own car such as Bonampak and Yaxchilán; however, recent road improvements have meant that even these once-remote spots are now quite accessible by car or *combi* (*see* p.437), and for places that are easy to get to by bus or *combi*, the advantages of a tour are questionable. You don't have to work out the route yourself, but cheap tours often only allow you a limited time at each place, which can be frustrating.

The 'standard' routes offered by all Palenque agencies are: 1-day tours of **Palenque ruins**, **Misol-Ha** and **Agua Azul** (from $6); 1-day trips to **Misol-Ha** and **Agua Azul**, sometimes including **Agua Clara** (from $6); 1- or 2- day tours to **Bonampak** and **Yaxchilán** ($35–$70) with the option of continuing to **Flores** in Guatemala; and **transport-only** trips to **Flores** (from $20).

Palenque agencies tend to stick to known itineraries (more adventurous agencies are based in San Cristóbal), but some offer options such as horse-riding or rafting, and if asked can arrange trips to remoter destinations such as **Naha**, **Pico de Oro**, or into Guatemala via **La Palma** in Tabasco. Some agencies theoretically offer trips to the ruins of **Piedras Negras** on the Guatemala side of the Usumacinta, but the best way to get there is with the **Vallescondido** restaurant (*see* p.469). The best agencies tailor itineraries to your needs, as long as you make up a group (min. 4 people; costs depend on numbers). For all such trips, contact an agency in advance.

For more on Bonampak and Yaxchilán tours, and on choosing tours in general, *see* p.458

Tour Agencies

Kichan Bajlum, Av. Juárez, corner of C. Abasolo, t 345 2452, *www.kichanbajlum. com*. Decent prices for standard routes and a flexible approach: routes can be varied on request.

Kukulcán Travel, Av. Juárez 8, by the bus depot, t 345 1506, *www.kukulcantravel. com*. Well-established agency that mainly sticks to the usual routes, but can arrange other trips.

Na Chan Kan, Av. Hidalgo, on the plaza, corner C. Jiménez, t 345 0263, *chiapas tour@hotmail.com*. Helpful agency, with better-than-average standard tours and many other destinations. There's also an office opposite the main bus station.

Paco Tours, based in El Panchán (*see* p.452). Not as cheap as some, but a knowledgeable guide, working on his own. As well as the usual destinations he offes bird-watching trips, jungle walks, horse-riding and more.

Services in Palenque

Banks: Banamex and Bancomer on Av. Juárez (corner of Aldama); both have ATMs. There are several *cambios* on Av. Juárez, and most **tour agencies** (*see* p.450) change dollars.

Health: Palenque's state **hospital** is on Juárez next to the bus stations, and there is a **24hr-pharmacy** opposite, next to the gas station.

Internet Access: There are several internet cafés along Av. Juárez.

Post Office: Av. de la Independencia, next to town hall, just off the Parque (*open Mon–Fri 9–1 and 3–6, Sat 9–1*).

Shopping

There are souvenir stalls at the ruins entrance, and in the ruins museum is **Amanecer**, an official Chiapas state handicrafts store. In town, the **Mercado de Artesanías** (corner of Juárez and Abasolo) has the best range.

Where to Stay in Palenque

Palenque accommodation ranges from tour hotels and upscale *cabañas* to comfortable lower–mid-range options and, since it's long been a backpackers' den, a big budget choice. Most hotels are in one of three areas: in the centre around the main square and Av. Juárez; in the wooded lanes of La Cañada (several on Calle Merle Green), and along the road to the ruins, where there are *cabaña* hotels and camp sites. At all the ruins road locations you have the attraction of a chorus of Howler Monkeys in the forest around you. Take bug deterrent if you stay on the ruins road.

Moderate

⊛ Chan-Kah Village >

Chan-Kah Village, Ctra de las Ruinas Km 3, **t** 345 1134, *www.chan-kah.com .mx*. Distinctive 'resort village' on the ruins road, with comfortable bungalows around a forest estate full of flowers and hummingbirds; there's a shaded terrace **restaurant**, a wonderfully lush garden and a fabulous pool that's almost an artificial lagoon. Some cabins are a little old – but its relaxing charm makes up for this.

Hotel Maya Tulipanes, C. La Cañada 6, **t** 345 0201, *www.mayatulipanes.com. mx*. Very popular hotel much used by international tour groups, with 72 high-standard (if bland) rooms with every comfort, a good **restaurant**, free WiFi in the patio, and a garden pool. In the lobby are reproductions of the reliefs from Pakal's tomb and the Temple of the Cross. Rates often drop to *upper-inexpensive*.

Inexpensive

Camping Maya Bell, Ctra de las Ruinas Km 6, **t** (045) 916 348 4271, *www. mayabell.com.mx*. The longest-running site on the ruins road is quite a solid operation, with smart cabins with bathrooms, fans and (in some) a/c. Also more basic, slightly cheaper *cabañas* sharing showers (all *inexpensive*), and dorm-style cabins, camping or hammock space (all *budget*). There's a pretty **restaurant** with plenty of vegetarian dishes, a pool and a spa. It gets full, so don't expect silence, but the setting is lovely, with a waterfall and the ruins close by. Note that as it's inside the national park you may have to pay the 20 pesos entry charge each time you come back from the town.

Chan-Kah Centro, Av. Juárez 2, corner of Av. Independencia, **t** 345 0318, *www.chan-kah.com.mx*. Under the same management as the Chan-Kah but more modest, this nevertheless enjoys a great location on the plaza and good views from its best rooms, with balconies. Rooms are smallish but well equipped, and a real bargain. Also one of the best restaurants (*see* below).

Hotel La Aldea del Halach Uinic, Ctra de las Ruinas Km 12.8, **t** 345 1693. Pleasant *cabaña*-style hotel on the ruins road: rooms are plain but spacious, all with a/c, good bathrooms and well-shaded terraces, and there's a **restaurant** (*moderate*) and pool. Prices are at the top of this band.

Hotel Kashlan, Av. 5 de Mayo 117, **t** 345 0297, *www.palenque.com.mx/kashlan*. Impossible to miss as you walk up Av. Juárez from the bus station, this big, friendly hotel has bright, clean rooms (*budget* if fan-only), a pleasant breakfast bar and an internet room. Some vegetarian dishes on offer in the restaurant (*moderate*).

Hotel Xibalba, C. Merle Green 9, t 345 0411, *www.hotelxibalba.com*. Far from resembling the Maya underworld this is one of the best-value La Cañada hotels, with big, light rooms divided between two buildings. All have good bathrooms, a/c, TV and other fittings, and the **Don Carlos restaurant** (*moderate*) is pleasant for breakfast. The owner also has a tour agency (Viajes Shivalva) which provides individual trips for hotel guests.

La Posada, Av. Nicolás Bravo 50, t 345 0437. Cheapest in La Cañada, with simple, comfortable rooms around a jungle-like patio. Several rooms with a/c are at the bottom of this price band; fan-only rooms are *budget*. The owners are very friendly and helpful.

Budget/Camping

Hostal Yaxkín, Av.Hidalgo/Merle Green, t 345 0102, *www.hostalyaxkin. com*. Recently-opened hostel in La Cañada whose owners are ready to go the extra mile for their guests. There are dorms and private rooms (*inexpensive* with a/c) and breakfast is included. The **restaurant** (*moderate*), bar, internet room and other common areas are attractive, spacious and lively.

 El Panchán >

El Panchán, Ctra de las Ruinas Km 4.5, *www.elpanchan.com*. Just by the entrance gate to the reserve a track turns south into a glade by a stream that's a private 'nature reserve' set up by the local Morales family. Amid the trees are five *cabaña* outfits offering everything from camping or hammock space through communal *palapas* to quite comfy private cabins (all *budget*); **Chato's Cabañas** and **Margarita & Ed's** (t 348 4205) are the most solid; Margarita, at the latter, is very hospitable and her rooms have good showers and a/c. **Restaurants** offer food from Mexican to Italian, Indian or vegetarian, and there are tour desks, a Maya steam-bath, internet access and a little pool. The layout doesn't allow total privacy, but the mellow feel and beautiful setting have made it first

choice for many travellers. You can book ahead at all the Panchán *cabañas*, or just turn up. Another *cabaña* operation, **El Jaguar**, has started up on the other side of the road.

Eating Out

Expensive

La Selva, Ctra de las Ruinas Km 0.5, t 345 0363. South of town near the ruins turning, this restaurant is surprisingly elegant, with neatly laid tables beneath a giant *palapa* or in a garden, smooth service and a pricey wine list. Its traditional food has less panache than the setting, but for a treat it's very comfortable.

Moderate

Chan-Kah Centro, Av. Juárez 2, corner of Av. Independencia. Of the hotel restaurants this wins for food and atmosphere, with tables on a balcony that offers a view of the hubbub below.

Mara's Café-Bar y Restaurante, Av. Juárez 1, corner of Av. Independencia. Facing the plaza, a big, pretty restaurant with outside tables and a generous mix of food and drink from breakfasts, sandwiches and classic Mexican snacks to larger feasts.

Restaurante Maya Cañada, C. Merle Green. La Cañada branch of Palenque's oldest restaurant, with a romantic terrace, good cocktails and ever-enjoyable local and Mexican standards. The original **Restaurante Maya**, a travellers' standby since 1958, is on the plaza in town (corner of Av. Hidalgo).

Budget

There are clutches of *taco*-stands on the plaza and Av. Abasolo, and *loncherías* along the south side of the square. The plaza is also the best place for *licuados* and juices. Towards the ruins, El Panchán (*see* left) has great bargain (and wholefood) meals.

El Sr Molino, Av. Juárez 120-C. Big restaurant on an airy balcony beside the 'rise' in Av. Juárez. Despite its basic, party-venue look the traditional food is very good, especially fish dishes, prepared with care – one more demonstration that in Mexican restaurants you can never go by appearances.

Getting to Misol-Ha and Agua Azul

Some *combis* from Palenque run direct to both falls; ask at *combi* stops. Other *combis* and second-class buses stop only on the Highway.

The turn-off for **Misol-Ha** is 19km south of Palenque. From there, it's 2km to the falls, not too hard a walk if you don't have a car. The turn for Agua Clara is another 33km south.

The turning for **Agua Azul** (called *Crucero Agua Azul*) is 8km from Agua Clara, 60km from Palenque. You may find local *combis* running to and from the Crucero (mostly at weekends), but otherwise, while the walk down is long (4km) but quite easy, getting back is a wearying, hot climb.

None of these places is good to visit in the rainy season and demands more caution than usual.

Tours

All Palenque tour agencies run day trips to Misol-Ha and Agua Azul, which have continued despite the recent problems. Many give you only a hurried stop at the former and around 4hrs at Agua Azul, so check; for flexibility, you need to make your own way. Some agencies still offer **horseback treks** at Agua Azul.

Misol-Ha and Agua Azul

🔧 Misol-Ha
Open daily 7–6; adm.

As Highway 199 winds into the hills south of Palenque it passes two of the most dazzling tropical landscapes in northern Chiapas, the waterfalls of Misol-Ha and Agua Azul. They are very popular day trips from Palenque, or stop-offs on the way south. Recently, political disputes have made visiting here a little more complicated, but without, usually, creating great difficulties or dangers for travellers.

Misol-Ha is the least problematic and in many ways the most attractive. The entry road runs out at the crest of a steep valley. A path winds down to the waterfall, a 35m drop into a deep-blue pool ringed by mahogany trees, *ceibas* and emerald-green vegetation. A rope slung across indicates where it's safe to swim. There's a precipitous path called **La Cortina** ('the curtain') behind the great sheet of water of the falls, where you get suitably drenched (local girls tackle it in high heels). On weekends or holidays big groups come to picnic and cool off, but on other days you may share the falls only with a few foreigners. If you wish to stay over, there are attractive *cabañas*.

Agua Clara
Two local communities charge adm for cars and visitors; there are no fixed times.

Another 33km on, another turn-off leads to another stretch of beautiful forest river at **Agua Clara**. Some *cabañas* were set up here a few years ago, but are very neglected, and there has been an angry dispute between Zapatista and non-Zapatista communities over access to the river. Anyone wishing to explore here should enquire first in Palenque or San Cristóbal on current conditions.

Eight km along the main road, a sign at another steep bend points downhill to **Agua Azul**. After 4km this road ends in a broad green valley floor by the largest of many pools in the Agua Azul river, a tributary of the Tulijá. Above this pool the river bubbles, crashes, divides and redivides through a water staircase surrounded by thick forest for 7km, through wide green pools, white-water rapids, whirlpools and quiet streams.

Agua Azul is one of the most celebrated natural beauties of Chiapas, and for years one of the local communities, also called

Visiting Misol-Ha and Agua Azul

Misol-Ha

Travellers sometimes pass these falls by in favour of those at Agua Azul, which are larger and better known. However, they're an easier ride from Palenque; also, they're a shorter hike from the main road, less crowded, have a much less hassled, less conflictive atmosphere and are far better for swimming.

Agua Azul

Once past the two entry controls, you come to a broad grass parking area and airstrip. If you drive, you'll be approached by kids wanting to watch your car, and insistent fruit and junk sellers. There are plenty of open-air cheap restaurants, especially by the lower pools.

Agua Azul, has made much of its money by charging tourists (sometimes aggressively) for access to the falls. In 2007–8, tensions arose over this 'monopoly' between Agua Azul – supported politically by the PRI – and an adjacent Zapatista community through whose land the entry road also passes. After some clashes and murky incidents in which tour buses were hijacked by masked groups (and each side put the blame on the other), an agreement of sorts was reached whereby both communities now charge entry to Agua Azul, at different points on the road. This kind of deal could change, of course, so a certain caution is advisable, although tour buses visit the falls regularly.

There are several points where you can swim, beginning with the lower pool itself, although the water is often murky. Great care is always necessary when swimming at Agua Azul, for as in any white-water river, currents can change in a few metres. Not far above the first pool is a cataract called the *Licuadora* ('Liquidizer'), where crosses commemorate people killed trying their luck too far. Swimming here is absolutely to be avoided. If in doubt, stick to the quietest pools and stay near the 'beaches'. Further up, the weekend crowds thin out a little. About a kilometre up is one of the most attractive spots, **La Selva**, with a ravishing lagoon, nicer restaurants than lower down and shady paths. The path goes on, increasingly steep but still populated, until at about 2km from the bottom it swings over to the right side of the river – by now a stream – via a broken-down but passable metal bridge. This is as far as most people go, but it's possible to go on for at least 3km, past more jungle pools and waterfalls.

Note that – politicial problems aside – in the whole region covered by this book, **thefts** are most frequently reported at Agua Azul. Robberies and occasional assaults on women seem most common on the 'empty' stretch of the path, beyond the rickety bridge. To explore this path it's best to go with a guide from one of the camp sites. Wherever there are plenty of people about, the danger of serious incidents is low, but petty theft is still a problem so look out for your things when swimming.

Where to Stay and Eat

Misol-Ha t (916–)
Cabañas Misol-Ha, t 345 0356, *www.misol-ha.com* (*budget*). The local *ejido* has a substantial tourism scheme (with website) centred on 19 nicely-decorated cabins, all with showers, fans and balconies, in a forest setting at the top of the falls, with great views. Some are family-size, with kitchens. There's also a pleasant **restaurant** and a shop.

Agua Azul
You can camp or park an RV by the bottom pool, but there are always people around. For some tranquillity, walk up 1½km to the main campsites (most called **Camping Agua Azul**). Some have cabin-style rooms (*budget*). Further on, **Hamacas Casa Blanca** also has cabins, and its owner is a forest guide. The Agua Azul sites are all fairly shabby, and you need to be careful about security (*see* p.454).

Yaxchilán, Bonampak and the Lacandón Forest

The Usumacinta valley southeast of Palenque is perhaps the part of the Maya world that shows the greatest contrast between the landscape over the last ten centuries and that of 1,500 years ago. By the time the Spaniards came it was taken over by scarcely inhabited forest; yet, around AD 800 this was one of the most thickly populated regions of Maya civilization, with communities trading and warring all along the river. Within the forest are two of the greatest relics of the Maya, **Yaxchilán** and **Bonampak**, with some of the finest of Mayan art. Bonampak is in the territory of the **Lacandón**, the forest Maya who until the 1970s kept all their non-Christian traditions and had scarcely any contact with the rest of Mexico. This is an area that is changing fast and has become vastly more accessible, with roads ever further into the Lacandón jungle. The trip to Yaxchilán and Bonampak remains a 'must' when travelling in the Maya lands, and still has a great feel of adventure.

Lacanjá and Frontera Corozal

Almost as soon as you leave Palenque the road begins to roll and climb, especially after the turn-off for Bonampak 8km south of the town, and runs on for mile after mile over the tops of ridges along the valley of the Usumacinta, like so many scales on the earth's surface. On either side the forest, once fabulously lush, has been cut back in great swathes by slash-and-burn *milpas*, empty patches of cleared ground and cattle *ranchos*. The *colonia* villages scattered along the road are, in the manner of settler communities in Mexico, gradually becoming more solid; **Reforma**, 42km from Palenque, now has the accolade of a bright new *gasolinera*. A road turns off the *Fronteriza* there for **Naha** and **Metzaboc**, home of the 'pure', most traditional Lacandón, deep in the woods. They get few

Forest People: The Lacandón

The Lacandón of the forests of eastern Chiapas were until about 40–50 years ago the most isolated of all the Maya communities, the one least touched by European civilization. They were the only Maya never conquered by the Spaniards, and so never Christianized by the Catholic friars. According to one theory they are descended from Maya who at the time of the Conquest fled into the forest to preserve their traditions. Their language, strangely, is closer to Yucatec Maya than the Chol of their closest neighbours, suggesting that at some point they migrated from the north.

The Lacandón survived by retreating into the remotest part of the Chiapas jungles. They lived very simply, relying on hunting and basic agriculture. In their own language they call themselves *hach winik* or 'true people', and always kept apart from the more settled Maya. Their beliefs have many equivalences with older Maya ideas, sharing a conviction that the whole world is alive around them. They venerated Yaxchilán, as the origin of the gods. Until recently they made their own distinctive leather drums and simple pottery, such as the 'god pots' with faces in which copal incense is burnt to summon up the gods. They also have – or had – enormous knowledge of the forest. The instantly recognizable characteristic of traditional Lacandón, though, is their appearance: they do not cut their hair, and wear long white smocks of coarse cotton. The impression could be of a bunch of hippies wandering round in hospital gowns.

The Lacandón also attracted great attention from anthropologists and researchers. They are most associated with Frans and Trudi Blom of Na Bolom in San Cristóbal (*see* p.496), who established a very personal relationship with them, and still today Na Bolom is a centre for aid and education programmes for the Lacandón.

Since the 1960s, and above all since the opening up of the road from Palenque in the mid-1990s, the Lacandón have been exposed to the modern world at a pace that's hard to comprehend. There are only about 600 of them, living in the villages of Naha, Metzaboc, San Javier, Bethel, Lacanjá and a few offshoots. Protestant missionary campaigns led to a split in the tiny community, as Naha and Metzaboc tried to keep to the old ways, and broke off relations with Lacanjá, where many are now 'Evangelicals'. The Lacandón no longer have the forest to themselves, as more and more other Maya and *mestizo* settlers have moved into the area. Relations with other communities are often bad, as Chol Maya villages nearby commonly complain that the Lacandón are privileged 'favourites' of foreigners and the Mexican government – as to some extent they are, since Lacanjá has a monopoly on access to Bonampak. This has provided a significant income for some, with a multiplication of tourist *campamentos* and *combis* and taxis running up and down to the ruins. This 'boom' might seem tiny by international standards, but it is a huge change for Lacanjá.

The Lacandón have undergone culture shock from many angles. In under ten years most men at Lacanjá have given up wearing their traditional smocks except for special occasions – or to please the tourists – and Lacandón ceramics have all but disappeared, since tourists prefer souvenirs that are easier to take home. Tourist expansion has further eaten away at community cohesion. And yet, some Lacandón still transmit a special sense of self and near-otherworldly calm, and are themselves determined to preserve what they can of their ways and their rare environment.

visitors, and the best way to go there is with a tour, especially those of **Na Bolom** in San Cristóbal, who have long-standing links with the community (*see* above). Otherwise, they may be willing sometimes to accept individual travellers. Both villages are next to lakes, an important source of food for the Lacandón. Village guides can take you around them by canoe, or you can go fishing or hunting. There are also more remote ruins nearby.

Along the main *carretera* more attractions are becoming accessible, such as another set of waterfalls at **Welib-Já**, 30km from Palenque, north of Reforma. Near the village of **Nuevo Francisco León** at km 61 on the *Fronteriza* are the spectacular falls of **Busil-Ha**, best visited via a stop at Vallescondido restaurant and *cabaña* hotel, where owner Willy Fonseca can also guide you to Piedras Negras on the Guatemalan side of the Usumacinta (*see* p.459).

Once you are 70km from Palenque, the forest is a little less battered, and becomes denser until you come to the first Lacandón village of **San Javier**, before a fork in the road at **Crucero San Javier** (135km from Palenque). The **Carretera Fronteriza** continues to the left, while the right fork runs toward Bonampak via the largest Lacandón village of **Lacanjá** (or Lacanjá Chansayab). Thanks to its government-sponsored privileges over access to Bonampak this has grown into quite a sprawling place, a curious, disorderly mix of a few remaining Lacandón palm-roofed huts, a much larger number of wood and corrugated zinc ones and one or two concrete buildings. An airstrip runs through the village, there's a basketball court, and several houses have satellite dishes. Look around, though, or walk a short way in any direction and you're soon reminded you're in a remote point in the forest. As the sun goes down nature takes over, with the electronic cacophony of jungle insects at dusk.

Lacanjá has become the principal place to stay in the Lacandón forest, with *campamentos* spread around the village, but some are dirty and poorly run. The best, such as **Campamento Río Lacanjá**, are in idyllic locations near the Lacanjá river, and offer activities such as kayaking, rafting and forest walks. If you have time, Lacandón guides can lead you to a beautiful lake, **Laguna Lacanjá**, 8km south, and the largely unexcavated, unexplored Maya ruins of Lacanjá.

The main *Fronteriza*, meanwhile, continues for another 25km from San Javier before passing a turn off to the left, which leads in 14km to the Usumacinta, the Guatemala border and **Frontera Corozal**, the base for river trips to Yaxchilán and across to Guatemala. A mainly Chol Maya community, Frontera has been given similarly exclusive rights over Yaxchilán access and the Guatemala crossing as the Lacandóns enjoy at Bonampak. Its hotel **Escudo Jaguar** has mushroomed, and the village now has a very well-defined main street, which runs straight down past the boatmen's co-operatives and the hotel to end at the walkway down to the still rather ragged *embarcadero*, the landing-stages by the river's edge. Beside the street, just back from the river

Museo Comunitario
Open daily 8–6

there is also an excellent free **Museo Comunitario**, which has an interesting exhibit on modern life in the area and a small display of Maya artefacts, including two superb stelae discovered at the small site of **Dos Caobas**, 12km to the south. This was a subordinate of Yaxchilán, and the stelae show Shield Jaguar II and Bird Jaguar IV (*see* p.460). As a rare concession, they have been allowed to stay in this local museum, instead of being taken off to Tuxtla Gutiérrez or Mexico City.

Getting to Yaxchilán, Bonampak and Lacanjá

Access to this area was transformed by the Zapatista conflict. In the early 1990s getting here, 150km from Palenque, involved bouncing for hours over a dirt track, or an expensive light-plane flight. Then, when the Zapatistas hit the headlines in 1994, it was noticed that there was a total lack of communications in the huge stretch of Chiapas that juts east into Guatemala. The Mexican army set about building a paved road along the track all the way around the frontier to Montebello, the **Carretera Fronteriza**, also labelled **Highway 307**. This has cut journey time from Palenque to Bonampak to 3hrs.

It also transformed access from Palenque to **Guatemala**. Crossings of the Usumacinta from the river village of **Frontera Corozal** were once purely 'informal', but there is now regular boat traffic, and Frontera has a Mexican immigration post. Most boats and all agency trips from Palenque head 30mins upstream to **Bethel**, which has a Guatemalan police post.

Even if you don't cross the border, you need to have your passport and Mexican tourist card with you, as police and army checks are relatively frequent. Like all forest trips, visiting Yaxchilán and Bonampak is more difficult (but not impossible) in the June–Oct rainy season.

Security on the Fronteriza

After a spate of robberies on the Palenque–Lacanjá road in 2002–3 the Chiapas state government ordered that all tours and buses should travel together in convoy with a police escort, forming up at the Cabeza Maya in Palenque at 6.30am and returning from Lacanjá and Frontera about 5–5.30pm. This system still operates, although sometimes only theoretically – on some days the escort fails to turn up. Tour agencies still travel in convoy and may exaggerate the dangers of the road in order to get you to put aside ideas of making your own way and take a tour instead. However, while no one should drive this road by night, by day it is now peaceful and trouble-free most of the time, and there are no special risks in driving down it by car. There's quite a steady flow of traffic, especially *combis*, which go up and down all day.

Tours

All Palenque agencies (*see* p.450–1) offer one-day (from $35) or two-day (from $70) trips to Bonampak and Yaxchilán, with the option of returning to Palenque or going on to Flores.

One-day tours can be very rushed, and one point against them could be that you have to get up very early, to join the convoy (*see above*) at 6.30am. **Two-day trips** leave at the same time but are generally much better. The usual tour consists of a drive by *combi* to Frontera Corozal, a boat to Yaxchilán and back, and a night in a camp or *cabaña* site at Lacanjá; on the second day you visit Bonampak before returning to Palenque. Meals, soft drinks and (where needed) camping equipment are included, but take water, sun block, bug repellent (essential), and a light for the camp site and examining the murals at Bonampak.

Tours are obviously useful if you don't have your own transport, and/or your time is limited. Compare agencies, and not just by price. Check what guarantee there is that a tour will leave when you expect it to (tours often require a minimum of 4–6 people, and agencies may take bookings, then cancel at the last minute), and whether there will be a guide and/or driver with you throughout. Many agencies now 'double up', taking one group to Lacanjá, leaving them there overnight at a campsite and going back to Palenque to pick up another group – a system that usually works fine, but obviously, the more direct service you have, the better.

Ask too which *campamento* is used at Lacanjá, whether adm charges are included in the price, and if any other 'extras' are provided, such as guides at the sites.

A few agencies will arrange longer tours on request, notably to **Naha** or **Pico de Oro**.

Travelling Independently

Combis now run frequently from Palenque, through the day, not just with the 6.30 convoy. **Transportes Chamoan** at Av. Hidalgo, off Av. Allende, has services more or less hourly to Lacanjá and several daily to Frontera Corozal, and **Cooperativa Río Chancalá**, Av. 5 de Mayo by Av. Allende, has *combis* to Lacanjá, Frontera and on to Benemérito. Fares are around $5. *Combis* that don't go direct to Lacanjá stop at Crucero San Javier, from where Lacandón *combis* and taxis will take you the 9km to Lacanjá or Bonampak. There are also a few second-class bus services. For points beyond Benemérito or further into the forest (such as Naha), finding buses or *combis* is a matter of looking around second-class bus depots or *combi* stops.

For travelling **by car**, the 307 road is well-maintained and in good condition certainly as far as Benemérito. A growing number of drivers now do the whole 'loop' to Comitán. Always fill up with **gas/petrol** in Palenque or Reforma, the last official fuel stop on Highway 307 until La Trinitaria, near Comitán (502km).

Boats to Yaxchilán

All visitors to Frontera Corozal must pay a basic *cuota* to the community, of 15 pesos each. The local boatmen are now quite organized. If not with a tour, you must buy a ticket: there are two main co-operative offices, **Pájaro Jaguar IV, t** 00502 5363 4166, *pajarojaguarIV@hotmail.com*, easy to spot beside the main road down to the river, and **Escudo Jaguar**, at the hotel of the same name (*see* p.469). If you don't find them, one of the *lancheros* will probably approach you anyway. Each uses similar set fares (sometimes negotiable). A *lancha* for up to four people costs about $40, four to six about $50. Fares to Bethel, Guatemala are similar.

Getting to Piedras Negras

Guatemalan authorities also allow visits to the Maya ruins of Piedras Negras across the Usumacinta, but this is a difficult part of the river and only some Frontera *lancheros* are willing to take it on. The best way to get there is with Willy Fonseca of Vallescondido (*see* p.469). Contact him in advance.

Yaxchilán

☺ Yaxchilán
open daily 8–5; adm

The first recorded monarch of Yaxchilán, venerated in later inscriptions as founder of the dynasty, was called Yat-Balam, and probably became *ahau* in AD 359. His name is often translated as 'Progenitor Jaguar', but could also mean 'Jaguar Penis', a good title for the founder of a Maya patriarchy. The site had been occupied much earlier. Its extraordinary location, dominating a bend in the river, gave It a powerful presence in politics along the Usumacinta. Instead of resting on artificial pyramids, its temples and palace-residences rise up in terraces on steep natural hills above the river. This location also brought it into permanent rivalry with Piedras Negras downriver, and the string of wars between them is one of the longest-running feuds in Maya history.

Yaxchilán has many of the most skilful of all Maya carvings and inscriptions, which have rendered up a great deal of information. So fine are the Yaxchilán carvings that many have been taken away: the lintels of Temples 21 and 23 were removed by Alfred Maudslay in the 1890s and are now in the British Museum, and others are in the National Museum in Mexico City. In place of some there are casts, which have been carefully done and are not a bad substitute. In the Usumacinta valley the strength or weakness of a community was measured by its war record, and Yaxchilán fought many battles with others neighbours as well as with Piedras Negras. At different times it battled with both Tikal and Calakmul, but in the later Classic era it seems to have been a Calakmul ally. For a long period in the 6th and early 7th centuries few monuments were created at Yaxchilán, a phenomenon which generally indicates a low point in a Maya kingdom's fortunes, perhaps because Piedras Negras had gained the upper hand. The two Yaxchilán rulers of whom most is known appeared at the end of this time, as the resurgent city entered a 'golden age', **Shield-Jaguar II** (*Escudo Jaguar*, more properly known as Itzamnaaj Balam II) and

Visiting Yaxchilán

The outboard-driven *lanchas* that take you to Yaxchilán from Frontera Corozal have palm-leaf canopies for shade, though ambient heat can be more noticeable than direct sunlight. The outward journey, with the current, takes about an hour; going back the *lancheros* work harder, and it takes longer. Either way they demonstrate a great knowledge of the Usumacinta, a powerful, big green flow with eddies and rapids.

When you reach the landing stage below Yaxchilán your *lanchero* will probably say he'll expect you back in 1½hrs; ruins enthusiasts may want to stay longer, so make this clear, and be ready to tip extra. Above the landing stage are an INAH ticket hut, toilets and a drinks stand. One of the watchmen may offer to guide you round the site, for $7–10.

his son **Bird-Jaguar IV** (*Pájaro Jaguar*). Between them they ruled for nearly 90 years. They were the first Maya kings anywhere to be individually identified, by Tatiana Proskouriakoff in the 1960s. Shield-Jaguar II became *ahau* in 681, apparently aged 34. Like his senior neighbour Pakal of Palenque he lived to a great age, 95, and is described as having led his warriors into battle even in his eighties. Even by the standards of Maya lords he and his son were prolific monument builders. Out of the effort to understand why they built so much, a dramatic story has emerged.

Like other cities Yaxchilán had a favoured style of monument, in this case the downward-facing stone lintels of temple entrances, which were decorated with intricately detailed carvings. They were designed to be 'read' by other members of the city's élite, who would pass beneath them. Although he reigned for over 60 years Shield-Jaguar II did not begin building large-scale monuments until after 720, suggesting he had first had to struggle hard to re-establish the city's strength and his own authority against external and internal enemies. Many of his monuments were accordingly highly militaristic, celebrating victories. The greatest monument of Shield-Jaguar II's reign, though, is Temple 23, built in 723–6. Its three wonderfully carved lintels – two of which are in London and the other in Mexico City – show the king's first wife Lady Xoc (or Kabal Xook) taking part in bloodletting rituals: one to celebrate the birth of the heir Bird-Jaguar in 709, in which she pulls a thorned rope through her tongue; a middle one, in which she summons up Yat-Balam, founder of the lineage, during Shield-Jaguar's accession rites in 681; a third one, in which, after shedding blood, she helps Shield-Jaguar prepare for battle. It was unprecedented for a woman to be given prime position in the portrayal of sacred rituals in this way. More unusual still, Xoc was not the mother of the child whose birth is marked in the first lintel (Shield-Jaguar should then have been 61, and she was probably a similar age). Bird-Jaguar's mother was a younger wife, known as Lady Ik-Skull or Eveningstar.

As at Palenque, monuments were used to reassert the power and legitimacy of the dynasty after a period of weakness, and to overcome political problems. Lady Xoc was a member of one of the

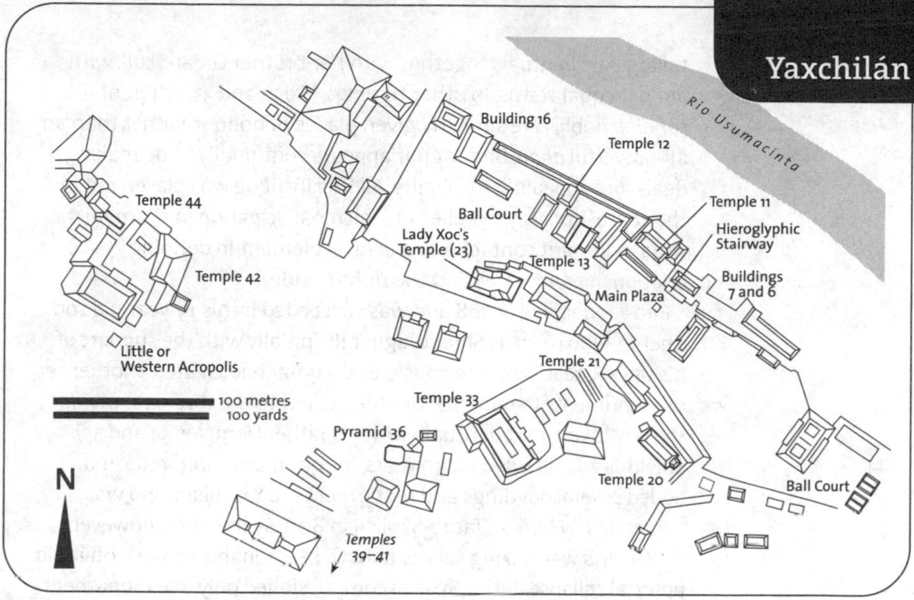
Río Usumacinta
Building 16
Temple 12
Temple 44
Temple 11
Ball Court
Hieroglyphic Stairway
Lady Xoc's Temple (23)
Temple 13
Temple 42
Buildings 7 and 6
Main Plaza
Little or Western Acropolis
Temple 21
100 metres
100 yards
Temple 33
Pyramid 36
N
Temple 20
Ball Court
Temples 39–41

most important lineages of Yaxchilán, while Ik-Skull was a princess from Calakmul. In choosing the young Bird-Jaguar as his heir Shield-Jaguar almost certainly passed over other, older sons who probably felt they had a better claim to the throne. It appears he was carrying out a balancing act. By creating a monument to Xoc – in which she herself celebrated the new prince – and paying her (and therefore her family) an unheard-of degree of honour, he could perhaps hope to have his foreign alliance and present his chosen successor without alienating his own aristocracy. This probably involved some practical concessions to Xoc's relatives.

His politicking seems to have worked only to a certain extent. Shield-Jaguar II died in 742, but Bird-Jaguar IV's formal accession did not come until 752, after a murky 'interregnum' during which it seems that another ruler may have been installed, perhaps with the involvement of the eternal enemy Piedras Negras. Bird-Jaguar IV's need to assert his authority was thus still greater than usual and, even before he was finally declared ruler he began a massive 'programme' of monument-building. In the great Stela 11, he had himself shown taking part in a 'flapstaff ritual' (a ceremony, still not fully understood, which involved a kind of banner and was held on the summer solstice) with the old king in 741; he also 'reinserted' his own mother, Ik-Skull, into his father's reign, in carvings that show her taking part in the same kind of rituals as were carried out by Lady Xoc in Temple 23. This suggests that Xoc's family, including his own half-brothers, may have been among his enemies. Bird-Jaguar also needed allies: rather than marry a foreign princess, he took as his principal wife a daughter of another of Yaxchilán's noble lineages, Lady Great-Skull, and the two of them are shown taking part in rituals together with her brother Great-Skull, with almost equal status. In other temples, like 21 and 33, different *sahalob* nobles are similarly given places of honour. Rather than an all-powerful *ahau*, Bird-Jaguar appears continually to be making deals and appealing for loyalty. All this intrigue was played out in the context of Mayan belief, in which participation in shamanistic ritual and spirit contact was a central element in defining relationships, loyalties and the right to rule.

Bird-Jaguar died in 768 and was succeeded by his 19-year-old son Chel-Te, who ruled as **Shield-Jaguar III**, initially with the support of his uncle Great-Skull. Previously, Bird-Jaguar had created another set of monuments to reinforce Chel-Te's claim to the throne, showing the boy taking part in rituals with his father (Temples 54 and 55). Shield-Jaguar III ruled for 30 years, fought many more wars and added several buildings and monuments to Yaxchilán, and was succeeded by his son Tatbu-Skull III in 800. By this time, however, Yaxchilán's warmaking seems to have been unable to stave off rapid political collapse. Tatbu-Skull III commissioned only one monument, the last Long Count inscription at Yaxchilán, dated 808.

Like other Usumacinta cities Yaxchilán was all-but abandoned within two centuries. Its temples were visited only by the Lacandón. It was revealed to the outside world in the 1880s by Maudslay and Charnay, after a Dr Livingstonesque encounter when they ran into each other at the ruins, each thinking they had found them first. Maudslay called the place *Menché Tinamit*, a name probably used by the Lacandón, but in 1901 Teobert Maler invented Yaxchilán ('blue-green stones'), which has stuck.

The Main Plaza

Its monuments aside, an essential attraction of Yaxchilán is its superb rainforest location. Above the river, the bluff divides into clefts, ledges and steep hills, reached by narrow paths through thick, high forest. Although the site has been excavated over many years, there are still a great many buildings half-lost in the undergrowth, and the forest seems ready to reclaim the whole site. In the tops of the trees, toucans and parrots are easy to spot, while in the background howler monkeys provide an extraordinary chorus.

As you walk through the trees from the entrance hut you come to a fork in the path, where a sign right indicates the *Pequeño Acrópolis* (the Little Acropolis, also known as Western Acropolis). If you take this path you can get the steep-climb part of Yaxchilán over first (and so do the rest of the itinerary here in reverse, to descend from Temple 33 into the plaza). If instead you stay on the main path, the first major structure you come to is the **Laberinto**, which is actually two buildings (**18** and **19**) linked together, a web of bat-filled passages – hence its name – that seems to have been a combined residential and ceremonial complex. Beyond it you enter the central plaza of Yaxchilán, which, in place of the usual artificial geometry of Maya plazas, follows the lie of the land, curving around the bluff. In the centre are some magnificent *ceibas*, the sacred world-tree of the Maya. A line of buildings closes off the plaza on the river side, while on the other more irregularly spaced structures climb the hills. On the left, one of the first is the east-facing **Building 16**, with a lintel showing Bird-Jaguar with a vision-serpent summoned up in a bloodletting ritual in July 741. A little further on is the small **Ball Court**. Next to it is **Temple 13**, built by Bird-Jaguar almost opposite Lady Xoc's monument **Temple 23** and dedicated to his mother Ik-Skull. Behind 13 is **Temple 12**, which has lintels from the 530s that list the first ten rulers of Yaxchilán. First carved for another building, they were probably reset here by Bird-Jaguar IV.

In the plaza there are several stelae: the largest is **Stela 1**, showing Bird-Jaguar IV in a bloodletting ritual accompanied by Lady Great-Skull. Beneath them there is the maize god, ready to receive the royal blood. On a platform towards the river is the oldest stela at Yaxchilán, **Stela 27**, erected in 514 and showing the city's founder Yat-Balam. The buildings just to the right, **Buildings 6** and **7**, are some of the oldest around the plaza that were not built over by Bird-Jaguar, from 500–550. More imposing is Bird-Jaguar IV's **Hieroglyphic Stairway**, an elaborate glyph text listing all the members of the dynasty of Yaxchilán, culminating, naturally, in himself.

Now lying on its side under a small *palapa* is one of the most important Yaxchilán stelae, **Stela 11**, originally erected by Bird-Jaguar IV high above the city near Temple 40 in 752. Still wonderfully clear, it shows Bird-Jaguar and the 93-year-old Shield-Jaguar II taking part in the flapstaff ritual in 741; the now-unseen other side shows Bird-Jaguar with three soon-to-be sacrificed captives. **Stela 3**, in poorer condition, shows Shield-Jaguar II, Bird-Jaguar IV – standing out with his giant thighs – and Lady Ik-Skull.

The Principal Temples

The temples with the most refined carved lintels at Yaxchilán are more or less in a line along the foot of the hill on the landward side of the plaza. If you take them from east to west or left to right, you come to them in reverse order. Furthest left is **Temple 20**, built by Shield-Jaguar III. In its three lintels he emphasizes the greatness of his father and his own right to the throne, and pays notable tribute to the lineage of his mother, Bird-Jaguar's queen Lady Great-Skull. The left-hand lintel, now faint, shows Bird-Jaguar subduing captives; the middle one shows him and Lady Great-Skull carrying out a bloodletting rite on the birth of Shield-Jaguar III in February 752; on the right Lady Great-Skull and her brother Great Skull are seen taking part in Bird-Jaguar's blood rite in 741 – the same as on Building 16 – with a vision-serpent between them.

Next to it is the remarkably well-preserved **Temple 21**, created by Bird-Jaguar IV himself. The imagery of the lintels seems deliberately to mirror that of Lady Xoc's Temple 23. On the left Lady Wak Tuun, one of Bird-Jaguar's 'junior' wives, is shown summoning up Yat-Balam in a vision rite, as Lady Xoc had done: she holds a bowl with the implements for bloodletting, while the vision arises out of the bowl where the strips of paper used to catch the blood are burnt. In the middle Bird-Jaguar himself and another wife, Lady Mut Balam, 'celebrate' the birth of the future heir Shield-Jaguar III in 752 in typical Mayan fashion, he by preparing to perforate his penis and she by passing a cord through her tongue. On the right-hand lintel Bird-Jaguar is shown standing over an unfortunate captured lord due to be sacrificed in his accession rites, also in 752. In front of the temple is the stunningly clear, narrow **Stela 35**, showing his mother Lady Ik-Skull performing a bloodletting ritual to mark his own birth in 709, at the same time as Xoc's spectacular bloodletting.

Lady Xoc's original monument, **Temple 23**, has fallen into ruin since Maudsley first explored it in the 1880s, so it's no longer possible on-site to compare its superb carvings with Bird-Jaguar's later efforts. There is no more graphic image of Maya blood rituals than the left-hand lintel (now in the British Museum), with Xoc pulling the thorn-spiked cord through her tongue, blood running down her cheek, while Shield-Jaguar II stands over her. One feature of these carvings is that Xoc's *huípil* in the bloodletting lintel, like those of Bird-Jaguar's wives in Temple 21, features a diamond design very similar to those still used by Highland Maya weavers today.

Between Temples 21 and 23 a once-majestic, partially-cleared stairway climbs up to the **Great Acropolis** or pyramid of Yaxchilán – a natural hill – topped by Bird-Jaguar IV's greatest building, **Temple 33**, still with a towering roof-comb. Almost certainly completed by his son Shield-Jaguar III, its remarkable carving is not only on lintels: some of the most spectacular images are on panels on the temple stairway, showing Bird-Jaguar IV playing the ball game, watched by two dwarves. In side panels he is accompanied by his dead father Shield-Jaguar II (step 6) and grandfather Bird-Jaguar III (step 8). Being dead, both play the game from *Xibalba*. Moreover, this appears to represent a specific game played in 744, during the 'Interregnum' before Bird-Jaguar was officially king, when through the game he summoned up his ancestors in his support. This is one of the most graphic images of the ball court as a portal to the Otherworld, with the ball shown as containing the soul of a sacrificial victim.

Temple 33's lintels show scenes around the accession of Bird-Jaguar IV. In the left-hand panel he is preparing for the accession rite in 752, attended by Lady Great-Skull; in the middle, he is with his five-year-old son Chel-Te, in rites to mark the anniversary of his accession in 757; on the right, he presides in a calendar ritual in 756, helped by a

Lady Xoc perfoming a bloodletting ritual in front of her husband Shield-Jaguar II, in October 709. From Temple 23.

sahal called Ah-Mac-Kin-Mo. A rich tomb, never identified, has been found beneath Temple 33. Inside the temple there is a headless statue, believed to be Shield-Jaguar II. It is revered by the Lacandón as an image of their creator-god *Hachakyum*, and they have a legend that when its head returns to its body the world will end.

The Southern Acropolis and Western Acropolis

Behind Temple 33 there are several still-semi-excavated structures, between which a real jungle path (one of the best places to look for monkeys and birds) leads down and then up again to the highest point in Yaxchilán, known as the **Southern Acropolis** and topped by three buildings, **Temples 39, 40** and **41**. This giant hill clearly had a powerful significance, and both Shield-Jaguar II and Bird-Jaguar IV dedicated temples there. Stela 11 originally stood in front of Temple 40. You are no longer able to climb up onto the Acropolis temples, but even from their base the view is fabulous, over the river and the great bed of forest stretching in every direction.

Another, equally rugged path leads down from there to the slightly lower hill of the **Western Acropolis**, an almost self-contained area with a compact plaza around **Temple 44**, completed in 732 and known as Shield-Jaguar II's 'war memorial', with carvings glorifying campaigns in his 50-year reign. Alongside it, **Temple 42**, built for Bird-Jaguar, has more finely-preserved carving. Another jungle walk from there leads back to the fork by the entrance path.

Bonampak

⊕ Bonampak
Open daily 8–5; adm

Bonampak, 9km south of Lacanjá, was a minor burg compared to Yaxchilán, to which it very probably often paid tribute. Its unique importance today comes from the fact that it has, in one temple, the only near-complete Maya mural paintings yet found anywhere, which justify the journey in themselves. Considering that nearly all large Maya buildings were painted in some way, it is extraordinary that so little has survived. The Bonampak murals portray Classic-era

13 Chiapas | Bonampak

court life with unparalleled vividness, giving a completely new image of Maya art and the abilities of Maya painters.

How the murals were found is part of their mystique. They were discovered by an American, Giles Healy, who in 1944 was sent to Chiapas to make a nature film. He had good relations with the Lacandón, and in 1946 they took him to Bonampak, then overgrown and unknown to archaeologists. Wandering around the site, he came across a smallish temple. He saw nothing special about it and, when he stuck his head inside, saw only darkness. Then he lit a torch, looked in again and realized, awestruck, that the walls were covered in paintings. The discovery of the murals caused huge controversy among Mayan experts due to their incontrovertible portrayal of war, torture and bloody rituals, at a time when it was often stated that the Maya were a pacific people.

Beyond the murals, relatively little is known about the history of Bonampak. It seems to have gained a position of power only very late and under only one of its *ahauob*, Chan-Muaan, the lord shown in the murals, who reigned from 776 until some time after 795. In earlier centuries it had been attacked by its larger neighbour Yaxchilán and at one time was a vassal of Toniná, but it is clear that by Chan-Muaan's time it had become a trusted

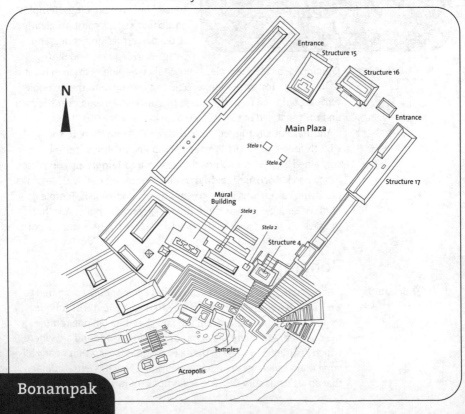

Bonampak

Visiting Bonampak

Only Lacandón vehicles are allowed to take visitors between Lacanjá village and Bonampak, and *combis* and taxis provide a regular shuttle service. The set price (around $4.50 per person) includes an entry charge paid to the Lacanjá community. This is in addition to the INAH admission fee ($2.50).

'subordinate' of Yaxchilán: his principal queen, who appears in the murals, was the sister of Shield-Jaguar III. Virtually all the structures that have survived were erected by Chan-Muaan. The murals refer to events from 790 to 792; the last recorded date at Bonampak came only three years later. The murals represent, therefore, a final, dazzling flourish of Classic Mayan civilization.

The Plaza and the Acropolis

The excavated area of Bonampak consists really of just one large plaza, which you enter, at the end of a deep green path, from the north side. On the left is **Structure 15**, a low platform with a broken stela, which like several monuments at Bonampak was deliberately mutilated at some point – possibly in unrest around the time of the dynasty's collapse, although it could also have been done much later by unknown occupants of the site. Although known for its murals, Bonampak also has some superb carvings, above all on three massive stelae that yet again glorify Chan-Muaan. **Stela 1** in the middle of the grass square, reassembled after being discovered broken into several pieces, shows him in triumph standing above an earth monster, his face a timeless image of power. Equally strong are the two at the base of the Acropolis, **Stela 2**, with Chan-Muaan about to perform a bloodletting ritual flanked by his wife and his mother, and **Stela 3**, picturing him seizing a captive.

Behind these stelae, banks of steps climb up to the **Acropolis** of Bonampak, a natural ridge, topped by a line of small temples, several of which still have fine stucco decoration. Once at the top, there's a fine view over the rest of the site.

The Murals Temple

The murals temple, surprisingly small, is to the right, looking from the plaza, now protected from the rain by a modern canopy. Only three people are allowed into each room at a time, and no photography is permitted. The rooms run in chronological order, left to right. **Room 1** on the left has in some ways the most fascinating images of all. They portray two separate events, which took place almost a year apart. The upper section of the wall in front of you and the side walls depict the presentation of Chan-Muaan's heir, on 14 December 790. On the right-hand wall Chan-Muaan himself sits on a dais, with his principal wife to his left and two other children. He appears to be talking to the man holding (pretty clumsily) the son and heir, on the main wall. He stands above a line of 14 nobles stretching round to the left wall, who, however, appear to be paying no attention to him whatsoever and to be far more involved in chatting among themselves. Above it all at the apex of the room are images of the Cosmic Monster, the ultimate spirit of the earth. Immediately apparent is one of the most striking and strangely unsettling features of the Bonampak murals, and of much Maya art: there seems to be no notion of 'genre', of division of subject matter. The murals portray great state occasions and bloody suffering, and yet at the same time seem to be distracted by everyday details and present some of their characters almost comically, as in the plump, garrulous lords. It's as if, rather than being separately reverential, awe-inspiring or comic, the whole of life had to be in the one picture.

The other scenes show a ceremony held 336 days after the first one, on 15 November 791. Above the door behind you, Chan-Muaan and two attendant lords are dressed in elaborate regalia of jaguar skins and green feathers to take part in a ritual dance, performed with Venus in the ascendant, probably to conjure up spirits to ensure that the young prince would be a great king and warrior. The dance itself appears on the lower panels all around the room, with the king and his two followers in the centre opposite the door. To the left are the musicians with their trumpets and maracas and by the door, there are dancers in monster costumes, representing the *wayob* or spirit companions summoned up in their dance.

Room 2 is the 'battle room'. Its glyphs relate the battle that took place on 2 August 792 and that Chan-Muaan was supported by his 'patron' Yaxchilán, but do not say who the enemy was. Bonampak was clearly victorious, taking many captives. Although it is now in poor condition the battle scene itself, around the facing, left and right walls, is extraordinary, the most horrific and complete image of Mayan warfare. On the left wall, Chan-Muaan's warriors hold up huge, fan-like battle standards. Everything else is a tangle of semi-naked bodies, slashing and slaughtering each other. Pride of place naturally goes to Chan-Muaan, on the far wall, seen grabbing a wretched captive by his hair. The small images in the apex of the roof represent the stars and so the omens for the day of the battle.

The most powerful image of all is on the wall above the door, showing Chan-Muaan disposing of his prisoners. This took place a few days after the battle. The king stands in the centre, attended by *sahalob* all in different regalia, and on his left stands a woman, presumably his queen and the sister of his ally Shield-Jaguar III. Below them is a scene of ferocious cruelty. To the far left a bending guard seems to be cutting off a prisoner's fingers, a torment inflicted on captives before final sacrifice. Alongside, prisoners, mutilated and stripped, beg for mercy; in the centre one has already been killed. Yet again, awesome, terrible images are combined with prosaic details, while the figure of the dying captive at Chan-Muaan's feet is astonishing, a demonstration of pictorial skill of a level that would not be seen in Europe for centuries.

Finally, **Room 3** portrays a ritual carried out by Chan-Muaan in his role as great shaman, probably not long after the battle. It is a powerful indication of the role of mystical dancing in Maya ceremonies. Parts are now faint, but the whole of the far wall is a riot of dancing figures, men in giant feathered back-frames and headdresses, with equally huge banners that stick out on either side of them. At the top dances Chan-Muaan; below him, two men hold another sacrificial victim by the hands and ankles, and seem almost to be throwing him up in the air towards an executioner who stands below the king. On the right-hand wall a strange procession carries a figure standing on a litter, perhaps representing one of the king's ancestors. To the left, Chan-Muaan's queen and other women of the royal house, on a dais, let blood by passing cords through their tongues. Above the door, the king stands in line with his *sahalob*. These ceremonies were probably carried out to give cosmic strength to the king's lineage and ensure continuity for his heir. Obviously, they were not successful.

Where to Stay and Eat

Busil-Ha/Nuevo Francisco León

Vallescondido, Carretera Fronteriza km. 61, t (916) 348 0721/(cell) 045 916 100 0399, *busil_h@hotmail.com* (*inexpensive*). This pretty restaurant by the road, between Palenque and Lacanjá (look for the km. 61 sign), serves great breakfasts/meals. Owner Willy Fonseca has also built impressive *cabañas* and is an expert **tour guide**, especially to Piedras Negras, with his own boats. Many activities are possible: ruins visits, jungle tours, and swimming at Busil-Ha falls.

Frontera Corozal

Escudo Jaguar, t 00502 5353 5637, *www.escudojaguarhotel.com* (*inexpensive*). Begun as a 'community hotel', this has grown into a subtantial place, with rooms with fans, and showers, in *palapa*-style buildings of varied sizes. Also rooms with shared facilities (*budget*), camping space and a big *palapa* **restaurant** (*moderate*).

Lacanjá

There are now around 14 sites in Lacanjá with visitor accommodation, all run by Lacandóns. Though all called *campamentos* most have cabins as well as camping space, and have tents for visitors who do not carry their own. All mainly deal with agencies, but will put up individuals. They vary a great deal, but these two are the best, both run with an awareness of what low-impact tourism means.

Campamento Río Lacanjá, t (967) 674 6660, *www. ecochiapas.com*. The most comfortable options in Lacanjá are the **Ya'axcan** *cabañas* here with bathrooms (*inexpensive*); there are also simpler 2–6 bed *cabañas* sharing well-kept showers (*budget*), all in the same idyllic location beside the Lacanjá river. From the site there's a nature walk through the forest, leading to an exquisite natural swimming pool. A little **restaurant** (*budget*) provides enjoyable meals. Bookings are made through **Explora** in San Cristóbal (*see* p.493), and kayaking, rafting, tours can be arranged. Booking advisable.

Campamento Tucán Verde, *www.tucanverde.com* (*budget*). Ismael Chansaap and his family take great care of their visitors, giving tours to the best forest swimming spots and unexcavated ruins, and an experience of Lacandón family life. There are simple cabins, sharing bathrooms, and camping space, and homely meals.

Getting to Montes Azules

Several companies run *combis* from Palenque to Benemérito, and some continue to Comitán; others run from Benemérito to Comitán. In Benemérito you can find local *combis* along the Pico de Oro road. But, the *cabaña* hotels are all off the main road, where *combis* usually leave you, so it is easier to reach them by car.
Benemérito is about 45km south of the Frontera Corozal turn on Highway 307 (200km from Palenque). About 8km south of the town at **Boca Lacantún** a paved road turns off the Highway for **Zamora-Pico de Oro** (30km), from where a 13km dirt track leads to Las Guacamayas. About another 50km further on, the Zamora-Pico de Oro road rejoins Highway 307 near **El Chajul**. From **Maravilla Tenejapa** (45km further west), there is a 12km dirt road to **Las Nubes**. The only **fuel** on this road is sold by unofficial village sellers.

Montes Azules, Las Guacamayas and Las Nubes

The *Carretera Fronteriza* rolls on south of Frontera Corozal, into territory that until about 1980 was almost a blank space on the map. **Benemérito de las Américas**, 50km further on, is a shabby settler town that acts as the region's main 'centre'. Recently, as this road has become better known and a bit more 'domesticated', a growing band of adventurous travellers are exploring the whole 500km-length of the *Fronteriza* route round to Montebello. The Marqués de Comillas area, the easternmost corner of Chiapas southeast of the Río Lacantún, is one of heavy recent settlement that is being rapidly deforested. Northwest of the Lacantún, however, there remains one of the largest stretches of rainforest in Chiapas, in the **Montes Azules** reserve. The biggest draw for travellers is **Las Guacamayas** ecotourism scheme near **Pico de Oro**, reached via a part-paved road off the *Fronteriza* south of Benemérito. *Guacamaya* means scarlet macaw, and this part of the Lacandón forest contains one of the largest populations of wild macaws in Mexico, as well as crocodiles, ocelots, monkeys and other wildlife. From Las Guacamayas you can explore the forest and kayak on the wide, placid river; nearby there are more scarcely identified Maya ruins. The road past Pico de Oro rejoins the *Fronteriza* near **El Chajul**, near which there is a luxurious *cabaña* hotel.

About 45km further west is **Maravilla Tenejapa**, from where a turn off leads back into the forest and to another of Chiapas' exquisite sets of thundering cascades and waterfalls at **Las Nubes**. There are plenty of great places to swim, the atmosphere is unhassled, and the friendly local community has a well-run ecotourism scheme. From Las Nubes, there's a short way left to **Montebello** (*see* p.510).

Where to Stay and Eat

Zamora-Pico de Oro

Las Guacamayas (Ara Macaw), Reforma Agraria, t 01 201 250 8004, *guacamaya escarlata@hotmail.com* (*inexpensive*). A comfortable ecotourism project, considering its location deep in forest on the Río Lacantún. Created in Reforma Agraria *ejido* as part of its macaw reserve, it now has professional staff, and so a more conventional hotel style. There are palm-roofed *cabañas* with hot showers and balconies, or dorm-style huts (*budget*), and even WiFi. By the river is a **restaurant** and boat jetty. As well as enjoying the magical setting you can go on forest tours with expert guides and kayak trips.

El Chajul

Ecoturismo Lacandonia–La Selva del Chajul, t (Mexico City) 55 5362 4339, *www.lacandonia.com.mx* (*expensive*). An upscale hotel in the depths of the Lacandón jungle, with five large cabins in seclusion near the Guatemalan border. The speciality is all-inclusive 'packages' combining a few days' stay with an activities programme.

Las Nubes

Centro Ecoturístico Causas Verdes-Las Nubes, Maravilla Tenejapa, t (963) 633 9777, *ecoturismo_nubes@hotmail.com* (*budget*). Pleasant cabins (sharing bathrooms), camping space and a **restaurant** beside Las Nubes falls, in a scheme set up by a Chol and Mam indigenous community. Activities include swimming below the falls, climbing, zip-lining and other tours.

The Highlands

...at times we had to go up on foot, at times on all fours...

Dominican friar Tomás de la Torre, travelling from Tabasco to San Cristóbal, 1540s.

The Chiapas Highlands are a giant castle of rock in the middle of the American isthmus, a world of peaks, crags, ridges and valleys abruptly different from the hot, flat plains only a short distance to the north. All the routes into the Highlands involve abrupt, winding climbs. Until the building of modern roads – within the last 50 years – the length and difficulty of this ascent long kept the mountains isolated in space and time from the rest of the world.

Fans of long mountain journeys can still enter the Highlands from the north on the old **Highway 195** road from Villahermosa via Teapa, one of the most dramatic mountain roads in Mexico. However, the recent projects of Mexican federal and Chiapas state authorities have been aimed at reducing further the Highlands' isolation – seen as a factor in political problems – and since 2003 most traffic has used the new *Supercarretera* that runs down from Coatzacoalcos in Veracruz state and crosses the spectacular **Puente Chiapas** bridge over the vast Nezahualcóyotl reservoir to approach Tuxtla Gutiérrez from the west. This is still only a two-way road for much of its length, and still has plenty of twists and bends – as does Highway 187, the newly-widened road that joins it from Villahermosa – but between them these roads have shortened journey times between the Highlands and central Mexico by a substantial five hours.

Approach the Highlands from Palenque, on the other hand, and you must still negotiate **Highway 199**, a sinuous road of endless green bends (the Chiapas state government also has a grand plan to build a new highway on this route, but it is not likely to be carried out soon). You begin to climb a short distance from Palenque, well before Agua Azul, and if you look back on the reverse bends, northern Chiapas soon appears spread out flat and green below and behind you. Just over halfway, 103km from Palenque, is **Ocosingo**, the largest town on this route and access point to the ruins at Toniná. From there the road rises up ever more steeply, through **Oxchuc**, into a final climb over a ridge at more than

2,000m before descending through pine woods into San Cristóbal. This 191km journey takes five hours. Ocosingo is the meeting point of the Highlands and the western Lacandón jungle, and the forests east of the town contain the original bases of the Zapatista movement, so this is the place where the political problems of Chiapas come closest, so to speak, to the main highway.

The Zapatistas and the Politics of Chiapas

The conflicts of Chiapas are about land, race, poverty and the way power is exercised in Mexico. They are also complex and often ambiguous, with fault-lines that are not always clear-cut. They are not simply to do with Chiapas being backward: rather, they are a product of modernity, of economic acceleration in the state as it becomes more and more part of the global economy. As is evident as you look around, there are a great many people, mostly Indians, who live by farming with minimal resources on poor land. Ever since the days of Porfirio Díaz, the officially recommended solution has been modernization: roads, schools, economic dynamism, progress. However, with each step in the intensification of commercial agriculture, rural poverty has worsened.

Since colonial times it had been customary for good land to be taken by *ladino* planters and settlers, while the Maya took whatever was left. The Highlands became permanently overpopulated, with many Indian families living on plots too meagre to support them. From the 1950s, encouraged by schemes declaring 'wilderness' areas open for settlement, many Highland Maya moved down from the mountains to 'colonize' the Lacandón jungles. They were joined by poor *mestizos*, also eager for land.

New tensions came with the greater commercialization of agriculture that began in the 1970s. In newly cleared forest areas, commercial farmers and cattle ranchers contended aggressively for land with poor settlers (*colonos*). A growing gulf appeared between those who had access to capital and the wider market – most but not all of them *ladinos* – and those who had not – most but not all *indígenas* (Indians) – many of whom were pushed into improvised villages at the fringes of established towns.

Central to the disputes that followed was the inoperativeness of law in land matters in Chiapas. Many *colonos* and poor communities in recently-settled areas never established clear legal title to their lands, so their rights to them could be challenged by anybody whenever the land become desirable. Instead of law, the key to land rights was political power in the municipalities, each of which had jurisdiction over scores of villages. However, local power in rural Chiapas was notoriously corrupt, dominated by farmers and ranchers bound up with the PRI, the party that had ruled the state and Mexico since 1929. Added to this was the unspoken racism of

Chiapas, and the way the Maya were traditionally disregarded in questions of legal rights.

Clashes were common well before Chiapas exploded into the headlines in 1994, with incidents of Indian peasants being expropriated, terrorized or murdered by farmers or their men, and of human rights abuses by state authorities. In Mexico's early-1990s boom too, breakneck economic liberalization lowered prices for anything poor farmers could produce, and increased those of goods they bought. The PRI élite believed it could keep this kind of problem in check by keeping it out of sight.

When the Zapatistas took over San Cristóbal de Las Casas and Ocosingo on 1 January 1994, the government of President Carlos Salinas appeared paralysed with shock. Morever, this group of ignorant Indians seemed far more agile than they could even hope to be – they were one of the first movements anywhere to make real use of the internet – with an enigmatic masked spokesman, Subcomandante Marcos, whose sharp, witty barbs against Mexico's status quo immediately hit home, made him a hero throughout the country and attracted worldwide attention. After a brief skirmish, the government was obliged to negotiate a ceasefire.

The PRI, the party of the Revolution, didn't like to appear as the oppressor, at least in broad daylight. More importantly, this first crisis also revealed one of the Chiapas conflict's most modern characteristics: the constant awareness on both sides of their international media impact. The 1994 rising triggered a collapse of the peso; ever since, a central concern of Mexican governments has been to keep Chiapas' problems out of the headlines. The Zapatistas for their part have relied on their favourable international image to ensure their survival. Hence neither has sought open confrontation, and the 'conflict' has gone on for years as governments and Zapatistas have stared at each other in a strange, often apparently immobile ritual dance.

Initially the situation seemed to demand more urgency. The last PRI administration of President Ernesto Zedillo committed itself to peaceful negotiations as the only means to a solution in Chiapas, while seeming to follow completely contrary policies on the ground. Troops were poured into the state, and a ring of roads and bases built around the Zapatista areas that would make any repetition of the 1994 events impossible; over the years these bases have become impressively permanent. Right-wing paramilitary groups emerged to oppose Zapatista land claims, often actively encouraged by the army and the state police. At times it seemed there was a deliberate policy of provoking the Zapatistas into violent action that would justify final repression. The Zapatistas, however, didn't take the bait, and adopted an almost Gandhian policy of passive resistance, sometimes being described as a 'moral presence' more than an armed group. In fact, for a guerrilla movement regularly pictured in combat gear, the Zapatistas have scarcely fired a shot since 1994. Violence in Chiapas has come overwhelmingly from paramilitaries.

In February 1996, after long negotiations in San Andrés Larraínzar, a solution seemed to be reached in the *Acuerdos de San Andrés*, the San Andrés Accords, in which government and Zapatistas apparently agreed a system of political and economic autonomy for Indian communities. These Accords have become the touchstone of any subsequent negotiations for the Zapatistas, but other than that only started a whole new argument. No government has been prepared to fulfil them in practice, and the Zapatistas have accused successive groups of politicians of never having negotiated in good faith, and hoping only to wear the movement down with time.

In the absence of an agreement the situation became increasingly murky. Zapatista villages set up their own autonomous communities, rejecting the authority of local municipalities, and flashpoints developed when the army, police or paramilitaries

Who was that masked man...

From their first emergence on the world stage in 1994 the Zapatistas have had a special image thanks to their choice of spokesman, *Subcomandante Marcos*. Conventional Mexican politicians had never stated their positions through jokes, parables, or quotes from an impressive range of world literature, or by comparing themselves to Speedy González. Marcos' musings and 'essays', published on the Net, sometimes maddeningly wandering, sometimes comic routines, have given the Zapatistas a unique appeal and tone, and helped them – and him – become figureheads of the international anti-globalization movement.

Marcos is *Sub-comandante* because the Zapatista *comandantes* are all Maya. In theory he is only spokesman and adviser to an indigenous movement. Inside Chiapas the names and roles of the *comandantes* – David, Tacho – are well known, even though, like Marcos, they are only ever seen in ski masks. To the media and the outside world, however, Marcos has often *been* the Zapatistas. From the first days in 1994 he was the ideal frontman: able to speak very well in English, French, Italian, Tzotzil and Tzeltal; witty, quick and able to charm as many news reporters as are put in front of him.

Mexican governments and other opponents of the Zapatistas have often presented Marcos as the real leader of the Zapatistas, manipulating his Indian followers. The 1990s PRI administrations also spent a deal of energy trying to find out who the masked man was. Eventually, they declared him to be Rafael Sebastián Guillén. If true (it has not been confirmed or denied, but seems fairly well established), Marcos is a former philosophy student from Tampico who got involved in Marxist groups in Mexico City in the 1970s, bummed around Europe and then disappeared into Chiapas. The government tried to use this discovery to demonstrate that behind the laughing exterior Marcos was just an old style Marxist-Leninist. This, though, missed the point, in that, whatever the ideological past of Marcos and his colleagues might be, they have shown a mental agility and openness to ideas far beyond Cold War stereotypes. Marcos is a very Mexican combination, part of a historic peasant struggle but with a head full of international mass culture. It is to a great extent thanks to him that the Zapatistas have appeared as not just a resistance movement of an ancient culture but very much part of the modern world.

Marcos may still be a star on T-shirts, but inside Mexico his appeal has waxed and waned. Some see him as a self-publicizing egomaniac whose meandering (and often hugely self-indulgent) 'statements' lead nowhere. Another of his quirks has been his occasional enigmatic 'disappearances' from public view, sometimes for months, which may have contributed to the immobility of the Chiapas situation – although Zapatista supporters point out that this subterranean pace reflects the genuinely open, decentralized nature of the movement, in which all major decisions have to be submitted to community consultation. For many the summit of Marcos' egomania was his anti-political 'Other Campaign' in Mexico's election year of 2006, which won him a new set of detractors. In late 2007 he announced another of his withdrawals into the forest, saying that an excessive focus on himself could have harmed the movement, and only reappeared in January 2009 at a 'Festival of Dignified Rage' held to mark the Zapatistas' 15th anniversary. Fifteen years is a long time to maintain any momentum. But, like the Zapatistas as a whole, Marcos has never lost all his charisma or the ability to surprise, and still comes up with acute insights. For his meditations and Zapatista statements, check *enlacezapatista.ezln.orgmx* or *submarcos.org*.

went in to dismantle them. The worst incident came in 1997, when 45 Zapatista sympathizers were murdered by paramilitaries at Acteal, north of San Cristóbal.

In Chiapas, therefore, still more than in the rest of Mexico, the ending of the PRI's 71-year rule with the election of President Vicente Fox in 2000 seemed to promise a new beginning. In his campaign Fox had said he could resolve the Chiapas situation 'in 15 minutes' and declared a willingness to negotiate with no preconditions, and as a sign of goodwill he reduced troop levels and withdrew troops from Zapatista villages, so allowing them their de facto autonomy. The new optimism reached a peak with the Zapatistas' "March on Mexico City' in March 2001, when the Zapatista *comandantes* even addressed the Federal Congress. The damp cloth came later, when the Fox government presented its own 'Law on Indigenous Rights'. The Zapatistas' central demand was that indigenous communities should be given inalienable rights to their own territory, but once again this was chipped away in laborious discussions over detail. The law was rejected by the Zapatistas and by Indian groups all over Mexico.

There have been no negotiations with Mexican federal or Chiapas state authorities since then. The Zapatistas produced their response in 2003: they reaffirmed that they no longer aimed to engage in armed struggle, and that while the *Ejército Zapatista de Liberación Nacional* (*EZLN*, Zapatista National Liberation Army) remained an army ready to defend their communities from any frontal attack, it had effectively 'set aside its weapons'. They were interested instead in civil construction: having been let down so many times they no longer expected anything from politicians, but would go ahead with building up their communities by them- selves. They intended to link each of the 2,000-or-so often tiny Zapatista villages around Chiapas to one of several hub-villages called **caracoles** (snails), the idea being that initiatives would spiral snail-shell-like back and forth between the centres and the villages. Disarmingly, they also say the snail image reflects the pace at which they're prepared to progress. Each *caracol* has a *Junta de Buen Gobierno* (Good Government Committee), and together the whole network is intended to become a separate system of direct democracy, outside of the state and municipalities.

Battered signs announcing *territorio zapatista* or *municipio autónomo* can be seen on many roads. *Caracoles* have built their own clinics and schools and are trying to develop fairtrade coffee cooperatives, and in parts of Chiapas – especially San Cristóbal – the Zapatistas seem to have become part of the scenery. However, the military presence around this 'anti-state' remains formidable, and confrontations still occur, usually in places far from media attention. The *Zaps'* economic base remains very weak. Since the 1990s' government funding has been pumped into Chiapas, as seen in its new roads, and official policy has continued to be the favouring of non-Zapatista communities, with the carrot of subsidies and state support. This has fuelled tensions at a local level, and much of the time the 'conflict' has become a tapestry of sometimes micro-sized – but still bitter – local disputes between Zapatista and anti-Zapatista communities, often over land.

The Zapatistas are committed to surviving, and some observers thought the best chance of a settlement that could ensure this would be in the election of Andrés Manuel López Obrador, candidate for the leftist PRD in the 2006 presidential election. However, after much deliberation Marcos ferociously denounced him as just one more untrustworthy politician, and spent the year touring Mexico in the 'Other Campaign', making contact with sympathetic groups and pouring scorn on all the candidates equally. While imaginative, this seemed to have limited impact, but when López Obrador lost the election by less than 1% of the vote it was felt that even this could have cost him the presidency. Many in Mexico's mainstream left once sympathetic to the Zapatistas have never forgiven Marcos, or the movement, for this, leaving it more isolated than ever before. In Chiapas the state government, led by the PRD since 2006, ignores the Zapatistas, to the extent of avoiding even mentioning their existence. Since they are non-violent, the Zapatistas have largely fallen off the international news agenda, but complain that they are subjected to steady low-level pressure. Their fear is that, if they are forgotten by the outside world, army and authorities may take the opportunity to finally snuff them out. The *caracol* of Oventic has taken the radical step of inviting in tourists to get a little more attention (*see* p.493), another new departure for a movement that has never been afraid to be inventive.

Ocosingo, Toniná and Laguna Miramar

Ocosingo is the main market town for a wide area of the lower Highlands. Its hub is, naturally, the plaza, four blocks downhill from the main highway, with the town hall and the 17th-century Dominican church of **San Jacinto**. The spectacular **market** is three blocks beyond the church. The Ocosingo valley is known for its cheese, the softish *queso de bola* ('ball cheese'), available along with fresh-grown coffee, spices and wonderful vegetables at the market. Around the market and plaza there are always women from nearby Tzeltal communities in their distinctive blouses, with embroidered lace trimmings that reflect Conquest-era Spanish styles.

Toniná

Toniná
Ruins open daily 8–5; museum open Tues–Sun 8–5; adm.

Inaccessibility long kept **Toniná** little known, but it is one of the most spectacular of Maya sites, as well as having been – perhaps – the last great Classic Maya city. Built in far more hilly terrain than any city further north, its architecture is almost bizarrely unique. Toniná had a very distinctive monumental style, creating massive statues of its rulers rather than flat stelae, and produced exceptional carvings, ceramics and reliefs, many now in its excellent **museum**. It is also one of the sites where dramatic finds, above all of stucco carvings, have been made only in the last few years.

Most of the visible structures of Toniná were built in the Late Classic, after 600, but beneath them are unexcavated buildings that are centuries older. Its location in one of the 'fringe' areas of Maya civilization meant that it came into frequent conflict with wealthier cities to the north and east and, above all, Palenque. Toniná's greatest ruler was called Baaknal-Chaak, who became *ahau* in 688 a year after the sacking of the city by Kan-Balam II of Palenque, during which his predecessor and probably father seems to have died. Baaknal-Chaak took revenge with a sustained challenge to the larger city, culminating in 711 with Toniná's finest moment when its warriors captured Kan-Hok-Chitam II of Palenque, plunging his kingdom into crisis. A superb relief panel from Toniná, now in the Tuxtla Gutiérrez museum, exultantly portrays Kan-Hok-Chitam as a bound and humiliated captive. Toniná took full advantage of Palenque's weakness to become a powerful force in the region. Its importance – with that of other Maya communities in central Chiapas – increased in the last years of the Classic era, as the 'Collapse' took hold further down the valleys. Toniná in fact has the last of all inscriptions in the Long Count calendar, and so can be said to represent the 'termination' of Classic Maya culture, from 909, two years after its nearest competitor far away at Uxmal and a full century after Palenque. A century later, Toniná was almost entirely abandoned, but some time after 1000 the site was occupied by a more primitive, non-Maya people: the Cheneks, who knocked the heads off many statues, perhaps to 'terminate' their magical power.

You approach Toniná along a green valley (past a huge military command centre), until you reach the site entrance, with a couple of restaurants and the museum. Initially you see nothing of the ruins, but walk along the 300m path and down a wooded dip and you come up into a very unusual **Sunken Ball court**, built into the temple platform. A panel has been found indicating it was dedicated by Baaknal-Chaak in 699. Then, if you turn back on yourself to the right, you see the great centre of Toniná. It is in effect one vast, pyramid-like structure, facing south, an extraordinary succession of stairways, levels and ledges sweeping up a giant hillside. With massive ramps of stone and steps, some with strange patterns in the stonework, it can look like an enormous abstract sculpture, or a dream-city out of Fritz Lang's *Metropolis*. There is no better example of the cult of awe and height in Maya building.

The **Great Plaza** of Toniná at the foot of the mountain-city allows its size to be fully appreciated. On the right at the lowest level is the entrance to the **Palacete del Inframundo** (Palace of the Underworld), a mysterious labyrinth of dark passages that appear to be leading somewhere but then do not, created to evoke *Xibalba*. Beyond that you begin the ascent: Toniná is a serious climb, as you zigzag your way up great walls of steps and stairways, interlocked and incorporated into the shape of the hill with enormous ingenuity. On the next level up is a fine stucco frieze of

Getting to Ocosingo and Toniná

Highway 199 runs along the western side of Ocosingo, and all buses stop along it. **First-class** OCC buses stop north of the centre on a steep slope, from where you walk uphill and then go left for the plaza. Most **second-class** buses stop at the top of the hill near the junction of the Highway and Av. Central. Walk down Av. Central to reach the main plaza.

Getting to Toniná

The Toniná site is 14km east of Ocosingo, with a paved access road. To find it **by car**, coming from north or south, look for signs just outside Ocosingo off Highway 199 on to the *Periférico*, which loops around the town to the east, where the Toniná turn-off is signposted. If you continue into town, turn off 199 down Av.1 Sur to the plaza, then go right by the church on to C.1 Oriente Sur, and follow this road out of town to the Toniná road.

Without a car, the way to get to Toniná is by **taxi**, which should cost around $13 (agree price first) if the driver waits while you visit the site.

Getting To Laguna Miramar

Tours to Miramar can be arranged on request through some of the San Cristóbal tours agencies (*see* p.493), but you can also get there independently. It's hard to make contact with the *ejido* in advance, but if you just turn up the site is rarely full. In the rainy season, from late June–Oct, all travel here is difficult.

Light-plane flights are run to Miramar from the **airstrip** at Ocosingo (near the Toniná road) by **Servicios Aéreos San Cristóbal, t** (963) 632 4662, *www.serviciosaereossancristobal.com*. They are often used by tours; for individuals, flights can cost from around $40 each way.

Combis and trucks run from the market area in Ocosingo to **San Quintín** (about 6hrs), from where it's a 1km walk to **Ejido Emiliano Zapata**. Ask for the *Presidente de Turismo*; fees (to enter the village, a place to stay, and for a guide) amount to about $16 a day. From the village it's a 7km walk (or drive) to the lake.

Miramar is in Chiapas' main 'conflict zone'. San Quintín, in a typical local disjunction, has supported the PRI, while one lake village, Benito Juárez, is Zapatista. The ecotourism scheme is run by Emiliano Zapata, which is slightly in the middle. San Quintín has an army post, and there are often checkpoints on the road. Foreigners are not stopped, but bags may be searched and your papers must be in order.

For more adventure there's also a 'river route' between Miramar and Las Nubes (*see* p.471). *Lanchas* run irregularly down the Río Jatate from San Quintín; ask at Emiliano Zapata about current possibilities.

13 Chiapas | Ocosingo, Toniná and Laguna Miramar

---

vision serpents and the city's lords. Above that and to the right is the **Palace** of Toniná. It has some similarities to the Palacio at Palenque, but is a great deal less elegant and open, as much like a bandit's lair as a palace – one of Toniná's hallmarks is the winding passageway, leading to hidden rooms. Behind it several buildings are currently being excavated, in one of which (*not open to view*) fragments of mural paintings have been found.

Another stiff climb takes you up to the most important section of Toniná, a broad flat level known as the **Fifth Platform**. Set into the middle of the immense bank of steps is a replica of the 'symbol' of Toniná, a massive, strangely oriental-looking statue-stela known as the **Zots-Choj** ('Bat-Tiger'), discovered on the very top level of the city in 1989. It dates from the 790s, but represents an early ruler called 'Jaguar-Bird-Peccary' who probably became *ahau* in 568. On the right of the Fifth Platform a tin roof protects some of the most remarkable of all Maya stucco carvings, discovered in 1992 (and originals, not replicas). Known as the *Frieze of the Dream Lords*, this combines, with the usual Maya parallels between this world and the next, images from the history of Toniná with others from the myth of the Hero Twins. It is split into four sections by a strange X-shaped frame, believed to represent a type of scaffold and portal to the

Otherworld on which sacrifices were sometimes put to death; in them are images of the four eras of creation that the Maya believed the world had passed through, the Suns of each cycle represented by human heads. Best-preserved is a frieze showing a skeleton figure, the image of one of the Lords of Death with whom the Twins struggled in *Xibalba*. At the bottom there is a rat standing upright, 'Precious First Rat', thought to be who first showed the Twins their ballgame equipment, and also a creature of the Otherworld.

In front of the frieze are two very large thrones, while behind it lies the huge **Temple of the Earth Monster**. On the front of the next rise there are more stucco carvings. This level, the **Seventh Platform**, is the last, in the middle of which is a small temple with wonderfully natural carved figures of Toniná *ahauob* and nobles around the base. Behind this there are still two more pyramids, the tallest of which really is the summit of Toniná, best reached by scrambling up a path at the back. At the very top there's a small inner sanctum, the **Temple of the Smoking Mirror**, near which the Zots-Choj was found. The summit is also the last place to look down and take in the whole astonishing structure, and the view for miles over the hills to the south.

Toniná's **museum** is a light modern building with some superb treasures. As well as the Zots-Choj himself there are *ahau*-statues in the same stocky Toniná style, hugely powerful but subtly carved. There are remarkable stucco panels, jewellery and superb painted ceramics with scenes of court life. Not the least awe-inspiring is a relief model of Classic Toniná, bringing out just how strange a fantasy-city this was. As it was an interlocking complex rather than a series of separate structures, its builders could extend even further the Maya liking for connections and cosmic symbolism; in the arrangement of levels and the number of doors, steps and temples, the whole city could be read as one giant representation of the calendar and Maya myths.

Laguna Miramar

Some 130km (but a five-hour drive) southeast of Ocosingo down a long, bumpy track off the Toniná road is Laguna Miramar, largest of the Lacandón jungle lakes. Marcos cited its beauty as one reason why he has stayed in Chiapas. Most of it is still lined by forest with some of the rarest Lacandón wildlife – howler monkeys, jaguars, dazzling birds – and the lake itself is full of fish, turtles and other aquatic life, and said to be wonderful for scuba diving. The *ejido* Emiliano Zapata operates a lakeside ecotourism scheme where you can stay, though conditions are very simple. Forest guides can be arranged, and there are canoes for hire. Different communities around the lake have varying attitudes to maintaining the forest, and some parts of the lake shore are becoming heavily deforested. Nevertheless, it's still an exquisite place.

Services

The bar-kiosk in the plaza also functions as a very basic information desk.

Banks: Banamex, on the plaza, and Banco Santander, C. Central Norte, both have ATMs.

Internet Access: several internet shops around the plaza.

Post Office: C. 1 Oriente, four blocks north of the plaza.

Where to Stay and Eat

Ocosingo

There are several more *budget* restaurants and pizzerias around the town plaza.

Hospedaje y Restaurant Esmeralda, C. Central Norte 14, **t** 673 0014, *info@ ranchoesmeralda.net* (*budget*). Just off the plaza, this likeable hotel has five simple but large and pretty rooms, sharing bathrooms. There's also a charming terrace **restaurant**, and staff are very friendly. Horse-riding trips into the countryside are a speciality.

Hotel Central, Av. Central 5, **t** 673 0024 (*budget*). Simple but well-kept hotel on the main plaza, with nice views from its best rooms, which also have showers, fans, TV and WiFi, despite the low prices. The **restaurant, Las Delicias** has a nice terrace.

Laguna Miramar

Emiliano Zapata's ecotourism scheme is 7km from the village, by the lake. There are *palapas* where you can camp or sling a hammock, some indoor beds, and a kitchen that provides simple meals (*budget*). Visitors should take food with them too. They also must observe a few rules: no alcohol is allowed, and there are rules on washing in the lake to avoid pollution.

San Cristóbal de Las Casas

Arrive in San Cristóbal from the sticky north on a morning in April or May and you immediately notice two things: the air and the light. Both are dazzlingly, crystalline clear and fresh. This is only one aspect of the weather in the valley of Jovel. On another day you can wake up amid a cold, damp fog, which turns to soupy humidity for a brief hour as the sun rises and burns off the mist, giving way to superb mountain sunshine through the middle of the day, only to be followed by what looks like a wet English afternoon as the sky clouds over before the day ends with icy, spitting rain. It's almost as if San Cristóbal were a volatile world in miniature. Another thing you may notice as you arrive are explosions. This is not because the Zapatistas have reappeared, but because in the Highlands it is traditional for celebrations to be marked with fireworks. There is always something being celebrated in the city.

Nestling in its valley between high peaks, with its arcaded porticoes, time-polished cobbles, Baroque churches, and centuries-old houses with orange-ochre walls and solid gateways, San Cristóbal is a city of deep shadows, patios and glimpses. It is perhaps the most atmospheric of all Mexico's colonial cities. While parts of Mérida can seem transplanted from Andalucía, San Cristóbal more readily recalls a Castilian hill town like Ávila or Toledo, hunkered down against the cold. It has a very Castilian stateliness. This is the capital of the Chiapas Highlands, where the Highland Maya – as well as forming an ever-growing proportion of the population of the city itself – come to buy, sell and interact with the outside world. Most still wear the traditional dress of each community. In some of the city's Spanish churches they worship in their own way, kneeling on the floor surrounded by candles and pine needles. Although San Cristóbal was founded as a colonial island in an Indian sea, the Maya are present in every part of the modern city.

All this one might expect, but what is more surprising is that San Cristóbal is the only city in the Mexican south that could be called chic. Artists, writers and intellectuals from Mexico City have treated it as a favoured retreat since the 1960s, and they have been joined by international bohemians on the Gringo Trail, and later by so-called *Zapatourists* seeking the aura of the Zapatistas. San Cristóbal has trendy coffee shops, and small stores where designers market their own jewellery and clothes. It has as many good bookshops as the rest of southern Mexico put together. This all adds to the mix. It confirms, perhaps, that this is a power point in the Maya sense, a place where Maya shamans, the Spanish Golden Age, backpackers, radicals from across the globe, *mariachis*, experimental info-technology and Mexican poets can encounter each other, in a rare mountain valley.

History

The first Spaniards to arrive in the valley of Jovel were the men of the expedition of Luís Marín in 1524, who after a hard fight with the Maya of Chamula and Zinacantán camped by the Río Amarillo, on the western side of the modern city, and commented among themselves that the location would make a fine site for a colony. It was four years later, however, that the conqueror of Chiapas, Diego de Mazariegos, founded the *Villa* (later *Ciudad*) *Real de Chiapa* on the same site. Capital-to-be of Chiapas within the Spanish Kingdom of Guatemala, it was a classic colonial city as ordained by the *Leyes de Indias*, with a grid and a plaza with sites marked out for a cathedral and Mazariegos' own residence, and two other main areas: around the Monastery of Santo Domingo, and to the south at El Carmen, both linked to the square by the same long straight street, now Av. Insurgentes and Av. General Utrilla. It was more than usually defensive, as the town was several days' journey from the next Spanish settlement and surrounded by only recently subdued Highland communities.

In 1537 the first friars arrived, of the Mercedarian order, and founded the Church of the Merced, to be followed in 1545 by the Dominicans under Bartolomé de Las Casas, who founded Santo Domingo. As the only Spanish town in a region with a large Indian population Ciudad Real was a major centre for the missionary orders, and the 17th century, above all, saw an enormous amount of church building in the city.

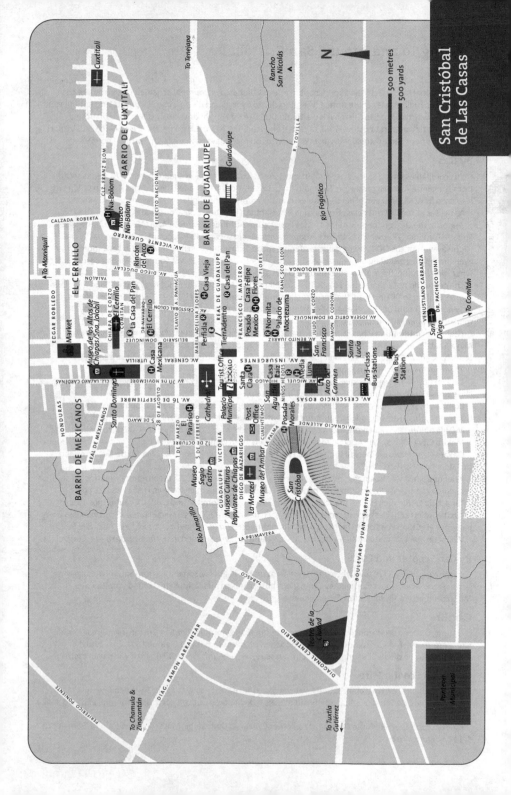

San Cristóbal
de Las Casas

N

500 metres
500 yards

Getting To and Around San Cristóbal

By Air

San Cristóbal has a neat little airport, built in one of Chiapas' development schemes. But, no airline has managed to run a viable service from it (it's often closed by fog) and it's only used by private and light planes.

The best way to fly to San Cristóbal is via **Tuxtla Gutiérrez**, a 1–1½hr drive away (*see* p.515). For around $30–40, Tuxtla's **airport taxi** drivers will take passengers direct to San Cristóbal. There is a scarce OCC 'airport shuttle' **bus** from San Cristóbal, with just two services on most days (5.30am, 3.30pm). Fare about $8.

By Bus

Bus companies have separate depots, but most are at least in the same area, where the Avenidas south from the centre meet Highway 190. The main **first-class station**, often called the **OCC** or **Cristóbal Colón** but also used by ADO, UNO and other companies, is at the corner of the Highway and Av. Insurgentes.

As well as at the OCC first-class tickets can be bought at **Ticketbus**, C. Real de Guadalupe 14.

Opposite the OCC on the south side of the Highway are **Autobuses Expreso Azul (AEXA)** and Transportes Rodolfo Figueroa **(TRF)**, which both have frequent *intermedio* services to Palenque ($5) and Tuxtla. By the Highway west of the OCC are the garages of more **second-class** lines, such as **Transportes Lacandonia**, with even lower fares, including long-distance. This can be confusing, but it leaves you spoilt for choice: no matter where you're going, there always seems to be a bus about to go there.

The depots do not exhaust the possibilities, for along the same stretch of Highway you will find gaggles of *combis* waiting to fill up a load, their drivers shouting 'Comitán, Comitán', 'Tuxtla, Tuxtla' or other places you may not have heard of. The other great *combi* point is at the other end of Insurgentes-Gral. Utrilla by the market, the place to find *combis* to Chamula and other Highland villages.

There is an **international bus service** to Panajachel and Antigua in **Guatemala**, the three-times weekly **Maya Shuttle** run with **ATC Tours** (*see* p.493). Fare to Antigua is around $70. Many other tour agencies offer tours to Flores in Guatemala via Palenque and Frontera, but it is better to start in Palenque (*see* p.437).

The main bus services from San Cristóbal are:

Cancún (*16–18hrs*): via **Palenque**, **Escárcega**, **Chetumal**, **Tulum** and **Playa del Carmen**, three ordinary first-class, one ADO GL daily from OCC, and three TRF. Fares $45–53.

Comitán (*1½hrs*), at least 15 first-class daily, of which several continue to **Ciudad Cuauhtémoc** (for Guatemala, *3hrs*). Fare to Ciudad Cuauhtémoc about $5. There are also frequent second-class and *combis*.

Mérida (*12½hrs*): via **Palenque**, **Escárcega** and **Campeche**, one first-class daily from OCC (6.20pm). Fare $34.

Mexico City (*13¼hrs*): two ADO GL, four first-class daily from OCC. Fares $57–67.

Oaxaca (*12hrs*): two ordinary first-class and two luxury services daily from OCC, via **Tuxtla Gutiérrez** and **Juchitán**. Fares $25–40.

Palenque (*5hrs*) via **Ocosingo**: eight first-class, one ADO GL daily from OCC, 1.10am–11pm, and frequent second-class. Second-class stop at **Crucero Agua Azul**, and there are many *combis*. First-class fare $9.

Tapachula (*7–8hrs*): eight OCC first-class, 12.05am–11.20pm, via **Comitán** and **Ciudad Cuauhtémoc**. Fare $15.

Tuxtla Gutiérrez (*1¼hrs*): one or more first-class each hour from OCC, 1.15am–10.45pm, and second-class every half-hour, via **Chiapa de Corzo**. There's also a near-continuous *combi* service (*see* above). First-class fare $3.

Villahermosa: two first-class daily from OCC via **Palenque** (*7hrs; $15*), and many *intermedio* and second-class.

By Car, Scooter and Cycle

To the east and west of town there are *gasolineras* on the Highway. Some trips from San Cristóbal are better made with a tour than your own transport, but a car is particularly useful around Comitán and Montebello, especially for visiting Tenam Puente.

Car Hire

Optima, C. Diego de Mazariegos 39, t 674 5409, *optimacar1@hotmail.com*. San Cristóbal's only car rental agency : efficient, friendly and, despite its monopoly, with decent rates (from around $27 a day). Further discounts may be offered for longer rentals, in low seasons (Feb–June, Sept–Nov), and if you pay in cash.

Cycle and Scooter Hire

San Cristóbal's shortish distances and low level of traffic make it easily cyclable. Try the following:

Los Pingüinos, Av. Ecuador 4-B, at north end of C. Real de Mexicanos, t 678 0202. Bikes for rent, and also daily small-group bike tours.

Croozy Scooters, Av. Belisario Domínguez 7, corner C. Real de Guadalupe. Motor scooters for rent from about $13 a day. *Closed Wed*

By Taxi

San Cristóbal has the usual abundance of **taxis**; city journeys cost about $1.60. Many drivers take on longer trips if you agree a price.

Orientation

The Pan-American Highway, **Highway 190 (Blvd Juan Sabines** in the city), runs along the south side of San Cristóbal. To the west it goes towards Tuxtla Gutiérrez and Villahermosa; to the east it bends south toward Comitán and to meet the Palenque road, 199. From the corner on the Highway by the OCC bus station, **Av. Insurgentes** leads up to the main square and the centre of town. Central San Cristóbal has a simple colonial grid, with streets with names; north–south are Avenidas, east–west are usually Calles. The only peculiarity is that streets change names on either side of the main axis from the plaza.

Most of the city is very walkable, but local *combis* can be useful for places such as Na Bolom that are far from the centre.

In 1712 Ciudad Real received a severe fright when a mass rebellion of Tzeltal Maya marched on the city from Cancuc, northeast of Tenejapa. In the 18th century it acquired many more of its patio houses, and more Baroque churches. From a Spanish city it slowly changed into one of *mestizos* and a tiny, Chiapas born white élite.

The sudden appearance of politics as the Spanish Empire crumbled caught this closed society almost by surprise. Under Spain Chiapas had always been part of Guatemala but, in 1821, the élite of Ciudad Real – which would become 'San Cristóbal' in 1829 – decided it would be more in their interests to join the new Mexican Empire. They encountered their first opposition from the ranching and trading families of Tuxtla, who objected to not being consulted, and so appeared the first signs of the dispute that would dominate official politics in Chiapas for the next century. In the civil wars of the 1850s and 60s the San Cristóbal élite, Catholic and conservative, supported the anti-Juárez camp and then Maximilian; Tuxtla and the Central Valley supported Juárez against the French. All these contests were irrelevant to the Mayan population, who took no part in politics except in brief outbursts such as the Cuzcat rebellion, a smaller version of Yucatán's Caste War, in Chamula in 1868.

Under Porfirio Díaz – a Juarista before he became dictator – San Cristóbal's pro-Maximilian conservatism led to it being suspected of disloyalty, and the state capital was transferred to Tuxtla in 1892. The Díaz era brought some other changes too: the first electricity arrived in 1908, and a municipal architect called Carlos Flores gave San Cristóbal a number of Victorian-era monuments.

Despite the 1910 Revolution San Cristóbal long remained a very traditional city, its Spanish-speaking people, known as *coletos*, renowned for insularity and conservatism. Change began to come with the first airstrip in the 1930s, and when the Pan-American Highway in 1947 at last gave San Cristóbal a land-link to the outside world that could be crossed in less than a day. The greatest

Conscience of the Conquest: Las Casas

Since the Mexican Revolution San Cristóbal has had included in its name that of its most famous resident (at least before Marcos), Bartolomé de Las Casas, first Bishop of Chiapas. Once called 'the conscience of the Conquest', with a breadth of vision that did not seem to fit his time or place, he remains an inspiration to many today.

Las Casas was born in Seville in 1484, and grew up in the years when the city was electrified by the news of Columbus' first discoveries. His father signed up on Columbus' second voyage, and, when he was 18, Las Casas, just after taking preliminary orders to become a priest, also embarked for America. In his first years in the colonies he does not seem to have had special opinions on the way they were run: his revelation, though, came in 1513, when he witnessed a massacre of Indians on Santo Domingo. Like other Spanish churchmen of the time he believed the American discoveries had come as a trust from providence, and that Spain had an obligation to carry the word of God to the newly found peoples. He proclaimed, though, that the way the colonists were making use of that trust was no more than a cover for theft, murder, greed and savagery. The civilizing mission was a lie and a sin.

He dedicated the rest of his life to making that point, in two ways: one, in practical work in often remote parts of the Americas; the other, by going to the top and buttonholing monarchs and ministers to plead the rightness of his cause. In 1515 he sailed back from Santo Domingo and rushed to get the ear of King Ferdinand on his deathbed, to no avail. Over the years he chased many more figures at the court, and in 1542 addressed his most famous work, the *Brief History of the Destruction of the Indies*, to the future King Philip II. Remarkably, he was rarely refused entry, and in 1542 Charles V actually let him revise the *Leyes de Indias* by which Spain's colonies were supposedly run. He even succeeded in getting some reforms implemented, although the real difficulty was in getting them to take effect on the ground.

Shortly afterwards Las Casas was offered the chance to return to America as Bishop of Chiapas. His time in Ciudad Real was actually short: not long after he arrived in 1545 he ordered that confession and absolution were only to be given to colonists who released all Indians from slavery, raising howls of *conquistador* protest. By 1547 he was back in Spain to explain himself. In 1550 Las Casas was called to take part in an extraordinary disputation in Valladolid. The subject was none other than the right of Europe to remake the world in its own image. His opponent was a rising star of the Spanish Church called Juan Ginés de Sepúlveda, a prototype of the intellectual who today works in defence industry think-tanks. Sepúlveda's argument was that the world was a kind of divine meritocracy: by their ignorance of true religion the Indians showed themselves to be inferior, and any violence used by Christians was therefore only a measured, justifiable response to the Indians' own violence and barbarism. Las Casas replied with example after example to show that the conquerors' actions were purely brutal with no 'measure' at all, so that any morality in the Conquest was sheer hypocrisy. The texts of this debate were then taken away, to be considered by Church and State. Las Casas continued to argue his case until his death, aged 82, in 1566.

recent change has been the Mayanization of San Cristóbal. Since the 1970s Highland Maya have flooded into the city, which has trebled in size. Community relations are now more fluid than they have been for most of the last 500 years.

The Zócalo

Whichever way you arrive in San Cristóbal, you are near-inevitably led to the gracious main square, the Zócalo, centred on a very Victorian-looking bandstand surrounded by neat rings of shrubs, iron benches and broad, shady trees. In among them are lines of shoeshine men, Indian women and kids who try to sell you woven belts and bracelets, and newsstands selling a wider range of press than is usual in southern Mexico. Alternatively known as

Plaza Mayor or just '*el Parque*', the Zócalo has a (virtually unused) official title of Plaza 31 de Marzo, the date of the city's foundation.

Contrary to normal Spanish colonial practice, the **Cathedral** does not stand on the east flank of the square but fills its north side. To the main plaza it presents only a giant, blank wall. 'Blank' here is not strictly the right term, for the most remarkable thing about the cathedral is its colour scheme: great bands of yellow and red ochre, with panels in black on the west façade, and details – Baroque columns and capitals, Mayan-looking flowers and Habsburg double-headed eagles – picked out in white. It was begun in 1528 as a simple church, but with the granting of a bishopric to Ciudad Real ten years later its status was elevated to that of cathedral. It was therefore begun well before the cathedral in Mérida, but its construction took much longer, and the façade was only completed in the 1690s. Inside, in contrast to the strong colours of the exterior, the cathedral is lofty and white, with gold trim around its columns. Within the side chapels there is a whole collection of Baroque altarpieces and 17th-century religious paintings by local artists such as Juan Correa and Eusebio de Aguilar.

Behind the cathedral, facing into the Zócalo, there is an entirely separate chapel, the very simple **San Nicolás**, from 1615. This density of religious buildings soon comes as no surprise in San Cristóbal, which is a city of churches, their doors thrown open by day in a way that makes them seem like a series of atmospheric alcoves beside the streets. Moreover, in virtually all of them there will be people quietly coming and going, and observing their devotions. This happens in two ways, especially in certain churches that are highly regarded by the Maya. The *coletos* sit and kneel in pews, in the normal way; the Indians go down on their knees on the marble floors before the altars, surrounded by an untidy circle of candles and pine needles, where they rock rhythmically while murmuring continuously in Tzotzil or Tzeltal. Suddenly, these very Spanish churches look as if they've been taken over by something very different, with a whole new set of religious references.

The plaza's east side is filled by **Los Portales**, a deep-shaded arcade which in Ciudad Real was the place where the Spanish gentlemen of the city gathered to find out what was going on. Facing the arcade across the plaza is the town hall, the **Palacio Municipal**, built by Carlos Flores in 1885–95 to replace a Spanish one destroyed in the Juárez-era wars in 1863. In a city where for three centuries the style of building had been 1550s Spain, Flores did his best to introduce the look of 1840s France.

On the south side of the Zócalo are San Cristóbal's oldest colonial residences. As in Mérida, the first solid building completed in the new town was not a church but the house of the chief conqueror, the **Casa de Diego de Mazariegos**, on the corner of C. Diego de

Mazariegos and Av. Miguel Hidalgo, from the 1530s. It has been greatly altered since then, but the main surviving part of the original house is the patio on Miguel Hidalgo now occupied by **La Galería** cultural centre, with a restaurant, a shop and an art gallery. More complete is the **Casa de la Sirena** ('House of the Mermaid'), now the Hotel Santa Clara, on the corner of Av. Insurgentes. It was built a few years later, for another *conquistador* called Andrés de la Tovilla, and its name refers to the carved mermaid on the corner above the square.

Av. Miguel Hidalgo north of El Carmen and its continuation Av. 20 de Noviembre as far up as C. Escuadrón 201 have been pedestrian-ized as an *Andador Turístico* or 'tourist promenade', with shops to match, part of what some see as a 'theme-park-ization' of San Cristóbal's genuine historic charms. At Av. 16 de Septiembre 16 is **La Casa del Jade**. As well as a smart shop with fine jade and amber jewellery, it has the **Museo del Jade**, with reproductions of jade artefacts from all Mexico's pre-Hispanic cultures, and a full-size reconstruction of the Tomb of Pakal from Palenque.

La Casa del Jade
www.eljade.com;
open Mon–Sat noon–8,
Sun noon–6; adm to
museum

Santo Domingo and the Market

From the Zócalo it's possible to head off in any direction, and San Cristóbal is a city that encourages strolling. It also encourages you to take your time, for it's a place of many small details. The doors of its colonial houses are smaller than those in Mérida, offering less of a view inside; a Castilian sense of enclosure, of retreating from the outside world, has long been considered a major element in *coleto* culture. Inside and behind the slab-like outside walls, the patios may be ramshackle, or magnificent.

Head north up Av. General Utrilla for an area that contains San Cristóbal's greatest monuments and its most spectacular cultural mix. Along the way are some of the grandest patio houses, many now hotels. Stay on the pavements and you're remarkably high up, 2ft above the street. This partly reflects the wet mountain weather, but also the fact that until the mid-20th century Indians were not actually allowed to mount the pavements within the city. Five blocks from the Zócalo, on the right, is the **Casa Utrilla** (no. 33), where the patio contains likeable cafés and a great bookshop.

The eye tends to be distracted across the street here, however, to the vibrant colours and tightly-packed stalls of the city's main **handicrafts market**. Looming up above it is **Santo Domingo**, the grandest church in the city, more elaborate than the cathedral. It was built as part of a monastery established in 1546 by Las Casas as the main house of the Dominicans in Chiapas, and its construction went on for decades. The main façade on Av. 20 de Noviembre, from the late 17th century, is astonishing, one of the greatest creations of Mexican Baroque: it's completely different from anything the Franciscans created in Yucatán, more Mexican but also more in touch with the late Renaissance. Rising through four tiers of columns, every inch is covered in extravagant decoration: fluted columns, flower patterns, bosses, lions, geometrical shapes and figures of saints. Once inside, the sense of the Baroque is even more overwhelming, since much of the interior – the altarpieces, the giant pulpit – consists of finely carved wood coated in gold leaf. The altarpiece of the *Santíssima Trinidad* (Holy Trinity), in a side chapel, is among the finest of all Mexican colonial carvings. Amid the Baroque gilt there may also be the smell of copal incense and the murmur of Tzotzil prayers, for Santo Domingo is highly venerated by the Maya from the outlying villages.

Forming the south side of the garden-plaza around Santo Domingo is yet another church, the **Templo de la Caridad**. This was begun in 1714 to give thanks to the Virgin of Charity for 'delivering' the city from the Indian rebellion of 1712. Ironically, still more than San Domingo it is now overwhelmingly an Indian church. Its interior is similarly Baroque, but with altarpieces in massive brown and gold wood rather than pure gilt.

The airy cloisters and monastery buildings north of Santo Domingo house cultural institutions, among them the **Sna Jolobil** weavers' cooperative (*see* p.495) and the **Museo de los Altos de Chiapas**, an informative museum (in Spanish only) on the region's post-Conquest history that also hosts exhibitions.

Museo de los Altos de Chiapas
open Tues–Sun 10–5; adm

From here it's impossible not to be aware that you are getting close to the general **market**, which, from its official location at the junction of General Utrilla and C. Edgar Robledo, extends over several blocks. The *combi* and pick-up traffic gets much thicker, as do the clusters of Chamulas and Zinacantecas padding by with babies on their backs and great bundles of beans, greens, potatoes or peppers. San Cristóbal's market is perhaps the most extraordinary bazaar in the whole of southern Mexico. On one street you might see heaped from end to end earthenware pots from Amatenango, all looking for a buyer; in the food stalls are the brilliant colours of avocados, lemons, squashes, and countless varieties of chillies, amid live animals, raw wool, and cut flowers. Buying, selling and talking goes on all the time, except when people break off to listen to one of the hucksters pushing magic remedies.

West of the market and Calzada Lázaro Cárdenas the atmosphere changes again in the **Barrio de Mexicanos**, founded as a district for loyal 'Mexican' warriors who fought with the Spaniards against the Maya, and now a very tranquil part of town. If instead you follow Av. General Utrilla through the market and stay on it as it becomes Calzada Salomón González Blanco (a dusty walk of nearly 1km, so consider a cab) you will eventually find the fascinating **Museo de la Medicina Maya** at no. 10, run by an organization devoted to studying and maintaining Maya healing and herbal medicine

Museo de la Medicina Maya
open Tues–Fri 10–6, Sat, Sun 10–4; adm

13
Chiapas | San Cristóbal de Las Casas

techniques. There are good English translations, and the little museum is engaging, inspiring and eye-opening.

El Cerrillo and Na Bolom

East of Santo Domingo, C. Comitán leads up into the district of **El Cerrillo** (the little hill), founded in 1549 for freed Indian slaves, though with its low houses and cobbled streets looping over the hill it looks more than anywhere else in the city like an old Spanish town. Popular with resident foreigners, El Cerrillo has contemporary art galleries, **Galería Studio Cerrillo**, C. Tonalá 19A and **Museo-Galería Elisa Burkhard**, C. Yajalón 2, and a **Jardín de Orquídeas** in a house garden at C. Tonalá 27. Calle Yajalón runs north out of town for about 2km to a curious 16th-century covered bridge, the **Peje de Oro**. The valley nearby is a nature reserve, and contains the Maya ruins of **Moxviquil**, first explored by Frans Blom.

Continue east up and over C. Comitán or the parallel streets and you will come to the house and museum of **Na Bolom**, a monument to two of San Cristóbal's most unusual residents, Frans and Trudi Blom. Frans Blom (1893–1963) was born in Denmark, but at an early age gave up on conventional living and began travelling, ending up in Mexico. Drawn to jungles, he worked at many jobs – oil exploration, rubber tapping – before developing an interest in archaeology. He joined Tulane University in New Orleans, and in the 1920s made the first surveys of many Mayan sites. In 1928 he made contact with the Lacandón Maya for the first time, staying with them for long periods. In 1943 he met Gertrude (Trudi) Duby (1901–93), and both recognized in each other the same passions. From Switzerland, she had been a left-wing activist in Germany; arrested by the Nazis in 1940, she had only been spared because of her Swiss nationality. Expelled to Mexico, she became fascinated by her new country, and met Blom on an expedition to the Lacandón jungle. Together, they developed their relationship with the Lacandón, and moved into this house in 1950, intending it to be both their home and a centre for the study of the anthropology, archaeology and environment of the Maya and Chiapas.

Na Bolom is now a cultural centre, supporting a range of development and ecology projects, and still has a close relationship with the Lacandón. There are rooms and a dining room open to non-guests (see p.496), and it offers a special range of tours.

A major attraction is the beautiful old house itself, with some of the most attractive of colonial patios. The garden contains nurseries and seed beds, used in preserving plant species and reforestation schemes. Still very present is the powerful personality of Trudi Blom, from her bedroom with the immaculately elegant clothes she wore for jungle trips, to the eccentric objects all around the house, the collection of Baroque

---

Galería Studio Cerrillo
www.studiocerrillo.com

Museo-Galería Elisa Burkhard
museoelisa.wordpress. com

Jardín de Orquídeas
Orchid Garden, open Wed–Sun 10–6, donations accepted

Na Bolom
Guided tours in Spanish and English daily at 11.30 and 4.30; times can change, so check; library has no fixed opening times, but open to non-residents; t 678 1418, www.nabolom.org; adm

religious images or her exquisite photographs of the Lacandón. In other rooms there are Maya artefacts excavated by Frans Blom, especially from Moxviquil, and mementos of his friendships with such figures as Diego Rivera. There is also a superb if now disorganized **library**. Across the street from the house there is a little crafts shop in a garden, **El Jardín del Jaguar**.

Guadalupe

Running east from the Zócalo, C. Real de Guadalupe is perhaps the foreign visitor's favourite street in San Cristóbal, with the biggest concentration of hotels, tour agencies, restaurants, bookshops, cafés and other places in which to enjoy one of the city's prime attractions – just being here. Its lower blocks are being pedestrianized as another *Andador Turístico*, but this doesn't seem to be changing the atmosphere much. **TierrAdentro**, at Real de Guadalupe 24, is a laid-back café-restaurant and a cultural centre that hosts Zapatista co-operatives and NGOs, and so a good place to get in touch with whatever's happening in the city as well as hang out over fruit juice or check email. If you've had enough of sitting around chatting, head up the hill of Real de Guadalupe to some good handicrafts shops. Walk up in the evening and you may hear music, for several *marimbas* and *mariachis* have little practice-halls along the street. On the parallel C. Francisco Madero there's a small but colourful fruit market, at the corner of Av. Diego Dugelay, while on C. María Adelina Flores (at no. 10) is the **Café Museo Café** (*see* p.498), with a 'museum' on the history of Chiapas coffee.

Real de Guadalupe and Madero both end at the hill of Guadalupe, where 79 steps lead up to the **Templo de Guadalupe**. It was built only in 1834, and so in some ways is a lot simpler than the older Spanish churches. As befits a shrine to the Virgin of Guadalupe, though, it's astonishingly colourful, and at the top of the hill you are rewarded with delicious fresh air and a great view back over the city.

Insurgentes and El Carmen

Thanks to the traffic from the bus stations, the streets south of the Zócalo are quite busy, with cheap hotels, untouristy shops and a small market on Av. Insurgentes. This district was, with the Zócalo and Santo Domingo, one of the three main areas of colonial Ciudad Real. Filling the block between Miguel Hidalgo and Crescencio Rojas is the building that was once Chiapas' Jesuit College, the 1681 **Antiguo Colegio de San Francisco Javier**, now used by a university. Nearby is the **Casa de Artesanías**, the official handicrafts showcase (*see* p.495). Two blocks further down Miguel Hidalgo the street is blocked by a large, squat four-storey belltower with a small arch attached to it, the **Arco del Carmen**. Also from the 1680s, this is the only remaining part of the Convento de la Encarnación, once one of the largest closed convents of nuns in the Americas, founded in 1597. The space alongside it has been tidied up to become a pretty small plaza, around which several old buildings have been converted to house the **Centro Cultural El Carmen**, with an exhibition hall and a pleasant café.

One block east on Av. Insurgentes, and still intact, **San Francisco** was also part of a larger unit, a Franciscan monastery founded in 1577 and demolished in the 19th century. The church is plain, with white walls and a gold altarpiece, but has in one transept an intriguing naive painting of a legend of the life of Saint Francis, with very vivid demon-toads. Next to San Francisco is a big building, surrounded by cheap *loncherías*, called the **Mercado de Dulces y Artesanías**, the 'sweets and handicrafts market'. This curious combination is just what you find inside, although many of its stalls are unused. **Santa Lucía**, two blocks down, is an 1884 wedding-cake church in blue and white; a further walk south and out along the Highway is **San Diego**, built by the Dominicans in 1650 to cater for Indians who were not allowed inside the city.

The Merced and Cerrito de San Cristóbal

The area west of the Zócalo also has its large religious building, **La Merced**, reached by heading down C. Diego de Mazariegos. In front of it there is a delightfully tranquil, park-like square. The Merced was actually the first church in San Cristóbal, begun in 1537 by Mercedarian friars, but little of the original structure remains. It was rebuilt in the 18th century, and the cloister alongside became an army barracks in the 1880s, when it acquired its turret-like sentry boxes and watchtower. It has been restored as a cultural centre, the major part of which is the **Museo del Ambar de Chiapas** on the first floor, with a shop with the best local amber below. As well as exhibiting beautiful samples of amber, it gives an information overload on one of Chiapas' most valued products.

Museo del Ambar de Chiapas
www.museodelambar .com.mx; open Tues–Sun 10–2 and 4–7; adm

Across the street on the corner of Av. 12 de Octubre is the **Museo de las Culturas Populares de Chiapas**, but this has closed for (probably lengthy) renovation. Of far more interest, a block north at C. Guadalupe Victoria 38 is the unique **Museo Sergio Castro**. This venerable house is the home of Sergio Castro, a remarkable character who has worked for years among the Highland Maya, especially in health promotion. He has amassed a fabulous collection of Highland weaving, as well as a prodigious knowledge of local traditions. You must call ahead for a 'tour', which he takes himself every day at 6–7pm, with very individual explanations in his rapid-fire but very clear English (or other languages).

Museo Sergio Castro
call for appointment, t 678 4289; adm

South of the Merced Calle Matamoros leads up to the second of the city's two main hills, the **Cerrito de San Cristóbal**. Streets like La Palma that wind around its foot are enjoyably peaceful. From the end of C. Niños Héroes, a ramp of steps zigzags up the hill. A prime attraction is the view, across to its 'twin' of Guadalupe. The **chapel of San Cristóbal** is small and intimate, but sadly no longer has its once-famous cross made of licence plates, donated by local cab drivers, which was stolen in 1996.

(i) **San Cristóbal**

in Palacio Municipal, on the Zócalo (open daily 8–8).

Tourist Information

t (967–)

Tourist Office staff are helpful, but still more useful are its racks of leaflets and flyers and ads offering rooms to rent. San Cristóbal's official tourism promotion has become high-tech, and around the centre you will see signs with a number to which you can send an SMS, and then get a return text with information in any language. If you use this a few times, even with a Mexican phone, it will be very expensive.

iPod Tours, Av. Belisario Domínguez 2-B, t 631 6367, *www.ipodtours.com.mx*. For around $10 a day (and a deposit) this friendly young company rent you an iPod with a 'multimedia tour' of San Cristóbal, and other local information, in a choice of languages.

Tours from San Cristóbal

San Cristóbal is the natural base for trips of all kinds around the Chiapas Highlands has many tour agencies and guides. As well as the 'well-trodden' routes such as Chamula, trips to more remote villages are available, but finding them can be a matter of asking around or checking flyers; Alex y Raúl (*see* p.494) and some agencies arrange trips on request. Plus there are any number of individual tours, especially horseback treks or bike tours, that you find out about from flyers at the tourist office or in restaurants.

The usual itineraries are:

Chamula and **Zinacantán**, sometimes with **Tenejapa**; from $10 per person.

Comitán and the **Montebello Lakes** (from $13).

Sumidero Gorge and **Chiapa de Corzo** ($11).

Palenque, **Misol-Ha** and **Agua Azul** (from $17).

Many agencies also offer horseback tours, trips to **Toniná** and to Palenque, **Bonampak** and **Yaxchilán**, sometimes with an option of longer camping trips,

and some include **El Chiflón** waterfalls in Comitán-Montebello trips. A few also offer **Miramar** (*see* p.411) and visits (with **San Andrés Larraínzar**) to the Zapatista community of **Oventic**.

Tours are most useful for getting to Chamula and Zinacantán or the Sumidero. Palenque, the waterfalls, Bonampak and Yaxchilán are better visited from Palenque, but some San Cristóbal agencies offer good jungle trips. In Comitán and Montebello it is better to travel independently. In choosing a tour similar considerations apply as in Palenque (*see* p.450): check what is included, as some tours give you much more.

Tour Agencies

ATC, Av. 16 de Septiembre 16, t 678 2550, *www.atctours.com.mx*. Adventure tourism specialist. As well as the regular tours they can arrange rafting, trekking and visits to remote parts of the state (ATC works with many foreign tour companies). They are also the local agent for the **Maya Shuttle** bus service to Antigua in Guatemala.

Chincultik, C. Real de Guadalupe 34, t 678 0957. Friendly agency offering local tours at decent rates, plus horse riding and buses to Guatemala.

Explora Ecoturismo y Aventura, C. 1 de Marzo 30, t 674 6660, *www.ecochiapas. com*. Although San Cristóbal-based, this lively agency offers memorable trips in five main areas: **Lacanjá**, where it handles bookings for the Campamento Río Lacanjá (*see* p.469) and offers rafting and Bonampak-Yaxchilán tours; kayaking and forest exploration around **Las Guacamayas**; rafting on the **Usumacinta** and **Grijalva**; rafting down **Río La Venta** gorge west of Tuxtla; and **caving** near Tuxtla. Trips are for 4–14 people, and individuals can usually join a group.

Ruta Nahual, C. Real de Guadalupe 123, t (044) 967 124 2110, *rutanahual@ hotmail.com*. Not just one more agency, as their speciality is guided 'ecotours' by bike or on foot around San Cristóbal (including night tours) and to Huitepec and other places around the city. Also bikes for rent. *Closed Mon.*

Independent Guides

Some of the best trips are made with independent guides. Guides advertise at the tourist office, but these two operate permanently.

⭐ **Alex y Raúl >** Alex y Raúl, t 678 3741, *alexyraultours@yahoo.com.mx*. In the Zócalo every day at 9.30am, by their *combi* in front of the Cathedral. Their guides are friendly, knowledgeable and have excellent contacts with local communities: their daily route is Chamula-Zinacantán ($10), but they're very flexible, and with advance notice can organize trips to other destinations – such as Tenejapa, horseback treks to Chamula, or the Zapatista villages of Oventic and San Andrés. Highly recommended.

Mercedes Tour: A San Cristóbal institution is the 'lady with the umbrella', waiting in the Zócalo every day at 9am, ready to take tours up to Chamula and Zinacantán. The 'lady' herself, Mercedes Hernández, an idiosyncratic but very energetic guide, has retired, but the service is carried on by Alberto Medina. Tours ($12) are now a bit more conventional.

Services

Banks: Mostly around the plaza; all have ATMs. **Cambio Lacantún,** C. Real de Guadalupe 12-A, is a private change bureau *(open Mon–Sat until 7pm)*.

Health: Chiapas uses a central phone number for all emergency services, t 066. One of several **24hr pharmacies** is on the corner of Diego de Mazariegos and Crescencio Rojas.

Internet Access and Phone Offices: Abundant internet shops along C. Real de Guadalupe. Recommended is **Fast Net CyberCafé,** C. Real de Guadalupe 7: fast connections and printing.

Post Office: Av. Ignacio Allende 3. Has **Mexpost** *(open Mon–Fri 8–7, Sat 9–noon)*.

Festivals

San Cristóbal has an intricate calendar of *fiestas* and celebrations. Every *barrio* has its *fiesta*, centred on the saint's day at the local church. In most, on the eve of the main saint's day the *barrio* is woken up early by a bigger than usual barrage of rockets, as an invitation to the *fiesta*, and all day people prepare the church and the image of the saint, leaving it garlanded in flowers, herbs, coloured paper and lace. This is an event in itself, as *marimbas* play at the church door. After dark come the *maitines*, when the *barrio* meets up to visit the saint in its full finery. There's a dance in the plaza outside, amid more fireworks. The morning of the main day is the most religious moment in the *fiesta*, when the saint is carried in procession, giving way to a lighter mood as music and fairground attractions pick up through the evening. The biggest city-wide events are **Semana Santa** *(Easter Week)* and **St Christopher** *(25 July)*, when crowds climb the Cerrito de San Cristóbal to watch the valley below explode with fireworks.

Other important dates are:

Corpus Christi, *late May.*

Santo Domingo, *8 Aug.*

All Saints' and the **Day of the Dead,** *1–2 Nov.* Cemeteries are visited.

Guadalupe, *12 Dec.* Everyone climbs the hill of Guadalupe.

Christmas and **Epiphany,** *6 Jan.*

Learning Spanish and Mayan Languages

San Cristóbal's atmosphere and low prices make this an enjoyable place to learn Spanish. Schools offer homestays with local families, or you can arrange your own accommodation; most schools offer a range of activities as well as the basic course. Some schools also give classes in Tzotzil and Tzeltal. There are also programmes with Zapatista communities outside San Cristóbal: for information, go to *www.schoolsforchiapas.org*.

La Casa en el Arbol, C. Real de Mexicanos 10, t 674 5272, *www.lacasaenelarbol.org*. Friendly, imaginative school with international staff giving classes in Spanish and also English, French, Italian, German, Tzotzil and Tzeltal. The school has links with a volunteering programme, *www.natate.org*, for anyone wishing to get closer to life in Chiapas.

Centro El Puente, C. Real de Guadalupe 55, t 678 3723, *www.elpuenteweb.com*. Courses with homestays at low prices. El Puente also hosts film screenings, art shows, an Internet café and **La Casa del Pan** restaurant (*see* p.498).

Instituto Jovel, C. Francisco Madero 45, t 678 4069, *www.institutojovel.com*. A highly-regarded, long-running language school. Culture workshops and Spanish for specialist interests (teachers, health care workers) are among the available options.

Shopping

With Mérida, San Cristóbal is southern Mexico's great centre for **traditional crafts**, above all **Highland Maya textiles**. You are offered small pieces of weaving, and the now-universal Zapatista dolls, all over the city by Indian women and children. The largest concentration is in the **Mercado Indígena** around Santo Domingo, where you can find belts and other things (and plenty of junk) as well as textiles. These are very varied: tablecloths, waistcoats, scarves and more, all colourful, although those produced for tourists may not be skilfully worked. Nor are they necessarily made by the people selling them, for textiles from Guatemala are now common in the markets.

Co-operatives like J'pas Joloviletik (*see* right) are the best places to find traditional local weaving of fine quality. Prices are higher than in the market, but one aim of the co-operatives is to ensure that Highland women gain a fair price for their skills and work.

Amber is a great speciality of Chiapas, and several of San Cristóbal's jewellery shops are run by original designers. Another feature of the city is its browser-friendly **bookshops**, most of which have stock in English and other languages as well as Spanish.

Recommended Shops

Arte de Sandía, C. 28 de Agosto 6. Bright, fun souvenirs and craftwork based on watermelons (*sandías*) and other fruity themes.

Casa de las Artesanías de Chiapas, Av. Miguel Hidalgo, corner of C. Niños Héroes. The official state handicrafts showcase covers all Chiapas, with work from other areas as well as the Highlands, at relatively high prices.

La Casa del Jade, Av. 16 de Septiembre 16. Part of the 'Jade Museum', with fine jewellery in jade and amber.

El Encuentro, C. Real de Guadalupe 63-A. Old shop packed with superior Chiapas and Guatemalan textiles, leatherwork and toys.

Flora María y Gabriela, Av. Miguel Hidalgo 4A, *www.floramariaygabriela.com*. Innovative jewellery, mainly by two sisters; more stylish than the souvenir-style shops, and made with amber and other materials. They also have an outlet in **TierrAdentro** café.

La Galería del Corazón Abierto, Av. Miguel Hidalgo 3-A. Part of the Casa de Mazariegos centre, owned by German artist Kiki Suárez (*www.kikitheartist.com*). As well as her own colourful work it has traditional crafts and modern work – especially jewellery – by other San Cristóbal-based artists.

Ixtle, Av. Miguel Hidalgo 13-B. More a design gallery than a jewellery shop, with innovative ceramics and other items as well as amber.

J'pas Joloviletik, Av. General Utrilla 43. Best of the weavers' co-operatives, packed with a fascinating range of work in many styles. It's entirely run by Highland women themselves.

Lágrimas de la Selva, Av. Miguel Hidalgo 1-C. Pretty shop specializing in Chiapas amber, with an in-store workshop that makes amber jewellery to order and to individual designs.

Librería Chilam Balam, Casa Utrilla, Av. General Utrilla 33. The town's most varied, engaging bookshop.

La Pared, Av. Miguel Hidalgo 2. Essential call-in for *gringo* travellers, with a wide-ranging English-language stock.

Sna Jolobil, Convento de Santo Domingo, Calzada Lázaro Cárdenas, *www.snajolobil.com*. 'The House of the Weavers' is the longest established Mayan weavers' co-operative and a fine showcase for Highland textiles. Prices are high but so is quality. *Closed Sun*.

Taller de Leñateros, C. Flavio Paniagua 54. Co-operative making handmade paper, notebooks and decorative pieces using traditional Mayan wood-working techniques.

Where to Stay in San Cristóbal

San Cristóbal is a city, like Mérida, where the traditional architecture of plant-filled patios makes for very characterful hotels. For once, a/c and pools are not major considerations; more important (especially Nov–Feb) is some form of heating: some hotels have rooms with fireplaces and provide wood. San Cristóbal hotels are exceptional value, and *moderate* or even *inexpensive* ones can be as good as *expensive* elsewhere. At the budget end, the city offers a big range of rock-bottom accommodation. Prices are lower outside Christmas, the Easter season and July–Aug.

There are also many rooms available in San Cristóbal to rent, often at very low cost. Good places to find them are the notice boards at the tourist office or TierrAdentro (*see* p.xxx).

Expensive

Casa Felipe Flores, C. Dr JF Flores 36, t 678 3996, *www.felipeflores.com*. An 18th-century patio house magnificently restored and decorated with antiques to create a truly distinctive guest house. It has a snugly intimate feel, with five elegant double rooms (the tower room is especially lovely). Ample meals are served, there's a lounge with plenty of books, and the house is hosted warmly by Nancy and David Orr, who are very helpful and can arrange very individual tours. Prices for some rooms are in the *moderate* band.

Parador San Juan de Dios, Calzada Roberta 16, t 678 1167, *www.sanjuandios. com*. This grand colonial *hacienda* on the north side of town has been opulently renovated by antiquarian Mario Uvence, also owner of Parador Santa María near Montebello (*see* p.511). Two rooms (*moderate*) and 10 suites (*expensive*) are spread around the *hacienda* buildings and gardens. The **restaurant**, **Agapandos** (*expensive*), serves refined Chiapas cuisine.

Moderate

Casa Mexicana, C. 28 de Agosto 1, corner Av. General Utrilla, t 678 0698, *www.hotelcasamexicana.com*. Owned by artists Gabriel and Kiki Suárez, this venerable mansion has been renovated and filled with artwork, photography and traditional crafts. The garden patio (with **Los Magüeyes restaurant**, *moderate*) is wonderfully lush, and rooms are pretty, if sometimes short on light. Rooms in an annexe across the street are in the same style, but larger.

Na Bolom, Av. Vicente Guerrero 33, t 678 1418, *www.nabolom.org*. Guest rooms at Na Bolom (*see* pp.490–1) are individually furnished with Mayan artefacts. Thanks to the house's long reputation they're in great demand and must be booked well ahead. Guests can choose from Na Bolom's special mix of tours and activities. The **restaurant** (*moderate*, open to non-residents) is the old dining room, where diners share the same big table to chat over meals of local specialities and organic garden produce.

El Rincón del Arco, C. Ejército Nacional 66, t 678 1313, *hotel_rincon@hotmail. com*. Off the beaten track (15-min walk from the centre), but one of the most individual old-house hotels. The best rooms in this rambling mansion are on the upper floor, overlooking the huge, exuberant garden, with fireplaces (wood is provided) and lovely views.

Tierra y Cielo, Av. Benito Juárez 1, t 678 1053, *www.tierraycielo.com.mx*. This very carefully designed boutique-style hotel has just 12 light, elegant rooms with superior modern fittings, WiFi and so on. Some, though, are a bit cramped, to fit into the old San Cristóbal house. There's also an ambitious modern **restaurant** (*see* p.498).

Villas Casa Morada, C. Diego Dugelay 45, t 678 4440, *www.casamorada.com. mx*. An unusual hotel in a quiet El Cerrillo street, with eight spacious suites almost like studio apartments. Each has a kitchen, but breakfast is provided. At the back, there are two family size 'villas' on a garden. Popular with academics and others staying for long periods: weekly rates drop well into the *inexpensive* band.

Inexpensive

Hotel Casa Margarita, C. Real de Guadalupe 34, t 678 0957, *www. mundomaya.com.mx/casamargarita*. A bright patio and attractive **restaurant** (*moderate*) are the first things you see at this likeable hotel. Free WiFi is provided, and there's a roof terrace for

⊛ **Casa Felipe Flores** >

relaxing afternoons. The charming owners have recently opened another hotel, **Posada Margarita**, at C. Dr JF Flores 39 (same details), with smarter, spacious rooms, several with fireplaces, and rates near the top of this band.

Hotel Jardines del Cerrillo, Av. Belisario Domínguez 27, t 678 1283, *www. hotelesjardines.com*. Bargain patio-hotel in a quiet area. Rooms are spacious and decorated with traditional art, and there's a **restaurant** (*moderate*). Other pluses include WiFi and a taxi-transfer service to Tuxtla airport. Around the roof terrace there are 'cabin rooms' with several beds in each, which are ultra-economical for groups and families. The owners have two more similar San Cristóbal hotels, **Jardines del Centro** and **Jardines del Carmen**, with the same website.

Hotel Palacio de Moctezuma, Av. Benito Juárez 16, t 678 0352, *www.hotelpalacio democtezuma.com*. Venerable but popular hotel with three flower-filled patios, and a little **restaurant** for breakfast. Rooms, all with TV, bathrooms and even WiFi, vary: fittings in some are elderly, but the hotel has loads of character. At slack times rates drop down to the *budget* slot.

Hotel Posada El Paraíso, Av. 5 de Febrero 19, t 678 0085, *www.hotel posadaparaiso.com*. One of the best patio hotels, and amazing value, with accommodation equal to that in a higher price slot. A classic old San Cristóbal house has been given a chic uplift, in powder blue and terracotta. Some rooms are small, and those by the street can be noisy, but they're all very comfortable. It also has a superior **restaurant**, El Edén (*see* p.497).

Hotel Santa Clara, Av. Insurgentes 1, t 678 1140, *hotelstaclara@hotmail.com*. Pride of place on the Zócalo goes to this venerable hotel, in the 16th-century Casa de la Sirena. It's a maze of timber staircases and balconies, with a pretty **restaurant**, and in one patio there's even a small pool. Character in buckets, but it's a bit neglected.

Budget

Hacienda Los Morales, Av. Ignacio Allende 17, t 678 1472, *www.hotel haciendalosmorales.com*. A great find: 17 'bungalows' around a hillside garden

overflowing with flowers, on the hill of San Cristóbal. While well used, they offer all basic services and have lots of space, fireplaces and terraces to take in the superb view. Entrance is through the patio and old house, a historic ex-pharmacy that's a semi-'museum', as well as a **restaurant** (*moderate*) that serves a great break-fast buffet, and is open for lunch Fri–Sun.

Hotel Posada Jovel, C. Flavio Paniagua 27, t 678 1734, *www.mundochiapas. com/hotelposadajovel*. Pleasant hotel with amiable staff and 30 rooms around a traditional garden patio, with a **restaurant** for breakfast. Rooms can be chilly at times but are attractively decorated. Free WiFi in the patio and lobby. Rates are lower for the non-ensuite rooms across the street.

Posada La Media Luna, C. Hermanos Domínguez 5, t 631 5590, *www.hotel-lamedialuna.com*. Another of San Cristóbal's big bargains, this patio house has been attractively renovated by its Italian owners. Rooms are pretty and have good bathrooms, TVs and other fittings, making them superb value; there's free internet, and WiFi in some rooms. Choose between ensuite rooms, an apartment with kitchen, or San Cristóbal's best cheap rooms, sharing bathrooms. There's also a small Italian **restaurant** and breakfast room.

Posada México, Av. Josefa Ortiz de Domínguez 12, t 678 0014, *www. hostellingmexico.com*. The best of the backpacker hostels, with dorms (about $8 per person), camping space, and double rooms, en suite or sharing showers. Rooms, over two houses with gardens knocked into one, are well-kept and airy; in cold spells they get chilly. But, breakfast is included, the owners are helpful, and there's a nice open kitchen, lounge with DVDs, internet, bikes for rent and parking.

Eating Out

The traditional cuisine of San Cristóbal, *cocina coleta*, is quite singular. The city has adapted to its American surroundings in some dishes – pumpkin soup (*sopa de flor de calabaza*), tamales – but dug its heels in with others, and continues to eat more Spanish-looking hams and

⭐ **Posada La Media Luna** >>

sausages, grilled meats and *estofado de carnero* (lamb stew, with chilli) than almost any other part of Mexico. Another tradition is wonderful breads. Among local dishes that are more Mexican than Spanish are *chalupas*, the equivalent of the Yucatán's *panuchos* and *salbutes*, small *tortillas* with a variety of toppings.

San Cristóbal's popularity as a multi-national bohemian focus has also had a big impact on its restaurants: it has the best vegetarian restaurants in southern Mexico. The biggest cluster of really cheap eating places is on Av. Insurgentes, near San Francisco.

Expensive

El Fogón de Jovel, Av. 16 de Septiembre 11, t 678 1153. Near the Cathedral, and the city's best known showcase for Chiapas' traditional food. It's very pretty, and popular with locals, but a kitsch element can override quality.

Tierra y Cielo, Av. Benito Juárez 1, t 678 1053, *www.tierraycielo.com.mx*. The most 'boutique'-style hotel (*see* p.496) has a smart restaurant, with a refined modern menu.

Moderate

La Casa del Pan, C. Dr Navarro 10 and C. Real de Guadalupe 55, *www.casadel pan.com*. The most celebrated vegetarian restaurant in town, run by American Kippy Nigh, author of several Mexican vegetarian cookbooks. The original Casa del Pan on C. Dr Navarro – pretty, mellow, and with a great organic bakery and crafts shop – is closed Mondays: the branch in **El Puente** language school, C. Real de Guadalupe, is closed on Sundays.

El Edén, El Paraíso, Av. 5 de Febrero 19. The restaurant in the Paraíso hotel (*see* p.497) has a similarly attractive, calming style. The hotel owners are Swiss, and the menu reflects this with a mix of Mexican and European dishes.

Glam, Av. Miguel Hidalgo 1. An adventurous departure on the Andador Turístico, with cool décor, enjoyable food that's a clever mix of Mexican and Asian styles and good cocktails.

Madre Tierra, Av. Insurgentes 19. A star among San Cristóbal's wholefood café-restaurants, with a lovely patio and an irresistible organic bakery, **Panadería Madre Tierra**, alongside. The menu is mainly vegetarian, but also offers some meat and fish choices.

La Paloma, Av. Miguel Hidalgo 3-A. Very pretty modern 'restaurant-bar-garden' in the patio of the Casa de Mazariegos, with a mix of sophisticated Mexican dishes and international variations.

Paris-Mexico, C. Francisco Madero 20. The name reflects its owners' origins, the Left-Bank-meets-Chiapas style, and the menu. Hence, there's warming French onion soup as an alternative to *fajitas*. (May) serve food after 11pm.

Perfidia, C. María Adelina Flores 23. Funky and friendly bar-restaurant hosting live music, art shows, and events. At other times, it's a relaxed spot to eat from a fine-value global menu with noodles and veggie choices. Free WiFi too. *Closed Sun.*

TierrAdentro, C. Real de Guadalupe 24, *www.tierradentro.com.mx*. Not so much a café, more a way of life: this café-cultural centre has tables in a big patio, around which it provides space for a bookshop, art space, Zapatista crafts co-operatives and human rights organizations. The café part offers a part-vegetarian organic menu, fine coffee and juices. Also free WiFi, concerts and events. It's also very friendly, hums with conversation, and is a great place to find out what's going on in town.

Trattoria Italiana, Av. Belisario Domínguez 8-B. Tiny but very popular Italian restaurant with great home-made pastas.

Budget

Café Museo Café, C. María Adelina Flores 10. Set up by a fairtrade co-op of small coffee producers to showcase their organic crop, this spacious café also has alcohol and good snacks. Attached is a **Museo del Café** (*adm*).

Restaurante Alameda, Casa Utrilla, Av. General Utrilla 33. Patio café with local dishes, salads and vegetarian snacks.

Restaurant Normita I, Av. Benito Juárez, corner of C. Dr JF Flores. For good local dishes in a warm, friendly environ-ment, you can't beat this little *comedor familiar*. Its *platos coletos* – spare ribs or grilled *chorizos* – and Mexican standards are enormously generous. There's a branch, **Normita II**, at Av. Insurgentes 5-A.

Entertainment and Nightlife

With so much street entertainment in *fiestas*, nightlife in San Cristóbal often consists of eating, drinking and talking, but there are buzzing venues too. Film screenings, performances and other events also happen in El Puente language school, **Perfidia** and **TierrAdentro** (*see* above). Apart from that, just follow the sound of *marimbas* and *mariachis*...

Grado Zero, Av. 5 de Mayo 2. International-style bar-club with high-energy DJs.

Iskra, C. Real de Guadalupe 53. The city's own microbrewery, with a bar-café that's a hub of the boho social scene, hosting live music of all sorts, and serving up great snacks with its beer and surprisingly good wine selection.

Kinoki, C. 1 de Marzo 22. An 'independent cultural forum' with a wholefood café, music and different films showing nightly.

Latino's, C. Francisco Madero 23. Live salsa-Latin bands, and open till 3am. *Closed Sun.*

Palenque Rojo, Teatro Daniel Zebadúa, Av. 20 de Noviembre. San Cristóbal's old theatre now hosts a rather tacky 'Maya dance spectacle' supposedly based on the wars between Palenque and Toniná. *Tues–Sun 8pm.*

Revolución, Av. 20 de Noviembre, corner of C. 1 de Marzo. One of San Cristóbal's foremost hang-out spots, a dark, friendly, laid-back bar with live music of some kind every night.

Around San Cristóbal: the Highland Villages

After a few days in the Chiapas Highlands, you can feel the place was invented by Jonathan Swift. In and around San Cristóbal there are people who wear blue, black and white and keep sheep (from Chamula), people who wear brilliant purples and reds and grow flowers (Zinacantán), people who make pots (Amatenango), others who are harder to identify. The Highland Maya communities have an intricate, complex culture, and from one hill to another you can encounter a different set of beliefs, legends and traditions: visiting the area is a fascinating, sometimes jarring venture into a world far from the routine ways of the 21st century.

Chamula and Zinacantán gave fierce resistance to the *conquistadors* in the 1520s, and were never totally subdued, settling into co-existence with the Spaniards of San Cristóbal, 10km away. For two centuries the missionary orders strove to stamp out 'paganism' in the Highlands and establish normal Catholic practice, but the Maya responded with what has been called 'passive resistance', intertwining their old beliefs with the new religion – some say throttling it – in a fascinating amalgam. Even so, the Highland peoples have considered themselves Catholics, for the boundaries between orthodox beliefs and others have never been defined.

There are many differences between them – including language, from Tzotzil to Tzeltal – but a pattern is common to all the traditional Highland communities. All have adapted Catholic saints and images to a very Maya veneration of the earth and sacred places. In each there is a ladder of social and religious authorities, called *cargos* (literally 'posts' or 'duties'), often referred to by a

Getting to the Highland Villages

It's very advisable to go with a **guide** when you first visit Chamula and Zinacantán. These villages may be well-touristed, but there is still so much that is alien, and so many places to which access is only possible with an introduction, that you will see and understand much more with someone to lead the way. All San Cristóbal agencies offer **tours**, but independent guides such as **Alex y Raúl** give the most personal service (*see* p.494).

If you do make your own way, *combis* are easy to find at the market in San Cristóbal (but they tend to head into town in the morning, and head back in the afternoon). **By car**, the road is also easy to find by following C. Guadalupe Victoria west out of San Cristóbal. Once you arrive, especially in Chamula, be ready for kids demanding to *cuidar el carro*, watch your car. Pick one, and make a deal.

Amatenango is in a different direction, off Highway 190 toward Comitán. Some agencies include it in tours to Montebello (*see* p.493), but it's easy to reach by car bus or *combi* on the Comitán route.

curious mix of Spanish names: *pasiones* ('passions'), *alfereces* ('lieutenants'), *mayordomos* ('stewards'). Each year's occupants of a post are chosen by the authorities of the previous year. Men (rarely ever women) begin by taking junior posts, if they gain sufficient respect, ascend to the most senior with age. Occupying an important *cargo* wins a man honour and prestige for the rest of his life. It is also expensive, for the *mayordomo* of a specific saint, for example, is responsible for maintaining the saint's shrine for a year and arranging the annual *fiesta* out of his own pocket, and must contribute to events like the Carnival. A complex system of loans has built up to allow men to take up their positions. Other important figures in the Highlands are the *ilol* or healers, often women as well as men. Another activity is the drinking of *posh*, powerful home-made cane hooch, knocked back in ample quantities to accelerate contact with gods and spirits – as similar brews were used by the Classic Maya – and also used in healing.

Although the Highland communities are often called villages, they cover wide areas. Chamula, the largest, has a total population close to 100,000, but only a part live in the 'ceremonial centre' of San Juan Chamula. The rest are spread across the mountains in tiny clutches of houses and fields called *parajes*. Nor is this world of traditions static or cut off from the world, for within their bodies of tradition each community has never ceased to evolve and adapt, so that if you visit a place like Chamula a few years apart you will always see significant changes. In the 1940s the Mexican government established an elaborate bureaucracy to deal with indigenous communities, providing privileged positions for chosen leaders, and in Chamula, especially, many elders were for years closely bound up with the PRI; on the other hand, one of the Zapatista *comandantes*, Ramona, was a Chamulan woman. The *cargos* system creates its own tensions, and is intolerant of anyone who rejects community authority. From the 1970s American Protestant missionaries made many converts in the region with their radical opposition to the old hierarchy (there are also 'autonomous evangelical' churches, who reject the Americans as well), which has led to bitter conflict and the expulsion of several thousand Protestants from Chamula. Many now live in the suburbs of San Cristóbal, or along the Comitán road southeast of the city. These are only some of the complexities of the Highlands.

If you can, it's a wonderful experience to get away from the ceremonial centres and drive a little way up the winding mountain tracks. On the tops of mountains or at the entrances of villages stand the green-painted crosses the Catholic Church long tried to present as a sign of the success of orthodox religion in the Highlands, but which are equally or more symbolic of the world-tree, surrounded by bromeliads and sprigs of pine. They are usually in pairs, representing God the Father and God the Mother.

Huitepec Nature Reserve

Huitepec Nature Reserve
Open Tues–Sun 9–4; adm

Pronatura Chiapas
www.pronatura-chiapas.org

About 3km from San Cristóbal the road to Chamula curves around the volcano of Huitepec, part of which is a 135-hectare nature reserve, rising from meadows and pines into cloudforest. All kinds of birds can be seen on the lovely 2km trail, including scarce forest species. **Pronatura Chiapas** provides guides and tours. Nearby a Zapatista community has set up its own reserve, accusing local authorities of having failed to protect the mountain.

Chamula

The ceremonial centre of **San Juan Chamula** is an untidy place, its sole focus a wide and sloping main square centred, naturally, on the church, which is all white but with bands of flowers painted around the portico. Around the sides of the square the church has been accompanied, just in the last few years, by a growing number of more substantial buildings, including a very solid town hall. Away from this hub, huts and houses straggle up tracks in no particular order. Until about 50 years ago there were no permanent buildings at all here except the church, and the population was dispersed in the *parajes*. The Chamulas are the sheep-herders of the Highlands. On Sundays, especially, most men and boys wear woollen smocks, in black or white, with the now equally 'traditional' addition of a stetson-style straw hat, and Chamula women virtually always wear their traditional black woollen skirts and blue or white blouses with embroidered strips round the edges (now made with synthetics).

As well as the town hall, there are many places around the square dispensing Coca-Cola and Pepsi. The Mayas' cola-fixation is much more peculiar than their dislike of having their picture taken. They believe that burping releases bad energies from the body, and formerly made a kind of natural lemonade to induce burps. Then, when they discovered how well modern gassy drinks can make the tubes gurgle, they took to them with devotion, and now have a consumption per head that must merit an entry to themselves in the annual corporate report. Several elders of Chamula have also done very well out of their neighbours by securing cola concessions.

Mayans, too, can take pictures...

Somehow or other, whether they read it in a guide book or were told it on the bus, virtually every traveller who arrives in San Cristóbal seems to have heard the story that the Highland Maya are afraid of cameras because they think they 'steal their souls'. For further colour, a dark warning may be added that someone was once killed at Chamula for nothing more than taking an innocent snap (the victim must have been pretty unloved, for no one has ever reported him/her missing). This all adds to the mystique around the Maya as being primitive and weird, and helps outsiders feel comfortably superior, but it is a gross distortion of what the Maya actually think.

The Highland Mayas' resentment of photography is due less to any idea of cameras 'stealing souls' than to the simple dislike of being used as decorative objects for no reward, and to their concept of *chu'lel* (vital energy). This is possessed by living creatures and inanimate objects alike, and any contact between people, with animals, or between people and the earth, involves an exchange of *chu'lel*. Picture-taking is rejected because it takes away *chu'lel* without asking – like walking into someone's house without knocking – and because the Highland Maya dislike all impersonal interactions. On a very practical level, the Maya are also acutely aware that their faces appear on all sorts of books and postcards, for which they receive no reward whatsoever. Impersonal picture-taking is just seen as exploitative.

And the Maya can use photography themselves. A remarkable project, the Archivo Fotográfico Indígena, has provided over 200 people from communities around San Cristóbal, most of them women, with cameras and support to enable them to take pictures of their own world for themselves. The results are extraordinary, from images of village life to much more idiosyncratic projects, and have been publicized in exhibitions and an impressive series of books. The AFI is based at a college by the Chamula road, CIESAS, Carretera a Chamula Km 3.5, t (967) 678 5670, *www.chiapasphoto.org*. It is open to visitors (*Mon–Fri 8–2*), but always call ahead.

With a good guide you may be able to visit first one of the 'shrines' of the different saints. It looks like another Chamula hut, except the door is garlanded in bromeliads and dried branches. Inside, the floor is carpeted in pine needles, and the Spanish-looking image of the saint is surrounded by flowers, leaves and yet more bromeliads – an air-feeding plant, and so held to be in contact with the spirits. The table in front of the image is packed with ceramic incense burners, often in the shape of cows or sheep, pouring out sweet copal incense. The Highland Maya dress their saints this way because they once worshipped in caves, and reproduce the environment of a mountain cave to create a sacred space. For the same reason they scatter pine needles around them when they worship in the ornate churches of San Cristóbal.

After that you return to the square and into the **church**, where, if you're not with a tour, the 'constables' charge about $1-2 for entry; put cameras in your bag to avoid misunderstandings. Inside, this is naturally the place where you most feel an intruder. Nowadays ever more lines of tourists tread gingerly between the candles, but nevertheless the church at Chamula can still be one of the strangest religious spaces anywhere in the world. The windows are often blocked by hanging plants; the floor is covered in pine needles, and images of saints extend in lines along each side, the main light given by hundreds of candles. There are no 'services' as such; all business is done on the floor. As you shuffle round, trying not to interfere, you trip over empty cola bottles. All of life is there: in one spot, a man prays alone with agonized intensity, rocking mesmerically back and forth, while next to him a family sits in its ring of candles and bottles, chatting or looking bored; elsewhere, two men giggle through a drunken conversation, after taking in a deal of *posh*. *Ilol* healers receive patients around the floor, holding their wrists and talking quietly in unhurried consultations.

museum
open daily 8–7; adm

Alongside the church there is a small **museum**, although it's not as interesting as the village around it. The **market** in the square covers all needs, and so most of the stalls have foods, fruit, pots and so on, but there are plenty with local weaving. Around the edges of the square there are a few simple *loncherías*. On a Sunday the raised section of the square will contain, sitting solemnly in line, the senior authorities of Chamula, in the hats that are a symbol of office, with bright coloured ribbons hanging over their eyes. This is another group who must not be photographed. Until very recently it was customary for any member of the community with a problem to present their case to the authorities in public in the plaza on Sunday, first greeting every one of them by going along the line kissing the ribbons of their hats as a sign of respect, but this has lately become far less common.

Zinacantán

San Lorenzo Zinacantán, like Chamula a Tzotzil-speaking community, is only 7km west, but feels remarkably different. The village itself is neater, with orderly streets and whitewashed buildings; the people seem gentler, and it's a less abrasive place to visit without a guide. The **church** (inside which you still mustn't take pictures) is a great deal brighter, exuberantly colourful, and less intense. The Zinacantecos' love of colour is visible in all kinds of ways. They grow huge quantities of flowers, particularly geraniums, chrysanthemums and carnations, which are now produced in industrial greenhouses and distributed across Mexico. For once the men's costume – sadly now becoming less common as everyday dress – is as colourful as that of the women, heavy purple or red smocks, embroidered with flower designs. Women, meanwhile, wear their hair bobbed up with flowers and ribbons, and shawls in rich purples, blues and reds laced with gold thread. They are all the brighter nowadays thanks to lurex and other synthetic threads, which have been taken up with enthusiasm by the Zinacantecas, delighted to obtain so much colour with so little effort. At *fiestas* or when they are performing rituals some men wear the full regalia of white shorts, red head-scarves, ribboned hats for the authorities, and leather sandals of a type near-identical to those worn by Kan-Balam on the reliefs of the Cross temples at Palenque.

Textile experts may bemoan the domination of synthetics, but the Zinacantecan women are far more interesting weavers than

13

Chiapas | Around San Cristóbal: the Highland Villages

those of Chamula, and their multicoloured products are the most popular Highland souvenirs. It's also much easier to visit weavers' homes here – Zinacantecas are keen businesswomen – and see them at work. The little **market** is next to the church. Nearby is the community **museum**, with weaving and relics of Zinacantecan life.

museum
open daily 8.30–5;
adm

On Sundays, Zinacantán's authorities do not sit in the open but in the chapterhouse beside the church, adorned with banners in gold, green and purple. This otherwise-hushed meeting is unmissable when the younger men accompany them to sing the 'Song of the Churchkeeper', the unearthly festival music of Zinacantán.

San Andrés Larráinzar, Mitontic and Tenejapa

Beyond Chamula the road winds north through fabulous scenery 16km to **San Andrés Larráinzar**, which produces some of the very finest Highland weaving, with an intricate, instantly recognizable style. There is a lively Sunday market, and an excellent co-operative shop by the road into town. San Andrés is also known for its Zapatista sympathies, and is usually included in trips to **Oventic**. A turn-off south of San Andrés curves east to **Mitontic**, a very pretty village winding up a hillside, from where a track, passable in a 4WD or *combi*, climbs and twists up to the summit of **Mount Tzontehuitz**, at 2,910m the highest peak in the Highlands and a sacred spot to the Maya, topped by a television relay station and a sheaf of Mayan crosses.

In another direction, east of San Cristóbal, a continuation of C. Real de Guadalupe twists for 25km to **Tenejapa**. About 4km from the city it passes a right turn to a favourite local beauty spot, the **Arcotete**, an imposing rock arch over the Fogótico river. Tenejapa's language is Tzeltal, not Tzotzil, but the dress of its *cargos* is similar to that of Chamula, with hats with bright ribbons. Tenejapan women are more distinctive, with *huípiles* with red and yellow patches and navy blue skirts. Tenejapa is known for its **market** on Thursdays, when many Chamula tours make a detour there.

The San Cristóbal Caves

At **Rancho Nuevo**, 10km east of San Cristóbal, where Highway 190 meets Highway 199 from Palenque, there is, on the north side of the road, a large and very solid army camp, and on the south side a turn-off into a beautiful pine wood. After less than a kilometre this track runs out at the **Grutas de San Cristóbal**, an extensive cave system, with awesome cathedral-like chambers. It's very cold inside, so go prepared.

Grutas de San Cristóbal
Open daily 8–5; adm.

The woods around the caves are popular for picnics, and horses can be hired (*about $10 per hour*) outside the cave entrance for rides along the forest trails. It's also possible to camp. Second-class buses and *combis* stop at the *grutas* on request.

Visiting a Zapatista Community

Zapatista villages have always had foreign visitors, committed volunteers who have come to help out. They have not, though, usually opened their gates to the just curious. But, in 2008 the *caracol* (*see* p.476) of Oventic, west of San Andrés Larraínzar, set up a *Comité de Explicación* or 'Explanation Committee' to receive tour groups – at least part-motivated by a need to remind the world they exist.

Visits normally begin with a stop in San Andrés, before winding up to Oventic. Like most *caracoles* it is a new village, created since 1994. Committee members still wear their ski masks, but there's no sense of aggression, nor any weapons around. The 'tour' begins with a brief talk by a member of the Explanation Committee; it's amiably low on rhetoric, and no question is off-limits. Then you can wander around Oventic, its schools, clinic and vigorously revolutionary murals, before leaving via the souvenir shop, where you can buy a real Zapatista wool ski mask.

Tours can be arranged through Alex y Raúl (*see* p.494) and some other San Cristóbal agencies, but need to be booked ahead.

Amatenango del Valle

The Tzeltal village of Amatenango, 38km southeast of San Cristóbal off Highway 190, is the *pueblo de alfareras*, the village of potters. For 1,000 years, or longer, its women have been dedicated to making earthenware pots and ornaments. The responsibility of the men, meanwhile, has been to find firewood to keep the open kilns going. They do so by hauling donkey-derby carts up the steep valley sides around the village, and then hurtling back down again with their load of wood at manic speed. In the process they have left the surrounding hills severely denuded.

As you approach Amatenango you see ranks of brown pots, jugs and jars for sale all along the main road. If you enter the village you will be found by a band of little girls, who will ask if you want to see how pots are made ('*¿Quiere ver como se hace la cerámica?*'). Once you accept an offer from one, she will take her catch back to the family *jacal* ('enclosure') to meet her mother. You are then sat down to watch while the girl models a small figure, maybe an animal, in about a minute. What you pay is normally up to you. More intriguing is the firing method, the preserve of the older women, a simple open-fired process. However, to see that you have to be insistent, as entertaining tourists seems to be kids' business.

The women of Amatenango have another completely distinctive style of dress: girls and younger women wear Tzeltal-style embroidered blouses and blue skirts; for older women there are heavy red and orange *huípiles*, long wool skirts with muted horizontal stripes, and an almost African-looking headdress.

Visiting the Villages

The best day to visit **Chamula** and **Zinacantán** is Sunday, which is both market day and the main day when the *autoridades* hold court in their squares. Thursday is market day in **Tenejapa**.

Photography

The attitude of the Highland Maya towards photography has been hugely maligned, but it is true that the worldwide tourist assumption that anyone can take a picture of 'the locals' without so much as saying hello is something they do not like. In all the villages, but especially Chamula, follow your guide's directions as to when you can take photos; in the market it's usually acceptable. There is an absolute ban on taking pictures inside Chamula church, and the '**constables**', young *cargos* in white smocks with big sticks, enforce this energetically. A tale has long gone around that foreigners have been killed at Chamula for taking pictures where they shouldn't. This is a folk myth, repeated in guide books. The constables will, though, grab a camera, take out the film or digital card (or, nowadays, may just delete every picture), and may give it back to you broken, with aggressive scowls.

For another take on the Highland Maya's complex attitudes to photography, *see* p.502.

Festivals

Given the importance of daily ritual to the Highland Maya, it's no surprise they keep up an elaborate calendar of celebrations. Easter is important in all the communities, but each has its own schedule of events, and usually one special *fiesta* when religious images, freshly dressed, are taken out in procession so that the world is 'reborn' for another year, with festivities building up over preceding days. The dates of some main village *fiestas* are:

Tenejapa: San Ildefonso, *23 Jan*.

Mitontic: San Miguel, *8 May*.

Zinacantán: San Lorenzo, *10 Aug*.

Chamula

Chamula has the most awesome cycle of celebrations, with over 20 festivals. **San Sebastián** (*20 Jan*), **Easter** and **San Juan** (*24 June*) are all important, but the greatest of all is the **Carnival** (*late Jan or Feb*). Its Tzotzil name, *K'in Tahimol*, translates as 'Festival of Games'. Whole books have been written about the interplay of beliefs within it. It lasts five days, corresponding to the five *uayeb* days at the end of the year in the *Haab* calendar, the unstable time when the world needs to be reborn. For the first three, officials of Chamula's *barrios* parade around the village with sumptuous banners representing the Sun and Christ, which in Chamula blend together. Around them, challenging them, dance the *max* or monkeys, representing the men of wood from the previous creation and symbolizing chaos and disordered nature. The disorder comes over clearly enough, as they look completely mad, in absurd 'uniforms' inspired by those of Maximilian's armies, long ago. Bands play a bizarre combination of instruments, performing the same meandering tune, the *Bolon Chon*.

All this is punctuated by plenty of eating, fireworks and noise. After three days of challenges to the Sun-Christ by the monkeys, the night of the third day sees the exhausted dancers and banner-carriers run up the hills on the outskirts of the village, as if the forces of chaos have won and banished the Sun-Christ. Then, on the fourth day, the *pasiones* and banners return to the plaza and perform the 'Path of Fire': a path of straw is laid from the church across the square and set alight, and the Sun-Christ banners are run along it through the flames three times. The Sun-Christ is thus reborn, and the universal order, to be celebrated on the last day, restored.

Around Comitán and the Montebello Lakes

Beyond Amatenango the scenery becomes less grandiose, as the true Highlands descend into a plateau, the *meseta* of Chiapas. Its main centre is the likeable country town of **Comitán**. To the south are two little-known Mayan sites, **Tenam Puente** and **Chinkultik**, and, 60km eastwards, the **Lagunas de Montebello**, a string of exquisite mountain lakes. Surrounded by almost sheer slopes, their deep, unpolluted waters have a superb richness of colour, the origin of their other name, the *Lagunas de Colores*. Most people come here in a day trip from San Cristóbal, but to get a real feel of the lakes it's better to stop over, in Comitán or one of the few places closer by.

Comitán

Comitán's official name is Comitán de Domínguez, after one of its most famous citizens, Dr Belisario Domínguez. He was the only member of the Mexican senate to denounce Victoriano Huerta as a murderer after the assassination of Madero in 1914. This was one of the utterly quixotic gestures that stand out in the murk of so much Mexican politics, as the good doctor was soon taken off and shot. His house is now the **Museo Belisario Domínguez**, primarily attractive as a virtually unchanged example of a gentleman's home from the 19th century, with charming, secluded patios.

Museo Belisario Domínguez
Av. Central Dr Domínguez 35; open Tues–Sat 10–6.45, Sun 9–12.45; adm

The other figure associated with Comitán was novelist Rosario Castellanos, who depicted the town of her youth in the 1930s in her book *Balún Canán* ('Nine Stars'), the Tzeltal name for Comitán. Somewhere beneath the modern town are the remains of a Maya settlement, and in a colonial-style building on the corner of the plaza and C. 1 Sur Oriente is the **Casa de Cultura**, with an attractive **Museo Arqueológico** with impressive finds from local sites, especially Tenam Puente. In the same building is a great café and the **Museo Rosario Castellanos**, with pictures of pre-1950 Comitán.

Museo Arqueológico
open Tues–Sun 9–6; adm

Museo Rosario Castellanos
open Tues–Sun 9–6; adm

The Plaza Central is naturally the centre of activity in Comitán, with cafés from which to watch whatever's going on. In the 19th century the town did well out of coffee and sugar, acquiring some Victorian-era architecture that can seem odd in the middle of Chiapas. In the plaza is a wrought-iron bandstand, where *marimbas* play several nights a week, and to one side is the neoclassical **Teatro de la Ciudad**.

South of the town a newly-improved road turns off west to eventually reach Tuxtla Gutiérrez, passing, 34km from Comitán, another of Chiapas' majestic ladders of waterfalls at **El Chiflón**. A popular visit for locals (included in some Montebello tours from San Cristóbal), the falls now have a *centro ecoturístico* alongside, with a restaurant and some comfortable *cabañas* (*inexpensive*).

Tenam Puente

Tenam Puente
Open daily 8–5; adm.

Tenam Puente was discovered by Frans Blom and Oliver LaFarge in 1925, but only opened to visitors in the 1990s. It is thought that like other Maya centres in the region it grew mostly in the Late Classic after 700, as the Highlands gained in prominence during the 'Collapse'. Its architecture shows influences of the Guatemala Highlands and the Petén, and it is suggested it was a point of contact between those areas and non-Maya lands to the west. It continued to be occupied long into the Postclassic, until about 1200.

Getting to and around Comitán

The **first-class bus station (OCC)** is on Highway 190 south of the centre at C. 8 Sur Poniente (a cab ride from the plaza). *Combis* and **second-class bus** companies also operate from the Highway, by the junction of C. 1 Sur Poniente. They run frequently to San Cristóbal and Tuxtla, and there are many *combis* to nearby villages. **Taxis** are plentiful, and cost around $1.40.

Getting to Tenam Puente and Chinkultic

Tenam Puente is well-signposted 10km south of Comitán on Highway 190. A paved road leads to the ruins (6km), via the village of Francisco Sarabia. *Combis* may only go only as far as the village, 2–3km from the site. 16km south of Comitán, just before La Trinitaria, is the turning east to Montebello. This road runs straight for 35km until you pass a turning north for **Chinkultic**, about 1km from the road. *Combis* from Comitán to Montebello (*see* p.510) pass the Chinkultic turn.

Orientation

Highway 190 (**Blvd Dr Belisario Domínguez** in town), runs along the west side of Comitán, and streets run off it into the grid to the east. The town has a fiendish street-numbering system. North–south streets are Avenidas, east–west are Calles. The grid axis is the junction of C. Central Benito Juárez and Av. Central Dr Belisario Domínguez (called Av. Central), at the **Plaza Central**. North of C. Central are C. 1 Norte, 2 Norte etc.; south are C. 1 Sur, 2 Sur, etc. Avenidas west of the Central are Av. 1 Poniente, 2 Poniente; on the other side are Av. 1 Oriente, 2 Oriente. As an additional help the grid is divided into quarters, so Av. 2 Poniente north of C. Central is Av. 2 Poniente Norte. Simple, really…. There are two big *gasolineras* on the Highway.

Tenam Puente's impact is in its spectacular hilltop location, and the way this is intertwined with its architecture. From the parking area you walk up into a giant central plaza, a broad, grassy heath. At one end is a **Ball Court**, with what almost look to be 'grandstands' at one end. The eye is drawn above all, however, to the vast horizontal ramp of stone that fills the whole east side of the square, the first level of the great **Acropolis**. In its day it would have been brightly coloured, but today is a mute grey mass of awesome slab-like wall and sweeping banks of steps. At the top of the first steep stairway you climb up on to a whole new plaza, big enough to contain another ball court, more pyramids and temples. Since the whole structure was built on one of the tallest ridges in the area, the views from the final pyramid are immense. On the front of **Structure 17**, near the upper ball court, there is a carving of a decapitated captive, very like some at Toniná. At the south end of the great platform is **Structure 7**, which Blom believed was the original location of a stela found at the site (now in the Tuxtla museum) with the date 790.

At the southern end of the Acropolis there is a small wooden cross. This is visited by processions in local *fiestas* for the day of the Holy Cross (3 May) and the Feast of the Assumption (15 Aug).

Chinkultic

Chinkultic
Officially open daily 8–5; adm.

Chinkultic is better known than Tenam Puente, as the original location of a celebrated carved ball court marker now in the National Museum in Mexico City. However, in 2008 a conflict arose between the INAH and Chiapas state and a local village *ejido* (not a

Zapatista community), who demanded some income from the site and closed off the entry road. This stand-off reached an entirely new level of bitterness when state police tried to break the blockade, shooting broke out, and several villagers were killed. This dispute has since dragged on for months and (contrary to claims by the state authorities) the site has stayed closed. A settlement could be reached at any time, but before trying to visit it's best to enquire at the Museo Arqueológico in Comitán on the current situation.

Chinkultic has fine carvings (many now in museums), but much about the site, in an area once considered remote within Maya culture, remains to be discovered. It was occupied for a long time – the ballcourt marker is dated 21 May 591 – but like Tenam Puente it seems to have developed most after 700, and most of its inscriptions are later (810, 844). In the 9th century its lords still erected monuments when lowland cities had given up doing so, suggesting this could have been one of the 'last redoubts' of Classic Maya culture. It was still occupied into the Postclassic, after 1200.

The site has no very impressive buildings, but is another with an astonishing location. It is divided between three principal groups. From the entrance a walk of about 300m takes you through meadows and forest and across a stream. As you descend a dip, ahead and above you see the group of pyramids known as **El Mirador**, high up on a lofty crag. Only when you're almost at the foot of the temples do you realize just how extraordinary their location is, since the pyramids stand on a neck of rock between two lakes, with almost sheer drops on either side. As a melodramatic, near-unreal setting for a sacred space it could hardly be bettered.

Near the entrance are two more excavated areas, **Group B**, with two platforms forming a plaza, and the **Ball Court Group** or **Group C**, with several exceptional stelae.

ⓘ **Comitán**
Palacio Municipal, Plaza Central (open Mon–Sat 9–1 and 5–8).

Services in Comitán
t (963–)

Viajes Tenam, Pasaje Morales 8-A, t 632 1654. Tours by reservation to Tenam Puente, Chinkultic, Montebello and Lagos de Colón. In the passageway alongside the town hall.
Banks: Several on the plaza or Av. 1 Oriente Sur.
Guatemalan Consulate: C. 1 Sur Poniente 26, corner of Av. 2 Poniente Sur, t 632 0491 (*open Mon–Fri 8–4.30*).
Internet Access: In Pasaje Morales, near Viajes Tenam, there are two cheap Internet cafés.

Post Office: Av. Central Sur between C. 2 Sur and C. 3 Sur (*open Mon–Fri 8–7, Sat 9–1*).

Where to Stay in Comitán
Hotel Hacienda de los Angeles, C. 2 Norte Poniente 6, t 632 0074, *www.hotelhaciendalosangeles.com.mx* (*moderate*). The plush option, in an old house recently rebuilt top to bottom to house spacious rooms with rather bland traditional décor but superior services (WiFi, big TVs, a small pool, comfortable **restaurant**). Service is attentive.

Posada el Castellano, C. 3 Norte Poniente 12, t 632 3347, *www.posada elcastellano.com.mx* (*inexpensive*). Pleasant hotel in an old house a few blocks from the plaza: rooms are dark, but they open onto a pretty patio, there's a café, and WiFi included. Prices only just above the *budget* band.

Eating Out in Comitán

Comitán's central plaza is very much the hub of local life and has a choice of restaurants around it, so it's rarely necessary to walk far. The restaurant in **Hotel Hacienda los Angeles** (*see* above) has a bit more refined cuisine.

Helen's Enrique, Av. Central Dr B. Domínguez, Plaza Central (*moderate*). Very enjoyable café-restaurant with terrace tables on the west side of the plaza.

Café Quiptic, Av. 1 Oriente, Plaza Central (*budget*). Charming café showcasing local organic coffee, in a great location in the porches of the Casa de Cultura. Also has great sandwiches and traditional snacks.

The Montebello Lakes

⭐ **Lagunas de Montebello National Park**

There are around 60 lakes in **Lagunas de Montebello National Park**, from large to tiny. At weekends and holidays families from Tuxtla or Comitán come to picnic and admire the views, but with so many lakes you can always find a spot to yourself. The landscape appears exaggerated for extra effect, as roads wind past precipitous slopes through pine forest and jungle, with the fabulous colours of the lakes always in sight.

Just inside the park a road turns off left, to the north, for 7km to **Bosque Azul**. This big lake is the busiest, on every tour itinerary, but not the most attractive. There is an unexciting restaurant, picnic tables, and a **campsite**, and rowing boats to rent.

On the main road, the first lake is **Laguna de Montebello** itself, after 3km. This is another large one, edged by a 'beach' area with picnic *palapas* and, usually, some local cowboys offering horseback rides. Another 3km east is the turn for the **Cinco Lagunas**, the 'Five Lakes', which meet through an astonishing landscape of forest ravines. There are well-built paths down to the water at most of them, and nearly always somebody offering to take you around the lakes on log rafts, a traditional form of transport here (*about $14 per raft, max. six on a raft*). Next is **Lago Pojoj**, 60m deep, in multiple shades of blue and easy for swimming. Again, 'rafters' are usually

Visiting Montebello

At the park gate there's an official entry charge of around $1.50 (20 pesos) per vehicle. There are also local men around offering to act as guides, but it's easy to find your way on your own. At various times there have been reports of robberies around the lakes, and to stop this the main lakes are usually watched over by state police and 'wardens' sent by the local *ejido* in Tziscao, which runs its own community development scheme. At the main lakes along Highway 307 (not Bosque Azul) and at the entrance to Tziscao village there will also be someone to levy the *ejido's* own charge of 5 pesos per person, which goes to the community and lake conservation. Once you have your ticket for the day, this is valid for all the other lakes in the *ejido*, you only have to hold it up at each entry point.

At the bigger lakes there are also people selling handicrafts and the community's own-grown coffee (a great bargain). And for more information, Tziscao has even set up a community website, *www.tziscao.com*.

Getting to and around Montebello

The road to the lakes is the southern end of Highway 307, the *Carretera Fronteriza* around the Guatemalan border from Palenque (*see* p.437). It is well-signposted east from Highway 190 about 16km south of Comitán, just north of La Trinitaria. This road leads straight across flat countryside in about 39km to the entry gate to **Lagunas de Montebello National Park**, 3km beyond the turn to Chinkultic ruins.

Línea Comitán-Montebello, t 632 0875, has frequent *combis* to the Lakes, 5.30am–5pm daily (last return from the lakes 5.30pm). Their garage is on Av. 2 Poniente Sur in Comitán, by C. 2 Sur three blocks from the plaza.

waiting to take passing travellers around. Pojoj has an island in the middle, and if you want to have a desert island for the day you can arrange to be taken across to it and then picked up later.

From there it's 5km to the only village in the lakes, **Tziscao**, on **Laguna Tziscao**. It's an untidy, amiable little place, with basic hotels and a little waterside community *parque*, with a restaurant and kayaks to rent. The lake – the south shore of which is in Guatemala – is wide and shallow, and turquoise rather than blue. Not far beyond Tziscao is a turn to **Dos Lagunas**, the last accessible lakes on this road. Beyond there, the *Fronteriza* road continues on towards Las Nubes and Lacanjá (*see* pp.470 and 455).

Where to Stay and Eat

Montebello Lakes t (963–)

Places to stay in this area cover the opposite ends of the scale. Most are on or near the road in from Trinitaria, just west of the national park entrance, or near the lake in Tziscao.

Off the Montebello Road

Parador-Museo Santa María, off the Montebello road 22km east of Trinitaria, t 632 5116, *www.parador santamaria.com.mx* (*expensive*). Strange to report, this remote part of Chiapas contains one of the most characterfully baronial hotels in Mexico. It's an 1830s *hacienda*, restored by antiquarian Mario Uvence and his brother, and filled with antiques, paintings and even a museum of Baroque religious art, in the former chapel. It would be ideal for a Zorro movie: each bedroom has different period furnishings, while facilities such as bathrooms are modern (with some quirks). The estate is pretty isolated, but horse riding and many other excursions can be arranged. As a concession to modernity a seductive

pool has been added; there's also a garden, a great bar-lounge and a lovely **restaurant** with home-baked bread. Sr. Uvence also owns Parador San Juan de Dios in San Cristóbal (*see* p.496)

Tziscao

To find the lake and the places to stay, follow the road through the village round to the left, and signs for the *Parque Ejidal*.

Hotel Tziscao, by the lake in Tziscao, t 633 5244, *htziscao@gmail.com* (*inexpensive*). Simple *cabañas* with showers, in a lovely location amid pines by the lake. Some cabins even have neat little terraces. The ladies who run it are sweet, and the **restaurant** offers cheap local classics (and cold beer). There are boats to rent on the lake. It fills up at Easter and in Mexican holidays, but prices may fall at other times.

Restaurante-Cabañas Playa Escondida, by the lake in Tziscao, t 634 9238 (*budget*). Near the hotel, with basic but decent two-bed cabins with showers, or very cheap ones with shared facilities. There's also a plain little lakeside-cabin *lonchería*.

Lagos de Colón and Lagartero

Further down Highway 190, south of Montebello and beyond La Trinitaria, a turning east leads in 10km to **Lagos de Colón**, a village spread along the series of beautiful lakes and rapids in the San Juan river that gives it its name. There are simple restaurants, and boats for hire. A fabulous walk from the village leads across rapids, rickety bridges, forest and maize fields to **Lagartero** (open access), a very old, Early Classic Maya site, with a few excavated pyramids.

Tuxtla Gutiérrez

Tuxtla Gutiérrez is only a big warehouse which stores products from other parts of the state.

Subcomandante Marcos

The Subcomandante wouldn't really be expected to think much of Tuxtla Gutiérrez, the largest city (population over 500,000) and seat of power and wealth in modern Chiapas. True to say, the state capital doesn't have many other fans either. Many Mexican cities seem forever marked by a particular time: Mérida has a permanent air of the 18th century; San Cristóbal is set in the 1560s; in Cancún it will always be the 1990s. In Tuxtla's case the period is one of Mexico's earlier booms, under Presidents Ruíz Cortines and López Mateos from the 1950s into the 1960s. Parts of central Tuxtla look like a showcase of angular 1950s high-rises, now revealing their age.

If you travel from San Cristóbal to Tuxtla you descend more than 1,400m over 80km. Tuxtla Gutiérrez sits in a wide, brown, hilly plain, at the foot of an immense wall of rock to the north cut through by the great gash of the Sumidero. Although the Central Valley of Chiapas is still part of the Highlands, its climate has a dry, Mediterranean heat rather than the chill of the real mountains.

Chiapas' authorities are always encouraging people to spend time in Tuxtla. It's an important transport hub, especially for people coming into the Mayan region from central Mexico, and many travellers find themselves staying a night. It has intriguing restaurants. Unless you have contacts here, though, its attractions are really three: its proximity to the old colonial town of Chiapa de Corzo and the Sumidero gorge; a fine museum, with artefacts from all over the state; and a remarkable zoo, the ZOOMAT.

History

Before the Conquest the Central Valley was inhabited by the Zoque and a now-extinct Nahua-speaking people called the Chiapa. Not much trace of them remains today. The main centre of Spanish settlement in the area was initially Chiapa de Corzo, then known as Chiapa de la Real Corona. At the time of independence San Marcos Tuxtla, founded around a Dominican

Teatro de la Ciudad

Museo Regional de Chiapas

CALZADA DE HOMBRES ILLUSTRES

Jardín Botánico

Parque Madero

C. 6 ORIENTE NORTE
C. 5 ORIENTE NORTE
C. 4 ORIENTE NORTE
C. 3 ORIENTE NORTE
C. 2 ORIENTE NORTE
C. 1 ORIENTE NORTE
CALLE CENTRAL NORTE
C. 1 PONIENTE NORTE
C. 2 PONIENTE NORTE

AV. 5 NORTE ORIENTE
AV. 4 NORTE ORIENTE
AV. 3 NORTE ORIENTE
AV. 2 NORTE ORIENTE
AV. 1 NORTE ORIENTE
AVENIDA CENTRAL OTE

C. 12 ORIENTE NORTE
C. 11 ORIENTE NORTE
C. 10 ORIENTE NORTE
C. 9 ORIENTE NORTE
BOULEVARD ANGEL A. CORZO

Las Pichanchas

María Eugenia

La Catedral

San Antonio

AV. 2 SUR ORIENTE
AV. 3 SUR ORIENTE
AV. 4 SUR ORIENTE
AV. 5 SUR ORIENTE

C. 7 ORIENTE SUR
C. 4 ORIENTE SUR
C. 3 ORIENTE SUR
C. 2 ORIENTE SUR
C. 1 ORIENTE SUR

Torre del Centro

Casablanca

Post Office

Palacio de Gobierno

Ayuntamiento

Las Canteras

PLAZA CÍVICA

Cathedral

La Casona

Museo de la Ciudad

AVENIDA CENTRAL PTE

CALLE CENTRAL SUR

Buses to Chiapa de Corzo

Buses to Zoomat

C. 3 PONIENTE SUR
C. 4 PONIENTE SUR
C. 5 PONIENTE SUR

AV. 1 SUR PONIENTE
AV. 2 SUR PONIENTE
AV. 3 SUR PONIENTE

Naturalísimo

BELISARIO DOMINGUEZ

C. 5 PONIENTE NORTE
C. 6 PONIENTE NORTE
C. 7 PONIENTE NORTE
C. 8 PONIENTE NORTE
C. 9 PONIENTE NORTE

AV. 5 NORTE PONIENTE

To 1st-class Bus Station

Real Avenida

Museo de la Marimba

Parque de la Marimba

Tourist Office

BOULEVARD DR CARLOS

Café San Carlos

To 2nd-class Bus Station

200 metres
200 yards

N

monastery (long demolished), was less important than San Cristóbal or Comitán. However, the Central Valley was becoming richer, producing cotton, maize, horses and cattle, which were traded with Mexico.

What politics there were in Chiapas were dominated by the fading aristocracy of Ciudad Real, San Cristóbal. When they decided to join Mexico in 1821, the ranchers and traders of the Valley rose against them, not so much because they preferred to stay with Guatemala but because they wanted their opinions to be heard. They were led by Joaquín Miguel Gutiérrez, who allied himself with the 'Federalists' in Mexico's endless civil conflicts and by a combination of war and politics firmly established a powerful role for Tuxtla within Chiapas. He was assassinated in 1838, but so revered was he in his home town that his name was attached to it, in 1849.

His role as leader of the Central Valley was taken up by Angel Albino Corzo, chief supporter of Juárez in Chiapas, who was also victorious over the conservatives and *Maximilianistas* of San Cristóbal. The Valley's growth in influence was formalized in 1892, when Tuxtla became the state capital in place of San Cristóbal.

The City Centre

In Mexican style the main square, the **Plaza Cívica**, is the hub of activity in Tuxtla. On one side is the **Palacio de Gobierno**, the state government, while on another is the **Ayuntamiento**. To the south across Av. Central, is the **Cathedral of San Marcos**, begun in the 16th century but rebuilt in the 1900s and only dedicated in 1982. The Plaza is a modern business-like space. The outdoor restaurants by the cathedral are a popular meeting place, while Av. Central is full of animation after dark, for Tuxtla has plenty of nightlife.

In the streets around the Plaza Cívica there are hotels and restaurants. A few blocks southeast, down Calles 4 or 5 Oriente Sur, is the huge **market**. West of the plaza along Av. Central, at the corner of Calle 2 Poniente Norte is the former Government Palace, built in the 1940s in a 'Mexican Revolutionary' style with diamond-pattern walls almost in imitation of Maya weaving, which now

Museo de la Ciudad
Open Mon–Fri 9am–8pm

houses the **Museo de la Ciudad**, with a mix of photos and artefacts donated by local citizens. Another six blocks west up Av. Central there is a prettier square than the plaza, **Parque de la Marimba**. The marimba is almost a symbol of identity for Chiapanecos, and the best *marimbas* in the state perform here for free, most evenings at around 8pm. On one side of the square, behind the tourist office,

Museo de la Marimba
Open Tues–Sun 10am–8pm; adm

there is now also a **Museo de la Marimba**, which tells you everything possible about marimbas and their history. Elderly exponents of the marimba often give recitals, and foreigners who show an interest are charmingly given a front seat.

Getting to and around Tuxtla Gutiérrez

By Air

Tuxtla's **Aeropuerto Angel Albino Corzo** has frequent flight connections with Mexico City, and offers the most convenient air route to San Cristóbal. **MexicanaClick (t** 01 800 112 5425), **Aviacsa (t** 01 800 284 2272) and **Interjet (t** 01 800 011 2345) provide most services.

The airport is 35km from the city near Chiapa de Corzo (and so only 50km from San Cristóbal). Driving to or from the airport can easily take 1hr, depending on traffic, so take this into account. An infrequent OCC **bus** runs *from* Tuxtla bus station *to* the airport (9am, 3pm, $6) but not in the opposite direction. A taxi to the airport should cost around $10. For arriving passengers *Transporte Terrestre* **airport taxis** are the way into town (about $14). Tuxtla airport taxi drivers are also very happy to take you to San Cristóbal ($30–40).

By Bus

Tuxtla Gutiérrez also has a gleaming new **first-class bus station**, used by OCC, ADO and other large companies (and often referred to as the OCC, Cristóbal Colón or ADO). It is part of a giant retail park, **Plaza del Sol**, on the west side of the city. **Taxis** are the only means of getting from there to the centre (about $2).

Tickets for all first-class buses can be bought at a **Ticketbus** outlet in the city centre at the corner of Av. 2 Norte Poniente and C. 2 Poniente Norte (*closed Sun*).

TRF, with *intermedio* and **second-class** routes around Chiapas, is on C. 4 Poniente Sur, corner of Av. 9 Sur Poniente. Other bus garages near junction of Av. 3 Sur Oriente and C. 7 Oriente Sur, and *combis* to San Cristóbal leave from here. Buses to **Chiapa de Corzo** go from the Av. 1 Sur Oriente near C. 5 Oriente Sur.

Main services from the OCC are:

Cancún (*19½hrs*): via **San Cristóbal**, **Palenque**, **Escárcega**, **Chetumal**, **Tulum** and **Playa del Carmen**, two OCC ordinary first-class, one ADO GL daily, two ADO GL via **Villahermosa** (*17–18 hrs*). Fares about $52–64.

Mérida (*14hrs*): via **San Cristóbal**, **Palenque**, **Escárcega** and **Campeche**, one OCC ordinary first-class, two ADO GL daily. Fares $39–54.

Mexico City (*12hrs*): seven ordinary first-class and five luxury buses daily. Fares $57–84.

Palenque (*6–7hrs*): via **San Cristóbal**, seven ordinary first-class (which stop at **Ocosingo**) and one ADO GL daily. Fares $11–14.

San Cristóbal (*1¼hrs*): one or more first-class each hour, 2.50am–11.55pm, including seven luxury. Fare $3–6. Some go on to **Comitán**.

Tapachula (*6–7½hrs*): via **Tonalá**, ordinary first-class hourly, and nine faster luxury services daily. Fares $18–21.

Villahermosa (*4–5hrs*): via **Cárdenas**, at least five first-class and two luxury buses daily, one daily via **Teapa** (*7hrs*). Fares around $16.

City *combis*

Little *combis* also provide sprawling Tuxtla's main local transport, so central streets are often snarled up with all-*combi* jams. *Combis* have route numbers, and some are particularly useful to visitors. Numbers ending in 1 or 01 run up and down Av. Central; routes ending in 7, 47, 49 or 72 go by the museum. *Combis* to the ZOOMAT leave from C. 1 Oriente Sur, by the corner of Av. 7 Sur Oriente. They normally have the number 60 and are marked 'Cerro Hueco'.

By Car and Taxi

Parking space is scarce in the centre. A **taxi** anywhere in the city should cost $1–2, and they are easy to find.

Car Hire

Tuxtla has several agencies, most on Blvd Belisario Domínguez, but renting here is relatively expensive. **AFA**, Hotel María Eugenia, Av. Central Oriente 507, t 611 3175, *www.afarental.com*. **Excellent**, Blvd Dr Belisario Domínguez 3470, t 671 6906, *www.excellent.com.mx*.

Orientation

Tuxtla Gutiérrez is a sprawling city, but most mid- or budget-range hotels are in the central area. It also has an archetype of the Chiapas street-numbering system. The city is a widely-spread grid. Streets going roughly east–west are Avenidas, north–south ones are Calles. At its centre is the **Plaza Cívica** (Zócalo), meeting point of Calle Central and Avenida Central, the spine that runs right through the city, also called at different points Blvd Dr Belisario Domínguez or Blvd Angel Albino Corzo. *Avenidas* north of Central are Av. 1 Norte, Av. 2 Norte and counting; to the south they are Av. 1 Sur, Av. 2 Sur, etc. *Calles* west of C. Central are C. 1 Poniente, 2 Poniente; to the east they are C. 1 Oriente, 2 Oriente. Each has a further 'locator', so that top left of the map you find Av. 2 Norte Poniente (Av. 2 North West), and bottom right C. 3 Oriente Sur (C. 3 East South).

Parque Madero and the Museum

From Plaza Cívica a longish walk or a *combi* ride will take you to **Parque Madero**, a formal but green park northeast of the centre. Through it runs a walkway, the **Calzada de Hombres Ilustres** ('Pathway of Illustrious Men'), lined with statues of Mexican Revolutionary heroes and cultural institutions, including a **Jardín Botánico** with examples of Chiapas' exotic plants, and Tuxtla's white elephant public theatre, the **Teatro de la Ciudad**. The prime attraction is the finely renovated **Museo Regional de Chiapas**. It covers the whole history of human occupation in Chiapas from distant prehistory, and is now well labelled (often with English translations). Preclassic exhibits begin with Olmec-influenced reliefs, and there are several items from Izapa, such as *El Danzante* ('The Dancer'), a stone jaguar-man from before 300 BC; there is also the stone with the very oldest date known in the Long Count calendar, from 9 December 36 BC, discovered, for reasons still not understood, in non-Maya Chiapa de Corzo. From the Classic era there are superb alabaster bowls, dramatic stelae, a beautifully modelled ceramic figure of a man sitting deep in thought and, on a different scale, the panel from Toniná showing the hapless Kan-Hok-Chitam II of Palenque in captivity. Another section, the *Sala de Historia*, deals with post-Conquest history, with fine relics of colonial Baroque.

Jardín Botánico
open Tues–Sun 9–6; adm

Museo Regional de Chiapas
open Tues–Sun 9–6; adm

The ZOOMAT

It never sounds good to say of a town that the best thing in it is the zoo, but Tuxtla's is something special. Its location is a delight in itself, on top of a forested hill south of the city, which catches a permanent refreshing breeze. Its full title is Zoológico Miguel Alvarez del Toro, after the pioneer ecologist and naturalist of Chiapas who founded it before his death in 1966. The extraordinary thing about the park he created is that every one of the several hundred animals, birds and reptiles inside is native to Chiapas.

The range is astonishing. Here you can see with ease all the most famous but elusive creatures of the region – jaguars, tapirs, exquisitely coloured quetzals – and many that are more obscure, like the yellow-necked toucan. It would of course be better to see them in the wild, but since that is unlikely this is the next best thing. There is every kind of forest cat, from pumas to *leoncillos*, crocodiles, anteaters, giant spiders and a special building housing normally invisible nocturnal creatures. Several animals that are no danger to anyone are allowed to run free, so that as you walk along you may spot, scurrying past you, creatures like the strange rodent-pigs called *guaqueques*, and peccaries. Even people blasé about zoos find this place a discovery.

The ZOOMAT
open Tues–Sun Sept–April 8.30–4, May–Aug 8.30–5; adm.

Tourist Information in Tuxtla Gutiérrez

ⓘ Tuxtla City
Tourist Office:
*Av. Central Poniente,
corner of Parque de la
Marimba (open daily
9–2, 4–8). Friendly,
helpful and with a good
stock of leaflets. Behind
it in the Museo de la
Marimba tickets are
sold for Circuito Tuxtla
city bus tours, which
run from the square.*

ⓘ Chiapas State
Tourist Office:
*Blvd Dr Belisario
Domínguez 950 (open
Mon–Fri 8–4). Also
helpful, but
inconveniently located
in official buildings at
the west end of
Av. Central.*

t (961–)

Tours

Tuxtla's limited tourist flow does not breed agencies in force, but those listed offer tours to the Sumidero, the ZOOMAT, San Cristóbal, Comitán, Montebello and Palenque. From Tuxtla the Sumidero is easy to get to.

Viajes Kali, Hotel María Eugenia, Av. Central Oriente 507, **t** 611 3175, *www.viajeskali.com.mx.*

Services in Tuxtla Gutiérrez

Banks: Several on the Plaza Cívica or nearby along Av. Central, with ATMs.

Health: Several large **pharmacies** on Av. Central, open 24hrs

Internet Access: Many very near the Plaza in Av. 2 Norte Oriente.

Post Office: Palacio Federal, plaza (*open Mon–Sat 9–6*). Has **Mexpost**.

Shopping

Instituto de Artesanías, Blvd Belisario Domínguez 2033, **t** 614 1833. This state-run centre combines a shop with high-quality craftwork from all over Chiapas, a bookshop and small museum (labelled in English).

Where to Stay in Tuxtla Gutiérrez

Moderate

Best Western Palmareca, Blvd. Dr Belisario Domínguez 4120-2, **t** 617 0000, *www.palmareca.com*. Well-equipped hotel with spacious rooms and suites, a pretty terrace **restaurant**, a pool in a sheltered garden and WiFi, a gym and other extras. It's on the Boulevard, some distance from the centre.

Hotel María Eugenia, Av. Central Oriente 507, corner of C. 4 Oriente Norte, **t** 613 3767, *www.mariaeugenia. com.mx*. The most comfortable option in the centre, with pleasant, functional rooms with good WiFi and other services, and an airy **restaurant**; also one of few central hotels with a pool.

Inexpensive

Hotel Casablanca, Av. 2 Norte Oriente 251, just off the Plaza Cívica, **t** 611 0305. Best of a bunch of low-cost hotels just east of the plaza: all tend to be noisy, but the location is useful. Rooms here are bright and have a touch of colour; prices are low, and fan-only rooms are *budget* level. Also (intermittent) WiFi.

Hotel Real Avenida, Av. Central Poniente 1230, by C. 11 Poniente Norte, **t** 612 2347, *www.realavenida.com.mx*. A modern hotel that's not as elegant as it thinks, but rooms have all the essentials, and are good value. There's free parking, and WiFi in the lobby.

Budget

Hotel Plaza Chiapas, Av. 2 Norte Oriente 299, **t** 613 8365. Noisy, but with simple rooms with good bathrooms.

Torre del Centro, C. 1 Oriente Norte 310, **t** 612 2755. A 1960s tower-block hotel, with rooms with decent a/c, TV and bathrooms, and the advantage of a view from the upper floors.

Eating Out

Expensive

Las Pichanchas, Av. Central Oriente 837, corner of C. 8 Oriente, **t** 612 5351, *www.laspichanchas.com.mx*. Showcasing the food and traditions of (non-Maya) Chiapas, this is a local landmark. Dinner comes with a floor show, a reproduction of the dance of the *Parachicos* from Chiapa de Corzo (*see* p.518). It's all a bit kitsch, but performed with great exuberance. The food is excellent, featuring local specialities such as *tasajo* (dry-cured beef) and *tamales* with *chipilín* (a spinach-like vegetable). Service is friendly and a feast here won't cost much over $20. There's also a branch at **Mirador Copoya** south of the city, with a panoramic view.

Moderate

There are several good outdoor eating options in the arcade beside the cathedral on the Plaza Cívica, with a view of the square. The thing to do is just walk along and pick one.

Las Canteras, Av. 2 Norte Poniente, near C. 1 Poniente Norte. Pretty restaurant serving local specialities.

La Casona>

La Casona, Av. 1 Sur Poniente 134, a block from the plaza. Pretty restaurant in a 19th-century house. The menu consists of both tasty Chiapanecan specialities – *tamales*, *tasajo* – and Mexican favourites. Charming service.

Naturalísimo – Nah-Yaxal, C. 6 Poniente Norte 124, off Av. Central Oriente, and Av. Central Oriente 523, by C. 4 Oriente Norte. Two central branches of a local chain of bright vegetarian cafés and health-food shops.

Budget

Jugos Chapala, Av. Central Oriente, by C. 2 Oriente Norte. One of a local chain of juice stands offering every kind of fabulously fresh juices, *aguas*, *licuados* and more. Several more on Av. Central.

Mesón del Quijote, Av. Central Oriente, between C. 2 and 3 Oriente Norte. Perhaps Tuxtla's star budget choice, with ultra-cheap set menus.

Around Tuxtla

Fifteen kilometres east of Tuxtla is the oldest Spanish settlement in Chiapas, **Chiapa de Corzo**. It has the attractive features that Tuxtla lacks: a charming central square, quiet streets, fine colonial architecture and a riverside location beside the Grijalva. The town and adjacent village of **Cahuaré** are the departure points for boat trips into the **Sumidero Canyon**, a dramatic gash in the landscape that extends north for 20km.

Chiapa de Corzo

Buses from Tuxtla bring you to the **Parque Central**, a wide colonial plaza with colonnades down two sides, restaurants and shops. On the side towards the river is a magnificent *ceiba* tree, which grew from a branch of one even larger, *La Pochota*, destroyed by fire in 1945. At the foot of this tree on 1 March 1528 Diego de Mazariegos founded *Villa Real de Chiapa*, as the first Spanish town in the region. He had just vanquished the Chiapa, whose capital was nearby. A mixture of legend and historical accounts states that their warriors threw themselves into the Sumidero rather than accept defeat, and they only survive in the name of the state and the town. In 1863 it saw a battle between Maximilian's army and the Juaristas, led by Angel Albino Corzo, the town's most famous son, and in his honour it was given its present name in 1888.

Next to the *ceiba* and dominating the view is Chiapa's most remarkable monument, the great brick **Pila** or well. It looks like

Festivals

Chiapa de Corzo is known for its spectacular *fiestas*, especially those that go on for a week around **San Sebastián** (20 Jan). The central figures are the *chuntas*, men dressed extravagantly as women – the town council awards a prize for the most impressive drag outfit – and *parachicos*, men in bizarre outfits of embroidered capes, *sarapes* and lacquered masks with white faces and staring blue eyes. Thought to represent the Spanish conquerors, they began as a way for lower-class *mestizos* to satirize them. The women meanwhile, dress up in dazzling flowered dresses in black, blue, red and gold. *Chuntas* and *parachicos* act as lords of misrule, dancing around the town, and the whole *fiesta* climaxes with a 'battle' of boats on the river. The *parachicos* also emerge at other *fiestas* (4 Aug, 17 Sept).

Getting to and around Chiapa de Corzo

Buses to Chiapa de Corzo, via Cahuaré, leave from Av. 1 Sur Oriente, near the corner of C. 5 Oriente Sur, in Tuxtla, roughly every 10mins 5am–10pm daily (return times can vary, so check). Buses stop frequently, so the journey takes 25–40mins; second-class buses between Tuxtla and San Cristóbal stop in Chiapa, and are faster.

something from the European Middle Ages, because it is: the finest example of Spanish *mudéjar* or Hispano-Moorish architecture in the Americas. Begun in 1562, it is actually a giant canopy over a well-head, with an inner gallery that's a deliciously shady spot in which to sit around the central pool.

Filling one side of the square is the town's other great colonial monument, the church and former monastery of **Santo Domingo**, built by the Dominicans' architect Friar Pedro Barrientos in the late 16th century. The church is huge, but made painted white and pinkish red. Walk around it to the left from the square and you come to the lovely **cloister**, which still has much of its delicate Renaiss-

Centro Cultural ex-Convento de Santo Domingo
open Tues–Sun 10–5

ance paintwork on ceilings and arches. Now the **Centro Cultural ex-Convento de Santo Domingo**, as well as tempor-ary exhibition spaces it has two permanent exhibits, one on the powerful work of local artist and engraver Franco Lázaro Gómez, who drowned aged 27 near Lacanjá in 1949, and the other the **Museo de la Laca**, devoted to the main craft of the women of Chiapa de Corzo, lacquerwork.

From one end of the church you can walk down to the landing stage by the river, with its line of restaurants. Nearby drinks-stands sell two Chiapan specialities: *pozol* is a mix of unfermented maize liquor and cacao, usually drunk from gourds; *tascalate* (better for the uninitiated) is a powder of ground maize, cinnamon, cacao, sugar and *achiote* pepper, beaten into water or milk.

From one side of the plaza Av. Julian Grajales leads up a steep crest to the colonial church of the **Calvario**, and Av. Miguel Hidalgo, which leads to the **Archaeological Zone** of Chiapa de Corzo, a Zoque site now under excavation and so closed to visitors

Where to Stay and Eat in Chiapa de Corzo

t (961–)

Chiapa de Corzo has an unusually good choice of pretty restaurants, which take full advantage of the town's colonnade-and-patio architecture. There are rows of terrace restaurants at the *embarcaderos* in Cahuaré and Chiapa (*moderate–budget*). The food is nothing special, but the riverside location exceptional.

 Hotel La Ceiba>

Hotel La Ceiba, Av. Domingo Ruíz 300. t 616 0389, *www.laceibahotel.com*

(*inexpensive*). A very attractive hotel, a few minutes walk north of the plaza. Rooms, in a converted old house, are decorated with local textiles and surround a lovely leafy patio with a pool. The similarly pretty **restaurant** (*moderate*) has enjoyable local dishes.

Los Corredores, Av. Francisco Madero 35 (*moderate*). A deliciously shady patio with bargain Chiapanecan specialities.

Jardines de Chiapa, Av. Francisco Madero (*moderate*). Another exquisite patio near the river and the square, this is just a little more expensive, and as such has rather superior local dishes.

13
Chiapas | Around Tuxtla

Getting to the Sumidero

Boats into the Sumidero leave from *embarcaderos* below the monastery in Chiapa de Corzo and in **Cahuaré**, beneath the bridge that takes the main road across the river. The various boatmen's co-operatives are now well organized: at each *embarcadero* there are desks where you can buy tickets to the *Parque Ecoturístico* ($20 adults, $15 children; park entry included) or for the more traditional *lanchero* trip into the gorge (about $11). Ticket desks are open daily 8am–4.30pm. At both *embarcaderos* there are attractive bars and restaurants.

The boats operate year-round, but at slack times you may have to wait for a boat to get a minimum load – which usually means at least eight people. Many *lancheros* also prefer to run passengers to the *Parque Ecoturístico* rather than continue on the full-tour route up the gorge. However, they'd rather have some work than none, and so even on quiet weekdays you rarely have to wait more than an hour. During weekends and holidays, boats run up and down continuously. The full Sumidero boat tour takes 2–2½hrs.

Independently, you can also get fine views over the canyon from the road that runs along the west of the gorge from Tuxtla's *periférico*. *Combis* go from second-class bus stations in Tuxtla, especially at weekends. All **tour agencies** in Tuxtla and San Cristóbal run trips here, sometimes including *Parque Ecológico* tickets.

The Cañón del Sumidero

Parque Ecoturístico Cañón del Sumidero
*www.sumidero.com;
open daily 9.30–dusk;
adm*

The Sumidero is an awesome rift in the world's surface, a seismic fault between one and two km wide, 20km long and with walls over 1,000m high. The Grijalva runs through the middle of it, but it did not create it. The river used to consist of some of the most dangerous rapids in the world, but in the 1980s the Chicoasén dam was built at the north end of the canyon, transforming it into a massive reservoir, thus making the current boat trips possible (*see* above).

To go into the Sumidero is to be swallowed up by it, as cliffs, crags and forested ledges rise up on either side. The gorge is lined by mangrove-like vegetation, and walls of rock. The canyon is full of wildlife; even crocodiles are quite plentiful. Waterfalls run down the cliffs, and favourite stops are the weird rock formations left over centuries, such as the **Arbol de Navidad**, which looks just like a Christmas tree, but is made up of layers of calcified rock.

The popularity of the Sumidero has been overexploited, although recently more is being done to preserve the cleanliness, and natural life, of the river. In a large area on the east bank of the gorge is the **Parque Ecoturístico Cañón del Sumidero**, an 'ecopark' created by the same organization that runs Xcaret on the Riviera Maya. Within it there is naturally lots to do: a forest walk, mountain-biking, rock climbing, 'enhanced' natural pools to swim in, restaurants, if all presented in the domesticated neat-and-tidy, nature theme-park style that will be familiar to anyone who has visited one of the group's other parks. If you have a car you can get another angle on the gorge, from above. A road runs from the Tuxtla *periférico* along the west side of the canyon, past *mirador* viewpoints with fabulous vistas. There is a restaurant at the end of the road.

El Triunfo Biosphere Reserve

Tuxtla Gutiérrez is also the main starting point for getting to the Biosphere Reserve of El Triunfo, 200km south in the highest ridges of the Sierra Madre, perhaps the most important of all Mexico's

Getting to El Triunfo

The main entry track runs from **Jaltenango**, 150km (by dirt road) south of Tuxtla, from where it's another 40km by dirt track to **Campamento El Triunfo**, in the cloud forest. The track that enters the reserve from Mapastepec on the Pacific side is rarely used.

The Campamento is the only visitor facility authorized in the reserve, and has *cabañas* and serves as a base for treks. Tours are available of from 4–10 days, for groups of around 4–10 people. These are real adventure trips, involving hiking, climbing and camping in the forest. They can be booked through the Mesoamerican Tourism Alliance (*see* p.106) and several other nature travel agencies, or for more information contact: **Ecobiósfera El Triunfo**, C. San Cristóbal 8, Fracc. La Hacienda, Tuxtla Gutiérrez, **t** (961) 125 117, *www.ecobiosfera.org.mx*.

forest reserves. It extends over 120,000 square km of tropical mountain, kept uninhabited by utter remoteness. This is where Chiapas' most reclusive species are still found – quetzals, ocelots, guans – and 392 bird varieties have been logged within it. Authorized treks can be booked through specialist agencies.

Pacific Chiapas

Chiapas' Pacific rim is separated from the rest of the state by its highest, least inhabited mountains, the **Sierra Madre**. As a result, its history has often followed a different course from that of areas further north. The Olmecs came down here, and later the area became a place of transit for a great many influences. It was not really part of Maya civilization in the Classic era, and this was the only part of Mexico's southern states that was absorbed into the empire of the Aztecs, who came here drawn by the region's fine-quality cacao, and also passed through on their way to attack Guatemala; a few years later the Spaniards did the same thing.

Anyone who travels down from Tuxtla or San Cristóbal has a choice of routes. Most impressive is Highway 190 southeast from San Cristóbal. Beyond Montebello you climb over hot, dry hills, but the road becomes more leafy as the Pan-American Highway separates from the Mexican highway to turn towards **Ciudad Cuauhtémoc**, for the crossing into **Guatemala**. This is no one's idea of a city, not much more than a dusty street; *combis* and taxis take you across the border to La Mesilla, from where buses run into Guatemala (for border information, *see* p.529). Back in Mexico, after **Motozintla** the road begins a staggeringly steep ascent into the clouds until, almost at the Pacific, you cross the Continental Divide with a thump at over 2,500m. You immediately start to descend, more precipitously than you came up, as the road switchbacks around jungle valleys and through cloudforest.

Highway 190 in the other direction, southwest from Tuxtla, is less extreme, but still has enough hairpins and ascents to qualify as a mountain road in any other country. About 40km west of Tuxtla a turn north leads to dramatic waterfalls at **El Aguacero** and the

Getting to Puerto Arista and Boca del Cielo

To reach either you must first get to **Tonalá**. Finding the *combi* departure points involves a bit of a trek: from Tonalá OCC bus station, turn left along the main street, Av. Hidalgo, and walk 12 blocks to C. 20 de Marzo. Turn right, and Puerto Arista *combis* are two blocks down on Av. J.M. Gutiérrez, near the market. The *colectivo* corner for Boca del Cielo is down another turn off Hidalgo, closer to the bus station at C. 15 de Septiembre. **Taxis** are cheap, and run up and down to the coast frequently.

Getting to La Encrucijada

The main entry point is via a turn off Highway 200 at Escuintla, 62km west of Tapachula, for **Acapetahua**, from where a road runs 17km to the landing stage at **Embarcadero Las Garzas**, where boats can be hired to go round the lagoons or to a remote beach at **Barra de Zacapulco**, with *cabañas* (*budget*) and a restaurant. Some agencies in Tapachula also offer tours. Local *lancheros* can also take you to **Campamento La Concepción**, the only authorized camp (with cabins) inside the reserve. Permits and reservations are essential, or it can be visited with nature tours such as those of MEA (*see* p.106). For more information contact the reserve office, **t** (918) 647 0084, *encrucij@conanp.gob.mx.*

Second-class buses/*combis* run from Tapachula to Acapetahua, from where there are *combis* to Las Garzas.

To get to the southern beaches around **San José el Hueyate**, turn off Highway 200 on the road for Mazatán, 14km west of Tapachula; from there a dirt road leads another 27km to the coast. *Combis* run from Tapachula to Mazatán, and from there to San José.

At **Barra San José** there are *budget* cabins to rent and basic restaurants, as well as a vast empty beach. Trips to the mangroves can be arranged with local boatmen.

---

spectacular gorge of the **Río La Venta**, a national park where rafting trips are being started up (by **Explora**, *see* p.493). From **Cintalapa** you climb again, and 23km further south the road splits: Highway 190 leads west into Oaxaca; Highway 195 remains in Chiapas to twist through ravines and rocky gorges, until you descend to the busy road junction of **Arriaga**, and a Mediterranean-like coastal plain.

Puerto Arista and Boca del Cielo

Tonalá, 23km from Arriaga, is a hot market town, the mango capital of Chiapas. It was an Olmec settlement, and in the plaza there is an Aztec stela found nearby. It's also the access point to Chiapas's beach villages, Puerto Arista and Boca del Cielo.

Ideas of them as sophisticated beach resorts need to be done away with. When you arrive in **Puerto Arista** you find, along the one, straight street by the beach, some surprisingly solid hotels, basic shops, weekend houses and any number of typical Mexican beach restaurants beneath huge *palapa* roofs, which only ever seem to get any customers during the Christmas and Easter holidays. The beach is grey volcanic sand, which means that it gets fiercely hot, but for anyone looking for somewhere simple and peaceful to flop for a while, this can be ideal.

Boca del Cielo is even more basic, a shark-fishing village 15km east. It sits opposite a long sand spit that forms a lagoon; the name, 'Heaven's Gate', refers to the point where this meets the Pacific breakers, attracting flocks of birds. Fishermen will take you to the *estero*, the sand spit, and back. One for serious sun-worshippers.

Where to Stay and Eat in Puerto Arista

t (994–)

Hotels are spread along the beachside road. You're usually spoilt for choice for places to eat, at least until about 8pm, but if everywhere is closed the Hotel Lizeth will usually grill some fish. Seafood can be spectacularly good here, as can fruit.

There are currently no permanent places to stay in **Boca del Cielo**, but ask around and you can often find beachside *palapas* to rent. Near the beach there are a few simple restaurants with freshly-caught fish.

Arista Bugambilias, Puerto Arista, t 600 9044 (*inexpensive*). Smart-looking apartment-hotel. Apartments with space for four, kitchens, living room and TV. They're a few years old and some are a bit neglected, but they're right on the beach.

Hotel Lizeth, Puerto Arista, t 600 9038 (*budget*). A friendly hotel where the road from Tonalá meets the beach, with light rooms. Some are fan-only, some have a/c, and most have a sea view.

La Encrucijada Mangrove Reserve

Lining the Soconusco coast south of Highway 200, La Encrucijada surrounds a 70km lagoon with Mexico's tallest mangroves, **Estero Las Palmas**. It's rich in birds, deer, forest cats, and especially turtles and crocodiles. The usual way to get there is via **Acapetahua**, 62km from Tapachula, but it's also possible to enter from the south via **San José El Hueyate**, which has long, long beaches at **Barra San José**. Local *lancheros* run trips, and treks can be booked through specialist agencies (*see* p.526). Plenty of bug repellent is essential: this coast is known for a special type of mosquito, the *zancudo*, and La Encrucijada is no-go area in the rainy season (June to October).

Tapachula

Graham Greene moaned about the heat in Villahermosa, but then he never got to Tapachula. Chiapas' second-largest city sweats, steams, and sweats again. It makes up for this by being the fruit-juice capital of the world. There are wonderful juice-stands on nearly every street, as well as young boys with hand-carts, selling natural *cerveza de raíz* (root beer), little fixes of coldness to take on the run.

Its position as a frontier town is essential to the identity of Tapachula. It once had the distinction of being a stateless city. In 1824, when the rest of Chiapas joined Mexico, Tapachula and the Soconusco decided to stay with Guatemala. To avoid a war neither was very interested in, the governments of Mexico and the Central American Confederation decided that neither one should own the town, at least until they felt like discussing it again. Sadly for anarchists everywhere, this 'experiment' was not a success. State-less Tapachula became a refuge for 'delinquents and destructive elements', while 'industry, agriculture and commerce' went to ruin. Finally, in 1842 General Santa Anna decided to make it part of Mexico, against apathetic protests from Guatemala. Later in the century the Soconusco's heat, rainfall and closeness to a coast

Getting to and around Tapachula

By Air

Tapachula airport is 18½km south of the city near Puerto Chiapas. **Aeroméxico Connect, t** 01 800 800 2376, and **Aviacsa, t** 01 800 284 2272, have daily flights from Mexico City. **Airport taxis** are the way into town (around $10).

By Bus

The **first-class bus station**, OCC/Cristóbal Colón, is on the main highway, C. 17, east of Av. Central by Av. 3 Norte. From there, it's a taxi ride to the centre. As a border station it has many services, especially to central Mexico, of which some of the most important are these:

· **Matamoros**, on the US border, opposite Brownsville, Texas (*30hrs*): for those arriving from Guatemala and wishing to travel straight through Mexico there is an ADO GL bus every night (5pm). Fare is about $120.
Mexico City (*18hrs*): six ordinary first-class and two ADO GL buses daily. Fares $62–73.
Oaxaca (*12hrs*): one standard first-class, one ADO GL daily. Fares $25–32.
Puerto Escondido (*12½hrs*) via **Huatulco**: one daily (10.45pm). Fare about $32.
San Cristóbal (*7–8hrs*): seven first-class daily via **Ciudad Cuauhtémoc** and **Comitán**. Fare about $16.
Tuxtla Gutiérrez (*6–7½hrs*): via **Tonalá** and other stops, ordinary first-class hourly and nine faster luxury services daily. Fares $18–21.
Veracruz (*13hrs*): one first-class, one ADO GL daily. Fares $43–51.
Villahermosa (*10–11hrs*): one first-class, one ADO GL daily, via Tuxtla. Fares $40–48.

There are regular **international buses: Trans Galgos Inter** (*www.transgalgosinter.com.gt*) runs three daily direct to **Guatemala City** (*5–6hrs*; fares about $18–21) and four that go on to **San Salvador**, El Salvador (*8–9hrs*; $35); **Línea Dorada** (*www.tikalmayanworld.com*) has a daily service to Guatemala City. The Costa Rican **Tica Bus** (*www.ticabus.com*) has a daily bus (7am) to **Panama**, taking four days. Fare is about $105.

Second-class buses have several depots. **Rápidos del Sur**, near the market on C. 11 Poniente, by Av. 12 Norte, has frequent buses north along the coast and to San Cristóbal and Tuxtla. Also near the market, C.5 Poniente is the big *combi* hub of Tapachula, where you can find *combis* to **Unión Juárez** and **Talismán**, which pass **Izapa**. **Omnibus de Tapachula**, C. 7 Poniente just off Av. Central, has services to the border at **Ciudad Hidalgo**.

By Car and Taxi

There are *gasolineras* on C. 17-Highway 200, either side of the city centre. **Taxis**, not local buses, are the key form of city transport, costing about $1.40 for any journey in town.

Car Hire

Some other agencies are based at the airport or in hotels.
Thrifty Car Rental, Av. 2 Sur 14, **t** 626 0982, *ofnatapachula@prodigy.net.mx*. Local franchise: also at the airport.

Orientation

Tapachula has a Chiapas street numbering system. Avenidas are north–south, Calles east–west. The city's peculiarities are, firstly, that Calles north of the central axis have odd numbers, while to the south they are even (but still have locators like C. 6 Poniente, C. 6 Oriente, etc.); Avenidas west of Av. Central are even, and to the east are odd. The main square, **Parque Hidalgo**, is not at the axis of the grid but in the northwest quarter. **Calle 17**, on the north side of the city is the local identity of Highway 200, the main east–west road.

made it the first area of Chiapas to be developed for modern agriculture, which brought in a new and varied population. The first coffee plantations were established by Germans, and under Porfirio Díaz Chinese and Japanese farmers were encouraged to settle here; a characteristic sight in the city are signs like *Taquería Yu Hang*. Modern Tapachula is Mexico's gateway to Central America, and hosts a big trade fair each March, *Expo Internacional Tapachula*, when all the hotels fill up. This idiosyncratic town need not just be a stopover, though: it is also an enjoyable base for

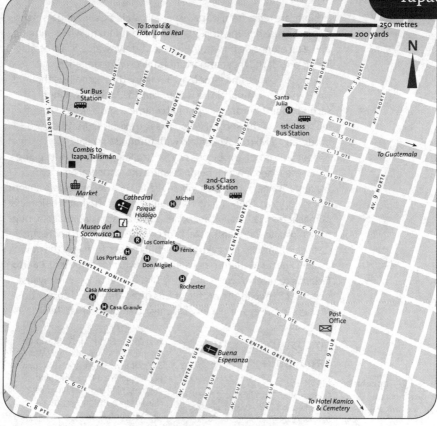

exploring the attractions of southeast Chiapas, which have recently expanded with the opening to visitors of idyllic coffee estates high in the mountains above Tapachula.

Parque Hidalgo and the Museum

Tapachula's main square has a character it owes to the heat, the city's early 20th-century prosperity and its peculiar role in the Mexican-Guatemalan economies. The heat is reflected in the line of terrace restaurants, which specialize in pint-size glasses of blended fruit – pineapple, mango, papaya, melon. The coffee boom is reflected in the town's tropical Art Deco architecture, especially the former town hall, now the **Casa de Cultura**. The all-white **Cathedral** alongside was built in the 18th century, but has been heavily renovated. Tapachula's relationship with Guatemala is seen in the square's tropical bustle, and its cranky range of shops. Along the top of the plaza is one of Mexico's largest concentrations of *taco*-stands, while in the middle a *marimba* plays every night.

Museo Regional del Soconusco

open Tues–Sun 10–5; adm

The old town hall also contains the **Museo Regional del Soconusco**, another museum that has been attractively renovated and is now one of the best local archaeological museums. Its star exhibits are relics from Izapa, especially **Stela 25**, showing a small human figure holding up a giant bird-like standard, while hanging in the air alongside him, pointing snout-downwards, is a crocodile. This is one of the most important Izapa carvings in terms of its mixture of Olmec and later Maya imagery; the crocodile is thought to be an early symbol of the *wakah-kan*, the Milky Way. On the second floor there are exceptional ceramics, and relics of later inhabitants of the Soconusco, such as an exquisite Maya carved bottle, and a Mixtec skull inlaid with turquoise mosaic.

Tapachula is not an obvious city for strolling, but it has intriguing parts. The **market**, which begins behind the cathedral on C. 5 Poniente, is one of the most vibrant of all Mexican markets, a chaotic tropical sprawl. There are no traditional handicrafts, but whole racks of machetes, walls of leather boots (some an amazing bargain) huge rolls of plastic sheeting, or stacks of coloured streamers for *fiestas*.

South of the city (by 27km), Tapachula's port, formerly the down-at-heel Puerto Madero, has been expensively made over as **Puerto Chiapas** to receive cruise ships, the first arrival of which may just herald a change in the profile of this often-unnoticed corner of Mexico. To the east are a few beaches, used by locals at weekends.

Tourist Information in Tapachula

ⓘ **Tapachula**
in the old town hall, on Parque Hidalgo (open Mon–Fri 9–3 and 6–9). Staff are not always well informed, but try hard.

t (962–)
Guatemalan Consulate: Av. 5 Norte 5, t 626 1252 (*officially open Mon–Fri 9–5, but may close for lunch*).
Mexican Immigration Office: C. Terminación Vialidad 435, Fraccionamiento Las Vegas, t 625 6618 (*open Mon–Fri 9–1*). Tapachula has special status as a frontier zone: on Highway 200 north of the city there are inspection points. If you enter from Guatemala and are given 15 days in Mexico, it's better to go further into the country to get an extension (not Tuxtla), rather than in Tapachula.

Tours

Crucero Tours, C. 1 Poniente 10, t 625 2257, *crucerotours@prodigy.net.mx*. As well as the usual travel services, this agency offers some adventure tours (on request), such as rafting.

Services in Tapachula

⭐ **Casa Mexicana**
>>

Banks: Near plaza or on Av. Central.
Health: Many 24hr **pharmacies**.
Internet Access: Katzuaki: Av. 2 Norte 6-D, off C. Central. More off the plaza.

Post Office: East of the centre at C. 1 Oriente and Av. 9 Norte (*open Mon–Fri 8–6, Sat 8–noon*). Restrictions apply to parcel mail from Tapachula, and anything bigger than a letter has to be checked by a customs agent.

Where to Stay in Tapachula

Moderate

Comfort Inn Tapachula Kamico, Prolongación C. Central Oriente, t 626 2640, *www.choicehotelsmexico.com.mx*. East of the city centre (not walking distance), this modern hotel has large, comfortable rooms, spread around a tropical garden with a fine pool, and a poolside **restaurant**.

Hotel Loma Real, Ctra Costera Km 244, t 626 1440, *www.hotellomareal.com.mx*. In lush gardens off Highway 200 in the northwest of the city. Spacious rooms and suites, and there's a gym, tennis courts, a pool and fine **restaurant**.

Inexpensive

Casa Mexicana, Av. 8 Sur 19, corner C. 2 Poniente, t 626 6605, *www.casa mexicanachiapas.com*. An excellent discovery in unfashionable Tapachula, this 'boutique hotel' is run with style, class and attention to detail, from the margaritas on arrival to the charming Mexican-with-a-twist decoration of each room, and yet prices remain within this band. Services such as WiFi are high-quality, and the patio contains a tiny pool, and an equally remarkable restaurant, the **Tapachtlán**.

Hotel Don Miguel, C. 1 Poniente 18, t 626 1143, *www.hoteldonmiguel. com.mx*. Good-value, centrally-located, conventional hotel, with well-refurbished rooms and good a/c – an appreciable factor in Tapachula.

⭐ **Tapachtlán >>**

Hotel Fénix, Av. 4 Norte 19, between C. 1 and 3 Oriente, t 628 9600. *www. fenix.com.mx*. Well-kept hotel with good a/c, WiFi and a pleasant patio. The **Hostal del Rey** restaurant (*moderate*) serves up good breakfasts.

Hotel-Posada Casa Grande, Av. 8 Sur 28, corner C. 2 Poniente, t 626 6701. Opposite the Casa Mexicana, this old patio house has only recently been turned into a B&B-style guest house. The atmosphere, and the rooms, are more homey than hotel-like, and it offers a taste of local life.

Budget

Hotel Rochester, Av. 2 Norte 6, near C. 1 Poniente, t 626 1406. Best budget option in the centre, with fan-only or a/c rooms with TV. Clean, and upper floors get plenty of light and air.

Eating Out in Tapachula

Moderate

Café Monaco, C. 1 Poniente, corner of Av. 4 Norte. Pleasant little modern café with light, health-foodish snacks, excellent juices and good coffee.

Los Comales, Parque Hidalgo, corner of Av. 8 Norte. Claims pride of place among the big, shaded terraces of the plaza: specialities include huge glasses of juice, but they also have enjoyable local and standard Mexican dishes and excellent breakfasts. *Open 24hrs*.

Tapachtlán, Casa Mexicana, Av. 8 Sur 19, corner C. 2 Poniente, t 626 6605. Tapachula has, in its hotel-gem the **Casa Mexicana**, one of the region's very best restaurants, with a real, young French chef, who produces irresistible dishes blending sophisticated skills with the finest tropical ingredients. Service, too, is exceptional. A reason to visit Tapachula almost by itself.

Cheap

If you walk around the plaza, along C. 5 Poniente, you'll be bombarded with cheap food on all sides. All around the centre there's also an irresistible assortment of *juguerías*, juice stands, selling *tascalate*, *pozol* and the local speciality *cerveza de raíz* (root beer) as well as standard juices.

La Flor de Michoacán, Av. 6 Norte, corner of C. 7 Poniente. A full listing of Tapachula's *juguerías* would be a study in itself, but this is one to recommend, with great ice creams, fresh fruit *aguas*.

Around Tapachula

Izapa

Izapa
open (officially) Wed–Sun 8–5; adm

This is far more ancient than any of the Maya cities described previously. **Izapa** was occupied from about 1500 BC, and its most important buildings were erected in the Early Preclassic, around 300 BC; by about AD 400 it had been abandoned. It is thus more contemporary with an Olmec city like La Venta than with Classic Maya cities. The Izapan culture – which extended as far as Kaminaljuyú, on the site of modern Guatemala City – was strongly influenced by the Olmecs, and did not use Maya glyphs. However, many elements of later Maya culture and myth are evident – early forms of the god Chac, or of *Vucub-Caquix* or 'Seven Macaws', the Celestial Bird, a symbol of nature challenging the gods that

Getting to Izapa and Santo Domingo

The Izapa ruins are on the road to Talismán 12km east of Tapachula. The main signpost and parking area is at Group C. *Colectivos* for Talismán leave about every 30mins from C. 5 Poniente. Tell the driver you want *Las Ruinas de Izapa*, and he'll let you off at Group C. To get back, flag down any Tapachula-bound *combi*.

The way to Santo Domingo is a continuation of the same road, via a fork left at Talismán through Cacahoatán. *Combis* run frequently from C. 5 Poniente to Unión Juárez and back.

appears in the *Popol Vuh*. Izapa has been called 'Proto-Mayan', the first stage in the emergence of a distinct Maya civilization.

The site is widely dispersed, with 80 structures in three visitable areas. *Combi* drivers drop you at **Group C**, the largest and the only one clearly signposted on the road. Here there is a plaza of several temple platforms, and badly deteriorated stelae and massive sculptures. Another feature of Izapa similar to Olmec styles is the many anthropomorphic images, particularly the huge toad-heads.

The southern groups of buildings are reached by heading back toward Tapachula for about 700m – a hot trek – to a signposted (and drivable) track south, a more enjoyable walk for about a kilometre through an overwhelmingly green landscape in which even the trees seem to sweat. At a three-way fork, take the centre path for the ruins. **Group A**, to the right, is a big open plaza, surrounded by largely unexcavated mounds and stelae. The carvings here are in a better state than in Group C; highlights are *Stela 4*, a very clear figure of a warrior, and *Stela 5*, with a bird-image believed to be *Vucub-Caquix*. **Group B**, a little to the east, is similar, with more toad-heads. Another Izapa special feature is the phallic 'headstones', in front of several stelae. After that, retrace your steps to the road, with another steamy walk in deep-tropical Mexico.

The 'Switzerland of Chiapas' and Santo Domingo

Beyond Izapa and directly north of Tapachula, on the very border with Guatemala, glowers the immense volcano of **Tacaná**, the highest mountain in Chiapas at over 4,000m high. Since its slopes are far cooler than the plain below, this was a favourite area for the

Visiting Izapa

This is one of the most rustic sites: each section is set on a small *rancho*, and the farmers are the caretakers. There's no set adm charge, but each farmer expects a tip, so you end up paying (a little) three times. Getting between the sections involves a steamy walk. Take water.

Where to Stay and Eat in Santo Domingo

t (962–)
Centro Ecoturístico Santo Domingo, t 627 0060, *www.centroecoturisticosanto domingo.com* (*inexpensive*). The hotel is across the gardens from the Casa Grande, a more modern building with ten spacious doubles and a bright breakfast room. The great attractions are the gardens, with pool, and the **restaurant** (*moderate*) on the balconies of the big house itself.

Ruta del Café: The Coffee Fincas of the Soconusco

Soaring up 2,000 metres, just 60km from the Pacific coast, the slopes of the Sierras behind Tapachula are clad with an explosive wealth of vegetation and produce some of the world's best coffee. European planters, mostly German and Swiss, set up coffee estates or *fincas* here around 1900, seeking altitude for better quality. Recently several, still owned by the founding families, have revitalized themselves by refocussing on premium quality and organic methods, and are open to visitors as the 'coffee route' or Ruta del Café. Two have very comfortable rooms, in cabins spread around each estate. Guests have a choice of walks, tours and adventures. In the old days it took three days to carry coffee from here, by mule, the 50km down to Tapachula; today, these estates still have the feel of a tropical Shangri-La.

To get to the Ruta you follow Av. 6 Norte out of Tapachula onto the Carretera de Nueva Alemania, which winds up through forest and villages until after 39km there is a turn right for **Finca Argovia**, at 600m altitude (combis from C. 5 Poniente go along the road, but not to the *fincas*). As well as *cabañas* or larger *casitas*, it has a lovely restaurant, using the estate's produce. Argovia grows flowers, especially orchids, as well as coffee and is the only completely organic *finca*, so its coffee grows amid wild plants; the sheer lushness is overwhelming. Another 5km along the road at Zaragoza is the entry to **Finca Hamburgo**. Much higher up, at 1,250m, this feels still more a world of its own; it is essential to notify them of your arrival so you can be collected (cars are left safely at Zaragoza), as the only way in is a 12km hill track that can take an hour to drive by 4WD. From the chalet-cabins at the top, the views across to the Pacific, above all at sunset, are unforgettable. The great restaurant, the Perleberg, has the same view (and even WiFi). Nearby is another organic estate, **Finca Irlanda**, with no regular rooms but an ecological reserve, rich in rare birds. It can be visited from Finca Hamburgo. All, of course, serve great coffee.

Finca Argovia, t in Tapachula 626 6115, *www.argovia.com.mx*
Finca Hamburgo, t in Tapachula 626 6404, *www.fincahamburgo.com* (both *moderate–expensive*)
Finca Irlanda, *http://fincairlanda.grupopeters.com*

region's mostly European and North American coffee planters to build their residences when they arrived in Soconusco in the early 20th century. Its label of 'Chiapas' Switzerland' is scarcely convincing but it is certainly very beautiful. On the way to the district's un-Soconusco-like main town of **Unión Juárez** is **Santo Domingo**, centred around a spectacular 1920s plantation house, the **Casa Grande**, a giant timber mansion with elegant verandahs and fabulous views that now houses a restaurant (*see* p.528). There's also a hotel and a museum on coffee production.

Into Guatemala

There are two crossing points across the Suchiate river into Guatemala from Tapachula – at **Talismán** (20km) to the Guatemalan town of **El Carmen**, and to the south at **Ciudad Hidalgo** (38km) to **Ciudad Tecún Umán** on the other side. Ciudad Hidalgo is the busier crossing, and recommended to drivers. If you are not on a through bus to Guatemala City, the same *combis* that take you to Izapa will take you to Talismán, and Omnibus de Tapachula run frequent services to Ciudad Hidalgo. At each crossing you can walk across, and on the other side there are buses to many points within Guatemala. For immigration requirements, *see* p.101.

Language

Several features of Spanish make it one of the easiest languages to pick up at least a little of from scratch. Firstly, it is phonetic, with very practical spelling that provides an immediate connection between how a phrase is written and the way it is pronounced. Stress is all-important in speaking Spanish in an understandable way. The stress is on the last syllable in words ending with most consonants, or on the penultimate one, in words ending in a vowel, an s or an n; where this pattern is not followed the 'new' stress is indicated by an accent, as in Mérida, Cancún (but no accent on Campeche). Secondly, basic Spanish grammar is very simple. Questions, in particular, are formed not by any changes in sentence order but by tone of voice: thus, the difference between *tiene mucho dinero* (he has a lot of money, statement) and ¿*tiene mucho dinero?* is just in how you say it, which anyone can understand. There are also particular advantages in Mexican Spanish for the absolute beginner. Most Mexicans speak more slowly than other Spanish speakers, and stresses are very strongly emphasized, making words recognizable and giving plenty of time to think about a response.

Anyone who already knows some Spanish from other countries will find many differences in the language of Mexico, above all if they learnt Spanish in Spain. Beyond individual words or phrases, most important is that Mexicans lay great store on politeness, and use forms of courtesy to an extent that would now be considered quaint in many other countries (Mexicans find Spaniards rude and aggressive, just by the way they speak). Expect to use polite phrases, even a simple *por favor*, a great deal. Also, use the polite form of the second person (*usted*) unless and until the other person makes it clear you've established your relationship sufficiently to call each other *tú*. The second person plural form is always *ustedes*, as a polite or a familiar term.

A useful phrase book is *Mexican Spanish* (Rough Guides). Books on 'Latin American Spanish' are likely to be no more use than a general Spanish phrase book, since there is no such thing as Latin American Spanish.

For vocabulary related to eating out and a menu decoder, *see* **Food and Drink**, pp.77–86.

Pronunciation

Vowels
a short *a* as in 'pat'
e short *e* as in 'set'
i as *e* in 'be'
o between long *o* of 'note' and short *o* of 'hot'
u silent after *q* and 'gue-' or 'gui-'; otherwise long *u* as in 'flute'
ü *w* sound, as in 'dwell'
y at end of word or meaning 'and', as *i*

Diphthongs
ai, ay	as *i* in 'side'
au	as *ou* in 'sound'
ei, ey	as *ey* in 'they'
oi, oy	as *oy* in 'boy'

Consonants
c before *i* or *e*, a soft *s* sound; otherwise as in 'cat'
ch like *ch* in 'church'
g before *i* or *e*, pronounced as *j* (*see* below)
h silent
j like the *ch* in 'loch', but harder; this sound does not exist in English
ll *y* or *ly* as in 'million'
ñ *ny* as in 'canyon'
q *k*
r usually rolled, which takes practice
v harder than in English; closer to *b*
x between consonants, hard like a *j* (*see* below for *x* in Mayan words)

Pronunciation of Mayan Names and Words

The most widely used spellings of Mayan languages are also fairly phonetic. Yucatec Maya is a language of very strong, throat-breaking consonants, and in a name like Oxcutzcab both c-syllables are pronounced with a powerful k-sound. Z indicates a real z sound, especially in the heavily voiced combinations dz and tz (although non-Maya Mexicans commonly say them with an s). The letter x normally indicates a sh sound, with a slight vowel sound before it when it comes before a consonant; thus *Xcambó*, *Xcaret*, are *Eesh-cambó*, *Eesh-caret*, and so on.

Chiapas Mayan languages are much softer and more whispering, and in names like *Chenalhó* the h-sound is very faint.

Frases Mexicanísimas

There are certain phrases that, within the Spanish language, are marked out as quintessentially Mexican. The following are a few that you will hear all the time, and might need to respond to:

ahorita The diminutive of *ahora* (now), theoretically meaning 'right now' but really referring to an indeterminate period of time, as in *ahorita viene*, 'she's coming right now', although she may be along in a minute, or in five hours, or *ahorita no sé*, 'I don't know at the moment' (but there's no guarantee I'll know in future either).

ándele An expression of encouragement, and/or amazement; also said when leaving, as in *ándele, pues* (let's be going).

bueno 'Good', but also the first thing Mexicans say when they answer the phone, with the stress almost transferred to the o.

¿cómo no? 'Why not?' or 'How could it be otherwise', roughly equivalent to 'of course', as when you walk into a deserted restaurant and ask if they're open, and the answer comes back *sí, ¿cómo no?*

mande Literally a polite word meaning 'command', but corresponding to 'Pardon me?'; when you ask many people a question they will automatically reply *mande*, so that you will then have to repeat the question, maybe in a more polite form.

órale An expression of amazement. 'Wow'.

Useful Words and Phrases

yes *sí*
no *no*
Hello *Hola*
Goodbye *Adios/hasta luego*
Good morning *Buenos días*
Good afternoon *Buenas tardes*
Good evening, Goodnight *Buenas noches*
I don't understand Spanish *no entiendo español*
Do you speak English? *¿habla usted ingles?*
Speak slowly, please *Hable despacio, por favor*
Can you help me? *¿Puede usted ayudarme?*
I (don't) like... *(No) me gusta...*
Help! *¡Socorro!*
Leave me alone! *¡Déjame en paz!*
please *por favor*
thank you (very much) *(muchas) gracias*
How do you do? *mucho gusto* (when greeting someone for the first time)
Well, and you? *¿Bien, y usted?*
What is your name? *Cómo se llama?*
My name is... *Me llamo.../Soy...*
you're welcome *de nada*
I don't know *no sé*
It doesn't matter *no importa*
All right *está bien*
excuse me, sorry *disculpe*
excuse me (to attract attention) *oiga* (polite)
I'm sorry *Lo siento*
be careful! *¡(tenga) cuidado!*
maybe *quizá(s)*
nothing *nada*
It is urgent *es urgente*
What is that? *¿Qué es eso?*
What...? *¿Qué...?*
Who...? *¿Quién...?*
Where...? *¿Dónde...?*
When...? *¿Cuándo...?*
Why...? *¿Por qué...?*
How...? *¿Cómo...?*
How much...? *¿Cuánto.../cuánta...?*
How many...? *¿Cuántos.../cuántas...?*
What time does it open/close? *¿A qué hora abre/cierra...?*
exit/entrance *salida/entrada*
I am lost *Estoy perdido*
I am hungry/thirsty *Tengo hambre/sed*
I am tired (man/woman) *Estoy cansado/a*
I am sleepy *Tengo sueño*
I am ill *No me siento bien*
here/there *aquí/allí*

near/far *cerca, cercano/lejos*
left/right *izquierda/derecha*
over there, that way *p'allá*
straight on *todo recto*
forwards/backwards *adelante/atrás*
good *bueno/a*
bad *malo/a*
slow *despacio, lento*
fast *rápido/a*
big *grande*
small *pequeño/a*
hot (food, drink) *caliente*
cold *frío/a*
I am hot/cold *tengo calor/frío*
Pull/Push (on a door) *Jale/Empuje*
toilets/toilet *servicios/lavabo*
men *señores/hombres/caballeros*
women *señoras/damas*

Numbers

one *uno/una*
two *dos*
three *tres*
four *cuatro*
five *cinco*
six *seis*
seven *siete*
eight *ocho*
nine *nueve*
ten *diez*
eleven *once*
twelve *doce*
thirteen *trece*
fourteen *catorce*
fifteen *quince*
sixteen *dieciséis*
seventeen *diecisiete*
eighteen *dieciocho*
nineteen *diecinueve*
twenty *veinte*
twenty one *veintiuno*
twenty two *veintidos*
thirty *treinta*
thirty one *trienta y uno*
forty *cuarenta*
fifty *cincuenta*
sixty *sesenta*
seventy *setenta*
eighty *ochenta*
ninety *noventa*
one hundred *cien*
one hundred and one *ciento uno*
two hundred *doscientos*

five hundred *quinientos*
one thousand *mil*
one million *un millón*
first *primero/a*
second *segundo/a*
third *tercero/a*

Time

What time is it? *Qué hora es?*
It's 2 o'clock *Son las dos*
...half past 2 *...las dos y media*
...a quarter past 2 *...las dos y cuarto*
...a quarter to 3 *...un cuarto para las tres*
noon *mediodía*
midnight *medianoche*
day *día*
week *semana*
month *mes*
morning *mañana*
afternoon *tarde*
evening/night *noche*
late night (around 1am–dawn) *la madrugada*
today *hoy*
yesterday *ayer*
tomorrow *mañana*
now *ahora*
later, after *después*
it is early *es temprano*
it is late *es tarde*
Monday *lunes*
Tuesday *martes*
Wednesday *miércoles*
Thursday *jueves*
Friday *viernes*
Saturday *sábado*
Sunday *domingo*
January *enero*
February *febrero*
March *marzo*
April *abril*
May *mayo*
June *junio*
July *julio*
August *agosto*
September *septiembre*
October *octubre*
November *noviembre*
December *diciembre*

Shopping and Sightseeing

I want, I would like... *Quiero...*
Where is/are...? *¿Dónde está/están...?*

How much is it? *¿Cuánto es?*
Do you have any change? *¿Tiene cambio?*
open/closed *abierto/cerrado*
cheap/expensive *económico/caro*
shop *tienda*
(super)market *(super)mercado*
bank *banco*
money *dinero/plata*
box office *taquilla*
newspaper (foreign) *periódico (extranjero)*
pharmacy *farmacia*
police/police officer *policía*
police station *comisaría*
post office *correos*
postage stamp *estampilla*
telephone (phone call) *teléfono (llamada)*
phone office *caseta*
hospital *hospital*
church *iglesia*
museum *museo*
theatre *teatro*
beach *playa*
sea *mar*

petrol/gasoline *gasoline*
garage *garaje*
This doesn't work *Esto no funciona*
road/street *carretera/calle*
dirt road *camino de terracería*
motorway *autopista, cuota*
Is the road good? *¿Es buena la carretera?*
breakdown *avería*
(international) driving licence *carnet de manejar/conducir (internacional)*
tyre *llanta*
tyre repair shopp *llantera, vulcanizadora*
driver *conductor, chófer*
speed *velocidad*
danger *peligro*
car park *estacionamiento*
no parking *estacionamiento prohibido*
give way/yield *ceda el paso*
stop *alto*
road works *obras*
army checkpoint *retén, control militar*
NOTE: most road signs will be in international pictographs.

Accommodation

Where is the...hotel? *¿Dónde está el...hotel?*
Do you have a (single/double) room? *¿Tiene usted una habitación (sencilla/doble)?*
...with twin beds *...con dos camas*
...with a double bed *...con una cama grande/de matrimonio*
...a family room *...un cuarto familiar*
...with a shower/bathroom *...con ducha/baño*
...for one night/one week *...para una noche/una semana*
Can I see the room? *¿Puedo ver la habitación?*
Are there rooms with more light? *¿Hay habitaciones con más luz?*
How much is the room per night/week? *¿Cuánto es la habitación por noche/semana?*
air conditioning *aire acondicionado, clima*
swimming pool *alberca, piscina*

Driving

to rent, hire *rentar*
car *carro/auto/coche*
motorbike/moped *moto*
bicycle *bicicleta*

Transport

aeroplane *avión*
airport *aeropuerto*
customs *aduana*
bus/coach *autobús/camión*
bus station *estación de autobuses/camiones*
bus stop *parada*
seat *asiento*
platform *andén*
port *puerto*
ship *buque/barco/embarcación*
small boat *lancha*
ticket *boleto*
I want to go to... *Quiero ir a...*
How can I get to...? *¿Cómo puedo llegar a...?*
When does the next (bus) leave for...? *¿Cuándo sale el próximo (autobús) para...?*
What time does it leave/arrive? *¿A qué hora sale/llega?*
Where does it leave from? *¿De dónde sale?*
Does it stop at...? *¿Para en...?*
How long does the journey take? *¿Cuánto tiempo dura el viaje?*
I want a (return) ticket to... *Quiero un boleto (de ida y vuelta/redondo) a...*

Glossary

aguada natural depression in the ground that retains water during the rainy season; the Maya reinforced them with masonry to create semi-permanent reservoirs.

ahau (pl. **ahauob**) king and chief shaman of a Classic Mayan city state.

alux Maya leprechaun-type goblin, benign or hostile according to whether offerings are made to them. In colonial times, they were believed to exact revenge on the Spaniards for the old Maya gods.

batab (pl. **batabob**) Maya community headman in colonial Yucatán, descended from the pre-Conquest aristocracy.

cenote a cave or sinkhole giving access to water through the dry rock of the Yucatán, or an underground cavern filled with water.

chultún artificial cistern: in Puuc regions and other very dry areas, large pits dug into the ground and lined with pottery, creating giant vats in which rainwater was collected to be retained through the dry months.

criollo in colonial and post-independence times, native-born Mexicans and Spanish-Americans of purely Spanish descent.

cruzob the followers of the rebellion of the 'Talking Cross' after the 1840s Caste War.

ejido rural community that owns lands in common, as recognized in the Mexican Constitution after the 1910 Revolution. *Ejido* land can be worked collectively, or as individual plots; areas such as forests are often managed by the community as a whole. Land can only be sold or redistributed by a vote of the whole community, although amendments to the Constitution associated with the NAFTA agreement have made it much easier to buy and sell *ejido* lands. An *ejidatario* is a member of an *ejido*.

encomienda under early Spanish rule, system by which areas of land and all the people in them were 'entrusted' (*encomendado*) to individual *Conquistadores*, who were theoretically responsible for ensuring that the areas were pacified and their inhabitants instructed in Christianity. In return they could demand labour or tributes from the local Indians, over whom they had almost absolute power. The system was modified from the 1550s, in case the *encomenderos* (holders of *encomiendas*) became so powerful as to challenge royal authority.

henequen type of agave cactus native to the Yucatán which, when stripped and carded, is used to make sisal rope.

ladino(s) in the colonial era and first century of independence, words used throughout the Yucatán, Chiapas and Guatemala to denote the Spanish-speaking community (*criollo* or *mestizo*) as opposed to the pure-Indian population. Now rarely heard in the Yucatán peninsula, as the ethnic divide has become far less marked, but retains some of its original force in Chiapas and Guatemala.

mestizo any person of mixed European-indigenous American descent.

milpa small field cleared for farming by slash-and-burn techniques, used for planting maize, in combination with small quantities of squashes, beans, chillies, etc.

multepal system of collective leadership seen in Postclassic Maya communities, with authority shared or rotated between lords.

sacbé Maya road of packed stone.

sahal (pl. **sahalob**) aristocracy of the Classic Maya cities, subordinate to the *ahauob*.

stela (pl. **stelae**) large, upright carved stones, installed as monuments in the main plazas or in front of major buildings in most Classic Maya cities. Commonly erected to mark significant events, they have often been the most important 'public record' found in the city of the community's history.

xibalba the Maya Underworld, one of the three levels of existence with the Earth and the Heavens. The realm of most of the gods with whom the Maya were in regular contact through shamanistic ritual.

Further Reading

Fewer books on Mexico and the Maya are available in Britain than in North America, but US editions are available via the internet.

The Maya

Coe, Michael D., *The Maya* (Thames & Hudson, 1966–96). A lively general introduction; also *Breaking the Maya Code* (Penguin, 1992). The fascinating story of the development of knowledge of the Maya.

Drew, David, *The Lost Chronicles of the Maya Kings* (Orion, 2000). A very readable, wide-ranging survey of Mayan history.

Gill, Richardson B., *The Great Maya Droughts* (Univ. of New Mexico, 2000). A challenging theory on the Maya 'Great Collapse'.

Houston, S. D., *Reading Maya Glyphs* (Univ. of California (US), British Museum (UK), 1989). A guide to really get to grips with the ruins.

Landa, Diego de, *Yucatán Before and After the Conquest*, trans. and ed. William Gates (Dover, 1978). A translation of Landa's *Relación*, an enormously detailed account of Mayan life as encountered by the Spaniards.

Martin, Simon, and Grube, Nikolai, *Chronicle of the Maya Kings and Queens* (Thames & Hudson, 2008). Wonderfully clear, incisive summary of current knowledge of Maya history, city by city, and recently revised.

Miller, Mary Ellen, and Taube, Karl, *An Illustrated Dictionary of the Gods and Symbols of Ancient Mexico and the Maya* (Thames & Hudson, 1993). Enables you to know your God L from the Lords of Night.

Proskouriakoff, Tatiana, *Album of Maya Architecture* (Univ. of Oklahoma, 1977). Superb, detailed reconstruction-drawings of Maya buildings.

Schele, Linda. Essential texts in bringing together modern knowledge of the Maya for a non-specialist public: with Miller, Mary Ellen, *Blood of Kings* (1986; Thames & Hudson, 1992); with Freidel, David, *Forest of Kings* (William Morrow, 1990), the first reconstruction of Maya history; with Freidel, David, and Parker, Joy, *Maya Cosmos* (William Morrow, 1993), on religion and belief; and with Mathews, Peter, *The Code of Kings* (Touchstone, 1999), with guides to buildings at Palenque, Chichén and Uxmal.

Schmidt, Peter, De la Garza, Mercedes, and Nalda, Enrique, ed., *Maya Civilization* (Thames & Hudson, 1998). Illustrated overview.

Tedlock, Dennis, trans., *Popol Vuh* (Touchstone, 1996). The best English version of the central book of Mayan mythology.

Webster, David L., *The Fall of the Ancient Maya* (Thames & Hudson, 2002). A stimulating analysis of just what Classic Maya culture was.

Post-Conquest History and Culture

Benjamin, Thomas, *A Rich Land, A Poor People* (Univ. of New Mexico, 1996). The history of Chiapas since the 19th century.

Clendinnen, Inga, *Maya and Spaniard in Yucatán, 1517–70* (Cambridge UP, 1989). A complete account of the Yucatán Conquest.

Collier, George A., ed., *Basta! Land and the Zapatista Rebellion in Chiapas* (Food First, 1994). Informative collection of essays.

Díaz, Bernal, *The Conquest of New Spain* (Penguin, 1963). Extraordinary soldier's tales.

Farriss, Nancy M., *Maya Society under Colonial Rule* (Princeton, 1984). Maya survival.

Krauze, Enrique, *Mexico: A Biography of Power*, trans. H. Heifetz (Harper Collins, 1997). A history of Mexico since independence.

Marcos, *Zapatista Stories* (Katabasis, 2002). *El Sub* presents his ideas through a series of whimsical fables; also *¡Ya Basta! 10 Years of the Zapatista Writings of Subcomandante Marcos* (AK Distribution, 2004).

Paz, Octavio, *The Labyrinth of Solitude*, trans. L. Kemp (Grove Press in US; Penguin in UK). The essential book on modern Mexico; read it after you've been there for at least a week.

Reed, Nelson, *The Caste War of Yucatán* (Stanford, 1986). Classic, readable narrative of the Yucatán's extraordinary conflagration.

Thomas, Hugh, *The Conquest of Mexico* (Pimlico, 1996). A complete overview.

Wells, Allen, *Yucatán's Gilded Age* (Univ. of New Mexico, 1985). The extravagant and ambitious Yucatán of the *henequen* boom.

Womack, John, Jr., *Zapata and the Mexican Revolution* (Random House, 1970). Fully informs you just who and what Zapata was.

The Modern Maya

Bruce, Robert D., and Perera, Victor, *The Last Lords of Palenque: The Lacandón Mayas of the Mexican Rain Forest* (Univ. of California, 1982). A detailed report of old Lacandón life.

Everton, MacDuff, *The Modern Maya: A Culture in Transition* (Univ. of New Mexico, 1991). Perceptive account of the Yucatán as it meets tourism, with superb photographs.

Foxx, Jeffrey, *The Maya Textile Tradition* (Harry N. Abrams, 1997). Wonderfully illustrated.

Laughlin, Robert M. and Karasik, Carol, eds., *Mayan Tales from Zinacantán* (Smithsonian Institution, 1996). Fascinating collection of mythology, dreams and folk tales.

Morris, Walter F., Jr, *Living Maya* (Harry N. Abrams, 1987). Beautifully illustrated account of the life of the Highland Maya.

Sullivan, Paul, *Unfinished Conversations: Mayas and Foreigners Between Two Wars* (Alfred A. Knopf, 1989). Based on time spent with the Santa Cruz Maya of Quintana Roo.

Travels

Canby, Peter, *The Heart of the Sky: Travels Among the Maya* (Kodansha, 1994). Fine book of encounters with the modern Maya.

Greene, Graham, *The Lawless Roads* (US title: *Another Country*, Penguin). For his fans only, written from a position of near-complete ignorance of the country.

Stephens, John L., with illustrations by Frederick Catherwood, *Incidents of Travel in Central America, Chiapas and Yucatán* and *Incidents of Travel in Yucatán* (Dover, 1969). Always enjoyable and still informative.

Tree, Isabella, *Sliced Iguana: Travels in Unknown Mexico* (Hamish Hamilton, 2001).

Captures a lot of the downright crankiness of modern Mexico, with style and humour.

Wright, Ronald, *Time Among the Maya* (Weidenfeld & Nicholson, 1989). A perceptive journey through all the Mayan countries.

Fiction

Castellanos, Rosario, *Nine Guardians* (Readers International, 1992). A translation of *Balún Canán*, by Chiapas' foremost modern writer (1925–74), on the intertwined worlds of Ladino and Indian as seen by a child in the 1930s. Also *City of Kings* (Latin American Review Press, 1993); *Ciudad Real*, a collection of stories about San Cristóbal; *Another Way to Be: Selected Works of Rosario Castellanos*, ed. Myralyn Allgood (Univ. of Georgia, 1990).

Greene, Graham, *The Power and the Glory* (Penguin). Some say this book is about Mexico, but it's really about GG's obsessions.

Uribe, Alvaro, ed., *Best of Contemporary Mexican Fiction* (Dalkey Archive Press, 2009). Interesting anthology of younger writers all working in Mexico today.

Birds and Wildlife

Useful, well-illustrated field guides include:

Howell, Steven N. G., and Webb, Sophie A., *Guide to the Birds of Mexico and Northern Central America* (OUP, 1996).

Howell, Steven N. G, *A Bird Finding Guide to Mexico* (Cornell University Press, 1999).

Reid, Fiona A., *A Field Guide to the Mammals of Central America and Southeast Mexico* (OUP, 1998).

Food and Drink

Coe, Sophie D., *America's First Cuisines* (Univ. of Texas, 1994). Fascinating study into the diet of Pre-Hispanic Mesoamerica; equally good is *The True History of Chocolate* (Thames & Hudson, 1996), with Prof. Michael Coe.

Morton, Lyman, and Rosario, Jorge, *Yucatán Cookbook: Recipes and Tales* (Red Crane Books, 1996). Bright and usable cookbook.

Nigh, Kippy, *A Taste of Mexico: Vegetarian Cuisine* (Book Publishing Co., 1996). Nigh's vegetarianized Mexican dishes are based on many years of living in Chiapas.

Index

Main page references are in **bold**. Page references to maps are in *italics*.

Abala 299
Acanceh 327–8
Acapetahua 523
accommodation 102–4
  useful phrases 533
  *see also haciendas; and under
  individual places*
Agua Azul 453–5
Agua Clara 453
Agua Grande 168
Agua Selva 429
airlines 95, 96–7, 125, 128, 257
Aké 246, **251–2**
Aktun Chen 187
Aktun Ha 191
Akumal **187**, 191, 192
aluxes 300
Alvarado, General Salvador 261
Amatenango del Valle 505
animal life 74–5
apartments 104
Aqua World 137
Arcotete 504
Arena 378–9
Arriaga 522
art and architecture 40–1, 67–8
Atlante 134
Aviario Xaman Ha 178
Azul 186–7, 343

Baaknal Chaak 478
Bacalar 342–5
Bahias de Punta Solimán 189
Balam Na 56, **334**
Balamkú 373–4
Balancán 432
Balankanché caves 66, **239–40**
ballgame 39–40
Banco Chinchorro 336, **338**
banks 93–4, 136, 147, 274
Barra San José 523
Barrera, Dr Alfredo 171
Barrera, José María 55–6, 332
bat cenote 368
beaches
  Cancún 130, 132, **133**
  Isla Mujeres 146
  Yucatán 245, 284
Becal 378

Becán 362–4, *363*
begging 110
Belize 335, 345, **353**
  getting there 101, 348
Ben Ha 203
Benemérito de las Américas 470
Biosphere Reserves 71
Bird Jaguar IV 460–2
birds 73–4
Blom, Frans and Trudi 25, 490
Boca del Cerro 432
Boca del Cielo 522–3
Boca de Dzilam 243, **293–4**
Boca Iglesia 153–4
Boca Paila 204
Bolonchén de Rejón 311, **399–400**
Bonampak 30, 455, 458, **465–9**, *466*
bookshops 114, 275
Bosque Azul 510
Buenavista 341–2
bullfights 90, 110–11
buses 97–9, 126, 128
Busil Ha **456–7**, 469

cabañas 103
Cabo Catoche 153
Cahuaré 518
Calakmul 29–30, 360, **367–73**, *371*
Calcehtok 66, **296–7**
Calderón, Felipe 64
Calkiní 378
Calotmul 241
Camino Real 378–80
Campeche City 380–92, *383*
  Alameda 387
  baluartes 385, 386, 387
  Casa Seis 385
  Casa del Teniente del Rey 387
  cathedral 385
  Dulce Nombre de Jesús 387
  eating out 391–2
  entertainment 392
  festivals 390
  Fuerte San José 388–9
  Fuerte San Miguel 368, 388–9
  getting to and around 382, 389
  history 381, 383–4
  Jardín Botánico X'much
  Haltún 387

Malecón 385–6
Mansión Carvajal 387
market 387
museums
  Arquitectura Maya 386
  Arte Popular 387
  Barcos y Armas 389
  Ciudad 386
  Cultura Maya 389
  Piratería 386
  Regional de Campeche 388
Palacio del Congreso 386
Palacio del Gobierno 386
Parque Principal 384–5
Plaza Moch Cuouh 386
Plaza del Patrimonio Mundial 385
Pozo de la Conquista 388
Puente de los Perros 387
Puerta de Mar 385
Puerta de Tierra 386
San Francisco 388
San Francisquito 387
San José 387
San Román 388
services 390
shopping 390
theatre 387
tour operators 390
where to stay 390–1
Campeche Playa 402
Campeche State *376*, **377–404**
  Chenes 42, **393–401**
  Edzná 393–6, *395*
  food and drink 80
  Gulf Coast 402–4
  Hopelchén 311, **397**, 400
  Petenes 42, **378–80**
  Santa Rosa Xtampak 398–9
camping 104, 286
Cancún *122*, *123*, **124–42**
  airport 125
  Av. Tulum 126
  Av. Yaxchilán 134
  Ayuntamiento Benito Juárez 133
  banks 136
  bars 141–2
  beaches 130, 132, **133**
  Boulevard Kukulcán 126, 129
  Cancún Center 130

Casa del Arte Popular
Mexicano 130
Ciudad Cancún 126, **133–4**, *135*
where to stay 138–9
clubs 141–2
eating out 139–41
El Crucero 134
El Meco 134
El Rey 132–3
Embarcadero 130
emergencies 136
entertainment 141–2
Estación Marítima 134
Estadio Andrés Quintana Roo 134
getting around 128
getting there 125–6
Gran Puerto Cancún 134
history 127–9
Hotel Zone (Cancún island)
124, 126, **129–33**, *131*
where to stay 138
Internet access 136
La Isla 129
market 134
nightlife 141–2
orientation 126
Parque de las Palapas 134
Playa Mujeres 134
police station 136
post office 136
Puerto Cancún 134
Puerto Juárez 134
Punta Nizuc 130
Punta Sam 134
shopping 136
sports and activities 137
Teatro de Cancún 130
tourist information 136
where to stay 137–9
Candelaria 404
Cañón del Sumidero 518, **520**
capillas de indios 67
Caracol 369
Cárdenas 429
Cárdenas, Lázaro 61
Carretera Fronteriza 457, 458
cars
driving in Mexico 99–100
driving to Mexico 91–2, 95–6
hire cars 99, 128
insurance 96
Cascadas de Reforma 432
Caste War **54–6**, 216, 260, 331, 332
Catherwwod, Frederick **24**, 268–9
caves
Balankanché 66, **239–40**
bat caves 368
Calcehtok 66, **296–7**
cave diving 116–17, 189, 190–1
Loltún 66, **316–17**

Ox Bel Ha 66, **190**
San Cristóbal 504
Xtacumbilxunaan 399–400
Celestún 285–7
cenotes **66**, 172, 190–1, 297
Azul 186–7, 343
bat cenote 368
Ben Ha 203
Cenotillo 240
Chichén Itzá 66, 231–2
Chihuan 240
Cristalino 186–7
Cuzamá 328
Dzitnup 66, **221**
Encantado 350
Holca 240
Ikkil 239
Kantum Chi 186
Samula 221
Valladolid 214
Xlacah 290
Yokdzonot 66, **240**, 241
Zací 217
Cenotillo 240
Centla Coast 411–12
Central Vallarta 171
ceramics 114
Chabihau 293
Chacchobén 342
Chacmultún 317–18
Champotón 401
Chamula 499–500, **501–3**, 505, 506
Chan Santa Cruz 56, 332–3, 346
Chan Chak Kaknal Ahaw 301–2
Chan Muaan 466–9
Chankanaab nature park 168–9
checkpoints 110
Chelem 291
Chemuyil 187–8
Chen Río 168
Chenes 42, **393–401**
Chetumal 345–53, *347*
Chiapa de Corzo 29, 68, **518–19**
Chiapas **434**, **435–529**
Agua Azul 453–5
Bonampak 30, 455, 458, **465–9**, 466
food and drink 80–1
Highlands 471–506, 473
Misol Ha **453**, 454, 455
Montebello lakes 506–7, **510–11**
Pacific rim 521–9
Palenque 436–52, *441*, *444*
politics 109–10, 472–7
San Cristóbal de Las Casas
68, **481–99**, *483*
Toniná 477–80
Tuxtla Gutiérrez 512–18, *514*
Yaxchilán 455, 458–9, **459–65**, *461*

Chicanná 364–6, *365*
Chichén Itzá 41–2, **224–38**, *228*, *236*
Chichén Viejo 237
Chicxulub 292
Chihuan 240
children 108
Chinkultik 506, **508–9**
Chiquilá 243
chocolate 276, 428
Chontal Maya (Putunes) 31, 225, 409
Chuburna 291
Chumayel 324
Chunchucmil 285
Chunhuhub 400
Chunyaxché 203
Chunzubul 177
churches 67–8, 113
Cinco Lagunas 510
Cintalapa 522
Ciudad del Carmen 402–4
Ciudad Cuauhtémoc 521
Ciudad Hidalgo 529
Ciudad Tecún Umán 529
climate 88
clothes 94
shops 114–15, 277
Cobá **206–10**, *207*, 227
Cocum 324, 325
coffee 529
Comalcalco 424–8, *427*
Comitán 506, **507**, 508, 509–10
community tourism 187
Conhuas 374
Conquistadores 46–51, 254–6
consulates 91, 108, 136
Contoy 147
Cortés, Hernán 46, 409
cost estimates 94
Costa Maya 336–41
Cozumel 142, 143, **158–69**, *159*
credit cards 94
crime 108–10, 454, 458
Cristalino 186–7
Cristo Negro 248
Crococun 169
Crucero San Javier 457
Cruzob (Cruz Maya) 56, 332–3, 335, 346
Cuauhtémoc 409
Cuba 101
Culubá 242
Cupilco 424
customs forms 92
Cuzamá 328
dancing 269
deforestation 70–1
departure tax 92
dialling codes 108, 118
Díaz, Porfirio 57–8

disabled travellers 92–3
diving 116–17
  cave diving 116–17, 189, 190–1
  see also sports and activities
dolphins 76, 146, **153**, 155–6, 185
Dos Caobas 457
Dos Lagunas 511
Dos Ojos 190
drinks 81–2
Dwarf of Uxmal 300
Dzibalchén 400
Dzibanché 354–6
Dzibilchaltún 66, **287–90**, *289*
Dzibilnocac 401
Dzilam Bravo 243, **293**
Dzitnup 66, **221**
dzulob 300

Echeverría, Luis 129
ecotourism 68–71, 105–6
Edzná 393–6, *395*
Ek Balam 222–4
El Aguacero 521–2
El Azufre 430
El Bajo 293
El Bosque 411
El Carmen 529
El Castillo 168
El Cedral 168
El Chajul 470
El Chiflón 507
El Cuyo 244–6
El Garrafón 146–7
El Meco 134
El Palmar 286, 402
El Remate 379
El Rey 132–3
El Tigre 404
El Triunfo Biosphere Reserve 520–1
El Uvero 338
electricity 110
embassies and consulates 91,
  108, 136
emergencies 108, 111
Emiliano Zapata **431**, 432
Encantado 350
encomienda system 49–51
entertainment 110–11
Escárcega 374, **404**
Estero Las Palmas 523

Faro Celarain Eco Park 168
Felipe Carrillo Puerto 332–6
ferries 101
festivals 88–90
fishing 117, 156, 165, 179–80, 245, 381
flamingo colonies 242–4, 285–6
Flamingo Lakes resort 293
food and drink 78–86
  menu decoder 83–6

shopping 115
football 134
Fox, Vicente 63–4
Frontera 411
Frontera Corozal **457**, 458, 469
fruit 83

Garrido Canabal, Tomás 61, 410, 431
gay scene 120
golf 70, 117, 134, 137, 165, 180, 277
Gran Cenote 190
Guatemala 101, 348, 458, 521, **529**
Guerrero, Gonzalo 48
guest houses 103

haciendas 102–3, 249, 250, **272–3**, 281
  Ochil 298
  Sotuta de Peón 298, **328**
  Temozón Sur 298
  Tres Ríos 173
  Yaxcopoil 297–8
hammocks 115, 276
Hampolol wildlife reserve 380
hats 115, 277
health 93, 111, 136
Hecelchakán **380**, 381
henequen 58, 260–1, 284
Hero Twins 33, **34**
Hidalgo, Miguel 52
Highland Maya 499–501, 502
hire cars 99, 128
Hochchob 400–1
Holbox 142
Holca 240
Holpelchén 311
homosexuality 120
Hopelchén 311, **397**, 400
Hormiguero 361–2
horse riding 117, 165
hostels 103
hotels 102–3, 104
  see also haciendas
Huimanguillo 428, **429**
Huitepec Nature Reserve 501
Hunucmá 284
hurricanes 88, 130, 346
hustlers 110

Ichmul 321
Ikkil 239
Independence 52–4
insurance 93, 96
Internet access 111
Isla Arena 378–9
Isla Contoy 147
Isla Holbox 152–7
Isla Jaina 41, **379**
Isla Mujeres 142–7, *143*
Isla de Pájaros 153
Iturbide, Augustín de 52

Iturbide village 401
Itzá 409
Itzamatul 250
Itzamkanaak 404
Izamal 246–51
Izapa 29, **527–8**

Jaguar Paw 369–70
Jaina 41, **379**
jaranas 269
jewellery 115

Kabah 309–11, *310*
Kan Balam II 438, 439, 443
Kan Hok Chitam II 439–40, 478
Kankiriché 299
Kantum Chi 186
kayaks 117
Kinich Ahkal Mo Naab III 439–40
Kinich Kak Mo 249–50
Kinichná 355, 356
Kohunlich 355, 356–8, 357
Kolem Jaá 430

La Encrucijada 522, **523**
La Malinche 46, **48**
La Selva 454
La Unión 350
La Venta 28, **417–20**, 429
Lacandón Maya 455, **456**
Lacanjá **457**, 469
Lady Xoc 460–1
Lafitte, Jean and Pierre 143, 293
Lagartero 512
Lago Pojoj 510–11
Lagos de Colón 512
lagunas
  Bacalar 341–53
  Lacanjá 457
  Mecoacán 411
  Miramar 479, **480**, 481
  Montebello 470, 506–7, **510–11**
  Silvituc 374
  Tziscao 511
  Yal Ku 187
Yucalpetén 291
Lake Chunyaxché 203
Landa, Diego de 51, 247
language 111–12, 530–3
  learning Spanish and Mayan
    112, 494–5
  menu decoder 83–6
Lanná 314–16, *315*
Las Casas, Bartolomé de 50, 482, **486**
Las Coloradas 243
Las Guacamayas 470
Las Nubes 470
Lerma 401
Limones 336
Loltún Caves 66, **316–17**

Lord Chak 301–2
Lords of Death 34

Madero, Francisco 59
Mahahual 336, **337–8**, 340
Malpasito 429
Mama 324
manatee reserve 76, 349–50
Maní 322–4
maps 90–1
Maravilla Tenejapa 470
Marcos, *Subcomandante* 475
María Carlota, Empress 260
markets 113, 115–16
Maroma 173
Maya **20–44**, 50–1
  art and architecture 40–1
  ballgame 39–40
  calendar 36–8
  Chontal Maya (*Putunes*) 31,
    225, 409
  collapse 42–4
  Cruz Maya (Cruzob) 56,
    332–3, 335, 346
  eras 23
  Highland Maya 499–501, 502
  Lacandón Maya 455, **456**
  names and spelling 27
  origins 28–9
  Postclasic era 44
  religion and mythology 32–6
  sites 21
    discovery and excavations 22–8
  society and culture 29–32
  warfare 38–9
Maya Koba 173–4
Mayan Beach Garden 340
Mayapán 44, **324–7**, *327*
Mecoacán 411
Media Luna 187
menu decoder 83–6
Mérida 253–**83**, *255*
  Altar de Patria 273
  Arco de Dragones 268
  Arco del Puente 268
  Arco de San Juan 270
  art galleries 267
  Ateneo Peninsular 264
  bars 283
  Bazar de Artesanías 270
  bus stations 257–8, 259, 270
  Calle 60 265–7
  Cámara House 273
  Capilla del Hospital de San
    Juan de Dios 263
  Capilla de los Apóstoles 263
  Casa de Cultura del Mayab 268
  Casa Frederick Catherwood
    268–9
  Casa de las Artesanías 268

Casa de los Artistas 267
Casa Molina 267–8
Casa de Montejo 263–4
  cathedral 262–3
  Centro Cultural Olimpo 263
  clubs 283
  courses 275
  eating out 280–3
  entertainment 283
  Ermita de Santa Isabel 270–1
  festivals 275
  Galería Mérida 268
  Galería Tataya 269
  getting around 258–9
  getting there 257–8
  history 253–6, 260–2
  Iglesia de Jesús 365–6
  Iglesia de las Monjas 268
  Iglesia de Santa Ana 267
  La Candelaria 270
  La Luz Galería 267
  La Mejorada 267
  MACAY 264
  Market District **269–71**, 276
  moonlight serenades 265
  museums
    Antropología e Historia 271
    Arte Popular de Yucatán 268
    Canción Yucateca 267
    Ciudad 270
  nightlife 283
  Palacio del Gobernador 263
  Palacio Municipal 263
  parks
    Centenario 269
    Hidalgo 265
    la Madre 266
    la Mejorada 267
    San Juan 270
    Santa Ana 267
    Santa Lucía 266–7
    Santiago 268
  Pasaje de la Revolución 264
  Paseo de Montejo 271
  Plaza Mayor 262–5
  Portal de Granos 270
  Prolongación de Montejo 273
  San Cristóbal 270
  San Ildefonso 262–3
  San Juan 270
  Santa Lucía 267
  Seminary of San Ildefonso 264–5
  services 274
  shopping 275–7
  Teatro Mérida 263
  Teatro Peón Contreras 266
  tours 274–5
  where to stay 277–80
  Yucatán State Congress 266
  zoo 269

Metzaboc 455
military checkpoints 110
Miramar 411
Miramar, laguna 479, **480**, 481
Misol Ha **453**, 454, 455
Mitontic 504
money 93–4
Mono Araña 210
Montebello lakes 470, 506–7, **510–11**
Montejo family 47–9, 254, 263–4
Montes Azules **470**, 471
moonlight serenades 265
Motozintla 521
Mount Tzontehuitz 504
Mujeres 142–7, *143*
Muna 299
Mundaca, Fermín 146
Murciélagos 190
museum opening hours 119–20
music 269
Muyil 202
mythology 32–6

Nacajuca 424
Nadzcaan 374
national holidays 112–13
newspapers 112
Nohoch Mul 209
Nohpat 309
Nuevo Francisco León 456
Nuevo Mahahual 337
Nuevo Yucatán 293

Ochil 298
Ocosingo 471, **477**, 479, 481
Ojo de Agua 153
Olmecs 28–9, 402, 409, 417–20
  sites 21
opening hours 94, 113, 119–20
Oventic 504
Ox Bel Ha 66, **190**
Oxchuc 472
Oxkintok 295–6
Oxkutzcab **320**, 321–2
Oxolotán 431
Oxtankah **353–4**, 355
Paamul **186**, 191
packing 94–5
Pakal the Great 438–9
Palenque 436–52, *441*, *444*
Paraíso 411
Parque Escúltorico Punta Sur 147
passports 91–2
Pat, Jacinto 54
Pedro Antonio de los Santos 341
Petenes 42, **378–80**
Peto 321
petrol 100
pharmacies 111
photography 113, 502, 505–6

Pico de Oro 411, 470
Piedras Negras 459
Playa Azul 411
Playa Bonita 401
Playa del Carmen 174–84, *178*
Playa del Secreto 173
Playa Varadero 402
Plumridge, Lieutenant 335
Pojoj 510–11
Polé 185
police 110, 136
politics 62–4, 109–10, 472–7
Pomoná 431–2
Porfiriato 57–8
post offices 113–14, 136
PRI 62–3
Progreso 290–2
Puente Chiapas 471
Puente de la Unidad 402
Puerto Arista **522**, 523
Puerto Aventuras **186**, 191
Puerto Calica 186
Puerto Ceiba 411
Puerto Chiapas 526
Puerto Costa Maya 336, 337
Puerto Morelos 169–73
Punta Allen 203–4
Punta Bete 174
Punta Chiqueros 168
Punta Herrero 338, 339
Punta Laguna 210
Punta Maroma 173–4
Punta Molas 168
Punta Morena 168
Punta Placer 338
Punta Santa Cecilia 168
Punta Solimán **189**, 192
Punta Sur 168
Putunes 31, 225, 409
Puuc Route **42**, **297–319**
    Chacmultún 317–18
    eating out 319
    entertainment 319
    Kabah 309–11, *310*
    Lanná 314–16, *315*
    Loltún Caves 66, **316–17**
    Sayil 312–13, *313*
    Uxmal 299–308, *301*
    where to stay 318–19
    Xlapak 131–14
Puyacatengo 430
radio 112
Rancho Loma Bonita 173
Rancho Nuevo 504
Rancho Sol Caribe 204
reefs 75–6
Reforma **432**, 455
Reforma 57, 58
religion 32–6

Reserva de la Biósfera Río
    Lagartos 242–4
Reserva del Mono Araña 210
restaurants 78–80, 110, 111
    menu decoder 83–6
    specialities 80–1
    Revolution 59–62, 261
Río, Antonio del 22, 23
Río Bec 42, *330*, **359–74**
    Balamkú 373–4
    Becán 362–4, *363*
    Calakmul 29–30, 360, **367–73**, *371*
    Chicanná 364–6, *365*
    eating out 367
    getting to and around 359, **360**
    history 360–1
    Hormiguero 361–2
    tour operators 366
    tourist information 366
    where to stay 366–7
    Xpuhil **361**, 401
Río Hondo 350
Río La Venta 522
Río Lagartos 242–4
Rivers Region 431–2
Riviera Maya *122*, 123, **169–210**
    Akumal **187**, 191, 192
    Cobá **206–10**, *207*, 227
    getting around 169
    Muyil 202
    Playa del Carmen 174–84, *178*
    Puerto Morelos 169–73
    Punta Bete 174
    Punta Laguna 210
    Punta Maroma 173–4
    Sian Ka'An **202–3**, 204–6, 339
    Tulum 193–201, *195*
    Xcaret 185
    Xel Ha 188–9
    Xpu Ha **186**, 190, 191–2
Ruta de los Conventos 322

Sabancuy 402
Sagrado 190–1
sailing 117, 165
Samula 221
San Andrés Larraínzar 504
San Antonio de Padua 246, 248–9
San Benito 293
San Claudio 432
San Cristóbal de Las Casas 68,
    481–99, *483*
    Antiguo Colegio de San
        Francisco Javier 491
    Arco del Carmen 491–2
    Barrio de Mexicanos 489
    Casa de Artesanías 491
    Casa de Diego de Mazariegos
        487–8
    Casa de la Sirena 488

Casa Utrilla 488
    cathedral 487
    Centro Cultural El Carmen 492
    Chapel of San Cristóbal 493
    eating out 497–8
    El Cerrillo 490
    El Jardín del Jaguar 491
    entertainment 499
    festivals 494
    galleries 490
    getting around 484
    Guadalupe 491
    history 482, 485–6
    Insurgentes 491–2
    Jardín de Orquídeas 490
    La Casa del Jade 488
    La Galería 488
    La Merced 492
    Los Portales 487
    market 488–9
    Mercado de Dulces y
        Artesanías 492
    Moxviquil 490
    museums
        Altos de Chiapas 489
        Ambar de Chiapas 492
        Coffee 491
        Culturas Populares 492
        Elisa Burkhard 490
        Jade 488
        Medicina Maya 489–90
        Sergio Castro 492
    Na Bolom 456, **490–1**
    nightlife 499
    Palacio Municipal 487
    Peje de Oro 490
    San Diego 492
    San Francisco 492
    San Nicolás 487
    Santa Lucía 492
    Santo Domingo 488–9
    Serrito de San Cristóbal 492–3
    services 494
    shopping 495
    Sna Jolobil 489
    Templo de la Caridad 489
    Templo de Guadalupe 491
    TierrAdentro 491
    tour operators 493–4
    tourist information 493
    where to stay 496–7
    Zócalo 486–8
San Felipe **243**, 244
San Gervasio 158, **162–3**
San Jacinto 477
San Javier 457
San José El Hueyate 523
San Juan Chamula 499–500,
    501–3, 505, 506
San Lorenzo Zinacantán **503–4**, 505

San Miguel de Cozumel 160–1, *162*
Sánchez Magallanes 412
Sanctuary of the Cross 332–3
Sanjuanistas 53
Santa Clara 293
Santa Elena 309
Santa Rosa Xtampak 398–9
Santo Domingo 528–9
Sayil 312–13, *313*
sealife 75–6
Señor 333–4
Seybaplaya 401
shark watching trips 155
Shield Jaguar II 459–60, 461
Shield Jaguar III 462
shopping 114–16
    textiles 71–3, 503–4
    useful phrases 532–3
Sian Ka'An **202–3**, 204–6, 339
Sierra Madre 521
Sierra de Tabasco 429–31
Sierrita 295
Sihoplaya 401
Silvituc 374
Sisal 284–5
skydiving 118, 180
snakes 75
snorkelling 117
Sotuta 324
Sotuta de Peón 298, **328**
sports and activities 116–18
    Cancún 137
    cave diving 116–17, 189, 190–1
    Costa Maya 339
    Cozumel 164–5
    Isla Holbox 155–6
    Isla Mujeres 148–9
    Playa del Carmen 179–80
    Puerto Morelos 171
    southern Riviera 191
    Tulum 198
stelae 41
Stephens, John Lloyd 24
Subteniente López 350, 353
Sumidero Canyon 518, **520**
swimming 137

Tabasco *406–7*, **407–32**
    Centla Coast 411–12
    Comalcalco 424–8, *427*
    food and drink 80
    history 409–10
    Rivers Region 431–2
    Sierra de Tabasco 429–31
    Villahermosa 412–23, *414–15*, *419*
    Yumká Nature Park 423–4
Tacaná 528
Tacotalpa 430
Talismán 529
Talking Cross 55–6, 335

Tankah **189–90**, 192
Tapachula 523–7, *525*
Tapijulapa 430
taxis 101, 128
Teabo 324
Teapa **429**, 430
Tecoh 327
Tekax 321
Tekit 324
Telchac 293
Telchac Puerto 293
Telchaquillo 327
telephones 108, 118
television 112
Temozón Sur 298
Tenam Puente 506, **507–8**
Tenejapa 504
Tenosique 432
Tepich 331
tequila 82
textiles 71–3, 114–15, 503–4
Thompson, Edward 25, 228, 232
Ticul 320–2
Ti'ho 253–4
Tihosuco 331
Tikal 29, 369, 370
time 108, 118
    useful phrases 532
Tipikal 324
tipping 118–19
Tixcacal Guardia 333
Tizimín 241–2
Tohcok 397
toilets 119
Toltecs 225
Tonalá 522
Toniná 477–80
Tortugranja turtle farm 146
tour operators 104–6
    Campeche 390
    Chetumal 351
    Mérida 274
    Palenque 450–1, 453, 458
    Río Bec 366
    San Cristóbal de Las Casas 493–4
    Villahermosa 421
tourist information 90–1
travel 95–101
    cost estimates 94
    useful phrases 533
    when to go 88
Tres Bocas 171
Tres Garantías 350–1
Tres Ríos 173
Tulum 44, **193–201**, 195
Tulum Pueblo **197**, 201
Tumba del Caracol 168
turtles 76, 146, 156, 245
Tutul Xiu 301
Tuxtla Gutiérrez 512–18, *514*

Twigge, Lieutenant 335
Tziscao 511

Uaymitún 292–3
Uchben Kah 341
Umán 294
Unión Juárez 529
Usumacinta valley 455
Uxmal 299–308, *301*
    Arch 308
    Ball Court 306
    Birds Quadrangle 303
    Cemetery Group 308
    eating out 319
    Governor's Palace 306–7
    Great Pyramid 307
    history 300–2
    House of the Macaws 307
    House of the Old Woman 307
    House of the Pigeons 308
    House of the Turtles 307
    La Picota 307
    North Group 308
    Nunnery Quadrangle 303–5
    opening hours 299
    Platform of the Stelae 308
    Pyramid of the Magician 302–3
    Round Building 308
    temples
        Centipede 308
        Phalli 308
        Venus 305
    Throne of the Jaguar 307
    where to stay 318–19

Vaca Ha 190–1
Valladolid 214–21
vegetarians 81
Villa Luz 430–1
Villa, Pancho 59
village accommodation 103
Villahermosa 412–23, *414–15*, *419*
    Avenida Francisco Madero 413
    Calle Juárez 413
    Calle Narciso Sáenz 413
    Casa de los Azulejos 413–14
    cathedral 417
    Centro Cultural 413
    CICOM 420–1
    eating out 423
    Embarcadero 417
    entertainment 423
    festivals 421
    getting to and around 416–17
    Laguna de las Ilusiones 420
    Malecón 415
    museums
        Antropología 420–1
        Cultura Popular 417
        Historia Natural 418

Historia de Tabasco 414
Palacio de Gobierno 415
Parque Juárez 413
Parque La Choca 420
Parque La Venta 417–20
Parque Tabasco 420
Parque Tomás Garrido
  Canabal 420
Plaza de Armas 415
Puente Gaviotas 415
services 421
shopping 421
Tabasco 2000 420
tour operators 421
where to stay 422
Zona Luz 412, 413–17
zoo 418
visas 91–2

water 120
Welib Já 456
Wet'n'Wild 137
whale sharks 155
where to stay 102–4
  useful phrases 533
wildlife 73–6
windsurfing 117
wine 81
women travellers 120

Xahuaxol 338
Xcacel 187–8
Xcalak 338, 340–1
Xcalumkin 380
Xcambó 292, 293
Xcaret 185
Xel Ha 188–9
Xicalango 403
Xiu 301
Xixim 286
Xlacah 290
Xlapak 131–14
Xoc 460–1
Xpu Ha 186, 190, 191–2
Xpuhil 361, 401
Xtacumbilxunaan 399–400
Xtampak 398–9
Xul Ha 343

Yaax Che Jardín Botánico 171
Yal Ku 187
Yaxchilán 455, 458–9, 459–65, 461
Yaxcopoil 297–8
Yaxuná 240, 241
Yokdzonot 66, 240, 241
Yucalpetén 291
Yucatán State 211–328, 212–13
  Aké 246, 251–2
  Celestún 285–7

Chichén Itzá 41–2, 224–38,
  228, 236
Dzibilchaltún 66, 287–90, 289
Ek Balam 222–4
El Cuyo 244–6
Izamal 246–51
Maní 322–4
Mayapán 44, 324–7, 327
Mérida 253–83, 255
Oxkintok 295–6
Oxkutzcab 320, 321–2
Progreso 290–2
Puuc Route 42, 297–319
Río Lagartos 242–4
Ticul 320–2
Tizimín 241–2
tour operators 274
Uxmal 299–308, 301
Valladolid 214–21
Yuknoom the Great 369
Yumká Nature Park 423–4

Zapata, Emiliano 59–61
Zapatistas 63, 64, 109–10, 472–7, 505
Zinacantan 503–4, 505
Zoh Laguna 361
ZOOMAT 516

Acknowledgements

Nick Rider

With full apologies to all those who helped me along the way but I cannot mention here for reasons of space, my warmest thanks and *más sincero agradecimiento* are due to: Manuel Díaz Cebrián, Lupita Ayala and Luís Rendón of Mexico Tourism in London; Cathy and Jo Matos and all their staff at Cathy Matos Mexican Tours, London; to Saúl Ancona and Alejandro Ceballos at the Yucatán state tourism office, Mérida, and to Eugenio Chamarro and Eduardo Alpay of the Tabasco state Secretaría de Turismo, Villahermosa. And also very warmly to Connie Leal of Mayan Ecotours and Alfonso Escobedo of Ecoturismo Yucatán, both in Mérida; to Alfred Rordame and Emily Navar at Macan Ché, Izamal; to Kristine Ellingson and Santiago Domínguez in Santa Elena; to Onny and Carmelo at Mawimbi, Holbox; to Sam Meacham of CINDAQ, Playa del Carmen, for essential information on the state of the Riviera Maya; to Paul Sánchez Navarro, Centro Ecológico Akumal; to Nancy de Rosa, of Villas de Rosa hotel and SAVE, Akumal; to Gilmer Arroyo Sánchez and Edith Contreras of Xiimbal, Felipe Carrillo Puerto; to Marcos Canté Canul of Xyaat cooperative, Señor; to Carol and Bob Wexler at Casa Carolina, Xcalak; to Ric Bertram and Diane Lalonde at Río Bec Dreams in Chicanná; and in Chiapas, to Nancy and David Orr of Casa Felipe Flores, César of Alex y Raúl, Ernesto Ledesma at TierrAdentro, Ernesto at Explora and especially Carlota Duarte of the Archivo Fotográfico Indígena, all in San Cristóbal, to Claudia Vírgen and the staff of Ecobiósfera El Triunfo in Tuxtla Gutiérrez, and to Andrea Medina of Finca Argovia and Ulises Hidalgo of Finca Hamburgo, both in Tapachula. And very special thanks and many *abrazos* go to Denis Lafoy, the Alonzo family at Mexico Rentacar, Ellyne and Chucho Basto at Cascadas de Mérida, Claudette and Sergio Terrazas, Sofi and Daniel Bosco at Hotel Marionetas and Tom and Donard at Luz en Yucatán, all in Mérida.

At Cadogan Guides I want to thank Rosemary Wilkinson, Louise Coe and Guy Hobbs, for seeing it all through. And special thanks of all sorts to Ethel, for sharing in the whole thing, whether it was taking notes in hotels, finding the way to lost ruins in Tabasco or enjoying the pool at Temozón.

Cadogan Guides

We would like to thank Thames & Hudson for permission to reproduce the Mayan glyphs on p.37, taken from Michael D. Coe's *The Maya*.

Mérida Mexico, 542 km
Palenque, Mexico 6 ½ Hrs

4th American edition published in 2010 by

CADOGAN GUIDES USA
An imprint of Interlink Publishing Group, Inc.
46 Crosby Street, Northampton, Massachusetts 01060
www.interlinkbooks.com
www.cadoganguidesusa.com

Text Copyright © Nick Rider 1999, 2002, 2005, 2010
Copyright © New Holland Publishers (UK) Ltd, 2010

Cover photographs: © Danita Delimont / Alamy (front), © Gonzalo M. Azumendi/Jupiter Images (back)
Photo essay photographs: © Secretaría de Turismo de Yucatán, except pp.1, 10 (Toniná), 11 (Uxmal Relief),
12, 14, 15 (Izamal) © Nick Rider; and pp.3,4,5,8 (beach near Tulum), 8 (Cancún Hotel Zone), 9, 13 (Cenote near
Tulum), 13 (Chaca Tree, Sian Ka'an), 15 (Colonial Houses, Campeche), 15 (Daily Market, San Cristóbal), 16
© Pictures Colour Library.
Maps © Cadogan Guides, drawn by Maidenhead Cartographic Services Ltd
Cover design: Jason Hopper
Photo essay design: Sarah Gardner
Editor: Guy Hobbs
Proofreading: Elspeth Anderson
Indexing: Isobel McLean

Printed and bound in Italy by Legoprint
Library of Congress Cataloging-in-Publication Data available

ISBN: 978-1-56656-795-4

To request our complete full-color catalog, please call us toll free at 1-800-238-LINK, visit our website at
www.interlinkbooks.com, or send us an e-mail: *info@interlinkbooks.com*